WHIRLWIND

Jefferson and Hamilton: The Rivalry That Forged a Nation

The Ascent of George Washington: The Hidden Political Genius of an American Icon

Almost a Miracle: The American Victory in the War of Independence

A Leap in the Dark: The Struggle to Create the American Republic

Setting the World Ablaze: Washington, Adams, Jefferson, and the American Revolution

The First of Men: A Life of George Washington

Adams vs. Jefferson: The Tumultuous Election of 1800

John Adams: A Life

Struggle for a Continent: The Wars of Early America

Independence: The Struggle to Set America Free

The Loyalist Mind: Joseph Galloway and the American Revolution

A Wilderness of Miseries: War and Warriors in Early America

WHIRLWIND

· · ·

THE AMERICAN REVOLUTION AND THE WAR THAT WON IT

JOHN FERLING

BLOOMSBURY PRESS

NEW YORK · LONDON · NEW DELHI · SYDNEY

To Catherine Hendricks, Matt deLesdernier, and James Sefcik,
friends who for years have been a source of help,
encouragement, and inspiration

Bloomsbury Press
An imprint of Bloomsbury Publishing Plc

1385 Broadway	50 Bedford Square
New York	London
NY 10018	WC1B 3DP
USA	UK

BLOOMSBURY and the Diana logo are trademarks of Bloomsbury Publishing Plc

Maps created by Gary Antonetti, Ortelius Design

ISBN: 978-1-62040-172-9

Typeset by RefineCatch Limited, Bungay, Suffolk
Printed and bound in the U.S.A.

CONTENTS

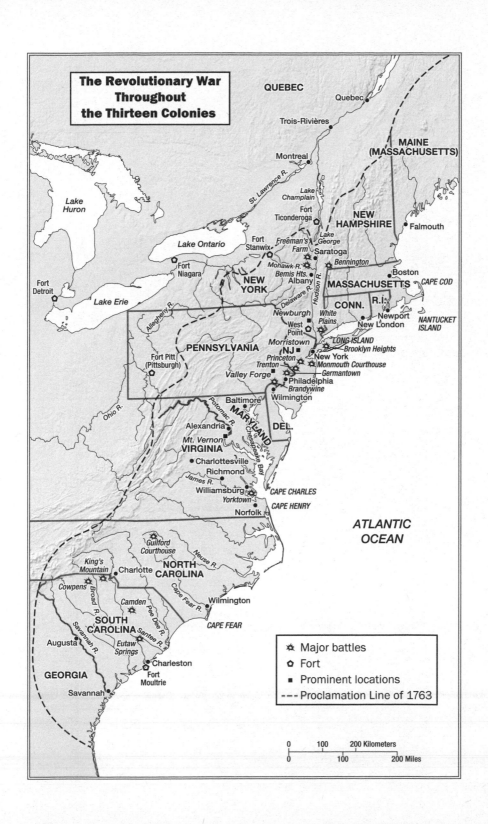

The Revolutionary War
Throughout
the Thirteen Colonies

QUEBEC

Quebec

Trois-Rivières

MAINE
(MASSACHUSETTS)

Montreal

St. Lawrence R.

Lake
Champlain

Fort
Ticonderoga

NEW
HAMPSHIRE

Falmouth

Lake
Huron

Lake Ontario

Fort
Stanwix

Freeman's
Farm

Lake
George

Saratoga

Bennington

Fort
Niagara

Mohawk R.

Bemis Hts.

Albany

Boston

CAPE COD

MASSACHUSETTS

Fort
Detroit

Lake Erie

NEW
YORK

Delaware R.

Hudson R.

CONN.

R.I.

Newburgh

White
Plains

Newport

New London

NANTUCKET
ISLAND

Allegheny R.

West
Point

Morristown

LONG ISLAND

Fort Pitt
(Pittsburgh)

PENNSYLVANIA

NJ

Princeton

Trenton

New York

Brooklyn Heights

Monmouth Courthouse

Germantown

Valley Forge

Philadelphia

Ohio R.

Baltimore

Potomac R.

Brandywine

Wilmington

MARYLAND

DEL.

Alexandria

Mt. Vernon

VIRGINIA

Chesapeake Bay

Charlottesville

Richmond

James R.

Williamsburg

Yorktown

CAPE CHARLES

CAPE HENRY

Norfolk

ATLANTIC
OCEAN

Guilford
Courthouse

Neuse R.

King's
Mountain

Charlotte

NORTH
CAROLINA

Cowpens

Broad R.

Camden

Pee Dee R.

Wilmington

Cape Fear R.

SOUTH
CAROLINA

Santee R.

CAPE FEAR

Augusta

Savannah R.

Eutaw
Springs

GEORGIA

Charleston

Fort
Moultrie

Savannah

Major battles

Fort

Prominent locations

--- Proclamation Line of 1763

0   100   200 Kilometers
0   100   200 Miles

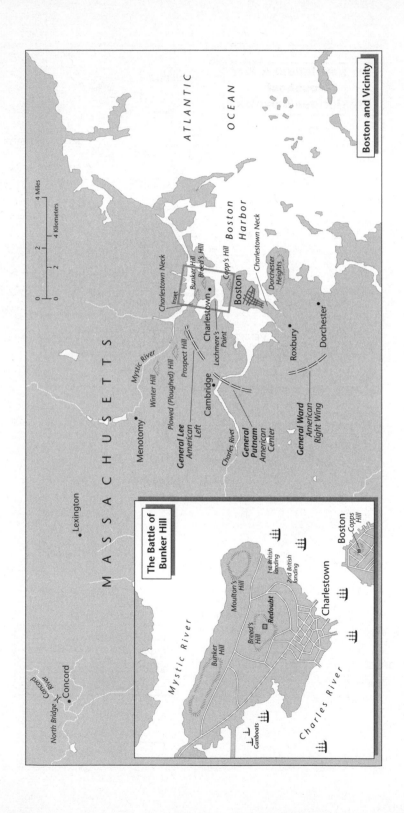

Boston and Vicity

ATLANTIC

OCEAN

M A S S A C H U S E T T S

Mystic River

Menotomy

Winter Hill

Plowed (Ploughed) Hill

Prospect Hill

*General Lee
American
Left*

Lexington

Concord

North Bridge

Concord River

Charles River

Cambridge

*General Putnam
American
Center*

*General Ward
American
Right Wing*

Roxbury

Dorchester

Charlestown Neck

Inset

Bunker Hill

Breed's Hill

Copp's Hill

Charlestown

Lechmere's
Point

Boston

*Boston
Harbor*

Charlestown Neck

Dorchester
Heights

4 Miles

4 Kilometers

0   2   4

The Battle of Bunker Hill

Mystic River

Bunker
Hill

Moulton's
Hill

Breed's
Hill

Redoubt

1st British
landing

2nd British
landing

Charlestown

Boston

Copps
Hill

Gunboats

Charles River

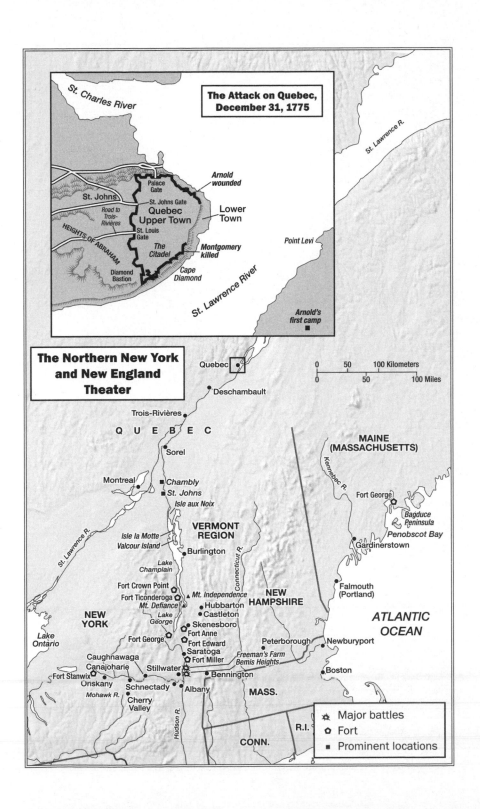

The Attack on Quebec, December 31, 1775

St. Charles River

Arnold wounded

Palace Gate

St. Johns Gate

St. Johns

Road to Trois-Rivières

Quebec Upper Town

Lower Town

St. Louis Gate

HEIGHTS OF ABRAHAM

The Citadel

Montgomery killed

Point Levi

Diamond Bastion

Cape Diamond

St. Lawrence River

Arnold's first camp

St. Lawrence R.

The Northern New York and New England Theater

Quebec

Deschambault

0   50   100 Kilometers
0   50   100 Miles

Trois-Rivières

Q U E B E C

MAINE (MASSACHUSETTS)

Sorel

Montreal

Chambly

St. Johns

Isle aux Noix

Kennebec R.

Fort George

VERMONT REGION

Bagduce Peninsula

Penobscot Bay

Isle la Motte

Valcour Island

Gardinerstown

Burlington

Lake Champlain

St. Lawrence R.

Connecticut R.

Fort Crown Point

Fort Ticonderoga

Mt. Defiance

Mt. Independence

NEW HAMPSHIRE

Falmouth (Portland)

Lake George

Hubbarton

Castleton

NEW YORK

Fort George

Skenesboro

Fort Anne

Fort Edward

Saratoga

Fort Miller

Peterborough

Newburyport

ATLANTIC OCEAN

Lake Ontario

Caughnawaga

Canajoharie

Stillwater

Freeman's Farm

Bemis Heights

Fort Stanwix

Oriskany

Schnectady

Bennington

Boston

Mohawk R.

Albany

MASS.

Cherry Valley

Hudson R.

R.I.

CONN.

☆ Major battles
⬠ Fort
■ Prominent locations

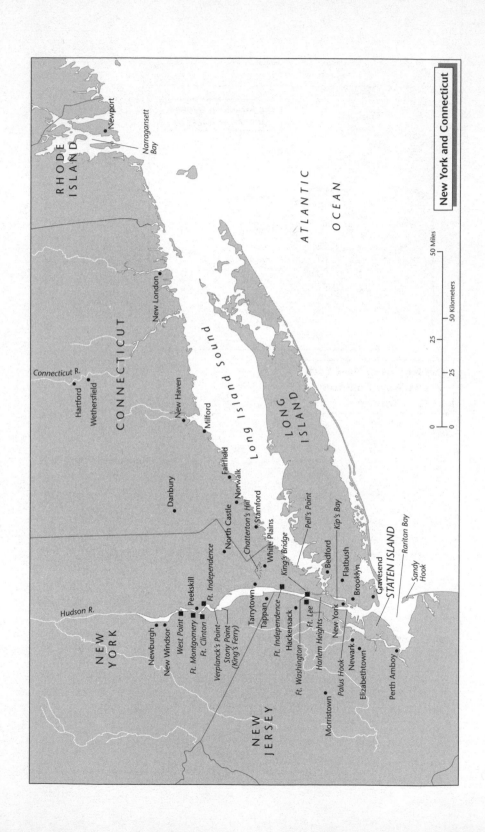

New York and Connecticut

RHODE ISLAND

Newport

Narragansett Bay

CONNECTICUT

New London

Hartford
Wethersfield
Connecticut R.

New Haven

Milford

Fairfield
Norwalk
Danbury
North Castle
Chatterton's Hill
Stamford
White Plains

LONG ISLAND SOUND

Long Island Sound

LONG ISLAND

Pell's Point
Kip's Bay

King's Bridge
Bedford
Flatbush
Brooklyn
Gravesend

STATEN ISLAND

Raritan Bay
Sandy Hook

ATLANTIC OCEAN

NEW YORK

Hudson R.
Newburgh
New Windsor
West Point
Peekskill
Ft. Montgomery
Ft. Clinton
Ft. Independence
Verplanck's Point
Stony Point
(King's Ferry)
Tarrytown
Tappan
Ft. Independence
Hackensack
Ft. Lee
Ft. Washington
Harlem Heights
New York
Palus Hook
Newark
Elizabethtown
Perth Amboy

NEW JERSEY

Morristown

50 Miles

50 Kilometers

0   25   25

0   25   50

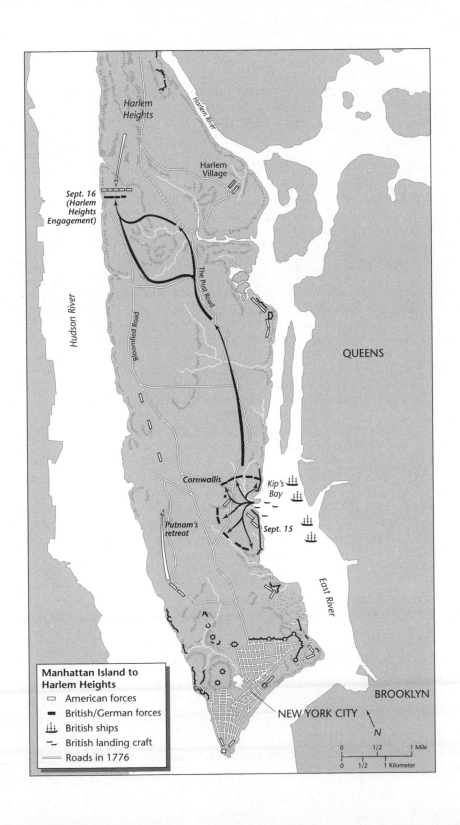

Harlem
Heights

Harlem River

Harlem Village

Sept. 16
(Harlem
Heights
Engagement)

The Post Road

Hudson River

Bloomfield Road

QUEENS

Cornwallis

Kip's
Bay

Putnam's
retreat

Sept. 15

East River

NEW YORK CITY

BROOKLYN

N

**Manhattan Island to
Harlem Heights**

- American forces
- British/German forces
- British ships
- British landing craft
- Roads in 1776

0   1/2   1 Mile

0   1/2   1 Kilometer

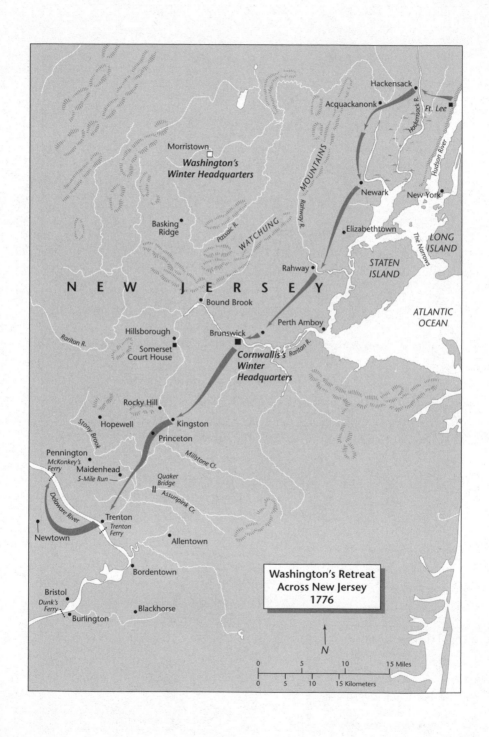

Hackensack

Acquackanonk

Ft. Lee

Hackensack R.

Morristown

Washington's Winter Headquarters

Newark

New York

Hudson River

Basking Ridge

Passaic R.

WATCHUNG

Rahway R.

MOUNTAINS

Elizabethtown

STATEN ISLAND

The Narrows

LONG ISLAND

N E W   J E R S E Y

Bound Brook

Rahway

Perth Amboy

ATLANTIC OCEAN

Raritan R.

Hillsborough

Brunswick

Cornwallis's Winter Headquarters

Somerset Court House

Raritan R.

Rocky Hill

Kingston

Stony Brook

Hopewell

Princeton

Millstone Cr.

Pennington

McKonkey's Ferry

Maidenhead

5-Mile Run

Quaker Bridge

Assunpink Cr.

Delaware River

Trenton

Trenton Ferry

Newtown

Allentown

Bordentown

Bristol

Dunk's Ferry

Blackhorse

Burlington

Washington's Retreat Across New Jersey 1776

N

| 0 | | 5 | | 10 | | 15 Miles |

| 0 | 5 | | 10 | | 15 Kilometers |

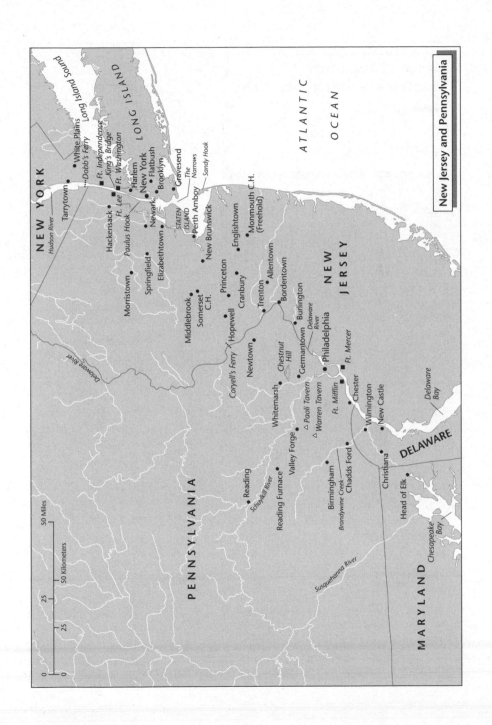

New Jersey and Pennsylvania

NEW YORK

Long Island Sound

LONG ISLAND

White Plains
Dobb's Ferry
Ft. Independence
King's Bridge
Ft. Washington
Tarrytown
Harlem
New York
Flatbush
Brooklyn
Gravesend
The Narrows
Sandy Hook

Hudson River

Hackensack
Ft. Lee
Paulus Hook
Newark
STATEN ISLAND
Perth Amboy
New Brunswick
Englishtown
Monmouth C.H. (Freehold)

Morristown
Springfield
Elizabethtown
Princeton
Cranbury
Allentown
Bordentown

Middlebrook
Somerset C.H.
Hopewell
Trenton
Burlington

NEW JERSEY

PENNSYLVANIA

Coryell's Ferry
Newtown
Chestnut Hill
Germantown
Philadelphia
Ft. Mercer

Delaware River

Whitemarsh
Paoli Tavern
Warren Tavern
Ft. Mifflin
Chester

Reading

Valley Forge

Wilmington
New Castle

Schuylkill River

Reading Furnace

Birmingham
Chadds Ford
Christiana

DELAWARE

Brandywine Creek

Head of Elk

Delaware River

Delaware Bay

MARYLAND

Chesapeake Bay

Susquehanna River

ATLANTIC OCEAN

0   25   50 Miles
0   25   50 Kilometers

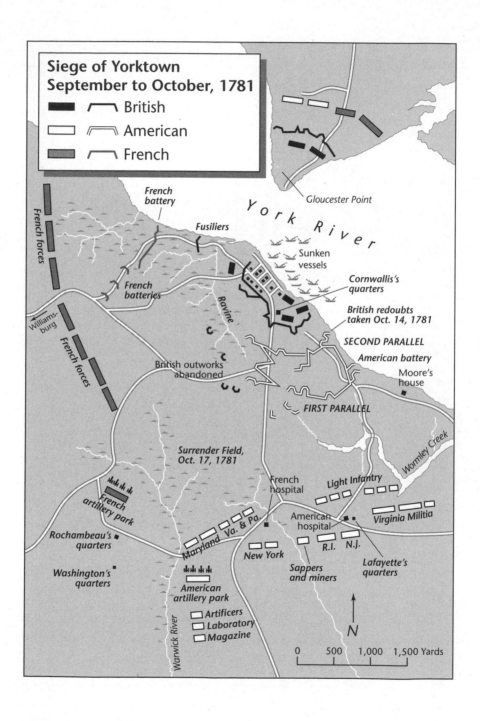

**Siege of Yorktown
September to October, 1781**

British

American

French

Gloucester Point

French battery

Fusiliers

Y o r k R i v e r

Sunken vessels

French forces

French batteries

Cornwallis's quarters

Williamsburg

Ravine

British redoubts taken Oct. 14, 1781

French forces

British outworks abandoned

SECOND PARALLEL

American battery

Moore's house

FIRST PARALLEL

Wormley Creek

Surrender Field, Oct. 17, 1781

French hospital

Light Infantry

French artillery park

Virginia Militia

Rochambeau's quarters

Maryland Va. & Pa.

American hospital

R.I. N.J.

New York

Washington's quarters

Sappers and miners

Lafayette's quarters

American artillery park

Artificers

Laboratory

Magazine

Warwick River

N

0   500   1,000   1,500 Yards

PREFACE

No event in American history has been more significant than the American Revolution. The colonial revolt appeared to rise up out of nowhere, and even after a decade of protest, a considerable portion of those who supported the insurgency opposed breaking with Great Britain and establishing an independent American nation. But independence was declared, and unlike any other nation ever created, the new United States was born with an exhilarating and explicit commitment to the natural rights and equality of its citizenry.

Independence may have been declared in 1776, but it still had to be won. Years of bloody warfare followed. The death toll was staggering, for soldiers and noncombatants. Of all the wars in the history of the United States, only the Civil War witnessed a greater percentage of deaths among those who soldiered. The ratio of mortality among American servicemen in World War I and World War II did not come remotely close to that of the Revolutionary War. This was also a war that America came very close to losing. At the start of the conflict's seventh year, in 1781, victory was far from assured. Looking back, it is astonishing that America emerged victorious from its long struggle and that the nascent United States—and the American Revolution—endured. Indeed, more than a few contemporaries were surprised that that United States survived its birth pangs.

As a professor, I taught the American Revolution course more than thirty times, and each time I vowed to someday write a history of that stirring event. It wasn't that the Revolution was in danger of being forgotten. Important events and people from the Revolutionary era are iconic in the national culture. The Founders appear on our currency, show up in television advertising, are the subjects of movies, are depicted in myriad statues, attract well over a million visitors annually to their homes, and of course have books written about them. Though Congress almost forgot to celebrate the first anniversary of its having declared independence, no one has forgotten it since, and it is annually commemorated just as John Adams said it should be:

with parades, picnics, games, and fireworks. Reenactors relive assorted Revolutionary War battles, usually on the preserved sites where the engagements took place; many museums feature artifacts from the period; everything from Washington's crossing of the Delaware to his wartime spy network have been the subject of recent television movies; and a few years ago a popular movie treated the South's partisan warfare. Nearly every American knows something about the American Revolution. It is part of our shared memory.

But memories are notoriously inaccurate, and when what is remembered is part of a nation's origin, there is always the possibility that some things— pleasant and unpleasant—may be forgotten or misrepresented. The job of the historian is to apprehend and assess past events and those who played a part in them, to come to grips with what occurred and the reasons for the occurrences, to understand who or what was responsible for what transpired, and to evaluate those who played leading roles in the upheaval. That is what I have attempted here with the American Revolution.

This book differs from most other histories of the American Revolution in several ways. It emphasizes that the colonial insurgency was caused, and driven, by economic factors and by the desire of colonists to exercise greater control over their destiny, which in itself often had an economic basis. I don't suggest that ideas about freedom and liberty were unimportant; ideas provided a prism for how the colonists saw themselves and the actions of leaders in the mother country. Nor was ambition insignificant. The desire to improve one's lot—whether economically or by gaining power and renown— shaped the conduct of a great many actors in the Revolution. Men such as Adams and George Washington spoke frankly of their yearning for honor and reputation.

But take away the economic incentives and, in my judgment, the American Revolution would not have occurred, at least not when it did. This is the story of merchants who sought the freedom to trade wherever a lucrative market existed and of those whose economic well-being was tied to that of the merchants—sailors, stevedores and longshoremen, artisans, shopkeepers, and farmers on an urban periphery. It is the story of great planters yearning for more lucrative investments in western lands and of small farmers eager to acquire new, fertile acreage for themselves or their children—all frustrated by decisions made in London. Obstructed by imperial policies—oppressed by a faraway government, the colonists would have said—Americans first sought greater freedom within the British Empire. When their hopes were frustrated, they moved slowly toward a more radical solution, American independence. While the more affluent colonists generally remained in control of the insurgency until 1776, many ordinary colonists came to see a connection between a better future for themselves and the reduction of the imperial government's sway over their lives. Less British control came to mean jobs, better incomes, a better life. Colonists came to see, too, that Britain's imperial leaders sought to protect and advance Great Britain's national interests, principally those of England. American interests were secondary. In fact, what at times was of paramount importance to Americans was thought in London to be contrary to British interests. In time, a majority of American colonists came to believe that severing ties with Great Britain was essential for American peace and prosperity.

Breaking with the mother country was not taken lightly. As one writer in 1776 warned, it was "a leap in the dark," a vault into fearsome uncertainty. But rage—a deep, abounding anger toward what was thought to be Britain's tyrannical designs and the haughty nabobs that held power and made imperial policy—pushed many to the precipice. Insurgents were also driven by a seething hatred of Royal officials in America, and especially of those colonists who served imperial interests. Those who wished to cut ties with Great Britain were spurred by the hope of replacing the perceived traitors of their native land with Americans who would serve the interests of America and its people.

But neither economics nor rage can fully explain the colonists' decision to go their own way. Americans in 1776 believed deeply that their revolt would usher in a better world—a freer, happier, and more peaceful world, in which individuals would exert greater control over their destiny. Some even dreamed that the American Revolution would spark change in the monarchies of Europe. For them, the American Revolution was but the first step in sweeping changes that lay on the horizon.

Some historians feel that the colonists were uneasy with imperial rule from the moment that the first outposts were established and that long-held vexations in their relationship with London were pivotal in bringing on the Revolution. That troubles existed is undeniable, but I believe that throughout history, most great revolutions have come as a surprise, and that subsequent generations, in trying to understand what occurred, discover roots that were not in fact the fulcrum for revolutionary behavior. John Adams expressed his surprise when the first colonial protests occurred in 1765, and in 1776 he said that he was astonished at the speed with which the sentiment for American independence had grown, even though he had been a leader in the fight to separate from the mother country. To him, the American Revolution was unexpected, as I think it was to most colonists. This book argues that the colonists were generally happy with the imperial relationship in the early

1760s, and for a considerable time thereafter. If Great Britain, in fact, had repealed most of its objectionable new colonial policies, as the First Continental Congress demanded in 1774, returning the Anglo-American relationship to where it had stood in 1763, Congress would not have declared independence.

This book also differs from most other histories of the American Revolution in that it treats the war as no less important than the political rebellion that led to the break with the mother country. Adams famously wrote to Thomas Jefferson in 1815, asking "what do we Mean by the Revolution? The War? That was no part of the Revolution." Some historians have taken Adams at his word, but I don't. I believe that Adams was incorrect. The War of Independence was no small event in the lives of the revolutionary genera-tion. In some way or other it touched everyone. People died, suffered life-changing wounds, lost loved ones, sacrificed, paid exorbitant taxes, and lived with shuddering anxieties. It was a radicalizing agent. Without the war, inde-pendence would not have been declared. The war changed people, and hostil-ities led to changes that in some instances were not immediately apparent. The war influenced how the Revolutionary generation saw itself and its world, and it was important in shaping what contemporaries wanted in post-Revolutionary America.

Unlike many histories of the American Revolution, this one focuses not just on the colonies but on the mother country as well. It examines the choices faced by imperial leaders and the reasons for their decisions. There were foes of Britain's policy toward the colonists at every step. I have assayed the alternatives proposed by the opposition and the role of popular opinion. British leaders made decisions about going to war, how to wage the war, and ultimately whether to make peace. What happened in London was crucially important in America, and it receives abundant attention.

Historians have never reached a consensus about when the American Revolution concluded. I agree with those who think it has never ended, given that the egalitarian and natural-rights ideas of the Revolution have inspired subsequent generations down to the present. Nevertheless, a history of the American Revolution has to come to an end somewhere. Some works have carried the story through the ratification of the Constitution and George Washington's inauguration as president in 1789, some through Jefferson's election to the presidency in 1801, and some through the War of 1812. This book concludes with the Treaty of Paris of 1783, a choice I made because the agreement to end hostilities brought to a close the sequence of events set in motion some twenty years earlier by British policies: American protests, then insurgency, and finally revolution and war. Furthermore, contemporaries looked on the period from 1763 to 1783—the span roughly formed by the onset of alarming imperial policies and the peace treaty that finally brought an end to a once seemingly endless war—as one long, interconnected epoch.

In a sense, half of this book deals with the period until the Declaration of Independence and the other half with the war and the changes brought about by the American Revolution. In fact, the colonial rebellion, the domestic revolution, and the armed conflict were intermingled, a disorderly jumble that I attempt to unravel.

Although the events of the American Revolution occurred a long time ago, this distant historical experience remains relevant today. The irresolvable issue down to 1776 was that of the power and sovereignty of Parliament and the British monarch, and much of the current partisan politics swirl around the extent of the federal government's authority. Many today view with alarm the scope of executive power, just as the Founders anguished over hereditary monarchy and its capacity for accumulating authority. Yet numerous others today see a powerful government in a positive light, much as many Founders came to feel that the central government needed greater power to meet urgent military and economic crises. Many now worry about government's regulation of the economy, as did colonists who thought that their well-being was jeopardized by imperial trade regulations and proclamations prohibiting western migration. Many colonists believed that Great Britain was irredeemably corrupt, and nowadays there are those who fear that America is in the maw of corruption and decline. Our current federal officeholders may be more unpopular at home than British officials were with colonists in 1776; in fact, two notable Revolutionary-era British officials, William Pitt and Edmund Burke, may have been more well liked by colonists than any current American official is by today's citizenry. America appears to some to be under the sway of a plutocracy at the moment, much as England was in the eighteenth century. Money now so dominates politics and politicians that some Americans wonder whether they are citizens or subjects, much as many colonists wondered at the time of the American Revolution.

The British Empire was awash with war. It waged four major wars in the seventy-five years before the War of Independence, a track record not unlike that of the United States during the past century. At the height of the Anglo-American crisis, Britain's rulers refused to bend and compromise, often contending that national weakness and deterioration were certain to follow any substantive concessions, and there are those today who argue that American conciliation toward adversaries is certain to be followed by national ruin. Troublingly, too, the British government went to war with the colonists in 1775 after cavalierly brushing aside those who predicted a long, difficult, and perhaps unwinnable war, the very sort of misjudgment that America's leaders made in two wars in the past half century. We can learn from history, from wise choices and dreadful decisions, from extraordinary statesmanship and inept leadership, and the American Revolution provides many examples of both good and bad.

Great societal forces are always at work in any big historical event. That isn't in dispute. Even so, I believe that people make history. What occurred in the American Revolution flowed from the choices that individuals made. Men and women decided whether to join the rebellion or to remain loyal to the king. Men did not always have a choice of whether or not to soldier, but if they wound up in the army or the militia and were faced with combat, they had to choose whether to fight or run, to try to kill or not to kill. Indian tribes had to choose between the belligerents, or to remain neutral. Even those who were not free, like most black Americans, sometimes had to decide whether to gamble everything on the risk of a flight for freedom. In reconstructing these events, I tried to keep in mind—and the reader must as well—that when individuals made their choices, they had not the slightest idea what the future held for them. I chose Howard Pyle's 1906 painting *The Nation Makers* for the book's cover because it depicts ordinary Americans marching into battle, and I believe that without the protests, the ideals, and the sacrifices of ordinary people, the American Revolution would neither have occurred nor succeeded. Nevertheless, there were leaders, and their importance cannot be overlooked. Samuel Adams played a crucial role in fostering and organizing Boston's protest, John Adams craftily managed Congress's slow passage toward declaring independence, Thomas Jefferson's eloquence sharpened the meaning of the Declaration of Independence, and General Washington's political shrewdness may have kept alive a fight that could have faltered and failed under another commander in chief.

Americans are familiar with the tarring and feathering during the colonial insurgency, though by and large the American Revolution is not widely remembered for its violence. Many of the most common images of the American Revolution have been purged of violence. Arguably, the most popular paintings are benign portraits of leaders, or of scenes depicting the British surrender at Saratoga or Yorktown, the committee charged with drafting a declaration on independence presenting its handiwork to Congress, General Washington being rowed across the Delaware River or kneeling and praying in the snow, or soldiers shivering in the cold. Pictorial images that show the landscape littered with bodies, such as those of Gettysburg or of Normandy's beaches—are noticeably missing from the American Revolution. But the American Revolution was indeed harsh and brutal. Soldiers who lay wounded on the battlefield were killed by the enemy; people were beaten and

sometimes tortured; property was confiscated and destroyed; large numbers
were jailed, executed, and driven into exile; soldiers were treated by their
officers in ways that approached barbarism; and soldiers in turn were known
to have harmed civilians, including molesting women.

While this is a book about the causes of the American Revolution, the war
that won it, and the meaning of the Revolution, it is also about the revolutionaries themselves. The book evaluates those who held high civil and military
positions, lesser-known individuals who joined the protests and managed
affairs at the local level, and above all, those who bore arms as Continental
soldiers and sailors or militiamen. This is not a book that spins fairy tales or
that depicts the Founders as unique geniuses. Even the most revered leaders
of the Revolution blundered from time to time. Historians have an obligation
to dispassionately assess causes and outcomes, conduct and performance,
and that is what I have attempted, letting the chips fall wherever.

The book's title is taken from a line in a letter that John Adams wrote to
his wife during the final, tempestuous weeks leading to the Declaration of
Independence. Adams told Abigail that judgment and courage were required
"to ride in this Whirlwind." When her little hamlet in Massachusetts was
overrun by a terrible wartime epidemic spawned by diseases in the nearby
army camps, felling one of her children and killing her mother, Abigail briefly
questioned the colonists' wisdom at having embarked on this "Whirlwind."
Borrowing from John and Abigail Adams and calling this book *Whirlwind*
seemed appropriate, for the Anglo-American troubles spawned a vortex that
swept up everyone and nearly everything in colonial America.

Forty years after the first shots were fired in the War of Independence,
John Adams asked Thomas Jefferson, "Who shall write the history of the
American revolution? Who can write it? Who shall ever be able to write it?"
Jefferson answered, "Nobody; except maybe its external facts." Thinking that
so much had occurred in secret that no historian could ever unravel what had
transpired, Adams and Jefferson touched on the problem that faces every
historian and biographer. They were both right and wrong. As with all historical events, some things can never be known by subsequent generations. But
thankfully, a trove of letters, diaries, journals, newspapers, and recollections
left by actors in the drama of the American Revolution has survived, and
those primary sources afford a glance behind the curtain. Despite the skepti-
cism of Adams and Jefferson, good histories of the American Revolution have
been written. My aim is to add some new perspective to that list.

Debts accumulate in the course of writing a book. I am particularly grateful
to Matt deLesdernier and James Sefcik, who over the years have offered

guidance on many literary and historical matters. I can't begin to count the ways that Catherine Hendricks has helped me, but for two things I am especially thankful: One cold winter morning, Catherine took my picture that appears on the dust jacket. She was also instrumental in helping me decide on both the book's title and its cover illustration. Keith Pacholl, Benjamin Carp, Arthur Lefkowitz, Jim Piecuch, Edith Gelles, David Waldstreicher, Andrew Clayton, Fred Anderson, and Lawrence Babits generously answered questions. Lorene Flanders, who has graciously supported my research and writing, provided an office that I used daily while working on the book. Angela Mehaffey and Margot David in the interlibrary loan office of the Irvine Sullivan Ingram Library at the University of West Georgia unfailingly met my frequent requests for books and articles, and Gail Smith in Acquisitions saw to the purchase of some items that were important to my work. Julie Dobbs helped me out of numerous scrapes with my computer and word processing program, and Chris Harris kept my laptop humming along.

Geri Thoma, my literary agent, supported my notion of doing this book and provided encouragement—and much more—in seeing to its inception.

This is my eighth book with Peter Ginna, a masterful editor who, along with criticism, provides encouragement and a storehouse of wonderful ideas.

This is my first with George Gibson, who was supportive, understanding, and helpful. It is my second with Rob Galloway, whose assistance throughout the lengthy process of bringing a book to the light of day was deeply appreciated. This is my third book with Maureen Klier, who has no equal as a copy editor, and my first with Laura Phillips, an excellent production editor.

Sammy Grace, Simon, Katie, and Clementine may never read this book, but they enrich my life, and that makes the often-trying work of writing a book a bit easier.

Carol, my wife, has always supported my writing, and her understanding and patience has been crucial to my literary and scholarly activities.

"I SEE NOTHING BEFORE US BUT ACCUMULATING DISTRESS"

SNOW BLANKETED THE GROUND and gray, wintry clouds slid past overhead. January 1, 1781, had dawned, the beginning of the seventh year of the War of Independence. General George Washington's spirits were as gloomy as the weather and as the "dreary station," as he called it, that was his headquarters.[1] He was in New Windsor, New York, a twenty-year-old farming community on the Hudson River, about ten miles north of West Point. As was his habit, Washington had selected a roomy farmhouse for his headquarters, though since his aides also lodged there and sundry officers came and went on a daily basis, the Dutch-style stone house soon took on a congested and confining air that contributed to his sagging spirits.

But Washington's despair was due to more than his environment. Just over two years before, he had thought that the war was nearly won, that Great Britain was ready "to give up the matter" and make peace "upon almost any terms."[2] Now, not only was victory uncertain, but also America's chances of winning the war seemed to be slipping away. The Americans and their French allies had not won a major victory in more than three years. Defeats had been piling up, especially in the southern theater, where during the past two years three American armies had been routed. The greatest disaster had occurred six months earlier, when Charleston fell and nearly seven thousand American soldiers were killed or captured. Rebel officials had been ousted in Georgia, replaced by the royal government that had existed before 1776. Many believed it would not be long before the British retook all of South Carolina and restored a second province to their North American empire. No one thought that North Carolina could be saved from the British armed forces if South Carolina fell.

Defeats sapped morale, but so too did the seeming endlessness of the war. In the fall of 1780, Thomas Jefferson, the governor of Virginia, faced what he

called a "dangerous fire" of insurrection, as dissidents who once had supported the Revolution now sought to prevent the mobilization of the militia in
some counties. Alexander Hamilton, one of Washington's young aides, railed
at the growing war-weariness, charging that Americans "are determined not
to be free." Fearing that the war might be lost, Hamilton wrote, "Our affairs
are in a bad way." In September 1780, Virginia's Arthur Lee, a veteran diplomat, returned home for the first time since before the war began and
discovered that many Americans had come to believe that a peace settlement
short of independence was likely an "inevitable necessity."[3]

Despondent members of Congress spoke of "the present deranged situation," "our distressed Country," and "our . . . numberless distresses." The
"state of our public affairs wear a most melancholy Aspect," said one, while
another confessed that the nation was "pressed with Difficulties." One
congressman sighed late in 1780 that recent months had "Exhibited a Scene of
Misfortunes scarcely to be Equaled in History." Not a few feared that the
congressmen who had opposed declaring independence in 1776 might soon
regain control of Congress. Another wondered if, like the "Stiff necked
Israelites of old," Americans would have to "wander in the wilderness" for
generations before finally gaining independence. In their exasperation, some
privately questioned the leadership of the army and Congress. One exclaimed
to a friend that "those men & things in which we have placed great confidence, have rendered us but little Service."[4]

Nor was it only American spirits that suffered. John Adams reported from
Paris that the steady diet of bad news from America had "spread an Alarm
here." France had aided the American war effort for nearly five years and had
been an ally in the war for three, but aside from swelling economic woes, it
had nothing to show for its sacrifices. Warning that the peace faction in the
French ministry was gaining strength, Adams left no doubt that allied military victories were essential if France was to remain a belligerent. Congress
knew that Adams was not exaggerating. The French minister in Philadelphia
had warned earlier that European developments might compel France to
leave the war at any moment. Adams also advised Congress that many of
Europe's neutral nations favored an international conference to mediate the
dispute and bring to an end hostilities that had played havoc with their
commerce. Such a conference, Adams cautioned, would pose the greatest
threat to American independence of anything that had occurred since hostilities began in 1775. Nor was that all. As France's determination flagged, the
Netherlands—unwilling to find itself at war with Britain without its French
ally—backed off on extending a much-needed loan to the United States. The
"TIMES ARE PREGNANT," Adams remarked on the cusp of 1781.[5]

Observing that the "history of this War is a history of false hopes," Washington took stock in bleak terms. The army's officers "are mouldering away by dayly resignations." The army had "no Magazines . . . and in a little time we shall have no Men." The soldiers, lean and haggard, and now in the grip of yet another hard winter, had not been paid in ages. With foreboding, Washington told correspondents that the "Enemy . . . are probably preparing to push us in our enfeebled state." As he looked to the future, Washington saw "nothing before us but accumulating distress."[6]

The afflictions of which he spoke quickly worsened. Soldiers in the Pennsylvania Line mutinied on New Year's Day 1781. Washington not only feared other rebellions within the Continental army; he nervously expected that the enemy "might take advantage of the Revolt" by striking the vexed American troops in the dead of winter. He was correct on the first count. Mutinous "Jersey Troops" rose up three weeks later "in imitation of the Pennsylvania line" and marched on the state capital. Brooding and anxious, Washington told Congress that these revolts might portend "an end to all subordination in the Army."[7]

A palpable apprehension gripped those in a position to know just how bad conditions had become. The chances of an American victory were vanishing, and if the war was not won, the hopes and dreams that had been placed in the American Revolution would also disappear. Nine days into 1781, James Madison, a young member of Congress, told Governor Jefferson that confidence in America's cause had reached "a very serious aspect." At about the same moment, James Lovell, a Massachusetts congressman, was more blunt when he sent the news to John Adams: "I can only say that we are bankrupt with a mutinous army."[8]

CHAPTER I

"I AM A BRITON"

ON THE BRINK

EMPIRES EXIST FOR THE BENEFIT of the parent state. That, and the fact that the colonists eventually came to appreciate this truth, goes a long way toward explaining the origins of the American Revolution.

Throughout the seventeenth and eighteenth centuries, the authorities in London, the seat of Great Britain's empire, portrayed imperial governance as for the equal benefit of all. For 150 years, most American colonists appear to have found the notion convincing.

During all that time, the great majority of colonists thought that life in America was good, a belief that was also widespread throughout Great Britain and beyond. People immigrated in droves to Britain's mainland colonies. The population in the thirteen colonies increased eightfold in the seventy-five years after 1700. People were drawn by the belief that more abundant opportunities, and fewer adversities, existed in the colonies than in their homeland. The lion's share of those who came were English, though in the eighteenth-century floods of Germans and Scots-Irish from northern Ireland crossed the Atlantic, and by the close of the colonial era, the non-English made up about 20 percent of the population.

However, not all who crossed to America came voluntarily. The largest share of eighteenth-century immigrants were African slaves, who by the 1770s totaled nearly one-fifth of the colonial population.

By then, some 2.5 million people lived in colonies that stretched from the rugged wind-swept shores of northern New England to the steamy marshes and pine barrens of coastal Georgia. Settlements in most provinces extended from the Atlantic to the barrier posed by the western mountains, often one hundred miles or more inland. Some 95 percent of the colonists dwelled in rural areas, primarily on farms.

Most farms in the five southern colonies—Virginia, Maryland, North Carolina, South Carolina, and Georgia—produced tobacco, rice, or indigo, cash crops grown for exportation, as they could not be grown profitably in Britain. Little that was grown north of Maryland was sent to England, as farms above the Potomac River yielded mostly the same crops that were raised in the mother country. Those who worked the land in the mid-Atlantic colonies (Pennsylvania, Delaware, New Jersey, and New York) mostly produced grains, shipping much of their corn and wheat to urban centers such as New York and Philadelphia, but also to markets in the Caribbean sugar colonies. Farmers in New England (Massachusetts, Connecticut, Rhode Island, and New Hampshire) also raised grains, but as the land and climate were less accommodating in the more northerly regions, many yeomen turned to perishable items—dairy products, for instance—that were sent to nearby local markets. However, New Englanders were exporters, too, sending rum, lumber, barrels, fish, and of course some grains to foreign markets.

The colonies existed under charters bestowed by the British Crown, documents that the colonists came to think of as inviolable constitutions. The charters stipulated the structure of government, which did not vary greatly from one province to another. In most provinces, the executive, or governor, was appointed by the Crown and wielded considerable power, including the authority to grant land, appoint militia officers and some judges, and determine who sat on the council, a body that frequently functioned as both the executive's cabinet and the upper house of the assembly. The lower house, which everywhere was modeled on the House of Commons, was a more representative body. Its members were elected by adult white males who met property qualifications. As property ownership was widespread in the colonies, a degree of popular participation in government prevailed that was unknown in the parent state, or almost anyplace else in the Western world. Through their control of appropriations and the power to block much that the governor might desire, the elected assemblies over time garnered steadily more sway over provincial matters.

Life in Anglo-America might have been good for most freemen, but it was not trouble-free, and some thought that it could be improved. The residents of the backcountry often bridled with discontent. Though in many colonies about half the population lived in the backcountry, by the late colonial era, the west was almost always underrepresented in the assembly. With justification, westerners felt the revenue from the taxes they paid was more likely to go toward providing services—erecting bridges or improving harbors, for instance—for easterners. Religion was another rub. After mid-century, many in New England, whose Puritan ancestors had fled to America to escape an Anglican Church they thought tainted with the teachings and practices of Roman Catholicism, feared not only the growing power of "priest-ridden"

Anglicanism but also that an Anglican bishop for America might soon be appointed. So powerful were these concerns that late in life John Adams remarked that the "apprehension of episcopacy" had shaken the attachment of many New Englanders to Great Britain. Nor were religious tensions confined to New England. The Anglican Church was the state church in every southern colony, which meant that it was subsidized by the taxpayers whether or not they were Anglicans. Non-Anglicans—mostly Baptists and Presbyterians—stridently objected from mid-century onward to what they regarded as ecclesiastical oppression. They wanted religious freedom— "Liberty of conscience" was "the sacred property of every man," said one dissenter—and they wished to be free of the obligation to pay for the support of a church they despised.

Historian Rhys Isaac wrote that in "the eighteenth-century world a man had to be either a master or a servant." For freemen, conditions may not have been as bleak as Isaac's assertion suggests. The overwhelming majority were farmers who exercised a remarkable degree of individual autonomy. Nevertheless, power was concentrated in a few hands. Merchants dominated the cities, which in turn exerted regional dominion. Planter aristocrats presided in the South. Gentlemen, those who through wealth, education, or family status were viewed as well-bred and had attained social esteem, wielded authority everywhere and over almost everything, so that in fact the great mass of people were dependent on a small percentage of the population. Legislatures, the judiciary, the militia and any army that came into being were the purview of gentlemen. Leading families dominated local affairs, a predominance that often translated into greater access to things of import- ance, including land. Appearances suggest that the colonists acquiesced in the distribution of power without objection, but appearances can be deceiv- ing, and the American political history that commenced in the 1760s provides evidence that the groups that were marginalized in the colonial era sought a share of the power that once had been wielded by so few. Indeed, commercial growth brought steadily more wealth into the colonies in the eighteenth century, but it also increased the number of landless and resulted in more apparent divisions between the rich and the poor, a reality accentuated by an increasing tendency of the elite to ostentatiously display their wealth, beha- vior that often led ordianry colonists to bitterly express their resentment.

Commerce was the engine that provided economic growth and prosperity, and commercial grievances grew in the colonies as the eighteenth century progressed. Imperial planners wished for the colonial economies to be accessories to, not competitors with, the economy of Great Britain. From the point of view of the metropolis, the empire was best served by a colonial economy that remained overwhelmingly agricultural while Britain shipped manufactured goods—chiefly cloth and clothing, but over time increasing amounts of luxury items—to colonial consumers. Early on, Parliament passed legislation that restricted the manufacturing of some items in the colonies. Other laws confined portions of the colonial commerce to the empire, though Americans could trade most everything with foreign countries so long as Britain's customs duties were paid. Still other mercantile legislation imposed prohibitively high levies on some foreign trade, such as on sugar imported from France's Caribbean colonies.

At first blush, the colonists appeared to suffer under oppressive restrictions, and there were problems, perhaps the worst during most of the colonial era being the specie-draining trade imbalances that went hand in glove with the imperial system. However, New Englanders, who, given the nature of the region's economy, were most likely to be victimized by imperial constraints, were aided by the fact that Britain never rigorously enforced its trade laws. What is more, Yankee merchants turned smuggling into an art form, so they could often trade where they pleased. In addition, colonial merchants everywhere enjoyed real commercial benefits from being part of the British Empire. American ships and cargoes were protected by the Royal Navy—which lowered their insurance rates—and many American merchants and planters could not have done business without the credit extended by English bankers.[1]

Many colonists doubtless found the imperial commercial policies to be infuriating, but greater numbers were more likely deeply troubled by Great Britain's chronic warfare. Imperial interests, and the ruling elite's gluttonous hunger for ever more riches, kept Great Britain at war for nearly half the time during the three-quarters of a century preceding 1763. When the mother country went to war, moreover, the colonists were dragged into the hostilities. While the colonies were sometimes asked to furnish soldiers, they were always expected to cease trading with the enemy. Prices and taxes rose during wartime, and in American cities civilian seamen often fell prey to press gangs that dragooned them into the Royal Navy. Massachusetts was nearly driven to bankruptcy by its sacrifices during Great Britain's wars with Spain and France in the 1740s. While inflation drove up prices ninefold in four years, the province raised thousands of men, some by conscription, to meet London's demands. Soldiers from Massachusetts helped the British take Louisbourg on Nova Scotia's Cape Breton Island, the great French fortified outpost that guarded the entrance to the St. Lawrence River and New France. More than a thousand Yankees died in the siege of Louisbourg and the occupation that followed in the dank, cold Canadian winter. Massachusetts rejoiced at the hard-won victory, which was seen as the first step in the removal of the hated French enemy from the northern flank of Anglo-America. But just as London never consulted the colonists about going to war, it did not ask their opinion about terminating hostilities or making peace, and in the treaty that ended the fighting, Britain returned Louisbourg to France in exchange for prizes that better served the interests of powerful factions in England. John Adams, an adolescent at the time, later recalled the fury of the residents of his hamlet—Braintree, Massachusetts—at Great Britain's coldhearted indifference both to the price paid by the Yankee soldiers and colonists and to New England's vital interests.

If the colonists anticipated a lengthy period of peace following that war, they were disappointed. Shooting began in the next imperial war six years later. Another Anglo-French war was likely inevitable, but this one was hastened by high rollers in Virginia who had invested heavily in the Ohio Company, an enterprise that sought to open and settle the broad, fertile stretch of land north of the Ohio River and west of the Appalachians. When France in 1750 deployed an army in what the colonists called the Ohio Country, Virginia's governor asked London how to respond. By 1753, the governor was instructed to inform the French that the Ohio Country belonged to Great Britain and to demand that the French army abandon the region. The governor needed a volunteer to deliver the message. George Washington, a twenty-one-year-old, stepped forward, eager for adventure and impatient to win renown.

There were three ways that an ambitious young Virginian with neither a formal education nor much money might rise to prominence. He could become a surveyor, achieve iconic status as a soldier, or marry well. Washington eventually did all three. He had begun to work as a surveyor at age sixteen. When the French spurned the message that Washington delivered in 1753, Virginia created an army—the Virginia Regiment—to win the Ohio Country through military action. Washington soon became the commander of that army. Once he was acclaimed a military hero, Washington married the wealthiest widow in Virginia.

In 1754, Washington, twenty-two years old and a lieutenant colonel despite his lack of military experience, led Virginia's army toward the Ohio Country just as the spring foliage was bursting out. His force of some two hundred Virginians and a few Indian allies struggled through the tangled, hilly woodlands of Maryland and what now is western Pennsylvania, advancing to within a few miles of the head of the Ohio River. When scouts returned with word that a party of French soldiers was just ahead, Washington had to make a rapid decision. War had not been declared. Moreover, his orders were to "act on the Difensive." But mad for glory, callow young Washington ordered an ambush. Creeping stealthily through the wet, dense forest, he discovered that the small French party was preparing breakfast; having no reason to suspect that danger lurked, their commander had posted no sentries. Washington ordered his men to encircle the French while the Seneca tribesmen with him formed an outer ring. Nerve-racking minutes passed while the men silently took their places. If Washington had second thoughts about striking, he did not turn aside. When all was ready, the young Virginian screamed the order to attack.

The surprise attack was a bloodbath. Some of the French soldiers were killed or wounded in the first volley. Others died trying to escape through the impenetrable two rings of soldiers surrounding them. The Indians scalped some of the wounded and decapitated one fallen soldier. Soon, this small patch of sunless forest was littered with the corpses of upwards of a dozen French soldiers. Once the carnage ended, Washington read the papers that he found on the body of the deceased French commander. This had not been a war party. The French were delivering a message to the English, much as Washington had done six months earlier when he had carried the communiqué of Virginia's governor to the French. Washington's rash act may have been a blunder, but he was ecstatic. He gushed, "I heard the Bullets whistle and believe me there was something charming in the sound."[2]

The French immediately retaliated, sending a large army after Washington from nearby Fort Duquesne (at present-day Pittsburgh). The French found their prey at Fort Necessity, a rude circular redoubt that Washington had hastily constructed in the Pennsylvania wilderness. The engagement that followed was one-sided. In half a day's fighting, one-third of Washington's men were casualties, including many who had suffered fatal wounds. Washington surrendered. After burying his dead, Washington was allowed to march his vanquished army back to Virginia, though he was required to leave his cannon in the hands of the French.

Worse was to come for the British. The following year, London dispatched an army of more than a thousand British regulars under General Edward Braddock to achieve what the Virginians had failed to accomplish. Accompanied by Washington and a force of several hundred colonials, Braddock plunged toward Fort Duquesne, taking the road the Virginians had cut the previous year. Braddock's army never reached the Ohio. At a spot not far from the decaying remains of Fort Necessity, it stumbled into a large force of French and Indians and Canadian militiamen. A slaughter ensued. Braddock was killed and two-thirds of his men died or were wounded. Braddock's pitiless defeat triggered declarations of war in

Europe's capitals, and before the conflict finally ended in 1763, it had become a world war.

The Seven Years' War—or French and Indian War, as Americans have been wont to call it—was long and grim. For years, nothing went right in the American theater. An attempt to retake Louisbourg ended in failure, as did a couple of bloody campaigns in New York. The citizenry's spirits were sustained by the authorities and their spokesmen, who drew on the deep reservoir of anti-Catholicism and anti-French sentiment in Anglo-America. The tide finally turned when William Pitt, who had served in several British ministries during the past dozen years, was called on to form a government. Masterfully, Pitt acquired continental allies to help with the fighting in Europe, sent twenty thousand British regulars to America, ordered the colonists to furnish an equal number of soldiers, and waged a withering war on the high seas that ultimately vanquished France's navy. In 1758, an Anglo-American force that included Colonel Washington and Virginia's army took Fort Duquesne. Quebec fell during the following year, and in 1760 the British took Montreal. British colonists exalted. France, labeled the pope's "proud Antichristian Whore" by many a colonial preacher, had been humbled.[3]

Some seventy-five thousand colonists had soldiered during the Seven Years' War. Year after year, Virginia fielded an army of more than two thousand men; Massachusetts raised even larger armies, usually about four times the size of Virginia's, until upwards of 60 percent of men of military age in the Bay Colony had borne arms. No one knows exactly how many Americans died, but the death toll certainly ran into the thousands. Perhaps hundreds of colonial soldiers died alongside Braddock, and in the following year, 1756, one-third of those in the Virginia Regiment commanded by Washington were killed or wounded. Hundreds from northern provinces, chiefly New Yorkers and New Englanders, died in the bloody assault on Fort Carillon (later Fort Ticonderoga) and the siege of Fort William Henry, and countless others perished in campaigns along the northern frontier and in Canada. Over three hundred men from Boston alone perished.

Mounting casualty lists were only part of the toll for the colonists. Commerce was interrupted, inflation was rampant, and labor shortages drove numerous urban businesses into bankruptcy. The cost to the colonies of waging the war was staggering. Virginia spent more than £600,000 prosecuting the war. Massachusetts spent even more. Two years before the war ended, Massachusetts already carried a public debt of £350,000, a sum that with interest would cost nearly double to retire. Taxes quickly soared to fearsome levels. "Taxes on taxes are multiplied" and caused "a heavy burden," sighed a Virginian. Another dryly noted that Virginia's assembly had levied "every kind of tax ever devised" to pay for the war. In the face of skyrocketing taxation and economic dislocation, property foreclosures climbed to unprecedented levels in some colonies.[4]

But Great Britain had gained a magnificent victory, as was recognized in the Treaty of Paris of 1763. Great Britain obtained all of North America east of the Mississippi River, as France relinquished its claims and Spain was stripped of Florida. France was gone from New England's northern border. No longer could it arm and incite the Indians, reducing the likelihood of recurrent frontier warfare, with all its terror, expense, and upheaval. Land-hungry colonists and land speculators rejoiced at the opportunities awaiting them in the newly won fertile country that splayed westward in trans-Appalachia. Most colonists appeared to swell with pride at being part of a triumphant empire, a spirit captured by an ecstatic American poet who rejoiced that the "glorious Conflict's done! And *British* valour has the conquest won!"[5] Americans euphorically pronounced themselves blessed to live in such a magnificent empire and under such an "indulgent Mother" country. Caught up in the rapture, Pennsylvania's Benjamin Franklin proudly boasted, "I am a Briton." Franklin had plenty of company. Many colonists still referred to England as "home." They exuberantly erected memorials to fallen British heroes, named towns for them, and mourned the death of their king, George II, who passed away in 1760. Spontaneous celebrations occurred when word arrived of the coronation of the new monarch, George III.[6]

After nearly a quarter century of war, peace had arrived. With no prospect of renewed hostilities clouding the horizon, Americans could at last get on with the business of living their lives unruffled by armed conflict and faraway governments. They were ready to enjoy peace and the fruits of victory. In one of countless exultant sermons on America's glorious future, a New England minister jubilantly proclaimed the commencement of the "Era of our quiet Enjoyment of . . . Liberties . . . till time shall be no more."[7]

CHAPTER 2

"LOYAL BUT JEALOUS OF THEIR LIBERTIES"

CHANGES IN IMPERIAL POLICY AND THE COLONISTS' THINKING, 1759–1766

THE COLONISTS LIKELY would have been startled had they been privy to the private discussions among the imperial leaders during the twenty or so years before 1763. The sense had developed among ministers that London must establish closer supervision over the colonies. This was not a new thought. The century-old trade regulations had been inspired by the desire to manage colonial commerce, and now and then during the previous one hundred years the need for greater control had been revisited. Before mid-century, for instance, some in London expressed concern that New England's economic development had made it "already the Rival and Supplantress of her Mother" country, and one writer warned that unless restrictions were put in place "the Independency of New England ... must be the Consequence: a fatal Consequence to this Kingdom!" [1] But talk of tighter controls usually ended in nothing more than the creation of a board with scant authority.

Lax enforcement had in part been due to a woefully inadequate bureaucracy for such a far-flung empire. Even more, the recurrent warfare got in the way. It was thought to be imprudent to demand that the colonists help win wars while at the same time tightening the screws on their freedom of behavior. But warfare cannot fully explain the failure to bring to bear British authority. During the more than two decades that Sir Robert Walpole served as prime minister—from the 1720s into the 1740s—Britain's government, though fully aware of widespread smuggling by colonial merchants, had chosen not to make an issue of it. Convinced that 50 percent of the money that resulted from American commerce would "be in his majesty's exchequer" within two years, Walpole thought it best to give the colonists "the utmost latitude." Adding that he did not wish to have the colonies "set against me,"

Walpole remarked that he would leave tighter regulation "for some of my successors, who have more courage than I have, and are less a friend of commerce than I am."[2]

By the mid-eighteenth century, anxiety had grown in London that generations of indulgence had led to a dangerous degree of colonial autonomy. With worry afoot that the colonists were becoming more American than British, the belief swelled that change was necessary lest the American colonists simply drift toward independence.

To be sure, in some ways the colonists were conspicuously different from the people in England. Roughly a fifth of the free population in colonial America hailed from non-English backgrounds and harbored no deeply held affections for Great Britain. Perhaps more troubling was the noticeable differences among those whose origins and traditions were English. By the late colonial period, many families in New England could trace their American roots back for five generations, and now and then one might run across a Virginian who was a sixth-generation American. Over time, the colonists' diet, patterns of dress, and housing styles had become subtly, sometimes strikingly, unlike those of the English. Moreover, while most at home were Anglicans, a substantial chunk of the colonists were Presbyterian, Congregationalist, Lutheran, or members of some small, unfamiliar sect. English visitors to the colonies attested that provincials used peculiar words, spoke in unfamiliar dialects, and gave words strange-sounding pronunciations. Borrowing from others in America, including Indians and the Dutch, the colonists alluded to "cribs," "bullfrogs," or being "bamboozled," terms that did not resonate with those in the old country. Some English words had taken on new meanings. A "pie" to an Englishman was a meat pie, but to a colonist it was a fruit pie; the term "dry goods" in England referred to corn or wheat, while to a colonist it meant textiles. In Massachusetts the word "daughter" came out as "darter," while in Virginia "first" might be pronounced as "fuust" or "hold" as "holt."[3]

Given the likelihood of unremitting Americanization, some imperial officials in the colonies advised that "Regulation & Reformation" of British control was "necessary Work."[4] However, no one painted a picture of immediate alarm. Near mid-century, two royal governors of Massachusetts depicted their subjects as Britain's most loyal colonists, and one predicted that any push for American independence was "some Centuries" down the road.[5] Benjamin Franklin said more or less the same thing. Soon after the Seven Years' War, he described the colonists' feelings for the mother country as the "best in the world," and he reminded imperial authorities that the Americans "cost you nothing in forts, citadels, garrisons or armies to keep them in subjection." Franklin added that the colonists felt "not only a respect, but an affection, for Great-Britain." He said that natives who emigrated from England to America were treated with "particular regard." An "Old England-man" enjoyed "a kind of rank among us," he maintained.[6]

Yet, many in London doubted that such affection could last forever. From reading history they knew that in antiquity many Greek and Roman colonies had ultimately thrown off their imperial yokes. Some were also influenced by the cyclical theory of history, all the rage at the time. It held that nations passed through the same cycles as humans. They began as dependent chil-dren, but on reaching what was characterized as an energetic young adult-hood, they wanted to break free of restraints and go their own way. In middle age, nations were experienced and enlightened. Finally, like people, nations fell into senescence and died.[7] To many English officials, the colonists appeared ominously close to the adulthood stage. The American provinces had grown into stable entities dominated by political and social elites who were keenly aware of their colony's unmistakable economic interests.

American conduct during the Seven Years' War not only quickened the feeling that the colonies were not sufficiently dependent but also provoked resentment in England. Not a few American merchants had blatantly violated imperial trade restrictions, and some had trafficked with the enemy. Late in the war, William Pitt had charged that America's "illegal and pernicious Trade" had enabled France "to sustain, and protract this long and expensive War."[8] Furthermore, while some colonies had raised substantial armies, others had not complied with London's requisitions for money and manpower.

As the Seven Years' War wound down, some in England so doubted the loyalty of the colonies that they urged that Canada be left to France. The empire would be better served in the peace settlement by taking Guadaloupe, they argued, in part because of its economic benefits, but to some degree from the belief that the colonists could be kept "in proper subjection" only if New France remained on New England's northern border. Otherwise, once the colonies understood that they no longer required British protection, they would break away.[9] The debate in England was loud and heated, even prompting Thomas Hutchinson, who in time would become a royal governor of Massachusetts, to claim subsequently that the controversy had planted the seed of American independence. Actually, the colonists had on their own already realized the potential for change should the French be driven from Canada. Near the outset of the Seven Years' War, John Adams, not yet an adult, had remarked that "if we can remove the turbulent Gallicks" from North America, the colonists would eliminate a great impediment to "setting up for ourselves."[10]

But nothing prodded imperial officials more strongly to action than their desire to protect English economic interests. By the end of the Seven Years'

War roughly one-third of England's trade—imports as well as exports—was with the colonies. The wealth generated by the colonies had been a factor leading to the war, as powerful figures in England had predicted national bankruptcy should the colonies be lost to France. Some had declared the American colonies more important to England than its European allies.[11] The long, costly war only accentuated the importance of the colonies. In 1763, with peace seemingly assured for a very long time, it was inevitable that entrenched interests in the homeland would feel that the time had come to stiffen control over the colonies.

A new ministry—the cabinet, or administration, which was representative of the majority faction within Parliament and consisted of all the ministers of the government—was formed in 1763. Its head, more commonly called the first minister rather than the prime minister in the eighteenth century, was George Grenville. Bent on doing what Walpole had thought was not worth the risk, Grenville set to work on more rigorously enforcing imperial trade laws. Acting on the belief that 90 percent of the tea consumed by the colonists was imported illegally, and that one-half of the foreign items sold each year in the colonies had been smuggled in—a Treasury study placed the value of European manufactured goods annually smuggled into the colonies at £500,000—Grenville took steps to overhaul the customs service.[12] There were to be more customs agents, the army and navy were to lend a helping hand, and a vice-admiralty court was created for trying suspected trade violators. It was situated in Halifax, Nova Scotia, so that prosecutors would be less likely to be frustrated by local juries; in fact, there were no juries whatsoever, as justice in this court was rendered by a judge. What is more, armed with court-ordered writs of assistance, or blank search warrants, customs officers could now comb through vessels and warehouses utilized by suspected smugglers. Had Grenville's government done nothing more than taking these steps to rigorously enforce imperial commercial policies, it would have created a stir, but the storm would have been confined almost solely to New England.

Wars, even those that are successful, bring on change, and change not infrequently creates anxieties and problems. Grenville faced two formidable problems occasioned by the recent war, and it was his ministry's attempt to cope with those quandaries—in league with enforcing the trade laws—that triggered a tempest. Waging the protracted worldwide war against France and Spain had been extraordinarily costly. Great Britain's national debt had nearly doubled in seven years, climbing to £146 million by 1763—so stupendous a figure that merely servicing the interest on the debt would have consumed some 60 percent of the national budget in peacetime. Grenville had to find revenue. Simultaneously, his ministry had to frame a policy for the immense trans-Appalachian territory that Britain had acquired in the peace settlement, a region inhabited by Indians and one that hordes of colonial settlers and speculators were eager to have opened.

Residents of the homeland already groaned under heavy, wartime taxes. When Grenville's predecessor imposed a cider tax in search of additional revenue, it sparked such angry demonstrations that the prime minister was forced from office. That was a factor in leading Grenville to cast his gaze on the colonies as a source of revenue. In what at first glance appeared incongruous, Grenville began his quest for American revenue by cutting taxes. He secured the passage of what was variously called the American Duties Act or the Revenue Act, though it was better known as the Sugar Act of 1764, legislation that replaced the Sugar Act of 1733. Designed to secure a monopoly for Britain's West Indian planters, the earlier act had imposed duties of up to 100 percent on imports of molasses, sugar, and rum from the foreign sugar islands in the West Indies. But rather than terminating the foreign trade, the excessive duties had encouraged colonial merchants to smuggle in the customary commodities. Grenville's Sugar Act of 1764 lowered duties—the rate on molasses was reduced from six pence per gallon to three—in the expectation that the streamlined customs service would collect revenue that had previously been lost through surreptitious trade.[13]

The Sugar Act was rife with provocation, and so too was a new British policy toward the American West. During the war, ministers, boards, and even George III had wrestled with what to do with the West, but no decision was made until the first months of Grenville's administration. What was decided amounted to a radical departure. The Proclamation of 1763 strictly forbade migration beyond the crest of the Appalachians "on pain of our displeasure," said the ministry in its pronouncement. Grenville's cabinet also unanimously agreed to keep an army in America, a decision that was unquestioned in Parliament.

The imperial government had never before prohibited western migration, nor had it ever kept a large standing army in the colonies in peacetime. The army was thought necessary for taking control of several vital harbors along the southern coast, for maintaining order in what had been New France—home to eighty thousand French residents—and as an indispensable part of Britain's Indian policy. The army was to protect the Indians from unscrupulous English fur traders and maintain peace between settlers and Indians, and it is not too much to say, as has historian Edward Countryman, that the Proclamation of 1763 offered the "last real hope that the Western Indians would be able to preserve their way of life." Whereas a few hundred regulars had been posted in the thirteen mainland colonies before the war, some eight thousand troops were to remain in America after the war. Most were to be garrisoned in a score of posts on the frontier. Parliament acquiesced, in part from the belief that France would eventually seek to recoup its losses from the late war, but also from a conviction that the colonists were to bear the burden of supporting the army.[14]

If all this was not enough, Grenville's government took one additional step. More than a decade earlier, London had restricted the use of paper money in New England and prohibited it altogether in the payment of private debts, a measure aimed at both preventing the depreciation of paper currency and protecting English creditors. The law was unpopular in New England, which had a chronically inadequate money supply, and in 1763 Grenville contemplated allowing a colonial paper currency controlled by London and secured by a fund created through an American tax. In the end, the prime minister backed off that idea. Instead, he secured passage of the Currency Act of 1764. Though aimed at Virginia, the law banned future issues of legal tender paper money or its use in any transactions, private or public, in the provinces south of New England. Grenville's intent was to eliminate paper money in those colonies. His law was no more popular south of New England than its predecessor had been with the Yankees. The elite throughout the colonies, in provinces with carefully supervised currencies and in those in which the amount of money in circulation and its exchange rate had been improperly managed, bridled at London's intrusiveness. More than a few northern entrepreneurs were roiled, as were southern land-speculating planters, by the realization that not only had Parliament made it more difficult to borrow and accumulate capital, but also that when confronted with a choice of protecting British investments in America or serving colonial needs, London cared more for those at home.[15]

George Grenville was just past fifty when he formed his ministry. He had sat in the House of Commons for more than two decades and held several ministerial posts, earning a reputation for honesty and industry. Contemporaries thought him a financial wizard and a competent manager of his cabinet and the House of Commons. They believed he would do well unless, as one observer put it, he and his ministers "thrust their hands in to some fire." To be sure, Grenville's policies were incendiary, and in the judgment of Edmund Burke, one of the more perceptive members of Parliament, the prime minister was ill-equipped for coping with much more than cobbling together a budget. Burke thought that Grenville might excel in coping with details, but lacking a "greater knowledge of mankind," he was blind to "the total circuit of our affairs." George III thought him "dillitory" and added that he had "never yet met with a man more doubtful." Nor have historians been kind to Grenville. They have portrayed him as "unimagina-tive," uninterested in learning more about Americans and the labyrinthine nature of the colonies, and unable to effectively manage the monarch. All in all, said one scholar, Grenville was "the wrong man in the wrong place at the wrong time."[16]

His faults were real, but making Grenville the scapegoat for all that went wrong would be bad history. England's indebtedness and the American West were pressing problems that cried out for attention. The Proclamation of 1763, much maligned by historians, was undertaken not just to conciliate the Indians but also to reassure the French and Spanish, who feared that London would follow its victory in the Seven Years' War with unbridled future expansion. Moreover, Grenville had held office just a short while before word arrived of Pontiac's Rebellion, a massive Indian uprising that began early in 1763 near Detroit. In less than sixty days, numerous British outposts fell and scores of British regulars, settlers, and traders were killed or captured. The bloody uprising convinced many in England, and some in America, of the wisdom of keeping a large army on the colonial frontier. Franklin, for instance, remarked that if united, the colonists could defeat the Indians in one campaign, but alas the Americans were disunited and required the pres-ence of the British army if the West was to be opened to settlement anytime soon.[17]

In fairness to Grenville, he never envisaged making the colonists pay for everything. He did not propose taxing them to cope with the debt problem, and he never suggested that they should bear the entire cost of maintaining the army in the American West. But heedful that England had lavished considerable treasure in winning the recent war, Grenville was convinced the colonists should pay something for the maintenance of what had been won for them. When he outlined his policies to Parliament, Grenville declared, "We have expended much in America. Let us now avail ourselves of the fruits of that expense."[18] But here was the rub. When young John Adams had dreamily reflected in 1755 on America's eventual independence, he had added, "The only way to keep us from setting up for ourselves is to disunite Us."[19] Grenville's initiatives had the opposite effect. They raised shared concerns from New England to the Chesapeake, making cooperation among the tradi-tionally uncooperative colonists far more likely.

There may never have been a good time for Grenville's new colonial policies, but his initiatives came at a decidedly inopportune moment. It was not uncommon for economic woes to follow a drop in military spending, and that occurred again in the wake of the Seven Years' War. America's cities were feeling the pinch by the early 1760s. Many businesses went bankrupt in

Boston, New York, and Philadelphia. Shopkeepers and artisans faced auster-
ity, and unemployment spread among sailors, dockhands, and laborers in
general. No city was hit as hard as Boston, which was confronted by a perfect
storm of troubles. In addition to the termination of military contracts, the
city faced soaring rates of taxation to cope with war debts and the need
to care for unprecedented numbers of war widows, their children, and the
poor. These tribulations beset Boston at a time when it faced increasing
competition from inland towns and regional ports and its population growth
had stagnated for nearly a generation.[20] But Bostonians, and northern city
dwellers in general, were not alone in facing adversity. Boom times for
tobacco had ended around mid-century. Not unlike many northern
merchants, numerous Chesapeake planters were being squeezed by their
English creditors.

How Grenville expected America to respond to his measures is not clear.
Prior to the passage of the Sugar Act, authorities in London had been advised
by Sir Francis Bernard, the royal governor of Massachusetts, that the "People
here are loyal . . . but jealous of their liberties." Whatever he meant by that,
Bernard went on to mistakenly state that the Yankees' "general Disposition"
was "to submit to regulations & requisitions."[21] By the time the governor
peddled his misguided advice, a consortium of Boston merchants had already
retained a team of lawyers, led by James Otis, to fight the issuance of general
writs of assistance, one of the Crown's weapons in the war against smuggling.
Otis, now thirty-five years old, had graduated from Harvard at age eighteen
and had been practicing law for a dozen years. A scholar-lawyer (he had
authored a tract on Latin prosody that was used as a text at Harvard), Otis
was widely regarded as an expert on common, civil, and admiralty law, a
splendid orator, and the leading lawyer in Massachusetts.

Otis's talent notwithstanding, the merchants' challenge to the writs failed
when Thomas Hutchinson, the chief justice of Massachusetts, ruled against
the plaintiffs. However, Otis's legal reasoning impressed others. Otis had
built his case not on the economic damage that might result from restricting
trade, but on questioning the hitherto orthodox premise that there were no
limits to Parliament's authority. The "Parliament of *Great Britain*," Otis
asserted, "is circumscribed by certain bounds," which it might not exceed; it
could neither act "against the fundamental principles of the British constitution" nor arbitrarily overrun the natural rights of life, liberty, and property.
In essence, Otis had asserted that the sanctity of natural rights was a rule of
law superior to parliamentary sovereignty.[22]

Three years after Otis's court argument against general writs, word of the
Sugar Act reached Boston. Along with it came accounts of an exasperatingly

long-winded "Budget Day" speech delivered by Grenville to the House of
Commons. For the first time, the prime minister mentioned a direct tax on
the colonists as part of his new colonial policies, though he said he would
take no action until he learned the feelings of the colonists. Otis—whom
Governor Bernard labeled a "Gentleman of great warmth of Temper & much
indiscretion"—was one of the first to respond. Declaring that the Sugar Act
had in six months "set people a-thinking" about the colonists' relationship
with the mother country "more than they had done in their whole lives
before," he published the thrust of his legal argument against the writs of
assistance in a pamphlet, *The Rights of the British Colonies Asserted and
Proved*. Otis's reasoning was at times convoluted, though the essence of his
argument was easily grasped: the Sugar Act was a tax disguised as a measure
to regulate trade. What followed was more important. Otis fleshed out his
earlier argument about limitations on parliamentary authority: "No parts of
His Majesty's dominions can be taxed without their consent," and the colonies had not consented because they were not represented in Parliament.
Therefore, Parliament had no legal right to tax the colonists. Otis warned
London that it was playing with fire. With considerable hyperbole, he claimed
that New England was the "center of motion upon which the wheel of all
the British economy in America turns." To all this he added a threat:
Massachusetts might engage in a trade boycott should the Sugar Act not be
repealed.[23] Not long thereafter, Otis followed with a series of essays in the
Boston Gazette in which he broadened the scope of his attack by indicting
Britain's mercantilist system for pinioning the colonists in a "dependent
state" by "shutting them out . . . from all the world."[24]

It is not difficult to see why John Adams, subsequently reflecting on the
coming of the American Revolution, concluded that not only had New
England's insurgency come alive in response to the Currency Act, but also
that Otis's courtroom presentation and pamphleteering had been so pivotal
that "Then and there the child Independence was born."[25] Adams may have
exaggerated, but he was correct that transforming thoughts about the colonists' place in the British Empire had their genesis in the early 1760s, and he
was on target in recalling that by 1764 some New Englanders—and especially
Boston's merchants, with whom as a rising young attorney he was in close
contact—had been disconcerted by the shift in imperial policy. In fact, during
1764 a spate of pamphlets and essays attacking the Sugar Act rolled off the
presses in New England. Like Otis, some authors abandoned the region's
traditional acceptance of Britain's right to restrict colonial manufacturing
and trade, inching toward a free trade position. Increasingly, too, some questioned the age-old view that English and American interests were identical.

Imperial policies, it was said, were the cause of chronic colonial trade imbalances and currency shortages. Stephen Hopkins, the governor of Rhode Island, authored an assembly-sanctioned pamphlet charging that imperial policy served the interests of West Indies planters and English merchants, manufacturers, and creditors while ignoring—and often harming—the interests of colonists in America.[26]

Before the end of 1764, New England's merchants, and those tied to them for their economic well-being, had become all too aware of Britain's more rigorous enforcement of its new colonial policies. Whereas previously a merchant who engaged in smuggling had avoided paying duties on a load from the foreign sugar islands, now that same businessman paid a levy of £250 on a typical cargo from the French West Indies. And that was the tip of the iceberg. The three-pence tax on foreign molasses spiked the price of New England rum, making it less competitive in foreign markets. Furthermore, the English sugar islands did not produce enough molasses to keep New England's distilleries operating at their previous levels. Rum, it was widely thought, generated the capital that drove New England's economy. Now rum's once-handsome profits were jeopardized. For Boston, which was already losing its dominance in the ship construction industry to Newburyport, the Sugar Act portended misfortune.[27]

However, as the impact of the Sugar Act was largely felt in the port towns, protest was not widespread. Only Massachusetts and New York took a stand against the act, and the latter alone protested that the parliamentary tax violated the rights of Americans. The lower house in Massachusetts had wanted to take a similar stand, but the upper house, dominated by wealthy conservatives led by Thomas Hutchinson—his legislative seat was one of four major offices that he held—blocked a muscular statement. Massachusetts ultimately objected on the grounds that the Sugar Act would have an adverse impact on its commerce. Most colonies said nothing one way or another. In London it seemed that few provinces were especially troubled by the mother country's more stringent commercial control.[28]

But the prospect of a direct tax was a different matter. Grenville had not kept his plans about a stamp tax a secret, and during 1764 he learned on good authority that the levy he was considering had provoked "a rouse." At least one royal official in America had advised that a tax "would cause a great Alarm & meet much Opposition," and in fact nearly half the colonies had remonstrated against parliamentary taxation. The earliest had come from the Massachusetts assembly, which had endorsed the instructions adopted by a Boston town meeting for the city's legislative delegation. Those instructions, drafted by Samuel Adams, expressed "Surprize" and the "deepest Concern" that the ministry was considering taxing the colonists. They additionally declared that a tax would be economically ruinous for the province and harmful to the commerce of the mother country. Embracing Otis's argument, the instructions added that such a step "annihilates our Charter Right to govern & tax ourselves." Submission to parliamentary taxation, it resoundingly concluded, would reduce the colonists "from the Character of free Subjects to the miserable State of tributary Slaves."[29] If Grenville read that statement, he had a preview of what the colonists would say time and again throughout the ensuing decade.

Most of the colonies had long retained emissaries, or agents, as they were usually called, in London to serve as their eyes and ears, and during 1764 Grenville discussed the pending stamp tax with four of them. Each warned of trouble if a direct tax was levied. One remarked that a parliamentary tax "would go down with the people like Chopt hay," and added that it would be extremely difficult to collect the revenue. However, Benjamin Franklin, who had spent most of the past seven years in London as the Pennsylvania assembly's representative in its campaign to change the province's government, told Grenville that neither an indirect parliamentary tax, such a sales tax, nor a requisition system—under which the Crown would determine what each colony owed and the provincial assemblies would decide how to raise the revenue—would provoke much opposition. Out of touch from having spent so little time in Philadelphia in recent years, Franklin badly misread the mood of his fellow colonists. They would not, he added, be "much alarm'd about your Schemes of raising Money on us. You will take care . . . not to lay greater Burthens on us than we can bear."[30]

Leaders often must make decisions on the basis of contradictory and incomplete information. Grenville was confronted with conflicting evidence, but truth be told, he had made up his mind from the outset to ask Parliament to tax the colonists. Listening to the agents was pure chicanery, a ploy to convince Parliament that the Americans had offered no serious alternatives. Grenville finally introduced his stamp tax early in 1765. Speaking to Parliament in what one observer called his "soft lisping eloquence," Grenville said the tax was essential to support the army.[31] The Americans, he said, should "take off that part of the burden from their mother country which concerned the protection and defense of themselves." After all, the colonists had been "nourished by our indulgence . . . and protected by our arms," and the West had been won for them by British arms. He added that the stamp tax rates were low and should not be a burden to the colonists, and he offered abundant statistics showing that the Americans possessed the means of easily paying the tax. His attorney general told the House of Commons that the colonists could "tax themselves" only through "a federal union—God forbid that," or through a requisition system that would inevitably produce charges of unfairness. Better that Parliament levy the tax, which he said it had every right to do. The few in Parliament who spoke against the tax did so mostly on economic grounds, asserting that it would have an adverse impact on commerce.

The Stamp Act became law in March 1765. Legal documents, newspapers, pamphlets, licenses, and bills of lading required stamps—that is, taxes in varied amounts had to be paid on those items. The law stipulated that the revenue was intended exclusively for America's defense and would be spent solely within the colonies. Once the Stamp Act was passed, Grenville asked each colony to designate a stamp master. The position struck many as a plum, for the chief tax collector could pocket 7.5 percent of the revenue he collected.[32]

About forty-five days after the Stamp Act became law, Parliament enacted the Mutiny Act—designated the Quartering Act by the colonists—which was destined to be the final installment of Grenville's American legislation. It not only directed the colonies to furnish firewood, salt, candles, bedding, cooking utensils, and a daily ration of beer or rum to the British soldiery posted within their jurisdiction, but it also authorized the seizure of vacant houses and barns for housing the redcoats.[33]

Shortly thereafter Grenville's ministry came to an abrupt end, having run afoul of the king because of unrest sparked by its domestic legislation, not its new colonial policies. On leaving office, Grenville advised the monarch not to permit succeeding ministers to "draw the line between his British and American dominions," lest it cost him "the richest jewel of his Crown."[34] Grenville was telling George III that the empire would be lost if some future ministry should concede that Parliament lacked authority to legislate for America. Not long would pass before he and his countrymen learned how America responded to parliamentary taxation.

As has been true of legislatures throughout most of American history, the provincial assemblies were controlled by conservatives who were not inclined to rock the boat. For two months after news of the Stamp Act reached the colonies, not one assembly condemned the law, not even those that had remonstrated against the proposed tax a year earlier.[35]

Virginia was the first to take a stand, thanks to Patrick Henry, only recently elected to the House of Burgesses. Neither part of the planter aristocracy nor well educated, Henry had latched onto practicing law at age twenty-four after failing at everything else he had tried. He entered practice after a few weeks' study and soon discovered oratorical skills that enabled him to captivate country juries; in three years, he won more than one thousand cases. At age twenty-eight, Henry joined the assembly. He was gifted with a political sixth sense and an intuitive feel for self-advancement, and just nine days after entering the legislature he glimpsed his opportunity to act. The assembly had met for weeks and had said nothing about the parliamentary tax. Nor did its leaders contemplate any action. Nearly two-thirds of the assemblymen had already left for home, including George Washington, a seven-year veteran of the legislature, who in late May was planting turnips and cultivating hemp at Mount Vernon when Henry acted.

Henry gathered about him some young assemblymen avid for insurgency against the legislative leadership and induced one of them to draft seven resolutions on the Stamp Act. On May 29, Henry—tall, thin, and sallow, with dark hair, sharp angular features, and mesmerizing blue-gray eyes— introduced five of the seven "resolves" with one of his patented fiery speeches, delivered in what a contemporary called his "homespun pronunciation," which many found strangely effective. A colleague who heard many of Henry's speeches referred to him as "a Son of Thunder." Twenty-two-year-old Thomas Jefferson, who was studying law down the street in Williamsburg, stood in the lobby just outside the legislative chamber and listened to this address. He thought Henry's "sublime eloquence" was such as he had "never heard from any other man." Years later, Jefferson acknowledged that Henry's oratory had shaped his thinking. While John Adams came to think that James Otis's rhetoric and essays had set the colonists on the road to independence, Jefferson subsequently came to believe that Henry's speech attacking the Stamp Act had been "the dawn of the Revolution."[36]

The first four resolves introduced by Henry stated that Virginians possessed all the rights enjoyed by the people of Great Britain, including the right to be taxed by themselves or their representatives, a prerogative that was "the distinguishing Characteristick of *British* Freedom." The fifth resolution, which passed by one vote but was later rescinded after Henry left Williamsburg, declared that only the Virginia assembly could tax the inhabitants of the colony and that "every attempt to vest such Power in any other Person or Persons ... has a manifest Tendency to destroy British as well as American Freedom." Newspapers throughout America published not only the four declarations the burgesses had approved, but also the rejected fifth resolution and the two others that Henry had never introduced. Articulate colonists across the land assumed that the Virginia Resolves, as they came to be known, consisted of seven bold statements, including the intrepid avowals that Virginia was "not bound to yield Obedience" to parliamentary taxes and that anyone who said otherwise "shall be Deemed, AN ENEMY TO THIS HIS MAJESTY'S COLONY."[37]

At the same moment that Henry introduced his resolutions, the Massachusetts assembly met, but its response was less spectacular. The popular party in Boston was in disarray. Otis, perhaps evincing the first signs of an emotional disorder that would overwhelm him within a few years, both renounced the positions he had taken a year earlier and became the helpmate of royal officials. It was the first of his several chameleon-like transmutations, and his bewildering behavior for a time left in a muddle those who wanted to protest the Stamp Act. In the end, the assembly, unable to take a forceful stand, merely appealed to the other colonies to send delegates to a national congress to consider how to respond to the parliamentary tax. Meanwhile, Andrew Oliver, the cold and aloof provincial secretary and member of the council, a man whose great wealth enabled him to live like a grandee, had been appointed stamp master. As soon as the stamps arrived, Oliver would begin collecting the duties, which would fall on many widely used items.

The assembly had done little to impede the Stamp Act, but plenty of Bostonians were prepared to do something. They were not revolutionaries at this juncture, but many were desperate, some were uneasy, and not a few were bitter. A 1764 census suggested that fully one-fifth of Bostonians may have been impoverished, and given London's tight-money policies and more stringent enforcement of the imperial trade laws, residents of the city— from wealthy merchants to industrious craftsmen to unskilled workers— already faced a grim future even before a stamp tax kicked in. For many, Britain's new colonial policies, like its recurring wars, seemed designed to serve the interests of a faraway government in which the colonists had no voice. Furthermore, innumerable Bostonians were contemptuous of men like Hutchinson and Oliver, champions of the Currency Act and now defenders of a stamp tax, and would have opposed anything these two supported. Much of the citizenry saw the two native-born Americans as toadies of their imperial masters, despicable men who smoothed the way for what a remote ministry and parliament wished, all too often obstructing those who sought to advance the interests of the province, and not infrequently going about their business with an insultingly haughty manner.[38]

Bostonians were separated by class needs and concerns, but many were drawn closer by a shared belief that British policies spelled danger. Commonality was helped along by the press, which since the writs-of-assistance furor had been filled with essays attacking imperial policy and those who made possible its implementation. Boston's inhabitants inter-mingled at work and church and in neighborhood taverns, clubs, and fire companies, where concerns were voiced and ideas swapped. Britain's policies were debated and a coherent response to them was fabricated through a maze of networks that ran to the Boston Caucus, a leadership council that traced its roots back some thirty years. Composed mostly of tradesmen who, according to John Adams, drank rum and "smoke[d] tobacco till you cannot see from one end of the Garret to the other," the Caucus hammered out what was to be brought before the Boston town meetings, where it generally had its way. However, the sanction of a town meeting was not the same thing as a provincial law. For instance, a May 1764 town meeting became the first political body in America to assert that Parliament could not constitutionally tax Americans, but the assembly refused to take such a radical stand.[39]

It was likely that somewhere in this shrouded political network the decision was made in the summer of 1765 to fight the Stamp Act in the streets of Boston. Some historians have guessed that the Loyal Nine, a secret society of politically active artisans and shopkeepers, plotted a strategy of street protest. Governor Bernard thought otherwise. He believed the principal instigators of the protest were those whom he identified as "abettors of Consequence," "Gentlemen of the first fashion," and "the richest Merchants in this Town." While Bernard believed that Ebenezer MacIntosh, a twenty-eight-year-old shoemaker and veteran on the French and Indian War, was the individual who organized Boston's angry and distressed workers and got them into the street, the governor was certain that he was "under the directions of Persons much his Superiors."

Historians have largely seen Samuel Adams and his confederates in the Loyal Nine as responsible for the Stamp Act protest, but Bernard was convinced that it was "Otis & his Gang" who were pulling the strings. Indeed, Bernard thought James Otis was the "great Leviathan" and "grand Incendiary" who was most responsible for carrying out the wishes of the disgruntled merchants by manipulating workers with "deception, inflammation, & intimidation." (Bernard told his superiors in London that in 1760, when Otis's father had been denied appointment to the highest judicial position in the colony, young Otis had publicly vowed to make the royal governor "repent it," threatening to "set the whole Province in a flame" in reprisal.) Bernard may have been on to something in seeing aggrieved merchants and their hirelings as the instigators of the protests, but neither he nor most of the conservative colonists understood that workers could think and act in their own interest. Their tendency was to see workers as "perfect Machines," puppets who went into action when the demagogic "Geniuses" blew the *Mob Whistle*, as horrid as the *Iroquois Yell*."[40]

Whoever was responsible struck before sunrise on August 14, hanging in effigy Andrew Oliver, the stamp master. A note on the effigy indicted Oliver for having "Betrayed" his country "for the Sake of Pelf." That evening, as the deep, sloping shadows of sunset stretched across the city, a large crowd surged into the streets, dragging the tattered effigy. The crowd flattened and burned a downtown building owned by Oliver and then marched to his house, where it "beheaded the Effigy," broke several windows, ripped apart a picket fence that surrounded the mansion, and completed the night's work by destroying his carriage house, phaeton, and lovingly tended garden. When the governor tried to call out the militia to disperse the crowd, he was told that most of the militiamen were members of the mob. The next day, the thoroughly frightened Oliver resigned as stamp master. For the near term, the Stamp Act was not enforced in Massachusetts. Crowd action had achieved what the assembly had shrunk from attempting.

Hutchinson had escaped, or so it seemed. But eleven days later, another mob, inspired by loathing for what many saw as an apostate who served only the city's elite and a distant British government, went after him. The angry throng descended on Hutchinson's six-pilastered brick mansion, crying, "liberty & property" and—if Governor Bernard was correct—bent on murdering this son of Massachusetts, who had, in the judgment of so many, repeatedly betrayed the citizenry of his native land. By the time the crowd's carnival lust for revenge and destruction was sated, the house and all its furnishings were ruined. Hutchinson had escaped by slipping out a rear door and sprinting to safety through neighboring yards.[41]

Samuel Adams had probably played a role in hanging Oliver's effigy and it is a good bet he was involved in the planning to get protestors into the street, a crucial step in politicizing the populace and lessening attachment to royal authority. In all likelihood, however, he had not countenanced the mob's violence, chiefly because he deemed it politically counterproductive. Adams had a passion for politics, perhaps fueled by poor success in other careers. After obtaining two degrees from Harvard, he failed at two business endeavors, one of which was the management of his father's brewery. By the time he ran the brewery into bankruptcy, Adams verged on pennilessness. At one time, Adams may have looked forward to a comfortable inheritance, but his father had been ruined through investments in a land bank that was opposed by Hutchinson and ultimately dissolved by Parliament. The calamity that befell his father was an object lesson to young Adams on the plight of provincials who lacked autonomy and the means of controlling their destiny. What is more, Adams faced years of struggle with what he believed were malicious royal officials who sought to seize his father's assets to settle land bank accounts. By the 1760s, Adams had gone through a number of public jobs, including town scavenger and tax collector, and his wife worked to supplement the family's income; acquaintances later recalled that the family was so poor at times that neighbors provided food and clothing for the children.

Along the way, Adams had immersed himself in politics. Full of antipathy for those colonists who served their royal masters, he unfailingly struggled to protect the slivers of provincial autonomy that existed. But more than enmity drove him. Adams longed to reestablish Massachusetts as a "Christian Sparta." His hope was to return to the piety of his Puritan forebears, resurrecting a more egalitarian society and one that was less susceptible to what he saw as the corrupting influences of commerce and market forces. Royal officials in Boston dismissed him as a "great Demagogue" and a man of "serpentine Cunning" given to "criminal" ploys in pursuit of his radical ends. There was some truth to that, but John Adams's subsequent characterization of Samuel Adams as courageous and "staunch and stiff and strict, rigid and inflexible" in defense of American rights" was more accurate. By the time of the Stamp Act, Samuel Adams had been engrossed in politics for twenty years. It was his life, and he had a knack for it. People were drawn to him. Vigorous and dogged, but warm and human, he was joyously social, mixing and mingling easily with the parishioners in the large church to which he belonged and, ever the organizer, creating and participating in singing clubs. Adams's features were strong and handsome, his manner assertive. He seemed gifted with a cunning hardness that the times demanded. His cousin John Adams thought him unique in his ability to understand the "Temper and Character of the People," and Samuel in fact could converse easily with people from every social and economic background. He understood their grievances as well as their longing for greater control over their lives and society, and he won their trust. Most Bostonians were not revolutionaries in 1765, but it is likely that Samuel Adams had already reached that stage in his thinking. For certain, he was willing to take extreme steps in defiance of parliamentary authority and against those officials who submitted to it.[42]

After the violence in Boston, several stamp masters in other colonies saw the wisdom of immediately tendering their resignations. Those who did not immediately renounce their posts were made to resign by mobs that destroyed their property or threatened to do so. Benjamin Franklin, who was still in London, had thought he was doing a friend a favor when he secured his appointment as Pennsylvania's stamp distributor. Instead, Franklin's friend was ruined politically for having accepted the post, the fate of most of the stamp masters. Franklin himself nearly lost his brand-new house during Philadelphia's stamp riots. As fires set by angry crowds cast an eerie orange glow in the night sky over Philadelphia, a mob descended on Franklin's residence intent on razing it. The throng would have succeeded had not friends and Franklin's wife, Deborah, stood vigil brandishing firearms.[43]

New York City pulsed with protest as well. Over two thousand people gathered at the Battery when the ship bearing that province's allotment of stamps arrived. The crowd was peaceful, and the stamps were eventually unloaded. However, a week later, on the day before the law was to take effect, protestors garbed in mourning clothes surged through downtown streets breaking lamps and windows, burning effigies, and threatening to demolish the property of both royal officials and stamp distributors. The following day thousands again took to the streets. Rushing the residence of Lieutenant Governor Cadwallader Colden, the mob broke into his coach house and destroyed two of his handsome carriages and two expensive sleighs; the rioters next turned on Vauxhall, the home of an important British army officer, pillaging it and wreaking considerable damage on the structure. In the days that followed, the captain of the ship that had brought the stamps to New York fled for his life, New York's stamp master resigned his commission—though not until after his house was badly damaged by a mob—and unruly crowds burned effigies of numerous officials, including George Grenville. Hastily assembled throngs of New Yorkers additionally compelled the stamp distributors for four other provinces, who had sailed from England, to resign their commissions when they disembarked in Manhattan's harbor.[44]

Angry mobs composed of workers throbbing with bitterness toward their social betters may have helped nudge New York's merchants to agree to fight the Stamp Act by boycotting British trade. On October 31, two hundred Manhattan merchants adopted a compact pledging not to import British goods after the end of the year. Albany soon joined in, and within a month Philadelphia, Boston, and a string of Massachusetts coastal towns had come aboard as well.[45]

Three weeks before the stamp tax was to go into effect, the national congress requested by Massachusetts in June convened in a more tranquil Manhattan. Nine colonies were represented in what came to be known as the Stamp Act Congress. Most delegates were extremely conservative. A majority of the congressmen from Massachusetts were political allies of the royal governor, and Timothy Ruggles—who was elected chairman of the Stamp Act Congress—would ultimately choose loyalty to Great Britain over allegiance to the United States. In the span of two weeks, the congress adopted several resolutions and petitions, each cautiously constructed. The congress acknowledged the colonists' "Allegiance" and "all due Subordination" to king and Parliament, but insisted that the colonists enjoyed the right of all Englishmen to consent to taxation. It added that the colonists had not assented to the Stamp Act, as they were not represented in Parliament, and given their distance from the mother country, they could never be represented in that body.[46]

On November 1 no stamps could be purchased. That in turn meant that no land could be sold, nor could ships sail, money be borrowed, debts be paid, courts convene, or newspapers be printed. Parliament's tax had been nullified, not because of the Stamp Act Congress or the Virginia Resolves, but as a result of popular uprisings throughout the land. During that autumn, protestors—now calling themselves Sons of Liberty—organized embargoes of British imports in Boston, New York, and Philadelphia. Protest leaders and dockhands, backed by crowds in the streets, watched vigilantly to see that no British ships entered their harbors and no vessels bearing stamps cleared the major urban ports with a cargo of exported goods. Commerce was shut down. Fortunes were threatened. Royal officials in the port cities saw their predicament as akin to a ticking time bomb. Wringing his hands, the comptroller of customs in New York told London that "the Mob" is "daily increasing and gathering Strength," given that there were so many unemployed sailors. Seafarers, he added, "are most dangerous . . . as their whole dependence for a subsistence is upon Trade." By December, customs officials had caved. Port officials in the major northern cities were permitting ships to sail without stamped paper, and by then the courts were operating and newspapers were publishing throughout the colonies.[47]

The colonies, as historian Edmund Morgan noted, had asked for no new freedoms, but "they wanted no less, either, and were willing to fight" to maintain what they had long enjoyed.[48]

In retrospect, American defiance of the Stamp Act may have presented Britain with its best chance to crush the rebellious spirit in the colonies. In 1765, the colonies were disunited. Political leaders were largely unaware of their counterparts in other provinces and possessed only the scantest idea of sentiment beyond the borders of their own colony. Hardly any provincial leaders exhibited anything close to a revolutionary mentality. In fact, those who held leadership positions in most colonies in 1765 were quite conservative in contrast to those who were predominant only four or five years later. No central body existed to coordinate America's defense. Furthermore, the militia had been largely inactive everywhere for the past several years, and no steps were taken during the Stamp Act furor to reboot it. Indeed, such war weariness had prevailed in many colonies long before the protracted Seven Years' War finally ended that it may have been impossible in 1765 to gin up the will to fight yet again. In contrast, Great Britain may have been better prepared to use force than it would be a decade later. The British army had not yet fully demobilized, and the Royal Navy, which had crushed its adversaries in the recent war, had not fallen into the state of disrepair that would soon plague it. Nor was there much likelihood that France or Spain, only recently defeated by Great Britain, would have contemplated intervention in the event of an Anglo-American conflict in the mid-1760s.

The first word of the colonial resistance to the Stamp Act, including accounts of disorder and the resolutions of several assemblies, reached London in mid-summer. It was greeted by surprise, followed by confusion and consternation, and considerable anger. The administration rapidly instructed officials in the colonies to maintain order and defend the authority of Parliament and king, and it authorized the army to use force, if necessary, to prevent further mob violence. All the while, however, perplexed officials in London sought to understand the breadth and depth of the colonial protest and the reasons for the American defiance. Their puzzlement only contributed to the uncertainty over how to respond. The irresolution expressed by one minister, the Duke of Newcastle, doubtless reflected that of many. On learning of the colonists' recalcitrance, the duke wrung his hands over what he called the "inconveniences" that would result both from trying to enforce the law and rescinding it.[49]

Reports on conditions in America arrived in London from stamp collectors who had been forced to resign and from many colonial governors. But the advice of General Thomas Gage, the commander of the British army in North America, was regarded as the most sound, as he presumably was detached and in the best position to judge what was occurring throughout the mainland colonies. With the assorted assessments in hand, the cabinet took up the colonial crisis at several meetings during the late summer and early autumn. Predictably, Gage's appraisal was crucial in shaping the ministers' initial thinking. Gage advised that the "general outcry" was not confined to one or two colonies but spanned the continent. He also emphasized that the colonists' objections had not arisen from their inability to pay the tax, but instead that the American protestors believed the act was "unconstitutional" and wished for "Independency" from the "Legislative Power of Great Britain."[50]

Gage's reports arrived at a time when the Duke of Cumberland, who had been brought into the cabinet following Grenville's fall, was serving as prime minister. The son of George II and captain-general of the British army, Cumberland had crushed the Scottish Highland uprising in 1745 with such ruthlessness that he thereafter was called the "Butcher of Culloden." Hardbitten through and through, Cumberland gave no hint of backing down in the face of the colonial protest. Pledging to enforce the Stamp Act, he summoned the cabinet to meet on the last day of October. His plan was for his lord chancellor, Lord Northington, to propose the enforcement of the legislation through "military force," if need be. The meeting never took place. The forty-four-year-old Cumberland dropped dead of an apparent heart attack that very day. Richard Jackson, Pennsylvania's agent in London and an individual with a keen understanding of sentiment in high places, thought that had Cumberland lived, the use of force would have been more likely than the repeal of the Stamp Act.[51]

In the aftermath of Cumberland's demise, more temperate sentiments slowly gained favor in England. No one reason can explain the change, though additional reports by General Gage were certainly influential. By late in the year, he was advising London that should the government decide to use coercion to suppress the protestors, "nothing but a very considerable Military force can do it." Furthermore, numerous essays appeared in the press that urged repeal, always avoiding constitutional issues and contending instead that the legislation was misguided economically. For instance, Thomas Pownall, a former governor of Massachusetts, predicted that repeal would bring peace to the colonies, for five of the seven issues that troubled the colonists were due to economic woes brought on by the tax. Using a variety of pseudonyms, Benjamin Franklin flooded London newspapers with political cartoons, letters, and news items—nine squibs and tracts in January 1766 alone—purporting to show that the colonial protest was caused by economic distress and warning that Great Britain faced untold dangers, even ruin, if it persisted in the enforcement of the law. His cartoon "Magna Britannia: her Colonies REDUCED," depicted merchant ships idled by the colonial boycotts and a crippled British Empire.[52]

The Marquess of Rockingham, who succeeded Cumberland as first minister and was in every way cut from different cloth than his predecessor, moved the government in a new direction. Rockingham was tied to business interests that had never cottoned to a tax certain to have an adverse impact on trade, and from the outset he leaned toward abandoning the stamp tax. He was aided by an orchestrated campaign by merchants distressed by the trade dislocations during 1765. They sent circular letters to more than a score of manufacturing towns, lobbied administrative officials, published essays, petitioned the House of Commons to repeal the tax, and organized demonstrations, including a parade through the streets of London by forty thousand artisanal manufacturers waving "black Flags" of mourning to show the hardships they endured in the face of the colonial boycotts. Rockingham also had his way because of the growing sentiment during the fall and winter that Great Britain could repeal the Stamp Act and still achieve its ends.[53]

Nevertheless, when Parliament convened some seventy-five days after Cumberland's demise, Grenville and others continued to press for strong measures. Rockingham's cabinet was divided and undecided. Some ministers agreed with Grenville that the "honor and dignity of the kingdom" required that the Stamp Act be enforced. Others were influenced by old and ill William Pitt, an iconic figure who was lionized throughout the empire as the architect of victory in the late war.

Pitt was regarded even by his enemies as having no equal as an orator. Characteristically adopting what one scholar called an "attitude of command," he was, according to a biographer, "a spellbinder at work, the skilled actor commanding" in a "musical voice" and a "magnetic presence." Contemporaries called him "as great a bruiser as any orator whatsoever," but also spoke of his "great dignity and temper" while addressing an audience, his "fulminating eloquence" and "florid eloquence," the "grace and force" of his speeches, his "excelling" style and "high invective." One called him the "most entertaining" of all orators at least in part because time after time he "outdid his usual outdoings."

Pitt spoke on the Stamp Act in January 1766. For two hundred years the House of Commons had met in what once had been a chapel in Westminster Palace. The chamber was small and cozy—"clubbable" in the words of one writer—easily accommodating the 150 or so of the 558 members who usually attended. A major speech by Pitt customarily drew well. On this day, the room was overflowing. An observer remarked that Pitt "rose and with a torrent of eloquence flowed like a spring-tide, and almost as long." Pitt did not deny Parliament's sovereignty, but he cried out that the imposition of a direct tax was dishonorable. An American revenue should be realized through the regulation of trade, not through taxation, he said. "The Americans have not acted in all things with prudence and temper," he acknowledged, but they "have been wronged. They have been driven to madness by injustice. Will you punish them for the madness you have occasioned?" To this, Pitt added: "I rejoice that America has resisted." Pitt meant what he said, but geopolitical considerations lurked behind his riveting oratory. He and others, including some who were never among his followers, then and later were as preoccupied by the prospect of Franco-Spanish unity as by the victimization of the colonists; they feared that the endgame of the new colonial policy would be an Anglo-American conflict that would benefit only London's European rivals, perhaps even resulting in the eclipse of Britain's naval supremacy. Grenville, in opposition to Pitt, voiced another concern. If Great Britain did not demand obedience, he said, "a revolution will take place in America."[54]

Never having wished for a confrontation with the colonies, Rockingham's resolve to seek repeal was strengthened by Pitt's moving assault on the act. It grew even stronger when the king not only authorized talks to bring Pitt into the ministry but also told Rockingham that he preferred repeal to enforcement. So far, the Stamp Act had produced barely £3,300. It was netting less than it cost to enforce. The administration decided on repeal accompanied by a declaration of Parliament's sovereign right to legislate for the colonies.[55]

The ministry laid the groundwork for rescinding the Stamp Act by holding hearings in the House of Commons early in 1766. Nearly thirty witnesses were called. The very first, Barlow Trecothick, a former Bostonian who had become one of the major figures in Britain's commerce with America, probably provided the most persuasive testimony. He estimated the American trade to be about £3 million and stressed its importance by demonstrating that Britain's trade elsewhere was declining. If that was not sufficient to get the attention of his audience, Trecothick added that American debts to British creditors ran in the neighborhood of £4.5 million. Prudence, he seemed to say, suggested that London should refrain from alienating the colonists.[56] The witness who ran a close second in importance to Trecothick was Benjamin Franklin, the best-known American in London. The ministry wanted Franklin to bolster its case. Franklin had his own ends. Now age sixty, he hoped for an appointment to an important office. He was just as eager to mend fences back home, repairing the damage caused by his earlier nonchalance toward British taxation. But pleasing the authorities in London while seeking redemption in Pennsylvania was a difficult juggling act.

Franklin helped Rockingham by testifying that the colonists had always thought Britain's government was the "best in the world," though he warned that continued attempts to enforce the tax would result in the mother country being "detested and rejected." If the army was sent to enforce the tax, he added, the soldiers "will not find a rebellion," but "they may indeed make one." When a member of the House asked why America should not pay for the costs Britain had incurred in defending the colonies, Franklin sounded very American. The last two wars had been waged "to protect your trade," he said. Furthermore, in the Seven Years' War the "Colonies raised, cloathed and paid ... near 25,000 men, and spent many millions." Trecothick had predicted that the colonists could live with an indirect tax. It was an idea around which many members of Parliament and of the ministry were coalescing, and Franklin embraced it as well. Franklin portrayed an indirect tax as akin to what today would be called a sales tax. Such a duty would be "laid on commodities. . . . If the people do not like it at that price, they refuse it; they are not obliged to pay it." In contrast, the Stamp Act was a tax "forced from the people without their consent."[57]

The ministry's proposal to repeal the Stamp Act produced in the House of Lords what a British historian called "one of the most important debates of the century." Those favoring repeal offered an array of arguments, but chiefly insisted that the tax could lead to the "gloomy prospect of the colonies throwing off all allegiance" and carrying on a war that might invite foreign intervention. Those opposed to repeal were just as adamant that appeasement would someday lead the colonies to sever their ties to the mother country. In the end, large majorities in both houses favored repeal, but only if it was tied to a declaration of Parliament's sovereignty. In March, Parliament repealed the Stamp Act and made further concessions, including a reduction in the duty on foreign molasses and some other non-English goods. It also enacted the Declaratory Act which stated that Parliament could "make laws for America . . . in all cases whatsoever."[58]

The Stamp Act's revocation, and the peaceful end to the plight of Anglo-American relations, was greeted with exultation and public celebrations throughout the colonies and with relief in many circles in England. A time of maximum danger had ended peacefully. Few doubted that something of great consequence had occurred. The crisis had altered thinking on both sides of the Atlantic, leaving considerable uncertainty in its wake, an unsettled feeling that was captured by an MP during the debates in the House of Commons: "Last year we were all asleep, now were awake, and like people just roused, a little disordered and in confusion."[59] But in London one thing had come into clearer focus: the belief that the colonists must bow to the unqualified will of Parliament. During the next two decades those who held power would never abandon that belief.

Meanwhile, the furor caused political earthquakes in some colonies. According to John Adams "every Man who has dared to speak in favor of the Stamps . . . has been seen to sink into universal Contempt and Ignominy." His was hardly an overstatement. Nineteen Massachusetts assemblymen who had opposed challenging the Stamp Act lost their seats in the next election. A month after Hutchinson's house was wrecked, Samuel Adams was elected for the first time to the assembly. Soon thereafter the assembly chose Otis as its Speaker and Samuel Adams its clerk. Not stopping there, the lower house ousted four Crown lackeys, including Oliver and Hutchinson, from the council. In the estimation of John Adams, the "little Tools and Creatures" of these Crown officers were now "afraid to Speak and ashamed to be seen."[60]

In Virginia, Patrick Henry leaped to prominence through his opposition to the British tax. A political unknown in May, Henry was almost immediately thereafter widely regarded as Virginia's leading advocate for the rights of colonists. Others, such as Richard Henry Lee, were transformed by Henry's new and exalted stature. Lee had entered the assembly in 1758 and for eight years had been unable to move up to a leadership position. His initial response to word of the Stamp Act was to unsuccessfully solicit appointment as Virginia's stamp master, but once aware of Henry's swift rise, Lee made an about-face. He not only denounced the tax as "pernicious to my Country" but also flayed the star-crossed fellow who had gotten the post as stamp distributor, charging that he sought to "fasten chains of slavery on this my native country." Before the end of 1766, Lee was a leader in the House of Burgesses, and he and Henry were widely seen as Virginia's leading reformers.[61]

The times were changing. Some, like Dr. Joseph Warren in Boston, concluded that the "Colonies until now were ever at variance and foolishly jealous of each other, [but] they are now . . . united."[62] Warren embroidered, though it was true that the provinces had seldom cooperated and now to some degree they had acted in concert, and with success. It was a lesson to be learned. Attitudes were changing too. A motion to spend £1,000 for a marble statue to Pitt was approved by the South Carolina assembly. A motion to erect a statue of George III died for lack of a second.[63]

Mostly, the colonists tried to understand what it all meant. John Adams thought the episode had made Americans "more attentive to their liberties, more inquisitive about them, and more determined to defend them." He and others also puzzled over the Declaratory Act. Some thought it a face-saving gesture that was not meant to be taken seriously. Some, like Otis, thought the declaration was meant to apply to things other than taxation. But the Declaratory Act made John Adams wonder "whether they will lay a Tax, in Consequence of that Resolution."[64]

CHAPTER 3

"A PLAN FOR GOVERNING
AND QUIETING THEM"

THE SECOND GREAT CRISIS,
1767–1770

WHEN CHANGE IS SLOW and its unsettling upshots are felt only gradually, apprehension and unrest may be minimal. But in the immediate aftermath of the Stamp Act's repeal, the colonists were confronted by an array of unsettling changes that aroused suspicion, provoked anger, and caused increasing numbers to rethink America's position within the British Empire.

Within four months of the Stamp Act's repeal, the king formed a new ministry. His action had nothing to do with the repeal of the tax, but grew from a belief that Rockingham's government was too weak to function adequately. Pitt, who took a peerage, becoming the Earl of Chatham, agreed to head the cabinet. The colonists were optimistic. They looked on Chatham as their friend, a view that seemed to be confirmed when he did not bring any shrill foes of repeal into his ministry. Within a few months, however, Franklin reported that the first minister was so "totally disabled" by illness that he seldom met with the cabinet, a turn of events that has left historians to wonder what might have been had Chatham remained healthy. But Franklin also noted a "general Clamour . . . and so much Ill-humour, against America" within Parliament that the course of history might not have been substantially different had Chatham been fit.[1]

The harsh feelings that Franklin detected grew from a simmering anger at the recent American protests, rancor that was stoked by more disagreeable news from the colonies. More than two hundred New York merchants had petitioned London to relax its regulation of colonial commerce, prompting an irritated Chatham to remark that America faced "a gloomy prospect," as he suspected that the entreaty by New York's businessmen would deliver them into "the hands of their enemies" in London. News from the colonies soon grew even worse. New York defied the Mutiny Act, refusing to supply or quarter the British soldiery within the province. Even Chatham, indisposed at his country home, railed at America's "ingratitude." He predicted that behavior of this sort by the colonists "will draw upon their heads national resentment" and a "torrent of indignation in Parliament." He was prescient.

In the void left by Chatham's lingering absence, the key figure in the formulation of the administration's response to what was occurring in New York—and of Britain's colonial policy in general—was Charles Townshend. Long an ally of Chatham and a veteran of several ministries, the forty-one-year-old Townshend had been brought into this cabinet as chancellor of the exchequer. He has been nearly universally condemned by historians, who have characterized him as an impetuous and capricious "charlatan" who ignored good advice. He "invariably played his own hand (and, as a rule, played it badly)," according to one scholar. A contemporary observer, whose viewpoint was widely shared, remarked that Townshend was "want of all principle . . . and therefore altogether incapable of doing great and national Good, and yet [his] great abilities put it in his power always to do mischief." Some thought him crazed by ambition and so consumed with longing to gain glory that he acted swiftly and recklessly, hopeful of winning accolades for resolving the American problem before Chatham could return to head the ministry. Townshend did act hurriedly, but his haste may have arisen from poor health, which had dogged him since childhood. Faced with a lifelong struggle with epilepsy, Townshend frequently lamented what he called his "crazy constitution." His was a lonely battle that left him fearful that his time was limited.[2]

What was clear was that within six months of forming his ministry, Chatham wanted to be rid of Townshend, convinced that his "incurable weaknesses" made him unfit for his "critical office." But Chatham was too ill to put up a fight. The monarch similarly lost confidence in Townshend. Cruelly referring to him as "vermin," George III remarked that Townshend was "so fickle that no man can depend on him."[3] Yet the king left the ministry under Townshend's sway, perhaps because, like nearly everyone else, he regarded the chancellor of the exchequer as a nearly unrivaled authority on money matters, and Britain was beset with financial troubles.

Townshend may have been worthy of the harsh words of his critics, but it was also true that he wielded power at a demanding time. Many who had voted to repeal the Stamp Act thirsted to demonstrate the parliamentary sovereignty expressed in the Declaratory Act, just as John Adams had feared would be the case. Furthermore, pressure to find other revenue spiked in 1767 after Parliament, faced with an ugly postwar depression and a ruinous harvest, reduced Britain's wartime land tax by one-quarter. All the while, alarming assessments rolled in from royal officials in America. In the wake of the Stamp Act's repeal, the governor of Massachusetts surmised that New England's radicals had been emboldened by Britain's "Weakness." General Gage reported that "the Colonists are taking large strides toward Independency." Gage further advised that "Britain by a speedy and spirited Conduct" should demonstrate that the colonies were unequivocally "depend-ent" on the mother country and "not independent States."[4]

Townshend could not have agreed more. He visualized the American assemblies as veritable nests of "factious men closely cemented together upon a fixed plan . . . to establish their popularity in their own country upon the ruin of the dependency of the colonies upon Great Britain."[5] For Townshend, and a great many others, the Stamp Act disorders offered proof that Britain must tighten the reins on the colonists. Townshend had supported repealing the Stamp Act, but only because he feared that the use of force at that junc-ture would "perhaps drive them [the colonists] to . . . extremities." Rather than unleashing the army, he had urged the formulation of a "proper plan . . . for governing them as well as quieting them," and he cautioned that unless such an imperial system was put in place, Great Britain would face an "extremely dangerous" American problem.[6]

But if Townshend acted to head off a problem that potentially lay down a long road, he succeeded in creating an immediate crisis. However impeccable his logic, his plan was grounded on a view of the past that was in the main illusory, and one with which few colonists would have agreed. Townshend's starting point was that America "ought to share" in meeting the costs of the army, a conviction that stemmed from his belief that the colonists owed all they had to the nurture provided by the mother country. He portrayed the colonists as "children planted by our care, nourished up by our indulgence," and "protected by our arms" until they had "grown to a degree of strength and opulence." His view that the mother country's benevolence accounted for the colonies' prosperity, even survival, was widely shared in England, but Townshend's outlook might in part have stemmed from the loss of his brother, a soldier in the British army who perished in 1759 while fighting the French in New York.[7] Townshend was also persuaded that disaster would follow should Britain ever back down, and his vanity, impetuosity, and misplaced self-assurance let him be goaded into boasting to the House of Commons in January 1767 that he could procure revenue from the Americans.

During the next several weeks Townshend pieced together his American policy, revealing it in the late spring in three separate bills. New York's defi-ance of the Mutiny Act was first on the agenda. His ministry had considered authorizing the governors to lodge troops in private houses, and it had given

some thought to fixing an impost on New York to generate revenue for billet-
ing the soldiers. In the end, Townshend settled on suspending the New York
assembly until the province complied with the Mutiny Act. Franklin, still in
London, was appalled, calling it "a very extraordinary Act." Colonial
governors were empowered to send assemblies packing, and had often done
so, and the Crown could veto bills passed by provincial legislatures, something it had done with some 5 percent of the legislation passed in the colonial
era. However, Townshend's step was out of the ordinary. Foreseeing an escal-
ation in which suspicion and fury were inexorably ratcheted up by the action
of one side and the response of the other, Franklin feared that Townshend's
"Imprudencies" would "Step by Step, bring on mischievous Consequences."[8]

Since entering the cabinet a year earlier, Townshend had searched for a
more efficient means of collecting custom duties. That led to the second
prong of his program, the creation of an American Board of Customs. It was
to include five commissioners, legal counsel, and a staff of clerks. In addition,
Townshend secured approval of the creation of three new vice-admiralty
courts, a step designed to streamline the prosecution of suspected violators of
imperial trade laws. In a move akin to throwing gasoline on a smoldering
fire, it was decided that the American Board of Customs was to be situated in
Boston.[9]

The final part of Townshend's scheme would carry out his boast of raising
revenue in America. His ultimate decision on colonial taxation evolved from
an unhurried rethinking of British interests in the trans-Appalachian west
and the role of the army in America. By 1767, Townshend realized that the
annual cost of maintaining the army in the west was about £700,000, an
amount that was more than double the original estimate and far beyond what
could be obtained from the colonists through taxation or what England
would wish to bear. In addition, Viscount Barrington, the secretary at war,
had come to question the wisdom of garrisoning several thousand regulars
deep in the American interior. Not only was it stupendously expensive to
supply and maintain a large army on the other side of the mountains, but also
the army had already demonstrated its inability to effectively regulate trade
with the Indians in such a huge territory. Besides, thinking of trans-
Appalachia as an "American desert," Barrington saw no reason to open the
region to settlement anytime soon. He preferred to keep the Proclamation of
1763 intact, leaving Canada, Nova Scotia, and Florida as Britain's only new
North American colonies. Barrington advocated returning control—and the
cost—of Indian affairs to the colonists and withdrawing the army to the
settled East, from which it could readily be redeployed in the event of troubles.
Although the troop withdrawal was postponed until the ministry embraced a

plan for the American West, the army's pending redeployment shaped Townshend's thinking concerning American revenue.[10]

The grounds for Parliament's unprecedented colonial taxation had always been British indebtedness and the necessity of supporting the army and supervising the frontier. Townshend abandoned those justifications. His Revenue Act of 1767 was a naked attempt to assert parliamentary sovereignty. Townshend never thought his taxes would raise more than £40,000, roughly a third of what Grenville had envisaged collecting from the Stamp Act, but he foresaw a steady revenue stream. He knew that the colonists had acquiesced in the Sugar Act, albeit unenthusiastically, and he was swayed by Franklin's ill-considered contention that his countrymen would not object to indirect taxes. It was something that neither Townshend nor Franklin would have believed had they taken seriously the Virginia Resolves or the declaration of the Stamp Act Congress.

His thinking shaped by these assorted ingredients, Townshend proposed taxes on all glass, lead, paint colors, and tea imported into the colonies from Great Britain. In addition to a new tax, his legislation (almost immediately referred to as the "Townshend Duties") candidly stated that the revenue was to be used for paying what at the time was called the civil list—the salaries of numerous royal officials in the colonies. As the colonial assemblies had long thought it their right to vote on the salaries of these officials, there could be no question that Britain was seeking to reduce the influence of the American legislatures. As if all this was not enough, the act formally authorized customs officials to use writs of assistance upon entering "any house, warehouse, shop, cellar, or other place . . . to search for and seize prohibited or uncustomed goods." This legislation was a ticking time bomb from the moment it was enacted by a huge majority in a Parliament that reflected England's simmering outrage, which Franklin had detected, in the wake of the colonial protest and riots against the Stamp Act.[11]

Townshend died scant weeks after his duties became law. His death, sudden and unexpected, left Lord Shelburne, the secretary of state for the Southern Department—whose jurisdiction included North America—as the most important minister with regard to colonial affairs. Shelburne's vision for trans-Appalachia could not have been more different from that of Grenville, Townshend, or Barrington. While Shelburne agreed with the withdrawal of the army to the east, he proposed the creation of two new colonies beyond the mountains, one around present-day Detroit and the other in the Illinois Country, which extended to the Mississippi River, and he recommended returning control of the Indian trade to the colonists. Rather than imposing parliamentary taxes on America, Shelburne would have financed western colonization by quitrents—a fee paid by landowners—and requisitions from colonial assemblies. Shelburne's imperial system would have continued the decentralization that had prevailed prior to 1763. Enough of his thinking was made public that it won applause from colonial land speculators, powerful men who understood that opening new colonies brightened the chances of selling their lands. Alas, in 1768 colonial affairs were transferred to a newly created ministerial office, the Secretary of State for the American Department—its head would be called the American secretary—and the post went to Lord Hillsborough. Shelburne's plans came to a crashing halt. As the 1760s came to an end, the American West remained largely closed to settlement.[12]

Word of the Townshend Duties did not arrive in America like a thunderclap. In fact, nearly a year passed before any colony responded in a meaningful way. The fiery spirit that had gripped Boston two years earlier seemed to have vanished. The Stamp Act had provoked troubling questions about London's intentions and the colonists' place within the empire, but it had not instilled a pervasive revolutionary mentality. Moreover, the non-importation agreements adopted to fight the Stamp Act had caused distress, especially in the port cities and particularly among the merchants, sailors, and dockhands. Grave concerns also existed about how London might respond to renewed protest. It had backed down once, though its retreat had been accompanied by a ringing declaration of Parliament's unlimited authority over the colonies. No one was certain whether that had been a face-saving step or whether Parliament felt a deep-seated commitment to such a doctrine, but unsettling rumors were issued from London that further defiance would call down the British army. Above all, the colonies could not have been more disunited. Protest by any province might be a very solitary act. The repeal of the Stamp Act had "hushed into silence" the insurgents, as John Adams noted, and it was not easy to reignite the popular protest.[13]

The Massachusetts assembly was not scheduled to meet until early 1768, and the royal governor dared not heed the pleas of Samuel Adams and others to convene a special session. In the interim, the best that Boston's leaders could do was obtain a call by a town meeting for the citizenry to voluntarily abstain from purchasing imported goods from Great Britain, and two meetings were required to get that measure adopted. Even then, it was to be a toothless, non-compulsory boycott of luxury items, none of which were subject to the Townshend Duties.[14]

A breakthrough of sorts came late in 1767 with the publication of John Dickinson's *Letters from a Farmer in Pennsylvania*, a tract that appeared in

installments in nearly every American newspaper late in the year and was
soon issued as a pamphlet. Though he called himself a farmer, Dickinson
was a thirty-five-year-old London-educated lawyer who lived in Delaware
and practiced in Philadelphia. He was also the head of one of the two political parties in Pennsylvania. Two years earlier, he had written against the
Stamp Act, asserting that parliamentary taxation would sow economic
misfortune among colonists as well as English merchants and manufacturers. In *Letters from a Farmer*, Dickinson shifted his emphasis, doubtless
because of the Declaratory Act. He assailed the Townshend Duties on
constitutional grounds. Parliament, he insisted, had no legal authority "to
lay upon these colonies any 'tax' whatever." It could not impose a direct tax.
It could not levy an indirect tax. It could not tax America. If Parliament
ever succeeded in taxing America, "our boasted liberty" would be "a sound
and nothing else," for the colonial assemblies would "not hold even the
puny privilege of French parliaments." None of this differed significantly
from the position taken two years earlier in the Virginia Resolves, but the
Letters appeared at a crucial moment of irresolution. Besides, Dickinson
was hardly an upstart. He was wealthy and respected, and no one thought
him a firebrand. His tone was moderate. He did not even argue that
Parliament had no authority over the colonies. In fact, he maintained that it
possessed the unquestioned legal authority to regulate imperial trade. He
had taken a middle ground between the seemingly immoderate positions of
a Patrick Henry or Samuel Adams on the one side and a Charles Townshend
on the other. What Dickinson had proposed could be embraced by the
more conservative colonists, especially by powerful northern merchants
who saw overwhelming advantages to America's commercial links with
Great Britain.[15]

The *Letters* were an immediate sensation, selling more copies than the
combined sales of the sixty or so prior pamphlets on the imperial crisis, and
transforming the previously unknown Dickinson into an American hero, a
turn of events that was not lost on ambitious politicians. In no time, engrav-
ings of Dickinson's image appeared in almanacs and pamphlets, his figure
was added to a waxworks museum in Boston, a ship was named after him,
and he was toasted at banquets from Savannah to north of Boston. What is
today Princeton University awarded him an honorary degree, and *Letters
from a Farmer* was published in England and France.

Within days of the appearance of the first portions of Dickinson's *Letters*,
Massachusetts finally did something. The assembly petitioned the king to
"afford us Reliefe" from the Townshend Duties. Soon thereafter it dispatched
a shorter but nearly identical letter to every provincial assembly requesting

that they, too, petition the monarch. Both the petition and the Massachusetts Circular Letter, as it was called, condensed Dickinson's argument—and for that matter the position taken by Pitt during the Stamp Act imbroglio—and asserted that while "Parliament is the supreme legislative power over the whole empire," there were limits to its authority. One limitation was a prohibition on taxing subjects without their consent. Hence, as the colonists were not and could not be represented in Parliament, the Townshend Duties "overleap[ed] the bounds" of parliamentary authority.[16] The petition and Circular Letter were at once gambits to foster colonial unity and to appeal to those in England who shared the views of Chatham.

Some in London saw that an amicable resolution of the issue of parliamentary sovereignty was impossible in the current environment, and the wisest among them understood that demanding acquiescence to the Declaratory Act "must totally destroy all connection with the colonies," as a former prime minister put it in 1768.[17] A handful in London saw the Massachusetts Circular Letter as a relatively moderate statement, one that neither questioned Parliament's power to regulate commerce nor the steps taken by Townshend to tighten the regulation of colonial trade.

Sometimes, history hangs on timing, sometimes on personalities. Both were at play in London's reaction to the Circular Letter. Had the Circular Letter been sent a few months earlier, it would have come to the desk of Shelburne, nearly universally regarded as a friend of America. Instead, Lord Hillsborough, the new American secretary, would determine the administration's response. No one knew what to expect of him. Hillsborough was a follower of the intransigent Grenville, yet he had opposed the Stamp Act and voted for its repeal. Massachusetts's agent in London reported that Hillsborough "had never discovered any particular affection for America," but Franklin did "not think this nobleman in general an enemy to America." Months after the new American secretary took office, Franklin still assumed his "inclinations are rather favourable towards us," though within the parameters of what Hillsborough "supposes [are] the unquestionable rights of Britain."[18]

Franklin soon ate his words. Hillsborough's response to the Massachusetts Circular Letter revealed that however well disposed he was toward the colonies, he would brook no questioning of Parliament's authority. If the American problem was to have any chance of being fixed peacefully, it required leadership by supple and adaptable statesmen who were open to new ways of thinking. Instead, at this critical moment the office of American secretary was occupied by a perversely implacable individual. Franklin eventually concluded that Hillsborough was "senseless," "wrong-headed," and "proud, supercilious, extreamely conceited." He was not alone in his harsh judgment. A personal friend thought Hillsborough close-minded and noted both for "a *petitesse* in his character" and his "little and confined" viewpoint." George III, with whom Hillsborough worked closely for years, subsequently concluded that among all the major ministerial officers of the time, none exercised "less judgment" than his American secretary.[19]

By mid-April 1768, when Hillsborough learned of the Circular Letter, the press in England was "in full cry against America," as Franklin disclosed, outraged by talk in the colonies of another boycott of British imports and fuming over attacks on the Townshend Duties in the American print media. At the same moment, however, word reached London that New York had capitulated in the face of Townshend's resolute stand, voting adequate funds for quartering the British army. Those developments strengthened Hillsborough's resolve, which already had been stiffened during his first one hundred days in office by the hard-liners who surrounded him, the sort who—again in Franklin's opinion—did not "dare tell him disagreeable Truths." Hillsborough's undersecretary of state, for instance, advised that "if the colonies see this country is earnest, they will probably . . . take the part of peaceable subjects in future."[20]

Townshend's duties were an egregious blunder. Hillsborough compounded the error. With revenue coming in from the Sugar Act and the buttressing of customs officials, he might have taken care to avoid a provocative response. Instead, the American secretary ordered that the Massachusetts assembly must rescind its Circular Letter or it would not be permitted to meet. Nor did he stop there. In a directive that soon was known as the "Hillsborough Letter," he warned that the same fate awaited any assembly that approved the Bay Colony's "seditious" assertion.[21] Not only had London refused to hear Massachusetts's petition, but also, for the second time in two years, the mother country was threatening to shut down colonial assemblies.

Three years earlier Franklin had told Parliament that the colonists were not rebels, but if imperial authorities acted imprudently, they might create an insurgency. His prediction was coming true. Within six months of the arrival of the Hillsborough Letter, nearly every colony had endorsed the Massachusetts Circular Letter and most had petitioned the king for redress. Furthermore, by roughly a five-to-one margin, the Massachusetts House refused to repeal its letter. The House was prorogued by the royal governor, an act that reenergized Boston's popular leaders to try again to institute a meaningful boycott of English imports. They sought a non-importation accord, and by late summer 1768—with Boston's shops groaning with unsold inventories of British goods—the idea was more popular. However, Boston's merchants would agree to stop importing British goods only if New York and Philadelphia joined in. New York was willing, Philadelphia was not. Seven long months were required to gain the Philadelphians' assent, though by March 1769, some twenty months after word of the Townshend Duties reached America, the three commercial hubs in the northern colonies had united in an economic protest, and they were joined by Virginia, Maryland, and South Carolina.

This was a more comprehensive, better-enforced boycott than the almost slapdash trade stoppage that had sprung up during the Stamp Act troubles, and at least in New England the rhetoric that accompanied it had a different dimension. Numerous essayists and the resolves of some country towns insisted that the region's economic troubles stemmed not just from taxes or high custom duties but also from the colonists' lack of economic independence. Some decried England's monopoly on sales to the colonies, which kept prices artificially and injuriously high for Yankee consumers; others were critical of the impediments on free trade, which depressed the value of the region's exports. Still others, restive with constraints on colonial manufacturing, saw the embargo as a heaven-sent spur for jump-starting local production. Some New Englanders even proudly wore homespun garments, both as a sign of adherence to the boycott and a not-so-understated endorsement of colonial manufacturing. Newport's well-heeled denizens conspicuously wore homespun gowns to elite balls, and in 1769 the graduates of Harvard, Yale, and Brown voted to attend their graduation ceremonies dressed in locally made clothes and to receive diplomas printed on paper produced in New England.[22]

In Virginia, the movement to institute a boycott was led by George Washington, heretofore little troubled by the new colonial policies. Washington had been elected to the House of Burgesses in 1758 while serving as commander of Virginia's army during the Seven Years' War. Neither a college graduate nor a lawyer, and unaccustomed to rapid-fire legislative floor debates, Washington remained a backbencher. He worked hard on behalf of his own pecuniary interests, tirelessly doing all he could to make sure that he received the bounty lands that Virginia's soldiers in the late war had been promised. Otherwise, he seemed resigned to be a secondary figure. He had neither been troubled by word of the Stamp Act nor taken part in the protest against it; if anything, he appears to have dismissed the legislation as an isolated blunder by imperial leaders. However, the Townshend Duties made it clear to him—and a great many other colonists—that London was pursuing a deliberate policy.

Washington opposed parliamentary taxation, though he was disturbed by other things as well. He was uneasy with the imperial restrictions that inhibited certain types of colonial manufacturing. As his slaves produced textiles, Washington was anxious lest an all-powerful Parliament might someday restrict their manufacture in the colonies, as it already prohibited the making of hats, woolen items, and certain types of iron. The day might come when he wished to engage in other types of manufacturing. However, Washington's principal grievance concerned the imperial land policy. He had soldiered and sacrificed for five years to win and open the western regions, and through soldiering he was due thousands of acres in trans-Appalachian bounty lands. Yet, as the decade wound down, that land—his land—remained closed to settlement under the Proclamation of 1763. Washington had not realized a farthing from the land for which he had paid dearly in service to his colony and empire.

Washington additionally festered with resentment at the manner in which Americans had been treated by British officials during the recent war. It riled him that British officers scorned their American counterparts as callow inferiors. He fumed at the British practice of treating every colonial officer, no matter his rank, as subordinate to the lowest-ranking British officer. By the late 1760s, Washington appears to have reached the point of longing for Americans to control their own destiny and to secure their own interests. In his heart of hearts, it is likely that Washington already dreamed of American independence. He never said that, but in private, he raged at "our lordly Masters in Great Britain" and he quietly told influential Virginia assemblymen that he was ready to soldier again if the British did not back down.[23]

In 1769 Washington urged boycott, not war. Even here, Washington thought non-importation was to his economic advantage, and he thought it would be beneficial to southern planters in general, as it would curb intemperate spending on consumer items and provide a shield against indebtedness. Like many another planter, Washington filled Mount Vernon with china, silver, furniture, and assorted ornamental pieces acquired from England, usually after ascertaining that what he was purchasing was in fashion in the mother country. Washington complained of being cheated by the English, but he never apologized for his acquisitive habits, and he never suggested that he was manipulated by English entrepreneurs who exploited his spendthrift ways. Others did, however. For instance, South Carolina's David Ramsay conceived a fanciful conspiratorial scenario in which diabolical English businessmen "encourage[d] our dissipation and extravagance for the twofold purpose of increasing the sale of [their] manufactures and of perpetuating our subordination."[24]

Working with his neighbor and fellow assemblyman George Mason, Washington had the boycott legislation ready for action when the House of Burgesses met in May 1769. First, the assembly passed another set of Virginia Resolves, which among other things defended its right to act in concert with other colonies in petitioning the king. In reprisal, the governor dissolved the House of Burgesses, but the members defiantly—and illegally—met in a private house in Williamsburg and adopted non-importation.[25]

Underlying the colonists' concern about taxation was a dread of losing the degree of autonomy they possessed and coveted. And the fuel driving the colonists' desire to maintain, even to increase, their autonomy was economic: profits, jobs, income, and opportunities.

In Boston, the yearning to maintain what long had been enjoyed fed the raging apprehension aroused by Britain's plans for tightening commercial regulation, a prospect that became reality in November 1767, when the customs commissioners sent by Charles Townshend arrived in the city. Reporting home that smuggling had reached epidemic proportions among Boston's merchants, the commissioners soon set to enforcing the trade laws. In no time, they were subject to intimidation. Small crowds gathered before their homes at night, and men armed with clubs called out threats and some-times broke windows. Larger crowds held rallies and hanged effigies of the commissioners on the city's Liberty Tree, the now-sacred elm from which Oliver's effigy had swung back in 1765. The worried commissioners beseeched Governor Bernard to provide protection. The chief executive's only option was to call for troops, a step he shrank from taking, partly from fear that it would inflame an already dangerous situation and partly from fear for his own safety. "I have conducted myself so as to be able to say, and swear to it, if the Sons of Liberty shall require it, that I have never applied for Troops," Bernard weakly responded.

For weeks, Bernard had reported that "a violent Opposition to the [Customs] Officers . . . is hourly expected." It occurred in June following their seizure of the *Liberty*, a vessel owned by John Hancock, a wealthy and influential merchant with close ties to the popular movement. In no time, a mob of thousands roamed the streets of Boston and pillaged property belonging to the commissioners. Confiscating the *Liberty*'s cargo was the last thing the commissioners did for a while. Fearing for their lives, they fled to the safety of Castle Island, south of the city on the shores of Boston Harbor, where they were eventually housed in Castle William. Seven months after their arrival, the commissioners had been put out of commission by a popular movement that controlled the city. Since shortly after they came to Boston, the commissioners had concluded that enforcement of the trade laws hinged on the presence of the army, and in February, the American Customs Board appealed to London to send several regiments to Boston. Their plea was underscored by Governor Bernard, who at wit's end worked up the courage to tell the ministry that troops were needed "to rescue the Government out of the hands of a trained mob, & to restore the Activity of the Civil Power."[26]

Around the time the commissioners beseeched London for help, Benjamin Franklin said of the imperial crisis, "the more I have thought and read on the subject the more I find myself confirmed in opinion, that no middle doctrine can be well maintained. I mean," he went on, one "of the extremes" must prevail. Either "Parliament has a power to make *all laws* for us, or it has a power to make *no laws* for us." Hillsborough had long since come to a similar conclusion. Indeed, Hillsborough was certain that behind the colonists' protests lay plans to foster a "struggle for independency." That was incorrect. Some colonists had probably always longed for independence and others, radicalized by events since 1765, had come to cherish the thought of breaking away from the mother country. But hopes for a total break with the mother country were not widespread in the colonies in 1768. However, it is not difficult to see how Hillsborough came to believe that the colonists were steely-eyed revolutionaries. He heard it often from royal officials posted in America. For instance, General Gage wrote home in 1768 that whereas the American insurgents had initially objected only to direct taxes, they now balked at all duties levied by Parliament. The rebels "mean to go on step by Step 'till they throw off all subjections" to Parliament, he advised. If successful, Gage added, the day will come when they will also "deny the prerogatives of the Crown."[27]

Early in June, after consulting with the king, Hillsborough directed Gage to deploy one regiment to Boston. Later, when he learned of the *Liberty* riots, the American secretary ordered two additional regiments to Boston. His intention was to break the back of the rebellion in Massachusetts, which he was convinced would quell "a like dangerous Spirit of Opposition" elsewhere. For the first time, but not the last, London acted against Massachusetts on the assumption that it was the epicenter of the American troubles and that the other provinces merely tagged along. Not for the last time, too, imperial authorities acted on the belief that in the face of a harsh response, the American insurgents "would be less bold."[28]

Britain's decision to send troops to the city did more to change the thinking of Bostonians than any step previously taken by London. Armies had atrocious reputations. It was not just that throughout history armies had often been the vehicle for establishing tyranny; soldiers had reputations for spreading mayhem and misery. Many in Boston spoke of the "British invasion." In fact, when the army's arrival was imminent, the city lit the beacon that it had historically used to alert the countryside of a threatened foreign invasion. In this instance, the troops on the way happened to be British, but they were still soldiers, thought to be an unsavory bunch deployed for a malign purpose—to beat down civilians. The thoughts of many in the city drew on an old Whig adage from early-eighteenth-century England: there was "little Difference between being oppressed by a Standing Army of Natives [and] a Standing Army of Foreigners."[29]

There was wild talk in Boston of armed resistance to the British regulars. Samuel Adams allegedly claimed that he could muster thirty thousand men "with their knapsacks and bayonets fixed" to "destroy every soldier that dares put his foot ashore."[30] Despite his supposed bravado, Adams soon was more circumspect. Some degree of unity had formed among the provinces, but hardly the sort of solidarity necessary for waging war against the mother country, and no one understood that better than Adams. He knew very little about sentiment throughout America or, for that matter, even in backcountry Massachusetts. However, he sensed that the presence of British troops could foster greater unity between the city and the countryside. Adams and his confederates turned aside all thought of armed resistance. Confident in their ability to maintain control, Adams and his colleagues in Boston's popular leadership backed as a first step a town meeting to discuss the city's response. It in turn called for an extra-legal colonywide convention to decide what measures, if any, to take when the army arrived. Nearly one hundred towns and eight districts were represented when the delegates assembled late in September at Faneuil Hall. The carefully managed convention spurned a call to arms. Instead, it petitioned the governor to reconvene the assembly and the king to protect them from arbitrary and illegal parliamentary measures.

That very evening fourteen vessels carrying 1,200 soldiers clad in the British army's familiar red coats sailed into Boston harbor, their way illuminated by fireworks arranged by royal officials. Residents of Boston could hear the strains of "Yankee Doodle" derisively played by a band of musicians aboard a troop transport. Two days later the soldiers disembarked to the pulsating sounds of martial music. They marched through mostly empty streets, only occasionally passing a scrum of grimly scornful and silent citizens. But march they did, loudly and conspicuously through the cobble streets to the Commons, where they paraded amid the clattering of arms and the barking of brusque commands. A large army of British regulars had come ashore without incident. When the last of the British soldiers arrived a few weeks later, some 2,200 regulars were in Boston, sent to keep peace and to ensure that British law was enforced.[31]

Bostonians had not resisted the landing of the troops, though they were not especially cooperative. The council supplied the troops with the items required by the Mutiny Act, but the local authorities did not bend over backward to provide housing, leaving a great many redcoats to endure Boston's painfully cold autumn nights in tents on the city's Commons. That only contributed to the friction between citizens and soldiers. Soon enough, incidents occurred. Citizens spat on soldiers, heckled them, and waylaid the unwary. The soldiers, harried and contemptuous, responded in kind. Now and then, a Bostonian was attacked, some were victims of thievery, and one rape was reported. Local newspapers described some episodes, and in October the *Journal of the Times* came into being. It resembled a newspaper but was the creation of the popular leadership, which used it as a muckraking vehicle for disparaging both customs officials and the soldiery. Crammed with stories of purported villainy by the redcoats, indiscreet readers must have been convinced that soldiers hourly visited mayhem on some unfortunate Bostonian.

Samuel Adams utilized the army's presence to mold a revolutionary mentality within Massachusetts. In numerous newspaper essays he asserted that deploying the troops in a peaceful city violated the English Bill of Rights. He charged, too, that sending the army to enforce an unconstitutional act offered proof that Britain had fallen under the leadership of evil men bent on establishing despotism. His refrain was that resistance alone would preserve American liberty. For many New Englanders, as for Adams—and because of Adams—Hillsborough's order to dispatch troops to Boston was a tipping point.[32]

Since the earliest troubles, articulate colonists had struggled to comprehend what lay behind the departures in imperial policy and what it meant for them. They saw things through the prism of ideas with which they had long been familiar, an outlook derived from the classics of antiquity and the writings of Enlightenment rationalism, though the political thought from the era of the English Civil War was especially influential. During the seventeenth century, English thinkers had formulated a reasoned theory of opposition to absolutism. Challenging the traditional argument that monarchical authority stemmed from divine right, the heart and soul of the contrarians' belief system was that kings derived authority from the people. John Locke, who was born shortly after the *Mayflower's* historic voyage, exerted a particularly profound sway on thought in the colonies. In *Two Treatises on Government* (1690), Locke argued that early humankind had left a state of nature to form governments for the protection of their life, liberty, and property. If government broke the contract between rulers and ruled—by depriving the citizenry of liberty or by seizing their property—the people might after a "long train of Abuses, Prevarications, and Artifices" legitimately revolt and change the government to prevent their enslavement. Joined to this outlook was the notion nourished by the Scottish Enlightenment, and notably by Francis Hutcheson, that the test of all institutions, and not least of government, was whether they contributed to "the *greatest happiness* for the *greatest numbers.*"[33]

Theorists who wrote in the Commonwealth period after the Civil War, including Algernon Sidney, James Harrington, and Henry St. John the 1st Viscount Bolingbroke, were crucially important as well, although the ultra-libertarian views of John Trenchard and Thomas Gordon, who authored scores of essays that were collected and published in 1721 as *The Independent Whig*, exerted the most profound influence in the colonies. Their tracts conveyed the notion that England remained threatened by a political absolutism and social decadence that endangered all to which the nation and its people had long been accustomed. In fact, these authors were extreme conservatives reacting against the forces of modernization—the Bank of England, stock markets, huge mercantile firms, commercialized farming, and a chronic public debt—but among colonists far removed from the mother country, the belief was spawned of an ineradicably corrupt and decaying English nation in which individual liberty, property, and happiness were under siege. Their dark picture of the hopelessness of life in an iniquitous England was the lens through which the best educated colonists viewed, and interpreted, ministerial actions after 1765.[34]

It is not likely that many farmers returned to their hearth in the evening after a long, tiring day of plowing fields or weeding rows of corn and thoughtfully perused Lockean treatises, or that many artisans, after hunching for hours over a workbench, read Voltaire by candlelight and greedily consumed the polemical tracts in the *Independent Whig*. Those who worked with their hands were more likely to draw on the Bible or the sermons of their ministers to understand the world around them. But many clergymen had read the ideology of dissent, and they preached of the dangers posed by centralized authority to the rights of the people. These ministers—subsequently dubbed the "black Regiment" by an American Tory—assailed parliamentary taxation, and in ringing homilies some drew a parallel between the unjust slavery in which the ancient Egyptians held the Israelites and the fate that awaited the colonists should they acquiesce in the imperial ministry's threatening intentions. Above all, they stressed that even before the first governments were formed, God had bestowed universal rights on humankind. Indeed, in the words of one historian, the idea that God-given "rights were a fundamental aspect of the human condition" was "irrefutable," and when carried to its logical conclusion, it meant that God expected even common people to stand vigil against tyrants and to judge whether their rulers governed for the common good. Political activists sometimes noted the clergy's importance in shaping popular opinion. John Adams thought it significant to the insurgency that clergymen "thunder and lighten every sabbath" and Thomas Jefferson spoke of sermons that coursed through the Virginia countryside "like a shock of electricity."[35]

Whatever their source for interpreting British actions, more and more colonists grew wary of royal authority after 1765. The Stamp Act had been a warning bell that alerted them to a threat to their liberty from London. Within another two or three years, suspicions of what was driving Parliament and the imperial leadership hardened among many Americans into a conviction that nothing less than a deep-laid plot existed to "complete our slavery."[36] Imperial taxation, the imposition of a standing army, a government that would not listen to petitions for redress, a commercial policy more intent on serving the interests of the powerful at home than the vital needs of colonists, and an unmistakable pattern of seeking to diminish the authority of colonial assemblies had awakened growing numbers to the existence of danger. But for many it was a long-playing affair in England that brought what appeared to be happening into sharp focus.

In the early 1760s, John Wilkes, a member of the House of Commons, published numerous attacks on the foreign policy of the king and ministry in his newspaper, the *North Briton*. His vitriol reached new heights in April 1763 in issue number 45. Wilkes hurled charges of corruption and unconstitutional behavior at the monarch and his ministers. With George III fuming, the Grenville ministry secured a search warrant to comb through Wilkes's property, and the House of Commons condemned his journalism as seditious and libelous. Faced with arrest, Wilkes fled into exile. Five years later, he returned to England. Petitioning the Crown for a pardon, Wilkes also declared his candidacy for a seat in the House of Commons. He won the election, but lost his appeal to the king and was imprisoned for his five-year-old "crime." From his cell, Wilkes appealed again, this time requesting his release to represent his district while Parliament was in session. Not only did the ministry reject his entreaty, but also the House of Commons expelled him, the first of three times that it refused to permit Wilkes to occupy the seat to which he had been elected. Throngs of Londoners took to the streets to protest what many saw as Parliament's unjustifiably harsh action. Countless numbers in the crowds wore blue cockades adorned with the lettering "Wilkes" or "45," in reference to issue 45 of his paper. In May 1768 one especially large crowd gathered in St. George's Fields outside the prison where Wilkes was confined to protest his treatment. Units of the army were summoned to maintain peace. A tense standoff ensued. It ended when the soldiers fired into the crowd. Upwards of a half-dozen citizens were killed and fifteen were wounded. Soon, the incident was known in London and America as the "St. George's Fields Massacre." The contingency of events is often crucial. News that Parliament had blocked the popular will and that the army had fired on civilians just outside King's Bench Prison reached the colonies not long after the draconian Hillsborough Letter and about the same moment that Britain's red-clad army marched into Boston.

John Wilkes was lionized in the colonies. Seemingly the very embodiment of liberty, and the victim of a British government indifferent to the popular will, Wilkes was toasted at dinners and Sons of Liberty gatherings. The number 45 became, in the words of one historian, "almost a sacred number." As the tempestuous 1760s neared its end, more and more colonists saw in the panoply of British actions since 1765 a "design . . . to enslave them."[37]

But not all who would one day become revolutionaries were yet radicalized. John Adams, an up-and-coming young lawyer in Massachusetts, may not have defended Britain's new policies, but down to 1770 and beyond he looked with equal mistrust on Britain's ministers and Boston's militants. Adams had written Braintree's remonstrance against the Stamp Act, secretly penned a Boston town meeting petition urging that the army be recalled, and clandestinely crafted communiqués and inflammatory propaganda pieces for protest leaders. When in 1768 he was offered an appointment as solicitor general (the royal governor's chief legal officer), Adams immediately declined. But he still respected Great Britain and believed its policies were misguided rather than tyrannical. Furthermore, having been privy to the inner circles of the popular leadership, Adams concluded that many of those activists nurtured a secret agenda, American independence, which he did not share. He was convinced that they plotted to "deceive the People" and "conceal[ed] . . . essential truth[s]." Making clear in the privacy of his diary that he did not welcome the sentiments of the radicals, Adams wrote of their conspiracies and "Crimes." He said of the path that Samuel Adams wished to take: "That way madness lies." Something else nagged at Adams. He was aware that royal officials had heaped "Curses, and Imprecations" on his cousin Samuel Adams and that James Otis had been reproached as "a reprobate, an apostate, and a traitor in every street in Boston." He knew too that Otis's legal practice had suffered as a result. Married with young children, still only in his early thirties and with a legal practice that was just getting off the ground, Adams did not want his career ruined by his political activism. On the other hand, he did not want it damaged by giving the appearance that he opposed the popular protests. When Samuel Adams in 1769 cautioned him that people were questioning his commitment to the cause, John hurried to a public rally of the Sons of Liberty.[38]

Benjamin Franklin played both sides as well. In his early sixties when the Townshend Duty crisis erupted, Franklin had lived comfortably in London for years. Relishing the social and intellectual opportunities offered in this cosmopolitan environment, Franklin desperately yearned to live out his life in the metropolis, and he hoped to never have to choose between London and Philadelphia. Franklin spent the latter 1760s warning administration authorities of the dangers in the course they were pursuing. He told them that "the Seeds of Liberty are universally sown in America" and he advised that harsh, intransigent rule would drive the colonists to "a Separation." Cautioning that force would be met with force, he reminded imperial leaders that in the last war Britain had been compelled to raise forty thousand men to subdue a single sparsely populated province, Canada. The solution to the crisis, he came to believe, was for London to acknowledge that the colonists owed allegiance only to the king, and he advised Hillsborough and others to "*Repeal* the LAWS [of taxation], *Renounce* the RIGHT [of Parliament to legislate for America], *Recall* the Troops, *Refund* the Money [raised thus far by taxation], and *Return* to the old" ways of the empire prior to the Stamp Act. He remained hopeful, though he was convinced that many in Parliament harbored an "inveterate Malice to the Americans." Franklin even imagined that many MPs wished to push the colonists to the brink in order "to hang" every American dissident.[39]

Given the gravity of the situation, contemplative Americans were not alone in pondering a way out of the morass. During 1769, feeling the pinch of the American boycotts and avid to avoid war, some within the ministry searched for a constructive resolution of differences, openly questioning Hillsborough's strident responses toward the colonies. But for a time, they were drowned out by a vengeful majority that coalesced around the idea of retribution against Massachusetts as a prelude to the withdrawal of the army and the repeal of Townshend's duties. A host of extreme measures were entertained. Interminable debates ensued. The ministers considered preventing town meetings in Boston, prohibiting some who were thought to be troublemakers from sitting in the assembly, issuing a new charter for the province, and prosecuting leaders of the popular resistance for treason. Discussions spun on for months, with perspectives changing according to the latest news from the colonies. The absence of violent protest in colonial cities aided those who favored restraint, as did the king's opposition to vengeful measures.

Ultimately, those opposed to punitive measures prevailed, convinced that recriminations against Massachusetts would, as the chancellor of the exchequer, Frederick Lord North, put it, only add "fresh grounds of dispute." That left the matter of taxation to be sorted out. London knew that in two years the revenue raised by the Townshend Duties was far short of what proponents had foreseen. Only about £17,000 had been realized, nearly all of it from the duty on tea. The taxes were a bust, and so too, given the boycotts, was the greater enforcement of the trade laws. In two years, the Townshend Duties had netted only about 20 percent of what had been projected; during the five years since the customs service had been streamlined, less than half the anticipated revenue had been realized. The cabinet divided not only over the wisdom of repealing the duties so long as the colonies questioned the Declaratory Act but also over whether to rescind all or only some of the duties. Testy meetings and fractious relationships eventually led to the resignations of some ministers, including the Duke of Grafton, who had emerged as prime minister following Townshend's death. During the summer of 1769 the king asked Lord North to reorganize and head the ministry.[40]

North had long been regarded as the monarch's spokesman in the cabinet. In time, he had come to favor repeal of all the Townshend Duties but that on tea. For North, the tea tax was crucial, mostly as a symbolic demonstration of Parliament's authority, though he did not wish to be deprived of the revenue it raised. Seeing his policy as conciliatory, North believed it would at once break the back of the boycotts while resolving Anglo-American difficulties for years to come. On March 5, 1770, North addressed the House of Commons, asking "how so preposterous a law" as the Townshend Duties had been enacted in the first place, and he added that it was his "wish to be thought . . . a friend to trade, a friend to America."[41] He asked the Commons to repeal all the Townshend Duties except that on tea. It obliged. Parliament had not backed off its avowal of authority over the colonies, but it had taken a more moderate approach than that favored by a majority of ministers only a few months earlier.

Colonial opposition to the Townshend Duties had been peaceful and mostly centered on petitions, newspaper essays, and non-importation agreements. Instituting and enforcing boycotts had never been easy. Some coastal towns never assented to the ban on British imports; some localities instituted embargoes, but, in the words of one scholar, they were "a farce." Even in Boston, the boycott was far from ironclad. It was so obviously porous that after a few months the protest leaders at a mass meeting took the administration of non-importation from a committee of merchants and put it in the hands of the "Body of the Trade"—called "the Body" by the citizenry—open meetings attended by upwards of 1,400 that functioned as a giant committee. Enforcement was more rigorous and compliance noticeably improved, particularly after it published the names of violators. Even so, when customs agents in the fall of 1769 leaked to an antiboycott newspaper the manifests of all cargoes that had entered Boston Harbor that year, it was evident that many of the most vocal proponents of the boycott—including John Hancock—had routinely disregarded the embargo they had allegedly championed.[42]

Tension remained high in Boston. Before mid-1769, reliable word from London was that some of the duties would be repealed, but Franklin and others advised that "nothing will bring on" the revocation of all the taxes "but our unanimous Resolution to consume no more of their Goods."[43] The presence of the army and customs officers added to the uneasiness that shrouded the city. Incidents were unrelenting, each with the potential for igniting a general explosion. Brawls between soldiers and Boston's sailors and dockhands were commonplace, someone tried to burn down the residence of a merchant who had been blacklisted by the Body, and James Otis somehow got into a fistfight with one of the commissioners of customs, paying for his pugnacity by suffering a thorough beating. But two especially violent occurrences in a nine-day stretch in the dead of winter in 1770 brought feelings to a fever pitch.

On February 22 a crowd gathered, hoping to intimidate Theophilus Lillie, a merchant who openly violated the embargo on trade with the mother country. Lillie in fact thumbed his nose at the Body, suggesting that its campaign to restrain trade amounted to "slavery." He was not easily frightened. His office had already been damaged by a mob, and a ship's captain had threatened to break his neck. On this day, the mob posted materials outside his office in hopes of discouraging Bostonians from purchasing any commodities from him. Its thirst for reprisal hardly slaked, the horde shoved off to the nearby home of Ebenezer Richardson, also a marked man, as he was known to have informed on smugglers. The assemblage shouted taunts and pelted the house with garbage. When it appeared that the mob might break into his dwelling, Richardson flung open an upstairs window and fired his shotgun into the crowd below. Two in the throng were hit, including eleven-year-old Christopher Seider, who was mortally wounded. Popular leaders, growing more desperate as both a partial repeal of the Townshend Duties and the demise of the boycott appeared likely, made young Seider a "little hero and first martyr to the noble cause." Thousands attended his carefully planned and lavish funeral.[44] A couple of days later, on Friday, March 2, a second inflammatory incident occurred. An unusually large brawl between soldiers and civilians took place at Gray's ropewalk. Upwards of seventy strong-willed men slugged it out with fists, clubs, even cutlasses. The bloodied combatants—and soon their friends—vowed to continue the fight after the weekend.

Three days later, on Monday, March 5—ironically, the very day that Lord North in London proposed the repeal of all the Townshend Duties save for the tax on tea—workers and not a few redcoats in Boston were ardent for battle. It was a bitterly cold late-winter day. Snow, old and dirty, stood everywhere. Low-lying smoke from thousands of fireplaces blanketed the town. Isolated incidents erupted on the threshold of evening. Once night descended, more fracases occurred, but all were small-scale affairs. Given the cold and the jet-black night, it was a good bet that things would wind down early on. Suddenly, however, at nine fifteen P.M. an alarm bell tolled. Residents were being summoned downtown. It was never clear who rang the bell, only that men scurried from their homes and grog shops thinking a fire alarm had been sounded. Within minutes a crowd of some two hundred men and boys had gathered on snow-covered King Street in front of the Customs House, which was guarded by a squad of eight nervous regulars and one officer. It was never made known who steered the crowd to this location, or why it lingered once it was evident that there was no fire, but royal officials subsequently thought that occurrences to this point were not accidental, and they may have been correct.

The crowd of would-be firefighters, curiosity seekers, and ruffians out to break heads soon turned into a mob, jeering and cursing the increasingly anxious soldiers. Some threw snowballs and pieces of ice at the redcoats. A few even recklessly dared the soldiers to shoot. Only a few minutes elapsed before the superheated situation predictably turned tragic, though exactly what happened was never established. In all likelihood, a lone soldier fired his weapon. It is possible that he deliberately squeezed his trigger, but more likely that, struck by a chunk of ice or a piece of cordwood and knocked off balance, he accidentally discharged his weapon. In a flash, one or two edgy soldiers responded with a shot of their own. A second later, the remaining men in the squad, probably thinking they had not heard their captain's order to fire, also shot into the crowd. Six civilians were wounded. Five others lay dead or dying in the frozen slush. All the victims were workers, and some were mariners and ropemakers, which helped fuel suspicions that the soldiers had deliberately drawn down on known antagonists. Most of those who had been shot were young, and some were only boys. The youngest to die was Samuel Maverick, a seventeen-year-old apprentice to a joiner; the oldest was Crispus Attucks, a forty-seven-year-old sailor who was part Indian and part African American, and who may have once been a slave. Attucks and two others died almost instantly. The two men who suffered mortal wounds lived on for a few hours. John Adams ever afterward called the incident the "slaughter in King Street," but almost from the moment the muskets were fired, most referred to the tragedy as the "Boston Massacre."[45]

Less than twenty-four hours after the carnage, the acting governor, Thomas Hutchinson, ordered the troops to quit the city. He did so under pressure from a town meeting attended by thousands. Samuel Adams met with Hutchinson and advised that nearly a thousand men, many armed, had left behind their shaggy winter farms and comfortable homes and were descending on Boston from nearby villages. The "country is in general motion," Adams claimed.[46] Hutchinson's knees buckled and his face went ashen, or so Adams claimed. Whether or not his fear was that obvious, Hutchinson capitulated in order to avoid almost certain additional bloodshed, and the consequences it would provoke. The last redcoat left Boston eleven days after the shooting, most having been transported to Castle Island, where they joined the customs commissioners in Castle William.

The popular leaders understood the propaganda value of what had occurred. An elaborate funeral for the victims drew thousands as church bells rang throughout the day. Soon thereafter, Boston's leaders published a lurid account of the massacre, replete with nearly one hundred depositions by eyewitnesses who laid all blame at the feet of the soldiers. (The accounts of twenty bystanders who absolved the soldiers of wrongdoing were omitted.) Boston's version of the incident was distributed throughout America and published in England. Scribblers in newspapers drew parallels between the St. George's Fields Massacre and the Boston Massacre, tracing the root of each tragedy to the oppressive government in London. What was more, each March 5 for the next five years commemoration services were held in Boston. Often, the oratory featured well-worn, blood-curdling accounts of the massacre, recounted in harrowing detail and accompanied by sprays of venom toward royal officials. Each year's principal speaker seemed intent on surpassing his predecessors in depicting the redcoats' heinous behavior. By 1772 listeners heard of "children subjected to the barbarous caprice of the raging soldiery [and of] our beauteous virgins exposed to all the insolence of unbridled passion." The orator selected in 1775 spoke while garbed in a Roman toga.[47]

The stationing of the troops in the city has been accurately described as "the turning point in the radicalization of Boston opinion," but beyond the city the "invasion" of Massachusetts Bay, and news of the Boston Massacre, aroused considerably less furor.[48] In fact, some colonists were coming to be as distrustful of the radical Bostonians as they were of a standing army.

In America and in England most still hoped for a peaceful resolution of Anglo-American differences, and most appear to have still believed it was possible.

CHAPTER 4

"I AM UNWILLING TO GIVE UP THAT DUTY TO AMERICA"

TO THE TEA PARTY, 1770–1773

LORD NORTH'S POLICY of partial repeal of the Townshend Duties appeared to break the back of the colonial protest against those taxes. American turbulence was a distant memory in London within a few months of the Boston Massacre.

Lord North might have seized the moment to seek a lasting solution to Anglo-American differences—to find some middle ground that would have mollified discontented colonists and won back their hearts while gaining at least grudging support within the mother country. North could not have known in early 1770 that he was presiding over the last opportunity to peacefully save the empire and prevent the American Revolution. Yet, even had he been blessed with clairvoyance, North possessed neither the clear-minded, farsighted qualities of a great leader, nor the courage, boldness, and fortitude that sets gifted statesmen apart from the commonplace.

North was thirty-seven when he moved into the cramped and as-yet-unnumbered residence on Downing Street that for a generation had been available to the head of the ministry. As a minister responsible for managing a department—especially as chancellor of the exchequer, where he coped with economic and financial matters—North's wit, charm, efficiency, perseverance, and industry had led to his success. But once he became the prime minister, his limitations were more apparent. Though he continued to excel at resolving small, isolated problems, it became clear in time that he had difficulty coping with larger, more complex issues. Indeed, he was given to indecision and vacillation when confronted with truly complicated matters. His inabilities were exacerbated by frequent bouts of poor health and episodes of melancholy that one cabinet member referred to as North's "distressing Fits." Attributes usually associated with great leaders were also conspicuously absent in his makeup. He was neither charismatic nor intimidating, and "dignity," "eloquence," and "grandiosity" were terms never used to describe him. Of average height, North was obese, awkward, and disheveled, and he slurred his words, because of his "Tongue being too large for his Mouth," according to one onlooker. His acute myopia led another to remark that North's "large prominent eyes rolled to no purpose." Observers spoke of him as "blubbery," and his features included what one described as a "wide mouth [and] thick lips." He was cruelly lampooned as "booby-looking." North doubted that he was up to the task of heading a government. He sought to persuade George III that he was not the man for the job, and on three occasions before war with America erupted, North unsuccessfully offered his resignation.[1]

The king believed in North. A cheerful, even-tempered sort who won over others with his self-deprecating wit, North had an ability to make coherent presentations that was seldom matched, and he exhibited something of a sorcerer's mastery when it came to managing debates in Parliament and the cabinet. Not a few—including Edward Gibbon, who dedicated one of the volumes of his *Decline and Fall of the Roman Empire* to North—were struck by the "lively vigour of his mind." Unwilling to let him go, George III co-opted North, piling sinecures on him, his wife, brother, and father, and even personally paying off a £16,000 debt accumulated by the minister. Through thick and thin, North stayed on.[2]

North's plan, to the degree that he had one, was to end the colonists' boycotts and avoid provocation. He thought that the earliest protests had been sparked solely by the issue of taxation and that the American problem would have been "easily ended" had no further levies been attempted following the repeal of the Stamp Act. North grasped that the imposition of the Townshend Duties not only had radicalized many colonists; it had produced greater unity among them as well. To a lesser degree, North sensed that the turbulent 1760s had recast Anglo-American differences from a disagreement over parliamentary taxation to a more virulent dispute over the limits of American autonomy.[3]

North hoped not to provoke the colonists, but he had no intention of surrendering to America's radicals, a message he sent early on by purging his cabinet of all who had favored total repeal of the American taxes. On the other hand, North did not surround himself with hard-liners. There were some, of course, like Hillsborough and Barrington, and once word of the Boston Massacre reached London, they pushed for unsparing reprisals against Massachusetts. Above all, they sought draconian changes in the colony's charter. They hoped to transform the Bay Colony's council from a "democratical" body into one appointed solely by the governor, to prohibit town meetings, and to put Boston's popular leaders on trial. But a majority of ministers understood that taking any of those steps would reignite Anglo-American tensions at the very moment the cabinet was striving to end the American embargo of British imports. North's government never brought the subject of retaliatory measures before Parliament. In fact, a perusal of the debates in the House of Commons during the first thirty months of North's administration might lead the reader to conclude that the American problem had vanished.[4]

An international crisis in 1770 that threatened to plunge Britain into war with Spain removed America from the spotlight. In addition, the moderates in North's administration were aided by news from the colonies. The non-importation campaign collapsed during that summer, save for embargoes of British shipments of tea, and those boycotts were far from airtight. In the next three years, nearly eight hundred thousand pounds of tea shipped from the mother country was unloaded and sold in the colonies.[5] North also got good news regarding the fate of the British soldiers charged in the Boston Massacre. Expecting the worst, he had feared his government would have to intervene to save them, a step certain to have a combustible impact in Boston.

Civil authorities had taken the soldiers into custody on the night of the tragedy, and a few days later John Adams and Josiah Quincy agreed to represent them. Adams always insisted that he had acted from a belief that the nine redcoats deserved a fair trial. He also appears to have quietly cut a deal with Samuel Adams, who hoped the soldiers would be convicted, but after having been defended by one of the city's best lawyers. Samuel Adams likely promised his cousin, who was ambitious and a political novice, a place in Boston's delegation to the provincial assembly in return for his taking the case. The younger Adams, who had been practicing law for a dozen years and had one of the heaviest caseloads among Boston's attorneys, proved an admirable choice—too good, in fact, from Samuel Adams's perspective. The captain who commanded the squad was acquitted, as were six of his men. Two were convicted of manslaughter, but they escaped punishment by pleading benefit of clergy, an ancient practice still permissible in English common law through which first-time offenders could escape harsh sentences.[6]

Boston remained quiet that year, and the next two as well. Through Thomas Hutchinson, who became the royal governor of Massachusetts early in 1771, the ministry learned that the "late incendiaries are much fallen" and "are nonplussed." Hutchinson accurately reported that schisms had opened within the ranks of the radicals, including a break between Hancock and Samuel Adams, and that Boston's moderate candidates had heavily outpolled their more radical opponents in the assembly elections of 1772. Six months after the Boston Massacre, and for a spell thereafter, Hutchinson believed—and so advised the American secretary—that affairs were leading toward a restoration of "a due sense of [America's] subjection to the supreme authority" of Great Britain.[7]

The one episode in this period with the potential for reigniting the crisis occurred in Rhode Island in 1772, where the Royal Navy had dispatched the *Gaspee* to snuff out illicit commerce. In June, while chasing a suspected smuggler in Narragansett Bay, the *Gaspee*'s commander, Lieutenant William Dudingston, ran his schooner aground. That same night a mob boarded the helpless vessel and, after a brief struggle in which Dudingston was wounded, burned the craft. Word of the incident once again put the hard-liners in the cabinet in a retaliatory mood. Some clamored for the revocation of Rhode Island's charter and the arrest of the culprits and their transport to England to stand trial for treason. North seldom acted in haste, however, and as the weeks passed, a majority in the cabinet came to see the wisdom of a restrained response. In August, the administration created a commission of inquiry. As that was likely to defer a final resolution of the matter for up to a year, North may have believed that a volatile situation had been defused, and in large measure it had, for ultimately no colonist was ever arrested for complicity in the destruction of the vessel or the wounding of its commander. In fact, the only person who was censured was Dudingston, for having acted overzealously. North's temporizing had led him to sidestep a potentially precarious crisis, though he did not entirely avoid damaging fallout. When word reached the colonies late in the year that the Crown's investigators were empowered to send any accused colonist to England for trial, it spawned alarm and outrage, even in colonies nowhere near Rhode Island, and resulted in a propaganda bonanza for some colonial activists.[8]

North's policy of dodging measures that might inflame the colonists seemed to be working. Boston was so quiet that the surprised pastor of one of the city's largest churches remarked that London's "temperate" efforts at "securing the Affections ... of the colonies" had resulted in a "Pause in Politics."[9] Yet while an unaccustomed tranquility prevailed, this period was important in fueling discontent among some colonists. One issue that festered and ultimately embittered many powerful colonists concerned imperial policy for the American West.

When Hillsborough supplanted Shelburne as the minister chiefly responsible for American affairs, plans for trans-Appalachia changed profoundly. Shelburne had favored the opening of the West and the creation of two inland colonies. Hillsborough not only opposed new colonies, he looked askance at interior settlement altogether and sought to prevent a westward readjustment of the Proclamation of 1763 line. Some at the time thought Hillsborough, an

Irish land baron, feared that opening the American West would siphon renters from his properties in Ireland. That may have been true, but the West was also a political battleground in England's factional strife. British land speculators envisaged great profits from opening new American frontiers. In contrast, British merchants and manufacturers, aware that there was no way to get goods to markets on the other side of the mountains, were apprehensive that colonists living in trans-Appalachia would of necessity become manufacturers in their own right.

Hillsborough had hardly taken office before he learned that imperial Indian superintendents had negotiated treaties with various Native American tribes that would permit relocating the Proclamation Line farther to the west. Hillsborough tried to block the treaties, but his hand was stayed by the cabinet, which among other things feared that spurning the accords would trigger an Indian war. Reluctantly, the American secretary consented to moving the Proclamation Line farther west; originally situated some two hundred miles east of present-day Pittsburgh, the line was now to cross the Ohio River more than one hundred miles west of the head of the Ohio. Encouraged, Virginia's House of Burgesses petitioned the Crown for permission to annex Kentucky and for legal title to nearly all the land in present-day western Virginia and West Virginia, some fifty thousand square miles, a domain that would double the land area of the Old Dominion. Older land companies were reactivated and new ones created for the coming bonanza, and not just in Virginia. Virginia's roster of investors included Washington, Thomas Jefferson, and several members of the influential Lee family, but Benjamin Franklin and numerous others from mid-Atlantic colonies also sunk money into land company stock.

Ultimately, all the American investors were disappointed. The winner, at least temporarily, was the Grand Ohio Company, a concern consisting mostly of well-connected figures within the mother country, which was awarded title to the newly opened lands. Shortly before the Boston Massacre, the House of Burgesses acknowledged the hopelessness of gaining Kentucky, and Virginia's royal governor announced that the province would grant no lands beyond the mountains until authorized by London to do so.

No one was more outraged than Washington. He had lost money. But that was not all. He watched helplessly as officials in London stripped the Ohio Company, in which he had long been an investor, of title to land that it had been awarded prior to the Proclamation of 1763. Title to the property went instead to a competing company in England. An indignant Washington raged at the imperial authorities' "malignant disposition towards Americans."[10] He may have been correct, but the Grand Ohio Company was also ultimately frustrated when the Board of Trade, which since 1763 had opposed inland colonies, ruled against it. The board's decision assured that all of trans-Appalachia would remain closed to settlement, just as it had been twenty years earlier when young Colonel Washington commanded a Virginia army that fought to open the region. Someday, somehow, the vast, fertile prairies beyond the mountains would be opened and land speculators would make fortunes, but when that occurred, the hopes of Virginia's landmongers would still rest in the hands of faraway imperial officials over whom the Americans exercised no influence.

An American who had spent time in London lobbying for one of the colonial-based land companies wrung his hands in hopelessness: "there has been Nothing Don . . . by the Grate ones butt Squbeling & fighting. . . . [T]he public Interest is Neglected to Serve privat-Intrest." He made that anguished comment in 1764, but years later it still rang true among frustrated land speculators in the colonies. In the aftermath of the land-rush episode, an embittered Washington felt that he would never gain title to the frontier lands that he thought were his, and he traced his vexation to the colonists being "stigmatiz'd" because they were colonists.[11]

When it came to land, nothing was more irksome to Washington than his travail in gaining the bounty lands promised in 1754 to those who served in the Virginia Regiment. Following the Seven Years' War, Washington used his influence in the House of Burgesses to move along the process, and in 1769 the governor and council designated a huge tract east of the relocated Proclamation Line—in what now is West Virginia—for the veterans. The legislature also approved a plan under which the bounty lands were to be divided according to rank among eighty-one officers and men. Washington not only was due to receive in excess of twenty thousand acres, but he also purchased the bounty lands of numerous cash-strapped veterans who had no intention of moving west. However, in the winter of 1774 the Crown stayed the governor's hand, preventing Virginia from awarding land to its veterans.[12]

Washington and others had yet another ax to grind with regard to land. The Proclamation of 1763 had promised a land bounty to all colonists who had soldiered in the Seven Years' War. Privates were to receive fifty acres, field officers five thousand acres. But in 1772 the imperial authorities inexplicably ruled that the land bounties were solely for British regulars. Thousands of colonists who had soldiered were instantly denied what they believed they had been promised. No one stood to lose more than Colonel Washington. He lost ten thousand acres, his bounty and the share of another officer that he had purchased. Washington was not alone among veterans who believed they had soldiered for Great Britain with "fidelity" only to be cheated by imperial authorities steeped in "malice" toward Americans.[13]

Land policy was not all that rankled Washington and numerous other planters. Tobacco prices had always fluctuated, but bad times set in after mid-century. Increasing numbers of Tidewater planters sank deeply into debt and many others, as historian T. H. Breen noted, "began to discuss tobacco in ways that they had not done before." Some now spoke of tobacco as a "worth-less weed" and a "precarious commodity" that seemed to have left Virginia in "a declining State."[14] For wealthy planters who doubted tobacco's future, the lure of speculation in the West was made even more attractive, and it was all the more frustrating to them that the West remained closed.

Chesapeake planters understood the vagaries of the marketplace, but with considerable justification they concluded that their problem stemmed prin-cipally from British mercantilism. Under imperial law stretching back several generations, American tobacco planters could sell their tobacco only within the British empire; they watched helplessly as English and Scottish merchants resold American tobacco at higher prices in European markets. When tobacco prices had been good, colonial planters had not complained. But when bad times set in and debts accumulated, imperial policy was seen as burdensome. In the 1740s the House of Burgesses first petitioned the Crown to be allowed the "free export of their Tobacco to foreign Markets directly." Their appeal was turned down. An English clergyman who visited America in 1759 discovered that Virginians thought it "a hardship not to have an unlimited trade to every part of the world." As the issue simmered in the Virginia assembly, Arthur Lee, brother of Richard Henry, authored a pamph-let in 1764 in which he said candidly that the best hope for Virginia's planters was to be independent of "the arbitrary impositions" of British mercantilism, which "fix, like cankers, on their estates, and utterly consume them."[15]

The debts of tobacco planters were piling up. The amount of money owed by planters to British creditors doubled in the ten years after 1766. By the mid–1770s at least fifty-five members of the House of Burgesses owed £500 or more; ten Virginia planters owed in excess of £5,000, the equivalent of four lifetimes of arduous labor by a skilled tradesman. Washington remarked with disgust, "Our whole substance does already in a manner flow to Great Britain." Later, looking back on the plight of those who raised tobacco, Jefferson wrote that the "debts had become hereditary from father to son, for many generations, so that the planters were a species of property, annexed to certain mercantile houses in London." Furthermore, the Currency Act exacerbated the planters' problems of meeting their debt obligations. Lack-ing cash, planters commonly sold some of their property, though English creditors often only agreed to the transaction if those assets were under-valued, a demand that in effect sometimes meant that debt-ridden colonists "pay perhaps double what they owe," as a Virginia newspaper essayist pointed out in 1766.[16]

Virginia's planters tried to save themselves by petitioning the Crown in 1772 to end the African slave trade within the British Empire. Shrinking the number of available slave laborers would have driven up the price of slaves while creating a shortage of labor in rice-producing South Carolina and Georgia. Many of Virginia's planters could have escaped their debts by selling their surplus chattel to the Low Country. But the Crown spurned Virginia's entreaty, prompting one planter to exclaim that never before had Virginians felt such a "galling yoke of dependence." Another declared that planters would be reduced to "madmen"—a code word for "revolutionaries"—unless the colonists could somehow make the imperial officials "lift that heavy finger from off our shoulders." To many, the king's conduct laid bare the reality that when the interests of English businessmen and financiers collided with those of the colonists, the Crown would always side with those in the metropolis against what Jefferson soon called "the lasting interests of the American states."[17]

In quiet Massachusetts, where ardor for protest had waned, Samuel Adams toiled feverishly to revive the rancor toward the mother country that had soared when the redcoats had marched into Boston. His was a ceaseless search for an issue that would reignite popular resistance. He authored news-paper essays comparing Governor Hutchinson to the worst despots of ancient Rome and depicting him as a traitor to his native land for carrying out London's wicked schemes. Adams also attacked Britain's plans to pay the salaries of government officials. A governor who was independent of the legislature was more likely to become a tyrant, he warned. Furthermore, what Britain was attempting violated the provincial charter. Adams called the Massachusetts charter a "Sacred Ark," a compact between the Crown and the people of the colony according to which the assembly alone was respons-ible for the salaries of executive and judicial officials. Desperate to keep alive a horror of standing armies, Adams not only had a hand in organizing the annual commemoration of the Boston Massacre, but also, through a series of newspaper essays, argued that the verdicts in the massacre trials had been wrongheaded. He warned that Lord North was seeking to "lull us into that *quietude* and *sleep* by which *slavery* is always preceded." He railed against parliamentary taxation and the vice-admiralty courts and cautioned that the Church of England soon would appoint a bishop for America, a step that presaged limitations on religious freedom. Shining through Adams's harsh rhetoric was his case for republicanism: public officials were the representatives of the people and they were to serve the people.[18]

Nothing worked. Massachusetts remained quiet. Hutchinson had once called Samuel Adams the "grand Incendiary," and that was how he appears to have been seen by many of his Yankee brethren who were happy with the return of Anglo-American tranquility. His radicalism even chased away John Adams, who resigned after one year in the assembly, troubled by what he regarded as false peril manufactured by Samuel Adams to foment unrest. Predicting that the imperial crisis would never resurface while he was alive, John Adams relished life in his "still, calm, happy" hometown of Braintree, where he could forget public duties and focus on his legal career. But Samuel Adams never stopped cultivating him. He called often on his cousin, utilizing every artful ploy to allay his fears, but mostly he postured as a moderate who abhorred violence and revolution.[19]

Samuel Adams never believed the imperial crisis was over, but keeping the flame of resistance burning was a daunting challenge. It was his genius to understand that support for opposition to the supposed threat posed by British policies had waned in part because of the lack of systematic organization. Adams grasped that the existence in Massachusetts of committees of correspondence—networks for interlinking Boston's popular leadership with residents of backcountry communities—might "awaken a sufficient Number" to maintain vigilance. The Boston Committee of Correspondence came into being in the autumn of 1772 and immediately reached out to farming towns in the hinterland. Ultimately, about 40 percent of the hamlets in backcountry Massachusetts formed their own committees of correspondence.[20]

Communication was largely one-way. Members of Boston's committee met for several hours one night each week, swilling beer, socializing, and compiling news, rumors, and hard information to send to their country cousins. Not everyone thought the endeavor would come to much. Governor Hutchinson labeled it "a foolish scheme" that was likely to make Samuel Adams appear "ridiculous." Some of the derision stopped when the committee prepared, and a Boston town meeting adopted, "The State of the Rights of the Colonists." Adams played the principal role in the preparation of this document, which in many ways foreshadowed the Declaration of Independence. It listed a dozen "Infringements & Violations of Rights" committed by the mother country, including parliamentary taxation, the use of writs of assistance, maintaining a standing army in peacetime, enhancing the jurisdiction of vice-admiralty courts, multiple violations of the colony's charter, and restraints on manufacturing. Adams sketched the colonists'

"Natural Rights . . . as Men," among which "are these: First, a Right to *Life*; Secondly to *Liberty*; thirdly to *Property*." To this, he tacked on a philosophical statement on the right of revolution. "All Men have a Right . . . in case of intolerable Oppression . . . to leave the Society they belong to, and enter into another."[21]

Hutchinson had sneered at Adams's dreams for the committees of correspondence, but the radical tone of "The State of the Rights of the Colonists"— which had been sent throughout the colony and endorsed by several towns—goaded him into a public rebuttal. Hutchinson called the assembly into session and addressed it early in January 1773, launching an exchange that Adams said proved to be "like Thunder in the ears" of most colonists. Seeing no shades of gray, Hutchinson advised that "no line . . . can be drawn between the supreme authority of Parliament and the total independence of the colonies." Either the colonists must adhere to the laws of Parliament or they must be independent of Great Britain. There was no alternative. And if it was independence that the colonists chose, their break with Britain would end disastrously, probably in their conquest by one or more European powers.

The assembly answered before month's end. With a straight face, the assemblymen said they were only mentioning independence because "your Excellency . . . has reduced us to the unhappy alternative" of having to discuss it. However, they did not advocate independence. The assembly offered an alternative to the stark choice that Hutchinson had envisaged. After once again denying Parliament's jurisdiction over the colonies, the legislators insisted that the king was the sole link of empire and they reiterated their loyalty to the Crown. But now that the issue of independence was on the table, the assembly asked Hutchinson—and, implicitly, other colonists throughout America—which was best, a "state of vassalage" to an "absolute uncontrolled power" of Parliament or independence from Great Britain.

During the exchanges, Adams pried from Hutchinson an admission that superior court judges were being paid by the Crown. It had been one of the worst-kept secrets in history. Under Massachusetts's charter, the salaries of the governor and royal officials who served in the province were to be paid by the colonial assembly, and in fact that had been the source of their compensation for eighty years. But in 1771, when the legislature had appropriated funds for the governor's salary, Hutchinson had vetoed the act, leading Adams and others to conclude that the British government was providing for him. By the next year, rumors swirled in Boston that London was also paying the salaries of royal judges in Massachusetts. The governor had long been thought a puppet of the monarchy, but concern over judicial integrity was new and especially alarming. While considerable ink had been spilled on the potential for the Crown to corrupt the judiciary, the issue never gained traction until Hutchinson's avowal that the salaries of the highest judges in Massachusetts were indeed being paid by the Crown. Thereafter, what had been mostly shrugged off as yet more grist for the mill in Adams's propaganda initiatives was suddenly taken seriously. The legislature, the Boston town meeting, and the Boston Committee of Correspondence denounced the British government's new policy as still another step in the monarchy's despotic conspiracy to snuff out the liberties of the colonists. Any judge who was compensated by the Crown, said the assembly, "has it in his Heart to promote . . . an arbitrary Government in the Province."[22]

Hutchinson "will not be thanked for this," John Adams immediately remarked when he learned of the governor's first speech to the assembly, and he was correct. Lord North and many in his ministry were furious. After all, as Hutchinson's biographer noted, the governor not only had brought into the open "the most sensitive issues of Anglo-American relations," but he had also permitted himself to be maneuvered into a confrontation "carefully staged for maximum publicity." His addresses and the assembly's answers were rapidly published and circulated throughout America. No one was more delighted than Samuel Adams, for the subject of independence at last had been openly broached, and colonists everywhere could puzzle over the grim choice that Hutchinson had offered.[23]

Around the time of Hutchinson's blunder, Benjamin Franklin somehow got hold of a bundle of purloined letters exchanged between Hutchinson and Thomas Whatley, who had been Grenville's secretary to the treasury. Franklin passed the letters on to Thomas Cushing, the speaker of the Massachusetts assembly, who showed them to Samuel Adams. For Adams, the missives were like manna from heaven. Hutchinson had said little in the letters that he had not said openly, but in one explosive sentence he remarked that the public good required that the colonists accept "an abridgement of what are called English liberties." Over a period of weeks, Adams prepared the public with a clever press campaign in which he promised revelations that proved the existence of a plot "to overthrow the Constitution of this Government, and to introduce arbitrary Power into this Province." With the citizenry panting to see the evidence, Adams at long last published the letters in June 1773, making sure they were disseminated throughout the colonies.

Hutchinson's candor about restricting liberty sparked revulsion and alarm far and wide. He was hanged in effigy in Philadelphia and by college students in Princeton, New Jersey; numerous essayists compared him to the worst scoundrels in antiquity. For many readers, Hutchinson's letters confirmed that London was bent on stripping the colonists of their liberty. Many must also have concluded, as did John Adams, that Samuel Adams's dire and incessant warnings had all along been accurate. John Adams said that for him Hutchinson's letters amounted to a "grand discovery." He now believed that the mother country posed a threat to the colonists' freedom. Where once he had thought Samuel Adams a dangerous radical bent on leading the colonists down a path to havoc, and likely doom, John Adams now looked on his cousin as "restrained [in] his Passions," a "cool, genteel and agreeable" leader driven by the purest motives.[24]

Around this moment Samuel Adams received another gift. Word arrived from Williamsburg that the Virginia House of Burgesses had created a standing committee to correspond with other colonies about real and potential threats facing the colonists. Virginia's action stemmed from the alarm sowed in 1772 by the revelation that the commission created to investigate the *Gaspee* incident was empowered to send suspected colonists to England to stand trial for treason. At the next meeting of Virginia's assembly, in January 1773, Thomas Jefferson, Patrick Henry, and Richard Henry Lee, seeing the action of North's ministry as a usurpation of the colonists' authority, took the lead in having the Burgesses transmit the Virginians' concerns to Massachusetts, as well as in establishing a committee of correspondence through which intercolonial communication and union might be facilitated. Boston's Committee of Correspondence responded promptly, and within a year every colony but Pennsylvania had created a committee of correspondence. Historically, the colonies had never had much contact; communications and commerce with the mother country had been more important. Now, the leaders in the colonies were in touch with one another, sharing ideas and information, sometimes seeking counsel, reinforcing suspicions of the British government, and as Samuel Adams remarked in his initial letter to Lee, firming up the belief that the "Colonies are all embarked in the same bottom. The Liberties of all are alike invaded by the same haughty Power." The committees of correspondence provided one another with critical reassurance, but more than anything, their collaboration was an important step toward concerted action.[25]

A year earlier, Samuel Adams, at age fifty, appeared to have passed his peak. The cause he had championed was moribund and his popularity in Boston had waned. Some feared that his radicalism spelled disaster for Massachusetts. Others, who shared Adams's misgivings about the mother country, wanted no part of what they believed were his democratic leanings. Adams had sunk to such a low ebb that he suffered a landslide loss in a contest for the office of Suffolk County register of deeds. Andrew Oliver, the lieutenant governor, could not have been more gleeful. Oliver even thought that his old, acrid rival was finished politically. Oliver's prophecy did not quite pan out. In the spring of 1773, soon after the confrontation with Hutchinson, Adams was reelected to the assembly, capturing 413 of 419 votes. Furthermore, while no one understood it to be the case that spring, the colonial insurgency was on the cusp of reawakening. It was about to become a truly revolutionary movement.[26]

Hillsborough was gone, forced to resign as American secretary after one too many blunders, and replaced in August 1772 by the Earl of Dartmouth, Lord North's half-brother. (Dartmouth's widowed mother had married North's father in 1736.) Although he had entered Parliament at about the same time as North, Dartmouth had never previously sat in a cabinet. In fact, Dartmouth had held no important post since he had played a visible role in the repeal of the Stamp Act. But North turned to him once Hillsborough was finished. Aware that Dartmouth was widely viewed in the colonies as a friend of America, North believed his appointment would signal a new ministerial course and contribute to the pacification of the colonists. Like North, Dartmouth thought it possible to "heal the Breach" with the colonists, mostly by taking pains not to ruffle feathers across the sea. Dartmouth believed that if calm prevailed for a spell, he might "obtain more in favour of the Colonies" on his side of the Atlantic.[27]

On learning of Hutchinson's misguided war of words with the Massachusetts assembly, Dartmouth sought to palliate the Yankees by taking the extraordinary step of writing to Massachusetts's Speaker of the House. He told Speaker Cushing that he was drafting the letter not as a minister but as a "simple Individual" who was "a hearty friend and well-wisher." His devout hope, Dartmouth said, was that the issue of Parliament's right to tax "should be suspended and lie dormant" until some threat to the empire arose "in which the Expediency and Necessity of such Exercise should be obvious to every considerate Man in every part of the Dominions of Great Britain."[28]

Despite Hutchinson's bungling and the hay made by the colonial radicals over his letters, Dartmouth remained optimistic. So did Franklin, who deep into 1773 was convinced that North's administration sincerely wished "to compose all differences with America."[29] North was never going to resolve all differences, but he was on a path that pointed toward a calm and peaceful relationship. Then something happened. After all the deliberate provocations in recent years, this occurrence was unplanned. Not for the first time in history, and certainly not for the last, the world shook as the result of a crisis brought on by the mismanagement of a commercial enterprise.

The East India Company, the second-largest financial institution in the country after the Bank of England, was in trouble. The far-flung company operated on three continents and trafficked in numerous commodities, though after mid-century, tea was its principal item of trade, accounting for 90 percent of company profits. By the time the Seven Years' War ended, the company was struggling. It blamed the government, as the company was required to ship its tea to England, where it paid both tariff and inland duties. But the company also had a long, troubled history of rapacious excess and corruption. Its highest executives lived like grandees, and long after the company fell on hard times, it continued to pay lavish dividends in excess of 12 percent. Matters came to a head in the 1760s, when the price of East India Company tea exceeded that of its great rival, the Dutch East India Company. Spying a golden opportunity, smugglers turned to the less expensive Dutch tea. In no time, nearly twice as much smuggled tea was being sold in England, Ireland, and America as was vended by the East India Company.

In 1767, the government had offered help by reducing the company's tax burden, but that was also the year of the Townshend Duties, which included a tax on tea sold in America. Non-importation agreements sputtered into being in the colonies. Company sales, already suffering from the illicit trade in Dutch tea, were further injured by the boycotts. Although the colonial embargoes were far from impermeable, by the end of the decade the amount of English tea entering through Philadelphia and New York had been cut by 99 percent. During 1772 only about 15 percent of the tea sold in the colonies was East India Company tea. By then the company was losing £400,000 annually, its warehouses were bulging with roughly three year's supply of unsold merchandise, its indebtedness skyrocketed, and it no longer could obtain loans. This giant enterprise verged on insolvency, an occurrence that could have brought down the entire British economy. Faced with the disquieting specter of a national economic catastrophe, North's administration was driven to find a solution.

Months of wrangling ensued. Divisions occurred principally over bailing out the company or prohibiting it from paying dividends until it was creditworthy. Unavoidably, too, the company's woes brought into play the matter of the existing duty on tea. The company was still selling copious amounts of tea in the colonies, though most thought it needed to sell more if it was to remain solvent. Some members of Parliament implored Lord North to repeal the tea duty, which would end both the boycotts and the smuggling. They acted not from a sudden empathy with the colonists' objections to parliamentary taxation, but because they represented merchants or feared economic chaos. Nevertheless, their pleas to repeal the tea tax offered North the face-saving means of terminating the attempt to tax the colonists, a step that might for years have preserved calm within the empire until a new generation came along to cope with Anglo-American relations. But North turned his back on the opportunity. "I am unwilling to give up that duty on America upon which the [colonial officials' salaries] are charged. . . . I see no reason for taking it off," he told Parliament in the spring of 1773. North risked all on the belief that American governors and judges who were unshackled from the colonial assemblies could enforce imperial law and maintain peace in the provinces. His gamble carried the day in the House of Commons by roughly a six-to-one margin.

The East India Company was bailed out by two pieces of legislation, the Regulating Act and the Tea Act. The company was permitted to sell tea in America directly through its agents rather than at public auction, giving it a monopoly over every step that ultimately culminated in the colonists pouring tea into their cups. Furthermore, the import duties paid in England were to be refunded on all tea subsequently shipped to America, a step that would reduce the cost of East India Company tea by roughly a third, making it cheaper than Dutch tea, even with the tea duty intact. There was virtually no discussion in Parliament or the press over how the legislation would be received in the colonies. It was as if no one anticipated that there might be a problem. After all, who could object to cheaper tea?[30]

Some observers understood what many in high positions in England could not seem to fathom. On very nearly the day the legislation passed, Franklin remarked that North and his followers "have no Idea that any People can act from any Principle but that of" their economic interests. Governor William Tryon of New York perhaps saw things with even greater clarity. He observed that there would be protests whether the tea duty remained or was rescinded. If maintained, radicals would continue to object to the tax. If repealed, merchants who made fortunes from smuggling would stir up a protest on some issue or other.[31] Tryon had put his finger on the crux of the American insurgency, at least at this juncture. Taxes were visible and unwanted, and an easy means of arousing protest. But for many, ranging from popular leaders to merchants, from sailors, dockhands, and skilled tradesmen, the paramount objective had always been to preserve, even to enhance, American autonomy. For them, Lord North's Tea Act was a fresh reminder that within the British Empire the great decisions were made in London.

By late summer the colonists knew of Parliament's action. They were also aware that the East India Company was filling the cargo holds of vessels destined for Boston, New York, Philadelphia, and Charleston with nearly as much tea as it had sold in America during all the previous year. Ten weeks or more passed before the ships arrived, ample time for filling the press with inflammatory pieces and for contemplating how to respond. Whereas passions cooled after 1770 and people had turned a deaf ear to radical exhortations in the wake of the *Gaspee* and Hutchinson Letters incidents, the populace was once again receptive to warnings of London's diabolical plotting. What is more, feelings ran deep that a tea tax to fund the civil list was nothing less than a plot to destroy the provincial assemblies. The traditional constitutional arguments were aired: the law was "designed . . . to establish *parliamentary despotism* in America." People were also warned that by lowering the existing tax, Parliament was trying to lull the colonists into paying an unconstitutional duty; if successful, more taxes would follow. Some in the popular movement played on the bestowal of monopoly rights on the East India Company, charging that a monopolistic company, not the free market, would dictate prices.

By mid-autumn, well before the first tea ships arrived, the citizenry was aroused as it had not been for years. It is possible that Britain's earlier capitulations, full or partial, stiffened their backbone. It was likely as well that the popular leaders had grown more adept at organizing and raising the consciousness of their followers. John Adams saw something else at work. Like Governor Tryon, Adams believed that at least some of the campaign against the legislation had been set in motion by merchants who smuggled in Dutch tea and feared the Tea Act would ruin their illicit trade. It was plausible, and just as likely, that sailors, dockhands, and shopkeepers whose livelihoods were dependent on the well-being of the existing tea trade had a hidden agenda in opposing the Tea Act.[32] Most Americans in 1773 were far from being revolutionaries, but with regard to the Tea Act, there were more white-hot radicals than there had been during the two previous imperial crises.

Not one leaf of the tea shipped to America late in 1773 was sold. Prior to the arrival of the *Polly*, the tea ship bound for Philadelphia, a mass meeting in the city adopted resolutions excoriating the Tea Act as arbitrary and unconstitutional. Serving as a template for other provincial bodies, legal and extralegal, Philadelphia's trenchant assertion was tantamount to the Virginia Resolves of this episode. The meeting additionally demanded the resignation of the tea agents, who were looked on as fiendish and indistinguishable from the earlier stamp masters. They immediately resigned. A month later, the *Polly* reached the Delaware River. Handbills circulated that promised to "make a Goose" of—that is, tar and feather—any river pilot who escorted *Polly* upriver, yet somehow the vessel reached Philadelphia. Another mass meeting convened, and it convinced *Polly*'s captain that his cargo was in grave danger. Choosing discretion over valor, he turned for England without attempting to unload the dutied tea. Somewhat the same scenario was played out in New York. In

Charleston, the royal governor ordered the removal and storage of the tea, but he dared not attempt to sell it.[33]

Things were different in Boston. The tea ship *Dartmouth* arrived while Boston slept on the inky-black Saturday night of November 27. Bostonians awakened the next morning to find the vessel berthed in the harbor. During the next three weeks *Eleanor* and *Beaver* also arrived. Between them, the three vessels carried 340 chests containing some ninety thousand pounds of tea. In the first days after *Dartmouth*'s arrival at Griffin's Wharf, the Board of Selectmen (the city council) pondered what to do, the Committee of Correspondence marshaled support among nearby towns, the council met with the governor, several town meetings convened, and one or two private citizens acting as go-betweens sought to broker a peaceful settlement. A sense of urgency prevailed. A century-old imperial regulation mandated that duties on taxable cargo must be paid within twenty days or customs officials were to seize the ship and sell the cargo at auction. The clock was ticking. If the matter was not resolved before December 17, *Dartmouth*'s tea would be sold and the tax revenue collected.

As days passed, Governor Hutchinson was exhorted from several sides to order the ships to return to England with the tea untouched in their cargo holds. He steadfastly refused. He had taken an oath to uphold the law. He knew as well that to fail to enforce the Tea Act would destroy his aspirations of advancement to a better position, possibly in London. A variety of other personal reasons may also have accounted for his intransigence: he had secured positions as tea consignees for his two sons; his salary now came from the tax on tea; and most of his liquid wealth—nearly £4,000—was invested in East India Company stock.[34] Atop these motives, Hutchinson may simply have hoped to settle old scores with Samuel Adams and assorted other radicals who had tormented him for years.

Numerous public meetings were held in November and December, usually at the Old South Church, the only building capable of accommodating the multitudes who attended. Those who gathered—Hutchinson labeled them the "rabble," chiefly "the lower ranks of people," though others said that "men of the best character and of the first fortunes" were present—heard fiery speeches and lively debates over whether or not to destroy the tea. But the events that were to unfold later in those last cold days of autumn hint that these meetings were primarily for arousing the populace in Boston and the backcountry, securing their support, and preparing them for what was to come. The crucial decision concerning what to do in the event that Hutchinson would not back down was almost certainly made soon after *Dartmouth*'s arrival, if not before, and it was made in secret. Once the decision was made, those in charge, including Samuel Adams, the Sons of Liberty, and leaders of the North End Caucus, prepared with something approaching martial precision. Between 100 and 150 men signed on for duty. All were thought to be reliable men who would not divulge to anyone what was coming. Each man was given a specific assignment. Some were to be lookouts or to carry lanterns, others were to operate hoists or wield axes. Three boats were to be used to convey the men to the tea ships, and a captain and a boatswain were assigned for each craft. Each man swore an oath of secrecy, to which the great majority remained remarkably true for the rest of their lives.

The popular leaders strung things out to the last possible moment, keen on convincing the public that the Boston Tea Party occurred only because Hutchinson left the patriots with no choice but to act. On Thursday, December 16, a raw, rainy day—and the last day before customs officials would be free to impound the tea ships—a final public meeting was called. At ten in the morning nearly five thousand men and women, mostly Boston's artisans and laborers, but some farmers and others from towns as far as twenty miles away, crowded into the cavernous Old South Church.

Candles burned throughout the meetinghouse, and a rank, stale odor hung over the sanctuary, for the building was packed with hardworking people who bathed once a week, if then, and most were clad in wet woolen or leather garments. The meeting began with speeches and discussion, creating the illusion that the citizenry was coming to a popular decision on the proper course of action. In late morning, it was agreed to send Francis Rotch (pronounced "Roach"), the twenty-two-year-old son of *Dartmouth*'s owner, to Milton, where Hutchinson, fearing trouble in Boston, had taken refuge in his country home. Rotch was to ask Hutchinson once again to send the three vessels, with the tea still in their holds, back to England. Milton was seven miles from Boston, so Rotch faced a fourteen-mile round-trip on horseback in addition to an audience with Hutchinson. That could take a while. The meeting adjourned until three P.M.

As the afternoon wore on, an even larger crowd drifted into the Old South. Three o'clock arrived, but Rotch had not yet returned. The audience waited impatiently, expectantly, as time dragged by. Darkness eventually gathered over the city. The wait went on. Finally, near six P.M., Rotch at last arrived back at the Old South, and was immediately escorted before the hushed gathering.

The moderator wasted no time. He asked Rotch for the governor's response. Rotch's answer was not a surprise. Hutchinson, he said, had refused the meeting's request. Samuel Adams responded that "nothing further could be done." The Bostonians, he said, "had now done all that they could for the

Salvation of their Country." Suddenly, a resounding Indian "War Whoop" pierced the air. Others remembered hearing shouts of "The Mohawks are come. Every man to his tent," "Hurrah for Griffin's Wharf," and "Boston harbor a tea-pot tonight." Cheers and thunderous applause could be heard blocks away.

Quickly, quietly, some men slipped out of the church. They hurried elsewhere to don disguises. They would call themselves "Mohawks" on this night, and most blackened their faces with charcoal and draped and tied blankets and shawls over their clothing, hoping to hide all telltale evidence of both their identity and their vocation. The subsequent claim that those chosen for the work ahead were "young men, not much known in town and not liable to be easily recognized" has a ring of authenticity to it.

But they could not hide what they were doing. The rain had long since stopped, and a bright moon hung over the harbor. Royal Navy vessels lay nearby. The sailors were aware of what was occurring on board the tea ships. However, Admiral John Montagu would not act unless ordered to do so by the civilian authorities. Hutchinson was miles away in Milton. The order to prevent the destruction of the tea never came.

The Boston Tea Party was completed with astonishing speed. The boarding parties could not have reached their destination much before seven P.M. All the men were back on shore before nine. Each man performed his preassigned task. For most, that meant hard, sweaty labor. The rapidity of the operation suggests that those who boarded the three tea ships knew their way around sailing vessels, and it is a good bet that most were accustomed to heavy work, for dozens of chests weighing four hundred pounds had to be hoisted from holds to decks, then smashed apart, and their contents thrown overboard into the dark, swirling water of Boston Harbor. When the work was done, the men were rowed in silence back to shore. The journey to safety must have seemed endless, but all made it. They left behind three undamaged ships, though all the tea had been destroyed, property that the East India Company subsequently priced at £9,659 (today's equivalent of several million dollars' worth of property).[35]

John Adams had not been let in on the popular movement's plans. Surprised the next morning to learn of the Boston Tea Party, Adams understood immediately that what he called "an Epocha in History" had occurred. That same bitingly cold morning, Admiral Montagu disembarked for a walk on the wharf. Seeing some Bostonians whiling away the time, he stopped and chatted, and asked them a salient question: who is "to pay the fiddler now?"[36]

CHAPTER 5

"BEHOLD AMERICANS WHERE MATTERS ARE DRIVING"

1774, YEAR OF MOMENTOUS DECISIONS

WORD OF THE BOSTON TEA PARTY was brought to London during the third week of January 1774 by the captain and crew of John Hancock's *Hayley*. Lord North received the tidings with a mixture of surprise and anger. He had thought a hostile reception in the colonies so unlikely that he had not even consulted the American secretary while the Tea Act was under consideration. Even given Boston's penchant for causing trouble, North had never imagined that the tea might be destroyed. The prime minister hoped against hope that Boston had been the exception and that elsewhere the tea had landed and was being sold. But mariners on the *Polly*, which tied up at a London quay six days later, came ashore with the news of what had occurred in Philadelphia. North and his monarch now understood that their American problem had returned, and that in fact it had never gone away.

Outrage over the Boston Tea Party swept England, and it grew as reports arrived of resistance to the Tea Act in each of the four tea ports. Most of the rampant fury in the English press was directed at Boston, the lone site of violence and always the vanguard—or so it seemed—of the colonial protest. As Massachusetts had been settled 150 years earlier by Puritan dissidents, newspapers rang out with allegations that the "turbulent" Yankee colonists had from the outset longed to be independent of England. Supposedly, they had only been awaiting a favorable moment before acting, and the removal of France from New England's northern boundary provided the long-anticipated signal to throw off British rule. Some screeds contended that New England's preachers, men with the contamination of Puritanism in their genes, were a pernicious influence behind the ongoing Yankee rebellion. Others blamed the "arch rebel" Samuel Adams and other "demagogues" for whipping up revolutionary fervor. Still others condemned the unsavory and unhappy merchants, portraying them as the "Milch-Cows" of the rebellion. Previous ministries were reproached, too, charged with having inspired the insurgency by capitulating in the face of earlier protests. While there was no consensus on who was responsible for the American troubles, the press at least agreed on two things: the time for toughness had arrived, and Boston must be severely punished. One writer proposed "a Cargo of American scalps" as payment for the destroyed tea. Another cried out for the authorities to "Hang, draw, and quarter fifty" of Boston's leading radicals.[1]

Panting for revenge, British officials first went after Benjamin Franklin, who was not merely a handy quarry, but he had recently acknowledged his culpability in passing along Thomas Hutchinson's pilfered letters to Boston's radicals. Already, Franklin had been pilloried in Britain's press as a two-faced traitor. Three days after the *Polly* docked, Franklin was summoned to a meeting of the Privy Council, which he believed had been called to consider Hutchinson's future. The unsuspecting Franklin arrived at the Cockpit, an indoor amphitheater within the government complex known as Whitehall, to discover instead that he was to be targeted for public humiliation. Franklin, who was almost seventy years old, was forced to stand for more than an hour and silently endure a tongue-lashing by Alexander Wedderburn, Britain's solicitor general. While the audience jeered and hooted, Wedderburn flayed Franklin, charging that he was not a gentleman, but a thief who had forfeited the trust of society. Above all, said the solicitor general, Franklin was "the true incendiary," the "first mover and prime conductor" behind the colonists' thirst to create "a Great American Republic." Forbidden to speak, Franklin stood silently, expressionlessly, listening to Wedderburn's vitriol and the taunts from the audience behind him. Franklin had to know that he was finished in England. His dream of living out his life in London had abruptly ended. Soon after his ordeal, Franklin informed the radicals in Boston of the "Bull-baiting" he had been made to endure, and he closed with a warning: *"Behold Americans where matters are driving!"*[2]

North's cabinet met on the afternoon of Franklin's ordeal to consider its response to the Boston Tea Party. The ministers were in no mood for concili-ation. They rapidly concurred that "effectual steps" must be taken "to secure the dependence of the colonies," but they were divided over what action to take. They met frequently during the next six weeks, sometimes in Whitehall, sometimes at the home of one or another minister. On occasion, the meetings lasted late into the night. They discussed what to do and the likely ramifica-tions of each course of action. During these deliberations, the ministers for the first time considered the use of force, brooding over whether a war against the rebellious colonies was winnable, how it should be waged, and above all if French and Spanish intervention was probable in the event of Anglo-American hostilities. Few, if any, in the cabinet imagined that defeating the colonists would be very difficult, and it was assumed that victory could be won quickly, before any foreign power intervened. History is filled with instances of leaders having underestimated their adversaries or misjudged the obstacles that would be faced in gaining victory. That Britain's ministers fell into the trap is indisputable, although their discussions about the use of force in 1774 occurred at a time before there was much evidence of colonial unity and prior to the first steps taken in America to prepare for war.

Although one or two ministers thought the time to use force had come, most did not. They agreed from the start that "we must risk something" or lose America, as North said straightaway at the first cabinet meeting, but their focus was on what steps to take short of war. Dartmouth alone urged restraint. No one agreed with him. His colleagues revisited measures that had been pushed by the hard-liners in the aftermath of the *Gaspee* incident, and this time, unlike in 1772, the cabinet was in an avenging mood. The majority would have preferred to seize and prosecute well-known popular leaders, though the ministers backed off when Wedderburn advised that hard evidence was lacking with regard to the complicity of any individuals in the Boston Tea Party.[3]

In the end, the administration coalesced around what North called the Coercive Acts and the colonists later labeled the Intolerable Acts. In late winter and early spring the first minister presented four bills to Parliament. The Boston Port Bill would fine Massachusetts for the destroyed tea and close Boston Harbor until restitution had been made. The Massachusetts Government Bill would change the province's nearly eighty-year-old charter; henceforth, the council would be chosen by the royal governor; town meetings were prohibited without the chief executive's authorization; and the executive's authority over the judiciary was broadened. The Administration of Justice Bill would empower the governor to transfer to other colonies, or to England, the trials of indicted government officials. The Quartering Act would authorize the commander of the British army in America to lodge his soldiers wherever necessary, including in private residences. The legislation augured a dramatic increase in the British government's authority while blatantly diminishing the ability of the Bay Colony's citizenry to control their lives and destiny. The bills, in fact, would do in Massachusetts just what the most radical colonists had been warning for a decade was London's intention for all America.

North's measures faced little opposition in Parliament or the press. The shopworn arguments about parliamentary supremacy were rehashed, but alongside them some supported coercion for reasons of British national security. Britain could maintain the favorable balance of power in Europe, it was asserted, only through the assets brought by the American colonies. Some also argued that time was against Great Britain. The moment was favorable for a showdown with the disunited colonists. This was the time to crush the spirit of American independence. If the opportunity was lost, disaster would follow. Said one MP, "If we do not ... get the better of America," within a few years "America will get the better of us."

Edmund Burke, who was coming into prominence in British politics, made the principal speech against the Intolerable Acts. It was the first of three important speeches on the American question that he would deliver in Parliament during a span of nineteen months. Burke, forty-five, paunchy and jowly with dark wavy hair, had come to London from his native Ireland more than a decade earlier to pursue legal studies. Instead, he became Rockingham's secretary and eventually won a seat in the House of Commons. Burke had risen from modest middle-class origins, but he was consumed with desire to be seen as part of the gentry. He lived well above his means, among other things purchasing a large country house just outside London, a step that plunged him into a lifelong indebtedness. To make ends meet—and because of his enormous energy and ambition—Burke not only took on the job as New York's agent but also turned to writing essays and editing the *Annual Register*, a compilation of the past year's important news stories.[4]

By 1774, Burke had served in the House of Commons for nine years, gaining attention chiefly through his literary skill and his powerful oratory. Prior to his speech on the Intolerable Acts, Burke had said little over the years about America, an omission for which he apologized in his remarks. But now, faced with the prospect of the enactment of a string of harsh, retaliatory measures against Boston and Massachusetts, Burke warned that coercion would lead to war and, in all likelihood, the loss of the colonies. Burke focused on the economic value of the colonies and what it might grow to be in the future. Britain's trade with its colonies, he pointed out, was basically equal to the trade that England had "carried on at the beginning of this century with the whole world!" Burke also maintained that Britain's revenue-raising policies toward America had been wrongheaded since 1765. Even had all the anticipated revenue been collected, it would have been a negligible amount. What is more, levying duties on the colonists for the purpose of making the point of parliamentary sovereignty had only aroused a "just alarm" among Americans. Burke called for the repeal of the Tea Act and advocated that Parliament "bind America" to England through commerce, the "corner stone" of the empire.

Burke additionally argued at length that coercion simply would not work. The American colonists were ardently attached to their rights and freedom, suspicious of the heavy hand of government, and very far away. Most of all, however, Burke perceived what few others saw: the colonists through their own governments had mounted a well-ordered insurgency in defense of their liberties. At least by implication, Burke was saying that if the colonists could organize so efficiently to resist British laws, they could in a worst-case scenario likewise offer a credible defense against British force. Burke's prescient warnings went unheard. With only about 20 percent of those in Parliament voting with him, each bill passed easily.[5]

North's administration had been driven by the belief that America must be subjugated. A few weeks after the last of the Intolerable Acts passed, the prime minister told Hutchinson, who had left his homeland for good and taken up residence in England, that the imperial government would neither "allow the thought that the kingdom" could not legislate for the colonies nor that its legislation would be nullified by the colonists.[6] North also told all who would listen that coercion would prevent a war, not cause one. Not every minister thought that would be the case. Some expected coercion to be met with defiance, which in turn would almost certainly mean war. Some doubtless already thought that war was inevitable, but choosing coercion rather than force in 1774 would allow time to prepare for military operations and make the public more amenable to hostilities when the time came. But most in North's ministry appear to have believed that the colonists would shrink from war, not only because they had to know that war with Great Britain would be cataclysmic, but also because as only Massachusetts was faced with punishment, the colonies would remain too disunited to respond with force.[7]

Boston's popular leaders were worried, but they appear to have worried less about the British government's response to the Boston Tea Party than about how their fellow colonists—including those in the interior towns of Massachusetts—would react to news of the destruction of the East India Company's property. Boston heard first from the Bay Colony's backcountry. Not everyone was happy. Some towns condemned the destruction of the tea, and a few even severed ties with Boston's Committee of Correspondence. Boston's radicals responded with a twofold strategy. They flooded the country with stories calculated to "put our Enemies in the wrong," as Samuel Adams remarked. It was alleged that Hutchinson could have saved the tea but instead had taken "malicious pleasure" in bringing on the crisis. The radicals additionally argued that the destruction of the tea was a last resort that had to be taken. Submission to the Tea Act would have meant capitulation to British

tyranny that the colonists had struggled for ten years to prevent. The propaganda campaign succeeded in convincing many that the destruction of the
tea had been fitting, although later in the spring, when Boston's Committee
of Correspondence pushed for another round of boycotting—it called its
proposed embargo the "Solemn League and Covenant"—only 7 of 260 towns
and districts in the interior signed on. Indeed, the plan to reenergize the
trade boycott failed to win adherence in Boston, and Samuel Adams and his
colleagues had their hands full in rebuffing a merchant-driven movement to
pay for the tea that had been destroyed.[8]

Boston's deft and anxious popular leaders had not waited to learn the reaction of the other colonies to the Tea Party. On the day after the tea was
destroyed, riders set off from the city with dispatches in their saddlebags
justifying the steps taken the previous night. Paul Revere, a durable thirty-
nine-year-old silversmith who had been among the "Mohawks," rode to New
York and Philadelphia, the first of five long rides that he would make to those
cities. He carried materials claiming that Hutchinson and his "Cabal" had
turned down every "conciliatory" offer made by Boston's citizenry. Ultimately,
Boston learned that the Tea Party had provoked little outrage in America.
Committees of correspondence from other colonies seldom mentioned the
destruction of the tea, and when they did, it was to acknowledge that it had
been "Justified by a strong Necessity."[9]

Thereafter, Boston spent the winter and early spring awaiting London's
reaction. The popular leaders expected the worst. Friends in England had
informed them of the fury that blanketed the land.[10] Late in the spring,
Hutchinson's successor as governor arrived in Boston. It was General Gage,
who would continue as commander of the British army in America while
serving as the new royal governor of Massachusetts. Soon, too, news of
the Intolerable Acts trickled in. Parliament's response exceeded what the
Bostonians had anticipated. Boston and the Bay Colony had been singled
out for punishment. No reprisals had been taken against the other cities
and colonies that had resisted the Tea Act. London was pursuing a divide-
and-conquer strategy, seeking to isolate Massachusetts.

Boston's popular leaders were under no illusion that the Bay Colony could
stand alone. Dispatch riders mounted up and sped off again, with hearty Paul
Revere carrying messages first to Rhode Island and Connecticut, then
making his second ride to New York and Philadelphia. The riders carried an
appeal from a Boston town meeting for food and assorted supplies. But that
was not all. Samuel Adams and other popular leaders in Boston urged an
immediate American-wide embargo of British imports. The entreaties for
provisions succeeded: aid—including livestock, rice, corn, grain, cabbage,

fish, and firewood—poured in from as far away as Georgia.[11] But Adams's hope for a prompt boycott of British commerce encountered trouble.

Although the Intolerable Acts provoked widespread outrage, most colonies preferred a national conclave that could fashion a unified American response rather than a knee-jerk embargo. Even neighboring Connecticut spurned the idea of instantly joining Massachusetts in a boycott and instead appealed to the other colonies to send delegates to a general congress. Momentum for a national meeting gathered rapidly in June. Some thought such a meeting was essential to restrain Boston's firebrands. Others hoped for a course of action that was less confrontational than a trade embargo. Still others supported an embargo but wanted guarantees that every colony and every port city would join in. Some thought that a display of American unity would induce North's ministry to back down, averting war. Not a few believed that a congressional defiance would result in war. Before agreeing to any provocative step they wanted to measure sentiment throughout the colonies. Above all, those who thought war was likely wanted assurances of American unity before embarking on hostilities.[12]

Samuel Adams was acutely worried. He had misgivings about a national congress. He wanted swift action, as the Boston Port Act had taken effect on June 1 and Boston Harbor was shut tighter than a drum. Adams knew that weeks, possibly months, would pass before a congress could meet. Still more time would be lost before it did anything, if it agreed to do anything. Adams recalled all too well that nine years earlier the Stamp Act Congress had not only failed to endorse a trade boycott but it had also pledged "all due subordination" to Parliament. However, this was a fight that Adams could not win, and in mid-June, with the notion of a general congress having taken on an air of inevitability, he reluctantly endorsed it.

Though disappointed, Adams took solace from the far-reaching passion aroused by the Intolerable Acts. North and south, colonists appeared to share fears that if the mother country succeeded in imposing these punitive measures on Massachusetts, someday London would single out other provinces for similar treatment. The Massachusetts Government Act—which abrogated the colony's charter—provoked the greatest fury and trepidation, for as an American pamphleteer said that year, colonial charters were "a solemn covenant between [the King] and our *fathers*." The earliest charters, moreover, had declared that the colonists were guaranteed the "liberties and immunities" of Englishmen "as if they ... were born within the realm of England." But if the Massachusetts charter—or any charter—could be rescinded with the stroke of a pen, how safe were the colonists' "rights of Englishmen"? How safe was freedom of worship in Pennsylvania, for instance, where for a century the inhabitants had been free "to worship God according to their understandings"? How safe was trial by jury? How safe was representative government?[13]

Actually, it was not only the Intolerable Acts that aroused a storm of indignation that summer. Just weeks after Parliament enacted the legislation to punish Massachusetts, it passed the Quebec Act, word of which reached the colonies at nearly the same time as that of London's coercive measures. Americans may not have conflated the parliamentary measures, as some historians have suggested, but the colonists learned of the acts at roughly the same time and some colonists were just as troubled by the Quebec Act as by the Intolerable Acts.

The Quebec Act guaranteed religious freedom in strongly Catholic Canada. The *Connecticut Courant* immediately declared that "the mask is at length thrown off." The mother country plotted the popish domination of Canada and religious "slavery" in New England. Furthermore, the Quebec Act established a government for Quebec with no elected assembly, a measure that alarmed colonists already uneasy over London's trampling of provincial legislatures. But it was the section on Quebec's boundaries that spelled danger to powerful, entrenched interests in the colonies. The act incorporated all land between the Ohio and the Mississippi (essentially today's Midwestern states of Ohio, Indiana, Illinois, and Michigan) into the province of Quebec. With the stroke of yet another pen, thousands of square miles of charter-based land claims of Virginia and Connecticut were jeopardized. Land speculators in Virginia, many of whom held key positions in the House of Burgesses, already saw themselves as helpless victims of imperial land policies. With the Quebec Act, their interests were yet again threatened by a faraway imperial government over which they had no control. The reaction of Virginia's Arthur Lee may have been typical among the well-heeled planters who hoped to make a fortune through speculation in America's western lands. Said Lee, "every tie of allegiance is broke by the Quebec Act, which is absolutely a dissolution of this government; the compact between the King and the people is done away with."[14]

For all of Samuel Adams's worrying, the American response to the Intolerable Acts was little short of a rebellion. In fact, the colonists' reaction in 1774 made possible the American Revolution.

Backcountry Massachusetts had remained largely quiet before the summer of 1774. The Intolerable Acts changed things. Nearly all the towns that in May had snubbed the Solemn League and Covenant adopted boycotts of British imported goods during the summer. One town called it a "Withdrawment of our Commerce." Many threatened to not merely publish "to the world" the names of violators, but to also break off all social and economic ties with transgressors.[15]

The outrage that swept these rural western hamlets grew from the draconian nature of the Intolerable Acts, the appointment of Gage as governor of the Bay Colony, and a deeply felt conviction that the colonists' God-given rights were being trampled by an unrighteous government. Passive until now, these farmers and artisans concluded that the time for petitioning was over and that the time to strike back against oppressive rulers had arrived. If any one thing set the Massachusetts hinterland on a truly revolutionary path, it was Gage's action on August 9. On that day, the governor announced the appointment of the new provincial council. Under the old charter, the elected members of the lower house annually selected the members of the council, which advised the governor and served as the upper house of the legislature. But the elected council was deposed by the Massachusetts Government Act. Now, the royally appointed governor was to unilaterally select the council. As nothing previously, this laid bare what many saw as a diabolical plot in London to strike at the heart of the Bay Colony's autonomy. But that was not all. The boiling anger of the citizenry was also fed by loathing for those whom Gage had appointed to the council. It was an all-consuming wrath born of festering hatred toward men who were thought to be selling out their coun- trymen, stoked by resentment of gentlemen who, through wealth and family ties, had long wielded local power, often with a palpable arrogance.

Crowds numbering in the hundreds, sometimes in the thousands, gathered in town after town and took whatever steps were necessary to force the resig- nation of the newly named councilors. The appearance of a gun-wielding mob usually did the trick, but on occasion guns were fired—though no one was shot—and property was damaged. The favorite horse of one appointee was either killed, painted, or maimed (the stories varied). It all happened quickly. By early September, every councilor had resigned or fled to Boston, usually never to return home. Several sheriffs and court officials had also been forced out of office and into exile, and newly fabricated county conven- tions had taken control. As historian Ray Raphael has written, by summer's end in 1774 "all traces of British authority had vanished from Massachusetts save for the military garrison in Boston."[16]

The events of that summer in Massachusetts were remarkable, but what occurred in Pennsylvania was truly astonishing. By early summer, all but two colonies had committed to sending delegates to the Continental Congress, as the national meeting of the colonies was being called, and it was known that the conclave was to gather in Philadelphia early in September "to deliberate on those general measures which the united interests of America may . . . require," as Maryland had proclaimed. Only Georgia, a tiny new colony preoccupied with the likelihood of an imminent Indian war, and Pennsylvania had not acted.[17]

Philadelphia dominated Pennsylvania, and the city in turn was controlled by merchants who long had flourished from a thriving trade with the mother country. There was strong resistance within the mercantile community to another trade embargo, and an equally fervid desire to maintain the Anglo-American ties that were thought to be crucial to prosperity. In these respects, Pennsylvania was not unlike New York and one or two other colonies. But politics that were unique to Pennsylvania always colored the actions taken, or not taken, by this province.

Since early in the Seven Years' War, the Pennsylvania legislature had been under the sway of the Assembly Party, a political faction created by Benjamin Franklin and Joseph Galloway. The two men could not have been more dissimilar, but those differences were critical to the success of their political partnership. Franklin, who was nearly twenty-five years older, was an artisan acclaimed by Philadelphia's tradesmen, while Galloway, a lawyer who had married into money, was well connected in elite circles and generally thought to be unrivalled as an orator. In time, Galloway was chosen Speaker of the House. After a bit more time, he and Franklin hatched the idea of seeking to have Pennsylvania made a royal colony. They came to their decision while Great Britain basked in the bright glow of victory in the Seven Years' War. They also believed that submitting to Crown rule would open to settlement, and speculation, lands controlled by the Penn family, the proprietary rulers of the colony since the days of William Penn. Many suspected, probably correctly, that Franklin and Galloway viewed royalization as the means for their personal advancement. Rumors circulated that Franklin hoped to become Pennsylvania's first royal governor and Galloway its chief justice. It was to campaign for having Pennsylvania made a royal colony that Franklin sailed for London in 1764. He was still there in 1774, ostensibly hopeful that royalization might yet come to pass.

From the outset, Franklin and Galloway understood that their success hinged, in part, on keeping the British ministry happy, a realization that led them—or at least Galloway—down a calamitous path. During the Stamp Act furor, Galloway made the Assembly Party into a cheerleader for the parliamentary tax. He paid a price. After seven years of undisputed legislative dominion, the Assembly Party faced tough competition from a new faction, the Proprietary Party. It was headed by John Dickinson, who, as "The Farmer," was emerging as the best-known political writer and most renowned politician in the colonies. Dickinson's party drew its support from among several contingents: those opposed to Britain's centralizing policies, including some merchants; Philadelphia artisans and shopkeepers who had come to believe that the Assembly Party ignored their social and political aspirations; and backcountry residents who wanted more equitable representation in the provincial assembly. Galloway further damaged himself and his party through his fealty to the Townshend Duties. Unable by the close of the 1760s to win reelection in Philadelphia, Galloway thereafter had to run in a district in Bucks County, north of the city. Galloway's problems notwithstanding, the Assembly Party still controlled the Pennsylvania assembly in 1774, though only because the seats in the legislature were unfairly apportioned. Philadelphia and the counties in eastern Pennsylvania, the core of the Assembly Party's strength, contained about 50 percent of the colony's population but nearly three-quarters of the seats in the assembly.

Galloway laid low during the Tea Act troubles, but when Paul Revere galloped into Philadelphia in May 1774 with Boston's appeal for a national trade embargo, Speaker Galloway spoke out against yet another cessation of trade. In part, he acted on behalf of some of Philadelphia's merchants, but Galloway also genuinely feared that a trade boycott would mean war with the mother country. Only the assembly could legally sanction a boycott. It was not in session and only the governor could summon it to meet. Governor John Penn refused to act, and Galloway was not about to urge him otherwise.

In Virginia, where something similar occurred, the burgesses, led by their speaker, simply convened on their own as a rump legislature and instituted a boycott. But with Galloway refusing to budge, a coterie of Philadelphia activists—including Thomas Mifflin and Charles Thomson, both prosperous merchants; Joseph Reed, a leading lawyer; and Dickinson—took the initiative. They organized mass meetings in the late spring. An outdoor meeting in June that was attended by thousands endorsed the colony's participation in a national boycott and called on Galloway to summon the assembly into session. When Galloway still refused to act, a subsequent mass meeting voted for the election of a provincial convention, an extralegal body certain to afford greater representation to the western counties and, in consequence, a smaller percentage of seats to the eastern counties. The message was crystal clear: if the conservative assembly would not meet and act, a more radical provincial convention—a revolutionary body—would take charge in Pennsylvania. Penn buckled. He called the assembly to meet in July in a special session.

The Provincial Convention met anyway, as the radical leadership was eager to keep pressure on the assembly. Convening in June, three weeks before the special session of the assembly was slated to begin, the delegates to the Provincial Convention gathered in Carpenter's Hall, a recently constructed Georgian brick building that served as a guild hall for tradesmen. The Convention adopted a series of resolutions and instructions to the colony's eventual delegation to the Continental Congress. While advocating that Congress adhere to a "plan of conduct" aimed at "restoring harmony" with the mother country, the delegates voted by "a great majority" that Pennsylvania join in a national boycott, should that be Congress's choice. It additionally denounced the Coercive Acts, as well as numerous imperial restrictions on American trade and all forms of taxation by Parliament. It concluded by preparing its preferred list of delegates to the Congress.

The members of the legitimate Pennsylvania assembly had hardly taken their seats on July 21 when the delegates to the Provincial Convention marched en masse to the State House and formally presented Speaker Galloway with their resolutions. The assembly paid no heed. It did agree to Pennsylvania's participation in the coming intercolonial congress, naming Galloway as one of its seven delegates and making sure that a majority of the delegation shared his outlook. Not one person on the Provincial Convention's list of delegates was chosen, including Dickinson, Galloway's longtime rival. Nor did the assembly's instructions to the delegates mention a boycott. Instead, the congressmen were urged to seek a redress of grievances, protect "American Rights," and pursue a course that aimed at "establishing that Union and Harmony which is most essential to the Welfare and Happiness of both Countries."[18]

Throughout that scorching summer, every colony except Georgia chose its delegates to Congress. The larger colonies voted to send five to nine delegates, the smaller provinces two or three. Most who were chosen were legislative leaders. Virginia, for instance, elected a star-studded delegation that included Patrick Henry, Richard Henry Lee, and George Washington. One of the few chosen to Congress who had not been a key political figure in his colony was John Adams. He had sat in the Massachusetts assembly for only one year back in 1771 and had never been in the forefront of Boston politics. In Massachusetts, an assembly committee that consisted only of Bay Colony legislators who had proven "their opposition to the British Aggressions" met covertly during three consecutive evenings to select the delegates. The assembly rubber-stamped the slate proposed by the committee.[19] Samuel Adams played the principal role in picking the delegates, and through his influence John Adams was added to the delegation. Wishing the Bay Colony delegation to give the appearance of moderation, Samuel could find no better choice than his cousin John, a leading Boston lawyer who had defended the

British soldiers charged in the Boston Massacre. Besides, Samuel must have imagined that John, a political novice, would look to him for guidance.

Fifty-six delegates attended what was to become known as the First Continental Congress. More than half were lawyers, nearly one-third had attended college, and five had studied abroad. Forty-nine had served in provincial assemblies and thirteen had been their Speaker. Close to half of the congressmen were slave owners. The average age of the delegates was forty-five.[20]

Those congressmen who arrived early visited with one another, eager to assess their counterparts. The delegates ranged from Anglophiles whose devotion to the king remained undiluted to those who secretly yearned for independence. As the congressmen sized up their colleagues, it soon was readily apparent that Congress was likely to agree to boycott British trade, but certain to divide sharply over the question of the limits of Parliament's authority. Above all, it was clear that if Congress was to accomplish much, and especially if the remarkable degree of American unity that had brought this gathering into being was to be maintained, all sides would have to make concessions.

On September 5, four months almost to the day since word of the Intolerable Acts reached Boston, the congressmen assembled at the City Tavern for their first meeting. They first had to pick a permanent site. Galloway offered the Pennsylvania State House; some who knew him, or of him, countered by proposing that all meetings be held in Carpenter's Hall. The First Continental Congress chose Carpenter's Hall. Many delegates saw this as a test vote to gauge the strength of the extreme conservatives.

After walking through a light rain to their meeting site, the delegates got down to business. They spent some time on procedural matters, including the thorny issue of voting. The larger colonies naturally wanted voting to be based on population, the smaller provinces demanded an equal voice. There was much speechifying, but the more radical delegates from other large colonies, particularly Massachusetts and Virginia, realized that they needed all the help they could get. Congress agreed that each province would have one vote, a practice that prevailed for the next fifteen years. The congressmen additionally agreed to an oath of secrecy and to meet in secret. The latter step was taken to encourage candid discussions and to keep vital information from local Tories, who could be counted on to pass it on to royal officials.

Before Congress could move on to the substantive issues that had led to its creation, express riders galloped into town on two successive days. The first brought word that the British armed forces had shelled Boston; the second reported "a rupture"—fighting between New England militiamen and British regulars. "God grant it may not be found true," a worried John Adams logged in his diary. Neither story was true. Five days before Congress convened, Gage had dispatched a large party of his soldiers on a mission to seize a stockpile of gunpowder stored in the Provincial Powder House six miles outside Boston. The operation had been carefully planned, and its success may have exceeded Gage's expectations. Not only were the colonists taken by surprise, but also, without a drop of blood having been shed, the regulars confiscated all of the 250 half barrels of powder stored in the arsenal. In the tense hours that followed the raid, rumors spread that the British army was about to march again, perhaps to raid other armories, perhaps to restore British authority in the Bay Colony's backcountry. Dispatch riders fanned out across New England to spread the alarm. Soon the news took on a life of its own, and word of what the British army might do turned into tales of what it had done.[21]

Within forty-eight hours, Congress learned that the news of "a dreadful Catastrophy" in and around Boston had been a mistake. Nevertheless, the more radical Yankees took heart from the initial response of their colleagues and that of the Philadelphians. As muffled bells rang throughout the city, the citizens had displayed "unfeigned marks of sorrow" for the Bostonians and, at least in the estimation of John Adams, nearly every congressman had considered "the Bombardment of Boston, as the Bombardment, of the Capital of his own Province." The curious incident appeared to demonstrate that if the British resorted to force, there would be a widespread willingness to take up arms against them.[22]

On the third day it met, Congress created what would be called the Grand Committee. Composed of two representatives from each colony, it was to define American rights and state how they had been "violated & infringed."[23] Congress anticipated a report within two or three days, but deep, bitter discord immediately surfaced within the committee on the issue of the extent of Parliament's authority over the colonies.

Congress did nothing while it awaited the committee's report. Soon a week had elapsed, then ten days. On September 16, Paul Revere, who by now must have been able to make the ride to Philadelphia blindfolded, arrived on his familiar mount bearing the Suffolk Resolves, a statement adopted by a convention of towns near Boston. The timing of Revere's arrival was not by happenstance. Samuel Adams and his confederates at home, chiefly Dr. Joseph Warren, had planned this all along in order to test, even to shape, sentiment in Congress. Warren, thirty-three years old, Harvard-educated, and a Boston physician—British officials called him the "rascally apothecary"—had joined the popular protest during the Stamp Act crisis. Not long passed before he was an insider, grinding out newspapers essays, plotting strategy, and ultimately serving as president of the provincial congress following its establishment in the fall of 1774. Just as Congress gathered in Philadelphia, delegates to the Suffolk County Convention met at Vose's Tavern in Milton and adopted nineteen resolves. They were presented by Warren, who, together with Samuel Adams and others, had drafted the resolves weeks earlier.[24]

A Massachusetts delegate described what became known as the Suffolk Resolves as "temperate and spirited," but more conservative delegates thought them dangerously inflammatory, even tantamount to a declaration of war. After stating that American loyalty to the mother country hinged on a compact, the Resolves denounced Britain's rulers for their "attempts ... to enslave us" and declared that "no obedience is due" to the Coercive Acts. For good measure, the resolutions assailed the presence of the British army, calling the soldiery "military executioners." The Resolves urged a boycott of trade with England and preparatory steps for war, though stipulating that the militia were to "act merely upon the defensive, so long as such conduct may be vindicated." Congress endorsed the Suffolk Resolves after only a brief debate.[25]

In light of actions that the First Continental Congress later took, and also refused to take, its rapid sanction of these resolves has left generations of baffled scholars scratching their heads. One delegate later claimed that many congressmen were stampeded into voting against their convictions from fear that the failure to endorse the Suffolk Resolves would lead to mob violence in the streets of Philadelphia. As Congress met in secret and no one outside Carpenter's Hall was aware of what the delegates were doing, the greater likelihood was that the more conservative congressmen were outmaneuvered by Samuel Adams. That was Galloway's take on what had occurred. Later, he said the radicals in Congress had been managed by "Samuel Adams—a man, who though by no means remarkable for brilliant abilities" was adroit "in popular intrigue, and the management of a faction. He eats little, drinks little, sleeps little, thinks much, and is most decisive and indefatigable in the pursuit of his objects." Adams, said Galloway, determined the policy and strategy of the radicals. Adams decided what he "wished to have done" by Congress, and for the most part he got his way.[26]

In fact, Samuel Adams did not always get his way with Congress (or even with his own colleagues within the Massachusetts delegation), and he alone did not craft the strategy of the more radical delegates. Like any good leader, he acted in concert with like-minded congressmen. But Adams was a master of timing, and given the response inside and outside Congress several days earlier to the fictitious report of the shelling of Boston, he saw that the moment was right to spring the long-ago drafted Suffolk Resolves. Adroitly, Adams understood the temper of this Congress. He knew that some delegates would endorse military preparedness in Massachusetts as a ploy to persuade the British government to back down, but he also was aware that a majority were sufficiently realistic to understand that a national boycott would lead to war. In short, Adams manipulated few, if any, of his colleagues into doing what they did not want to do. Congress endorsed the Suffolk Resolves because the overwhelming majority agreed with their hard line. When Congress approved the Resolves, John Adams sighed in relief that he at last was "convinced ... that America will support ... Massachusetts."[27] Samuel Adams was aware of that prior to the submission of the Resolves.

Galloway, however, was correct in his appraisal of Adams's political skill. Realizing that many congressmen looked on everyone from the Bay Colony as a wild-eyed revolutionary, Samuel Adams cautioned his colleagues in the Massachusetts delegation to say little, and when they did speak to temper their comments. Adams let like-minded friends from other colonies, especially those from Virginia—where there had been no tea parties, riots, or massacres—take the lead in introducing measures and advocating their adoption. In all likelihood, that was the tack that Adams took with the Suffolk Resolves.

After affirming the Resolves, Congress did nothing more until, on September 24, the Grand Committee finally produced its long-anticipated report on American rights. To this point, the delegates had politely settled whatever differences had cropped up, but the debate on the Grand Committee's recommendations was fevered.

It may not have been a coincidence that Richard Henry Lee chose this moment to move the adoption of a boycott of British imports that would take effect on December 1. There was little doubt that Congress would approve non-importation, but Lee and Samuel Adams may have wanted the vote taken before ill feelings growing out of the wrangle over the Grand Committee's report could sow additional divisions in Congress. Lee introduced his motion on September 26, and it was approved the same day. However, when a New England delegate followed with a motion to also terminate all exports to the mother country, southerners objected. They had put in their tobacco, rice, indigo, and sea-island cotton crops before learning of the Intolerable Acts, in some instances even before they were aware of the Boston Tea Party. As they were just now about to harvest what they had planted, non-exportation would deny them an income for an entire year.

Several southern delegates expressed fears that such a move could drive many debt-ridden planters into bankruptcy. The debate that ensued was fierce and nasty. This first North-versus-South clash in American politics spun on through two tense sessions, and at the end of the second day, the issue had not been settled.[28]

Galloway may have felt that he was outmaneuvered in Congress by Samuel Adams, but he was no babe in the woods when it came to politics. He had meticulously scrutinized his colleagues and cultivated those who shared his outlook, and three weeks into the meeting he had established himself as the leader of the more conservative delegates. Furthermore, just as Adams had seized the right time to bring up the Suffolk Resolves and non-importation, Galloway saw the fracas over non-exportation as the moment when he should introduce the conservative plan for resolving the imperial crisis.

On September 28 Galloway took the floor and spoke for two hours, possibly the lengthiest speech made during the First Congress, and one in which he summoned all his rich oratorical skills. In the early portion of his address, Galloway argued that Great Britain had steadily nourished the colonies, bringing them to an incredible level of wealth and freedom. Even greater good fortune awaited an America that remained united with the mother country, as it could rapidly expand to the Pacific Ocean and even overwhelm Spain's colonies in Central and South America. Unimaginable riches would flow to the colonists.

But all would be lost if America went to war with Britain. With certitude, Galloway argued that the colonists alone could not win such a war. Defeat, he added, would result in harsh retribution. Victory was possible only with French assistance, the consequence of which would be that Americans would find themselves under the thumb of an autocratic Catholic monarch. If by some miracle the war was won and true independence leading to the creation of an American nation was achieved, that Union could not last long. It would break up into several small nations, which would frequently make war against one another. Most likely, the northern country would invade the southern country. Finally, Galloway was the first in a long line of conservatives to warn of the danger of social and political radicalism imbedded within the insurgency. An independent America, he cautioned, would be a democratic America, a nation in which the wealthy would be heavily taxed, wealth would be redistributed, and sweeping social changes would occur.

To safeguard the good and prevent the bad, Galloway offered a compromise plan that straddled the constitutional positions taken by London and the colonies. Labeling it his "Plan of Union," Galloway proposed the creation of an "American Branch" of the imperial government. It was to consist of a national legislature—not unlike the Continental Congress—that would be the third branch of Parliament and a president general appointed by the king. Congress and the executive would "exercise all the legislative rights, powers, and authorities necessary for regulating and administering all the . . . affairs of the colonies." Furthermore, no imperial legislation enacted by the Commons and Lords in London would become law unless assented to by the American Branch.[29]

Galloway argued that his plan met the objections of both sides. Parliament would be sovereign, yet no taxes or other legislation pertaining to the colonies could take effect without the colonists' consent. Galloway's proposal frightened the more radical delegates. John Adams later said it posed "the most alarming" threat to "effective and united action" prior to independence. But Galloway's plan was seconded by John Jay and some thought it the "perfect" solution to the imperial dilemma. It garnered support among northerners and southerners, and it is possible that a majority of the congressmen favored its adoption. However, what counted was the vote not of delegates but of delegations and by a vote of 6–5, Congress tabled Galloway's plan. (Rhode Island's two congressmen divided, preventing the province from casting a vote.)[30]

The more radical congressmen had opposed Galloway for several reasons. A constitutional debate might tie up Congress for months, and still more time would pass while it was debated in London. All the while, Massachusetts—under the thumb of the Royal Navy—would be unable to import or export a thing. Such a long, painful delay could destroy the unity that had so painstakingly been constructed within the Bay Colony, and if unity unraveled in Massachusetts, it might break down everywhere. Besides, radicals longed for greater American autonomy than Galloway's plan would have provided. In the end, the radicals were aided—perhaps even saved—by Galloway's sullied reputation. He was widely thought of as a Tory, one who was blindly loyal to the mother country, and as John Adams discovered after only a few days in Philadelphia, a "Tory here is the most despicable Animal in the Creation. Spiders, Toads, Snakes, are their only proper Emblems."[31]

Once Galloway's proposal had failed, the sessions seemed less acrimonious. Having gotten nearly all that they wanted, and having prevented what they did not want, the more radical delegates were more accommodating, eager to cement American unity. Congress took several substantive steps during its final month. It completed its work on the boycotting of the mother country by agreeing not to import any items from England or Ireland, any East India Company tea "from any part of the world," molasses or coffee from British islands in the West Indies, to "neither import nor purchase any slave," and to "wholly discontinue the slave trade." What is more, Congress voted for non-exportation to Great Britain, Ireland, and the British West Indies beginning a year down the road, on September 1, 1775, a compromise that would enable southerners to prepare for it. After March 1, a ban on the sale of British goods already ordered or acquired by American merchants was to take effect. Congress additionally created the Continental Association to enforce the trade boycott. Every city, village, and county throughout America was to create an Association committee that was to be elected by those who were qualified to vote for representatives in the provincial legislature. Congress also agreed to boycott the trade of any province that refused to adhere to the embargo.[32]

During this period, Congress returned to the Grand Committee's report, debating it for three weeks before agreeing, on October 17, to the Declaration of Colonial Rights and Grievances. Much of the grievance portion of the document rehashed innumerable statements by colonial assemblies going back to 1765. In addition to stating that the colonial assemblies alone could tax the colonists, it assailed the peacetime deployment of the British army in the colonies, the Intolerable Acts and the Quebec Act, London's policy of making judges dependent on the Crown, the dissolution of colonial assemblies, and the "contempt" with which Crown officials had treated the colonists' "humble, loyal and reasonable petitions," and it denied that the mother country possessed the authority to transport colonists to England to stand trial for treason. Regarding the rights of the colonists, Congress declared that "they are entitled to life, liberty and property, and they have never ceded to any sovereign power whatever, a right to dispose of either without their consent." The moderates won out on the touchy issue of the limits of Parliament's authority. Congress adopted the position that John Dickinson, the Farmer, had taken in 1767. In order to secure "the commercial advantages" and "commercial benefits of its respective members" throughout the British Empire, the congressmen declared, "we cheerfully consent to the operation of such Acts of the British Parliament, as are *bona fide*, restrained to the regulation of our external commerce."[33]

The last sensitive issue concerned ordering military preparations. Richard Henry Lee brought it up, proposing that Congress both direct each colony to ready its militia and furnish arms and ammunition to the citizen-soldiers throughout the colonies. The conservatives recoiled in horror, arguing that such pugnacity would foil the steps that Congress had taken to gain peaceful redress and reconciliation. Patrick Henry fought his timorous colleagues. "Arms are Necessary, & . . . Necessary Now," he said, though for the benefit of his more squeamish colleagues he added that a "Preparation for Warr is

Necessary to obtain peace." In the end, Congress agreed to half of Lee's recommendation. It merely asked the colonies to ready their militias.[34]

Before concluding, Congress drafted addresses to the British people, the inhabitants of Canada, and the king. Congress pointed out that the colonists sought no new rights, longed for peace and reconciliation, and appealed to the monarch to use his "royal authority . . . for our relief."[35]

Numerous appeals to the king had been made previously. None had ever been answered. But given American unity and the gravity of the situation, some in Congress hoped for a positive response. However, many were certain that it was a futile gesture. The last step taken by Congress was to agree to meet again the following May in the event that the Anglo-American troubles had not been resolved.

When Congress adjourned late in October, the most radical delegates departed Philadelphia convinced that war was inevitable. But they understood that Americans could not start the war. The preservation of American unity hinged on the soldiers of the mother country firing the first shot.[36]

CHAPTER 6

"Blows Must Decide Whether They Are to Be Subject to This Country"

The War Begins

Congress had met behind closed doors, and the congressmen had taken a vow of secrecy, but someone had been blabbing. The Earl of Dartmouth, the American secretary, had been kept abreast of what was occurring. The most likely suspect was Joseph Galloway, who may have tattled to his friend William Franklin, Benjamin Franklin's son and the royal governor of New Jersey. Young Franklin in turn probably passed along the information to Dartmouth, which included damaging revelations of the bitter divisions among the congressmen.

Dartmouth had despaired when he learned in early October that Congress had endorsed the Suffolk Resolves. "They have declared war on us," he said immediately.[1] However, once aware of the Galloway Plan and its narrow defeat, Dartmouth saw a glimmer of hope for Anglo-American reconciliation if the ministry could exploit the disparate viewpoints in the colonies. Dartmouth urged Lord North to send a commission to America to open negotiations. North had no interest in bargaining, though given his close ties to the American secretary, the prime minister agreed to take the matter to the monarch. Although George III had questioned neither Parliament's authority over the colonies nor the wisdom of sending troops to Boston in 1768, for the most part he had come down on the side of leniency when responding to colonial provocations. The Boston Tea Party brought about a sea change in his attitude. Thereafter, the monarch was stern and unbending, regretted the earlier appeasement of the colonists, and saw no alternative to using force to bring his rebellious subjects in line. The colonists were in "a State of Rebellion," he said before Congress met, adding even then that "blows must decide whether they are to be subject to this Country or independent." On another occasion he had remarked that the "dye is cast," the "Colonies must submit or triumph. . . . [W]e must not retreat." Not surprisingly, the king rejected discussions with the colonists. "I do not want to drive them to despair but to Submission," he told North.[2]

Once formal word of the steps taken by the Continental Congress was received in December, the ministers took up the American crisis but deferred a decision on how to respond until after the holidays. They chose this course because the monarch insisted that "reason not passion" must be their guide. But opinion in England was hardly dispassionate. Throughout the Christmas season and into January, most of the press and numerous pamphleteers assailed the "wicked and treasonable" colonists. Samuel Adams came under fire, but no one was savaged like Franklin, who was limned as "Old Doubleface" and "Judas."[3]

Dartmouth aside, the ministers required no exhortations to be firm. They reached a decision on how to respond to the defiant colonists in the course of three meetings in January 1775. From the outset, all signs pointed toward the use of force. The ministers were influenced by numerous Crown officials in the colonies who painted a picture of a widespread and intractable insurgency that could be put down only by armed forces.[4] The most influential was General Gage, who had been in Boston since June. The time for "Conciliating, Moderating, Reasoning is over," he advised. "Nothing can be done but by forcible Means." The "popular Fury was never greater," he went on. He reported that the Yankees were preparing for war. They "threaten Resistance by Arms," he warned, adding that backcountry inhabitants had vowed "to attack any Troops who dare to oppose them." Although he acknowledged that the Yankees might field a capable army, Gage left no doubt that the rebellion could be crushed militarily. The Americans would "be lyons whilst we are lambs but if we take the resolute part they will be very meek," he had long insisted, and now he predicted that a successful "first strike" would "be fatal" to the rebels. Even if the rebels persisted after the first engagement, the troops "would be able to overcome them, no doubt, in a year or two." If the ministry took in what Gage said about the projected ease of crushing the rebellion, it ignored what he said about the need for a great many troops to do the job. "If Force is to be used . . . it must be a considerable one," he counseled, adding that he would need 20,000 British troops—he had only 4,521 at the time—and those must be supplemented by several thousand troops obtained from somewhere in Europe. Sending a sufficient army, he said, would "save both Blood and Treasure in the End." But if too few were sent, it would only "encourage Resistance."[5]

The ministers had contemplated war a year earlier, in the immediate aftermath of the Boston Tea Party. In its deliberations in January 1775, the ministry went back over the same ground and in greater depth. Overconfidence was rife. The colonists had militias, but there was no American army and no colonial soldier had ever commanded an army of the size that would have to be created. It was implausible that America's untrained and undisciplined soldiers would be a match for Britain's professional troops. Indeed, the consensus among Britain's officers who served in the colonies during the Seven Years' War had been that the Americans were a "poor species of fighting men." Some in the cabinet may have agreed with many in the House of Commons who openly derided the colonists as lazy and cowardly, even that it was "romantic to think they would fight." One British general publicly remarked that he could march from one end of America to the other with an army of five thousand; another was known to have observed that "the native American is an effeminate thing, very unfit for and very impatient of war." An MP exclaimed that "a good bleeding" would "bring those Bible-faced Yankees to their senses." In addition to their alleged shortcomings as soldiers, the colonists had no navy and no manufacturing sector that could arm and clothe those who served. It was doubtful that the colonists under the best of conditions could finance a war, but with the Royal Navy blockading the coast and shutting down American trade, it was inconceivable that the colonies could wage a war of any length. Furthermore, the thirteen colonies had long been so disunited that to many it seemed unimaginable that any degree of solidarity could be sustained in the face of adversity.

The cabinet mulled over two troubling questions, though both were ultimately brushed aside. Some ministers wondered whether the British army could campaign in the backcountry, where it would not only lack naval assistance but also have to maintain long supply lines in hostile territory. Those fears were laid to rest largely by the belief that simply taking control of the coastal cities would bring to heel the colonists in the hinterland. Some in the cabinet also found the possibility that France and Spain might aid the colonists, or even enter the war as America's allies, to be unsettling. However, few thought Britain's European rivals would act swiftly. They would watch and wait, and while they did so, Britain's military would suppress the colonial rebellion. The American war would be over while Versailles and Madrid were still contemplating belligerency.[6]

Foreseeing that the ministry would opt to use force and that the monarch would be cool toward opening negotiations, Dartmouth in November—prior to the first cabinet sessions—conceived a last-ditch effort to avert a war. He saw Benjamin Franklin as his only hope. Dartmouth knew enough about Franklin to realize that he remained ambitious and he wanted to live out his life in London. If Franklin could be persuaded—"baited," might be a better word—to propose terms for reconciliation, the king might yet agree to pursue negotiations along those lines. Even if talks with the colonists never led to an accord, the slightest sign that London was willing to yield a bit might drive a wedge between the various factions in America, shattering colonial unity and sapping the will for armed resistance.

Dartmouth selected two English Quakers with ties to Pennsylvania to approach Franklin. After meeting with them, and at their behest, Franklin responded with what he called "Hints ... of Terms" that might resolve the crisis. Franklin proposed that Massachusetts or the Continental Congress make restitution to the East India Company for the property lost in the Boston Tea Party; that the conditions of Britain's regulation of imperial trade be decided through Anglo-American negotiation; that the restraint of colonial manufacturing be "reconsider'd"; that British troops could henceforth be deployed "in any colony [only] with the Consent of its Legislature"; that the Tea Act and Coercive Acts be repealed; and that in wartime, the king might requisition revenue from the colonial assemblies.[7]

Straightaway, Dartmouth saw that Franklin's terms would go nowhere with North's ministry. But he did not give up. He had his intermediaries arrange for Lady Caroline Howe, the sister of General William Howe and Admiral Richard Howe, to invite Franklin to her home to play chess. Franklin accepted the invitation and enjoyed himself so much that he returned for a second match and, on Christmas night, for a third game. During the last visit, Admiral Howe himself dropped in, "accidentally" bumping into Franklin. Howe apologized for the treatment that Franklin had endured in the Cockpit a year earlier and said that if the Pennsylvanian played along, he could "expect any reward in the power of government to bestow." If Franklin had not previously known that he was being used, he surely did now. He would not sell out America, perhaps because it was his native land, perhaps as he sensed that he had a brighter future there than in England. Franklin held fast to the decision he had likely made at the time of his savage humiliation in the Cockpit: he would leave England and cast his lot with the colonies. Over the next few days, Franklin drafted another set of conditions for settling Anglo-American differences. Largely scrapping his original proposals, Franklin submitted to Howe a list of terms that essentially dovetailed with the demands of the Continental Congress.[8]

Dartmouth now realized that peaceful reconciliation was hopeless. Nevertheless, he proposed one last time in the cabinet meetings that commissioners be sent to America to open negotiations. It was a futile gesture. The cabinet adhered to the hard line from which it had never budged throughout the month of discussions, its inclinations bolstered by the support of the

monarch, who later declared that no nation had ever entered into more justifiable hostilitics than did Great Britain in 1775. With the use of force agreed
to, North's ministry in January bolstered the Royal Navy and voted to bring
Gage's manpower strength up to 7,500. This was only about one-third the
number of redcoats that the general had said he would need and a fraction of
the manpower he had envisaged as necessary for putting down such a widespread rebellion, and it would take months to get these reinforcements to
him. Its final decision was to order the arrest of the leaders of the rebel
government in Massachusetts and to command General Gage to use force to
suppress the rebellion.[9]

In a cruel turn of fate it fell to the gloomy American secretary to dispatch
the order to Gage. Thus Dartmouth, nearly the lone voice among the ministers in opposing war, wrote and sent the directive that would launch
hostilities. On January 27, 1775, he ordered "a vigorous Exertion of . . . Force,"
adding for good measure that Gage was to be "active & determined," and not
to hesitate to send his army into the interior of Massachusetts to smash the
rebellion. What is more, Gage was to "arrest and imprison the principal
actors & abettors in the [Massachusetts] Provincial Congress."

From word of the first American protests against the Stamp Act in 1765 to
the receipt of the promulgations and entreaties of the Continental Congress a
decade later, Britain's leaders had never sought to redress the colonists'
fundamental grievances. With a fatal intransigence, they had refused to
reconsider the framework through which power and wealth flowed within
the British Empire, and in 1775 they gambled that they could salvage
everything by bludgeoning the colonists into submission in a war they were
convinced would be short and easy. After all, as Dartmouth stated to Gage in
a remark that summarized majority sentiment in the ministry, the colonists
were "a rude Rabble without a plan, without concert." Success should come
from "a single Action." It was even conceivable that American resistance
would end "without bloodshed" once those Yankee farmer-militiamen
glimpsed the unnerving sight of British regulars bearing down on them.[10]

Given the lag time in communicating from one side of the Atlantic to the
other, Lord North knew that Gage would not receive Dartmouth's order for
four weeks or more. (Bad weather that winter played such havoc with shipping that ten weeks elapsed before Gage received his orders.) That gave the
prime minister ample time to unveil the administration's response to events
in America, though in all that he said to Parliament in January and February,
North never divulged that Gage had been ordered to use force.

Parliament's final peacetime debate on the American question was
launched by a dramatic address by the Earl of Chatham, five days after

Dartmouth penned his secret order. As he was old and ill, this was to be Chatham's last great speech. He counseled against war. The Americans would not back down, he said. They were driven by a sense of honor and the belief that their rights as Englishmen had been violated. It had taken an army of forty thousand men to defeat the French in America, but an even larger army would be required for suppressing the colonial rebellion, if it could be put down. A better course than war was to "restore America to our bosom" through dispelling its "fears and . . . resentments." Chatham essentially urged Parliament to acquiesce in the wishes of the Continental Congress, for he asked his colleagues to remember that "taxation is theirs, commercial regulation is ours." Specifically, he advocated for the removal of the army from Massachusetts and the repeal of the Tea Act and Coercive Acts.[11]

North answered in two long addresses in February. In the first, he revealed that reinforcements were being sent to Gage and vowed to redress American grievances once order was restored. In his second speech, on February 20, he offered what soon was popularly called the North Peace Plan, although the prime minister never for a moment expected that his supposed concessions would assuage the colonists. In fact, he told the king that his actual strategy was to win public support in England for the war that was coming once the Americans had spurned his offer. North's so-called conciliation would have permitted the colonial assemblies to decide what sort of tax to levy once Parliament had stipulated the amount of revenue to be raised by each colony. (One member of the House of Commons who saw through North's chicanery said that the prime minister was really saying: "give us as much money as I wish, till I say enough, or I will take it from you.") Desultory debate followed off and on for a month. In the early going, the highlight was an exchange between Baron Camden and the Earl of Sandwich, the first lord of the Admiralty. Camden warned that Great Britain could never subdue more than two million free people who lived behind a coastline that stretched over 1,800 miles and were united in quest of "liberty and justice." Sandwich responded that the "American heroes" were "raw, undisciplined, cowardly men" who would take flight at the "very sound of a cannon." Erroneously charging that Franklin had written Chatham's recent speech, Sandwich went on to label the Pennsylvanian "one of the bitterest and most mischievous Enemies this country had ever known." Franklin, the guest of Chatham, happened to be seated in the gallery that day and heard this latest blast directed his way by a high British official.[12]

Edmund Burke's remarks were the most thoughtful offered that month in the House of Commons. In the second of his three major speeches on America prior to independence, Burke, like Chatham had earlier, advised that the colonists would not back down. The "fierce spirit of liberty is stronger in the English Colonies probably than in any other people of the earth." The time had come to rethink the relationship between colonies and the parent state. Though guarded and opaque, Burke hinted at something of a federal system in which the largely autonomous colonists were bound by loyalty to the king. Above all, however, he dreamed of a return to pre–1763 practices, a time before "little minds" had threatened the dissolution of "a great empire" through attempts to levy parliamentary taxes on the colonists.[13]

In the end, by a nearly four-to-one margin, the House of Commons turned its back on those who opposed war and endorsed the purported concessions offered by the prime minister. Parliament had committed the nation to the war that the ministry had already covertly ordered.

There were colonists who believed that the mother country would back down in the face of the resolution and unity exhibited by the Continental Congress, and some hoped the appeal to the monarch would lead him to intercede, pointing the way to an accommodation. Few were so sanguine, however, and the colonists prepared for the worst. Long before Congress adjourned, Massachusetts was readying its militia. The colony's Provincial Congress directed each town to organize and regularly train its militia, and as speed would be essential in responding to a threat by the British army, it further stipulated that "one-third of the men of their respective towns, between sixteen and sixty years of age, be ready to act at a minute's warning." These men would come to be known as "minutemen." In the other colonies, militia training—or at least some degree of organizing—followed the Continental Congress's "earnest" admonition that in each province "a Militia be forthwith appointed and well disciplined." By early 1775, militiamen were training on muddy drill fields in Rhode Island, New Hampshire, Connecticut, Maryland, South Carolina, and Virginia. The latter also created companies of riflemen. They were to consist of those who could "procure Riphel Guns," were capable marksmen, and were distinguished from other militiamen in that they were to wear "painted Hunting-Shirts and Indian Boots." Connecticut, which had ordered three days of training each month for its militiamen, also commissioned two independent, or volunteer, companies. Independent companies similarly sprang up in several counties and towns in Virginia, including one in Alexandria that George Washington helped drill and outfit. Virginia and Massachusetts also began producing gunpowder, and some colonies looked into the possibility of acquiring ordinance and munitions from western Europe.[14]

While some men drilled, others sat on the Continental Association committees that Congress had ordered into being to enforce the trade boycotts. Hundreds of committees sprang up in the weeks following Congress's adjournment; twenty-eight were up and running in Connecticut within two months. For the most part, they variously styled themselves as committees of observation, inspection, or safety, though some called themselves "committees for the detection of conspiracy."[15] Several colonies created large committees consisting of dozens of members, a step deliberately taken to deepen support for the insurgency. New Jersey and Pennsylvania both had more than five hundred Association committeemen, and some three thousand manned the approximately three hundred committees that came into being in the four New England colonies. Boston's committee consisted of sixty-three members, including representatives from the Loyal Nine and assorted caucuses.

The Association committees acted with such zeal that the value of British imports during 1775 was just 5 percent of that of the previous year. Taking to heart Congress's instructions to "observe the conduct" of the citizenry, many committees searched for enemies of the American cause, hoping to identify them through the use of loyalty oaths. Those who refused to sign the oaths were considered Loyalists or Tories. They were placed under surveillance in some locales, disarmed in others, jailed in rare instances, not infrequently harassed and threatened, and here and there "ordered to depart." Joseph Galloway, now retired, savaged the committeemen as being "drunk with the power they had usurped" and said they "aimed at a general revolution."[16]

The Association committees were a vital stage on the road to revolution. As historian T. H. Breen has observed, they fostered the "sobering lesson . . . that the people were ultimately accountable for the common good." In addition, as most committeemen had never before held power, each had to know that his days as a suddenly influential local figure would come to an end the moment the American insurgency ended. Some were radicalized through their service on committees, while at the same moment the committees—bodies in which power flowed up from the people—provided a legitimacy to the insurgency. Whether by accident or design, Congress's creation of the Association put in place a structure that nourished intemperate feelings toward the mother country. Within six months of the meeting of the Continental Congress, it was apparent that in much of the country the populace harbored a far more radical outlook than had most of the congressional delegates and that the citizenry was in control of local government throughout America.[17]

Other changes were apparent as well. Shortly before Congress adjourned, the annual October assembly elections in Pennsylvania swept anti-British representatives into control of the legislature. The new majority dumped

Galloway from the speakership that he had held for years, immediately added John Dickinson to the province's delegation in Congress, and ultimately approved the steps Congress had taken. Refusing to concede defeat, Galloway made one final effort to prevent a war that he feared would be catastrophic. He and Governor John Penn drafted a petition to the king. However, whereas Galloway once had been assured of having his way in the Pennsylvania assembly, that no longer was the case. Galloway's once subservient assembly repudiated the appeal to the monarch by a vote of 22–15.

In New York, where the port city was heavily dependent on British trade, much of the elite feared a rupture with the mother country, anxiety that was also widespread among those who held power throughout the hinterland. During that fall and winter, only three of New York's thirteen counties adhered to the Continental Association. What is more, New York's colonial assembly refused to endorse the actions taken by Congress, balked at electing delegates to a second intercolonial congress that was to meet in May if necessary, and adopted a servile appeal to the king similar to the one that Galloway had sought in Pennsylvania. In the spring, however, more radical New Yorkers—acting through an extralegal Committee of sixty—responded as Philadelphia's radicals had a year earlier. They bypassed the assembly and held elections for a provincial convention. The colonial assembly last met on April 3, 1775, about the time that the provincial convention met and elected delegates to the next congress.[18]

During this period, the final flurry of peacetime pamphleteering occurred. A bevy of Tories assailed Congress and were in turn answered by Whigs. Vitriol flowed, but little new light was shed on Anglo-American differences, and it is unlikely that many minds were changed. As was often true of pamphleteering, readership was probably small, and in Massachusetts the turgid, legalistic essays of John Adams, who wrote as "Novanglus," and Daniel Leonard, a conservative Taunton lawyer who used the pen name "Massachusettensis," must have assured a limited audience.[19] In New York, Alexander Hamilton defended Congress, calling those who assailed it "bad men" with "mad imaginations" who engaged in "sophistry" to "dupe" and "dazzle" the American public. Hamilton's tracts were less sophisticated but more readable than Adams's, which was all the more remarkable considering that the New Yorker was a nineteen-year-old college student. Remarkably, too, Hamilton served up something novel in the literature of the American insurgency to this point. He may have been the first in print in America to maintain that Britain could not win a war with the colonists. He predicted not only that France and Spain would assist the colonists, but Hamilton also envisioned that by using what were called Fabian tactics, America could prevent a British victory. The colonists could "evade a pitched battle" and instead "harass and exhaust the [British] soldiery." Attrition suffered by the superior redcoat army would eventually force Britain's leaders to abandon the war.[20]

Galloway wrote the pamphlet that gained the most notoriety. In *A Candid Examination of the Mutual Claims of Great Britain and the Colonies*, he broke Congress's code of silence, revealing the terms of his plan of union and its narrow defeat by those who favored "measures of *independence* and *sedition* . . . to those of *harmony* and *liberty*." Virtually alone among the pamphleteers, Galloway also offered more than the vilification of his political enemies and the monotonous rehashing of familiar issues. His was a thoughtful essay on the need for a strong central government both within the empire and within America. As historian Merrill Jensen observed, Galloway "was concerned with the same problem and used many of the same arguments" that were employed by the authors of *The Federalist Papers* more than a decade later. For Galloway, however, his essay had calamitous personal consequences. His betrayal of congressional secrets resulted in death threats. Tired and frightened, he retreated to the safety of Trevose, his estate well north of Philadelphia, and when hostilities erupted, he quit the assembly in which he had sat for two decades, unwilling to hold office in a colony that was at war with the mother country.[21]

Perhaps the pamphlet that came closest to expressing the outlook of most Americans—more so than the steps taken by the compromise-driven Congress—was authored by Thomas Jefferson. Jefferson penned his essay in the summer of 1774 to instruct Virginia's delegation to the Continental Congress, taking the trouble in large measure because he badly wished to be included among the delegates. Illness prevented him from attending the Virginia Convention that selected the congressmen, and Jefferson was not included in the delegation. But several members of the convention saw to the publication of what he had written, and at year's end it appeared in print as *A Summary View of the Rights of British America*.

Jefferson's handiwork stood out for several reasons. It was composed in a crisp, lucid, and flowing style that made it one of the more readable pamphlets. In addition, he took issue with the nearly universal belief in England (and among Tories) that the mother country had nurtured the colonists from infancy. In Jefferson's version, several generations of Virginians, with next to no help from England, had repeatedly fought and defeated the Indians, opening one new western frontier after another. America was made by American colonists, he insisted. He denied that Parliament had any authority over the colonies, including the regulation of trade or restraints on manufacturing. Americans, he said, had a "natural right" to "a free trade with all parts of the world"; he labeled bans on manufacturing "instance[s] of despotism." The most cogent portion of his essay was his charge that the monarch was complicit in Britain's iniquitous designs on America. Abandoning the customary servile language the colonists used when writing of the monarch, Jefferson alleged that the king had strayed beyond his legitimate executive role to cooperate with Parliament in its "many unwarrantable encroachments and usurpations," especially its "wanton exercise of . . . power" in sending troops to the colonies in peacetime and disallowing legislation enacted by colonial assemblies. He excoriated George III both for having ignored the colonists' petitions for redress and for his blind indifference toward American interests, including the Crown's refusal to permit the colonists to migrate across the Appalachians. The monarch's behavior, Jefferson wrote, threatened to leave his reputation as "a blot in the page of history."[22]

No one knows how many colonists read Jefferson's pamphlet, though large numbers of congressmen and provincial assemblymen probably perused it, and most may have read it after hostilities began. Timing is everything in politics, and for many readers Jefferson's powerful language, captivating story of American prowess, and direct confrontation with the monarchy stood out a crucial moment.

The pamphlet that may have reached the largest audience at this juncture was *Strictures on "A Friendly Address to all Reasonable Americans."* It was written by Lieutenant Colonel Charles Lee, a native of Great Britain and for two decades an officer in the British army. Lee had resigned his commission and moved to Virginia in the early 1770s. Spurred by the likelihood of hostilities, his tract—which appeared a few months after Hamilton's—contended that the colonists could win a war against the mother country. British soldiers were overrated and often led by incapable officers, he asserted, adding that the colonists could quickly raise and train a viable army. Furthermore, Americans would have a psychological advantage. They would be fighting for something tangible and invaluable: their liberty.[23]

As wintry March gave way to April's softer spring weather in 1775, nearly six months had elapsed since the adjournment of Congress. America and the colonists had changed during that period, and the political changes in the year since news arrived of the Intolerable Acts had been especially breathtaking. Royal authority had disappeared throughout much of the American landscape, the importation and sale of British goods had ended, and citizen-soldiers were training. A transformation appears to have occurred as well in the thinking of many colonists. The emphatic good will, even deep affection, that once had existed toward the mother country had been replaced by a sour mistrust that often bordered on loathing. Whether or not they fully under-stood it, the colonists were coming to see themselves more as Americans than as British-Americans, and increasing numbers were, like Jefferson in *A Summary View*, no longer willing to acquiesce in "160,000 electors in the island of Great Britain ... [giving] law to four [sic] millions in the states of America." Most may not yet have come to long for American independence, but the vast majority desired greater independence from the sway of the mother country and were willing to fight for it. Once again, it may have been Jefferson who best captured the spirit of the moment. The colonists, he had written, felt that submission to what they saw as tyranny was "not an American art."[24]

General Gage had all along been making preparations to use military force against the colonists. He had long since requested additional troops, and during the summer of 1774, with the First Congress looming, he had deployed regiments from Halifax and New York to Boston. At that juncture, Gage may have acted more from hope that his steps would induce the colonists to back down, but after Congress embraced the Suffolk Resolves, he expected war. He began to fortify Boston, digging trenches and gun emplacements, and exer-cising his men. But Gage was not going to start the war. He was a soldier. He awaited orders, knowing they would come and certain they would direct him to use force. In the meantime, he assembled a network of spies and sent out reconnaissance parties to learn as much as possible about the country surrounding Boston.

Numerous incidents occurred between soldiers and civilians in the city during that winter—one altercation ended with several soldiers tarring and feathering a citizen—but Gage miraculously defused each episode before serious trouble resulted. Nevertheless, Gage came close to igniting the powder keg on February 26 when he sent to Salem 240 regulars under Lieutenant Colonel Alexander Leslie. They were on a mission to seize eight cannon that British intelligence learned had been sent from Europe to the coastal town. Warned that the regulars were coming, a tense standoff took place when the redcoats were greeted (surrounded, in fact) by local militiamen who had been joined by Marblehead militiamen and minutemen from as far as twenty-five miles away. Either because he was outnumbered or had orders not to fire the first shot, Leslie ultimately marched his men to their ship and sailed empty-handed back to Boston.[25]

Six weeks later the inevitable occurred. On April 14 the HMS *Nautilus* arrived in Boston with Dartmouth's orders to use force, drafted more than seventy-five days earlier. Gage was not surprised. He in fact had already prepared plans to destroy a rebel arsenal in Concord. He had considered other arms depots, but settled on Concord. Assuming that the countryside would be alerted and that minutemen would descend on Concord to save the ordnance, Gage knew that speed would be crucial to his success. Concord was only twenty miles from Boston, and a spy in the village had passed on information about the location of stockpiles of cannons, mortars, tents, lead balls, medicine, linen, rum, grain, vegetables, and salt fish in and about the town.[26] Gage's intelligence had additionally reported that Samuel Adams and John Hancock were in Lexington, which the British strike force would pass through en route to Concord, and Dartmouth had ordered the arrest of the leading rebels. Expecting the operation to proceed under a cloak of secrecy, Gage was confident that he could rapidly get his men to Concord and back to Boston. Immediately after the *Nautilus* docked in Boston Harbor, Gage set April 19 as the date for his lightning strike.

Gage's force could march across Boston Neck to Roxbury, skirting the Back Bay before turning north and heading through Cambridge toward Lexington and Concord. Or, the regulars might proceed to the Charles River, only a few blocks from their barracks, where the Royal Navy would be waiting with longboats to convey them to the northern shore. The latter option was thought to be the speedier of the two, and it was the one that Gage fixed on.

Unfortunately for General Gage, he was not alone in using spies. The rebels had their own surveillance network, and through an array of clues—and loose lips—they learned when and where the regulars were going, though not which of the two routes Gage had chosen. But they posted Paul Revere in Charlestown and contrived a simple system of signal lights. Lanterns were to be placed in the belfry of Christ Church (also called North Church), the meetinghouse with the tallest steeple in Boston. If one lantern was hung, the regulars were taking the land route via Roxbury; two lanterns would indicate the soldiers were being rowed across the Charles. It was a clear night. Revere saw two lanterns. Not long after the British soldiers had moved out of their barracks, Revere set out on his most famous ride, spurring on Brown Beauty, reputedly the fastest horse about, to alert Hancock and Adams—who were indeed in Lexington—and the militiamen in both that village and Concord. Others riders also mounted up and sped away along other routes to sound the alarm in towns throughout the hinterland.

Gage had dispatched a formidable force of more than nine hundred men—some infantrymen and some grenadiers, the elite of the British army. Filing out of their quarters about ten P.M., the soldiers had been ordered to walk in small parties toward the river, the better for muffling noise and not arousing the suspicions of any Bostonians still awake at such a late hour. All went well until the regulars reached the Charles River. The navy had sent out too few boats. More had to be found. Four hours were lost. It was nearly ten A.M. before the soldiers completed the crossing of the river and started again on their march, slogging along roads made soft from spring rains, past silent fields and dark trees that had stood stark and bare since late in the previous autumn.

Revere arrived in Lexington around midnight and the alarm bell began to ring its tidings of impending danger. Hancock and Adams tarried until nearly dawn, but ultimately fled to the safety of Woburn, northwest of Lexington. Revere, meanwhile, had set off from Lexington for Concord. He never made it. He was captured by a British patrol. Though released after a brief time in custody, his role of spreading the warning on this historic night was over. Dr. Samuel Prescott, a Concord physician who had been visiting his fiancé in Lexington, carried the news back to his village that the redcoats were coming.

The regulars reached Lexington around four thirty. In the first orange streaks of daybreak, they could see some sixty militiamen arrayed on Lexington Common. It is a mystery why the commander of Lexington's militia, Captain John Parker, a tall, forty-six-year-old farmer-mechanic who had fought in several engagements in the Seven Years' War, had not marched his men to Concord to join with other colonists to defend the arsenal. Parker may have kept his men in town to protect the inexplicably dawdling Hancock and Adams, though it is more likely that he and his men had remained in Lexington in the hope of defending their families. It is also puzzling why only some 40 percent of Lexington's militia of 144 men had turned out and were posted on the common when the redcoats arrived. Gut-wrenching fear probably kept most away. After all, the militiamen were not hardened soldiers. Until a few hours before, they had been farmers working their fields or tradesmen toiling at their workbench. Aside from Captain Parker, few, if any, had experienced combat. Standing up to formidable, well-equipped British regulars not only was a daunting prospect, but it was also illegal, and no one on Lexington Common on that chilly spring morning could have known what lay ahead in America's relations with Great Britain.

Lieutenant Colonel Francis Smith, whom Gage had put in command of the operation, detached six companies totaling 238 men to clear the village green. He gave the assignment to Major John Pitcairn of the Royal Marines. As the regulars advanced, Captain Parker, anxious and uncertain, in all likelihood not feeling very brave but trying to stand tall in his soiled and well-worn daily work apparel, supposedly told his men: "Stand your ground. Don't fire unless fired upon. But if they want to have a war let it begin here." Pitcairn, immaculately turned out in his gaudy, impeccably tailored red uniform, rode to within a few feet of the citizen-soldiers and in the curt, biting manner and tone customarily used when ordering about cowed subordinates, brusquely bawled a command: "Lay down your arms, you damned rebels." Parker had no wish to defy the British officer, much less to order his men to fire on the King's soldiers. Had he done so, Parker would have been taken into custody and charged with a capital crime. Parker ordered his men to step aside. He did not direct them to surrender their arms. None did so.

At this moment, already fraught with unbelievable tension, someone squeezed off a shot. Perhaps a militiaman fired; maybe it was a soldier. Later, some said they thought the shot was fired by someone hiding behind a nearby stone wall. No one then or later knew for sure who had fired the first shot of the Revolutionary War, or whether the gun had been discharged deliberately or by accident.

What was clear was that once the gunshot rang out, a volley of shots was fired into the ranks of the militiamen. Jitters may have led some redcoats to fire, but others deliberately charged toward the citizen-soldiers, the faint light of sunrise gleaming off their shiny bayonets. It took only a minute or so for the officers to restore order, but by then eight colonists were dead and nine others had been wounded. Two regulars had been shot, one in the hand, one in the leg.

Though speed was imperative, a considerable period passed before the regulars resumed their march to Concord, six miles on down the road. Much of that time was squandered in the futile search for Adams and Hancock. As it was apparent that the element of surprise had long since been lost, several officers who suspected rough going ahead urged Colonel Smith to return to Boston. He refused. Orders were orders. But he sent to Gage a request for reinforcements. The regulars reached Concord in mid-morning, some twelve hours after setting out from their barracks in Boston.

The regulars entered Concord without incident. The town's militia had long since been called out, assembling on their training ground across the Concord River, nearly a half mile north of the heart of the village. Outnumbered nearly three to one, they were in no position to offer resistance. Besides, their commander, Colonel James Barrett, a sixty-five-year-old miller who wore his leather apron this day as he commanded his troops, was no more eager than Captain Parker to order his men to fire on British regulars. Throughout much of the morning, the impatient militiamen remained at a distance, leaving the redcoats to work unhindered under a bright spring sun. But as the soldiers toiled industriously to destroy powder and ordnance in the arsenals, minutemen continued to arrive. As the size of the colonial force swelled, many of the militiamen implored Barrett to act. Barrett held firm until around eleven A.M., when it not only became apparent that his force was probably larger than that of the enemy and when a column of white smoke was spotted rising above the town. Although the regulars were only burning wooden gun carriages, the militiamen feared that the village had been torched. At last, Barrett ordered his men to advance toward the center of Concord.

As they approached the North Bridge, which spanned the gently flowing river, the militiamen saw 115 British infantry posted on the other side. The regulars were scattered and relaxing. On spotting the approaching rebels, however, the British soldiers hurriedly assembled at the foot of the bridge. If the Americans were to reach the center of the village, they would have to fight their way through the king's soldiers. Barrett ordered his men to advance. Men on both sides were anxious and excited. Both Barrett and the British commander called on those on the opposite side to disperse. No one backed off. Suddenly, a shot was fired. It came from within the British ranks—again, whether by accident or design know one ever knew. In an instant, the nervous redcoat commander ordered his men to fire. Colonial citizen-soldiers began to fall. Only then did Barrett give the order to fire. Twelve regulars were hit, three fatally. Badly outnumbered, the redcoats broke and ran. The militiamen did not pursue them. Having at last done something, and ascertained as well that Concord was not burning, they retreated to their training ground.

By then, Colonel Smith had done all the damage in Concord that was possible, and he shortly ordered his force to begin the trek back to Boston. They set off down what to that day had always been known to Bostonians as the Concord Road. After April 19, 1775, it would be called "Battle Road." For Smith and his exhausted men—already that day they had marched twenty miles and labored in Concord for a couple of hours under a warm sun—their ordeal was just beginning.

By the time the redcoats began their return march, more than a thousand American militiamen had gathered in Concord. Their numbers grew throughout the afternoon, eventually reaching about 3,600. The colonial force fanned out with febrile intensity, taking positions down Battle Road. Men hid behind stone fences, unpainted barns, leafless trees, and haystacks. Smith sent out flanking parties to root out the militiamen, but he had too few men to do an adequate job.[27] It was a bloodbath. Every few minutes during the fourteen-mile march to Lexington, the redcoats ran into another ambush, though sometimes the militia stood and fought. Not a few of the regulars were surprised by how well the rebels were led and by the valor of the citizen-soldiers. The militiamen were not an "irregular mob," one British officer accurately remarked. He thought they must have been commanded by officers who had learned the art of war while fighting the French and Indians. "They have men amongst them who know very well what they are about," he said of the colonial force. The militiamen had performed well under fire, testimony to their leadership, days spent on the drill field during recent months, daring born of the knowledge of the enemy's vulnerability, conviction bred by rage toward Great Britain, and understanding that were indeed fighting to protect nearby loved ones.

At times, it seemed that every redcoat would be a casualty before the force could reach Boston, and that might have been the outcome of the bloody day had these frightened soldiers of the king not been joined in Lexington by the reinforcements that Smith had called for at daybreak. Around seven A.M. Gage had ordered a brigade under Lord Hugh Percy to march for Lexington. Impeded by one thing or another, the first units in Percy's force of more than one thousand men did not set off until about two hours later; others began their march throughout the morning. All the men in Percy's brigade had finally reached Lexington in mid-afternoon, only shortly before the battered, retreating regulars from Concord also arrived. The British force now totaled roughly 1,800 men.

The presence of a larger enemy force notwithstanding, the militia persisted in fighting, and some of the hottest action of the day occurred late that afternoon. The Americans suffered heavy losses at Menotomy, about halfway between Lexington and Boston, losing twenty-five killed and nine wounded; the regulars lost forty dead and eighty wounded in the brawl at Menotomy. Further down the road, at Cambridge, the fighting was no less intense, for several regiments of militia from Cambridge and Brookline joined their comrades. Faced with somehow getting across the wide Charles River in the face of growing numbers of the enemy—an unlikely prospect—Percy changed his plans on the spot. He abruptly ordered his men to march eastward, hopeful that with his artillery he could fashion a defense perimeter in the hilly terrain of Charlestown. That might permit him to hold off the militiamen until the rapidly approaching night came over the region, and by the next morning's dawn he could be reinforced and protected by the heavy guns of the Royal Navy. The regulars barely made it to safety. Fresh units of militia from Marblehead and Salem were streaming in to join the fight. Had they been thrown into the fray, it appears likely that the entirety of the two forces that Gage had dispatched during that blood-stained day would have been destroyed. But the commander of those troops, Colonel Timothy Pickering, a lukewarm rebel who yearned for a negotiated solution to the Anglo-American breach, withheld his men. The redcoats slipped through. As darkness closed in, the regulars took up positions at a place that the colonists knew as Bunker Hill. Percy and his men were safe for the time being.

This nightmarish day for the proud British army had at last drawn to a close. Later that night, Gage received the appalling butcher's bill for the day of fighting. To his horror, Gage learned that 65 of his men were dead and 207 had been wounded, the equivalent of nearly one-third of the initial force he had dispatched and roughly 15 percent of all the men sent out that day were casualties.

Americans bled as well. Ninety-four militiamen from twenty-three towns were casualties, including fifty who were known to have died. In addition to the colonial soldiers, civilians also perished when regulars stormed houses along Battle Road in search of ambushers—civilian and militia—whose firing "galled us exceedingly," in the words of a regular. Afterward, a militiaman who entered a home found carnage beyond belief. The dead were everywhere and the "Blud was half over [my] shoes," he said.[28]

Years later, Captain Levi Preston of Danvers was asked why he had risked his life in fighting the regulars that day. Was it because of the Stamp Act? No. The Tea Act? No, again. Was it from reading Locke, Trenchard, and Gordon. "I never heard of these men," he responded. Then why did you fight? He answered, "[W]hat we meant in going for those Redcoats was this: we always had governed ourselves and we always meant to. They didn't mean we should."[29]

CHAPTER 7

"GREAT BRITAIN IS EQUAL TO THE CONTEST"

WAR BRINGS CRUCIAL CHANGES IN 1775

GEORGE WASHINGTON'S RESPONSE to Great Britain's use of force captured the rage that reverberated throughout the colonies. A "Brother's Sword has been sheathed in a Brother's breast," he exclaimed when the news reached Mount Vernon. John Adams discovered the depth of the fury and sense of betrayal expressed by Washington in the course of his journey from Massachusetts to Philadelphia just days after the fighting. "Never was there such a Spirit," said Adams, and adding, "The military Spirit which runs through the Continent is truly amazing." He, too, was in its grip. "Oh that I was a Soldier!—I will be.—I am reading military Books.—Every Body must and will, and shall be a soldier," he declared.[1]

Most of the delegates to the First Continental Congress had feared war. Like Adams, all who came to Philadelphia for the Second Continental Congress, which convened on May 10, supported the war. Those who had attended the First Congress had anticipated meeting for only a few days or weeks, but all knew that the Second Congress would be prolonged, leading its members to rapidly shift from cramped Carpenter's Hall to the larger Pennsylvania State House. Congress took over a chamber on the ground floor that had previously been home to the colony's assembly, which in turn moved to a room upstairs.

Sixty-five delegates were seated, nine more than in the First Congress, due in part to Georgia's participation, but also because a couple of colonies sent larger delegations. The congressmen rapidly discovered a "perfect unanimity" on the need to meet British force with force. Referring to Galloway and others who had shrunk from taking up arms, one congressman exulted that the "Tory Ministerial faction" had been replaced by delegates who embraced a "virtuous patriotism." Another gloated that the "little, dirty, ministerial Party

. . . is humbled in the Dust." These congressmen were angry, a mood captured by John Dickinson, who remarked that London's answer to the previous fall's petition for redress had been "written in Blood." These delegates saw themselves as Americans committed to fighting for an America that they cherished. New York's Robert R. Livingston, though every bit as conservative as Joseph Galloway, declared that he was "resolved to stand or fall with my country."[2]

Leaving nothing to chance, the popular leaders in Massachusetts had spread the word throughout the colonies—and to Congress—that British regulars had fired the first shots in both Lexington and Concord. Paul Revere and other riders fanned out to convey lurid accounts of British barbarism. Colonial newspapers soon ran stories blaming the bloodshed on Lexington Common on "a wicked ministry" and British regulars whose conduct had been more despicable than that of "the vilest Savages of the Wilderness." These charges were supplemented by depositions taken from eyewitnesses, militiamen, even captured British soldiers. Many Lexington militiamen claimed that the regulars had opened fire on them "whilst our backs were turned." Onlookers said the soldiers had begun shooting after Major Pitcairn thundered: "Fire! Fire, damn you, fire!" The Massachusetts Committee of Safety got its story to the American people before the British published their version, and to good advantage. The New England narrative was unquestioned. From settlements in the pine barrens of the South to those along the North's craggy coast, a boiling fury greeted the news of what the mother country had done. No one expressed the popular mood better than the *Cape Fear Mercury* in Wilmington, North Carolina: "Let it be delivered down to posterity, that the American civil war broke out on the 19th day of April, 1775.—An epoch that, in all probability, will mark the declension of the British empire!"[3]

If the members of Congress shared their countrymen's outrage and willingness to wage war, the congressmen were deeply split over what they wanted from the conflict. At one of the Second Continental Congress' initial sessions, South Carolina's John Rutledge asked the question that would harry the delegates for the next fifteen months: "do We aim at independency or do We only ask for a Restoration of Rights & putting Us on Our old footing"— that which had existed before 1763?[4]

At the outset, a majority in Congress sought reconciliation with the mother country. Some were surprised when Dickinson, who had been Galloway's great rival in Pennsylvania politics for the past decade, supplanted his old foe as the congressman most vocal in wishing to maintain ties with Great Britain. Before the war, Dickinson had been viewed as a radical, though in reality he wished no less than Galloway to maintain the colonists' ties to the mother country. There were significant differences, however. Dickinson saw a pernicious corruption in England that Galloway could not discern; Galloway had sought to maintain imperial ties through an imaginative—if politically inexpedient—constitutional realignment, while Dickinson at some point had come to understand that war alone would force concessions from London. Dickinson prayed that London would yield and that the Anglo-American union could be preserved. Like Galloway, he dreamed of the tantalizing prosperity that would flow to the colonists if the empire remained intact, and he, too, thought that maintaining ties with Great Britain was crucial for the prevention of radical political and social change in America.

There were those in Congress who doubted that reconciliation was possible, and the more radical among them already thought it undesirable. In their heart of hearts, these delegates favored independence, though none dared say so. To openly advocate separation from the mother country was to risk shattering the brittle unity essential for waging war. Yet, some in Congress and throughout the colonies had come to seek American independence from a conviction that their liberty and property could be saved from British tyranny and corruption only by severing all ties and going their separate way. Others had come to see how the economic interests of the colonies differed from those of the parent state, how indifferent London was to provincial interests, and how unlikely it would be for the colonists to secure their ends within the British Empire.

What is more, the long quarrel with England not only had nourished the realization of how unlike life in America was from that in the British homeland, but as historian Gordon Wood has written, it "brought to the surface the republican tendencies of American life," including its egalitarian proclivities and self-governing practices. The reproof of the British monarchy in Jefferson's *A Summary View*—published four months before the fighting along Battle Road—resonated with many. What John Adams said privately a short time later likely also reflected the thinking of numerous colonists. Adams spoke of wanting American governments chosen in annual elections by "Freeholders," a practice that would offer hope of avoiding dominion by the "Dons, the Bashaws, the Grandees, the Patricians, the Sachems, the Nabobs"—the titled aristocracy that controlled all things social and political in England. Many who were not uncomfortable with the thought of an independent America had unthinkingly grown to be Americans, not merely English living in America. They were Americans who had come to understand that colonial dependency meant an intolerable second-class status, and they yearned to strike out on their own and seek their American destiny.[5]

But there were other avenues that led colonists to cherish American independence. Some thought American society less decadent than that of

England, which was supposedly haunted by pervasive degeneracy. For others, the hardships borne through repeated boycotts and by soldiering demonstrated that the colonists were willing to sacrifice individual interests to the greater national good, a virtue thought to be essential for the success of republicanism. American independence was alluring to those consumed with bitterness from slights and wrongs suffered at the hands of Royal officials, vexation bred by having to fight Great Britain's wars, and the ambition of many colonists to wield greater authority than would ever be possible within the British Empire. Insurgency had already fed the aspirations of some, raising them to committees of safety, to provincial assemblies, to Congress, to high rank in the revived militia. Few were prepared to relinquish their loftier standing, and many wished for something even greater.

By summertime in 1775 John Adams had emerged as the leader of the covertly pro-independence faction in Congress. His ascendancy was little short of breathtaking. Adams was probably the least politically experienced delegate in the First Congress, having served only a portion of a one-year term in the Massachusetts assembly several years earlier. He had come to Congress the previous fall expecting to be overawed by savvy and seasoned politicians, not to mention by the best and brightest men that America had to offer. He soon came to see himself as their equal, if not their superior. A Harvard graduate who in a dozen years had reached the pinnacle of the legal profession in Boston, Adams was obviously bright, but also incredibly industrious. And he was remarkably ambitious. Even as a young adult, he had filled his diary with references to his longing to achieve fame, to be seen not only as "a great Man" but also as one who would gain "Immortality." Though captious and contrary, vain and short-tempered, Adams was also a wonderful conversationalist who liked being with others. His colleagues in Congress found him approachable, none seemed to think him duplicitous or dishonest, and, for the most part, even those with whom he disagreed found him to be friendly. He may in fact have made more lifelong friends among his colleagues than anyone who served in Congress at this juncture. In time, his colleagues also came to see him as the most knowledgeable congressman in matters of political theory and diplomacy, and though he had never soldiered, the delegate with the best grasp of munitions, weaponry, and logistics. Not surprisingly, after a couple of years many looked on Adams as possessing "the clearest head and firmest heart of any man in Congress." He was an exceptional individual who had found his place. According to Thomas Jefferson, Adams was the "ablest advocate and defender" of American independence.[6]

*   *   *

When Rutledge asked his crucial question about whether this was a war for reconciliation or for independence, Dickinson was the first to respond. In a lengthy speech, he staked out his position as leader of the faction that favored reconciliation. Dickinson acknowledged that the king had turned a deaf ear to earlier congressional and provincial entreaties, but he implored his colleagues to petition George III once again, and he urged that the appeal be delivered to London by congressional agents authorized to negotiate. The time was right, he insisted, as the colonists were united and the British army had just been mauled along Battle Road. The monarch might see the disaster that had befallen Gage's force as a forerunner of worse to come, prompting him to intercede. Many in Dickinson's camp hoped the king would summon Chatham to form a new ministry, the first step leading toward favorable terms for reconciliation. In the meantime, the colonists must keep the heat on London by pursuing the war.

Though Dickinson supported the war, he feared a protracted struggle, knowing that if the hostilities dragged on, momentum would build for declaring independence. He candidly prayed that the "evil Day" of American independence would never arrive. Dickinson additionally questioned whether America could win a long war. With stunning clarity, he laid out the unavoidable woes that would accompany a lengthy war: Battles would be lost; soldiers would perish on the battlefield; camp diseases would stalk soldiers and civilians, inflicting heavy tolls on both; New England would be invaded from Canada; slaves in the South would rebel or run away; supplying an army throughout North America would be a daunting task; the Royal Navy would be a "forbidding" adversary. As Great Britain was better equipped for protracted hostilities, the longer the war continued, the greater the certainty that Americans would "taste ... deeply of that bitter Cup" of adversity. Should America lose such a war, it would suffer fearsome reprisals. The key to the length of the war, said Dickinson, was in America's war aims. If America fought for independence, the war would be unavoidably long and hard, and its outcome unpredictable. But if the colonists fought to be reconciled with the mother country, the war would be shorter. Dickinson's prescription was that the colonists wage a defensive war and that Congress adhere to the demands spelled out in the Declaration of Colonial Rights adopted by the First Congress—reconciliation, but on America's terms. If those were America's war aims, said Dickinson, attrition would compel London to negotiate within a year or two.[7]

Not a few congressmen thought the idea of yet again petitioning the king "gives ... disgust." After heated debate, Congress deferred a decision on Dickinson's proposal until it could tend to a thousand and one other thorny issues. For instance, Congress had just learned that separate armies raised in Massachusetts and Connecticut—one led by Benedict Arnold, the other by Ethan Allen—had seized the British installation of Fort Ticonderoga on Lake Champlain, where they had captured a treasure trove of artillery. Flushed with success, Arnold and Allen had also taken Crown Point, another lightly held British installation twelve miles north of Ticonderoga, and they now were talking of crossing into Canada. Congress found all this to be deeply troubling. For one thing, the two New England armies had conducted operations on New York soil without that province's consent. For another, disaster awaited if each colony acted on its own. There had to be a central direction to the military effort. Congress resolved the matter by keeping the ordnance confiscated at Ticonderoga, but it left no doubt that it was responsible for American strategy. Its first step was to order the two New England forces to stay out of Canada.[8]

The question of an American army was the paramount military issue that faced Congress. A New England army was already in existence. The militiamen who had fought along Battle Road on April 19 had dogged the regulars all the way back to Boston. During that night, as they took up positions on the periphery of the city, those weary citizen-soldiers had been joined by other troops from Massachusetts, as well as units from Connecticut, New Hampshire, and Rhode Island. By sunrise on the 20th, thousands of armed colonists were encamped on Boston's doorstep, and their numbers grew during the next few days. The army peaked at about sixteen thousand before leveling off at some twelve thousand men. Newspapers dubbed the force the Grand American Army. In fact, there were really four separate armies, one from each of the New England colonies, though as these soldiers were on Massachusetts soil, Artemas Ward, commander of the Bay Colony's army, was the titular commander.

When Congress convened, the Yankee delegates immediately beseeched their colleagues to create a national army. They noted that New England lacked the means of feeding and paying such a large army, and that it was only right that every colony share the burden. There were other issues as well. The Grand American Army already lacked tents and was desperately short of arms and munitions, and even at this early juncture there were troubling signs of a breakdown in discipline. It was readily apparent too that not every field grade officer was capable. Some thought it essential to create a new army led by accomplished officers, men who owed their appointment to talent, not politics. Some thought that General Ward must be replaced by a tough, unsparing commander who could root out unqualified officers and make soldiers of the men in the ranks.

A month dragged by before Congress got around to the question of a national army, prompting an exasperated John Adams to sigh that Congress was an "unwieldy Machine." Samuel Adams, similarly irritated, attributed its unhurried pace to the wish of every congressman to speak at length on every issue. On June 14, John Adams could wait no longer. He moved that Congress create a national army. For once, the delegates acted swiftly. That same day, Congress voted to establish the "American Continental Army"—or what soon, and lastingly, would simply be called the Continental army—and it directed that men be raised by each province for one year's service. Immediately thereafter, Adams recommended the appointment of George Washington as its commander, and Maryland's Thomas Johnson formally nominated him.[9]

Washington was blessed by not being from New England, as Congress thought someone from outside that region would be best for recruiting a national army. But far more than that contributed to Congress's interest in him. Washington had as much military experience as any native-born colonist, and more command experience than most, having led Virginia's army for nearly five years during the Seven Years' War. He had learned how to lead men and to make life-and-death decisions, and he had gained an understanding of wielding power from his experience as commander of the Virginia Regiment. Some of that experience had been painful, for Washington had made mistakes in his early command. He had earned criticism for his all-too-frequent absences from the army, his having tolerated sybaritic habits among the officers, and his having quibbled endlessly with his colony's chief executive.

But at age forty-three and in robust health, Washington seemed suited for the rigors of the job and likely to be around for the long haul. He was physically imposing. At a time when the average man stood five feet seven inches tall, Washington was nearly six feet four, and at a bit over two hundred pounds, he was lithe and trim. Many observers described him as graceful and without peer as an equestrian, that century's benchmark for athleticism. Having served in the Virginia assembly for seventeen years, he understood politics and legislative bodies. Even more important, as a member of the Continental Congress since its inception, his colleagues—knowing this day might come—had scrutinized and spoken with Washington, interviewing him before the fact, so to speak. They could not know everything about Washington, but most had come to think of him as "Sober, steady, and Calm," dignified, "sensible . . . virtuous, modest, & brave," and no "harum Starum ranting Swearing fellow." His fellow Virginians advised the other congressmen that Washington was honest and virtuous and that there had been no hint of scandal on his command in the last war. He exuded undoubted qualities of leadership. Washington was peerless when it came to gravitas, and he struck many as tough and indomitable. (Years later the painter Gilbert Stuart, who had an artist's eye for divining character, remarked that had Washington been born in nature, "he would have been the fiercest man among the savages.")

If observers sensed rugged, hard, and forceful qualities in him, onlookers were also impressed by his tact and politeness, for Washington was schooled in the rules of well-mannered behavior fashionable among Virginia's patrician planters. (Finding Washington to be dignified and polished, Abigail Adams later that year remarked that "the Gentleman and Soldier look agreeably blended in him.") While people could not forget that he had been a soldier—Washington wore his uniform to each session of Congress lest anyone failed to remember—his years in the military had encompassed only one-sixth of his adult life. Since leaving Virginia's army in 1758, Washington had been a planter-businessman. His scores of slaves produced tobacco and wheat at Mount Vernon, his sprawling estate on the Potomac River, or toiled in his fishing or textile enterprises, and like many planters, Washington speculated in western lands. That he was not a professional soldier put Congress at ease. The delegates, and ultimately most of the citizenry, rightly thought of Washington as an individual who had temporarily set aside his civilian pursuits to answer the call to duty and who, when the emergency passed, would lay down his arms and return to farming. That the delegates were reassured was crucial, but Congress was choosing a military commander to lead the colonists in war, a war that had to be won or every congressman would pay a terrible price. At bottom, Washington inspired confidence. As one observer put it in the summer of 1775, Washington "has so much martial dignity in his deportment that you would distinguish him to be a general and a soldier from among ten thousand people. There is not a king in Europe that would not look like a valet de chambre by his side."[10]

Congress discussed the selection of a commander in chief for a day and a half before it appointed Washington. With Washington out of the chamber—he had excused himself—the delegates likely questioned Virginia's congressmen to see what they could learn. The Virginians probably glossed over Washington's numerous mistakes and striking lack of success as commander of the Virginia Regiment between 1754 and 1758, and instead emphasized his courage and firmness, the knowledge he had acquired in organizing and administering an army, and how he had learned to lead men. Some time must also have been spent in discussing the possible political fallout that could be expected from dumping General Ward and in pondering whether Yankees—

the only soldiers in the army at that moment—would follow a southern commander.

Washington followed his appointment with a little speech to Congress. He announced that he would serve without pay, asking only that his expenses be covered. In another address a few days later, he enunciated his conviction that military officials must be subservient to civilian authority. No public official ever got off on better footing. Before he ever reached the front, Washington was applauded throughout the land not only for the sacrifice he was making but also for his enlightened views.

Once Washington was commissioned, Congress selected the other general officers. John Adams thought it his most unpleasant experience as a congressman, for the colonies both wrangled over the ranking of those chosen and battled to have their favorite sons selected. The hope that politics would be divorced from the proceedings proved illusory. Adams feared that not a few of the chosen would be incompetent, and time proved that he was prescient. Washington asked Congress to appoint Charles Lee and Horatio Gates, both veteran British officers who had immigrated to Virginia, and it complied. Ten additional men were chosen, all from New York and New England. Only one among them, Nathanael Greene of Rhode Island, is now nearly universally thought by military historians to have been an exceptional strategist and leader, though two others—John Thomas and Richard Montgomery—showed flashes of greatness before perishing during the initial year of the war.[11]

Washington remained in Philadelphia for a week after his appointment—among other things, he had his will prepared—but on June 23 he was at last ready to ride to Boston to assume command of the Continental army. In the subdued light of early day, every congressman stepped outside the State House for the brief, simple ceremony. There might have been a speech or two, after which Washington, who was not given to shaking hands, bowed to those who had been his colleagues and were now his bosses. Then, as a little martial band played and a few companies of Philadelphia's militia stood poised to march with him to the edge of town, General Washington—who, discordantly, was going off to wage war against tyranny with two of his slaves in tow—easily sprang on his great white charger and began the long ride into an impenetrable future.[12]

Soon after tending to the army, Congress acted to keep the Indians neutral in the war. It named commissioners to confer with the Native Americans and approved a statement that was to be read to the leaders of the assorted tribes in the meetings that were sometimes called "treaty councils." Addressing them as "Brothers and Friends," Congress asked that the Indians "open a good ear and listen to what we are now going to say. This is a family quarrel. . . . You Indians are not concerned in it. . . . We desire you to stay at home, and not join on either side." (On occasion, Washington subsequently met with Indian chieftains to urge neutrality, though his tone was more tart: "Brothers, I am a Warrior. . . . 'Tis my business to destroy all the enemies of these states and to protect their friends," he said without mincing words.)[13]

Neither Congress's message nor the work of its commissioners likely did much to persuade the Indians to stay out of the war. That the colonists' war with Britain sowed confusion and divisions among the Indians, and that the British did not initially attempt to rouse the Indians to take up arms, were more important factors in keeping the frontiers relatively peaceful in the early years of hostilities. The principal exception was in the Southern back-country. During the first summer of the war, General Gage urged London to have its Indian agents incite the Cherokees and Creeks to "make a Diversion" along southern frontier, a strategy aimed at reducing Southern assistance to the Continental army. The Creeks wanted no part of it, but in the spring of 1776, the Cherokees, already angered by encroachments on their lands, took to the warpath. It was a misguided step. Armies of militiamen, raised in Virginia and the Carolinas, swept across a wide expanse of Cherokee country, burning towns and crops. By autumn, Cherokee power had been broken and other tribes were discouraged from acting. In the aftermath of what colonists called the Cherokee War, British influence in the South declined and for some time thereafter the frontier in the region remained relatively quiet.[14]

Meanwhile, a second great battle had been fought on Massachusetts soil. This action occurred prior to Washington's arrival, and it had a profound impact on both sides. The engagement took place on the watch of Artemas Ward. Swayed by Washington's later unkind comments about him, many historians have dismissed Ward as ineffectual. However, he performed capably during the brief time that he commanded the Grand American Army. He did not take hurried or imprudent actions, as some subordinates wished. He secured his incredibly long siege lines—which extended in an arc from north of Boston to the city's southwestern periphery—thoroughly reconnoitered the region, hastily put together an efficient intelligence network, and kept his men well fed.

In mid-June, Ward received intelligence that the British army planned to strike soon against the colonial siege lines near Roxbury, occupy Dorchester Heights, and launch a surprise attack against the rebel center in Cambridge. Discussions along these lines were in fact occurring at Gage's headquarters, though no decision had been made. All that Ward could know was that if Gage launched such an initiative, and if it succeeded, the siege of Boston would be over. Ward responded on the night of June 16 by sending 1,200 men under Colonel William Prescott to occupy Bunker Hill in Charlestown. Ward envisaged the step as a defensive move to protect the left flank of his main force in Cambridge. For reasons that were never clear, Prescott, who had served with distinction in the Seven Years' War, disobeyed his orders. Probably falling under the spell of Israel Putnam, who joined him with 250 men from Connecticut and lusted for action, Prescott posted his men not on Bunker Hill but farther to the southeast, atop Breed's Hill. From there, unlike on Bunker Hill, rebel artillery could menace British vessels both in the nearby Mystic River and in Boston Harbor. Prescott's insubordination changed the equation. Instead of being confronted with a rebel defensive installation on Bunker Hill, Gage was faced with an intolerable threat to his supply lines, which ran from Boston Harbor back to the homeland.

When Gage discovered that the rebels had worked through the velvety black night to construct a large quadrangular-shaped redoubt—its two lengthiest sides ran 132 feet—and a far-reaching breastwork (a 6-foot-tall earthen wall) along the summit of Breed's Hill, he knew instantly that he would have to try to retake the hill. Probably around the same time, Ward learned what Prescott had done. Angry, but feeling that he had no choice to reinforce Prescott, Ward ordered all the New Hampshire regiments to Breed's Hill.[15]

As Charlestown and the two hills above it were situated on a peninsula between the Charles and Mystic Rivers, the British might have scored a nearly bloodless victory by simply having the Royal Navy seal narrow Charlestown Neck, the lone exit to the mainland. But after the slaughter along Battle Road, Gage thirsted for revenge. Furthermore, still convinced that militiamen would be no match for regulars in a formal engagement, Gage believed that if he administered a thorough drubbing to the rebels at Bunker Hill—as everyone would mistakenly refer to the site of the American redoubt and the looming battle—it would break the colonists' will to persevere.

Gage assigned the task of taking Bunker Hill to General William Howe (the brother of Lady Caroline, Benjamin Franklin's chess partner), a forty-six-year-old veteran of thirty-years' service. Seen by his superiors as resourceful and intrepid, Howe always seemed to draw the most dangerous and crucial assignments, and he invariably responded capably.[16] On this occasion, Howe was given 2,300 infantry, roughly the same number as his enemy on the heights. Under a hot sun that beat down through a bright blue sky scudded with fleecy white clouds, Howe marched his men through the streets of Boston to the Charles River, where they boarded barges. As they crossed to Charlestown, the navy laid down a shuddering bombardment that set the small village ablaze and killed some rebels in and around the redoubt. The redcoats landed unopposed about two thousand yards down the beach from the burning town. To reach the crest of the hill, the soldiers—who were weighted down with nearly fifty pounds of equipment in addition to the twelve-pound Brown Bess musket they carried—faced a climb of some five hundred yards, ascending treeless farmland dotted with rail fences and stone walls.

British soldiers and officers were trained to fight in the European way of war. Armies, typically arrayed in three rows, slowly marched toward each other on an open battlefield. At a distance of fifty or sixty yards, the men in the front rows fired at their foes; as each man in the front row knelt to reload—which took around fifteen seconds—the men in the second row fired, then dropped to a knee and reloaded while those in the third row discharged their flintlock muskets. Although Howe would face a hidden and entrenched enemy, he never thought of fighting this day in an unconventional manner. He was unfazed by the knowledge that in 1758 an Anglo-American force had attacked a similarly fortified French force at Fort Carillon (later renamed Ticonderoga) and the results had been disastrous. The redcoats had suffered more than two thousand casualties, the greatest loss suffered by any British army on any American battlefield during the Seven Years' War. But Howe, like Gage, reasoned that the Americans on Bunker Hill were untrained amateurs, not professional French soldiers. Howe opted to go by the book.[17]

The regulars, resplendent in their bright red uniforms, began their measured uphill march at about three P.M., stepping off in their customary battle formation. Awaiting them inside the redoubt, or crouched below the long breastwork and hiding behind stone walls, wooden fences, barns, even bales of hay, were rebel soldiers clad in homespun; many wore the wide, floppy wool hats they donned when plowing and hoeing their fields. Incredibly, Dr. Joseph Warren, the Boston physician and president of the Massachusetts Provincial Congress who earlier had helped Samuel Adams draft the Suffolk Resolves, had joined the soldiers in the rebel lines. It was a mad act. A widower with four small children, Warren was unarmed, had never enlisted in the Grand American Army and, according to one observer, was dressed not like a soldier but as a man on his wedding day. The soldiers who surrounded Warren were, like the regulars, armed with notoriously inaccurate smooth-bore muskets. Like all in the rebel army, these men possessed precious little ammunition, in part the legacy of Gage's raid on the Provincial Powder House during the previous September. To conserve their powder and balls, the soldiery on Bunker Hill were under orders not to fire until the regulars came within fifty yards.[18]

The regulars advanced slowly up the gently sloping hillside, marching alternately over lovingly tilled, verdant tracks and ragged, overgrown fields that sported grass up to five feet tall. They came steadily, unwaveringly, ever closer to the rebel lines. At seemingly the last breathless moment, the Americans opened fire. The volley blew apart the redcoats' line. When those in the back stepped into the breach, they too were cut down. For a few dreadful moments the survivors kept coming, stumbling over the bullet-riddled bodies of their fallen comrades. But soon enough the advance of the long, red line stopped. The carnage was unimaginably heavy. A Bostonian, a civilian, who watched the action as if it were a spectator sport, spoke of the "majestic terrors of the field" and described what he witnessed as "most awful and tremendous." Lucy Trumbull, whose brother John would soon be a famous American painter, "became deranged" by the horrific violence that she observed, and she would never again see war as "glorious."[19]

Howe spent thirty minutes reassembling his decimated lines before he ordered his men into hell a second time. "Aim at the handsome coats," some American officers advised, but most appeared to have sighted in on the bright white shoulder belts that crossed in the middle of the regulars' chests. Not a few rebels deliberately drew a bead on British officers. When the advancing regulars came within twenty-five yards of the summit, the rebels in the redoubt and behind the breastwork unleashed a volley that to one redcoat resembled "a continual sheet of lightning" accompanied by a roar like "an uninterrupted peal of thunder." The regulars had marched into a murderous crossfire. The rebels nearly "picked us all off," one British soldier said later. The destruction was horrific. Men fell by the score. Major Pitcairn, who had disarmed Lexington's militiamen two months earlier, was among those mortally wounded, brought down by four bullets. Stopped in their tracks, the regulars fell back once again.

Some British officers appealed to Howe not to try again. By now, Howe's aide-de-camp had been killed and every member of his staff was dead or wounded. Shaken but unbowed, Howe did not listen to the entreaties to call off the attack. He summoned reinforcements. Once they were in place, Howe gave the order to move out a third time. Atop the hill, Colonel Prescott knew that his force's ammunition was nearly spent. When he saw the red line advancing yet again, Prescott supposedly told his troops: "Men, you are all marksmen; do not any of you fire until you can see the whites of their eyes." With incredible aplomb, his men followed orders, waiting and watching as the regulars, armed with muskets and glittering bayonets, came closer, so close that the men in the two armies could have conversed without raising their voices. Then, after what must have been an agonizing wait, the regulars were close enough. They were only fifteen yards away. Prescott cried out the order to fire.

Regulars fell right and left. But they kept coming. Suddenly, the shooting by the rebels all but stopped. They had run out of powder and lead. The redcoats sprinted for the redoubt. Most of the Americans broke, taking flight down the back side of the slope. Not all made it to safety. The regulars atop the hill poured a merciless fire on their fleeing enemy. Some Americans never had the chance to make a run for it. The British soldiers were on them too quickly. Fierce hand-to-hand combat followed, with men on both sides wildly swinging their muskets like clubs. The Americans trapped on the ridge were outnumbered, outgunned, and doomed. The regulars shot them out of hand, if they did not bayonet them. One of those who perished was Dr. Warren, shot in the face at close range.[20]

Three hours after this blood-soaked engagement began, it was over. Bodies littered the landscape. The tall grass on the hillside the regulars had climbed was streaked red, testimony to the price the soldiers had paid and the vengeful folly of their leaders. The toll on both sides was heavy. The Americans had suffered 160 killed and at least 271 wounded. But that paled in contrast to the damage suffered by the enemy. Gage had taken his hill, but in the process 226 of his men had died and 928 more were casualties. Nearly one in four men in Gage's army, including 40 percent of his officers, had died or been wounded. This was a catastrophic day for the British army. Another such victory would "ruin us," remarked one British general, while a veteran redcoat officer said that the shocking scenes of "that day will never be out of my mind till the day of my death." Gage, abashed and more mortified than he cared to acknowledge, simply said: "The [American] People Shew a Spirit and Conduct against us, they never shewed against the French."[21]

Word of Bunker Hill swiftly led Congress to rethink an earlier decision. Thirty days before, Congress had stopped the Massachusetts and Connecticut forces that had taken Ticonderoga and Crown Point from making an incursion into Canada. One day after learning of Bunker Hill, Congress ordered an invasion of Canada, doubtless thinking that if the shocking toll suffered by Britain's army along Battle Road and on Charlestown's hillocks was followed by the loss of Quebec, London might agree to the demands of the First Continental Congress.[22]

Congress took several additional steps that to some degree were influenced by Bunker Hill. On the day that Washington left for the front, Congress began work on a document that was tantamount to a declaration of war, but it did not approve what came to be known as the Declaration on the

Causes and Necessity for Taking Up Arms until about ten days after learning of Bunker Hill. The reconciliationists saw to it that the document stressed that the colonists had "not raised Armies with ambitious Designs of separating from Great-Britain, and establishing Independent States." Nevertheless, the language was tough and unsparing. After assailing Parliament and portraying the mother country's use of force as "cruel" and conceived for the "Purpose of enslaving these Colonies by Violence," Congress declared that "Our cause is just. Our union is perfect. Our internal Resources are great, and, if necessary, foreign Assistance is undoubtedly attainable." America did not wish war, Congress added, but Americans preferred "to die freemen rather than to live Slaves." Three weeks later Congress contemptuously rejected Lord North's so-called peace plan, terming it "villainous" and "unreasonable."[23]

Congress took another important step at this juncture. It once again petitioned the king. Over the objections of the more radical delegates, Congress had agreed in May to appeal to the monarch to redress American grievances, but the committee charged with drafting the supplication toiled for several weeks before it reported. Its deliberations were slowed in part by a wrangle over whether Congress should send envoys to negotiate with the king's representatives. Benjamin Franklin, who arrived home from London during the spring and was promptly added to Pennsylvania's delegation—and to the committee that dealt with the petition—led the fight against sending negotiators across the sea. No one knew better than Franklin the intrigue and mischief that London was capable of when it came to negotiating, and he correctly feared that should talks ever begin, the ministry would use them to irreparably divide Congress.[24]

Early in July, Congress took up the committee's draft petition to George III. These were Congress's stormiest sessions since the fight the previous autumn over the limits of Parliament's authority. Though John Adams detested the notion of yet again appealing to the king, he could not prevent Congress from taking the step. However, Adams fought to root out all evidence of servility in the petition's language. Adams thought Dickinson's draft petition was filled with "Prettynesses [and] Juvenilities" that would weaken support for the war in America and lessen opposition to hostilities in England. Dickinson and his followers fought back, desperate to make clear to the king that the colonists remained loyal to the Crown. Given the British army's drubbing on Bunker Hill, the reconciliationists cherished the hope that the monarch, if not frightened away by Congress's bellicosity, might repudiate North's administration and see to the formation of a government that would negotiate an accommodation.

After an especially tempestuous session, Dickinson confronted Adams in the shady State House yard. In what Adams recalled as a "violent . . . rough and haughty" manner, Dickinson declared that should "you New Englandmen" obstruct "our Measures of Reconciliation," he and his followers would "break off, from you" and "carry on the Opposition by ourselves in our own Way."[25]

In part, Dickinson was bluffing, but he got much that he sought. After two turbulent days, Congress agreed to what became known as the Olive Branch Petition to the king. But Congress refused to send envoys to London. Instead, it sent the entreaty to the monarch in a sealed envelope and entrusted the son of Pennsylvania's proprietor with the task of getting it across the sea and delivering it to Arthur Lee with the seal unbroken. What is more, Lee was not authorized to engage in any talks with the Crown. He was only to present the petition to the American secretary.

Dickinson's success had come grudgingly. "I dread like Death" petitioning the king, John Adams remarked, but "We cant avoid it. Discord and total Disunion would be the certain Effect of a resolute Refusal to petition." Nevertheless, Adams drew hope from his conviction that the petition would be meaningless and that in time a congressional majority would come to see reconciliation with Great Britain as unlikely, even undesirable. That would take time, however, and in the meantime, concessions would have to be made to Dickinson and his adherents. Adams put it this way: Congress's "Progress must be slow. It is like a large Fleet sailing under Convoy. The fleetest Sailors must wait for the dullest and slowest. Like a Coach and six—the swiftest Horses must be slackened and the slowest quickened, that all may keep an even Pace."[26]

Lord North and the king initially doubted the first sketchy—and dreadful— tidings of the action along Battle Road, but soon enough they and their countrymen knew it was true. A burning rage toward the colonists swept the land, prompting Edward Gibbon, an MP and later a renowned historian, to remark that the "nation . . . is in a manner unanimous against America." North summoned his cabinet and at two meetings it was agreed to send around five thousand more regulars to North America, so that by autumn there would be some thirteen thousand troops in Boston, nearly a threefold increase over the number posted in the city when the Intolerable Acts had been passed. The ministers also agreed to once again augment the British fleet in American waters. They sought, too, to bring the Iroquois into the war and ordered the royal governor in Canada to raise an army of six thousand for retaking Fort Ticonderoga.[27]

North thought he had done all that was needed, but a month after these actions were taken, news of Bunker Hill reached London. The response of William Eden, an undersecretary of state, was probably typical: The British army had taken the hill and won the battle, "but if we have eight more such victories there will be nobody left to bring news of them." Awakened to what his government had gotten itself into, North declared that this had to be treated as a "foreign war." In other words, this was a conflict on a magnitude with Britain's wars against European powers, and in fact the prime minister must have now presumed that the odds of French and Spanish involvement had increased drastically. His ministry agreed to dispatch still more troops to North America, which meant launching a recruiting campaign to spur enlistments. North, who in January had thought the rebellion could be suppressed by seven thousand troops, now planned on deploying thirty thousand regulars in the mainland colonies. But bad news continued to cascade on North. By autumn he knew that the Iroquois had declined to enter the war and that no army would be raised in Canada. North and the king opened negotiations in Europe to hire foreign soldiers.[28]

The woeful news from Massachusetts resulted in important personnel changes as well. The king had long since soured on Thomas Gage, convinced that only a defeatist could send such disagreeable messages about the likely difficulty of crushing the rebellion. Immediately after learning of Bunker Hill, the monarch decided that Gage had to go, and North recalled him. General Howe, who had led the assault on Bunker Hill, was named commander of the British army in North America. Soon thereafter, Lord Dartmouth was dropped as American secretary. Dartmouth had been long out of step with his colleagues, and his plea for an alternative to a military response following Lexington and Concord was the final straw. He had lasted as long as he did because of his familial ties to the prime minister, but faced with a long and difficult armed conflict, North wanted a steadfast supporter of the war as American secretary. He turned to Lord George Germain.[29]

North's choice was not universally applauded. Six feet tall and powerfully built, Germain was an imposing figure who had soldiered for years and had twice suffered wounds in combat. Nevertheless, he was "a man with a past," as one historian put it. Germain had risen to second in command in Britain's army in the European theater during the Seven Years' War, but charges of cowardice and disobeying orders during the Battle of Minden had led to his dismissal from the army. Though ridiculed and disgraced, Germain never abandoned his dream of redemption. After holding several inconsequential posts, he won a seat in Parliament, where he hewed to a hard line toward the colonies, steadfastly advocating the use of force to crush the rebellion. Some came to think of him as an expert on America, and not a few were swayed by his formula for winning the war in a single campaign: recruit as many Canadian troops as possible, strike in New York and New England, isolate the Yankees from their brethren to the south, and score a decisive military victory that would force the colonists to submit. But many opposed Germain's selection to be American secretary, some from an inability to forgive his earlier failings, some from a fear that his obsession with personal absolution would color his judgment in making military decisions, and some from a loathing of a man they found to be cold and unapproachable. Still others despised his homosexuality, which Germain scarcely attempted to hide, and the more intolerant among them cruelly portrayed him as the "buggering hero." North, however, was among those swayed by Germain's unbending firmness. The first minister summoned him on board, convinced that Germain above all others was the man who could "bring the colonists to their knees."[30]

North learned sometime during the summer that some sort of petition was to be sent to the king. The prime minister and his king might have waited to read it before acting. Instead, on August 23—one day before Arthur Lee presented the Olive Branch Petition to the American secretary—the monarch issued a proclamation (prepared for him by the cabinet) that charged the colonists with being "traitorously" engaged in an "open and avowed rebellion," which now included "levying war against us." The royal decree was tantamount to a declaration of war.[31]

As Parliament had adjourned in May before word of the fighting on the day of Lexington and Concord reached England, the MPs had been unable to comment on the ministry's decision to use force against the colonists. But late in October the king rode with great pomp at the head of a procession of majestic carriages from St. James's Palace to Westminster to convene a new Parliament. As custom dictated, he opened the session with a formal address, most of which concerned the American war, though he added little to his August proclamation. The "deluded multitude" of colonists, he said, was in the thrall of demagogues who promoted "this desperate conspiracy" with the objective of establishing an "independent empire." The monarch vowed to bring "a speedy end to these disorders" through "decisive exertions" of force. Enigmatically, George III mentioned giving "authority to certain persons on the spot" who would be "so commissioned" to restore colonial allegiance, an avowal that wishful thinkers took to mean that the monarch planned to send commissioners to America to negotiate with the colonists.[32]

On the whole, there was no mystery to what the king had said, and his bellicose remarks sparked a passionate debate in Parliament. Foes of the war denounced North for much that had gone wrong. One MP called him a "blundering pilot." Several excoriated his hard-line approach, predicting it would in the end lead to the loss of America and Britain's ruin. Lord Shelburne questioned the king's failure to respond to the Olive Branch Petition. There were even some who, while guarded in their comments, said that the war would surely be lost in the event that Great Britain's principal enemies, France and Spain, entered the war on the side of the American rebels.[33]

During this war of words Edmund Burke made the third and last of his major speeches on America prior to independence. Speaking for nearly four hours, Burke raised doubts that victory could be achieved under any circumstances, and certainly not with the number of troops that North was prepared to deploy in America. He predicted that continuing the war would only further radicalize the Americans, leaving them unwilling to accept terms for reconciliation that they would have found enticing in peacetime. In time, the colonists would be driven to declare independence. The surest way to peace, and to maintaining the empire, he concluded, was to suspend hostilities and immediately offer genuine concessions. Those terms should include renunciation of Parliament's authority to tax the colonists (though not its jurisdiction over trade); recognition of the authority of the Continental Congress to legislate for the colonies; repeal of the Townshend Duties and Coercive Acts; revocation of all legislation prohibiting manufacturing in the colonies; and pardons for all colonists who had borne arms in this war.

Furthermore, Burke proclaimed what Dartmouth had long understood and what America's radicals most feared. Aware of the divisions among the rebels, Burke told the Commons that an offer of generous terms "would be the truest means of dividing America." Once colonial unity was sundered, he added, Congress would have to accept peace.[34]

Aside from Britain's mercantile centers—such as Bristol, which Burke represented—most in England were more interested in revenge than accommodation. Few ministers had ever been disposed to negotiate with the Americans, and most now thought that to offer to talk in the aftermath of two humbling military encounters would be humiliating. Germain, in his maiden speech as American secretary, answered Burke. The Americans, he said, would treat Burke's negotiating points as "gratuitous preliminaries" and would demand more concessions. Ultimately, negotiations "would put us on worse ground." War offered the only means of maintaining control of America, said Germain, and he assured Parliament that Great Britain was "equal to the contest." The government had the votes. Parliament spurned the antiwar forces, and Burke, by large majorities.[35]

Following the last of the votes, North took the floor and proposed passage of the American Prohibitory Bill. Though the war was now seven months old, so far only Massachusetts had been blockaded, a step that went back to the Intolerable Acts. North's legislation would change that. Every colony would be subject to a naval blockade. By frustrating all hope of foreign assistance, North believed that the colonists' "treasonable commotions" would be brought to an end. There were few doubters.[36]

While Parliament heard the king, Congress grappled with difficulties raised by hostilities. Several unexpected problems arose in the army. First, Washington stunned Congress with an appeal for pay raises for his officers, who had served for less than six months and had never come under fire while part of the Continental army. Washington warned that unless this step was taken, an alarming number of junior officers would leave the army. Washington had acted in order to mollify disgruntled officers, but he also had hidden motives. He sought an officer corps drawn from the elite within American society, in part because he thought it essential for establishing the "Subordination & Discipline" necessary for building an effective army. In addition, Washington—and Congress, as soon would be apparent—thought a rigidly disciplined army whose leadership was drawn from the socially superior would be an unlikely force on behalf of radical social and political reform. Despite the fulsome rhetoric of sacrificial service—especially when recruiting enlisted men—it was a harsh reality that not many men from the upper strata would serve if they could not live close to their accustomed level.[37]

Washington got what he wanted, but the prospect of losing his officers had not been his only crisis. One month after taking command, he was confronted with a critical shortage of powder and lead. Munitions were so low that each man, on average, would have only nine bullets, insufficient for making any kind of stand should the enemy attack. A desperate Washington exhorted Congress to somehow solve the problem, wistfully advising that solutions that "appear chimerical often prove successful." Congress, which strangely had done virtually nothing to procure munitions during the first four months of the war, responded by allocating funds for the purchase of weapons and ammunition from European suppliers. But that would take time. In the end, it was simply America's good fortune that the enemy did not attack that summer or fall.[38]

Still another emergency arose when the enlisted men, who had signed on for one year's service, left for home in droves the moment their enlistments expired in December. Most were yeomen who worried that their lands would go to ruin if left untended for a second consecutive year and also feared losing their property if their farms generated no income for the tax collector. In a matter of days, the army declined by almost 80 percent, prompting Washington to carp about the "dirty, mercenary" character of these men, a criticism he had not made about the officers who had threatened to leave. Faced with recruiting an almost entirely new army, Congress and several colonial governments proffered everything from cash and land bounties to blankets, shoes, hats, stockings, and shirts as incentives to enlist. The entice-ments worked. By February 1776 the Continental army had grown back to 12,510, about where it had been in the fall. Washington said later that he had spent many a sleepless night while having "one Army disbanded and another to raise" within sight of the enemy.[39] Once again, however, luck had been on his side. The enlistment crisis occurred in the winter, when the British were unaccustomed to fighting. What is more, Bunker Hill appeared to have trans-formed General Howe. He now was less resolute, more cautious. Even if Howe was aware of his enemy's plight, he gave no thought to attacking.

The army was not Congress's only concern that autumn. It created an American navy. By the time Congress acted, at least six colonies had already established navies, even if they consisted of nothing more than row galleys. In addition, Massachusetts had licensed privateers to hunt for royal naval vessels and merchant ships transporting supplies to the British armed forces in Boston, and before summer ended, Washington had outfitted schooners to prey on enemy supply ships off the New England coast. The first British naval vessel was seized by American sailors just three weeks after Lexington and Concord, and "Washington's Navy," as some called it, captured fifty-five prizes in six months. The seizure of the ordnance brig *Nancy* in November—with a cargo of two thousand muskets, eleven mortars, over sixty thousand pounds of shot, and one hundred thousand flints—awakened Congress to the damage that might be wreaked on the British on the high seas.[40]

But it was not only the taking of the *Nancy* that spurred Congress to act. Late in October, word arrived in Philadelphia that a Royal Navy squadron had carried out a devastating raid on Falmouth, Massachusetts—now Portland, Maine—in reprisal for the tiny village's having fired on a British vessel. An eight-hour bombardment had reduced the town to ashes. With residents of every coastal village fearing that they would be targeted, Congress appropriated nearly one million dollars to purchase four existing frigates and construct thirteen others, and to raise two battalions of marines.[41]

Hard on the heels of news of the calamity at Falmouth came a bombshell from the South. Congress had long known that Virginia's royal governor, the Earl of Dunmore, had vowed to resist the rebels, and in the fall he raised a small force of Tories and got hold of a sloop, a schooner, and upwards of 150 regulars. Throughout October, Dunmore conducted successful raids against small bands of Virginia militiamen. Emboldened, early in November he issued what became known as Dunmore's Proclamation, a promise of freedom to all rebel-owned slaves who could escape their patriot masters and join his band of troops. Within a week, five hundred slaves fled behind Dunmore's lines—including one-third of the chattel who labored at the Williamsburg residence of Peyton Randolph, president of the First Continental Congress. More than five hundred additional bondsmen showed up and enlisted for service during the next thirty or so days, some reaching Dunmore on foot, others by boat. For many, the trek proved fatal; one-third or more quickly fell victim to smallpox. Numerous other slaves who bolted for freedom were apprehended by rebel patrols. Some were executed, while other luckless captives suffered hideous punishments. One fifteen-year-old girl was subjected to a flogging of eighty lashes, after which hot embers were put onto her slashed back. Still others yearned to flee to Dunmore but were restrained by fear or family ties. Even so, as historian Edward Countryman pointed out, Dunmore's proffer of freedom had inspired "the largest single escape from slavery in the whole history of British America to that point."

If Dunmore's offer sparked hope among the enslaved, it sent ripples of terror among whites. Planters feared losing their property, and nearly all white Virginians, whether or not they were slave owners, were acutely worried by the prospect of slave insurrections. A Virginia congressman called Dunmore a "monster" and the colony's only newspaper labeled him the "*king of the blacks.*" Washington somehow found it logical to refer to Dunmore as an "Arch Traitor to the Rights of Humanity." More perceptively, the American commander told Congress that at the moment, Dunmore was "the most formidable Enemy America has—his strength will increase as a Snow ball by Rolling."

Before Congress could act, a Virginia force defeated Dunmore in early December in the Battle of Great Bridge, an action fought just below Norfolk. The overconfident Dunmore—whose force of approximately six hundred included regulars, sailors from the Royal Navy, Loyalists, and some three hundred members of what the former governor called the "Royal Ethiopian Regiment": runaway slaves wearing white sashes that bore the inscription "Liberty to Slaves"—attacked a larger Virginia militia force protected by a strong line of earthworks. Dunmore had blundered egregiously in leaving his fortified position to take the offensive. Upwards of one-third of his force were casualties, prompting the rebel commander to call his victory "a second Bunker's Hill affair, in miniature, with this difference, that we kept our post."

Thereafter Dunmore was limited to an occasional skirmish, including one in Norfolk early in 1776 that resulted in the destruction of some nine hundred homes, warehouses, and businesses. News that the town had been torched spread rapidly from colony to colony. The razing of Norfolk, blamed on Dunmore and popularly conflated with the leveling of Falmouth, contributed to the image of the British as barbarians. In fact, as Virginia's authorities eventually discovered, more than 95 percent of Norfolk's structures had been sent ablaze by the rebel militia, information that was not noised about. Unaware of what had actually occurred, Samuel Adams predicted that news of Norfolk's fate would provoke such disgust that it would be crucial to "accomplish[ing] a Confederation" of independent states. Around the same moment, Edward Rutledge, a South Carolina congressman and slave owner, observed that Dunmore's Proclamation had done more "to work an eternal separation between Great Britain and the Colonies, than any other expedient, which could possibly have been thought of."[42]

In quickening the desire for independence, nothing reshaped thinking so profoundly, and so quickly, as the war. From the outset, John Adams had expected hostilities to change the outlook of the colonists, and by year's end there were almost daily reminders that his countrymen were changing. Not a few would have concurred with the Virginia assemblyman, once an advocate of accommodation with Britain, who now said that should Lord North ever come to the colonies the lowliest American would gladly "piss upon him." Samuel Adams might have agreed, though his response was more refined. Not even the most "industrious and able" colonial radical could have done as much as had the war to change attitudes, he remarked in the autumn of 1775, and he also predicted that things were leading to one of "the grandest Revolutions the World has ever yet seen."[43]

A further sign of deep change was apparent hard on the heels of Adams's remark. Soon after hostilities erupted, the Massachusetts provincial congress—eager to "form for ourselves a constitution worthy of freeman," as one Yankee put it—asked Congress's advice on how to proceed. Antipathy toward Great Britain was only part of the reason for wanting to change. The inhabitants of western counties, who were being asked to bear arms, were demanding a new government under which they would be more equitably represented and taxed. But the reconciliationists in Congress, who looked on changing provincial governments as synonymous with independence—and who in most instances were loath to lessen the eastern counties' lock on the colonies—prevented Congress from authorizing sweeping change. However, a new wind was blowing as 1775 neared an end. Within days of learning that the king had declared the colonists rebels, Congress received requests from

New Hampshire and South Carolina to create new governments, and Congress assented. The two provinces were authorized to establish whatever sort of government they wished through a "full and free representation of the people."[44]

The year 1775 had been filled with momentous events. More could be expected in 1776. As the new year approached, Congress impatiently awaited word from Canada, where a large American army had been campaigning since late in the summer. The delegates knew, too, that it could not be long before they learned of the king's response to the Olive Branch Petition. Franklin thought it doubtful that the monarch would offer meaningful concessions. It was more likely, he said, that Britain would continue to wage a war that was guaranteed to incite the colonists' "enmity, hatred, and detestation" for all things British. His view was shared by the young Virginian Thomas Jefferson, who likewise suspected that the king would never yield on any major points. And if George III refused to budge, said Jefferson, it would "undo his empire."[45]

CHAPTER 8

"The Birthday of a New World"

America Declares Independence

ALL AMERICANS ANTICIPATED crucial events in 1776, but no one expected such a string of pivotal occurrences to happen in January. By month's end, the series of momentous developments had made a congressional declaration of American independence seem more likely than ever before. In February, in fact, John Adams wrote home to his wife, Abigail, that there was now "no Prospect, no Probability, no Possibility" of reconciliation. He did not know when independence would be declared, only that separation from the mother country was virtually assured.[1]

On January 7 the text of George III's October war speech to Parliament arrived in Philadelphia. In an instant, all that the reconciliationists had banked on went up in smoke. "It is decisive," remarked a Rhode Island congressman. With the monarch already seen by Congress as the last link in America's ties to the British Empire, Samuel Adams rejoiced that the only conclusion his countrymen could now reach was that war "Guilt must lie at [the king's] Door."[2]

Two days later, Thomas Paine's *Common Sense* was advertised for sale in a Philadelphia shop. It was the most important pamphlet published during the American Revolution. In terms of its political ramifications, no publication in America equaled it until *Uncle Tom's Cabin* appeared three quarters of a century later. Nearing his fortieth birthday and down on his luck, Paine had moved from England to Philadelphia in 1774 to start over, purportedly by opening a school for girls. He never got around to that. Trained as a skilled tradesman—off and on, he had worked as a staymaker, a pursuit he hated, and he had also taught school and worked as a tax collector, neither of which he apparently cared much for either—Paine belatedly discovered that he could make a modest living as a writer, and he took to grinding out essays on every conceivable topic, including some that attacked imperial policies. It soon was clear that Paine was no ordinary scribbler. His animated essays were electrifying. As 1775 proceeded, and Congress remained in the vicelike grip of those who yearned to be reunited with the mother country, some Philadelphia radicals, and possiby a few frustrated congressmen, privately urged Paine to write a pamphlet assailing reconciliation and advocating American independence. Paine consented, and within two months he completed an eighteen-thousand-word tract.

Though little in *Common Sense* was new, Paine had written a masterpiece. He pulled together ideas he had heard in Philadelphia's taverns and coffee-houses, and threw in some things that were staples of English radicalism. Aside from its timing, what set apart Paine's pamphlet was its inviting literary style. It was free of suffocating jargon and indecipherable Latin phraseology, and it boiled with rage toward Great Britain, a sentiment that had gathered impetus in the colonies throughout 1775. Paine consciously sought a wider audience than the small, educated elite, and he found it. Dickinson's *Letters from a Farmer* had been the bestselling of the some 250 pamphlets published in the ten-year-long imperial crisis, but within only a few months *Common Sense* had sold nearly one hundred times more copies, and many who never read it themselves heard at least portions of it read on village greens, in the ranks of the army, even by pastors in the pulpit. Twenty-five editions of the tract appeared in the colonies in 1776, where sales totaled between 120,000 and 150,000 within a few months and—as a result of its success in England and France—may have reached 500,000 before the end of the year.

Paine opened with a discourse on government in which he asserted that the people were capable of governing themselves, after which he pitched into Great Britain's government as an abomination. Monarchical rule, not to mention the "aristocratical rule" of a titled nobility, was not geared for securing the needs and freedom of the people. When kings were not creating sinecures for sycophants—paid for with taxes imposed on the citizenry—they were making wars, which led to still more taxation. England's government was bad enough for those living in the homeland, but it was a "second hand government" for the colonists. "England consults the good of this country no further than it answers to her own purpose." It moved from one war to the next, dragging the colonists along into the carnage, making peace on whatever terms it desired, and all the while exploiting American commerce and industry for its own purposes. "I challenge the warmest advocate for reconciliation to show a single advantage that this continent can reap by being connected with Great Britain," Paine declared. Contrarily, American independence held the promise of peace and prosperity. " 'TIS TIME TO PART."

Some American insurgents—Jefferson and John Adams for instance—appear to have understood early on that they were part of an epic historical event. So did Paine, and he proclaimed it in ringing, even mystical terms. American independence, he believed, was foreordained, and it had fallen to this generation to consummate it. "The time hath found us," he stated. Furthermore, Paine cast what was happening as more than a protest against taxes. " 'Tis not the concern of a day, or year, or an age; posterity are virtually involved . . . and will be more or less affected even to the end of time, by the proceedings now." Paine told those who were making sacrifices and faced with great peril that they were part of a sacred cause, a people confronted with challenges and opportunities that fell to few generations. On the brink of a "new era for politics," this generation of colonists had it in their "power to begin the world over again. . . . The birthday of a new world is at hand." Liberty, said Paine, "hath been hunted round the Globe" and annihilated almost everywhere, but this generation in this American Revolution could save freedom for America and for those who would flock to the "asylum for mankind" that an independent America would become. Truly, the "Sun never shined on a cause of greater worth."[3]

For the first time, said a congressman, someone had dared to publicly use the "frightful word *Independence*." Paine had excited a clamor. *Common Sense* was being "greedily bought up and read by all ranks of people," noted one delegate. General Washington acknowledged that the pamphlet was "working a powerful change . . . in the Minds of many men."[4] No one knew that better than the reconciliationists in Congress, and with mounting desperation they fought back. Spurred not only by the threat posed by Paine's ringing message and burning vision, but also by the king's allusion to "peace commissioners" in his October speech, those who yearned to be reconciled with the mother country responded.

Led by James Wilson, a congressman who had emigrated from Scotland to Pennsylvania a decade earlier, the four mid-Atlantic delegations sought to have Congress declare its "present Intentions respecting an Independency." Knowing that Congress was not yet prepared to sever all ties with Britain, they believed that a disavowal of independence would lay the groundwork for talks with the envoys that George III had tantalizingly appeared to promise. Wilson prepared a statement denying that Congress ever intended to establish "an Independent Empire" and insisting that the colonists, who were fighting this war in defense of their constitutional rights, wished to "continue connected . . . with Britain." Wilson's proposal aroused heated debate, during

which Dickinson once again called on Congress to send two or more envoys
to London to seek to open talks with the monarch. Congress had spurned a
similar proposition the previous summer, and it remained adamantly
opposed to sending anyone to London to conduct diplomacy. Moreover, in
February 1776 it was neither in a mood to tie its own hands with a statement
repudiating independence nor to appeal yet again to a king who had rebuffed
his colonies so harshly already. Wilson abandoned the fight.[5] The reconciliationists had lost control of Congress.

But if the reconciliationists were no longer in control, those who favored
independence were not yet in command. Events were shaping the actions of
Congress, and events would ultimately determine what Congress would do.
For instance, even as it debated this latest sally against independence by the
reconciliationists, Congress learned through London newspapers that Lord
North was sending massive military reinforcements to North America and
that some were to be deployed in the southern colonies.[6] With heavy fighting
looming, Congress was unwilling to take any step that might be seen as a
show of weakness.

Nothing struck Congress with greater force than word of the fate of its
invasion of Canada. That campaign had been sanctioned the previous June
with the idea that it could be wrapped up before Canada's dreaded winter set
in. Responsibility fell to the Northern Department of the Continental army,
which was commanded by General Philip Schuyler, a wealthy New Yorker
with about as much military experience as Washington. As Canada was
lightly defended, and most of its residents were of French descent with little
apparent love for Great Britain, Congress was confident of success. All the
more so, in fact, as there were nearly three thousand Continentals in New
York for Schuyler to draw from, and Ethan Allen—who had displayed his
mettle in taking Fort Ticonderoga—would be available as well, along with his
band of frontier vigilantes known as the Green Mountain Boys.

However, as was customary in this war, problems cropped up immediately. Recruiting and logistical difficulties caused delays. Worse, Schuyler
repeatedly fell ill—so often in fact that some came to suspect that his maladies were psychosomatic and that he lacked the "strong nerves" necessary for
high command. Washington was among those who harbored doubts, and
deep into August, with Schuyler's force yet to set off, the commander created
a secondary force to advance on Quebec. Washington chose Colonel Benedict
Arnold to lead the force. The thirty-seven-year-old Arnold, who once had
owned an apothecary shop in New Haven, Connecticut, had eventually sunk
his capital into a small fleet that carried out a lucrative trade throughout the
Caribbean and Central America. A man on the make, like numerous other

officers, Arnold had entered the Continental army soon after the successful campaign to take Fort Ticonderoga back in May. He was glib and intelligent, and he exuded the qualities of a gentleman. But a steely combativeness and an ability to make men follow him shone through as well, and it was those attributes that Washington found especially compelling.

The high command sent out a notice asking for volunteers with backgrounds as "active Woodsmen" to serve under Arnold. Countless numbers of soldiers stepped forward, claiming intimacy with frontier life. Most had fibbed, but Arnold did his best in picking the 1,050 men who made up his newly minted army. Washington's thinking was that while Schuyler advanced toward Quebec by proceeding northward up the Champlain Valley, Arnold would make his way to Quebec through Maine. If Arnold arrived first and discovered that the British soldiery had gone west to contend with Schuyler's force, he was to attack Quebec. Otherwise, Arnold was to await Schuyler's arrival.[7]

At about the same moment that Arnold set off from Massachusetts, General Richard Montgomery, Schuyler's second-in-command, learned that his commander had been laid low yet again with a "Barbarous Complication of Disorders." That was the final straw. Montgomery, who had served for sixteen years as an officer in the British army before emigrating to New York in 1771, took charge and launched the invasion that was supposed to have begun weeks earlier.[8] Montgomery's force quickly reached Fort St. Johns, a British-held installation on the Richelieu River above Lake Champlain. But despite the Americans' three-to-one numerical superiority, two months passed and snow was in the air before Fort St. Johns fell. Plagued by supply problems, a shortage of artillery, and a callow, untrained, and undisciplined soldiery—"a set of pusillanimous wretches," according to their commander— Montgomery had experienced a portent of things to come. It was mid-November before Montreal was taken without a fight and early December before Montgomery reached Quebec. By then, disease, desertions, and the expiration of enlistments had reduced his army by nearly 75 percent.

Arnold was waiting outside Quebec for Montgomery, having somehow survived an incredibly arduous six-week trek through the wilds of Maine. In the first days of its expedition, Arnold's inexperienced soldiers lost much of their food and blankets when numerous bateaux capsized in Maine's swirling rivers. Within ten days the men were exhausted and hungry. Soon they faced heavy snow and even an autumn hurricane that destroyed much of their remaining food. A month into the campaign, an entire battalion deserted. Arnold's depleted force reached Quebec in mid-November, but the citadel was too well defended for him to consider an attack.

When Montgomery joined Arnold a few miles upriver from Quebec, American troop strength was 1,325, about one-third the number that had once composed the twin invasion forces. Montgomery sought to lure his adversary outside Quebec, but General Guy Carleton, Canada's governor, would have none of that. He had roughly three hundred fewer men than the Americans, but he possessed sufficient supplies to endure a prolonged siege. Carleton waited. Montgomery could not wait. The tour of duty for most of his men would be over at year's end, and given what they had gone through since late summer, Montgomery knew that virtually none would reenlist. He decided to strike on the night of December 31, though he had to know that the odds against success were enormous. The British occupied a walled city atop a tall, steep promontory, and they possessed superior artillery. Montgomery gambled that there were too few enemy troops to defend such a large area. If he could surprise his adversary and muscle his way inside Quebec's walls, his soldiers might possibly set the city ablaze. The weather cooperated. A raging snowstorm swept in. Montgomery hoped the British would not expect an attack in such dreadful conditions.

While a keening wind drove the snow, Montgomery launched his surprise attack deep into the night. But Carleton and his troops were not surprised, and in the first minutes of fighting, Montgomery was killed and Arnold seriously wounded, having taken a ball in his lower left leg. The attack quickly fell apart. Almost five hundred American soldiers were killed or captured. After their successes on Battle Road and Bunker Hill, the colonists had suffered an egregious defeat.[9]

News of the disaster took three weeks to reach Philadelphia. Some congressmen wanted to pull out of Canada immediately, but most were anxious to stay the course. Most hoped that a siege might lead to Quebec's fall before the Royal Navy could get relief ships through the ice-clogged St. Lawrence River sometime in the spring. Congress ordered that seven regiments be raised and sent north, and it authorized cash bounties to help with recruiting. It also sent a team of commissioners that included the aged Benjamin Franklin on an arduous trek to Canada for a firsthand look.

The repulse of Montgomery's attack was bad enough, but Congress may have been even more shaken by the woes that had afflicted Montgomery's force and doomed the campaign. The American soldiers had endured shortages of food, clothing, and weapons, especially artillery. The lesson that many congressmen drew was that America must secure foreign assistance, or its cause was hopeless. In fact, without help from abroad, the war probably could not be waged for long. Yet, no European country would help America so long as its goal was reconciliation, for those European nations—as Paine had counseled in *Common Sense*—would be "sufferers" from a "strengthening of the connection between Britain and America."[10] Only through declaring independence could America hope for ample help from France and possibly Spain.

Like other war-related events, the Canadian debacle produced unforeseen changes. In November, Congress had refused to send an agent to France in the hope of opening trade, fearing it might harm the chances of reconciliation. Thirty days later, early in December, a French agent arrived in Philadelphia. It was Julien de Bonvouloir, a French army officer who posed as an Antwerp merchant. Within hours of disembarking, he was meeting secretly at night at Carpenter's Hall with select congressmen, who divulged an eagerness for arms, munitions, and military engineers. Soon after Christmas, around the time Bonvouloir departed for his return trip to France, two French businessmen from Nantes, Pierre Penet and Emmanuel Pliarne, alighted in Philadelphia. They too spoke in secret with congressmen about conducting business with the colonists, but as they were not agents of the French government, the talks went nowhere. Penet and Pliarne were idling away their time awaiting a vessel to carry them home when the news of Quebec arrived. Within hours, Congress granted contracts for the two French businessmen to traffic in "all Sorts of Goods & Military Stores," as one gleeful congressman noted.[11]

Things were happening fast now, so rapidly that to those congressmen who favored separating from Britain, as well as to those who were opposed, it must have seemed as if they were caught in a churning vortex. In fact, John Adams wrote home that to sit in Congress at this juncture required "Temper . . . Understanding and . . . Courage . . . to ride in this Whirlwind."[12] Late in February, Congress learned of the American Prohibitory Act, which mandated that on March 1—only a day or two away—all colonial vessels bound for or departing from American ports were subject to seizure by the Royal Navy. This was total war, and for many it confirmed their worst notions of the mother country—what John Hancock, now the president of Congress, called the "Strain of Rapine and Violence" that had corrupted Great Britain. It pushed Congress to take several pivotal steps. Congress threw open American ports to ships from throughout the world, an act that officially brought to an end the colonists' compliance with Parliament's regulation of colonial trade, to which the First Congress had consented in its Declaration of Colonial Rights and Grievances.[13]

Samuel Adams was certain that what Congress had done meant that a declaration of independence could not be long in coming. John Adams thought independence had already come. If "This is not Independency . . .

What is?" he asked. Growing numbers of congressmen reported home that the desire to declare independence was growing. Congress was not yet prepared to take that step, but on the cusp of spring it agreed to two measures that it had previously hesitated to take. It legalized privateering and it sent Silas Deane—until recently a Connecticut congressman—to Paris to seek to establish commercial ties and secure sufficient quantities of arms and munitions for an army of twenty-five thousand. Deane was also to inquire whether France might consider an alliance "for Commerce, or defense, or both" should Congress declare American independence.[14]

Deane sailed immediately. Had his voyage begun a week later, he could have carried some good news to Paris. The nearly yearlong siege of Boston, begun on the night of Lexington and Concord, had ended spectacularly for the Americans. Washington had taken charge of the siege in July 1775. Two months later, he brought before a council of war a plan for attacking Boston. Washington's officers nearly unanimously rejected his scheme, convinced that assaulting the entrenched British defenders would result in a Bunker Hill–type catastrophe for the Americans. They urged a continuation of the siege. Washington unhappily consented, but during the winter, he sent Henry Knox, commander of the Continental army's artillery regiment, to fetch the British ordnance that had been captured at Fort Ticonderoga months before. After an epic crossing of the steep, icy Berkshire Mountains, Knox brought to Boston thirty-nine field pieces, two howitzers, and fourteen mortars. With their arrival, Washington's artillery arm had swelled by more than fourfold.[15]

Washington quickly summoned another council of war. After considerable discussion, the generals agreed to occupy Dorchester Heights. It was on the west side of Boston, but like Bunker Hill, artillery on its summit would command Boston Harbor. Howe would have to attack or relinquish the city. If Howe attacked, according to the plan that Washington devised, a force of four thousand carefully chosen men would charge across the frozen Charles River from north of Boston and strike the handful of redcoats left behind to defend the city. Once the redcoats were finished off, the Continentals were to destroy the enemy's supplies. The plan involved considerable risks, especially landing men in Boston, which at least one general protested "would most assuredly" result in "defeat and disgrace." But Washington yearned to attack and he carried the day, arguing that if successful, the daring assault might "put a final end to the War."[16]

The Continentals commenced a thundering bombardment of Boston on March 2. During the third night of shelling, the Continentals furtively occupied Dorchester Heights. When the British awakened on the morning of March 5—ironically, the sixth anniversary of the Boston Massacre—they discovered that three thousand American soldiers were dug in on Dorchester's ridgeline and the Continental army's artillery was trained on the vessels of the Royal Navy in Boston Harbor.[17]

Although the American force on Dorchester Heights was greater than the one Ward had put atop Bunker Hill, Howe's first inclination was to fight. Stormy weather forced a day's delay. Howe reconsidered. Since late the previous summer, he had planned to evacuate Boston and campaign for New York instead. All that had kept him in Boston was the long wait for troop transports. As those vessels had begun to arrive, Howe decided to offer Washington a deal. If the Americans would permit the British to depart unmolested, Howe would leave Boston intact. Otherwise, he would burn it to the ground.

Now it was Washington who faced a difficult decision. He might conceivably destroy all or most of Britain's army in America. On the other hand, the destruction of Boston might so frighten the leaders in New York and Philadelphia that they would turn against the war. Washington agreed to Howe's offer, and on March 17 the British army sailed from Boston. As no one on the American side had been aware that Howe had long planned to quit Boston, Washington was showered with praise for having liberated the city. Hailing the American commander a conqueror, Congress struck a medallion in Washington's honor. Harvard College awarded the general an honorary degree. It was indeed a magnificent conclusion to the British army's eight-year-long occupation of Boston. In fact, just two years after word had arrived in Massachusetts of the Intolerable Acts, not one royal official, civil or military, was left in the province. And this stunning turn of events had come at a crucial moment, only a few scant weeks after the citizenry had learned of the failed Canadian campaign.[18]

Word that the British army had abandoned Boston spread across an American landscape in which loyalty to the mother country was vanishing like snow under a warm sun. The rising death toll among militiamen and Continentals, combined with the suffering and anxiety of civilians in coastal hamlets, led Benjamin Franklin to discern "a rooted Hatred" for England among colonists who a dozen years earlier had displayed so much love for their mother country. Franklin's observation was correct. Hostilities had inspired a loathing for Britain that now burned with a white-hot intensity. Tories often bore the brunt of the bitterness. Some were assaulted, even tortured, by mobs, and some suffered the loss of their livestock at the hands of what one called "surly and savage" bands of rebels. Furthermore, by early 1776, committees of safety nearly everywhere were publishing statements that evinced a new mind-set, a growing sense of identity as Americans. One after another, these committees

spoke of being "a true friend to *America*" or "friends to *American* liberty";
some boasted of "the liberties of my country," while others denounced Great
Britain's "wicked system" that threatened "the destruction of *American*
liberty." Veneration of the British monarchy had disappeared. George III's
birthday was no longer celebrated, his portrait had been removed from nearly
every government building, and toasts to him ceased to be offered at public
dinners. Within only weeks of the publication of *Common Sense*, the new
American world that Thomas Paine had envisaged was on the verge of being
born.[19]

The final public debate on whether the colonies should remain part of the
British Empire played out in the press during the spring. The foes of separation focused largely on the uncertainties and dangers that would accompany
independence, a sentiment captured by a Philadelphia wordsmith who said
that severing ties with the mother country would be a dangerous "leap in the
dark." The proponents of parting company stressed that the realities of war
made independence a necessity. Paine, writing as "The Forester," denounced
reconciliation as a "false light" and declared that London's use of force "hath
cut the thread between *Britain* and *America*."[20]

Sentiment in Congress had already changed dramatically, but public
opinion was running breathtakingly far ahead of that among the delegates in
Philadelphia. South Carolina, freed by Congress the previous autumn to
replace its colonial charter government with one of its own choosing, adopted
a new constitution immediately after word of the American Prohibitory Act
reached Charleston. Although the word "independence" was not included in
the new constitution, the province's chief justice, William Henry Drayton,
ruled in April that South Carolina was "independent of Royal authority." His
judgment was based on a Lockean belief that the king's jurisdiction had
ceased because he had "broke the original contract" to protect the natural
rights of the colony's citizenry. When John Adams heard the news from the
Low Country, he exclaimed that it was proof of America's "sure steps to [a]
mighty Revolution," and he predicted that South Carolina's "Example . . . will
Spread . . . like Electric Fire."[21]

Adams could not have been more accurate. By early May, Georgia, Rhode
Island, and both the Carolinas had freed their delegations to Congress to
declare independence. The seething anger that the colonists already harbored
toward Great Britain spiked even higher in May, when word arrived that the
king had hired German mercenaries to help crush the rebellion. Some
thought it London's most infamous act. John Hancock called the king's action
the "last Extremity." Another New England congressman raged that this was
a foretaste of Britain's plan to arm "every other butcher the gracious King . . .

can hire against us." The Germans—or Hessians, as the colonists called them, for the principality from which they came—were reputed to be Europe's most brutal soldiers. Moreover, whereas many thought it possible that England's soldiers might show some restraint, given their former bond with the colonists, Americans expected only heartless cruelty from the Hessians. Jefferson, home on leave from Congress when the news arrived, found that around Charlottesville, Virginia, "nine out of ten are for" independence.[22]

It was in this frame of mind that Virginia's provincial convention in mid-May instructed its congressmen to move that Congress "declare the United Colonies free and independent States, absolved from all allegiance to, or dependence upon the Crown or Parliament of Great Britain." Some committees of safety had already urged American independence. For instance, the Charlotte County, Virginia, committee had declared that "all hopes of a reconciliation . . . are now at an end" and appealed to Congress to "immediately cast off the *British* yoke."[23]

Congress was getting there. Nevertheless, while news of the fervor for independence "rolls in upon Us . . . like a Torrent," as John Adams remarked in May, Congress could not have mustered a unanimous vote in favor of making the break, and unanimity was thought to be essential on this most crucial of all questions. New York and Pennsylvania, and possibly others, would "obstruct and perplex the American machine," an unhappy Virginian noted. The Pennsylvania assembly was impeding a break with the mother country by categorically instructing its congressmen not to vote for independence. Hope of change in that province collapsed when the pro-independence forces narrowly failed to win control of the assembly in the province's annual by-election in May. That nudged the pro-independence faction in Congress into action to shatter Pennsylvania's chronic obstructionism. In mid-May, while John Dickinson was at home tending to personal business, Congress adopted a resolution offered by John Adams that urged all colonies to create new governments capable of meeting "the exigencies" of the times. For good measure, it added that it was unreasonable for Americans to any longer adhere to a government whose authority was derived from Crown-issued charters. Congress had come so close to actually declaring independence that a Maryland delegate happily pronounced: "The Dye is cast. The fatal Stab is given to any future Connection between this Country & Britain."[24]

Congress's daring move, which would have been inconceivable only a short time before, provoked change. It was followed by a mass meeting in Philadelphia on May 20, which not only called on the Pennsylvania assembly to countermand its instructions to its congressional delegates but also voted that a convention be called for the purpose of writing a constitution for the province. The assembly backed and filled briefly, but during the second week in June it rescinded its instructions against independence. It was the last thing the assembly ever did. It never met again.[25]

John Adams had taken the lead in pulverizing the impediment in Pennsylvania. Similarly, he took the lead that spring in acting to placate those who feared that republicanism would result in radical political and social changes. In the First Congress, Joseph Galloway had warned that an independent America would be a republican—probably a democratic—America characterized by rampant domestic upheaval. In January, Thomas Paine's ruminations on governance in *Common Sense* had quickened the worries of some. Paine had proposed independent state governments consisting of unicameral assemblies, but no executive authority. Many of the more conservative colonists feared that unrestrained excess would result if those who held power were not curbed through a system of checks and balances. Many colonists were comfortable with breaking away from Great Britain, but uncomfortable with major transformations in colonial society. They especially wanted some assurance that their wealth and property would be secure.

Adams shared their concerns, remarking in private that Paine's nostrums would cause more harm than all the Tory treatises combined. Early in the spring, Adams committed to paper his plan to assure the "dignity and stability of government," and in April it appeared in print as *Thoughts on Government*. Adams's proposal, featuring a bicameral assembly, a strong executive, and a separate judicial branch, offered numerous bulwarks to prevent rulers from acting in a fit of passion, and also to hamper the possibility of swift and dramatic change. Adams's constitutional expedients reassured conservatives that "ambitious innovators" would be curbed and convinced many that it was possible to create an independent American nation in which much from the colonial past could be preserved.[26]

Momentum for independence had gathered with breathtaking rapidity since late in the previous autumn, but more than anything it was military reality that provided the final push for Congress to act. For months, Congress had known that the military reinforcements raised by Lord North in the wake of the fighting in Massachusetts were on the way. The first units, in fact, had arrived in March on the North Carolina coast, signaling that what had hitherto been almost solely a northern war was about to spread in earnest to southern provinces. London had ordered a campaign to pacify the southern colonies, swayed by the Crown-appointed governors in the region who unanimously insisted that the South teemed with Tories wanting only arms and assistance from the British army to subdue the rebels. Sir Henry Clinton, who commanded the southern venture, arrived "big with expectations." He also had 3,300 troops, a formidable fleet, and ten thousand muskets for the Tories. Clinton's optimism evaporated as soon as his flotilla docked. He discovered that North Carolina's Tories had been defeated two weeks earlier in a decisive engagement at Moore's Creek Bridge near Wilmington. Forced to improvise, Clinton decided on an operation to take Sullivan's Island at the mouth of Charleston Harbor. If successful, he not only would booste morale among the shaken Tories, but from his base, weapons could be funneled to those in the province who were prepared to fight the rebels. By June, Congress knew that the king's armed forces were poised for action in South Carolina.[27]

Nor was that all. Congress expected that Howe, with the army that had evacuated Boston, would land in New York in May or June, provoking by far the greatest test yet faced by the Continental army. Some thought that declaring independence prior to the looming campaigns in both the North and South would give the soldiery something positive to fight for. Others feared that further "Delay shall prove mischievous." They were apprehensive lest a crumpling defeat, or multiple setbacks, might dampen ardor for making the break.[28]

But it was not the projected campaigns that stirred Congress so much as more doleful news from Canada. In the wake of the ill-fated New Year's Eve attack, Congress had sent reinforcements and removed General David Wooster, Montgomery's successor as commander of the rebel siege force outside Quebec. At age sixty-five, Wooster was thought too old for the challenge. General John Thomas, thirteen years Wooster's junior and an officer who had performed well during the long siege of Boston, was appointed in his stead and hurried to Quebec. Thomas took over an army in perilous shape. The team of commissioners sent earlier by Congress to investigate described the soldiery as "broken and disheartened . . . without discipline . . . without pay . . . and reduced to live from hand to mouth." Both Thomas and Congress prayed that the besieged British force inside Quebec would run out of food and capitulate to the woebegone American army before the Royal Navy could save them. That did not happen. A royal flotilla of twelve ships carrying 5,100 redcoats arrived on May 6. The very sight of the rescuers led General Carleton to sally from behind his walled fortress and launch an attack. The American soldiery buckled in a flash, triggering an every-man-for-himself flight; so eager were the soldiers to reach safety that they abandoned their ill comrades. It was an army that had "dwindled into a mob," according to one officer. Thomas finally established control and stopped the retreat, but soon thereafter he succumbed to smallpox.[29]

New Hampshire's General John Sullivan succeeded Thomas. A thirty-six-year-old lawyer with no prewar military experience, Sullivan was precisely the sort of political appointee that John Adams had hoped to be rid of when the Continental army supplanted the Grand American Army. However, New Hampshire had demanded that it, too, be permitted to name one of the original general officers, and it backed Sullivan. Now, in May 1776, Sullivan hurried north with nearly six thousand men. At Three Rivers—roughly the midpoint between Quebec and Montreal—Sullivan ordered an attack. The victim of both poor intelligence and his own recklessness, Sullivan had thrown his raw soldiers into a wrongheaded attack on an enemy force three times larger and consisting mostly of British regulars. Predictably, the engagement did not go well for the colonists. Indeed, Carleton had it within his power to destroy the entire American army on Canadian soil, but he failed to seize the opportunity. Sullivan wiggled out of what had appeared to be a fatal trap; he and his men retreated from Canada—and did not stop until they reached Isle aux Noix, an island on the Richelieu River below Fort St. Johns and not far above Fort Ticonderoga. Sullivan may have been safe for a time from the British, but disease engulfed his army on the swampy, mosquito-infested island, killing hundreds within two weeks. The father of one soldier who died and, like his comrades, was buried in one of the two mass graves dug by the healthy, poured out his sorrow and rage when he learned of the fate of his child. His son had perished "defending the just Rights of America" against "that wicked tyrannical Brute (Nea worse than Brute) of Great Britain," he wrote in his diary.[30]

By early June, as it awaited Howe's army, which was bearing down on New York, Congress learned that the situation in Canada was "in a very bad way." Within a few more days, it was aware that Sullivan had failed egregiously and that his army might yet suffer a defeat even worse than that which had befallen Montgomery. The news should not have come as a surprise. Franklin and his fellow commissioners had previously reported to Congress that the American army in Canada was rotten to the core. Many officers were "unfit," the soldiery untrained, undisciplined, unpaid, woefully provisioned, and ill-equipped. "[C]onfusion . . . prevails thro' every department," they concluded. After ten months, the Canadian campaign was over. The Americans had lost over a thousand men killed and captured, and countless others were crippled from wounds or frostbite. "Our Affairs are hastening fast to a Crisis" that will "determine for ever the Fate of America," remarked the badly shaken president of Congress.[31]

The two Canadian disasters provided a clear lesson for many disquieted congressmen: the Continental army needed foreign help. With a British army in South Carolina, another about to strike at New York City and the Hudson, and a third possibly poised to invade northern New York from Canada, there was no time to waste. Many in Congress who had yearned to be reconciled with the mother country were driven by the demands of the war to consider severing all ties. As summer came on, they joined with colleagues who had long dreamed of independence, whether from a loathing of Britain's new colonial policies, a sense of having been betrayed by the mother country ("Even brutes do not devour their young" was how Paine put it), restless personal ambition, economic incentives, an ever-growing realization of American distinctiveness, a compulsion to replace servility and the dependence on monarchy with the idealistic goals of a republican people, a yearning for America's destiny to be shaped by Americans, or dreams of social and political change that was possible only in an independent America.[32] Inexorably, the war had been driving the colonists, congressmen as well as people from every walk of life in every colony, toward independence. Now the war dictated the timing of independence, for the Canadian misfortunes pointed to the very real possibility that the war could never be won and that without foreign help it almost certainly would be lost.

It had come to this. A bit more than a decade earlier, when the Stamp Act was enacted, a colonial rebellion had seemed unimaginable and any assumption that a revolution for American independence was imminent would have been treated as utterly preposterous. With a few exceptions, such as Samuel Adams, those in the forefront of the colonial protests down to, say, 1774 were, as historian Jack Rakove has observed, "as unlikely a group of revolutionaries" as can be imagined. Moreover, a widespread revolutionary mentality had emerged only slowly. British policy had stirred the American protests and British leaders alone could have averted a revolution. Instead, by the time the First Continental Congress met, Britain's unyielding policies had caused a majority of colonists—leaders and followers—to sour on Great Britain. Most sought much greater American autonomy than any British government was prepared to concede, but powerful entities within the colonies—including merchants hungrily searching for new and valuable markets and those with capital to invest, whether in manufacturing or trans-Appalachian land— were coming to see that their interests could be better fulfilled through separation from the mother country.

But it was not only the most influential who understood that a better day would dawn when a government three thousand miles away exerted less control, or no control, over America. Small farmers and would-be yeomen who craved new fertile lands for themselves or their children, and those who earned a living from myriad occupations tied to maritime endeavors, had come to believe that their well-being would be enhanced if Americans exerted greater control over America's destiny. In the wake of the First Congress, twenty year old Alexander Hamilton had perfectly summarized the colonists' viewpoint in his maiden effort as a pamphleteer: The "best way to secure a permanent and happy union, between Great-Britain and the colonies, is to permit the latter to be as free, as they desire."[33]

From the outset, a handful of British leaders, especially those surrounding Chatham, understood that something along the lines that Hamilton suggested offered the best hope of peacefully resolving the Anglo-American crisis. Chatham was also aware of the cautionary note sounded by Franklin in his 1766 testimony to the House of Commons: there was no mood for a revolution in America, but if Britain's leaders acted irresponsibly, they would provoke an American revolution. Chatham's solution in 1766—one that the First Congress would have accepted eight years later, and which Franklin proposed in 1775—was that Parliament surrender its claim to a right to tax America but continue to regulate all imperial trade. Chatham, and Franklin, grasped what too few British leaders understood. If the colonies and homeland were inextricably linked economically, their ties would be binding.

No other peaceful solution existed, but there was never the remotest possibility before the war that Parliament would yield a scintilla of its sovereignty. Hard-line conservatives, as is nearly always their proclivity, feared that any concession would be seen as weakness and dishonor. As early as the Stamp Act, the most conservative figures in England had insisted on standing firm "for the honour of the Crown, the dignity of P[arliament]." Others worried that unless the colonists were kept closely in check, their cooperation could not be guaranteed in time of crisis with Europe's powers. From the beginning, England's rulers were haunted by the belief that without America, England would be doomed to a second-class status. Unless Parliament tightly controlled the colonists, an MP cautioned in 1766, "Old England will become a poor, deserted, deplorable kingdom." In 1767 a pamphleteer asserted that it was the colonists' contribution to the "power and wealth of this nation" that ensured "a balance of power [in Europe] more in favour of Great Britain." Any loosening of the ties with America, warned a member of the House of Lords in 1775, would cause Britain to fall "to half her greatness." As "America is the hen that lays her *golden eggs* for Britain," said an English scribbler that same year, it was "by the American continent only that the balance of power can be any longer in [Britain's] hands." Lord North subscribed to this notion, and while presiding over the response to the Boston Tea Party, he advised his cabinet that "all is over" should England "retreat."[34]

With London never budging from its implacable opposition to rethinking the contours of the imperial relationship, it can in retrospect be seen with clarity that the imperial crisis was all along headed toward the abyss. In the wake of the Boston Tea Party, the only option that Parliament and the prime minister—and their king—could see was that America must surrender, whether peacefully or at the point of a gun. War had become inevitable more than a year before the first shot was fired. Short of a quick and total British military victory, hostilities made a declaration of American independence inescapable.

Richard Henry Lee, more or less the head of Virginia's delegation in Congress, waited nearly three weeks after receiving instructions from the Old Dominion's provincial convention to propose that Congress declare independence. On June 7, the day that Congress directed its president to inform General Washington that the army in the Northern Department was "almost ruined" and the military situation was "truly alarming," Lee introduced a resolution calling not only for American independence but also for steps to be taken to secure foreign alliances and adopt a constitution for the American confederation of states. Congress debated the resolution for two days. A few delegates—their numbers had shrunk precipitously—rehearsed the familiar arguments against independence. Some delegations pointed out that they still had not received authorization to declare independence. It soon was clear that Congress must wait a bit before acting. The nine-hour debate ended with Congress agreeing "to postpone the final decision to July 1," but also to create a committee "to prepare a declaration of independence."[35]

Congress almost always created committees that included representatives from each section. For this assignment, it selected two New Englanders—John Adams and Connecticut's Roger Sherman—and two from the middle colonies: Franklin and New York's Robert R. Livingston. That meant the fifth member would be a southerner. As Lee had introduced the motion for independence, he would in all likelihood have been selected, but he wanted to return to Williamsburg to participate in writing Virginia's constitution. In his stead, Congress selected Thomas Jefferson, a Virginian with a deserved reputation as a writer.

Jefferson, who was thirty-three in 1776, had been born with advantages. The son of a self-made planter aristocrat, he inherited thousands of acres and roughly a score of slaves. After graduating from the College of William and Mary, he briefly, and profitably, pursued a legal career. But Jefferson never warmed to practicing law, and he abandoned it immediately on marrying into considerable wealth in 1772. Jefferson had served in the House of Burgesses since 1769, where he had been active in the successful campaign to have the legislature vote to end the slave trade in Virginia, a step that was ultimately disallowed by the king. Jefferson thought slavery injurious to both blacks and whites. The latter suffered because slavery retarded the economy and led to the concentration of wealth and power in the hands of a planter oligarchy, relegating the many to a state of dependence on the few. Although his views were still in gestation, by 1776 Jefferson longed for broad social and economic changes, a transformation that would provide greater opportunit- ies for all free men than could ever exist for colonists within the British Empire or in an aristocratic society such as Virginia's. Jefferson believed that "dependence begets subservience and venality, suffocates the germ of virtue, and prepares fit tools for the designs of ambition."[36] For him, the American Revolution was about securing independence from Great Britain and, once independent, instituting fundamental political, social, and economic changes.

A *Summary View* had brought Jefferson notoriety as a foe of imperial policy and established his reputation a gifted wordsmith. On the day that Jefferson entered Congress in June 1775, a Rhode Island delegate gushed privately that "the famous Mr. Jefferson" was his new colleague. Jefferson literally stood out in Congress—he was six feet two inches in height. Slender, with sinewy arms and sandy red hair, Jefferson struck others as pleasant- looking, if not exactly handsome. Manifesting a "laxity of manner," he impressed acquaintances as amenable and hospitable, though, above all, it was his intellect that made the greatest impression. According to a later observer, Jefferson in social situations "spoke almost without ceasing. . . . It was loose and rambling, and yet he scattered information wherever he went, and some even brilliant sentiments sparkled from him." Yet, somewhat shy and uncomfortable as a public speaker, and above all anxious to avoid confrontation, he seldom joined in congressional debates. But given his intel- ligence and literary talents, Congress had frequently turned to Jefferson when forming important committees, and his fellow committee members found him "frank, explicit, and decisive."[37]

The Committee of Five, as the members of Congress took to calling the panel charged with drafting a declaration on independence, met immedi- ately. Its members probably first discussed the framing of the document. Was it to be akin to a lawyer's brief? What must be included? What might best be omitted? What should be its proper length? Someone had to be chosen to write the draft of the declaration. Years later, Adams recalled that the committee had asked him to take on the task but he had refused, begging off because of his heavy workload and as he had made many enemies in the course of leading the fight for independence. Jefferson, however, remembered that his colleagues on the committee had straightaway asked him to prepare the draft. Circumstantial evidence points to Jefferson's memory being better than Adams's.[38]

Working in his second-floor apartment at Seventh and Market, Jefferson wasted no time. He could not afford to. Congress was to take up the question of independence in eighteen days. Jefferson completed his task within seven. He showed it to Adams and Franklin, who recommended only a few changes, mostly stylistic, before presenting it to the full committee. Sherman and Livingston appear to have suggested virtually no changes. The document that would go to Congress was the handiwork of Jefferson.

Jefferson later remarked that Congress wanted a document that captured the "tone and spirit" of how Americans felt about the mother country and its king.[39] In striving for what it wished, he drew on his storehouse of knowledge from Enlightenment philosophers, English Whig polemics, the pamphlet literature that had been part and parcel of the imperial dispute, and sentiments he had heard expressed repeatedly in Congress. Given the striking similarities in what he wrote and what was included in the Virginia Declaration of Rights—recently drafted in Williamsburg and published in a Philadelphia newspaper on the day Jefferson probably began writing—it seems indisputable that the composition adopted by his colony's provincial convention also influenced his thinking. This was especially true of the portion Jefferson penned on the natural rights of humankind. Among other things, Virginia's document stated that "all men are born equally free and independent, and have certain inherent natural rights . . . among which are the enjoyment of life and liberty, with the means of acquiring and possessing property."[40]

Jefferson's document was divided into four sections. It opened with a brief preface declaring that the time had arrived to "dissolve the political bands" with the mother country. The best-remembered section followed, Jefferson's lyrical passage on egalitarianism and natural rights, including the right to revolution:

> We hold these truths to be self-evident; that all men are created
> equal; that they are endowed by their Creator with inherent and
> inalienable rights; that among these are life, liberty, and the pursuit
> of happiness; that to secure these rights, governments are instituted
> among men, deriving their just powers from the consent of the governed;
> that whenever any form of government becomes destructive of these
> ends, it is the right of the people to alter or to abolish it, and to
> institute new government, laying its foundation on such principles, and
> organising its powers in such form as to them shall seem most likely to

effect their safety and happiness. Prudence indeed will dictate that governments long established should not be changed for light & transient causes, and accordingly all experience hath shewn that mankind are more disposed to suffer, while evils are sufferable, than to right themselves by abolishing the forms to which they are accustomed. But when a long train of abuses and usurpations, begun at a distinguished period, & pursuing invariably the same object, evinces a design to reduce them under absolute despotism, it is their right, it is their duty, to throw off such government, & to provide new guards for their future security.

That melodic paragraph was followed by a bill of indictment cataloging the despotic acts of Britain's rulers and denouncing their refusal to receive the colonists' petitions for redress. Jefferson marshaled twenty-one charges of illegal and tyrannical actions by the king, a shameful record that marked him as "unfit to be the ruler of a people." Parliament was never mentioned by name, but the draft included nine accusations leveled against "their legis-lature." His compendium of grievances covered ground that for the most part would have been familiar to any informed colonist, ranging from "imposing taxes on us without our consent," swiping at customs officials, making war on America, burning towns, fomenting slave insurrections, having "plundered our seas," and dispatching foreign mercenaries "to compleat the works of death." Several involved infringements on the rights of colonial assemblies or threats to the independence of the American judiciary. Jefferson additionally excoriated the monarch for having perpetuated the slave trade and, by implication, the institution of slavery itself within the colonies, each of which he labeled an "assemblage of horrors." Nor did Jefferson distinguish between the natural rights of blacks and whites. His draft accused the king of having "waged cruel war against human nature itself, violating it's most sacred rights of life & liberty in the persons of a distant people."

The final section—the actual declaring of independence—was a slightly expanded rendering of the resolution that Lee had introduced earlier that month.[41]

Jefferson wrote in wartime and his was a war document. Not wishing to alienate the friends of America within the mother country, Jefferson had denigrated Britain's rulers but not its people, even acknowledging the "native justice & magnanimity" of Britons. He aimed the document as well toward those in Europe who might provide assistance, mentioning that the declaration contained "facts . . . submitted to a candid world." The reality of war may have led him to recast the familiar triad of life, liberty, and property. His draft spoke of "life, liberty, and the pursuit of happiness." Jefferson may have taken this tack since it was already clear that this was likely to be a protracted war in which many propertyless men would be called on to serve. Jefferson was of course conscious that the Declaration of Independence would accompany the birth of a new nation. He set forth the noble ideals on which the new nation would stand, enumerating those freedoms that Paine in *Common Sense* said had been "hunted round the Globe."[42]

Other congressmen might have written a document that squeezed in much that Jefferson included in his draft, but it is not likely that any could have matched the magical literary qualities of his composition. With peerless eloquence—and in simple and uncluttered language—Jefferson's Declaration of Independence glided effortlessly, like a vessel on placid water. There was a rhapsodic quality to his handiwork, for he was a penman with a genius for the cadence of the written word, a writer conversant with music who had a feel for what one scholar has called the "rhythmical pauses . . . comparable to musical bars." That is one reason why the document was read by successive generations, and is still read today, unlike every other document produced by the Continental Congress and its successor between 1774 and 1789. But it was not solely Jefferson's adroitness as a penman that accounted for the magisterial nature of the document. Like Paine before him, Jefferson evoked the colonists' pain, disappointment, reproach, sense of betrayal, and anger. More important, he embraced the hope and expectations that had swelled in the hearts and minds of the colonists by 1776, including the widespread desire for a more egalitarian society.[43]

Nothing in the Declaration provoked more questions than what Jefferson meant by declaring that "all men are created equal." Though aware of queries, he never provided an answer. Jefferson knew that egalitarianism was a radical idea, one of the most profoundly revolutionary sentiments within the draft. For Jefferson, the American Revolution was about more than breaking with Great Britain. Separating from Britain was merely the prelude to seminal changes that were to follow. It may be, as has lately been argued, that Jefferson knowingly sought political equality for all. It may be, as has also recently been asserted, that he was more committed to social equality. Possibly, he yearned for both political and social equality. A student of ideas who understood the power of concepts and beliefs, it may have been Jefferson's intention to unleash the idea of egalitarianism and let it tear "through American society and culture," as one scholar has written. Whatever Jefferson's intention, in the minds of most Americans, the Declaration of Independence made egalitarianism the fundamental tenet of the American Revolution.[44]

* * *

Congress had to declare independence before it could consider the document that would announce the step, and on July 1, as previously scheduled, it commenced what John Adams called "the greatest Debate of all."[45] The sun shone heavily on Philadelphia that humid morning. Long before Congress convened, the temperature was soaring steadily toward the nineties. Nevertheless, Congress adhered to its custom of keeping all windows shut, both to preserve secrecy and to muffle outdoor noise. After Congress formed into a committee of the whole and Lee's resolution was read, John Dickinson was the first to take the floor. Undeterred by the stifling heat, he spoke for nearly two hours, making one final stand against independence, though at the outset he acknowledged the futility of his effort. He presented all the stock arguments that the congressmen had heard "an hundred Times for Six Months past," as a weary delegate remarked. Although Dickinson acknowledged that the colonists had been repeatedly wronged by London, he insisted that red-hot wartime passions were driving Congress to a take a step that was not in America's best interest. Greater prosperity and a better chance of lasting peace would come from remaining tied to Great Britain. Dickinson thought a war for reconciliation would be brief and that in all likelihood London would offer attractive peace terms within a year or two. However, should independence became the aim of the war, London would fight tooth and nail, and this would become a protracted struggle. As he had a year earlier, Dickinson warned that victory in a lengthy war was far from certain. Even if it acquired an ally, America would face long odds. Outnumbered, unable to adequately furnish its army with arms and munitions, and lacking the financial resources needed for a long war, America would "brave the Storm in a Skiff made of Paper." Prolonged hostilities might end in America's defeat or a stalemated conflict. In the latter event, the war might be ended by a peace in which the European powers partitioned America: France might regain Canada and some of trans-Appalachia; Spain might reacquire its former provinces, and more.

When Dickinson concluded, John Adams responded with a rebuttal of nearly equal length, and one that also consisted of reasoning that had been "repeated and hackneyed" in Congress time and again. No record of Adams's speech has survived, but he must have addressed each point made by Dickinson, accentuated the benefits of independence, and most assuredly contested his rival's contention that the "Book of Fate" portended a "dreadful" future for an independent America. Adams, too, surely must have asserted that victory was possible only with the assistance of France, but that Versailles would not provide plentiful aid unless the colonies declared independence.[46]

As Adams spoke, the puffy white clouds of morning turned gray, giving way to a menacing black sky. At first, rumbling thunder could be heard in the distance, but it crept steadily closer until it boomed resoundingly over the city. Large raindrops splattered on the tall windows. In only a moment the rain came in torrents, lashing the State House. The temperature fell in the once sweltering congressional chamber. Candles were lit in the rapidly darkening room. Adams continued speaking through it all. Never known as an exceptional orator, he nevertheless was an experienced lawyer who had argued countless times before juries, and on this day he summoned all his skills as a public speaker. A New Jersey delegate, new to Congress, was so swept up that he called Adams the "Atlas of American independence," while a Southerner exclaimed that he "fancied an angel was let down from heaven to illumine Congress."[47]

With the room more bearable, and the congressmen fully aware of the importance of the moment, delegate after delegate followed Adams with brief speeches, each doubtless hoping to say something memorable. None succeeded. The last congressman concluded nine hours after Dickinson had launched the debate. Night was gathering over Philadelphia when the hungry delegates were at last ready to vote on the question of independence. Actually, two votes were necessary. The first would be a procedural vote on recommending the question out of the committee of the whole; the second would be on the motion to declare independence. The first vote disappointed those who sought unanimity. In a vote that was thought to foreshadow that on independence, Pennsylvania and South Carolina voted against sending the question to the floor; furthermore, one of Delaware's three congressmen, Caesar Rodney, was at home and the other two had deadlocked. New York's delegates, still not having received instructions, abstained. Hence, the result was 9–2, hardly the long-sought unanimity. Before the decisive vote on independence could be taken, South Carolina's Edward Rutledge urged a postponement until the following morning, hinting that his delegation might change its mind overnight. The drained congressmen happily acceded.[48]

A soft rain was still falling the next morning when Congress assembled to vote for American independence. Rodney was present. A messenger had been dispatched to New Castle, Delaware, to alert him to return hurriedly to Philadelphia. Rodney had ridden on horseback throughout the night in the soaking rain, reaching the State House shortly before Congress convened. With Delaware now certain to cast its vote for independence, many delegates, like John Adams, expected the final tabulation to be one of "almost Unanimity." Presumably, either Pennsylvania or South Carolina, or both, would spoil the hopes of those who longed for perfect unity.

But the roll call was a surprise. South Carolina switched its vote, as Rutledge had forecast. When it was Pennsylvania's turn, two of its seven delegates, Dickinson and Robert Morris were either absent or abstained from voting. They were unwilling to vote for or against independence. Three of the remaining five in Pennsylvania's delegation—James Wilson, John Morton, and Franklin—voted for independence. On July 2, American independence was declared by a 12–0 vote.[49]

Immediately after the vote, Congress took up the document that Jefferson had drafted, poring over it for some ten hours between midday on July 2 and near noon on July 4. The congressmen proved to be good editors. Though Jefferson was roiled by the changes to what he had written, his unsparing colleagues by and large did him a favor. They shortened the document by a third, so that the public saw a leaner Declaration of Independence. Congress added bite to at least four charges leveled against the king, corrected one or two factual errors, tinkered with the timbre of the section directed toward France and Spain, and in a couple of areas softened or set right what Jefferson said about the mother country. Jefferson had at one point not only called the English an "unfeeling" people, but, as in A Summary View, he had also reiterated his conviction that the colonists had established, secured, and expanded their settlements without British help. Both sentences were excised. Altogether, Congress made some forty changes to Jefferson's draft, but only one was truly regrettable. On the night before the climactic vote, Rutledge must have secured an agreement to delete Jefferson's unmistakably anti-slavery paragraph in return for South Carolina's vote in support of independence. In its role as editor, Congress consummated the deal by striking Jefferson's assault on the African slave trade and his assertion—filled with profound meaning and promise—that the king had abridged the "most sacred rights of life & liberty" of Africans by "captivating & carrying them into slavery." Expunging that momentous passage would have a telling impact on the course of American history and the lives of millions who would have to live as slaves within the United States.[50]

Once the editing was complete, Congress on July 4 voted to accept the emended document. At last, independence had been declared. John Adams was surprised by the "Suddenness . . . of this Revolution," but Samuel Adams feared that much "has been lost" by waiting fifteen months after hostilities commenced to declare independence. Had the break come earlier, the American army that invaded Canada might have been equipped and armed by France, and it might not have suffered such an inglorious fate.

No one in Congress was so deluded as to believe that declaring independence was the end of the story. The war still had to be won. The new nation could not be "saved by good words alone," said Massachusetts's Robert Treat Paine. To that he added, "our hands are full; may God . . . support us."[51]

Nevertheless, most congressmen were euphoric and understood they had just been part of a great historic event. John Adams captured their exhilaration. What had been done, he said, would forever be recognized as "the most memorable Epocha, in the History of America," and it would be "celebrated, by succeeding Generations . . . as the Day of Deliverance. . . . It ought to be solemnized with Pomp and Parade, with Shews, Games, Sports, Guns, Bells, Bonfires and Illuminations . . . from this Time forward forever more."[52]

CHAPTER 9

"THE AMERICAN CAUSE IS IN A CRITICAL SITUATION"

THE NEW YORK CAMPAIGN IN 1776

ON THE DAY CONGRESS took up the question of independence, John Adams predicted an imminent British invasion of New York. Later that same day, July 1, Adams and his colleagues learned that a British armada of more than one hundred ships had been sighted off Long Island.[1]

America's high command had expected the British army to return following its evacuation of Boston, and nearly everyone suspected that taking New York would be its objective. In fact, most presumed that the battle for New York City would be only the first step in Britain's plans. Thereafter, the enemy would seek to gain control of the Hudson River, the spine of the early United States. If Britain captured control of the river, it would sever ties between the four New England provinces and the nine states to the south, and it would win the war.

In January, more than two months before General William Howe quit Boston, General Washington had dispatched General Charles Lee to put New York "in the best posture of Defense." Lee had spent nearly twenty years in the British army before retiring and moving to Virginia a few years prior to the start of the war. Gifted with a first-rate mind and perhaps the best education of all the American general officers, Lee had additionally, and meticulously, studied military theory and tactics. The same age as Washington, Lee was tall and so thin that he struck others as emaciated. Nearly everyone also thought him habitually unkempt. (Abigail Adams described his appearance as "careless.") Lee never married and appeared to prefer his dogs to people—he traveled with a pack of canines and told acquaintances that he spoke "the language of doggism"—leading nearly everyone to think him eccentric. He had a proclivity, too, for annoying others. Acerbic and opinionated, and given to lengthy monologues, Lee could quickly wear out his welcome. But there was a war on and Lee was widely regarded as the "best qualified" American general, as John Adams put it, an observation with which most of his colleagues in Congress would have concurred.[2]

Washington likewise thought Lee a trusted and able officer, and without a doubt the man with the experience and savvy for devising a plan for defending the city and Manhattan Island. Within a month of his arrival in New York, Lee had a plan ready for Washington's consideration. Knowing that "whomever commands the Sea must command the Town," Lee came up with a plan that called for plentiful artillery batteries and the sinking of chevaux-de-frise—the hulks of ruined ships with tree trunks and limbs attached—obstacles whose purpose was to obstruct the Royal Navy's navigation of both the East River on Manhattan's east side and the Hudson on its west. He fortified King's Bridge in the northern reaches of the island, as it would be the Continentals' lane of retreat if necessary, ordered the construction of redoubts in Brooklyn Heights, and urged that Loyalists living around New York be arrested and disarmed. But perhaps the heart of Lee's plan was an intricate system of street defenses within the city. Never imagining that the Americans could keep the regulars from taking New York, Lee's goal was to "cost the enemy many thousands of men to get possession of it." His plan was to compel the British to fight street by street, combat for which they had neither training nor experience. Lee had fashioned a strategy designed to force the enemy to pay a price that would make the bloodbaths along Battle Road and on Bunker Hill seem minuscule. Devised six months prior to independence, Lee's plan was predicated on the notion that London would conclude that a war to suppress the American insurgency was not worth the cost. The losses incurred in the fighting for New York would lead London to meet Congress's terms for reconciliation.[3]

Washington arrived in New York in April with his army in tow. He appears to have initially concurred with Lee's master plan. But uncertain of his authority, and far from the august commander in chief he would later become, Washington often deferred to local authorities, and New Yorkers feared that the strategy Lee had mapped out would result in the destruction of the city. As April turned into May and New York remained uncommitted to independence, Lee's plan for fighting within the city was eviscerated. What is more, in July two British frigates, the *Phoenix* and *Rose*, successfully sailed up the Hudson, easily overcoming the rebels' river defenses. At that point, it should have been clear that defending an island against an enemy with a powerful army and total naval superiority was an invitation to catastrophe.[4]

Washington was aware of the dangers, but he believed that Congress wanted him to stand and fight, and he spoiled for a fight. Washington was convinced that France would risk providing plentiful help only if the British continued to suffer heavy losses, and he was persuaded that the army he had meticulously built during the past year would perform far better than the armies that had been sent to Canada. His Continentals were well trained. They would be well entrenched. Washington envisaged—in fact, he was obsessed with—winning his own Bunker Hill showdown with the enemy.

The British fleet that brought the regulars to New York was the largest expeditionary force that Great Britain had ever assembled; it would not put together such a force again until World War I. There were 130 ships in the armada, and Howe anticipated having thirty-two thousand men, several times the number he had possessed in Boston.[5] But Howe's first objective did not involve fighting. He and his brother Richard, the admiral who had sought to negotiate with Franklin early in 1775, were the so-called peace commissioners of whom the king had spoken in October and the reconciliationists had never stopped hoping for. After learning of the redcoats' disastrous engagements along Battle Road and on the slopes of Bunker Hill, Lord North had warmed to the idea of negotiating with the colonists. He realized that making concessions on parliamentary sovereignty could not be on the table, but the prime minister appeared willing to talk with the Americans about nearly everything else. North had inserted in the king's speech the sentence about "certain persons . . . so commissioned," and he saw to the appointment of Admiral Howe as the peace commissioner. It was North's hope that the admiral would be in America and negotiating as early as January. However, politics intruded. Some in the ministry, led by Germain, the new American secretary, objected to sending any commissioner. Others thought Howe the wrong choice. Tireless wrangling also ensued over the commissioner's instructions. Matters were not resolved until May. It was finally agreed that both General and Admiral Howe were to serve as commissioners, but their instructions constrained them from entering into talks until the rebels laid down their arms and acknowledged the supremacy of Parliament. In short, the commissioners were not being sent to parley, but to accept the colonists' surrender.[6]

In July, the Howe brothers sent an adjutant to meet with Washington. Predictably, the talks were unproductive. Admiral Howe also wrote to Franklin in Philadelphia, who responded that "Reconciliation . . . [is] impossible on any Terms given you to propose."[7] Through an emissary, the commissioners ultimately hinted to Congress that they were prepared to make concessions. Congress was skeptical, but feared public outrage should it refuse to talk. Franklin, John Adams, and Edward Rutledge were dispatched to Staten Island in September to meet with Admiral Howe. After walking between two lines of redcoats who looked to Adams "as fierce as ten furies," and dining with the admiral on ham, mutton, and tongues, the three congressmen sat down to talk. It did not go well. Howe did not offer a single concession. Moreover, Franklin straightaway told him that the love the Americans had once felt for Great Britain had been "obliterated" and that his countrymen could never again "expect Happiness . . . under the Domination" of the former mother country. Adams told Howe that America had undergone a revolution and that its citizenry was united in wishing to be part of an independent United States.[8] These "peace negotiations" were over. There would be no more for six long years.

During the weeks following General Howe's arrival in early July, Washington prepared for the blow that was coming. He committed a string of blunders in the process. In addition to passively permitting the obliteration of Lee's well-grounded plan of defense, Washington in mid-July sent home hundreds of cavalrymen provided by Connecticut, telling them "they could not be of use."[9] Having had no experience with mounted troops in the Seven Years' War, Washington failed to understand what assets that light horse could be in combat and as intelligence gatherers. Washington's next error stemmed from uncertainty over where the British invasion would occur. He thought the enemy would most likely strike first at New York City, though he worried that the initial onslaught might come miles to the north at King's Bridge. Persuaded, moreover, that the British army could not survive on Manhattan unless it possessed the lush farmlands on Long Island, Washington also thought that the redcoats might land near Brooklyn, just across the Narrows from Staten Island. In the end, Washington tried to cover all bases. He divided his army in the face of a superior foe, the very thing that every military manual cautioned commanders never to do. Washington posted half of his forces in the city and the remainder on Long Island, assuring that his army would be outnumbered wherever the British chose to fight.

The summer was nearly gone before General Howe was at last ready to open his campaign. His belated start was not due to sloth. What he had thought would be a brief stay in Halifax, following his departure from Boston in March, had dragged on for weeks. As fewer than a quarter of the transports sent from England with food, horses, and munitions had reached Nova Scotia prior to his arrival, Howe and his men were compelled to await shipments of the supplies needed for launching a major campaign. Nearly two months passed before he set off for New York. When he docked on Staten Island, deep into the sweltering summer, Howe discovered that neither the German mercenaries nor General Clinton's army had yet reached New York. Incredibly, 125 days passed between the embarkation of the Hessians in

Germany and their rendezvous in August with the British army near Manhattan. Clinton, meanwhile, was supposed to have completed his mission in the Carolinas in the spring. But it was June before he tried to take Sullivan's Island at the mouth of Charleston Harbor, and he failed in his endeavor. Leaving the Carolinas and Georgia in rebel hands when he sailed north, Clinton finally reached New York around the same time as the Germans. The tardy arrival of Howe's full complement of troops set back the start of the campaign for New York until late summer, a delay that in the long run would have a critical impact on the course of the war in 1776.[10]

Deep into the summer, Howe at last commenced the New York campaign. He opted for a landing on Long Island, and on August 22 about fifteen thousand regulars under Charles, Earl Cornwallis, went ashore at Gravesend, a tiny township consisting mostly of scattered farms six miles south of the little village of Brooklyn. Howe was supremely confident, in part because he was up against a foe led by an amateur. During the summer a military aide close to him had referred to Washington as "a little paltry Colonel of the Militia at the Head of a Banditti [of] Rebels," and there is no reason to suspect that Howe did not share that point of view. In fact, Washington's string of misguided actions likely confirmed Howe's thinking. Having already divided his army, Washington changed commanders on Long Island on the eve of battle, inexplicably removing General Sullivan and replacing him with Israel Putnam. Washington had also failed to properly reconnoiter the area, and he took no steps to prevent Putnam from scattering his men along a six-mile-long ridge line in the Guana Heights, a distance that was far too long for an army of seven thousand men to defend against a considerably greater adversary.[11]

The British rapidly exploited the rebels' mistakes. Soon after sunrise on August 27, Cornwallis commenced a diversionary attack on Putnam's lines. Meanwhile, the main British army—ten thousand men in a column that stretched two miles—marched noisily for hours along roads that the American high command had left unguarded. Dogs howled at the redcoats, who were also unavoidably kicking up a thick cloud of dust. That enemy force almost certainly would have been spotted had the Continentals possessed cavalry units, but as it was, the undetected redcoats circled the left wing of the rebel lines. In mid-morning, the flanking army, led by Howe himself, launched a surprise attack on the rear of Putnam's force. Some of the startled American units fought with valor. Others disintegrated quickly as panicky soldiers dashed madly away. Many of the fleeing rebels were hunted down and killed out of hand; not a few drowned attempting to swim across Gowanus Creek. By day's end, American losses stood close to 1,300—including three generals who had been taken prisoner—nearly 15 percent of the force that Washington had committed to Long Island.[12]

All who escaped—and the reinforcements that Washington implausibly committed following the debacle—wound up in the Brooklyn redoubts. If the 9,500 American soldiers in Brooklyn thought they were safe in their entrenchments, their optimism was misplaced. A numerically superior British army was on their front; the Royal Navy, sailing unhindered on the East River, was at their rear. Had Howe moved rapidly, he could have inflicted a cataclysmic blow to the rebel army. But Howe was different after Bunker Hill, no longer so daring, never again wishing to risk a repeat of the carnage he had witnessed that terrible June day in Charlestown. It was also possible, as one of his subordinates later said, that Howe's real talents had always been in executing the plans of others and that, in reality, he was deficient in the "great qualifications" required of the commander of an army.[13] Whatever the reason, with victory at hand—albeit probably a bloody victory—Howe paused. He sought better intelligence, more men, more supplies, more time before reaching a decision. Ultimately, he decided against assailing the rebel redoubts. As there was no way that the rebels could resupply their men in Brooklyn Heights, Howe believed he could conquer his adversary bloodlessly through a siege operation. If Howe succeeded, Washington, in his first engagement in the war, would have lost approximately 40 percent of his army.

Fully aware of the danger, Washington knew that he must seek to remove these men from Long Island. He called a council of war, which met as a nor'easter pummeled the region. Washington prevailed against the wishes of a handful of his generals, some thinking an attempted rescue too risky and some concurring with Putnam, who insisted, "Give an American army a wall to fight behind and they will fight forever." Acting that same night— while Britain's navy was immobilized by high winds—Washington sent a flotilla of small craft across the river to fetch his trapped soldiers to Manhattan. It was a perilous undertaking, but it succeeded, thanks in part to a fog so dense it swallowed the sight of everything more than a dozen feet away. In the lemon-colored light of early dawn, the last man, and the last of the invaluable artillery, came off Long Island. The Continental army had lived to fight another day.[14]

The army may have survived, but Washington was shaken to the core, and his thinking changed in substantive ways. He lost confidence in Putnam. Washington may have thought him too old—at fifty-eight, Putnam was about fifteen years older than most of the general officers—or he may simply have concluded that while courageous and adept at fighting Indians, Putnam was out of his depth when it came to commanding a large army against British regulars. Furthermore, where the commander had once believed that he had fashioned an army fully capable of standing up to Britain's professional soldiers, Washington now confessed his "want of confidence in the Generality of the Troops." He rethought how to wage this war, concluding that henceforth he must fight "a War of Posts." He would eschew risky large-scale offensive operations and avoid "put[ting] anything to the risqué unless compelled by a necessity into which we ought never to be drawn." His thinking pointed toward what strategists—and young Alexander Hamilton in his essay twenty months earlier—called a Fabian strategy. From this point forward, said Washington, he would pick when and where to fight, never hazarding his entire army in an engagement. He would bring the enemy to its knees through the attrition of men and treasure in the course of a long war.[15]

If Washington meant what he said about never being maneuvered into having to risk his entire army, it logically followed that his army must abandon New York City. To remain in the city was to be "cut [to] pieces," he acknowledged. He preferred to quit it and burn it—so that Howe would be denied its "great conveniences"—and retreat to Harlem Heights, where he could make a Bunker Hill–type stand with a portion of his army before retreating across the Hudson or escaping via King's Bridge. But he would not give up the city unless his general officers concurred, in part because his orders from Congress were that major decisions were to come through councils of war and in part from fear that he would lose the support of Congress if he did not defend New York. However, he worked on his generals as well as on Congress, and by September 14 both had consented to the evacuation of the city, though Congress ordered that it not be destroyed.[16]

More than two weeks had passed since the escape from Long Island. During that time, while awaiting a congressional sanction, Washington had once again divided his army, leaving about 3,500 men in the city and scattering the remaining 75 percent or so, though most were posted in Harlem Heights. As previously, Washington knew the British would be coming after him, but he was unaware of when or where they would strike. Howe's next hammer blow, it turned out, came on September 15, one day after Washington felt free to abandon the city, but before he could act.

Howe struck at Kip's Bay on Manhattan's east side, roughly midway between the two main contingents of the Continental army. Following a pounding bombardment directed at a brigade of rebels that Washington had posted earlier at the site, the British landed roughly thirteen thousand men. They came ashore unopposed, as the thunderous barrage had put to flight the Americans positioned along the shoreline. Once ashore, there was nothing to stop the British from advancing swiftly to the west side of the island, barely more than two miles away, taking control of every road in the process and sealing the thousands of Continentals in the city at the southern tip of Manhattan. Indeed, the rebel soldiers did not even begin their march out of the city until four P.M., hours after the first redcoats disembarked, and the Continentals faced a twelve-mile march to reunite with their comrades in the northern reaches of Manhattan Island. For the second time in two weeks, the British had it within their power to score a huge victory. But for a second time, the British army let a golden opportunity slip from its grasp. Britain's commanders remained exasperatingly hidebound to the ways of European warfare, unable to think outside the box, unwilling to attempt the unconventional, averse to risk taking. Hours passed before the redcoats moved off the beach, and when they finally set out, they marched up the island's east side while the once seemingly trapped rebels took roads along the west side. The long column of American soldiers escaped, though in making their hasty getaway, they decamped without their cannon.[17]

Britain's leaders may have been tied to convention, but Washington was fighting for his life and desperate enough to act audaciously. Four days after the Kip's Bay landing, New York City was put to the torch, with about a quarter of the town destroyed. It stretches credulity to believe that Washington had not set loose the firebugs, as seventeen men were apprehended setting blazes or in possession of torches and other incriminating combustibles. Some who were taken into custody were executed, including Nathan Hale, who on the day after the fire went to the gallows charged with spying.[18]

Washington had erred frequently during the campaign for New York, but in the month following Kip's Bay his judgment was so clouded that it nearly proved ruinous to himself and the army he commanded. His army was posted in Harlem Heights; Howe was nearby and with a considerably larger army. Still consumed with scoring a Bunker Hill–success of his own, Washington appeared to want a showdown, although Howe's behavior at Dorchester Heights and Brooklyn Heights suggested that he had no intention of obliging the American commander. In fact, there was no need for Howe to order another bloody assault against well-defended lines. He could deal with the rebels far more easily. Howe had only to utilize his army and the Royal Navy to seal all possible escape routes from the island of Manhattan and Washington's army would be trapped. Washington was fully aware of the extreme danger that he faced, but he made no attempt to steal away. Washington even admitted that when the British sprung the trap, he would face three options, all bad. If "cut off"—his term for being ensnared—the rebel army would be confronted with "the necessity of fighting [its] way our under every disadvantage," or of "surrendering . . . or starving."[19]

Washington remained immobile. Even in the face of evidence that his adversary was preparing to tighten the noose, Washington did not try to escape Manhattan Island. He had been pushed to the limit for weeks, and his judgment was likely undermined by physical and emotional exhaustion. What is more, anguished by his army's poor showing, surrounded by callow officers whose advice had often been flawed, and nagged by the belief that Congress expected him to make a stand, Washington admitted he did "not know what plan of conduct to pursue." There may be another explanation for Washington's bizarre behavior. The tone of Washington's letters suggest that he had slipped into the grip of a black depression that left him at a standstill. "I am bereft of every peaceful moment" and devoid of "all comfort and happiness," he wrote. Never had he been so unhappy. "Such is my situation that if I were to wish the bitterest curse to an enemy on this side of the grave, I should put him in my stead with my feelings." Vowing "not to be forced from this ground while [he had] life," he at times sounded like a man who believed his time was about up. In the throes of despondency, he appeared to think that should he go out in a blaze of glory at the head of his army, it would be a "credit to the justice of my character."[20]

Washington was saved by General Howe and General Lee. Typically, Howe delayed. Washington thought his adversary's slowness "perplexing." He also thought Howe's next move would be to attack the entrenched rebels in Harlem Heights. Instead, on October 12, four long weeks after the landing at Kip's Bay, Howe moved to entrap Washington by attempting to put ashore a force on the mainland above King's Bridge at Throg's Neck. The British plan was well conceived. Had it succeeded—and been followed by swiftly securing all roads between Long Island Sound and the Hudson—Washington, his army, and quite possibly the Revolutionary cause would have been doomed. But poor maps and faulty intelligence foiled the undertaking. High tide revealed that the landing site was separated from the mainland; the regulars might have slowly waded to the coastline, but casualties would have been heavy. Howe reloaded his men on naval craft and began the search for another place to go ashore.[21]

Two days later General Lee, who had been sent by Congress to defend South Carolina against Clinton's force, reached Washington's headquarters. Congress had rushed him to New York following his return from Charleston. "I wished so ardently" for his presence beside Washington, a Pennsylvania congressman remarked, adding: "I am Confident he will be better than 10,000 men to our Army." Lee immediately saw what Washington could not see, and he urged the commander to get his army off Manhattan. Washington listened and he posted contingents of Continentals at every conceivable site where Howe might try again to land. The very next morning, while the main body of Continentals was marching off the island, four thousand British troops disembarked at Pell's Point on Pelham Bay, not far from Throg's Neck. The regulars landed in a region where Washington had just deployed four regiments of Massachusetts soldiers under Colonel John Glover. The redcoats outnumbered the rebels by six to one, but the Yankees, hidden behind stone walls, fought just as Putnam said that Americans would fight. Glover's men soldiered with tenacity, pinning down their adversary for hours until Washington's army was off the island of Manhattan.[22]

The Continentals marched northward, past overgrown umber fields and shaggy farms that evinced the impact of war. The British came after them, but the rebels—who had abandoned nearly everything but their weapons in the hasty retreat from Manhattan—moved twice as rapidly as their pursuers. Late in the month, at hilly White Plains, Washington with Lee's approval—an assent that seemed crucial to the commander—fell back on his Fabian strategy. Given nearly a week to prepare, the Americans utilized the terrain to fashion an exceptionally strong position, one in which a successful flanking maneuver by Howe was out of the question. Washington put only a small portion of his army at risk and he dared Howe to attack it. Howe did just that on October 28. The intense fighting in the Battle of White Plains lasted throughout the day. As the sun pitched over the western horizon, the shooting stopped. The British had been unable to break through and they had lost nearly three hundred men, roughly twice the rebels' losses. Howe initially planned to renew the fighting the next morning, but bad weather set in, halting further action for two days. Given time to think it over, Howe on November 1 ordered his army back to Manhattan.[23]

Washington quickly summoned a council of war. It agreed to divide the army in four parts. Washington was to take two thousand Continentals to New Jersey, where, augmented by militia, he would stand sentinel against an enemy incursion. General William Heath was given three thousand men and sent to Peekskill to guard the Hudson. Lee, with seven thousand men, was to remain at White Plains, from where, if necessary, he could hurry east to defend New England, west to aid Heath, or south to join with Washington. The only real debate likely concerned the remaining portion of the Continental army.

When Washington evacuated Harlem Heights, he had left a thousand or more soldiers at Fort Washington, a pentagonal earthwork situated near the northern end of Manhattan at the island's highest point and the Hudson's narrowest point. Following the successful passage by the *Phoenix* and *Rose* in July, construction of the fort had been concluded and additional obstacles were sunk in the Hudson. But even if the installation at Fort Washington could prevent the Royal Navy from sailing the Hudson—and no one knew for certain that it could—it should have been clear that the fortress could not be held indefinitely. Winter was coming and there were no barracks; further-more, there was no well to sustain the soldiers during a siege. Washington told the generals that he expected an attack on the fort, but that in a worst-case scenario, he thought the defenders could escape across the Hudson. He insisted on maintaining Fort Washington. Lee and one or two other generals recommended it be relinquished, but a majority at the council of war concurred with the commander, who enlarged the detachment at Fort Washington to more than three thousand men.[24]

By the time Washington reached New Jersey, on November 13, he had learned that in recent days three additional British warships had sailed unscathed past Fort Washington. That suggested to Washington the useless-ness of the facility. He conferred that same day with General Nathanael Greene, who weeks before had been given responsibility for the fortress. Greene was certain that another Bunker Hill would result should Howe attack, and Washington committed another colossal blunder in permitting himself to be swayed by his subordinate. He later claimed that Greene's counsel had been "repugnant to my own judgment." While possibly accurate, it was no less true that Washington could not shake the spell that Bunker Hill held on him. What is more, he told his brother at this juncture that he was "wearied almost to death with the retrog[r]ade Motions"—that is, the constant retreating—of his army. Washington was more willing to have Howe attack Fort Washington than he subsequently acknowledged.[25]

Washington later contended that he spent three sleepless nights wrestling with whether to retain Fort Washington. The decision "caused [a] warfare in my mind," he said. If so, Howe ended Washington's brooding vacillation by attacking on November 16. Howe deployed thirteen thousand men, giving him better than a fourfold advantage. The British and Hessians had to climb steep and rugged precipices, surmount countless obstacles prepared by the defenders, and advance under heavy fire from rebels who waged a valorous and desperate fight for nearly two hours. Once the infantry reached the summit, the artillery was brought up. The Americans were doomed and they knew it. Five hours after the engagement started, the fortress that Greene had thought impregnable surrendered. In addition to the 149 rebel soldiers killed and wounded, the British took 2,870 prisoners, a considerable percentage of whom would die in captivity, many after enduring appalling suffering in the enemy's squalid prisons. Howe lost less than 4 percent of his men, a fraction of the cost he paid for taking Bunker Hill.[26]

Washington had made a grievous error in defending Fort Washington, but what followed was even more incxcusable. In the wake of the calamity on the east side of the Hudson, Washington permitted four full days to elapse before ordering the evacuation of Fort Lee on the New Jersey side of the Hudson, an installation that doubled as a large supply depot. It cost him dearly. On November 20, General Cornwallis, whom Howe had vested with responsibility for pursuing Washington, crossed the Hudson with six thousand assault troops, scaled the tall, rugged Jersey escarpment, moved speedily in the face of virtually no resistance, and seized Fort Lee. For a force as ill-provisioned as the Continental army, the losses were staggering. Cornwallis captured twelve cannon, six mortars, four thousand cannonballs, 2,800 muskets, four hundred thousand cartridges, five hundred entrenching tools, upwards of three hundred tents, one thousand barrels of flour, and untold amounts of baggage. In one week, the rebels had lost 146 pieces of artillery.[27]

"A Shudder went thro' the Continent," according to one congressman, when the citizenry learned of the November debacles. Samuel Adams glumly acknowledged that perhaps a majority in the mid-Atlantic states were now "determined to give it up." Some heaped the blame for America's plight on the reconciliationists in Congress, arguing that had they not delayed the declaring of independence, French aid might have been forthcoming that could have turned the tide in New York.[28]

Washington feared that his abilities would be questioned, and he did not have to wait long before discovering that some had lost confidence in him. Ten days after Fort Lee was taken, Washington learned that both Lee and Joseph Reed, once his secretary and all along his closest confidant in the army, thought him "curs'd with indecision" and convinced that his dithering would result in "eternal defeat."[29] For one as proud and ambitious as Washington, their lacerating criticism was mortifying. In the long run, however, Washington's awareness of their disapproval, as well of course as the pulsating anguish that he felt from his string of defeats, helped bring about substantive changes in his leadership.

Washington's first objective was to safeguard his army. He was up against a brave and experienced soldier. The thirty-six-year-old Cornwallis had spent nearly half his life in the army, studied in a military academy, and served with distinction in the European theater in the previous war. Cornwallis was perilously close by with a force that had rapidly swelled to 10,000. Washington had come to New Jersey from White Plains three weeks earlier with 2,000 Continentals and had been joined by about 1,500 militiamen. Washington ordered General Horatio Gates, who now commanded what still was euphemistically called the Canadian army, to send his Pennsylvania and

New Jersey regiments from northern New York. Similarly, Washington commanded Lee to march to New Jersey with as many of his men and those under Heath as could be spared. But as the enlistments for many soldiers expired on December 1, Washington had no idea how many men were coming or when they would arrive.[30]

Under a low granite sky, Cornwallis set off after the rebels on the day after he took Fort Lee, hoping to destroy Washington and, if fortune smiled, to take Philadelphia as well. The Americans had a day's head start, having already crossed the Hackensack River. Retreating southward from the hamlet of Hackensack, Washington's small force moved more rapidly than Cornwallis's large, plodding army, whose progress was hampered when the rebels felled trees and demolished bridges in their path, and when Washington posted pickets who lay in wait to force the enemy into small, vexing, time-consuming clashes. At times, Washington and Cornwallis were separated by as much as ten miles. On other occasions, the rear of the rebel army was leaving a small town while the redcoats' advance units entered it from the other side. At every step, Washington had to decide whether to break off and race for the safety of the Watchung Mountains at Morristown or to stay between Cornwallis and Philadelphia. Several officers urged the first option. Washington ignored their counsel and continued retreating to the south, hopeful that with Lee's troops he might make a stand somewhere in New Jersey. That was probably not a good idea, as he almost certainly would have been badly outnumbered and his chances of escaping would have been prob-lematic. He abandoned that option when, eight days into his retreat, Washington learned that Lee had not yet left White Plains. Astonished and suspicious—and above all furious—Washington resumed his retreat to the Delaware River, which his grimy, unshaven men crossed early in December, many making the passage at night in the eerie orange-yellow glow cast by fires set for illumination on each shore.[31]

The regulars ended the chase at the Delaware. Howe, who arrived on the scene and took command during the first week in December, chose to quit the campaign until spring. His decision leaves one to wonder if the war would have differed significantly had the start of the New York campaign not been pushed back because of Howe's springtime supply problems and subsequently further delayed by the tardy arrival of the Hessians and Clinton's force. Had Washington crossed the Delaware with his bedraggled band in, say, September instead of December, would Howe have taken Philadelphia—only a day or two's march away—and destroyed the rebels in his path as well?

But Howe, looking over the frigid, slate gray Delaware River in December, worried about his overextended lines, the impending onset of winter weather, and the very real difficulty of getting an army across the wide river in the face of determined resistance. Howe still had a considerable numerical superiority, though Washington's army was growing. Within a few days of crossing the Delaware, Washington's force had doubled to a bit over six thousand men. More militiamen had turned out, Gates' detachment was in camp, and twenty-six days after receiving the order to come south, Lee's men at last arrived too, though without their leader. En route, Lee unwisely chose to stay apart from this army in a tavern in Basking Ridge, New Jersey. Tipped off to his whereabouts by local Tories, a British scouting party captured him. Lee was a prisoner of war and would play no role in the Continental army's actions during the next fifteen months.[32]

Despite its many setbacks and often lackluster performance, the Continental army had survived 1776. But the "American Cause" was "in a critical situation," General Greene told Congress a few days before Christmas, and he pointed to what Samuel Adams had noted weeks before: the number of "disaffected" civilians was "dayly increasing."[33] Congress was quite aware of the crisis. Before it was clear that the enemy was suspending operations for the winter, Congress had fled Philadelphia for safer Baltimore.

Congress took two important steps before fleeing. It put Robert Morris in charge of an executive committee that was to see to the needs of the army. Given $200,000 and a free hand to draw on the Loan Office, Morris immediately dispatched to Washington all the provisions he could find. While it was on the run, Congress additionally granted Washington "full power to order and direct all things relative to . . . the operations of war." Two weeks later, on December 27, Congress stopped just short of vesting the commander in chief with dictatorial powers. Given the imperative need for "vigorous decisive Conduct" by the army's commander, Washington for a period of six months was authorized both to take whatever steps he deemed necessary within the army and to arrest those who were "disaffected to the American Cause."[34]

The gnawing popular disaffection also required immediate attention. Collapsing morale would make the recruitment of a new army in 1777 infinitely more difficult. In the emergency, officers in the highest echelons of the army turned to Thomas Paine in the hope that he could replicate the success of *Common Sense*. Paine was handy. Having joined a Philadelphia volunteer military company in July, he was with the army during its long, harrowing retreat across New Jersey. According to legend, Paine composed his initial tract in what would become *The American Crisis* by using a drum for a desk and a campfire for illumination. In actuality. Paine was furloughed to Philadelphia to facilitate his writing. Working in what he called "a rage" and "a passion of patriotism," Paine completed his radiant essay within ten days and it was published in a Philadelphia newspaper before Christmas. No writer ever began a piece with a more captivating hook:

> These are the time that try men's souls. The summer soldier and the sunshine patriot will, in this crisis, shrink from the service of their country; but he that stands it *now*, deserves the love and thanks of men and women.

Paine went on to vilify the king, lionize Washington, and exhort his readers to persevere in quest of their glorious cause. This essay may not have equaled the success of *Common Sense*, but many contemporaries thought Paine's composition "rallied and reanimated" the people, helping to restore hope and supplant irresolution with firmness.[35]

The black crisis of late 1776 was provoking change. To some degree, Washington, too, was reshaped by his recent tribulations and failures. Chastened by defeats and the errors that had contributed to those mortifying routs, Washington was now more inclined to trust his own judgment and to look askance on the advice of those around him who had so often been wrong. At times during the retreat he met individually with his general officers rather than in a formal council of war, and when the officers were formally convened, Washington increasingly thought of their opinions as advisory, not as binding. He also exerted more pressure to bend his subordinates to his way of thinking. Furthermore, by this juncture Washington had learned who usually offered good advice and whose counsel was often unsatisfactory.[36] One thing about Washington had not changed: he was a fighter. He loathed retreating and ached for action, and even more so now, as he knew there was a desperate need to restore faith in the cause. But that was not all. Washington was also eager to rekindle popular confidence in his leadership.

During the retreat, Washington had considered making a defensive stand, but in December he glimpsed another option. When Howe put his army into winter quarters, he divided and scattered his forces through four cantonments in New Jersey. Three were situated within a few miles of Washington's army, which was spread along the south bank of the Delaware. One enemy post was garrisoned by 1,500 Hessians in Trenton. Thinking it an inviting target for a surprise attack, Washington appears to have begun plotting an operation at least as early as the second week of the month, though he did not present it to a council of war until December 22. The officers approved his plan. It called for Washington to lead 2,400 men across the Delaware on Christmas night and to approach Trenton from the west. A second force of 800 Pennsylvania militiamen under General James Ewing was to cross the river directly south of the village. Colonel John Cadwalader was to lead 1,800 men across the Delaware twelve miles below Trenton. Cadwalader's job would be to seal the roads leading out of Trenton and prevent the enemy in the other cantonments from coming to the aid of their beleaguered comrades.

Christmas Day was cold but clear in the early hours, though late in the afternoon the weather began to fall apart as a whistling cold front blew in. First it rained, then sleet and snow pelted the area. All the while, the wind howled. Washington's men faced a march about as long as that made by the redcoats sent to Concord on the first day of the war—ten miles to the west to the site where they would cross the river, then nine miles back to Trenton. They went across the swirling, ice-clogged river in sturdy Durham boats ordinarily used for transporting heavy cargo to and from Philadelphia. On this night, the craft conveyed horses, eighteen burdensome pieces of field artillery, tons of ammunition, and the men.

The best-laid battle plans seldom unfold as intended, and this was no exception. No one could have foreseen the dreadful weather, though it in fact cut both ways. The terrible conditions diminished the enemy's expectations of an attack and muffled the sound of the approaching rebel army. On the other hand, only Washington's division overcame the storm-tossed river and made it to the other side, though he and his cold, weary men reached Trenton far behind schedule and had to launch their attack much longer after daybreak than the commander had wished.

The actual attack was brought off almost as mapped out on the drawing board. When the rebel artillery opened fire, the unsuspecting Hessians were still in their quarters. As they rushed into the streets, columns of Americans surged into the little village from three sides, trapping many of the enemy in a triangulated fire. In what now was lightly falling snow, the Germans tried to organize a counterattack, but were overwhelmed in a brief, savage fight. Less than sixty minutes after it began, the battle was over. Hessian losses exceeded one thousand men and a vast array of small arms, ammunition, and much-needed artillery. Fewer than ten Americans perished. It was a magnificent rebel victory, and it would have been greater had Cadwalader crossed the river and sealed the exits, preventing the escape of some five hundred of the Hessians.[37]

Trenton was to have been Washington's last action before he, too, went into winter quarters. However, when he learned from Cadwalader—who at last had crossed the Delaware—that the enemy troops that Howe had posted in Burlington and Bordentown were fleeing in disarray, Washington glimpsed the possibility not merely of another victory at the expense of the Hessians, but also of driving the British entirely out of New Jersey. His officers, some of whom found their confidence in Washington's judgment rekindled by the victory at Trenton, supported another shot at bearding the lion in his den. In perhaps his most audacious, and certainly his riskiest, gamble of the war, Washington crossed the Delaware yet again.

Unavoidable delays slowed the second crossing and Washington's last soldier did not alight on Jersey soil until December 31. Once in Trenton, Washington learned two things: his Hessian prey had escaped and reunited with Cornwallis near Princeton, only ten miles away, and Cornwallis was coming after him with a force of eight thousand men. Washington did not run. Yet again abandoning his Fabian strategy, Washington summoned Cadwalader's division. As January 2 dawned, dismally gray and cold, Washington's army had swelled to nearly seven thousand men. The American commander posted some men along the Trenton Road. Their job was to slow the enemy's advance and do as much damage as possible. The remainder, with thirty field pieces (several times the number Prescott had possessed on Bunker Hill), occupied the sloping ground above the Assunpink Creek. There, with their back to the Delaware River, these anxious men awaited the Second Battle of Trenton. Henry Knox acknowledged the army's "hazardous" position, and two of the soldiers described their situation as "most awful" and "momentous." One of the officers said that if ever there was "a crisis in affairs of the revolution, this was the moment."[38]

Cornwallis had a fight on his hands as he descended the Trenton Road. Early in the march, the British encountered pickets who fired on them, then vanished into the thick forests lining the road. For the regulars, it was unnerving, and deadly. Later, American units, sturdily positioned in the woods alongside the road, fought without flinching, though they were outnumbered by as many as six to one. Washington's strategy worked. Only an hour of daylight remained when Cornwallis at last reached the Assunpink. To get to Washington, Cornwallis's men had to first cross the creek. They never made it. Cornwallis ordered an assault, then another by his shock troops. The regulars struggled valiantly in the face of the murderous fire poured down on them. An American soldier, looking down in disbelief on a creek whose crystal blue water had turned a ghastly red and on a bridge and creek bank that were littered with bodies, called it a "great Slaughter." As night stole over the region, the fighting ended. Already, nearly five hundred of Cornwallis's men had been killed or wounded. Cornwallis did not despair. Washington was trapped. "We've got the Old Fox safe now. We'll go over and bag him in the morning," he allegedly predicted.[39]

But Washington's army escaped the trap, just as it had earlier broken out of snares in Brooklyn and Harlem Heights. During the bitterly cold night, the Americans slipped away, not across the Delaware River, but toward the north.

They were guided by Joseph Reed, who had studied in Princeton and was familiar with the back roads in the region. When Washington's army reached Princeton in the first soft glow of sunrise, Cornwallis had only just discovered that his quarry had made its getaway. On reaching Princeton, Washington's much larger force collided with seven hundred regulars who were just stepping off toward Trenton to reinforce Cornwallis. A torrid fight ensued. Washington personally led his men and at times was no farther from the gun-wielding, red-clad regulars than is a batter from the pitcher on a baseball diamond. Somehow, Washington survived unscathed. Successful in that short, savage battle, Washington pushed on into the village itself. More heavy fighting raged in the town and on the campus of what now is Princeton University, leaving a bitter pall of smoke hanging over the buildings where young scholars had only recently studied. With numbers on their side, a rare occurrence in this war, the Americans inflicted heavy losses. Some 450 redcoats were killed, wounded, or captured in the brief, sharp engagement at Princeton.[40]

Washington had gambled and won spectacularly, but he wisely opted not to roll the dice again and send his weary troops up against Cornwallis, who he knew would be marching for Princeton. Leaving behind the fresh smell of carnage, Washington marched his army to hilly, safe Morristown, where it entered winter quarters.

The historic campaign of 1776 was over at last. The final days, between December 25 and January 3, had been catastrophic for the British. Their losses totaled approximately 1,730. American losses were about 155.[41]

In retrospect, 1776 was the year in which Great Britain perhaps had its best chance to destroy the American rebellion. Instead, it had failed to win the war, and as 1777 dawned, the United States witnessed a palpable resurgence of optimism.

CHAPTER 10

"ACROSS AMERICA IN A HOP, STEP, AND A JUMP"

THE CAMPAIGNS OF 1777

As 1777 DAWNED, the United States, nearly two years after hostilities erupted, was better prepared for waging war. Its generals, from Washington down, were more experienced, and morale had soared as a result of the daring strikes at Trenton and Princeton, leaving congressmen to excitedly—and hopefully—insist that the "face of affairs is greatly changed." That was partly due to France. Though not openly allies, the French followed Julien de Bonvouloir's return home by beginning to clandestinely funnel aid to the Americans. Early in the year, a Carolina congressman exclaimed that the "French begin to shew their teeth." He cataloged the arrival from France of two hundred field artillery pieces, thirty thousand muskets, tons of powder, and five hundred thousand livres. The Continental army was thought to be stronger, too, and not solely because of French aid. It had been transformed from a citizens' army of short-term volunteers to a standing army.[1]

When Washington's army of one-year enlistees vanished at the end of 1775, he appealed to Congress to lengthen the period of enlistment. To make men "well acquainted with the Duties of a Soldier" and to "bring [a soldier] under proper discipline & Subordination ... requires time," he had counseled. Congress, awash with forebodings of standing armies, had not listened. But in the fall of 1776, with its second army about to disappear in the face of a large British force that was within a day's march of Philadelphia, Congress agreed to a three-year period of enlistment, though men could still engage for shorter stretches. Congress offered enticing cash and land bounties to persuade men to sign on for lengthier service and states pitched in as well. One-third of those who enlisted in Massachusetts in 1777 agreed to long-term service. In time, Washington would command battle-hardened veterans. Congressional acquiescence to Washington's wishes substantively transformed the Continental army. Previously, the soldiery had been something of a cross-section of the population of freemen in America, but farmers and tradesmen faced with creditors, tax collectors, and maintaining farms and shops were unwilling to serve for years. Beginning in 1777, young, poor, single men who owned no property made up the backbone of the army, and Congress had to proffer cash and land bounties to get them. As Congress assigned each state a quota of troops to provide, some resorted to conscription to raise their share. Not every state met its quota. Congress hoped to put 75,000 men under arms in 1777, but the army peaked that year at 39,443.[2]

Although the United States may have been stronger, it faced a formidable foe, and one that in some respects was more powerful than during the campaign of 1776. Worried about French intervention the previous year, London had kept much of its fleet in home waters, so that less than 40 percent of the Royal Navy crossed to North America. But Britain's successes in Canada and New York led the government to believe that the French were disillusioned with the rebels and would remain neutral. North's government committed six additional ships of the line to America in 1777. It also sent over another six thousand redcoats, a number that came close to offsetting the losses sustained in 1776. Lord Germain, fed up with Guy Carleton's lack of daring and aggressiveness, cashiered him as commander of Britain's army in Canada, replacing him with General John Burgoyne, who was brimming with passion for action.[3] Germain also conceived a well-informed strategy for gaining control of the Hudson River and winning the war.

Back in November, while Earl Cornwallis was chasing Washington across New Jersey, General Howe had crafted the initial plan for Britain's campaign in 1777. Howe envisaged a feint at Philadelphia, a move that he hoped would force Washington to remain in Pennsylvania. With Washington out of the picture, Howe planned to send ten thousand men to retake Rhode Island—and bottle up hordes of Yankee soldiers in the process—while another army of comparable size advanced up the Hudson to Albany, where it would rendezvous with the redcoats who were to invade New York from Canada. With the Hudson in hand and New England forced into the backwater of the war, the united British army would sweep across the Delaware River and reclaim the mid-Atlantic and southern colonies.[4] Germain endorsed the plan. But the events at Trenton and Princeton, and a nagging conviction that the British army was insufficient for carrying out the original plan, led Howe to rethink matters. He sent two additional plans to Germain. Both centered on taking Philadelphia and leaving the army descending from Canada to its own devices.[5]

Working through Howe's assorted plans, as well as one submitted by Burgoyne, Germain put together his own plan for a campaign in 1777, which he submitted to the monarch and the ministry. It was approved, though along the way Germain had to make compromises, and as always, he gave his commanders considerable latitude in implementing strategy. Burgoyne, with an army of regulars, Hessians, Canadian volunteers, and Indian allies, was to invade northern New York. While Burgoyne advanced on Ticonderoga with the main army, a smaller joint force of regulars and Indians was to create a diversion in the Mohawk Valley to siphon off enemy troops from Burgoyne's path. The two British forces were to combine after Burgoyne took Ticonderoga and jointly advance to Albany. Howe, meanwhile, was free to go after Philadelphia, though the administration made it clear that taking the Hudson was to be the focal point of that year's operations. Authorization for Howe to campaign for Philadelphia was based on the sensible assumption that he would launch operations in the spring so that he could complete the job in Pennsylvania by early summer. By the first week in May, Howe knew what his government wanted. Yet he disregarded its wishes and ignored the army descending from Canada.[6]

Howe remained inactive until June, when he wasted still more time by unavailingly marching his army to Somerset, a few miles above Princeton, in the hope of luring Washington into battle. Wiser than in 1776, and no longer concerned that Congress was breathing down his neck, Washington was not about to be drawn into an unwanted action. He remained inactive. Howe returned empty-handed to New York, where both Cornwallis and Sir Henry Clinton, the second-ranking officer in Britain's army in America, inveighed against a campaign for Philadelphia and urged that the army proceed toward Albany to rendezvous with Burgoyne. Howe did not listen. He stubbornly held to his plans to campaign for Philadelphia.[7] By the time he departed, Burgoyne's army was already in New York and in trouble.

Once the ice on the St. Lawrence River broke up in late April, Burgoyne was on his way. Ten years older than Washington, Burgoyne hailed from the gentry, though by marrying the fifteen-year-old daughter of an earl, he got one foot in the door of Britain's aristocracy. He had entered the army when he was fifteen, but on a couple of occasions had left the military to cope with debts that piled up from his compulsive gambling. As a soldier, Burgoyne performed with courage and valor, and his rise in the ranks was nothing short of meteoric; he vaulted from captain to brigadier general in six years. He was bright, charming, energetic, reputed to be a daring thinker in the field of military science, able at networking, and a consummate master of politics within the military establishment. Along the way, he had acted in and written plays for the theater, and he brought to bear the skills of a thespian in selling himself to key officials in London as a more forceful and intrepid warrior than Generals Carleton and Howe could ever hope to be. Some saw through his performance and lampooned him, dubbing him "General Swagger" and "Julius Caesar Burgonius." At least one observer judged him "more sail than ballast." However, perhaps from desperation after the disappointments of 1776, Germain bought what Burgoyne was selling.[8]

Burgoyne left behind 3,800 men to defend Canada, nearly four times the number that had repulsed the rebel invasion in 1775. He also relinquished 675 men to Colonel Barry St. Leger, who was to command the Mohawk Valley enterprise. That left Burgoyne with 7,250 regulars, about 15 percent fewer than he had expected London to furnish for the invasion force. Nor was that his only disappointment. He had looked forward to being accompanied by 1,000 Native Americans, but only half that number stepped forward to join him. Furthermore, on landing at Quebec, Burgoyne found only 300 men under arms in Canadian militia and Loyalist units. He had anticipated seven times that number. Burgoyne was neither the first nor the last British general to be led astray by the belief that large numbers of zealous Tories would take up arms to fight for their king. Curiously, he was not terribly dismayed, as he confidently looked forward to an avid turnout of Tories once he crossed into New York.[9]

Burgoyne's first objective was to retake Fort Ticonderoga, which Germain had thought Carleton would capture the previous summer or fall. That the installation was not yet in British hands was due in part to Carleton's unhurried and cautious habits, though the Americans had played a substantial role in keeping their enemy at bay. During the retreat from Canada in the spring of 1776, Benedict Arnold had conferred in Albany with General Schuyler, the commander of the Continental army's Northern Department. Reasoning that Carleton would have to construct a large fleet to transport his considerable army and its supplies up Lake Champlain to get at Fort Ticonderoga, Schuyler and Arnold planned the construction of a sufficient number of rebel crafts to challenge their foe. Arnold and Schuyler never imagined that they could defeat the British; instead, their object was to delay the enemy's advance, forestalling any attempted invasion of New York until 1777. During the interim, the defenses at Fort Ticonderoga were to be strengthened, with an eye on making the fortress impregnable.

In the course of sixty-eight days during the summer of 1776, while Washington awaited Howe's blow to fall in New York, an American squadron consisting of fifteen vessels—gondolas and row galleys—was constructed near Fort Ticonderoga. The little fleet was launched on September 1. More than a month passed before Carleton's navy with twice as many vessels—and twice the firepower—was completed and ready to sail. The first major clash occurred at Valcour Bay, with Arnold in command of the rebel defenders. It was a standoff, but during the next few days Carleton's warships repeatedly scored wins. The Americans lost two-thirds of their fleet and suffered a 25 percent casualty rate during the October fighting. But the month was nearly over and the season's first snow had fallen before Carleton was ready to test Fort Ticonderoga's defenses. After a brief probe, he concluded that it was too deep into autumn to launch an attack, or a siege, and early in November the British fleet sailed empty-handed back to Canada. Not a few historians have concluded that "the American cause . . . was saved" by the stout-hearted actions taken by Schuyler and especially Arnold.[10] Their vision and daring had prevented Carleton from invading northern New York at the very moment that Howe was invading southern New York, twin blows that might have proven fatal to the American Revolution. Fort Ticonderoga was still in American hands at the close of 1776 and the British—under Burgoyne— would have to take it before they could invade New York in 1777.

Taking Fort Ticonderoga was Burgoyne first objective when he set off up Lake Champlain in late May. The British commander was clearly more ener- getic than Carleton, and he displayed a degree of confidence seldom visible in his predecessor. However, only scant days into his campaign, Burgoyne received shocking news. In a communiqué from Howe, Burgoyne learned for the first time that the main British army was headed for Philadelphia, not Albany. Burgoyne now knew that he was on his own.[11]

A rebel army of 3,800 men under Major General Arthur St. Clair awaited the British invasion force at Fort Ticonderoga. St. Clair had soldiered in Britain's army in the previous war, serving under William Howe. But follow- ing his marriage to a woman from Boston, St. Clair resigned his commission and settled in the colonies. After joining the Continental army in 1775, he had fought in Canada and at Trenton and Princeton. St. Clair did not assume command at Ticonderoga until Burgoyne had begun his descent southward. Although Ticonderoga was widely reputed to be invulnerable, with some even calling it America's Gibraltar, St. Clair discovered that it was in a woebe- gone state. The British had permitted it to decay before 1775, and General Schuyler, who had been responsible for the installation for the past two years, had done little to rehabilitate it. In addition, St. Clair found that he had less than a six-week supply of food. A siege would doom him. Furthermore, a mile to the southwest stood Mount Defiance. Although it towered over the fort, Schuyler had left it undefended, acting on the belief that the enemy could never get artillery to its steep summit. St. Clair was not so sure.[12]

Burgoyne's force arrived at the end of June, and within a week his Hessians had artillery atop Mount Defiance. St. Clair, backed by a council of war, ordered a retreat. Hardly a shot had been fired and Fort Ticonderoga was back in British hands. The redcoats also gained more than fifty precious pieces of heavy artillery that St. Clair had abandoned when he took flight. Burgoyne kept his army moving, and within two weeks he also took Fort Anne, several miles farther south. Schuyler was at home in Albany, ninety miles away, when he learned of the debacle. He rode to Fort Edward, halfway to Ticonderoga, and from there wrote to Washington that the army—wherever it was, for he had no idea where St. Clair had gone—was "weak in Numbers, dispirited, naked ... destitute of provisions ... with little Ammunition, and not a single piece of Cannon."[13]

A few days later, St. Clair's army, which had split into two divisions when fleeing Ticonderoga, reunited at Fort Edward. Schuyler took command. Soon, too, he learned that reinforcements were coming. Washington had ordered 1,900 men to march for northern New York, and militiamen were on the way as well. By early August, Schuyler's force had grown to 6,359.[14]

For all of Burgoyne's bluster and bravado about acting boldly and resolutely—he "promises to cross America in a hop, step, and a jump," a doubtful detractor in London had noted earlier—the British commander did not move from Fort Anne for three weeks. Though unaware of the true state of his enemy in mid-July, Burgoyne knew the rebels were divided, in disarray, without artillery, and outnumbered. The ease with which he had taken Ticonderoga also led him to the conclusion that the rebels "have no men of military science." Burgoyne had to realize that every day he delayed was a day when more militiamen might arrive in the enemy camp. Given what he knew, Burgoyne might have sent his light infantry forward. Unencumbered by heavy artillery and the need to maintain an elaborate supply network, it could have lived off the land as it swiftly advanced. To have done so would have been quite risky, but Burgoyne had promised to be a risk taker. Instead, he turned cautious. Day after day passed while Burgoyne gathered supplies for his army and brought up his cumbersome train of artillery. In the past month, his army had swept across 150 miles; in the next month, it advanced only 22 miles.[15]

Meanwhile, Schuyler was an uncharacteristic whirlwind of activity, working tirelessly to find supplies and putting his men to work destroying bridges, felling trees across roads, constructing interlaced timber barriers, burning crops, driving away livestock, diverting some streams and plugging up others. He was "let[ting] the forest fight for him," as Washington had advised, forestalling the day when his army would have to fight Burgoyne, hopeful that in the meantime his force would continue to grow.[16]

When Burgoyne at last began to move again, his progress was slow—very slow. His snail-like pace arose from the demands of moving and provisioning

1,500 horses and an army half the size of the population of Boston, and from the grueling, time-consuming work of clearing the obstacles put in his path by the enemy. Furthermore, the men had to construct forty bridges and a two-mile-long causeway over a morass. By the second week in August, Burgoyne was ready to cross the Hudson for the final descent toward Albany, fifty miles away. He still expected to reach his objective before the end of the month. But every day seemed to bring a new problem.

On July 27, Burgoyne's Indian allies murdered Jane McCrea, who lived on New York's frontier. The rebels immediately seized on the propaganda possibilities of this wanton act. A widely printed statement from American headquarters excoriated the British army for "barbarously" turning loose the "savages" to perpetrate unspeakable atrocities. Remaining mum about the fact that McCrae was engaged to a Loyalist officer serving with the British, she was portrayed as a "lady lovely to the sight" who had been "scalped and mangled." Fear already suffused New York's frontier. Now anger welled up and militiamen poured forth to defend home and hearth.[17]

Burgoyne may have thought things could not get worse, but they did. With his supply lines stretching back 150 miles to Montreal, and with comestibles scarce because of Schuyler's scorched-earth policy, Burgoyne was growing desperate for food. He detached 750 Hessians to seize the large rebel supply depot at Bennington, about twenty miles east of the Hudson. That mission turned into a ghastly replay of Gage's foray to Concord some thirty months before. Encountering a numerically superior force of New Hampshire militia, the Germans were routed, and so too was a relief detachment. Altogether, Burgoyne lost 900 men. He already had left behind some 1,400 men to hold Crown Point and Ticonderoga.[18]

A few days later Burgoyne got still more bad news. Colonel St. Leger would neither be joining him nor containing enemy militiamen in the Mohawk Valley. The Indians with St. Leger had scored a bloody victory in an ambush at Oriskany, killing, wounding, and capturing more than 450 Tryon County militiamen. It was the only success he could point to. Otherwise, his expedition had failed, in part because the anticipated outpouring of New York's Loyalists had not occurred. Around the time that Burgoyne captured Fort Ticonderoga, St. Leger attacked Fort Stanwix, a rebel-held installation on the Mohawk River. Failing to take his prize, St. Leger settled in for a siege. While the siege dragged on, Schuyler sent a relief force led by General Benedict Arnold, recently ordered north by Washington. Arnold spoiled for a fight, but was disappointed. On the eve of battle, he sent ahead a Tory—who may have acted in return for having been pardoned from a death sentence—to spread the tattle that Arnold's once-diminutive force had grown to considerable proportions. St. Leger's Indian allies believed the story and deserted en masse. Now actually heavily outnumbered, and seeing that he could never reach Burgoyne, St. Leger retreated to Canada in August.[19]

A retreat to Canada might also have been advisable for Burgoyne. Autumn beckoned as he approached the Hudson and faced his most difficult decision. Once he took his army across the river, he would cut his umbilical cord to Ticonderoga and Canada. Furthermore, once he crossed the Hudson, the enemy might prevent his passage back across the river. Burgoyne's men were often hungry and bone-tired from weeks of arduous labor in New York's close, sultry forests. His army was depleted, few Tories had turned out, the Indians were abandoning the campaign, and Howe had forsaken him. But Burgoyne kept going. On September 14 his army crossed the Hudson, using a bridge of boats to get across. After all the boastful assurances he had made in London, perhaps he dared not throw in the towel in the face of adversity. Or perhaps his stubborn advance owed more to his total ignorance of the enemy—its size, its composition, its leadership, even its whereabouts. Burgoyne had to have guessed that his adversary was growing stronger. Seventy days had passed since the fall of Ticonderoga, more than ample time for swarms of militiamen to reach the front. Maybe he still scoffed at the military skill of rebel leaders. If so, he might have been disabused of such a notion had he known that the enemy army was no longer led by Schuyler, an amateur soldier, but by Horatio Gates, who had once been an officer in the British army.

Shock and outrage in Congress had greeted the news of the loss of Ticonderoga. It was the latest in a string of disasters on Schuyler's watch, and for many congressmen it was the final straw. Samuel Adams railed at this general who never seemed to be with his army; with Schuyler in command, said John Adams, catastrophes were to be expected. They wanted Schuyler out and Gates in.[20] From the outset, the Adamses represented the majority opinion in Congress, though fear of a political earthquake in New York prevented the delegates from immediately showing Schuyler the door. But on August 4, with even New York deserting him, Congress by an 11–1 vote recalled St. Clair and replaced Schuyler with Gates.[21]

Born in England to a family of commoners, Gates gained the assistance of well-connected aristocrats who secured his appointment as an officer in the British army. He served for eighteen years, nearly all of them in America and much of them in staff positions. During the 1755 Anglo-American campaign to drive the French from the head of the Ohio River, he met Washington and others who would subsequently become Continental army leaders. He left the British army in 1763, despairing of promotion above the rank of major, but also disenchanted with England because of his growing political radicalism. In 1772 he moved to Virginia and settled on an estate about fifty miles from Mount Vernon. Three years later, when the Continental army was created, Washington successfully beseeched Congress to include Gates in the initial batch of general officers. Gates participated in the siege of Boston and the preparation of defenses in New York before being named to replace Sullivan as commander of the so-called army in Canada.

Forty-nine years old in 1777, Gates did not match what many thought a soldier should look like, and, to be sure, he bore no resemblance to General Washington in appearance or manner. Overweight, not more than average height, slightly stooped, and seldom seen without his spectacles, Gates looked smaller and older than he really was. Burgoyne, in fact, once remarked that Gates resembled an "old midwife," and the troops under his command affectionately referred to him as "Granny Gates." Gates's polite, engaging, and mild-mannered demeanor won him an abundance of friends. But his years as a soldier had left their stamp on him. Few could match him when it came to cursing, and his conversations were sprinkled with ribald stories, leaving one shocked onlooker to observe that Gates's salty language would make "a New Englandman's hair almost stand on end." Gates was also ambitious and extraordinarily political. With success, he did what he could to cultivate congressmen and secure command of the Northern Department. Samuel Adams was among the adherents that he won in Congress. The situation in New York was "Bad," though "not ruinous," Adams thought, and he added that Gates's record of outstanding leadership "affords a flattering Prospect" that Burgoyne could be stopped short of Albany.[22]

Gates took command of the army nearly four weeks before Burgoyne crossed the Hudson. Schuyler's delaying efforts were crucial to what lay ahead, but so too was Gates's leadership. He restored morale in the dispirited army and persuaded Yankee militiamen to join him, something they had been loath to do while the imperious and aristocratic Schuyler was in charge. Now the army really grew, and not solely because of the New England militia. It was Gates who had authored the sensational piece on the murder of Jane McCrea. Following its publication, New York militia poured in. More than a week before Burgoyne crossed the Hudson, Gates posted his force at Bemis Heights and awaited the arrival of his adversary. The American army was anchored by the Hudson on one side and steep, craggy bluffs on the other, and it was well entrenched. Gates's defensive position resembled Washington's at White Plains, though on a more massive scale. Howe, despite enjoying a numerical superiority, had been unable to break through Washington's lines. Numbers were not on Burgoyne's side: Gates's force was nearly twice the size of Burgoyne's. What is more, Gates had another eight thousand men in reserve that he could call on. Given the immense size of his army, the terrain, and his more abundant artillery—nearly all of which had been provided by France, as had 90 percent of the weaponry and ammunition in the rebel force—Gates had advantages that the rebel forces at Bunker Hill and on the slope overlooking the Assunpink could only have dreamed of. In retrospect, Burgoyne's force was doomed the moment it crossed the Hudson.[23]

Burgoyne's only chance of reaching Albany was by fighting his way through Gates's force. It could not be done. He tried twice, in engagements fought two weeks apart and known to history as the Battles of Freeman's Farm and Bemis Heights, or by some as the First and Second Battles of Saratoga. As the first clash neared, General Arnold, now part of Gates's army, beseeched his commander to attack the advancing redcoats rather than waiting behind his fortifications for the blow to fall. Gates, wisely, wanted no part of such a strategy. He had a better understanding of how to use militiamen and a thorough grasp of the virtues of defensive tactics against an army of European regulars. Gates's judgment was sound. Burgoyne could not break through, and roughly 20 percent of the British force was lost in the engagement, twice the percentage of American losses.

Arnold refused to acknowledge that Gates had been right, and his simmering anger, stemming from a multitude of issues, finally combusted a few days following the battle. Arnold confronted Gates at headquarters in a heated clash that observers characterized as "passionate" and conducted in "a very high strain." Both men used "high words and gross language." Gates may have been furious, but he admired Arnold's abilities as a leader and a fighter and wanted his presence in the looming second battle. However, a few days after their tempestuous session, Arnold sent Gates a malign letter filled with affronts, including charges that Gates had lost touch with his troops and was jealous of Arnold's abilities. Arnold predicted that if Gates did not take the offensive, Burgoyne would exploit his weakness and succeed in escaping back to Ticonderoga. That was too much. Gates removed Arnold from command.

Then, when Burgoyne made his second attempt to break through, in the Battle of Bemis Heights on October 7, Arnold lost control of himself. In the words of a biographer, Arnold, "Jaw thrust out, bulldog fashion, and pale eyes afire . . . harshly shouted that no man would keep him in his tent that day." Some said that he was under the influence of strong drink, others that a dose of opium led him to act, and still others attributed his action to temporary insanity. Whatever the cause, Arnold rode into the battle and seized control of an American brigade. The men followed him, as always. He performed with valor and succeeded in driving the enemy from an important redoubt before suffering a gunshot wound in the leg.

Once again, Burgoyne failed to break through Gates's defenses. This time, Burgoyne lost more than 30 percent of his force. Some historians think that Arnold's intrepid conduct was the key to the American victory, and even Gates was moved to report to Congress on Arnold's "gallant" behavior under fire. But Gates did not think that Arnold's exploits decided the battle, and the evidence substantiates the commander's conclusion. The American defenders simply possessed too many advantages for Burgoyne to overcome, whether or not Arnold was a part of the Battle of Bemis Heights.[24]

Between the two bloody clashes, Burgoyne sent two messages to Sir Henry Clinton in Manhattan asking for help. Clinton's response was one of the more mysterious occurrences in this war. He did nothing to rescue Burgoyne's belea- guered army until after the second battle, when he gathered a small flotilla that sailed only about fifty miles above New York City in a halfhearted—and unsuc- cessful—move to draw off some of Gates's units. After the second losing battle, Burgoyne called a council of war. Many wished to abandon their baggage and make a run for Ticonderoga or at least Fort Edward; some thought in terms of an every-man-for-himself flight. But Ticonderoga was fifty-five miles away. It was an option certain to end in catastrophe, and it was rejected. The army withdrew to nearby Saratoga. The campaign to reach Albany was over. The Americans had "yarded Burgoyne," as the New Englanders put it.

Burgoyne languished in Saratoga for a week, hoping against hope that Clinton would rescue him. The week was an unmitigated nightmare. It was piercingly cold. It rained intermittently. Food was in short supply. American snipers took a deadly toll. Horses and cattle died. An inescapable stench permeated everything. The camp was a squalid hellhole. The soldiers were wet, muddy, tired, defeated.[25]

On October 14, with no sign of Clinton, Burgoyne waved a white flag. His once-promising campaign had ended disastrously, victimized by Howe's decision not to come north, Schuyler's adroit use of the only weapons at his disposal, and Gates's cautious by-the-book defensive campaign. Nor was Burgoyne blameless. He had not only left behind far too many men in a Canada that was unlikely to be seriously threatened, but when audacity was needed, he had also turned uncharacteristically wary. Above all, however, there was the matter that had been raised in the ministry's prewar discus- sions about using force. Some officials had warned that it would be extraordin- arily difficult, perhaps impossible, to successfully campaign in America's backcountry. Their nagging doubts had been swept aside by a majority filled with the arrogance of power. Burgoyne and his men paid the piper.

Talks between Burgoyne and Gates dragged on for three days. Initially, Gates demanded unconditional surrender. Burgoyne haggled, buying a few more days. Gates worried constantly that a relief expedition might arrive from New York. Eventually, Gates's fear that his prey—his prize—would slip from his grasp led him to negotiate a less-than-satisfactory "convention." The word "capitulation" was not included in the document. The terms stipulated that the captured regulars could sail for Great Britain after taking a pledge to never again soldier in America in this war. The Loyalists and Canadians were to be guaranteed safe passage to Canada.[26]

The next day, October 17, 1777, company after company, brigade after brigade of British and Germans soldiers—described by one witness as "poor, dirty, emaciated men"—gloomily marched to the despondent beat of drums and stacked their arms. Rebel musicians, kept out of sight but not of earshot, played "Yankee Doodle." The surrender of 5,895 enemy soldiers took four hours to complete. When it was done, the captives began the long march to Boston and a future that was more uncertain than suggested in the Convention of Saratoga.[27]

No one was more surprised than Washington when Howe did not in "good policy" seek to "form a junction up" the Hudson with Burgoyne. The commander's aide-de-camp, Alexander Hamilton, no doubt reflected his boss's outlook when he said that should Howe "cooperate with Burgoigne, it would demand our utmost efforts to counteract them." In June, Washington had marched his Continentals north of Manhattan in preparation for a campaign to prevent the British from taking control of the river from Albany to New York City. Several weeks later he learned that Howe was coming after Philadelphia, a revelation that led Hamilton—and perhaps Washington, too—to conclude that Howe was "fool enough to meditate" abandoning Burgoyne.[28]

Historians have shared Washington's disbelief at Howe's strategic decision. Their views, of course, were colored by knowledge of Burgoyne's catastrophic defeat at Saratoga. Howe did not know what would be the outcome of Burgoyne's campaign, having formulated his plan for the campaign of 1777 before the British army departed Canada. Furthermore, waiting to embark for Philadelphia until he learned that Ticonderoga had fallen, Howe knew when he set out on his campaign that Burgoyne had gotten off to an exceptionally good start.

Given what he knew in the middle of the summer of 1777, Howe's decision to make Philadelphia his objective was not as incomprehensible as it later seemed. Howe's starting point was the belief "that the defeat of the rebel regular army is the surest road to peace."[29] He cherished the hope that Washington would have to fight to protect such an important city as Philadelphia, and given his adversary's copious mistakes the previous summer, Howe did not doubt that he could destroy Washington's army if he could only get it onto a battlefield. Furthermore, Howe presumed that the seizure of both New York and Philadelphia would sow enormous economic hardship throughout the mid-Atlantic backcountry, a region in which support of American independence had been only lukewarm before July 1776. Howe, as has often been alleged without compelling evidence, might even have imagined that the psychological blow of losing the city that was home to Congress would have a crumpling effect on the rebels.

Howe could have marched his army from Manhattan to Philadelphia, a distance of one hundred miles. But worries over the maintenance of such an extended supply line led him to spurn an overland passage. Instead, Howe went by sea, expecting a swift, easy passage to the Delaware Valley. Howe loaded sixteen thousand men into a fleet of 267 ships. The armada weighed anchor on July 23, weeks after Germain had hoped that Howe's army would have already completed its mission in Pennsylvania and started northward for Albany. The voyage was a nightmare. Unable to draw favorable winds, the fleet remained at sea for more than a month. Having suffered from blinding heat, worm-infested food, and tainted water, the soldiers were in no shape to campaign when they at last landed on August 25 at Head of Elk, Maryland, about fifty miles southwest of Philadelphia. Howe was compelled to wait nearly two weeks for his men to regain their stamina before he could set off for Philadelphia. What is more, as some 350 of his horses perished during the grueling voyage, Howe's force was largely deprived of its cavalry arm.[30]

Washington had never planned to resist the enemy's landing. Initially, he may have been undecided on how best to respond to the invaders, but at some point in the three weeks following his arrival in Wilmington and Howe's nearly simultaneous landing at Head of Elk, Washington decided to abandon the Fabian strategy that had served him well and to fight a pitched battle. In some respects it was a surprising decision, as not even his aide Alexander Hamilton believed that Howe could be prevented from taking Philadelphia.[31]

Several factors may have influenced Washington's thinking. He had ample time to prepare for battle, even to choose the location of the encounter, and his army of sixteen thousand was the same size as his adversary's. In addition, much might be gained should Howe be made to pay a heavy price for taking Philadelphia. In combination with Burgoyne's looming disaster— of which Washington was fully aware—London might be led to make peace. Or France, seeing the ultimate defeat of the rebels as now increasingly unlikely, might be drawn into the war. One of Washington's young officers thought his commander had "made a sacrifice of his own judgment upon the altar of public opinion."[32] What he was saying was that Washington had chosen to fight because he feared Congress would be unhappy if he did not make a major effort to save Philadelphia and prevent the congressmen from having to flee yet again. That was not improbable. Nor was it inconceivable that Washington, who had begun to expect that Gates was on the cusp of scoring a huge victory over Burgoyne, might have been driven to fight from fear that another American general would win the laurels for American success in 1777. Washington would also have been less than human had he not wondered if the Congress that had dumped Schuyler in favor of Gates might turn on him should he not stand and fight Howe's advancing army.

Washington's showdown with Howe came on September 11, a warm, late-summer day. Washington posted his army behind Brandywine Creek along the road to Philadelphia and awaited his enemy's attempt to slug its way through. But Howe did not cooperate. He chose a strategy identical to the one he had pursued on Long Island a year earlier. While making a feint at the center of Washington's line, Howe attempted to flank the right wing of the Continental lines by getting his army across Jeffries Ford. The British commander very nearly succeeded, because, as on Long Island, Washington once again had failed to adequately reconnoiter the field. The American commander went into the battle unaware that the Brandywine could be crossed north of the battlefield. Intelligence of Howe's flank march repeatedly reached Washington during the battle. Time and again, however, he dismissed the reports as inaccurate. Once, he laughed openly as the information was communicated, and for an agonizingly long time he continued to reinforce the center of his line. Furthermore, although Washington in the wake of his New York disasters had learned of the need for cavalry and had persuaded Congress to authorize four mounted regiments consisting of three thousand troopers, he failed to utilize his horse soldiers as a mobile strike force on the Brandywine, a step that could have delayed or stopped Howe's advance before it became a grave threat.[33]

Washington's army was saved largely because it was a more experienced force than the one on Long Island and did not disintegrate in panic when it was surprised. Though outnumbered by nearly two to one, the Continentals on the American right fought courageously, holding off the enemy until Washington, hours into the fray, finally comprehended the threat and rushed in reinforcements from the center of his line. The fight continued for several additional hours. Washington was in the thick of it during those final hours, and he was desperately vulnerable. As the sun laid heavy on what only days earlier had been bucolic Pennsylvania farmland, Washington had ridden at a gallop, spurring his horse to leap over fences, to take command in the imperiled sector. The American right held. Howe was stopped.

But mortal danger still stalked the Continentals. Late in the day, redcoat and Hessian grenadiers fought their way across the creek and through the now-depleted rebel center. The British were close—perilously close—to overcoming the Americans' weak left wing. If they succeeded, the center of the rebel lines would be enveloped, and Washington's entire force would be threatened with a crippling defeat. But in the muted light of dusk, the Americans once again stood and fought with tenacity and valor, mounting a stout resistance until the sinking sun brought an end to the day's fiery encounter. A British sergeant thought Washington's army would have suffered a "total overthrow" had there been one more hour of daylight. Some Americans said nearly the same thing. No one can know what would have occurred in another hour of fighting. What is known is that Washington did not wish to risk a second day of battle. Under the cloak of darkness, he withdrew his army from the Brandywine that evening.[34]

Soldiers on both sides thought it one of the hottest clashes they ever experienced. Battles tend to be confusing to participants, who are assaulted by a colossal din, gruesome sights, and, above all, blinding terror. Of all the descriptions of the chaotic awfulness of the Battle of Brandywine left by the men who fought in it, perhaps that of Private Elisha Stevens best captured the horror: "The Battel was ... Cannons Roaring muskets Cracking Drums Beating Bombs Flying all Round, men a dying wounimeds Horred Grones which would Greave the Heardist of Hearts to See Such a manner as this."[35]

Following his close brush at Brandywine, Washington reverted to his Fabian strategy, though he repeatedly told Congress that he was anxious to fight again. He left the impression that he planned to assail the redcoats as they sought to make a cumbrous crossing of the Schuylkill River en route to Philadelphia, but Washington did little more than order three divisions—perhaps 20 percent of his army—to harass the rear of Howe's advancing force. (At Paoli, the division led by General Anthony Wayne was surprised in a midnight attack that resulted in the loss some four hundred rebel soldiers and nearly all its weaponry, as those who escaped abandoned their arms when taking flight.) Washington's bluster about another major battle was largely in response to criticism within Congress of his performance at Brandywine, sniping that had gotten back to him. Despite what he was telling Congress about his plans for another battle, Washington quite properly had no intention of hazarding his army in another showdown, especially as he now was certain that Howe could not be prevented from taking Philadelphia.

Howe's army maneuvered for two weeks, a large and inviting target. When it slowly crossed the Schuylkill, the bulk of the Continental army was twenty miles away. Washington hinted to Congress that he had been let down by his intelligence apparatus.[36]

Once the redcoats crossed the Schuylkill, the way to the city was clear. Washington dispatched Hamilton in the still, dark hours of early morning on September 22 to alert the congressmen. They "decamped with the utmost precipitation," according to an amused Philadelphia Tory—so quickly, in fact, that one frightened Yankee congressman even forgot to saddle his horse before setting off. They were taking flight for York, 75 miles west of Philadelphia; to avoid capture, most congressmen made a circuitous horse-back ride of nearly 150 miles. Four days later the campaign-weary British and Hessian soldiers marched into Philadelphia as a martial band played "God Save Great George Our King." General Cornwallis was given the honor of leading the army, which was accompanied by numerous Loyalists, including Joseph Galloway, the onetime leader of the Pennsylvania assembly, who had sought a compromise solution at the First Continental Congress. Galloway had remained on the sidelines during the first eighteen months of the war, but after New York City fell in 1776, he opportunistically proclaimed his loyalty to the mother country and offered his services to the Crown. Among other things, Galloway mobilized Pennsylvania's Loyalists to assist the British army, and it was through the guidance of the Tories that Howe learned of the crossing at Jeffries Ford.[37]

Howe possessed Philadelphia, but at the outset little of his army was garrisoned in the city. Large numbers of men were sent off to clear the Delaware River of underwater obstacles and take three rebel forts that had been constructed or improved during the past fifteen months. The river had to be opened if the army was to be supplied via Britain's Atlantic lifeline. Some eight thousand additional men were posted at Germantown, just north of Philadelphia, from which they could forage and guard the approaches to the city. Washington had initially withdrawn nearly to Reading, but he soon marched his men to Skippack, a safe distance above Germantown.

Two months or more of the campaign season remained, and Washington was eager to exploit it. Soon after the Battle of Brandywine, he began to consider the prospect of replicating his surprise attack at Trenton. He asked two governors to provide militia and implored Gates to send him his rifle-men. (Gates, who received the request between the two Battles of Saratoga, wisely refused.)[38] Within hours of the British army's triumphal parade through the cobblestone streets of Philadelphia, Washington was aware that Howe had divided his army. Two days later Washington summoned a council of war and proposed a "vigorous" surprise attack on the enemy posted in Germantown. The council declined, at least until sufficient reinforcements were available. During the next three days Washington's force was bolstered by the arrival of Continentals and green Virginia militiamen, bringing his total to eight thousand Continentals and three thousand militia. Washington now had a numerically superior force. He did not summon another council of war. Washington spoke privately with each general, after which he announced his intention of attacking.[39]

Washington drew up a more complicated plan than he had devised for his attack at Trenton, in large measure because, unlike the tiny New Jersey hamlet, Germantown stretched for nearly two miles. Washington planned for his army to make a night march of sixteen miles in four columns, each approaching the target from a different direction. At five A.M. the four would attack. Success hinged on perfect timing and surprising the enemy. Washington was frustrated on both counts. A thick fog rolled in during the night, which not only slowed the march but also caused some officers, who were unfamiliar with the roads to begin with, to take wrong turns. Not all the men had arrived when Washington—who knew nothing of the progress of the columns aside from the one he accompanied—cried out the order to attack. Having been tipped off by Loyalists and captured Continentals that something was coming, the British may have been startled when rebel soldiers suddenly came charging and screaming out of the murky darkness, but unlike the Hessians at Trenton, they were not unprepared.

The odds against a substantial American victory were enormous. Two-thirds of the American soldiers arrived thirty minutes late, the Maryland and New Jersey militia never found Germantown, and Pennsylvania's militiamen, pinned down by a ridiculously small number of Hessians, contributed next to nothing. Furthermore, a major blunder by Washington helped foil his chance of success. He squandered an entire brigade for an hour in a needless, and fruitless, attempt to destroy a bit more than one hundred redcoats lodged in the Chew House, a dwelling on the battlefield. Some four hundred men under Washington were lost while inflicting only four casualties. Furthermore, Howe outgeneraled Washington yet again in this engagement, regrouping his men and launching a counterattack on rebel lines that had become far too elongated, and sowing terror among the exhausted and surprised Americans. Panic also set in after rebel units, confused in the limited visibility caused by the smoke and fog, mistakenly fired on one another. In a flash, about three hours into the fray, American resistance collapsed. Washington was unable to rally his men. He later persuaded himself that victory was at hand when his men lost their will to fight, but in all likelihood that was not the case.

Washington's hopes of scoring another victory akin to his brilliant stroke at Trenton had gone amiss. Furthermore, at Germantown the Americans had lost more than one thousand men, twice the losses suffered by Howe. No one factor foiled the rebels, but several British and not a few Continental field-grade officers thought that Washington's fixation on taking the Chew House had ruined the Americans' chances of success.[40]

It was early October and the weather was likely to be suitable for campaigning for a while. Some congressmen hoped for robust initiatives that would take a toll on the regulars, and some thought "a Winters Campaign . . . necessary to accomplish something decisive." However, Washington remained inactive, even though at month's end he had eleven thousand men fit for duty. Throughout October and November the British struggled to invest the rebel-held Delaware River forts, leading Howe to summon 4,500 men from New York to help finish the job. Deep into November the rebels continued to control the Delaware River, displaying incredible endurance given the conditions they faced. Private Joseph Plumb Martin, an American soldier at one fort, later recalled having spent the "cold month of November, without provisions, without clothing, not a scrap of either shoes or stockings to my feet or legs." Day after day, he and his comrades were subjected to a nearly round-the-clock shelling by scores of heavy field artillery and Royal Navy vessels. He claimed to have gone two weeks without sleep. That must have been an exaggeration, but there can be no doubt that he was sleep deprived, and what sleep he had was when lying on the chilly, muddy earth. All the while, the "enemy's shot cut us up," he went on. "Our men were cut up like cornstalks," many "split like fish to be broiled." In the end, Martin survived and what remained of his unit escaped, leaving behind a decimated "fort . . . as completely ploughed as a field."

Washington, who seldom any longer called councils of war when he was bent on going into action, convened his generals late in October to discuss matters. Predictably, his generals urged him to remain on the defensive, though they voted to ask the victorious Gates to send twenty of his regiments to Pennsylvania. (Gates partially complied, but as he was under orders to retake Ticonderoga, he felt unable to send all the men requested.)[41]

Congress was frustrated, and all the more so once the British finally cleared and opened the Delaware River during the last week in November. A week later Congress sent three of its members to headquarters to meet with Washington. After apparently advising him that "Congress are exceedingly dissatisfied with the Loss of [the] Forts," the congressmen raised the possibility of the army "storming the Lines and Redoubts" of Howe's army in Philadelphia. It was the very sort of endeavor that Washington had been keen on in Boston eighteen months before, but he dismissed such an undertaking now on the grounds that his officers were opposed. The congressmen additionally suggested a winter campaign. The officers were not in favor of that either, the commander said. The congressmen returned to York empty-handed, but not before they expressed their displeasure to Washington at what they saw as a lack of "proper discipline" in the army and a "general discontent" that they had discovered among the officers. The congressmen closed by telling Washington that they wanted the army to display a greater "Spirit . . . to promote the public service."[42]

Washington guarded his personal feelings about taking the field that autumn or in the coming winter, but there can be little doubt that he was eager to get into winter quarters and shore up his army. Washington's unwillingness to fight may have rankled many congressmen, but his was a prudent course. It was wildly improbable that an assault on the entrenched regulars in Philadelphia could have achieved anything of value, and it might have had catastrophic consequences. Similarly, to have attacked the redcoats attempting to clear the Delaware River would have contributed to their woes, but it was beyond the rebels' capability to deny them success, and any such campaign would have been extremely risky. Washington chose caution, unwilling to undertake a "hassardous" enterprise that might "disgrace" his army and jeopardize the chances of France's entry into the war.[43]

By the time the congressional delegation departed, Washington was ready to go into winter quarters. He envisaged disseminating his army throughout numerous camps well to the west of Philadelphia, reasoning that the men would be safer, healthier, and more easily fed in such an arrangement. But officials from Pennsylvania and neighboring states pressured Washington to put the army into a lone cantonment near Philadelphia, hopeful that it could protect farmers from any pillaging redcoats and cover Lancaster, where the Pennsylvania state government had moved, and York, now home to Congress. Washington complied, but he was furious and his anger was evident in two responses to Congress. No army, he said, could provide "protection to every Individual and to every Spot of Ground in the whole of the United States." In wartime, some are "exposed . . . to ravage and depredation." His first object was to preserve the army so it could continue the fight. To this he added: It "is a much easier and less distressing thing, to draw Remonstrances in a comfortable room by a good fire side" than like a soldier "to occupy a cold, bleak hill, and sleep under frost & snow without Cloaths or Blankets."[44]

When he laid aside his pen, Washington marched his army to a place called Valley Forge.

CHAPTER 11

"THE CENTRAL STONE IN THE GEOMETRICAL ARCH"

THE WAR IS TRANSFORMED IN 1778

THE THREE-YEAR-OLD WAR changed dramatically in 1778 and the Continental army, which was settling in at Valley Forge at the beginning of the year, also experienced profound changes.

Valley Forge has often been depicted as a forbiddingly remote and desolate site, and in fact on first seeing it, one of Washington's officers grumbled that it was situated in a "wasted" region. But several thousand commercial farmers worked the land in the two surrounding counties, and four vibrant market centers—Lancaster, York, Wilmington, and Reading—were within seventy-five miles of Valley Forge. The site itself, just west of the Schuylkill and some twenty miles northwest of occupied Philadelphia, was heavily forested, but that was one of its virtues, as wood was plentiful for fuel and constructing housing. When Thomas Paine visited the camp in its early days, he found the soldiers working like "a family of Beavers," cutting down trees and erecting "a Curious Collection of Buildings in the true rustic order." Within six weeks, every man was housed in this "log city," as one called it, twelve enlisted men to each fourteen-by-sixteen-foot hut, and far fewer officers in comparably sized accommodations. The general officers found more comfortable lodging in private residences.[1]

Although the Valley Forge winter has often been depicted as bitterly cold and snowy, southeastern Pennsylvania in 1778 experienced one of its mildest winters. Yet, if the extremes of the season were embellished in popular lore, the often told stories of the suffering experienced by America's soldiers at Valley Forge were all too true. The winter may have been less severe than normal, but it was winter in Pennsylvania nonetheless, and according to Washington, three thousand men entered Valley Forge "barefoot or other-wise naked." Devoid of coats and blankets, and huddling in inexpertly and hastily built huts that were drafty and leaky (and in almost every instance without a chimney that drew properly), the men had marched into a death trap. Their already appalling condition was exacerbated by episodic food shortages. The army had begun to experience scarcities of food during the month before it entered Valley Forge, and on three occasions during the first sixty days in the cantonment—each lasting a week to ten days—the supply of comestibles dipped below what Washington referred to as the "fatal crisis" level.

Not surprisingly, disease stalked the camp. Typhus, assorted fevers, and pneumonia took an incredible toll. Some 2,500 of Washington's Continentals perished that winter, roughly one in five of those who had entered Valley Forge just before Christmas. (In contrast, one in thirty American soldiers died in combat in the Battle of the Bulge, one of the nation's costliest engagements in World War II.) Close to 7 percent of the American soldiers who died in the eight-year-long Revolutionary War perished at Valley Forge. Ever after, Washington was convinced that Great Britain would have won the war had Howe attacked that winter. It was not that Howe was unaware of conditions at Valley Forge. The Tory Joseph Galloway, through a bevy of remarkably accurate intelligence reports, kept the British high command informed about the plight of the American army and its vulnerability. But Howe never moved.[2]

The disaster that befell the hapless soldiers was not due to any single factor. Both the army and Congress were part of the problem. The army was an administrative nightmare. Eighteen months after assuming command, Washington's army, in the words of one scholar, was "plagued by incompetent staff, poorly defined departmental responsibilities, and intersecting chains of command."[3] Congress had done nothing during the first thirty months of the war to improve a quartermaster service that was never noted for efficiency. Indeed, Congress had permitted the post of quartermaster general to go unfilled for six months prior to the army's arrival at Valley Forge. During the Valley Forge winter, the supply system was plagued by shortages of wagons, horses, and drivers and by corrupt businessmen and teamsters who embezzled the army. Goods that were shipped were sometimes intercepted by British-raised Loyalist units, and the Royal Navy's raids on coastal towns and Hudson River villages resulted in the destruction of goods that might have been shipped to Valley Forge. Nor was the weather a friend of the supply system. Hard freezes at times shut down river traffic, but it rained more than it snowed, and pernicious downpours not infrequently turned America's unpaved roads into a fetid ooze that rendered them impassible. These complications were exacerbated by still other problems. The region about Philadelphia had not only been picked over by two large armies between August and December, but the British army also seized numerous Continental army magazines, many containing thousands of barrels of flour. Finally, many farmers with marketable commodities preferred to sell to the British, either because they were "toriestically inclined," as one American general thought, or because the redcoats paid specie instead of depreciated Continental dollars.[4]

There were times during this protracted crisis when Washington thought he had little chance of "holding the Army together much longer." Early in the winter, he told Congress that it must do something, and swiftly, or the army would "be reduced to one or other of these three things: Starve—dissolve—or disperse." Congress responded by appealing to the states to aid the beleaguered soldiers. Most made a stab at providing assistance. Washington could hardly have been more active himself, and he occasionally took the uncustomary step of micromanaging the acquisition of supplies. He sent officers to search for designated items in New England, New York, Maryland, and Virginia, made others responsible for repairing tents, and sent out still others to drive cattle to camp. Washington was always reluctant to impress property from civilians, but in this crisis he did not shrink from seizing goods. He ordered his generals to sweep the countryside with forage parties of a thousand or more men, taking what farmers would not sell to the army and leaving families with just enough to get through the winter. General Greene said that he acted like a "Pharoh," adding: "I harden my heart . . . to forage the country very bare." Greene thought the use of strong-arm tactics saved the army.[5]

Another factor in the army's salvation was seldom if ever mentioned by Washington and his generals, but more than one European officer serving with the Continental army was struck by the endurance of America's soldiers. "No European army would suffer the tenth part of what the Americans suffer," said the Marquis de Lafayette, who went through the Valley Forge ordeal.[6] The perseverance of the Continental rank and file remains something of a mystery. Merciless military justice doubtless contributed to their submissiveness, but these soldiers also must have carried on because they were committed to the cause.[7]

One thing that sustained Washington during this perilous winter was his belief that France's entrance into the war was imminent, and he hoped against hope that it would be accompanied by a Franco-American alliance.[8] He knew that French belligerency would change the dynamic of the war in countless ways, but above all, it would mean that if Great Britain had been unable to quash the American rebellion before France was in the war, it would be next to impossible for it to do so thereafter.

Soon after the war's first battles, France's foreign minister, Charles Gravier, comte de Vergennes, went to work on his monarch, Louis XVI, to persuade him of the wisdom of providing weapons, munitions, and other essential items to the Continental army. Vergennes's thinking was that France could only benefit from Great Britain's woes. Within six months of Bunker Hill, Julien de Bonvouloir was meeting with congressmen in Philadelphia. Three months later, Silas Deane sailed for Paris in search of aid. The first shipment of French goods crossed the Atlantic long before 1776 ended. It came clandestinely, disguised as a commercial enterprise carried out by the fictitious Roderigue Hortalez and Company. The furtive nature of the business arose because France was not yet prepared to enter the war. It first wished to strengthen its navy, and above all, it was anxious to determine whether the Americans possessed the will to fight and to persevere.[9]

If greater foreign aid was part of what Congress sought in declaring independence, it had gotten exactly what it wanted. However, Richard Henry Lee's June 1776 motion for independence had called for more than just support. It urged Congress to "take the most effectual measures for forming foreign alliances." When Congress appointed Jefferson's committee to compose the Declaration of Independence, it additionally created a committee to prepare what came to be known as the Model Treaty, a template to guide American diplomats. Franklin and John Adams, the key figures on the panel, were leery of military alliances, fearful that they would result in the United States being dragged into Europe's never-ending wars. They hoped that France would recognize the United States, as that might pave the way for recognition by other European nations, which in turn might lead them to throw open their ports to the United States. While Washington at times displayed his amateurishness as a soldier, Adams and Franklin revealed their diplomatic inexperience—or perhaps chutzpah—in thinking that France would recognize the United States and provide open aid without a military alliance. Congress adopted the Model Treaty, which essentially was a guide for American envoys to follow in securing commercial treaties, and it named Franklin, Deane, and Arthur Lee as commissioners to seek the commercial pact with France.[10]

America's three envoys were in Paris before Christmas 1776. Within sixty days they had arranged the sale of Chesapeake tobacco in France and the purchase of uniforms, weapons, and frigates for the American armed forces. But whereas French bankers and businessmen eagerly worked out transactions, the government hesitated to make any commitments. Given the drubbing that France had suffered in the Seven Years' War, Vergennes and his king wanted allies if and when their nation again faced Britain in a war. Furthermore, given the Continental army's dismal showing during the Canadian and New York campaigns in 1775 and 1776, the French were in no hurry to jump into the conflict. News of the surrender of Fort Ticonderoga without a fight in the summer of 1777 caused further disillusionment, though Vergennes remained sufficiently confident to extend a loan to the United States in the autumn.

Only days after signing off on the loan, the foreign minister learned of the surrender of Burgoyne's army. Saratoga changed the landscape, though it was not solely the tidings of that epic American victory that nudged Vergennes toward an alliance. Already stirred by Washington's daring exploits at Trenton and Princeton, Vergennes was equally impressed by what he called the American commander's "spirit of enterprise" in launching the surprise attack at Germantown. Convinced that the combination of the dispatch of massive amounts of assistance, the commitment of a French fleet to American waters, and Washington's bold leadership virtually assured a pivotal Franco-American triumph, Vergennes moved rapidly to gain his monarch's approval of an alliance with the United States. No time could be wasted. It was widely known that Great Britain was preparing to offer peace and reconciliation to its former colonies. In fact, within two weeks of learning of Burgoyne's fate, Lord North had sent an envoy to Paris to open discussions with Franklin, talks that the Americans did not hide. The tipping point had been reached. If France was to be the beneficiary of the American rebellion, it must seize the moment.[11]

On the day before Washington's army marched into Valley Forge, the French initiated low-level talks with the American commissioners. By early January serious discussions were under way. Few differences separated the two parties and each was eager to sign. On the night of February 6, 1778, treaties of commerce and alliance were signed in Paris without ceremony at the Hotel de Lautrec. The latter accord stipulated that in the event of war between France and Great Britain, the allies would "make it a common cause and aid each other." Each party also pledged that it would not make peace with Great Britain "without the consent of the other." The commissioners told Congress that they had been treated with "the greatest Cordiality" by French officials and that "no Advantage has been taken" of them. Later in the week that the alliance was consummated, Franklin responded to an old friend in London who had implored him not to ally with France. Franklin explained that "when your Nation is hiring all the Cut Throats it can collect of all Countries and Colours to destroy us, it is hard to persuade us not to ask and accept of Aid, from any Power that may . . . grant it." To that he added: "The Americans are received and treated here in France with a Cordiality, a Respect and Affection, they never experienced in England."[12]

Long before London learned of Burgoyne's surrender, and even before word arrived that he was in trouble, foes of the war in Parliament were questioning the strategy behind the campaign of 1777. Some with no military experience saw what Howe had been unable to see. Contending that Burgoyne's "army was not equal to the task," they predicted that the "gallant general" was being "sent like a victim to be slaughtered."[13]

News of Burgoyne's surrender not only proved them correct but also touched off a feverish panic. Sensing that France would enter the war, many imagined that Great Britain was doomed to "a petty state of the second class, of no importance, and disgraced." The anxiety aroused by Saratoga was accompanied by a flood of recriminations. Lord North, Germain, and the generals bore the brunt of it. This latest military disaster also led increasing numbers of MPs to question the war. Some called for scaling back the object-ive of the war, which to this point had been America's "unconditional submis-sion." Some, like the Earl of Chatham—Pitt—went further and venomously pronounced the war a "mad project" and "a wanton waste of blood and treas-ure."[14] No one wanted to say that the war was unwinnable, but that was implicit in the remarks of some MPs, and it is a question with which histori-ans have wrestled.

Prior to hostilities, nearly every minister and most MPs had thought victory was certain, and many had presumed that defeating the rebels would be easy. Obviously, they were wrong on several counts. The Americans were neither meek nor cowards: their militiamen and Continentals would stand and fight against British regulars. The colonists achieved greater unity than the officials in London had ever imagined was possible; the active support of those colonists who remained loyal to the mother country had been disap-pointing; and while it was true that the colonists could not adequately arm and clothe their soldiers, France had provided clandestine help.

North's ministers had accurately predicted that Britain would easily achieve naval supremacy, but they underestimated the damage that American privateers could inflict and, more egregiously, London erred badly in believ-ing that the Royal Navy could establish an ironclad blockade. Britain's navy simply never possessed the number of vessels needed for closing traffic along the vast American coast. Little thought had been given to the logistical diffi-culties this war might present, but each year Britain had to ship across the Atlantic more than three million pounds of food (for men and horses) and ton upon ton of clothing, camp equipment, munitions, and weaponry to sustain the army. It was a daunting challenge. Some supply ships never made it across the sea, falling victim to Atlantic storms or American privateers. Some vessels that made the crossing arrived with badly damaged cargoes. Getting supplies to America was only part of the problem. Coordinating shipments from England with the plans made by the army's commanders three thousand miles away in America was at best a shot in the dark.[15] But as London took stock early in 1778, no military problem approached that of how to successfully campaign in America's huge and hostile backcountry. The disasters along Battle Road, at Trenton-Princeton, and at Saratoga convinced many that this war could not be won.

North's ministry, and Germain, survived the growing disillusionment brought to a head by Saratoga and Howe's failure in 1777 to inflict mortal damage on Washington's Continentals. That the government weathered the storm was due largely to George III, who wished to continue the fight. Lord North, shaken and despondent, tried yet again to resign, but the king would not hear of it. The monarch steadied his prime minister and North's administration not only continued but also defeated several attempts in the House of Commons to repeal the harshest and most objectionable American measures.

Though North's government endured, the king demanded that the ministry reconsider how best to wage this war. The discussions were lengthy and filled with detours, especially after word arrived of the Franco-American alliance. In the end, the cabinet concluded that Britain lacked the manpower to suppress the colonial rebellion—having been unable to put down the rebels in thirteen of its colonies, London now faced the necessity of protecting all twenty-six provinces within its Atlantic empire—but that with redemptive strategic changes American independence could still be prevented. During the winter of 1778 North's administration set in motion several crucial steps. With French entry into the war thought to be inevitable, ten thousand redcoats were to be redeployed, mostly to the Caribbean to defend Britain's valuable sugar islands. That necessitated an even greater dependence on German auxiliaries. Before the year was out, the Hessians made up fully one-third of Britain's military force in North America; and within three years, nearly 40 percent of those fighting under Britain's flag were Germans. The British army in America also began to recruit Tories in earnest. Fewer than one thousand Tories appear to have been raised during the first three years of the war, though beginning in 1778 several units of Loyalist provincials came into being. It has been estimated that by the end of the war, some nineteen thousand colonists had served in the Loyalist corps. (Indeed, it is likely that there were times during the next two or three years when nearly as many Americans were serving in the British army as in the Continental army.)

The army was to be additionally expanded through the conscription of England's poor and unemployed, and to facilitate a bountiful harvest of draftees, the military's long-standing physical standards and age requirements were relaxed. The government also launched a stupendous program of ship construction and initiated forced impressment of men into the Royal Navy; within two years the number of ships of the line had increased by a third and the navy's seamen had nearly doubled. The navy, moreover, was ordered to largely confine its activities to prohibiting the flow of goods into and out of North America, tightening the porous blockade through which French goods had flowed almost unimpeded into the hands of the rebel forces. Furthermore, the government replaced General Howe—accepting his proffered resignation with alacrity—and appointed in his stead Sir Henry Clinton, a forty-eight-year-old widower who had soldiered since he was fifteen, and who had arrived in America in 1775 as the third-ranking British general officer behind Gage and Howe.[16]

London additionally scuttled the strategy it had pursued since 1776. It wrote off the conquest of New England and the mid-Atlantic provinces. Henceforth, British armed forces were to concentrate on the pacification of its four former southern colonies, Georgia, South Carolina, North Carolina, and Virginia. The South was of crucial economic importance to England, and given its large number of Anglicans and slaveholders, imperial officials believed the region abounded in Tories, who were to be actively recruited for the army. No decision was made with respect to arming slaves—who made up more than 50 percent of the South's population—but it was understood that even as noncombatants, the bondsmen could assist the army in numerous ways, including growing food and providing labor. If the new southern strategy succeeded, Great Britain could still come out of this war with a large and potent empire, one that included Canada, the trans-Appalachian west, the four southern colonies, Florida, and several precious colonies in the West Indies. At war's end, there might be a United States, but it would consist of no more than nine states surrounded by the British Empire. There was reason to believe that, in time, the American citizenry, hemmed in and impoverished, and facing a dismal future, would come to see the merits of reconciliation with their former mother country. In March, thirty days after the Franco-American alliance was sealed, Germain instructed the army's commander in America to invade Georgia in the autumn and, if possible, South Carolina as well before the end of the year.[17]

Lord North had never been as certain as most within his cabinet that the American rebels could be brought to heel through the use of force, and his doubts had only grown since that bloody day on Battle Road. Now, even though it was his government that conceived the new military strategy in the winter of 1778, the prime minister continued to fear the worst. He was convinced that if France entered the war, Britain would lose not only all of its American colonies but most of its possessions in the West Indies as well. The losses would be worse than a calamity. As Christmas 1777 approached, North explored a radical departure in Britain's imperial policy, one that might forestall France's entry into the war, prevent the dreaded disasters that Chatham and Burke had long ago forecast, and bring an end to the war before the southern strategy was instituted.

Beginning a month before the first meeting between the American commissioners and their French counterparts, and for seven weeks thereafter, North met quietly with the king and several undersecretaries and subministers, but never with his cabinet. He also sent three individuals to Paris to conduct secret talks with the commissioners, for the most part to see what the Americans wanted and what they might accept. The news was not cheery. The American envoys steadfastly demanded that London recognize American independence before discussions began, and Franklin in particular seethed with anger toward the former mother country. According to North's emissary, Franklin nearly "lost his Breath" raging against the British "system of devastation and Cruelty," and capped his rant by speaking of "English men [as] Barbarous!"[18]

Five days after the Franco-American treaties were signed in Paris, North finally shared his thinking with the cabinet. Unlike 1774 and 1775, when Dartmouth's calls for restraint had been unanimously rejected, the cabinet approved the prime minister's plan to repudiate much of Britain's prewar American policy, though predictably Germain sourly condemned the proposed changes as certain to result in a "disgraceful peace." Expecting "to be roasted," North next divulged his about-face in a two-hour speech to the House of Commons on February 17. To North's surprise, the House listened respectfully as he disarmingly confessed that the use of force had "turned out differently from his expectation," though he added that Britain was "in a condition to carry on war much longer." He expressed his hope of maintaining a "lasting bond of union" with the colonies, and to achieve that end, North asked Parliament not only to renounce its right to tax the colonists but also to approve the dispatch of peace commissioners free to enter into virtually unfettered discussions with the Continental Congress, as if it was "a legal body." Parliament consented.[19]

North had to know how doubtful it was that Congress would spurn an alliance with France that held the promise of victory and independence. But he made his best effort, and in directives prepared for the commissioners, the prime minister outlined a string of bold and striking concessions that went beyond the demands made prior to hostilities by the First Continental Congress. The commissioners could agree to

> suspend all American legislation enacted since 1763;
> never keep a standing army in the colonies in peacetime;
> never change a colonial charter without the consent of the colonial assembly;
> give Americans preference when filling colonial offices;
> eliminate Crown officers to which the colonists objected;
> staff the American customs service solely with Americans;
> consider colonial representation in Parliament; and
> help the colonists with the reduction of their war debts.

Virtually all that would remain of the pre-1763 imperial system were the hazy prerogatives of the monarch and Parliament's authority to regulate imperial commerce.

However, before the cabinet completed its work, Germain and his unbending allies scuttled whatever slim chance of success the commissioners might have had. They inserted into the commissioners' instructions what was tantamount to a death clause. The commissioners were not to negotiate until the colonists renounced their "pretensions to independence" and asked for the king's forgiveness. North offered little resistance. Perhaps he knew that the cabinet could not be prevented from sanctioning such a course. Or, sensing the hopelessness of the undertaking, North may have been willing to permit responsibility for the foreseeable failure to fall on Germain. The cabinet went through the motions of naming the members of what became known as the Carlisle Commission, but North—and Germain—must have known that it would be dead on arrival in America. The war would continue and it now would be a conflict with the United States and with France.[20]

Word of both the negotiations in Paris and North's pending peace plan reached North America in the spring. While Washington welcomed the French alliance, he was apprehensive that it might undercut the willingness of the states to continue to furnish men and supplies. But he was more alarmed by North's peace offering, which he said was "more dangerous than their efforts by arms." Remembering the strength of the reconciliationists in Congress two years before, Washington feared that the combination of growing war weariness and North's shrewd move to "ensnare the people by specious allurements of peace"

would lead to the resurgence of a spirit of reconciliation. Washington's prefer-
ence was clear. "Nothing short of Independence . . . can possibly do." French aid
"has saved us . . . thus far," he said, and continued sacrifices, fighting, and
foreign aid would "free us entirely."[21]

Washington need not have worried about Congress. It ratified the French
treaties within days of their arrival. The alliance gave "a most happy tone to
all our affairs," Washington exalted, adding that the "glorious News . . . must
put the Independency of America out of all manner of dispute." The congressmen saw things in a similar light. Some mistakenly thought England would
immediately recognize American independence rather than risk war with
France and the United States. Others, like Washington, suspected the war
would continue, but now "America will be in a Situation to prosecute the War
with Ease."[22]

By the time Washington and Congress rejoiced, the winter supply crisis at
Valley Forge had passed, but other problems remained. Some concerned the
officer corps. The enlisted men had signed on for three years' service, but the
officers were free to quit the army as they pleased. At Valley Forge, the officers
resigned in droves. Washington estimated that upwards of three hundred
officers departed. Fifty in Nathanael Greene's division quit on the same day
in December. Some departed in anger, fuming that the civil authorities had
left the soldiery "badly fed and almost naked." Some were embittered at
having been passed over for promotion. Rancor over promotions was endemic
in the army, once prompting John Adams to observe that the officers "quarrel
like Cats and Dogs . . . Snarling for Rank and Pay like Apes for Nutts." But
more than indignation drove officers away. Some simply had experienced all
the adventure they could ever want. And, with prices zooming into the stra-
tosphere as a result of wartime inflation, many officers were no longer able to
adequately support their families. Not a few were implored by desperate
spouses to come home.[23]

Both Congress and Washington realized that changes must be made if the
Continental army was to survive as an effective force. In November, Congress
had told Washington of its displeasure with the army, and in January it sent a
delegation to Valley Forge to bring about a "reformation." What was called
the Committee at Camp encountered a masterful politician in General
Washington. One of Washington's strongest assets was his judicious sense of
deference to civilian authority. Perhaps because he had sat in both Virginia's
House of Burgesses and the Continental Congress, he readily understood
legislators and the legislative process, and he was all too aware that congressmen represented myriad interests from throughout thirteen disparate states.
However maddening it must have been at times for Washington, he was

patient with Congress and strove to avoid any hint of imperiousness in his behavior. But while deferential, Washington had to look out for the interests of the army, to hold it together, to satisfy strong-willed officers, and ultimately to win the life-and-death struggle against America's enemy. From his earliest days in command in Boston's siege lines, Washington had demonstrated remarkable manipulative skills in bringing Congress to the army's way of thinking, and he did so once again when the delegates that composed the Committee at Camp arrived at Valley Forge. Washington greeted them with his own list of recommended changes, compiled in a twenty-eight page document written largely by Colonel Alexander Hamilton. Some of the congressmen were friendly from the outset, others were malleable, and in the end all submitted to nearly every wish that Washington expressed. Significant changes resulted.

To prevent the further emasculation of the officer corps, Washington lobbied for half-pay pensions for life for his officers, a customary practice in the British army. Congress would not go that far, but it agreed to half-pay pensions for seven years following hostilities and for benefits for the widows and orphans of officers. Both Washington and Congress wanted a better-trained army. The general proposed the creation of a mounted military police, and Congress soon authorized a constabulary that would be known as the Maréchaussée Corps. For its part, Congress had dispatched Friedrich William Augustus, Baron von Steuben—whom it believed to be a Prussian aristocrat and veteran soldier who had served under Frederick the Great—to Valley Forge to help overhaul the army. Washington did not give him that much latitude, but he charged Steuben with "establishing regulations for manoeuvres"—that is, drilling the soldiers. Steuben may have embellished his status in the old country, though he had indeed soldiered in Europe and, in Washington's estimation, he succeeded in rapidly instilling a new "spirit of discipline." Steuben did even more. In his fractured English—the lion's share of the language that he knew consisted of expletives—Steuben educated the officers on the importance of spending time with the men, visiting the sick, learning what they were eating and how it was prepared, taking part in the drills, and how to conduct safer and faster marches.[24]

Washington did not get all that he wanted from Congress. He hoped for a national policy of conscription, but Congress declined. Nor would Congress consent to his request for more draconian punishments, including increasing the number of lashes from one hundred to five hundred when flogging deserters and disobedient soldiers. However, Congress agreed to improve the pay of both officers and enlisted men, to devise a "settled rule of promotion" for field grade and general officers, and to reform the supply service.[25]

Collaboration between Washington and the congressional committee had been surprisingly smooth given the disaffection within Congress. November's restiveness over Washington's leadership had grown to a "loud bellowing" during the winter. The unrest was fueled by Washington's uncertainty at Brandywine, the supposed botch he made of the attack on Germantown, his failure to resist Howe's final drive into Philadelphia, his unwillingness to do more to impede the enemy during its campaign to clear the Delaware River of rebel obstructions, and a misplaced belief on the part of some that the misery at Valley Forge was due largely to the shortcomings of the army's leadership. Critics accused Washington of indecisiveness, of surrounding himself with sycophants, of over-reliance on the advice of General Greene, of an arrogance that allegedly alienated many young officers, and of administrative ineptitude. So skeptical had some become of Washington's generalship that his opinions were "treated with ... much indecent freedom & Levity" within Congress, according to its president. Some wanted to remove Washington and replace him with Horatio Gates, the hero of Saratoga. Some of the harshest judgments—which may or may not have reached Congress—were offered privately by generals and officers at headquarters who observed Washington up close. They assailed Washington as ignorant and vain, "a weak man," "only fit to command a regiment," and "totally unfit for his situations." General Johann de Kalb, who had soldiered in Europe for a quarter century, called the American commander the "weakest general" under whom he had served and said that if Washington ever accomplished anything "sensational he will owe it more to his good luck or to his adversary's mistakes than to his own ability." Even Hamilton thought the public's perception of Washington as a great general was "unfounded."[26]

Washington was largely unaware of the carping among the officers, though he was alerted to the criticism in Congress by members of the Virginia delegation. He also learned from a wine-soaked officer that General Thomas Conway, a French volunteer, had allegedly written to Gates that "Heaven" had heretofore saved the American cause from the repeated failures of "a weak General." Thin-skinned and in the midst of a crisis-laden winter, Washington jumped to the conclusion that his detractors were part of a vast conspiracy that included congressmen, army officers, and influential civilians and that General Gates was a part of the "malignant faction." Washington was wrong. Although some historians have accepted the notion of an organized plot—calling it the "Conway Cabal"—solid evidence is lacking that the disgruntled ever coalesced in a formal intrigue or that Gates was part of any plot to overthrow Washington. (Though to be sure, Gates did nothing to dash the hopes of those who longed for a new commander in chief.)[27]

The episode caused Washington many sleepless nights, though in the end he not only survived the tempest but also emerged even stronger. It is doubtful that Congress ever came close to replacing him. Some whose confidence in Washington had been shaken were likely restrained both by fears of the political fallout that would result from his removal and concern that his dismissal would leave the country and its army in "the State of a Rudderless Ship in a boisterous Ocean." The hand of others may have been stayed by the realization that the great majority of Continental army officers were devoted to Washington or by a foreboding that the overthrow of the commander would have an adverse impact in France, which was verging on entering the war. But most stuck with Washington because they believed in him. They recognized that Washington was not a professional soldier, and that was precisely what they wanted in their commander. He had never abused his power and he had worked well with Congress and state officials. Nor was there any hint of popular disaffection with the commander. In addition, most understood that in going up against Howe in 1776 and 1777, Washington had faced a stronger foe than Gates had confronted.[28]

The season of suffering at Valley Forge, and the accompanying alarm that the army might come apart before winter ended, was transformative. Having experienced the travail firsthand, army officers drew closer to Washington, both in admiration of his steadfast struggle to pull them through the dire crisis and in appreciation of his advocacy of their demands. Their anguish and suffering also instilled among officers a conviction that they more than others were sacrificing to win independence, a view that left many with a sense of pronounced separateness from all other Americans. Even Washington privately complained of the contemptible smugness with which many state officials—far from the front lines—looked on the army. Furthermore, the conviction took shape within the officer corps that the new nation required a strong central government, one better able to wage the war and advance the national interest of the new United States. After 1778 many officers in the Continental army wanted an independent America modeled on their values of honor and duty, a view that led them to look askance at self-seeking individualism and emphasize instead that individual happiness must be subordinate to the well-being of the community.[29]

Having stared over the precipice of waging the war without Washington, Congress now exalted him as never before. According to Benjamin Rush, a former congressman, signer of the Declaration of Independence, and the army's surgeon general, "state necessity" led Congress to launch a concerted campaign to make Washington an iconic figure. John Adams concurred, remarking that Congress concealed the commander's blunders from the public and inflated his achievements and that it "agreed to blow the trumpet of panegyric in concert, to cover and dissemble all [of Washington's] faults and errors, to represent every defeat as a victory and every retreat as an advancement, to make [him] ... popular and fashionable with all parties in all places and with all persons, as a center of the union, as the central stone in the geometrical arch."[30]

To a degree, Congress had recognized a spontaneous, perhaps inevitable, process among the population to fasten on General Washington because it needed an icon, but congressmen were aware too that powerful forces within the army's officer corps had begun to boost the commander in chief as a national figure around which the citizenry could rally. As early as 1776 some Americans had already spoken of Washington as "our political Father and head of a Great People." During the winter of 1778, Henry Knox orchestrated the first public celebration of Washington's birthday, a gathering by the troops and officers on the snowy lawn of Washington's headquarters at Valley Forge. That crisis-laden winter also witnessed the publication of an almanac in nearby Lancaster, Pennsylvania, that referred to Washington as "the Father of His Country"—the king of England was "the Father of His People"—an expression thereafter used on occasion during the war. Poets, preachers, writers, and orators lauded him, songs celebrated him, it became fashionable to toast Washington at public gatherings, and from 1779 onward his birthday was widely observed. Washington's image was displayed on coins (some of which had previously depicted the king), his picture appeared here and there in courthouses, and three counties and two towns were named for him. But Congress had not simply responded to others; it was intent on creating a groundswell of support for Washington. At a time when there was no president and no politician of national stature on whom the people could focus their hopes for the cause of independence, Congress felt the need for a leader figure. From this moment forward, civil and military leaders celebrated Washington as the indispensable man of the American Revolution, the key to victory and the glue that held together the fragile new nation. And from the spring of 1778 onward, Washington was seen as beyond reproach.[31]

As the warm spring sun heralded the advent of a new campaign season, Washington exuded confidence that his army had been transfigured both by Steuben's "indefatigable Exertions" and the miseries the soldiery had endured at Valley Forge. Speaking of his eagerness for the battlefield, Washington ruminated on attempting to retake either Philadelphia or New York. In the end, however, he listened to a council of war that preferred keeping the army within its "secure, fortified Camp," responding only to whatever steps the enemy took. With France's entry into the war seen as imminent, most generals thought it unwise to engage in a risky undertaking when the army might soon be able to act in concert with its new ally. That was also part of the reason for Washington's chilly response to calls by General Gates and many congressmen, including nearly all the New England delegates, for an invasion of weakly held Canada. Calling the notion "a child of folly," Washington insisted that only the defeat of the British army could end the war.[32]

This war, like most, was characterized by unforeseen twists and turns, and perhaps no other year during the Revolutionary War exceeded 1778 for missed opportunities and major changes. As North had expected, and feared, France declared war late in the spring, prompting his government to order its new commander in America, General Clinton, to abandon Philadelphia, taken only nine months earlier at a cost of nearly two thousand British soldiers. Clinton was additionally ordered to relinquish ten thousand of his men, nearly half his army—they were to be sent to Canada, Florida, and St. Lucia in the Caribbean—leaving him with 13,661 and compelling him to forswear hopes of taking the offensive.[33]

Unaware of Clinton's orders, Washington thought the arrival of a new commander meant that the enemy was at last about to do something. On June 18, he learned what Clinton planned. As dawn was breaking over Philadelphia, the British army marched out of the city and crossed into New Jersey, beginning a long overland march to New York. Eager to have at his adversary, Washington put his army in motion too, shadowing the redcoats and trying to decide what sort of fight he wanted. A heat wave had settled over the region. Every day the temperature soared to near one hundred degrees. The two armies, each with about ten thousand men, slogged across the scorched and sweltering landscape.

Six days into the march, Washington conferred with his generals. Even more so than at the council of war six weeks earlier, an overwhelming majority advised against attempting anything greater than harassing activities by perhaps a tenth of the army. The generals knew that a French fleet had put to sea. Its destination was unknown, but if it was sailing for the United States, the generals saw no reason to risk a major engagement prior to its arrival. One of the officers who was most outspoken in urging caution was Charles Lee, recently released in a prisoner swap after well over a year in captivity. Early in the war, Washington had scrupulously adhered to Lee's advice. No longer, however, for Washington remembered all too well what he had thought was Lee's deliberate betrayal in the crisis of late 1776. Not all of Washington's generals were happy with the council of war's recommendation of caution. Some dissenting generals urged a bolder approach, condemning what they saw as the excessive circumspection that had carried the day in the council of war. Its advice, one said, "would have done honor" to a "society of midwives." Washington listened to their argument and changed step. He decided to do what he probably had wanted to do all along. He opted to risk more than half his army in an attack on the two-thousand-man rear guard of Clinton's force. Washington put Lafayette in command of the operation.[34]

Only twenty years old and woefully inexperienced, Lafayette immediately botched things when he took the field. Either on his own or at the urging of officers who had little confidence in Lafayette's abilities, Washington suddenly replaced Lafayette, giving Lee—the highest-ranking general officer—responsibility for the attack. On the breathlessly still, hot morning of June 28, the British resumed their march, setting off from Monmouth, New Jersey. Simultaneously, Lee moved out under a pale blue dawn sky, his units' heat-heavy flags hanging limp as the men marched. Unknowingly, he was advancing into an even more precarious situation than the most wary of Washington's generals had imagined. Once again, Washington had failed to reconnoiter the area. As Lee moved on, he discovered that three deep ravines sliced through the countryside. In a worst-case scenario—say, the need to suddenly fall back—Lee feared that the ravines might hamper both his withdrawal and the speedy arrival of reinforcements.

Lee's anxiety was not misplaced. When he attacked, Lee had nearly a three to one numerical advantage. But Clinton, who was no less eager than Washington for a major engagement, rushed in units to buttress the beleaguered tail of his army and to counterattack. Lee's numerical superiority vanished. By late morning, the numbers were in Clinton's favor. When Lafayette, in command of one of the three American divisions, made a precipitous withdrawal—which some of his fellow officers thought unnecessary—the rebel lines buckled. Although Lee had not ordered a retreat, one was occurring, at least on some parts of the battlefield. Unplanned pullbacks in the midst of combat are every commander's worst nightmare. A withdrawal in one sector can imperil units on another part of the battlefield, and the sight of comrades falling back can sow panic throughout the lines. Fully aware of the sudden danger, Lee ordered a retreat. His plan was to fall back behind one of the ravines and make a defensive stand.[35]

Washington was more surprised than angry when told of the retreat. But he was suspicious, and he spurred his horse toward the front lines to see for himself. Officers who Washington met along the way misleadingly told him that Lee's retreat was unnecessary. Washington, known for his volcanic temper, worked himself into what one witness described as "a great passion." It was his first battle since the furtive winter plotting, and things were going awry. When he finally reached Lee, Washington "swore . . . till the leaves shook on the trees," according to an officer who was present. He relieved Lee of command and took charge himself. Next, Washington did precisely what Lee was attempting to do. He withdrew his army behind the last of the ravines and made a desperate stand.[36]

Lafayette together with Hamilton, who had hitched his wagon to the commander's star, later told the public that Washington's "calm courage," his "coolness and firmness," had saved the day. Washington's bravery and leadership under fire were beyond question, but he had not assumed command of an army in disarray or on the verge of collapse. He summoned reinforcements, which evened the odds, and he also benefited from Clinton's inexperience in leading armies in battle, readily apparent when the British commander failed to employ many of his available troops.[37]

The Battle of Monmouth was the longest one-day battle of the war, it featured the largest artillery exchange of any engagement, and it was the last major clash fought in this war in a northern state. It was also one of the war's most desperate fights. There were times on this heat-seared day when it appeared that the British, who made repeated attempts to break through, would succeed, inflicting a crushing defeat on the Americans. But the men in the American army, crouched behind fences and hedgerows, grimly fought for hours in the blistering heat, thwarting one assault after another while their artillery comrades raked the advancing enemy with a deadly fire. The courage and tenacity of America's common soldiers was crucial to the staving off the British assaults. As at Brandywine, the tinge of gathering darkness brought an end to hours of inconclusive combat. Washington prepared for more fighting the next day, but when he awoke in the creeping light of early morning on June 29 the American commander discovered that Clinton's army had stolen away during the night.[38]

Again and again, the British had suffered from bad timing. In the wake of Monmouth, it was the Americans' turn. A week following the battle, and after Clinton's army had safely reached New York, the anticipated French fleet arrived off Sandy Hook, only a few miles from Monmouth. Under the command of Vice Admiral Count d'Estaing, the imposing flotilla consisted of twelve ships of the line, four frigates, and over four thousand marines. Had d'Estaing sailed only slightly earlier, or crossed more quickly, Clinton's army would have been trapped and beyond salvation. In that case, the war almost certainly would have ended in an allied victory in 1778, for it was improbable that Great Britain would have continued to fight after losing two huge armies within the space of ten months.

Washington was disappointed, of course, but he thought there was still hope of gaining a decisive victory that summer. He proposed a joint campaign to retake New York. With the Royal Navy scattered up and down the Atlantic coast, d'Estaing's fleet would be unmistakably superior to the few British ships left near New York; augmented by an outpouring of militiamen, the Americans would have the greater army. Washington was convinced that the "ruin of Great Britain" would be "reduced to a moral certainty." Alas, d'Estaing's pilots ascertained that New York's channel was too shallow for France's heavy warships.[39]

Washington's dream died, but he had another idea. He proposed a joint campaign to retake Newport, Rhode Island, which had been captured by Howe in December 1776. With the odds again in favor of the Allies, Washington once more was "certain of success." D'Estaing agreed. Retaking Newport was important in itself, but if the British garrison of 6,700 redcoats could be captured as well, this, too, might be a war-ending victory. The French fleet sailed immediately, Washington detached troops to join the one thousand Continentals already in Rhode Island, and Massachusetts called its militia to duty.[40]

The bright promise of July went awry in August. Washington was part of the problem. He had put the troublesome John Sullivan—who had failed egregiously in Canada—in command in Rhode Island back in the days when it was in the backwater of the war. Now, with the campaign looming, Washington might have replaced Sullivan with Horatio Gates, who wanted the assignment and was enormously popular in New England. The American commander chose not to do so. According to the ever-loyal Nathanael Greene, Washington shrank from giving a "doubtful friend" the opportunity of winning still more laurels. Predictably, Sullivan botched this assignment too, so angering d'Estaing that the Americans had to send in emissaries to calm him.

Sullivan was not the only obstacle to victory. Massachusetts was unaccountably slow in fielding its militia, affording Admiral Howe time to gather a fleet and sail for Rhode Island. Howe arrived off the coast during the second week in August and the two naval squadrons squared off. The Americans had frequently been the beneficiary of the weather, but not in the Rhode Island campaign. A hurricane blew up, scattering both navies and so damaging the French fleet that d'Estaing called off further campaigning and sailed for Boston to make repairs.[41]

Early in November 1778, d'Estaing sailed from Boston for the Caribbean and Washington, without objection from Congress, scattered his army for the winter between Danbury, Connecticut; West Point in the Hudson

Highlands; and Middlebrook, New Jersey, where he established his headquarters. The campaign of 1778 was at an end, but so, too, was the bloody and arduous first phase of the Revolutionary War. In many ways, even greater perils to securing American independence lay in wait during the second half of this war.

CHAPTER 12

"THE LONGEST PURSE WILL WIN THE WAR"

REFORM AT HOME WHILE THE WAR TAKES A NEW TURN

THE REVOLUTION HAD BEGUN IN AMERICA before the first shots were fired at Lexington and Concord. The war escalated change, and independence ushered in still more changes. By the time Washington's army went into winter quarters late in 1778—thirty months after independence had been declared—the America of the colonial era had begun to be transfigured.

The overwhelming majority of those who exercised control throughout the states in 1776 desired some political changes. Above all, they wished to end forever the status they had faced within the British Empire, a stature that one rebel had summed up by describing the colonists as a "servile and dependent" people. Their wish was to become citizens, not subjects.[1] They thought of themselves as republicans and spoke of establishing a republic. While the word "republicanism" meant many things to many people, nearly all thought it included opposition to monarchy and titled nobility. On the eve of independence, John Adams—in a private letter to Patrick Henry—captured the sense of America's republicans when he said the revolution was about establishing "a more equal Liberty, than has prevail'd in other Parts of the Earth."[2]

If there was to be no monarch or nobility, who was to govern in the newly independent states and nation? Adams remarked that the "People will have unbounded Power," but he also spoke of "qualified Freeholders" as voters, an indication that he did not envisage that all adult white males (much less females or free blacks) would have suffrage rights. Nevertheless, Adams anticipated a new national state that would be strikingly unlike the colonial America that had been tethered to Great Britain. For Adams, the American Revolution was about independence from Great Britain and what he called the "Purification" of America—the eradication of "Vices" left over from

British rule and "an Augmentation of our Virtues." The foremost vice, which had provoked resentment in Adams throughout his adult life, and especially once he became a successful Boston lawyer, was that a handful of old, wealthy families monopolized important offices. Sometimes, one individual held numerous high offices. Adams thought that merit, not old money or ties to the powerful in London, should be the basis of holding office. Furthermore, it was bad enough to see his ambitions blocked by the scions of those "opulent, monopolizing" clans, but he was enraged by the "Scorn and Contempt and turning up of the Nose" that these people exhibited toward an accomplished and educated man like himself who descended from the "common People." More than a decade before the Declaration of Independence, Adams said that those who rode the coattails of their "Ancestors' Merit" had no right "to inherit the earth. . . . All men are created equal."

Despite his grievances, Adams acknowledged that greater equality of opportunity existed in the colonies than in England or Europe, and that was the principal American virtue of which he spoke. For Adams, and many like him from every social class and every colony, the American Revolution was about opening doors for the ambitious and the talented so that they could ascend as far as industry and merit could take them, something that was unimaginable in an aristocratic-dominated nation, or in the colonies of such a nation.[3]

The American insurgency had for the most part been managed by the colonial assemblies and the Continental Congress. Elected legislators had petitioned the king, approved boycotts, chosen the members of Congress, mobilized militias, and created extra-legal provincial governments. More often than not, the assemblymen in every colony had been well-to-do gentlemen and luminaries in their cities and towns. Once the question of independence was settled, the matter of the shape of the new nation emerged, at that point chiefly in the form of writing and ratifying the first state constitutions. For the most part, those elected officials who had been prominent in the American protest, and who favored independence, crafted those first constitutions.

Thomas Paine, in *Common Sense*, said that he had heard some say they dreaded independence from fear that a tyranny of the people would be substituted for British tyranny.[4] To be sure, Joseph Galloway had warned the First Congress that such an outcome was unavoidable should the rebellion lead to independence. The new state constitutions did indeed institute significant changes that ultraconservatives such as Galloway found abominable. Only Virginia and Delaware retained their pre-Revolutionary property qualifications for voting. Most reduced the requirements, broadening the electorate.

Some states eased the property qualifications for holding office, but most retained them and some set steep prerequisites for sitting in the upper house or the governor's chair. Every state prohibited plural officeholding.

State governors were vested with far less power than their predecessors in the colonial era. Elected by the legislatures for only brief terms and seldom given appointment powers, the executives existed mostly to enforce the wishes of the assemblies. Power was shifted to the legislatures, and especially to the lower houses, whose members were elected annually. Several states stipulated that population was the basis of representation in the lower houses, and almost everywhere, the people living in the backcountry were better represented than they were before 1776. All but three states embraced bicameralism, as John Adams had recommended in *Thoughts on Government*, usually fashioning upper houses that represented property, not people. The upper house was the conservatives' bulwark against radicalism. It was theoretically conceived to be the chamber for the most talented men, and its members were to check the excesses of the lower house and, not coincidentally, protect the interests of the wealthy.[5]

Pennsylvania, once under the thumb of Galloway and others who had fought against the break with the mother country, adopted the most radical constitution of all. The state's constitutional convention was attended by ninety-six democratically elected delegates, for all free adult males who paid taxes and renounced allegiance to Great Britain were eligible to vote. The result was the most sweeping turnover in political power experienced by any state. Galloway, of course, was not part of that state's constitutional convention, and indeed few who had sat in the assembly were elected. Nor were many merchants or lawyers chosen. Craftsmen were plentiful, but most delegates were farmers, many of them immigrants or the sons of immigrants, and not a few came from western counties. The convention was dominated by a brewer, a clockmaker, a physician, and a mathematics tutor who earlier in the summer had publicly cautioned against trusting the "Great and overgrown rich" to draft the constitution, as any document they embraced would chiefly serve their interests while ignoring "the common interests of mankind." Pennsylvania's convention produced a constitution that put in place not just republicanism but also democracy. All free, adult male taxpayers could vote or hold office in the unicameral assembly. The people were put in charge of the state, and few institutional impediments existed to prevent them from taking whatever course they wished.[6]

More conservative Pennsylvanians and some outsiders, such as Adams, recoiled in shock. Adams called the constitution "fatal" and a "curse," but his anti-democratic sentiments were only part of the reason that he privately condemned the constitution. Adams also feared that it would provoke such divisiveness that Pennsylvania might drop out of the war or at the very least be "rendered much less vigorous in the Cause." Divisiveness did result, as conservatives within Pennsylvania—such as Benjamin Rush, who charged that the constitution was fit for a Philadelphia "dung cart"—denigrated the drafters of the document as uneducated and incompetent. But what they really objected to was the threat that democratization jeopardized the hegemony of Pennsylvania's elite. Conservatives immediately embarked on a campaign to overturn the constitution, which, as it turned out, was a foretaste of the postwar conservative reaction to undo many of the changes unleashed by the American Revolution.[7]

Outside Pennsylvania, those who had been without a voice in the political process before independence often had little or no voice in what went into those original constitutions. Many who were excluded had a different vision of the American Revolution from that of, say, John Adams. They, too, embraced independence and republicanism, but for them, this was a revolution about redressing their powerlessness in American society.

Two months before independence, John Adams remarked that "mighty Revolutions make a deep Impression on the Minds of Men and sett many violent Passions at Work."[8] He believed there was a dark, malevolent side to human nature, and he was convinced that, among many citizens, malign passions had been stirred by the intemperate rhetoric and menacing actions that had accompanied the insurgency, leading many otherwise good people down the wayward path of extremism. For Adams, the baleful fanaticism to which he alluded was the tinge of political radicalism in quest of sweeping change.

The aspirations of many were doubtless shaped by inspiring screeds such as Thomas Paine, who articulated radical ideas, but Adams's dark appraisal ignored the fact that many colonists simply hungered to improve the quality of their lives. Just as Adams had come to see the American Revolution as the means of redressing the oppressive restraints on opportunity that existed in colonial America, many who were propertyless and lived on the margins of deep poverty—people who could neither vote nor hold office—saw in the Revolution the means of deep change that would never be possible for Americans living within the British Empire. Those colonists did not require ten years of protest to make them realize that they were victims of their powerlessness. The viciousness of their assaults on Hutchinson and Andrew Oliver in 1765 laid bare long-standing frustrations and anger. But the ensuing decade was nevertheless crucial for shaping their thinking, for deepening their understanding of themselves as victims of economic inequality, for creating an awareness of ways to participate in public affairs, and for quickening the belief that change was possible.

Their outlook was shaped by many things, and certainly by far more than Adams realized, though he acknowledged that there were "secret Springs of this surprising Revolution," which historians one day would have to unearth.[9] It now seems likely that just as committees of correspondence had made leaders such as Richard Henry Lee and Samuel Adams aware that others in distant provinces felt similar grievances and harbored hopes of like expectations, small farmers in the countryside and workers in the cities likewise came away from meetings, from service on committees, or from marching side by side on city streets with the realization of shared affronts and common aspirations. Social settings and churches were also important sites for the dissemination of radical ideas. According to one historian, "taverns were where republican concepts gripped men's imaginations and unleashed new levels of participation." They "served not only as centers to pass judgment of local leaders but as places where abstract concepts and grievances could be translated into terms familiar and immediate to the lives and labor of ordinary colonists."[10]

Ideas that were in the air were contagious. Dock jockeys and tenant farmers may not have read John Locke, but what historian Bernard Bailyn called the "logic of rebellion" that abounded in radical tracts seeped beyond the libraries of the elite, sweeping "past boundaries that few had set out to cross, into regions few had wished to enter," as he put it. Whig ideas that meant one thing to a John Adams sometimes meant something different to the politically impotent. It depended on the prism through which one viewed events.[11] The assorted strands of English radical thought, especially ideas about liberty, natural rights, representation, tyranny, power, and powerlessness aroused in many without power the conviction that they, too, had legitimate political rights. For them, the American Revolution was about securing those rights and gaining the power to advance and protect their interests.

Two sources of ideas were especially influential. Thomas Paine's *Common Sense* focused on independence, but he also nurtured the idea that those who rule do so in their own interest, and that those without influence were devoid of freedom and security. Paine also endowed the colonial rebellion with a mystical aura. The American insurgency, he said, aimed at nothing less than the creation of a new world. After reading Paine, many who had been without influence would come to see the American uprising as more than a struggle against British taxation and tyranny. It was a fight for their empowerment, a struggle so that they too could exercise greater control over their destiny. The Declaration of Independence fixed the idea that the new American nation was committed to equality and natural rights for all. As historian Gordon Wood observed, both Paine and Thomas Jefferson left their readers aware "for the first time ... that their culture was exclusively man-made."[1][2] Many who had previously been without influence came to believe that they, too, had a right to a share of power so that they might participate in the making of their world and society.

The printed word, as well as events such as the Boston Massacre, shaped and transformed attitudes, but nothing was more important than the war in bringing into better focus the way Americans saw themselves and their world. In one way or another, the war touched virtually every American. By the end of 1778, thousands of men had already soldiered in the Continental army and countless others had served as militiamen. Innumerable families had sent loved ones off to war. Some who soldiered did not come home in one piece. Many never returned at all. Hard-pressed families watched property get confiscated by soldiers, faced heavy wartime taxes and rising prices, and experienced chronic scarcities of cherished commodities. Congress and state officials repeatedly told the citizenry, and Washington often told his soldiers, that the new national fight was a glorious cause waged against tyranny and for freedom. Some who believed the rhetoric, and made sacrifices on behalf of winning independence—for themselves as well as their country—expected an American victory to usher in a better way of life than had existed in the colonial era, one in which they were empowered to participate in shaping the world around them.

Much of the fight to shape American society occurred following the war, configuring partisan politics for fifteen years or more after peace finally came. That is not to say, however, that the war failed to immediately sow some profound changes. For instance, Virginia faced the necessity of raising prodigious numbers of men in this protracted war, far more than had been required of the province in any of its previous wars. Congress annually set the Old Dominion's quota of men to be furnished to the Continental army at upwards of three thousand. In addition, Virginia fielded a separate army to fight the British and Indians in the trans-Appalachian West, and it required all other able-bodied free white males between the ages of sixteen and fifty to serve in the militia, portions of which were mobilized frequently throughout the war. It did not take long before discontent was evident. During the war's first months, anger surfaced over the selection of militia officers, what was widely seen as the exorbitantly high pay for those officers and the inconsequential pay of the common soldiery, the exemption from military duty of overseers of slaves, and the practice of many wealthy planters of declaring themselves to be overseers to escape from having to bear arms. The swelling patriotism that had spurred recruitment at the outset of hostilities had faded by 1777, forcing the state to resort to conscription, a practice that aroused protests and led to mass desertion. Raising and furnishing armies and militiamen was expensive. Taxes skyrocketed, which provoked rancor. Militiamen who had been summoned to duty time and again—including in the planting season or at harvest time, sometimes for what turned out to be false alarms, sometimes for service out of state—were particularly restive. After five years of war, mutinies among militiamen flared.

Virginia's leaders were in a bind. They knew that the insatiable maw of war required, as one leader remarked, "nothing less than furnishing . . . by any means" adequate numbers of men. Nothing else would "ensure Success." What is more, the leaders' heads were on the line in the event of defeat. The need to make changes if victory was to be achieved forced concessions from Virginia's ruling planter elite. Before the war ended, Virginia revamped its tax system, shunting aside its regressive poll tax and replacing it with taxes levied on the assessed value of property set by elected officials. Under what historian Michael McDonnell called this "radical, even revolutionary innovation," the wealthy henceforth paid more, the marginal less, in taxation. Furthermore, the legislature terminated the age-old requirement that dissenters pay taxes to the established church. In addition, much-hated conscription was suspended in favor of inducing enlistments by offering recruits a slave between the ages of ten and forty, and the slaves who were offered up were to be taken, if need be, from planters who owned twenty or more slaves.[13]

The changes that occurred in America during the first couple of years after independence, or even by war's end, were not sufficient to please everyone. Nevertheless, change—real, substantive change—had occurred. British rule was over, royal officials were gone, power was exercised by Americans, often by very different Americans than before the war, and not just in democratic Pennsylvania. From northernmost New England to the steamy Low Country, significant changes had taken place in the composition of the state legislatures within a decade of independence. Nearly everywhere, the percentage of extremely wealthy delegates was cut by at least half, their places taken more often than not by small farmers who held up to 50 percent of the seats in some assemblies. Men from elite families had occupied nearly half the seats in the New York and New Jersey assemblies on the eve of independence, but fewer than 15 percent a decade later. In South Carolina the percentage of wealthy delegates dropped from four-fifths to one-third and in Virginia from 50 to 30 percent. Everywhere, power shifted from the coast to the interior. Contemporaries were fully aware that striking changes had occurred. In the mid-1780s, a conservative Yankee remarked disdainfully that "men of sense and property have lost much of their influence" and that "blustering ignorant men" now had power in their hands. But a more radical Georgian exulted that his state had become "the most compleat democracy in the known world" and a Virginian of like mind was delighted that his state's assemblymen were "not quite so well dressed, nor so politely educated, nor so highly born" as before the war. The new assemblymen, he said, were "the People's men."[14]

Change was hastened by the departure of the Tories. Thousands who opposed the Revolution fled their homes. Many left the mainland colonies altogether before July 1776. Thereafter, in the course of the war, countless numbers found sanctuary in areas occupied by the British army, principally New York, Charleston, and Savannah. While loyalism cut across social and economic lines, a disproportionate number of the approximately sixty thousand who ultimately joined the exodus had wielded enormous influence before the Revolution because of their wealth or their family's influence. Their departure shattered previously influential groups and left abundant political offices to be filled by new men. During 1779, after four years of war, James Warren, who had worked closely with the Adamses to further the insurgency in Massachusetts, commented none too charitably that across America men "who would have cleaned my shoes five years ago" now wielded considerable influence.[15]

Virginia's Thomas Jefferson, who was committed to greater political and social change than his friend John Adams, returned home from Congress in the late summer of 1776 to seek reforms that would lay "the axe to the root of the Pseudo-aristocracy" that had long dominated his state. He urged legislation to give fifty acres of land to each free, landless man, a step that would have resulted in universal manhood suffrage in Virginia. That did not fly in an assembly filled with land speculators, but Jefferson, working with others, took the next best step. The assembly turned Kentucky into a county, a step that held the promise of making available cheap and abundant land in the bluegrass country following hostilities. Jefferson additionally secured the assembly's approval to modernize the state's laws, a project that took years to complete. The Committee of Revisors, of which he was a part, ultimately secured approval of a reformed criminal code that reduced a staggering list of capital crimes to just two: treason and murder. In addition, the laws of entail and primogeniture, both staples of aristocratic dominance that over time contributed to the concentration of property in fewer and fewer hands, were repealed. The committee's recommendations for greater religious freedom aroused fierce resistance—Jefferson later called it "the severest contest in which I have ever been engaged"—but after years of struggle, it, too, was finally enacted. Thereafter, no one was compelled to attend or support any church, nor were any to be persecuted for their religious beliefs, or lack thereof.[16]

America was being transformed and more change was coming. Above all, ideas had been planted in the souls of the Revolutionary generation that would fuel still more alterations. These included that all men should enjoy liberty; all possessed the same natural rights; this was a generation destined to remake the world; what was secured in the Revolutionary War was to be bequeathed to those who were yet to be born; those freedoms, rights, and opportunities for which the Revolutionary generation was struggling were being earned through selfless sacrifices, including the shedding of abundant bloodshed. Ideas are powerful, and no idea that flowered during the American Revolution was more potent than that of human equality. The sense that no one was greater than others, that all men were created equal, came to be, in the words of one historian, "the single most powerful and radical ideological force in all of American history."[17]

But while to many it must have seemed that the Revolution had unleashed a whirlwind of change, not all lives experienced an immediate transformation. In the spring of 1776, with independence on the horizon and constitutions soon to be written, Abigail Adams implored her congressman-husband to "Remember the Ladies, and be more generous and favorable to them than your ancestors." She was not beseeching John to ask Congress to enfranchise women, but urging that the "new Code of Laws" about to be written should moderate the unrestricted power that husbands exercised over their wives. "Do not put such unlimited power into the hands of the Husbands," she implored, adding: "Why then, not put it out of the power" of husbands "to use us with cruelty and indignity with impunity." Her husband's response was "I cannot but laugh." A bit later, Hannah Corbin, the sister of Richard Henry Lee, suggested to her brother that if "no taxation without representation" was a principal to be honored, propertied women had "as legal a right to vote as any other person." Her hope was not realized. Women did not vote or hold office, they were not organized, and no one had publicly called into question ingrained assumptions regarding the traditional spheres of women. Women were to marry, have children, and manage the household. That premise had not been debated before the Revolution and it was not debated during the Revolution.[18]

While the status of women went unchallenged, Revolutionary America witnessed an impassioned scrutiny of slavery, the first since the practice of bringing enslaved Africans had haltingly sprung into existence more than a century earlier. The American Revolution was not solely responsible for the questions that were raised about slavery's morality and usefulness. The Enlightenment sparked rethinking about human rights and inhuman practices, and fostered a belief that all of humankind had the potential for improvement. For the first time, too, questions were being raised about whether slavery was an efficient labor system. Furthermore, Quakers and evangelical Christians questioned the ethics of slavery.[19]

The slave trade was not infrequently attacked in the colonial press prior to the war, and on occasion slavery itself was assailed. Eleven years before hostilities began, during the protest against the Sugar Act, Rhode Island governor Stephen Hopkins publicly denounced the "arbitrary and cruel" practice of slavery. In that same year, James Otis, in his pamphlet on British taxation, condemned slavery as "vile and miserable" and challenged the notion that it was "right to enslave a man because he is black." Throughout the long colonial protest inaugurated by the Stamp Act, American insurgents so often spoke in defense of liberty against Britain's conspiracy to enslave them—as a sampler, George Washington wrote that "the trueborn Sons of America" could distinguish "between the Blessings of Liberty and the Wretchedness of Slavery"—that some found it no longer possible to reconcile themselves to the existence of slavery. For instance, Arthur Lee censured slavery in the *Virginia Gazette*, asserting that freedom was the "birth-right of all mankind, of Africans as well as Europeans." Benjamin Rush argued in 1773 that blacks and whites were equal, and that the "vices which are charged upon the Negroes" were the "genuine offspring of slavery." Thomas Paine, in the second essay that he wrote after arriving in Philadelphia—penned a year before *Common Sense*—produced one of the first abolitionist tracts to be published in the colonies. Paine pointedly inquired how a "Christianized people," who professed a faith grounded on a love of others, could "be concerned in the savage practice of slavery."[20] Nor was it a matter of rhetoric only. Connecticut and Pennsylvania prohibited the slave trade in the early 1770s, Rhode Island restricted it, and in 1771 the Massachusetts assembly passed legislation prohibiting it, which Governor Thomas Hutchinson refused to sign into law. Of no little importance, slavery was ruled illegal within England in the Somerset decision handed down in 1772.[21]

But it was the war—as will be seen subsequently—that actually touched the lives of countless numbers of free and enslaved African Americans. Some would soldier, perhaps as many as forty thousand would take flight in hopes of escaping their masters, thousands more would be taken out of the United States by their Loyalist owners, untold numbers would die as a result of the conflagration, and some would pass from slavery to freedom because of the Revolutionary War. The revolution and the war had an effect on whites as well. In a revolution supposedly against tyranny and for liberty, natural rights, and equality, the surprise was not that some whites were prompted to reconsider slavery, but that more were not moved to do so. Nevertheless, the Founding generation, touched by ideas and the experience of war, would take steps in the immediate aftermath of hostilities that it believed would bring about the gradual end of slavery in America.

In the midst of the revolutionary transfiguration, a constitution was drafted for the nascent United States. Like the Declaration of Independence and the Model Treaty, it, too, stemmed from the resolution that Richard Henry Lee introduced in May 1776. In addition to independence and foreign alliances, Lee proposed that Congress prepare and send to the states for ratification "a plan of confederation." Congress responded to Lee's resolution by appointing three committees, one for each item in the resolution. The independence and diplomatic committees were small, but the constitution-writing panel consisted of one representative from each state. A third of its initial members opposed independence, including John Dickinson, who was chosen to prepare the draft. After July 4, however, Dickinson dropped off the committee and out of Congress. His draft would never have been accepted anyway, as Dickinson's document recommended sovereign authority for the national government and checks on the supremacy of state legislatures. Americans in the first blush of a revolution against the centralization of British authority were in no mood to create a centralized national government with nearly untrammeled authority over the states.

Decentralization was about the only thing a majority of the committee members seemed to agree on. Its sessions were bitter and acrimonious, and when the issue of taxing slaves came up, it was greeted by talk of disunion. Should slaves be taxed, warned Thomas Lynch Jr. of South Carolina, "there is an end to Confederation." The threat of fatal divisions led to the suspension of the committee's activities during the war crisis in the second half of 1776. Work was not completed on the constitution—which was called the Articles of Confederation—until the following spring, and even then Congress hesitated to send it to the states for ratification until after America's dramatic victory at Saratoga in the fall of 1777. The constitution divested the national government of strong powers. More or less a copy of the Continental Congress, the congress that was to come into being under the Articles would have no power to tax or to regulate commerce. It could only requisition money from the states. What Congress sent to the states for ratification in 1777 was a constitution for a confederation of equal and independent states, as each would continue to have one vote in Congress. Ratification by all thirteen states was required, a process that would not be completed until 1781.[22]

Another change had occurred, one that threatened to undermine the war effort, jeopardizing all the dreams of what the American Revolution might bring about. By 1779 the economy was in deep trouble. The initial eighteen months or so of the war had been a relatively prosperous time. If military supplies were to be had, trade was essential, and the brisk commerce that resulted drove up prices that had collapsed in the wake of the prewar embargoes. By the end of 1776 the prices that many farm products fetched were 150 percent higher than those in 1770. Artisans did well too, and the war enabled some high rollers to flourish. For instance, General Philip Schuyler, one of the wealthiest New Yorkers, had by the end of 1776 sold goods and services to state and national governments that today would be valued in the millions of dollars. The war stimulated domestic manufacturing, and purchasing American-made goods became the patriotic thing to do, as was wearing homespun clothing. The army had an insatiable appetite for nearly all things—shoes, clothing, food, wagons, carts, barrels, boats, axes, grubbing tools, rum, lumber, gunpowder, and guns. Some goods that wound up in the homes of Americans, or in the army's camps, came from trade in Europe or had been seized from British ships by privateers, but much originated on domestic farms or was made by American tradesmen and laborers.

During the first year and a half of the war, the states had issued millions of dollars of money and Congress had put into circulation about twice the amount of all the states combined. The economy was booming, and the influx of the money further stimulated the boom. However, hurriedly dumping all that money into circulation virtually guaranteed currency depreciation. It commenced about the time that Washington's army was retreating across New Jersey late in 1776. At first, depreciation was a minor problem. But the war continued with no end in sight, and in time governments could not raise enough money to finance the war. Both the states and Congress issued paper money that they could not back.

The "presses can scarcely be found to strike money fast enough," was the response of Washington's military secretary in 1779. Congress urged the states to impose wage and price controls and to prohibit the exportation of essential goods. Some states complied, but others did not, and many citizens disobeyed the regulations that were enacted. Around that same time, Congress stopped printing money. It opened loan offices, hoping people would purchase Continental certificates bearing 6 percent interest. But with the value of money collapsing and the outcome of the war far from certain,

Anno quinto

Georgii III. Regis.

C A P. XII.

An Act for granting and applying certain Stamp
Duties, and other Duties, in the *British* Colonies and Plantations in *America*, towards
further defraying the Expences of defending,
protecting, and securing the same; and for
amending such Parts of the several Acts of
Parliament relating to the Trade and Re-
venues of the said Colonies and Plantations,
as direct the Manner of determining and recovering the Penalties and Forfeitures there-
in mentioned.

WHEREAS by an Act made in *Preamble.*
the last Session of Parliament,
several Duties were granted,
continued, and appropriated, towards defraying the Expences
of defending, protecting, and
securing, the British Colonies
and Plantations in America :
And whereas it is just and necessary, that Provision be made
for raising a further Revenue
within Your Majesty's Domi-
nions in America, towards defraying the said Expences :
We, Your Majesty's most dutiful and loyal Subjects,
the Commons of Great Britain in Parliament assembled,

4 A 2   have

5

The Stamp Act of 1765 (Library of Congress)

The Boston Massacre engraving by Paul Revere (Library of Congress)

Samuel Adams (left) and James Otis (right) (Courtesy of DEA Picture Library)

John Adams (left) and Joseph Galloway (right) (Library of Congress)

Benjamin Franklin (left) and John Dickinson (right) (Library of Congress)

Battle of Bunker Hill by Howard Pyle (Delaware Art Museum)

The title page of Thomas Paine's *Common Sense* (National Archives)

Thomas Paine (left) (Library of Congress), Thomas Jefferson (middle) (Library of Congress), Patrick Henry (right) (United States Senate)

The Philadelphia State House, 1776 (Library of Congress)

George Washington (left) (The White House Historical Association) and Henry Knox (right) (National Park Service)

Horatio Gates (left) (Library of Congress) and Alexander Hamilton (right) (Hulton Archive/Getty)

The Declaration of Independence (Library of Congress)

Declaration of Independence by John Trumbull (United States Capitol)

Thomas Hutchinson (left) (MPI/Getty Images) and the Earl of Chatham, William Pitt (right) (Library of Congress)

Frederick Lord North (left) and Lord George Germain (right) (Library of Congress)

Edmund Burke (left) and King George III (right) (Library of Congress)

Colonel Benedict Arnold (left) and General Charles Lee (right) (Library of Congress)

Major General Nathanael Greene (left) (Photo by Universal History Archive/UIG via Getty Images) and Richard Henry Lee (right) (Creative Commons 2.0, Flickr user cliff1066)

Captain John Paul Jones (left) (United States Senate) and General Daniel Morgan (right) (Independence National Historic Park)

General William Howe (left) and Admiral Richard Howe (right) (Library of Congress)

Sir Henry Clinton (left) (Library of Congress) and Thomas Gage (right) (Yale Center for British Art, Paul Mellon Collection)

General John Burgoyne (left) (Hulton Archives/Getty Images) and General Charles Cornwallis (right) (Photo by DeAgostini/Getty Images)

Lieutenant Colonel Banastre Tarleton (left) and General Philip Schuyler (right) (Library of Congress)

Marquis de Lafayette (left) and Comte d'Estaing (right) (Hulton Fine Art Collection)

Comte de Rochambeau (left) (National Archives) and Admiral de Grasse (right) (Library of Congress)

Washington and Lafayette at Valley Forge by John Ward Dunsmore (Library of Congress)

Surrender of Lord Cornwallis by John Trumbull (United States Capitol)

American Commissioners of the Preliminary Peace Agreement with Great Britain, 1783–1784, London, England (unfinished) by Benjamin West. From left to right: John Jay, John Adams, Benjamin Franklin, Henry Laurens, and William Temple Franklin, Secretary to the American Delegation (The Henry Francis DuPont Winterthur Museum, Wilmington, Delaware)

General George Washington Resigning His Commission by John Trumbull (United States Capitol)

few people risked investing in the securities. Meanwhile, Congress relinquished to the states the responsibility of paying the army, and it urged that
they not only resort to "speedy, vigorous & repeated Taxation," but that they
also confiscate and sell Loyalist lands and houses. State taxes skyrocketed.
During 1779 the states levied upwards of one hundred times the taxes they
had imposed in peacetime. Before the year was out, most states began to
appropriate property belonging to Tories. Labeling Thomas Hutchinson and
Andrew Oliver, among others, as "Notorious Conspirators" and "open
avowed enemies," Suffolk County, Massachusetts—which included Boston—
seized and sold thirty-five parcels of property; Dutchess County in New York
impounded and sold 469 tracts. But the transactions were in depreciated
currency, so that the property sold on average for only about a quarter of the
assessed value.

There was no end in sight. By 1779 the value of Continental currency had
shrunk to three cents to the dollar, wheat and salt sold for about forty times
what they had gone for two years earlier, a hat could cost as much as $400,
and the price of a horse had risen twentyfold. When it reached the point that
the army's Quartermaster Corp had to spend $100 million to obtain the same
amount of supplies that had cost $10 million early in the war, Washington
cogently summed up the sorry state of the economy and its impact on the
army: how can the war be waged when a "waggon load of money will scarcely
purchase a waggon load of provision."[23]

In December 1778 Washington journeyed to Philadelphia at the behest of
Congress. It wanted to know what Washington had in mind for the coming
campaign. He came willingly, even eagerly, as he wanted to make sure that
Congress understood the economy's adverse impact on the army. Washington,
who had not been away from his army during the past thirty months, spent
forty-three days in Philadelphia. What he saw of Congress and the civilian
sector caused him greater alarm than anything he had seen since the dark
days of 1776. Night after night, he was the guest of affluent Philadelphians.
They were living comfortably and their tables groaned with food and wine.
For them, the war was far, far away. Their chief preoccupation appeared to be
how to further enrich themselves. Washington could not believe what he saw.
At a time when common soldiers faced deprivation and danger, and officers
were either quitting the service or—as Washington said—staying on and
"sinking by sure degrees into beggary & want," Philadelphia's merchants and
financiers regularly attended concerts and plays, and hosted lavish dinner
parties. Many lived lives of "idleness, dissipation & extravagance" with
nothing on their minds but their "insatiable thirst for riches," Washington

remarked. Driven by "avarice, & thirst for gain," many of the leading Philadelphians viewed "the War for their own private emolument." Washington now suspected that "various tribes of money makers" in other cities saw things in the same light. A few days in Philadelphia convinced him that the American Revolution was in "eminent danger." Unless "things [were brought] back to first principles . . . inevitable ruin must follow."

His judgment of Congress was just as bad. Virtually none of the men who had been his colleagues in 1774 and 1775 still sat in Congress. Some, like Franklin and John Adams, were abroad on diplomatic assignments. Most, like Jefferson, had gone home to serve their states. A handful had forsaken public service altogether. With little knowledge of economics, Washington initially jumped to the conclusion that America's economic plight was due to what he believed were the mediocrities who now dominated Congress. "[P]arty disputes & personal quarrels are the great business of the day whilst . . . a great & accumulated debt—ruined finances—depreciated money—& want of credit . . . are but secondary considerations," he said. Washington added that while first-rate "characters . . . sleep at home," America was "sinking into irretrievable . . . ruin."[24]

Gradually, Washington saw that America's tribulations were due to more than the presumed lack of talent in Congress. This appears to have been the moment when he concluded that a decentralized political system would doom America to a second-rate status and might rob it of victory in this war. He told others that a nation must work like the "Mechanism of a Clock." In his metaphor, each state represented the small working parts of the clock; the national government was the "great wheel, or spring which is to set the whole in motion." The states were "useless"—that is, their interests would never be secured—unless the clock (the United States) was "kept in good order." Washington was too good a politician to openly assail the Articles of Confederation, which was winding its way through the ratification process. Instead, he privately urged that "our Men of abilities . . . come forth to save their Country." Pointedly, he asked that "Jefferson & others" not stay at home and "let our noble struggle end in ignominy."[25] The war was far from over, Washington cautioned. Whereas a year earlier Lord North's ministry may have been willing to make peace "upon almost any terms," the "present state of our Currency" had raised Great Britain's spirits, leading it to continue the fight, hopeful that the American war effort, like its economy, would collapse. The time had not yet arrived, Washington warned, when America's "ablest men" could "set down under our own Vine and our own fig Tree" and live idly. Jefferson got the message. He did not return to Congress, but he agreed to stand for election as governor of Virginia, and that summer he was elected by the state legislature.

Congress's real reason for summoning Washington was to discuss the campaign of 1779. During the fall, Congress had once again been beseeched to sanction an invasion of Canada. Such a venture was pushed loudly by Lafayette and General Gates, and embraced by nearly every congressman from New England and New York. Washington, however, was no more keen on invading Canada than he had been during the Valley Forge winter, and in November—a few weeks before coming to Philadelphia—he made his feelings known to Congress. Such an operation, Washington counseled, was fraught with danger and too risky to contemplate at this juncture. Over and above the inherent perils in getting the invasion force to Quebec and scoring a victory, Washington contended not only that the cost of such an operation might prevent more crucial initiatives, but also that peeling away some of the soldiery outside Manhattan might give Clinton a free hand to act. In a confidential letter to Henry Laurens, the president of Congress, Washington raised further objections. He claimed that the plan to invade Canada had originated in Versailles, which envisaged an American conquest as the first step toward France's reacquisition of the region. That, said Washington, would not be in the best interest of the United States.[26]

Only Washington knew how much of this he believed, or whether his opposition to the proposed invasion stemmed from hidden motives, including his concern that General Gates, his enemy, would almost certainly be chosen to lead the campaign. One thing is certain. His principal object was the retaking of New York, and he wanted his army to be in position and strong enough to act should d'Estaing suddenly return with the French fleet. Washington was convinced that victory over the British occupiers was possible if the allies acted in concert, and he further believed that a decisive victory in New York would end the war. The idea of retaking New York had hardened into an obsession with Washington.

Congress was no longer willing to buck Washington, not on questions of strategy nor, for that matter, on much else. Given Washington's objections, it spurned the Canadian project, asserting that "the arms of America should be employed in expelling the Enemy from her own shores, before the Liberation of a Neighbouring Province is undertaken."[27] But if invading Canada was not to be considered, and a campaign to retake New York hinged on the uncertain prospect of the French fleet's arrival, what, if anything, would the army do in 1779? Congress's early-winter discussions with Washington revolved around two possibilities.

At the tag end of 1778, Great Britain had launched its southern strategy, dispatching a force of 3,500 men—including four Loyalist battalions—to reclaim Georgia. That province, the newest and smallest of the thirteen states, was defended by only about 850 men, two-thirds of them Continentals, the remainder militiamen. They were commanded by Brigadier General Robert Howe, whom Congress had put in charge of the army's Southern Department two years before. Though badly outnumbered, Howe put up a fight. It did not last long. Before sunset on the day that the British went into action, nearly every American soldier had been killed or captured and Savannah once again was in British hands. Within a brief time, too, Britain's royal governor had been reinstated, the assembly was back in the hands of Tories—who immediately repealed all the laws that the rebel legislators had enacted since 1776— and several companies composed of Loyalist militiamen were under arms. When the British army had disembarked on the Georgia coast under a warm December sun, it had offered freedom to slaves who fled their rebel masters. In not long, upwards of 1,500 former slaves had decamped behind British lines and were serving the soldiers as cooks, laundresses, nurses, and butchers. By the time Washington and Congress began discussions in January 1779, the portion of Georgia in and around Savannah was again a royal colony.[28]

Congressmen from Georgia and South Carolina immediately demanded that a new army be established in the Southern Department and that some units under Washington be detached southward. While South Carolinians figured they would be Britain's next target, congressmen from throughout the South wrung their hands at the prospect of the liberation of slaves, a step that would ruin planters, sow divisions, devastate morale, strengthen the British army, and possibly trigger slave insurrections. With considerable myopia, Washington discounted the threat posed by the British in the South. To win the war, he said, the enemy had to destroy the Continental army, not take "defenseless Towns." He jealously guarded the men under his command. Congress found men elsewhere and sent them southward, slowly building an American force in South Carolina and the Georgia backcountry.[29]

New York's congressmen had an agenda as well. Most would have preferred a Canadian campaign, but when Congress rejected that undertaking, the New Yorkers called for action against the Six Nation Iroquois Confederacy and its Tory allies on the northern frontier. Neither in New York nor anywhere else had the frontier ever been entirely peaceful once Anglo-American hostilities erupted. Settlers—whom General Gage once characterized as "Licentious Ruffians" who in their insatiable desire for land repeatedly perpetrated "violences"—had time and again made inroads on the Native Americans' lands, often arousing a forceful response. After 1775, encroachments by frontiersmen were especially common in Kentucky and just above the Ohio River, a region far west of the extinct Proclamation Line. Raids by one side were answered by counterraids from the other side. Furthermore, not long elapsed before British Indian agents began working zealously to bring tribes north and south into the war. Native American militants throughout Indian country preached not only the necessity of relying on British assistance but also that the Revolutionary War offered a golden moment for concerted action. After all, as Great Britain was willing to provide supplies and support, there would never be a better time for recovering what had been lost in previous generations. Similarly, leaders within some states, aware that the British army was in the fight of its life east of the mountains, saw an opportunity for making gains at the expense of the Indians. It was a toxic brew of hate, passion, and avarice, and not long elapsed before it boiled over.

Virginia, fresh off its success in the Cherokee War, spied an opportunity in 1777 to "quiet . . . our frontiers" and "add to the Empire of liberty an extensive and fertile Country." (Those were Jefferson's words.) An army under George Rogers Clark was dispatched to capture Detroit and solidify the state's claims to the vast territory that many Virginians believed London had attempted to take from them in the Quebec Act in 1774. Clark never captured Detroit and his marauding force most certainly did not bring quiet to the frontier. It, in fact, lit up violence from Kentucky to the Mississippi River, from the Ohio River to the Great Lakes. Yet, though Clark failed to achieve his original objectives, he had, in the words of historian John Selby, "kept the British and Indians in the West sufficiently off balance to prevent them from mounting a campaign that could distract American armies in the East," or even from acting in strength until it was too late for them to achieve their ends or affect the outcome of the war.[30]

Virginians had helped make the Ohio Country a bloody ground, but by 1779 perhaps no frontier had experienced more bloodshed than that of New York. This frontier was the homeland of the Iroquoian-speaking peoples who made up the Iroquois Confederacy. At the outset of the Revolutionary War, their leaders had told colonial commissioners at a parley in Albany that they would remain neutral. "We mind nothing but Peace," they said, and they fully intended to honor their pledge. But Indians, like the residents of the states, were changed by the war. In time, some tribesmen within the Confederacy, like Thayendanegea, or Joseph Brant, as his British friends called him, concluded that the American patriots had started "this Rebellion to be sole Masters of this Continent," a turn of events that spelled disaster for all Indians.

Brant, who was thirty-two when the war began, had been born in the Ohio Country, near present day Cleveland. His parents were Mohawks—one of the six tribes in the confederacy—but a grandparent likely was English. During his adolescence, Brant was taken under the wing of Britain's first superintendent for Indian affairs, who saw to his formal education and conversion to Christianity. Brant grew to be a tall, spare, handsome young man who struck observers as courteous, grave, dignified, intelligent, and rugged. He also became the owner of a substantial amount of property, including a successful farm that was home to him and his wives. (He married three times, as his first two wives died young of tuberculosis.) The Revolutionary War did not radicalize Brant. He had grown more militant in the years leading to the war as a result of mistreatment by colonial authorities in and around Tryon County, in New York's Mohawk Valley. Certain that he would lose his property and face continuous harassment and discrimination should Great Britain lose the war, Brant hurried to Canada to fight against the colonial invaders in 1775. Following Montgomery's defeat in the attack on Quebec, Brant accompanied several English officials to London. He remained in the metropolis for four months, a visit capped by an audience with Lord Germain, who assured his guest that "the King their father" would crush the rebellion and redress the Indians' grievances. Brant believed him, and he returned home more than ever convinced that the interests of the Iroquois would be served better by preserving ties with Great Britain.

Brant landed in America in the summer of 1776 and fought with the British in the New York campaign. While Washington retreated across New Jersey that autumn, Brant visited one Iroquois town after another to urge that neutrality be cast aside. He also met with Tories who lived on New York's northern frontier and appealed to them to take up arms. Most Iroquois turned a deaf ear to him. But Brant was undeterred. He formed what came to known as Brant's Volunteers, a mix of Mohawks and Loyalist vigilantes. Beginning in 1777 he and his confederates roamed Tryon County, plundering little hamlets and isolated farms and driving off settlers who refused to declare for Britain. Brant—bold and charismatic, and to many a man who saw the meaning of the colonial rebellion with crystal clarity—snatched the leadership role from the hands of the sachem chiefs.

Burgoyne's campaign sparked greater activism among the Iroquois, and upwards of three thousand served with him or Colonel St. Leger in their disastrous endeavors. Saratoga did not bring peace to the region. In the summer of 1778, Brant's Volunteers and other pro-British bands resumed their destructive sorties throughout the Mohawk Valley. At times, more than eight hundred Indians, Loyalists, and British regulars—described by the victims as a "Banditti of thieves & Robbers"—composed the parties carrying out the attacks. They struck screaming the "dreadful yells of Indians," according to one of their victims; terrified settlers, clustered inside small forts and safe houses, could hear "Cries of Murder" on the outside. Homes were razed, farms plundered, livestock destroyed, farmers tortured and maimed, sawmills and gristmills leveled. The hamlet of Cherry Valley, fifty miles west of Albany, was struck at dawn on a rainy November 1778 morning. It was the seventh village to be destroyed in a span of some sixty days, and the settlement widely thought to be the most secure. What occurred there was soon commonly, and accurately, characterized as a massacre. Sixteen Massachusetts Continentals, part of a regiment sent to garrison the local stockade that had been built the year before, were killed, along with thirty-two residents, including nine members of one family. Most of the civilian victims were women and children, as were a considerable percentage of the seventy taken captive. Long before Washington came to Philadelphia, New York was seeking help in coping with the raiders.[31]

During his initial discussions in Philadelphia, Washington had been a roadblock to those congressmen who urged action in the South or in Canada, but from the outset he welcomed doing something to pacify the northern frontier. A successful strike against what he called the "repeated incursions of the Savages" would pacify New York's frontier, and that in turn would free up desperately needed men and materials for his cherished attack on New York City. Within three weeks of his arrival in Philadelphia, the decision had been made "to carry the War into the Indian Country."[32]

Washington called on General Sullivan, who had failed so often in the past, to lead the campaign against the Iroquois. As a diversion, one division of Continentals took steps that gave the appearance of preparations for an invasion of Canada through the Connecticut Valley. Meanwhile, three divisions of Sullivan's force readied an advance on Iroquoia from eastern Pennsylvania and via the Susquehanna-Chemung and Allegheny Rivers. The feint was critical to the success of the undertaking, as the authorities in Quebec fell for it; they gathered a large force inside the walls of their citadel and awaited an attack that never came. Thus, the Indians were left to fend for themselves against a massive and heavily armed force that totaled some four thousand soldiers. Sullivan's orders were clear. He was to wreak "the total destruction and devastation of their settlements" and "capture . . . as many prisoners of every age and sex as possible." Furthermore, Sullivan was not to agree to any peace terms until the "total ruin of their settlements is effected."[33]

The American army—in what became known as Sullivan's Expedition—faced virtually no opposition. Realizing the folly of standing and fighting against overwhelming odds, the warriors—including Joseph Brant—fled, and they were accompanied by residents of entire settlements. Proceeding with grim efficiency under late summer's cerulean skies, the army destroyed town after abandoned town. Nothing was spared. Day after day, the soldiery left in its wake acrid gray-black smoke from the fires set to domiciles, vegetable gardens, and shimmering green and amber fields of corn and grain. Forty hamlets ceased to exist, some 160,000 bushels of corn were laid waste, and four thousand Iroquois retreated into Canada, where they faced a harsh winter without adequate food.

But in the long run, the apparent success of the operation proved to be illusory. While the frontier remained largely tranquil for the remainder of 1779, the Indian warriors were unscathed and eager for revenge. The bloodletting along New York's scarred frontier resumed early in 1780, preceded by a letter that Brant wrote to the enemy authorities: "You have exceedingly angered me. . . . I shall certainly distroy without distinction."[34]

While Washington read Sullivan's dispatches, he waited impatiently for the French fleet and dreamed of attacking New York. It was not to be, and Washington's army remained largely inactive throughout 1779. The British were not especially active either. General Clinton holed up in New York City awaiting reinforcements, having been promised six thousand fresh troops by London. But like the French fleet for which Washington was expectantly waiting, the supplemental redcoat regiments never arrived, and Clinton filled out the year with small operations. In May, he sent six warships and 1,800 men to wreak havoc along the Virginia coast. The raiders destroyed shipyards, captured or destroyed 130 vessels, burned six million pounds of tobacco, razed warehouses, ransacked numerous plantations, and liberated some 1,500 slaves. Clinton had manifold motives. In addition to seeking the destruction of tobacco that was being exchanged in Europe for war materials, he hoped to tie down men in Virginia who might otherwise serve under Washington or elsewhere in the South, and he wished to plant seeds of doubt among at least some of the residents of the Old Dominion about continuing the war. His raid succeeded on all counts.[35]

Hard on the heels of the destructive Chesapeake raid, Clinton utilized the same armada to seize rebel posts at Stony Point and Fort Lafayette at Verplanck's Point, only a dozen or so miles below West Point on the Hudson. The delighted British commander gleefully proclaimed that his counterpart must be "distressed." He was correct. Washington knew that the installations would serve as a base for gathering supplies and "a new door to distress and disaffect the country." Mostly, however, Washington feared for the safety of West Point, which if lost could give the enemy its long-sought objective of controlling the Hudson River and severing New England's link to the mid-Atlantic and southern states. Washington's fears were well placed. Clinton was indeed laying the groundwork for an advance on West Point, an operation that would compel Washington to stand and fight, and in fact Washington marched most of his men into the Hudson Highlands and readied them for a possible battle.[36]

Clinton never came. Some Americans, Horatio Gates among them, believed the British could have taken West Point had they moved quickly. Rumors buzzed that Clinton "knew not what to do" and that he was inactive "from indecision and a fluctuating state of mind." Actually, he was awaiting the phantom reinforcements. Clinton, in 1779, was akin to someone trying to fight with one arm tied behind him. British forces in the American theater had shrunk by some fifteen thousand men during the past twenty-four months, and the British navy in North American waters had declined precipitously as well, as steadily more ships were redeployed to the Caribbean. Clinton's only other action that summer was to order raids in Connecticut that resembled the spring foray into Virginia. New Haven, Norwalk, and Fairfield took the brunt of the blows, each suffering significant damage. Clinton hoped the raids might "stir Mr. Washington," as he put it, but otherwise he never imagined that the forays would be pivotal. Clinton was uncomfortable with this sort of war, thinking it better suited to pirates than to a proud army. And when the year came to an end, Clinton, sounding much like Washington, reflected that "Another year . . . of this destructive war" had passed without it having resulted in "a single event to better our condition or brighten our prospects."[37]

Washington could point to Sullivan's Expedition among his actions during the year, though its success was fleeting. Furthermore, having demonstrated his proclivity for surprise attacks in past campaigns, Washington pulled off another in July 1779. Fearing an erosion of morale, and deeply worried about the security of West Point, he organized a daring attack to retake Stony Point. Anthony Wayne, whom Washington regarded as not just intrepid but also an inveterate risktaker, was to lead 1,350 men in a midnight assault on the installation garrisoned by 700 redcoats. The assault force advanced quietly under a moon sheathed in clouds. To avoid shooting one another, the American soldiers were ordered to attack with unloaded guns. They carried muskets with bayonets, as well as swords, knives, and spontoons (half-pikes), and they were prepared to fight with their fists. When Wayne shouted the order that launched the attack, the British were taken by surprise. But the British were soldiers, and they fought desperately for survival during the hour-long battle. The Americans fought just as tenaciously, prompting Washington to say later that the Continentals "behaved like men . . . determined to be free." The Americans killed or captured all but 25 of the British defenders while suffering about a hundred casualties. Whatever the value of the fort (and it was not inconsequential), the victory was a propaganda coup that buoyed sinking

244

WHIRLWIND

morale. General Gates summed up the ecstatic mood: "American Arms have now reached the Summit of Military Fame." To that, he added: "George the 3d may seek another Continent . . . for he has lost This."[38]

Gates was a bit too optimistic. There were no more American victories that year, or for the next twenty-seven months. One major setback occurred before 1779 ended. It was in the South. If Washington persisted in underestimating the importance of the war in South Carolina and Georgia, southerners did not. Southern congressmen and officials in Charleston begged French diplomats to urge d'Estaing to sail for Savannah. He did just that. Early in September d'Estaing arrived off Tybee Island, just below Georgia's capital, and rapidly prepared to act, for he was under orders to return soon to France. If optimistic before his arrival, d'Estaing was startled to discover that the new commander in the southern department, General Benjamin Lincoln, had barely one thousand Continentals with him. D'Estaing came close to abandoning the operation to retake Savannah, but he stayed, fearing he would be disgraced at home if he did nothing. He called on Lincoln to bring every Continental from South Carolina, raise militia, and summon the rebel soldiers strung out along the Carolina-Georgia frontier.[39]

While he awaited his allies, d'Estaing brought his ships, armed with heavy cannon, up the Savannah River to the city and positioned them within range of the British lines. All the while, more and more of d'Estaing's allies gathered. After three weeks, the Franco-American force had swelled to 7,722 men, about 40 percent of them French marines. As the Americans brought up their heavy artillery, struggling to move the cumbersome guns through coastal Georgia's reluctant sandy soil, d'Estaing demanded the surrender of the British garrison within Savannah. Talks began, and continued for several days. The discussions went nowhere. The delay in launching the attack was a boon to the British defenders under General Augustine Prevost. Not only did reinforcements from near Charleston drift in while the talks spun on, but also Prevost put his men—and Savannah's slaves—to work digging an intricate defensive system of épaulements and traverses. Prevost had only about half as many men as his enemy—his numbers included two hundred armed blacks and a handful of Cherokees—but when the siege began, they were extremely well entrenched.

On October 4, nearly a month after arriving on Georgia's coast, d'Estaing at last opened fire on the city's besieged defenders. Day after day of shelling followed. Houses and buildings were leveled or burned. Frightened residents cowered in basements or sought refuge beneath the tall riverbanks, sharing space with huge wharf rats and enduring a blistering sun by day and nights quick with autumn's chill. Countless civilians, including many slaves, perished during the merciless bombardment. D'Estaing's real prey—the British soldiery—escaped largely unscathed, safe in their redoubts and trenches. After nearly a week, d'Estaing saw that continued shelling was useless. He ordered an attack. The assault began at daybreak on October 9. It was suicidal. In fact, it was a Bunker Hill in reverse. The charging allied troops were repulsed at every point of attack. D'Estaing suffered two wounds, though neither was fatal. But 117 of the men in the Allied force died and 707 were wounded. The British lost fewer than 100 men.[40]

The Americans had failed to retake Savannah and had little to show for 1779, the fifth year of what many were beginning to think was a never-ending war. Convinced that time was on his side, Washington had largely remained idle, gambling on the possibility of a pivotal allied campaign to retake New York. A few weeks after this difficult year wound down, with the economy in ruins and signs of war weariness abounding, Washington at last appeared to conclude that perhaps time was his enemy's ally, not his. "In modern wars," he wrote, "the longest purse must chiefly determine the event." That spelled trouble for the United States. Its purse could never match that of its former mother country and, for that matter, Washington did not think France's could either. Something else worried Washington. He feared that America's lack of success since 1777 might drive France to seek a peace.[41] That meant that the new year, 1780, could well be the war's most crucial.

CHAPTER 13

"Whom Can We Trust Now?"

A Year of Disasters, 1780

AMERICA HAD SUFFERED no major military disasters in 1779, but it had accomplished nothing toward winning the war. Nor did the new year start happily. Most of the Continentals went into winter quarters with Washington at Morristown, New Jersey. In popular lore, Valley Forge was the army's worst winter, but for those who were there, the winter of 1780 was worse. Veterans remembered it as "the hard winter." Morristown's first snow that winter fell in December, and thereafter it snowed every three or four days, including an early-January blizzard that raged for thirty-six hours. With the temperature seemingly stuck below freezing, snow drifts grew to depths of twelve feet. Thanks to French aid, the men were better clothed than they were two years earlier, and each had a blanket, but the soldiers' quarters remained primitive and the incredible cold forced men to sleep huddled together in an often-futile effort to stay warm.

Episodic food shortages also bedeviled the men. Private Joseph Plumb Martin once went four days without a meal, during which he saw some comrades "roast their shoes," gnaw on tree bark, and dine on unwary dogs that visited the camp. When food was available, it seldom included meat. Corn, rice, and bread were the staples, prompting Washington to comment that his soldiers had to "eat every kind of horse food but hay." In February, General Greene feared that the army was close to "disbanding for want of provisions." He added with disgust that a nation of farms "overflowing with plenty" was "suffering an Army employed for the defense of every thing . . . to perish for want of food."[1]

As at Valley Forge, there was no single cause for the scarcities. Devastating droughts during the previous summer and fall had reduced the harvests, and the persistently bad winter weather played havoc with the flow of that which was available. Those problems were exacerbated by the supply system. Congress had earlier sought remediation by relinquishing the job of supplying the army to the states, but that only complicated matters. Raging that America's governance system was "a many headed Monster," Washington yet again wondered if the war would be lost because "our measures are not under the influence and direction of one council, but thirteen." The winter crisis aroused worries of mutinies, and an uprising did occur within the Connecticut line in the spring that led to attacks on some officers, including the nonfatal bayoneting of a colonel. But Washington appears to have been more fearful of a British attack, which, as at Valley Forge, he believed would result in "a most serious calamity." The British never attacked, though at one point General Clinton dispatched a raiding party of three hundred men, who were to storm the camp and seize Washington. It was foiled by the very snow that, among other things, gave Washington such grief.[2]

The tribulations of Morristown were extreme, but hardly a time existed in this war when the Continental army soldiers were free of troubles. Private Martin, who had enlisted in 1776 and reenlisted for the duration a year later, in time came to wonder at his "imbecility" in having rejoined the army. Many of his comrades had similar thoughts about continuing to serve, and not a few of them tried to get away. The army's desertion rate varied according to circumstances. It spiked in 1776 at around 20 percent, ran about 7 percent during the Valley Forge calamities, and from 1779 onward hovered between 1 and 3 percent, brought down in part because the army's leadership learned to be more generous in granting furloughs during the winter season. The reasons for the enlisted soldiers' discontent are not difficult to discern. Food was at best adequate and often fell short of that mark, housing was rudimentary, warm clothing and blankets were not always available, and the demands of work or duty were incessant. There was wood to cut, a camp to be cleaned, latrines to be dug and covered, clothes to be washed, food to be prepared, cooking and eating implements to be cleaned, cartridges to be made, and weapons to be cared for, along with inspections, roll calls, drills, and sentry, guard, and patrol duty. Forage parties were put together on nearly a daily basis. Other units were sent out almost every day to harass enemy foragers. Still others were dispatched to search for deserters. Livestock had to be driven to camp, slaughtered, and butchered. And the days were long. Reveille was sounded when there was sufficient light to see a thousand yards; the workday did not end until sundown, if it ended then, for every night some men were assigned sentinel duties. There is "no cessation of duty," one weary soldier complained, and another said he faced "one constant drill" year round. A soldier who had lived on a farm before the war recalled harvests as the most demanding time of the year, but he allowed that the labor of gathering crops "is nothing to be compared to the fatigues I undergo Daily" in the army.[3]

Enlisted men served under a stringent code of military justice. Soldiers were punished for desertion, disobeying orders, thievery, falling asleep on duty, plundering civilians, and countless other offenses. Punishments were often barbaric. Men faced floggings of up to one hundred lashes for many infractions, with the number of stripes depending on the severity of the wrongdoing and whether it was a repeat offense. Punishments also included being made to ride the wooden horse, run the gauntlet, or endure the piquet (suspension by one arm for a protracted period). Some behavior—homosexual acts, for instance—could result in the soldier being drummed out of camp, a step tantamount to a dishonorable discharge. Execution by the hangman or firing squad was the most extreme punishment, and upwards of one hundred soldiers are believed to have met this fate. After 1778 most death penalties were carried out by excarabineers, or executioners, in the Maréchaussée Corps. All penalties were meted out following a hearing, or court-martial, in which the judges were at all times officers. But some punishments were outside the official code of justice. There were instances when officers abused soldiers— slapping, punching, or even clubbing them with the stock of a musket. Nor was it unheard of for an officer to take the punitive step of simply, and arbitrarily, assigning a man extra work, an unsavory task, or a hazardous duty.[4]

Atop deprivation, cruelty, and abasement, the soldiers faced danger. The war claimed an appalling toll. In addition to untold numbers of militiamen, sailors, and privateers who perished, some thirty thousand of the one hundred thousand who served in the Continental army died in the course of this long, bloody war.

As in all wars, men died of accidents and suicide. Less than a third of deaths within the Continental army were battle-related. The overwhelming majority of those who perished were victims of disease. Roughly an equal number of those who died from illnesses were prisoners of war and soldiers in Continental army cantonments. Washington understood that there was a relationship between hygiene and health, and he sought to teach his officers the importance of clean camps. Even so, disease was an ever-present danger in camps, where underfed, overworked, poorly housed, and inadequately clad men lived in close quarters. Diseases such as dysentery, typhus, diphtheria, malaria, and pneumonia stalked the soldiery. Smallpox had struck the northern armies in 1775 and 1776, but beginning in the winter of 1777, Washington mandated the variolation, or inoculation, of his soldiers who had never suffered from the disease. The step was so successful that it became a regular feature of army life during the winter months, with the result that smallpox, the scourge of armies since time immemorial, was a relatively minor problem in the last years of this war.[5]

The army at Morristown was considerably different from the original Continental army. A small percentage of the men were draftees, as some states resorted to conscription to meet their quotas; those who were drafted were usually unmarried militiamen who were obliged to serve shorter terms of duty, seldom exceeding a year. At its inception, the army had no cavalry, but by 1780 there were troops of light horse, as well as engineers, a geographer, surveyors of roads with topographical staffs, chasseurs or light infantry for carrying out raids behind enemy lines, military police, a regiment for repairing equipment and maintaining ordnance, sappers (for digging entrenchments) and miners (for constructing subterranean tunnels), and Washington's Life Guard, a company of one hundred men who protected the commander in chief. Most of the Continentals carried French-made muskets, the artillery included some two hundred field pieces furnished by America's ally, and much of the clothing and most of the blankets were also of French origin. Few of the enlisted men were property owners or skilled craftsmen. Most were young and single. Some of the officers were French, Prussian, or Polish. Not a few enlisted men were recent immigrants, principally from Ireland, Germany, Scotland, and England, leading one soldier to remark that he heard so many languages and dialects that he suspected a few of his colleagues might be from "some undiscovered country."[6]

The army was strikingly different too in that by 1780 a considerable number of soldiers were African Americans. Neither the army nor Congress had always welcomed their service. When Washington took command in 1775, he found a handful of blacks in the army, New England men who had earlier enlisted in the Grand American Army, some after having fought as militiamen on the first day of the war. Washington had not wanted them or any other black men in the army. He had feared that the arms they bore would find their way into the hands of insurrectionary slaves, and he had also been apprehensive that the presence of blacks might hinder recruiting or encourage the British armed forces to enlist slaves and free blacks. After six months at the helm, Washington changed his opinion, possibly from having discovered that blacks could perform as ably as whites, but Congress still held to the commander's initial view. At the end of 1775 it decreed that the African Americans already in the army could reenlist but that "no others" could serve.[7]

During the Valley Forge crisis in 1778, Rhode Island—with Washington's unspoken blessing—defied Congress by announcing its intention of raising a regiment of blacks. In no time, 250 African Americans enlisted, including both free blacks and slaves. The latter joined with their master's blessing after the owner was granted compensation in the amount of $400; the bondsmen were enticed to risk life and limb after being promised freedom at war's end. Connecticut, Massachusetts, Virginia, New York, and Maryland followed Rhode Island's example, though some—Virginia, for instance—admitted only free blacks and specified that they were to be drummers, fifers, or pioneers (artisans armed with axes and saws). By around the time of the Battle of Monmouth, some 775 African Americans were in the Continental army and some were noncommissioned officers. Steadily larger numbers of blacks entered the army from 1779 onward, until ultimately about five thousand African Americans had enlisted in the Continental army. By war's end, blacks accounted for approximately 5 percent of all the men who had soldiered as Continentals, and they served in integrated units, something that would not occur again in the United States Army until the Korean conflict 175 years later.

No southern state had authorized arming slaves, but in the wake of Savannah's capture late in 1778, Colonel John Laurens, a South Carolinian serving as an aide to Washington, persuaded his father, Henry Laurens, the president of Congress, to seek congressional authorization for raising "able bodied Negroes." By the following March, Congress was close to adopting a resolution recommending that Georgia and South Carolina raise three thousand slaves for the army; while the slaves would not be paid for their service, the congressional measure would have compensated slave owners for the loss of their property and at war's end freed the slaves who had soldiered and awarded them $50. Low Country planters were so aghast that South Carolina's Council threatened to drop out of the war if the measure was adopted. The elder Laurens urged Washington to back the resolution, thinking his endorsement alone could persuade South Carolina to comply. Young Laurens and Alexander Hamilton, his fellow aide, also urged Washington to act, with Hamilton insisting that "negroes will make very excellent soldiers" as their "natural faculties are probably as good as ours." But Washington refused to get involved, largely from fear that doing so would encourage the enemy to actively recruit blacks, but he also shrank from acting from a foreboding that it would lead South Carolina to abandon the war and the United States.[8]

Women could not serve in the army or militias, but they were in camp nonetheless. The wives and daughters of numerous field grade officers came to camp annually while the army was in winter quarters, enjoying several months of parties, dances, courtships, and formal dinners in the company of officers while the enlisted men huddled in their dark and austere huts only a short distance away. Washington welcomed the presence of these women, but he did everything he could to keep the spouses and girlfriends of the enlisted men away from the army, issuing more than two dozen general orders on the topic. His refrain was that women in camp would drain the army's all-too-often bare pantry. Washington made considerable headway against unmarried women, but ultimately tolerated the presence of the soldiery's wives. It was either accept them or chance losing their husbands to desertion.

The number of "camp followers," as they were called, averaged about 3 percent of the number of soldiers, so that two hundred to three hundred women were customarily in camp. As most soldiers were young and single, a significant number of married soldiers must have been joined by their spouses. The women were required to be immunized against smallpox and, unlike the spouses of officers, these women went to work. They cooked, sewed, washed, made soap, herded sheep and cattle, milked cows, nursed the ill, and sometimes foraged for food. At times, the army even hired them to perform these essential tasks on a grander scale. One observer described these camp women as "beast[s] of burden, having bushel baskets on their backs, by which they were bent double." He added that most were "barefoot, clothed in dirty rags." Another said these women dressed "some in rags and some in jags, but none in velvet gowns." Washington sought to prohibit them from following the army when it marched off to battle, but some tagged along anyway. Some came under fire while lugging water to thirsty soldiers and to artillerymen who had to swab the barrels of their field pieces between rounds. Some, like "Molly Pitcher," the mythical artillerist at Monmouth, might have participated in the fighting.[9]

Only a fraction of American women ever entered a camp, but large numbers on the home front supported the war effort. Sometimes calling themselves "daughters of liberty," made bullets, sewed, knitted, and spun fabric for the faraway soldiery. A New Yorker wrote that while women did not bear arms, they were "armed with spinning wheels." A Yankee farm girl who carded wool for the soldiers said that the labor made her feel "Nationaly." Other women showed their support for the war by wearing homespun. "I chuse to wear as much of our own manufactory as pocible," a young Bostonian remarked. Philadelphia's Esther DeBerdt Reed, the wife of Joseph Reed, Washington's former secretary, found ways to directly support those who were bearing arms. In June 1780, after publishing a broadside in which she urged women to be "really useful," Reed organized the Association, a body of female volunteers who made clothing and candles for soldiers, organized drives to gather essential items, and appealed for funds that were to be used to acquire shirts for the soldiers. In a few weeks, her efforts netted $300,000 from 1,600 donors, which resulted in the purchase of two thousand shirts. The Association eventually had chapters in six states, and it spurred churches here and there to join the effort to help the soldiers.[10]

The burden of the war fell on both sexes, which may have been a factor in Abigail Adams famously asking her congressman-husband to "Remember the Ladies" in the "New Code of Laws" that independence would necessitate. Like thousands of women whose husbands were away at war, Abigail Adams was left at home alone to cope with the children, the family's economic concerns, and the travail caused by the war. After assisting refugees from occupied Boston during the first months of fighting, the war came to her doorstep when camp diseases—ranging from smallpox to assorted fevers—spread from the siege lines in Boston to Braintree. Casualty rates were appalling. "Some poor parents are mourning the loss of 3, 4 & 5 children, and some families are wholly stripped of every Member," she reported to her husband in Philadelphia. She came to believe that the plight of civilians caused by the "desolation of War" and the "Havock made by the pestilence" equaled the distress faced by the soldiery, and in fact civilian deaths in Braintree late in 1775 may have been proportionally greater than the death rate among soldiers besieging Boston. The war had taken over her life, leaving her "melancholy" with "Anxieties upon my mind," and wondering if having "mount[ed] the Whirlwind" would in the long run prove to have been worthwhile.

Abigail tended many who fell ill and comforted others who lost loved ones, including her sister-in-law, the wife of John's youngest brother, Elihu, a militiaman who died of a camp disease during the siege of Boston. Abigail in fact took in one of the children of her newly widowed relative. Other duties were thrust on her. She performed tasks that before the war had been handled by her husband, including dealing with a tenant living in one of the Adams's two houses. It was an experience that did not go well. "I have met with some abuse and very ill treatment," she reported to John, adding: "I want you for my protector and justifier." The unpleasantness she encountered with the surly renter paled next to the anxiety and grief visited on her by the war. During the first months of hostilities, the war was on her threshold, and it was terrifying. Rumors persisted that the regulars were about to march from Boston and strike Braintree, making her neighborhood part of the immediate military front. That never occurred, but her residence was near Dorchester Heights, and when the Continentals occupied it in March 1776 and shelled Boston, the sounds of the bombardment reverberated through Braintree. "The House this instant shakes with the roar of Cannon," she wrote to John, adding, "No sleep for me to Night." In the morning she wrote to her husband once again, saying, "my Heart Beat pace" with the cannonading throughout the dark, restless night. For several days, she lived with the prospect of a nearby engagement on the order of Bunker Hill, an action that had destroyed adjacent Charlestown. She was spared that fate, but so long as the armies were in and around Boston, diseases continued to extend into neighboring hamlets. When her mother fell victim to a malady, Abigail faced an inconsolable grief. "Woe follows woe, and one affliction treads upon the heal of another," she cried. The "Hand of God presseth me soar," she wrote to John. "O my bursting Heart."[1]

Abigail Adams was separated from her husband for all but about twelve months during the decade between 1774 and 1784. Most women whose husbands went to war faced a separation consisting of months, perhaps a year or two. Many of these women were compelled to take on the duties ordinarily performed by their spouse—"to plough and hoe . . . and raise bread," as a Virginian put it, but also to market what was grown and to manage the family's finances—in addition to their customary responsibilities of caring for children and the house. A Connecticut woman whose husband was serving at Fort Ticonderoga noted that her "duties were not light" and left her with "no time for aught but my work." Even Abigail Adams, who was far more affluent than most, took on assignments that she had never previously faced. The Adamses' prewar income had come from the farm and John's law practice; the high cost of wartime labor stripped the farm of much of its profitability, and for all practical purposes, John never again practiced law after the summer of 1774, when he attended the First Continental Congress. Abigail never walked behind a plow, but she learned how to supervise those who were hired to tend to the farm, and in time she grew to be a successful manager of the couple's financial resources. She bought and sold land, and invested in bonds and securities, and in the end she succeeded in preserving the family's solvency despite the severe economic dislocations brought on by the war.

For some women, the experience of taking charge of family and farm was transformative. Early in the war, one woman wrote to her husband at the front about "Your farming business"; in time, she subtly shifted to writing about "our farming business." For women whose husbands were away, the war brought loneliness, endless toil, uncertainty, and apprehension, and for some it brought the grim news that their loved one had either died or been seriously wounded while serving his country. For the handful living near the front lines, or in the no-man's land of civil warfare in, say, New Jersey in 1776 or South Carolina after 1780, there was the churning fear of mistreatment, including molestation, at the hands of an armed soldier.[2]

The war wore on women, as it did on men, and though fervor for the ideals of the American Revolution may not have vanished for those of either sex, the protracted nature of these hostilities tested their willingness to sacrifice. Sarah Hodgkins was twenty-four years old and married to an Ipswich, Massachusetts, shoemaker when the war began and her husband, Joseph,

enlisted. Sarah was caught up in the patriotic fervor at the outset of hostilities, but as the war continued seemingly without end, and Joseph reenlisted
time and again, Sarah's patriotic intensity waned. At home with seven
children—one of whom died during the conflict—she eventually expressed
her disappointment with Joseph's unremitting service, notifying him that he
had a "duty to come home to [his] family." Telling Joseph that she felt like a
"widow," Sarah finally said, "Let some body else take your place." He did,
though not until he had served for four years. For all her support of the war
effort, Abigail Adams came to share Sarah's frustration. In 1782, three years
after she had last seen her husband, Abigail told John that she felt "deserted,
unprotected, unassisted, uncounseled." She added that his absence was
nothing less than a "moral evil," for in the "holy [marriage] ceremony" he
had agreed to the vow "What God has joined Let no Man put asunder." Two
additional years passed before they were reunited.[13]

The wives of husbands who chose loyalty to the king faced even greater
trials. Many Tory families were driven from their homes and forced to flee to
strange surroundings. None fell further than Grace Galloway. At the time of
her marriage to Joseph, some fifteen years before the war erupted, she and her
husband were widely thought to be the wealthiest family in Pennsylvania.
They owned five houses, including a mansion on a spacious Bucks County
estate. But she lost everything in the course of the war—her houses, their
contents, even her friends. After the British army abandoned Philadelphia in
June 1778, Grace was forced to spend her last years living alone in a tiny back
alley apartment while her husband was in London desperately trying to
persuade the British to continue to wage the war. Saying that she was
"undone" and "coud Not forgive" Joseph for having picked the wrong side,
she acknowledged that she was "easey Nay happy not to be with him." She
died alone in Philadelphia not long after the war ended.[14]

Morristown was not America's sole source of anguish at the outset of 1780.
Fearing that Britain's success in Georgia would set Clinton's sights on neighboring Charleston, Congress funneled men and supplies to General Benjamin
Lincoln in the weeks that followed the failed attempt to retake Savannah.
Lincoln, in fact, tirelessly cautioned Congress that should Charleston fall, all
of Georgia and South Carolina would be lost, and if the enemy captured those
states, North Carolina would be doomed as well. What is more, there was
reason to believe that South Carolina was especially vulnerable. It contained
the largest slave population of any state—two-thirds of its inhabitants were
held in bondage—and its resolve was questionable. The previous spring
General Prevost had marched an army from Savannah to the gates of

Charleston and threatened to reduce the city if it did not surrender. It was a bluff. Prevost had little artillery and only 2,100 men, fewer than the militia that was defending the city. Nevertheless, Governor John Rutledge proposed that his state would remain neutral for the duration of the war if Prevost would only lift his siege. Perhaps unwisely, Prevost refused the proffer, after which South Carolinians with more backbone (and likely more zeal for independence) took control of matters, and the British force withdrew to Georgia.[15]

Congress's concern that Clinton planned a campaign to take Charleston was well placed. At Christmas 1779, the British commander loaded 8,700 men (together with 5,000 sailors and 396 horses) onto ninety transports in New York and sailed southward. Hoping to capture the city and defeat a large rebel army in the process, Clinton declared on the eve of sailing: "This is the most important hour Britain ever knew." It was hardly an overstatement. Success in Charleston was thought to pave the way for pacification of the entire state, and with South Carolina's fall, Great Britain would have returned half of the southern colonies to the imperial fold.[16]

Clinton's destination was not a well-kept secret. While the British armada was at sea, Washington ordered the entire Virginia line serving under him— some 2,500 men—to march for Charleston. Congress directed additional Continentals posted in the Upper South to hurry to Lincoln's side. The congressmen also arranged for the transfer of arms and equipment to the Low Country and set three Continental frigates sailing for South Carolina. General Lincoln's numbers had been steadily increasing since October and by mid-March, as the time for fighting approached, there were 4,300 Continentals in and around Charleston. Still, that was well below the number of British soldiers that were coming, prompting Lincoln to urge South Carolina to consider "arming some Blacks." South Carolina refused his entreaty. Though unhappy, Lincoln anticipated that in time he would achieve parity if not numerical superiority, for he expected that his regulars would be augmented by thousands of militia drawn from Virginia, Georgia, and both Carolinas. In addition, he knew for certain that he had six frigates and assorted smaller vessels—totaling 260 guns—and forty artillery pieces between Fort Moultrie and Sullivan's Island.[17]

Clinton's men disembarked onto blessed land on February 11, ending a nightmarish six-week journey that matched what Howe's men had faced on their voyage to Pennsylvania thirty months earlier. Nearly all the horses had perished (many had suffered broken legs and were thrown overboard) and some of the siege artillery had gone to the bottom of the storm-tossed Atlantic. The British force that came ashore included numerous Americans who had enlisted in Loyalist regiments, units that the British had not begun to raise in earnest until after Saratoga. In all, some nine thousand Tories were serving in such units by 1779, about 50 percent of the number of Americans serving in the Continental army at that moment. Roughly one man in five who stepped off onto South Carolina's sandy soil was a member of Loyalist unit.[18]

The British force landed unopposed below Charleston. Its advance on the city was painstakingly slow, in part because of dogged harassment by American cavalry, but also because of the uneasy realization—as one soldier noted—that the army was marching through tall marsh grass inhabited by "crocodiles sixteen feet long ... wolves and several species of venomous snakes." Four weeks were consumed in covering twenty miles. Along the way, Clinton was joined by Savannah's garrison of redcoats, swelling the size of his army to eleven thousand men.[19]

Lincoln believed he was ready for the enemy force. The forty-seven-year-old Lincoln had served briefly as a Massachusetts militiaman in the Seven Years' War, but had not tasted combat. Following that war, he held a string of local and provincial offices, including a seat in the assembly. He was named a general in the Massachusetts line early in 1776, but remained in the war's backwater until the Saratoga battles, when he had performed well before suffering a gunshot wound that shattered his ankle. Many in Congress respected Lincoln's administrative and leadership skills, and thought him prudent and tactful, qualities that could be especially useful when dealing with prickly state officials. Although afflicted with narcolepsy, which sometimes caused him to abruptly fall asleep, the ailment had never been a hindrance in carrying out his responsibilities. Congress selected Lincoln as Robert Howe's successor following the loss of Savannah.[20]

Lincoln had long known that the enemy was coming after Charleston, and for weeks he had presided over the construction of a defensive system. It was Bunker Hill on a massive scale. Eschewing any thought of meeting Clinton in a set-piece battle, Lincoln believed he could thwart an attack or survive a siege. Lincoln ordered the building of an outer wall beyond Charleston, running between the city's canals and the Ashley and the Cooper Rivers, as well as "wolf traps"—camouflaged deep pits—redoubts and deep ditches. Within those defenses, Lincoln assembled hundreds of pieces of artillery and mortars.[21]

Clinton had all along envisaged a siege operation. It was how he would have responded to a Franco-American attempt to retake New York, and he expected the same response from the rebel commander in Charleston. Actually, Lincoln had options. He might have retreated into the interior, somewhat as St. Clair had done in abandoning Fort Ticonderoga, and sought to win his own Saratoga-style victory in the Carolina backcountry. Or he might have made a stand behind the Ashley River, as Washington had done at the Brandywine, inflicting heavy casualties before retreating to safety and leaving the city to the enemy. But Lincoln was under severe pressure from local and state officials to fight to save the city. What is more, he must have questioned whether South Carolina would have the will to continue the struggle, even to remain in the Union, should Charleston fall. Furthermore, Lincoln believed that he could save the city. Once it had become crystal clear that Clinton's target was Charleston, Lincoln had yet again pleaded for reinforcements and, in April, Washington ordered 1,400 Maryland and Delaware Continentals under Major General Johann de Kalb to march southward.[22] On the cusp of the engagement, Lincoln looked forward to having roughly the same number of men as Clinton, perhaps more, and considering the formidable defenses that had been erected, he did not think the British could breach his lines. The key to his thinking, however, was that the royal fleet—which included five ships of the line, three other large vessels with nearly fifty guns apiece, and four frigates—could not get into Charleston Harbor and blast away at the city from that side. Not only had a chain of obstructions been installed, but also Fort Moultrie, a forty-gun installation that had thwarted British vessels in the 1776 attack, would once again be pounding away on the slow-moving royal ships.

Things quickly went wrong for the Americans. On March 20 the royal fleet overcame all obstacles and took control of Charleston Harbor. Nine days later the British army crossed the Ashley on Charleston's southwest side, sealing off nearly every exit from the city. Only two escape hatches remained open. One was Lampriers Point, a fortified area across the Cooper River from Charleston, which in a worst-case scenario afforded a route that the army might use to bolt to freedom. The second was at Monck's Corner, situated at the forks of the Cooper River above the city, where Lincoln had posted Brigadier General Isaac Huger with five hundred cavalry and militia. From the start, however, Lincoln saw Huger's mission not so much for the purpose of keeping the area open for a breakout as for assuring that Monck's Corner remained ajar as an entry portal for men and supplies coming to the rescue of the besieged city. Precious few men or provisions ever passed through the aperture. Aside from Charleston's militia, units of citizen-soldiers in South Carolina did not turn out. Governor Rutledge had done all in his power to get the militiamen under arms, even threatening to confiscate the property of those who refused to serve. But the men stayed at home. They feared the city would be a cauldron of smallpox, though their enmity toward Charleston and

Charlestonians was perhaps a greater factor. These militiamen were from Carolina's backcountry, a region that for generations had been victimized by colonial assemblies dominated by Charleston's planters and merchants; now, they were unwilling to risk their lives to save those who had for so long willfully discriminated against them. While South Carolina's soldiery was nowhere to be seen, militia sent from Virginia by Governor Jefferson were on the way to South Carolina and so, too, were the Continentals under de Kalb that Washington had ordered south. However, neither of these bands of troopers ever reached Lincoln. In mid-April, Huger's force was cut to pieces in a surprise attack, and Monck's Corner was shut by the British. Soon thereafter General Cornwallis, second in command to Clinton, rushed forces across the Cooper and took possession of Lampriers Point. Once it fell, no reinforcements could get into the city and Lincoln's army could not get out.[23]

The American army in Charleston was trapped, every bit as much as Burgoyne's army had been ensnared at Saratoga three years earlier. Lincoln later said—much as had Washington during his worst days during the New York campaign in 1776—that his "insufficiency" had arisen from "want of experience." To be sure, he made many of the same errors that the novice Washington had made. Lincoln was fatally indecisive, wavering uncertainly over whether to run or to defend the city during the three weeks between the arrival of the enemy army and the closing of the last exit. Washington had worried that a retreat from Manhattan would alienate Congress; Lincoln permitted himself to be overawed by South Carolina's leaders, who not only demanded that he hold out to the "last extremity" but also verbally abused those generals who in councils of war advocated quitting the city. Some who held office in South Carolina even treacherously warned that if the city was abandoned without a fight, they would aid the enemy while it pursued the retreating Americans.[24] Washington was saved because he had been fortunate enough to have the counsel of Charles Lee. Lincoln was served by lesser lights. He listened to them and he was doomed.

The British cannonading of Charleston began during the first week of April. After five days of shelling, Clinton paused to demand that the Americans surrender. Lincoln refused. "Duty and Inclination point to the propriety" of defending the city, he responded. During the next two weeks the redcoat siege lines moved steady closer. Clinton was patient and methodical, too much so for many of his soldiers, who were fed up with the southern heat and bugs, and to awakening every morning and finding rattlesnakes nearby, or so one disgruntled soldier claimed. Two weeks into the bombardment, the rival commanders once again parleyed. Clinton said that only Lincoln's unconditional surrender could save the city from "havock and destruction." Lincoln again declined to give up the fight, prompting Clinton in a mix of amazement and perturbation to remark, "I begin to think these People will be Blockheads enough to wait the Assault." The British resumed firing. It continued around the clock. Soldiers under fire spoke of the "red hot shot" that set fires. Paradoxically, the nights were "dreadful" but "glorious," as shells "like meteors" filled the sky. It was "as if the stars were tumbling down," said a soldier. Upwards of a dozen Continentals died daily from what Lincoln called the "murderous fire." Civilians perished too, some after being plundered by starving soldiers who skulked about during the stygian nights in search of food. Whether citizen or soldier, terror and discomfort were ever-present companions. Sleep was well-nigh impossible, the heat, mosquitoes, and sand flies nearly unbearable. After several additional days of blasting away, Clinton for a third time demanded unconditional surrender. On this occasion, the British commander declared that if the rebels continued to hold out, he would not be responsible for "whatever vindictive Severity exasperated Soldiers may inflict" on the residents of the city and its defenders following the inevitable surrender.[25]

With Hessian jaegers only thirty paces from the American defenses, Lincoln was ready to talk. Perhaps to his surprise, Clinton was willing to negotiate, a change brought about his receipt of information that a French fleet had sailed for North America. More than ever, Clinton wished to wrap up the siege and get most of his men back to New York. The talks dragged on for two days. Finally, on May 11, Lincoln agreed to surrender, pushed at last to capitulate by the threat of mutiny by Charleston militiamen who had had enough. The terms were harsh. Although the militiamen were permitted to go home as "prisoners on parole"—that is, they pledged never again to bear arms in this war—the regulars laid down their arms and marched into captivity.

Charleston was the greatest defeat suffered by the Americans in this war, nearly matching the British debacle at Saratoga. Some 225 Americans died at Charleston—about 50 fewer deaths than Clinton's army suffered—and 6,700 men (including 7 generals) were taken prisoner. The Americans also lost their frigates, nearly five thousand muskets, and four hundred pieces of artillery. Two signers of the Declaration of Independence, Thomas Heyward and Arthur Middleton, were captured when the city fell and sent to Florida for incarceration. In five years of war, England had not been overwhelmed with heroes, but it made up for lost time. When news of Charleston's fall arrived in London, crowds poured into the streets for "exuberant and wild" celebrations, and some observers thought Clinton suddenly became "the most *popular* man in England."[26]

Taking Charleston was only the beginning of Britain's campaign to restore South Carolina as a royal colony. Two ways existed for trying to achieve this end. One was to hold Charleston, blockade the coast by land and sea, and wait for the upcountry inhabitants and the Low Country planters to be so squeezed economically that they would conclude the rebellion was no longer worthwhile. It would take time, but the price in blood would be low. Clinton, however, was under pressure from Germain to act aggressively and he thought that the state could be returned to the British fold quickly. After all, the large and powerful British army was poised to grow even stronger as Tories came forward in abundance to soldier. Furthermore, the rebels no longer had an army in the state. For that matter, there was nothing worthy of being called an American army south of Washington's Continentals in New Jersey.

Nor was that all. Clinton was eager to utilize South Carolina's large population of African Americans that the rebel authorities had refused to use in Charleston's defense. Angered that both free blacks and slaves were enlisting in the Continental army, Clinton during the previous summer had issued what came to be known as the Philipsburg Proclamation. He threatened to sell into slavery all captured African American soldiers. But in its better-remembered portion, Clinton had also promised to emancipate at war's end all slaves who fled behind British lines. A bit later, using the slogan, "Freedom and a Farm," Clinton proposed that, following the war, liberated blacks would be resettled on land taken from the defeated rebels. Until Charleston fell, the Philipsburg Proclamation was of little consequence. Thereafter, even Clinton was astounded by the number of slaves who fled their masters. Within forty-five days of taking the city, more than one thousand slaves fled behind British lines, and more came during the summer and fall. One British officer said that on seeing any detachment of redcoats, "all the negroes, men, women, and children . . . quitted the plantation and followed the army."

As transforming raw recruits into disciplined soldiers was a lengthy enterprise, Clinton used most of the runaways as support personnel rather than as soldiers. The British commander set them to work on plantations producing supplies for the army, assigned them to infantry units as menial laborers, gave the skilled workers among them to the Royal Artillery or set them to work constructing and repairing forts, sent a few to work as orderlies in hospitals, turned to some to provide help as guides, employed a handful as cooks, and utilized some to raid plantations and liberate still more chattel. A bemused German officer said that the freedmen eagerly volunteered to plunder the homes of their former owners. Many, he said, "clothed themselves piecemeal" with the booty they took, including silk britches, elegant shirts, dressing gowns, hats, and even wigs.[27]

Clinton got things off to a spectacular start in the days immediately following Lincoln's surrender. The British commander sent out columns in every
direction, and by the end of May his troops occupied posts from Georgetown,
sixty miles above Charleston on the coast, through Camden and Ninety-Six
deep in the backcountry, and on to Augusta on the Georgia–South Carolina
border, an arc extending nearly 175 miles. Early in June, Clinton returned to
New York, leaving Cornwallis to complete the job. Clinton envisaged that
Cornwallis, with British regulars and battalions of Loyalists, would subdue
the interior while Tory militiamen, functioning as a home guard, protected
local officeholders installed by the army. Ordering Cornwallis not to depart
South Carolina until pacification was complete, Clinton left him with about
three thousand men and directions to recruit Tories who were thought to be
eager to serve the Crown. Within a month of Charleston's fall, more than two
thousand South Carolinians had volunteered to bear arms for the mother
country and approximately the same number had taken oaths swearing allegiance to Great Britain. Within six months, upwards of six thousand Southern Loyalists—mostly South Carolinians, but some Georgians and North
Carolinians as well—were under arms and assisting the British army, many
in provincial regiments that also included northern Tories who had signed on
for service a year or two earlier. Before departing, Clinton offered pardons to
all who pledged allegiance to the king. The response was gratifying. Unable
to leave well enough alone, Clinton issued a proclamation a few days later
that in effect characterized all who refused to take a loyalty oath to the king
as rebels. Clinton had made neutrality impossible. He additionally erred by
maintaining military rule for the province rather than reinstituting a central
civil government. Subsequently, many officials in London and Tories in South
Carolina concluded that the "dread of remaining under Military Law" had
alienated a considerable portion of the population and retarded efforts to win
back the loyalty of the inhabitants.[28]

Cornwallis wasted no time in setting off to track down the few men that
Lincoln had posted outside Charleston or those who had arrived too late to
get into the city. When intelligence reported that some 340 Virginia
Continentals under Colonel Abraham Buford were still in South Carolina,
though hurrying home, Cornwallis dispatched his green-clad British Legion,
a Tory regiment organized two years earlier and composed largely of
Pennsylvanians recruited during the British occupation of Philadelphia.
Consisting of infantry and cavalry, the Legionnaires were led by Lieutenant
Colonel Banastre Tarleton. The son of a well-heeled Liverpool merchant,
Tarleton had joined the British army in 1775 after studying at Oxford. In his
five years of service in America, he had acquired a reputation as a hard and

daring soldier who shrank from nothing that could win him laurels. Typically, Tarleton responded with eager readiness to his assignment to find Buford's Virginians. Setting off primarily with his cavalrymen, Tarleton and his force covered 105 miles in fifty-four hours, despite the oppressive heat.[29]

Tarleton caught his prey late in May in the Waxhaws, a region close to the North Carolina border. Buford had time to form a defensive line, but it was no match for a cavalry charge. The speed of Tarleton's 270 mounted troopers was stunning. Churning up a dense cloud of dust, the horse soldiers were on the Virginians before the rebels squeezed off a second shot. Some of the Virginians were trampled. Others were cut down by riders swinging sabers. Resistance ended in seconds. The Virginians cried out "quarter," the universal plea for mercy. Their entreaties went unheard. In a spasm of violence, Tarleton's vengeful Tories dismounted and assailed their helpless foes. Before order could be restored, more of the vanquished had been killed or wounded, some suffering terrible, maiming injuries. In all, 263 Virginians were casualties on that bloody day, some three-quarters of Buford's men. In war, some engagements go unremembered. Not this day of horror. From this day forward, Southern rebels called the leader of the British Legion "Bloody Tarleton," "Butcher Tarleton," or "Bloody Ban" and spoke bitterly of "Tarleton's quarter."[30]

Congress learned in June of both Charleston and the Waxhaws disaster. Initially, many thought the news of Charleston's surrender a "Puff," a deception to "foment Discontents and Mutiny in the federal Army." Soon enough the congressmen knew the truth, prompting a New Jersey delegate to admit that "no greater Stroke has befallen us." As never before, he added, the United States must undertake "more active and thorough Exertions . . . to recover and repair" the damage. Some worried about morale at home, others about the impact of the debacle in Charleston on opinion in France, without whose support the war could not be waged. What Congress did know, or thought it knew, was that Cornwallis was "making a rapid March through S. Carolina," and within days he was "expected to penetrate into N. Carolina." The congressmen knew, too, that something must be done to stop him.[31]

It did not take Congress long to settle on Horatio Gates to command the Southern Department. Though hailed as the hero of Saratoga, Gates in the three years since Burgoyne's surrender had never been given an independent command. He wanted this post, however, and lobbied Congress for it. His record was obviously sparkling, and above all he was popular with militiamen. Yankee militiamen had rallied to his side in 1777, and expectations soared that South Carolina's stay-at-home troopers would also turn out to serve under him. In mid-June, Gates was named commander of the southern army. A friend in Philadelphia captured the mood when he wrote to Gates: "Our affairs to the Southward look blue—so they did when you took the command before the Burgoynade. I can only say, *Go & do likewise.*" Unlike in the Saratoga campaign, Gates would not have much to work with. There were few Continentals in the South, and Washington refused to give up any more of his men. Having learned that France was sending an army to America, Washington wanted to keep his army intact and prepared for a joint operation to retake New York. If he surrendered any men to the southern theater, Washington told Congress, he would be "condemned to a disgraceful and fatal inactivity." Washington's comment, coming from general who had been largely inactive for three years, must have perplexed many in Philadelphia.[32]

Gates arrived in North Carolina and took command of his army in the last days of July. Disconcerted by what he found, Gates told a friend that his army was tiny and that he lacked money and supplies. If that was not bad enough, Gates also deduced that southerners were "apparently Deficit in Public Spirit." That was not entirely true. Soon after leaving Philadelphia, Gates had sought militia from Virginia and North Carolina, and he appealed to the governors of those two states, Thomas Jefferson and Abner Nash, to provide him with every conceivable sort of item that an army might use. Knowing that Virginia would be next on Cornwallis's list should he break through North Carolina, Jefferson sought to comply, even sending along tomahawks. Though he had been reluctant to provide troops to Lincoln, fearing they would be needed in the event of another British raid on Virginia, Jefferson quickly promised that two thousand militiamen would march to Gates's assistance. Jefferson shrank from confrontation and was habitually deferential toward Washington, but this crisis was so grave that he dared write to the commander in chief, telling him that it was the sense of Congress and Virginians that the commander must yield some of his army for the defense of the South.[33]

Reinforcements trickled in to Gates's camp, but toward the end of July he continued to characterize his army as "a scene of . . . multiplied and encreasing wants." Twenty-five percent of the militiamen ordered south by Jefferson had not arrived and those that had, said Gates, were "not so completely supplied as I either wish'd or expected." Some were without arms, others had defective muskets, still others had no bayonets, and none came with cartouche boxes for carrying ammunition. The army lacked tents, and Gates was told that only twenty horses could be found for his cavalry. Plus, the army was short of food. For weeks prior to his arrival, Gates reported, the men had episodically gone without meat and corn, surviving by pillaging green vegetables from unhappy neighboring farmers. "I have before me the most unpromising prospect my Eyes ever beheld," Gates forlornly stated.[34]

Military intelligence plays a crucial role in decisions of whether or not to act, and generals find it helpful to know the trustworthiness of those providing the information. Gates knew nothing about those who furnished two key items of intelligence. He was told that there were seven hundred British troops at Camden, an outpost some forty miles below the North Carolina border that was situated on the road from Charlotte to Charleston. Gates was also informed that "shoals of militia"—presumably the hitherto elusive South Carolina trainbandsmen—were near Camden and awaiting the arrival of an American force.[35] Gates would have had good reasons for doing nothing at this juncture: his officers were strangers, he was new to the South, and he faced no immediate threat. Instead, he acted without delay. He ordered his army in motion only two days after he assumed command at Hillsborough, North Carolina. The reasons for Gates's unwise haste can only be surmised. Obviously, he glimpsed an opportunity for scoring an important victory, something on the order of his own Trenton, a triumph that just might lead the enemy to abandon all its interior posts and pull back to Charleston. Gates must also have believed that success alone could bring out the militia, whose presence would be critical for his future activities. What is more, with Washington, his rival for glory, and his nemesis, seemingly perpetually wedded to a defensive strategy, Gates may have itched to win a great victory through an offensive action.

Taking the field so hurriedly was a blunder. Gates compounded his mistake by turning a deaf ear to his officers who urged that he take the longer of the two routes to Camden, proceeding through Salisbury, Charlotte, and the Waxhaw Creek settlement, in all of which he could have found stores of food. He opted instead for the shorter route, though it required a march through a barren and war-ravaged region devoid of even the opportunity to forage. It was not long before Gates realized his mistake. With his men surviving on green corn and unripe peaches, Gates's ire was on display in letters written to Jefferson and Nash during the march. He scolded the governors for their "unpardonable Neglect" of their "half Starved Fellow Citizens" and importuned them to send flour and "Droves of Bullocks." Seventeen days of marching under Carolina's merciless August sun finally brought the army to the cusp of Camden. By then, half of the Virginia militiamen were gone, many having quit in disgust at the deprivation they experienced, and Gates compounded their loss by detaching four hundred others to assist a partisan leader on what turned out to be a wild goose chase after a British supply convoy.[36]

Gates had acted on the assumption that only seven hundred British were at Camden. His intelligence had once been correct. However, by the time the Americans completed their two weeks' march, Cornwallis had arrived with reinforcements. Gates learned of that turn of events only when he reached the outskirts of Camden. Instead of the six-to-one numerical majority Gates had anticipated, his force was only slightly larger than that of his adversary, and the British had more regulars, more artillery, and five times as many mounted troops, including those under Tarleton. Fighting was not a good option, but given the enemy's strength in horse soldiers, retreat might have been riskier than battle. Gates elected to fight. He gave his men a meal of mush and molasses. It was good going down, but within a couple of hours nearly every man suffered exceedingly from abdominal cramps and diarrhea. Already exhausted and malnourished, Gates's soldiers were in no condition for battle, but fighting was inescapable.

Under a full moon on the night of August 15, the Americans set off for Camden. Unbeknownst to them, Cornwallis was also advancing, hoping to surprise his foe. The two equally startled commanders encountered each other at Saunders Creek just above Camden. The next morning, as the sun rose red and hot in the eastern sky, Cornwallis and Gates arranged their troops for battle. It was then that Gates committed his last, and perhaps greatest, error of this mistake-laden campaign, a colossal blunder that has baffled historians ever since. Fully aware that Cornwallis had aligned his men with the regulars on the right wing, Gates mysteriously chose to place his callow militiamen on the left of his line; the least experienced of his men would have to absorb the blow of battle-hardened redcoats, while his Delaware and Maryland regulars would face Cornwallis's unseasoned Tory recruits. After the recent massacre perpetrated by Tarleton's Loyalists in the Waxhaws, Gates may have believed that his militia were less fearful of British regulars than of Cornwallis's Tories. Or, his experience at Saratoga may have led Gates to an unshakable confidence in the capability of militia. He may have reasoned that if the militia stood firm, his regulars might meanwhile break through the Tory line, turning the enemy's flank and enveloping Cornwallis's entire force.

Instead, the rebels suffered a disaster. The engagement opened when Gates ordered the militia to attack. Few of these soldiers were seasoned. They advanced timidly and confusedly. The few rounds they fired did little damage. Cornwallis ordered a counterattack. For green militiamen, the sight of the advancing enemy soldiers—their bayonets gleaming in the day's early sunlight, the sound of the redcoats loudly chanting traditional battle huzzahs, an awareness that their own firing was not stopping the enemy advance, and the realization that comrades were being hit by enemy fire, some suffering ghastly wounds—was too much for inexperienced troops. The American left, the militia line, collapsed. The Virginians broke first. Some men threw down their weapons, joining comrades who were fleeing for safety in a frenzied panic; their loss of nerve sparked alarm among the North Carolinians, who joined the flight to escape the battlefield. Some of the frightened militiamen ran before firing a single shot. The Continentals on the right fought valiantly until, deep into the engagement, Cornwallis was able to throw more units against them. Overwhelmed and faced with the prospect of being surrounded, the Continentals broke. It was not an orderly retreat. Leaving the wounded behind, they, too, raced in search of any available sanctuary. A rebel officer said later that their flight had occurred "Like electricity"; it "operate[d] spontaneously." Seldom in this war had so many Americans acted in such an unsoldierly manner. Yet, worse was to come. When Gates could not stop his panicked men, he also fled, riding past his leaderless soldiers, who straggled on foot. All feared being overtaken by the enemy, especially by Tarleton's British Legion. Gates did not stop riding until he reached Charlotte, sixty miles away.

In time, when the army's losses were assessed, all knew that the magnitude of the defeat at Camden had been enormous. More than six hundred American soldiers were lost; some, like General de Kalb, died fighting after Gates had taken flight. All the artillery was lost, as were hundreds of muskets and the entire baggage train of the army. For the second time in ninety days—and the fourth time in eighteen months—a southern army had suffered defeat. Moreover, the Battle of Camden was the first time in this war that the British had scored an important victory deep in the American interior.[37]

Exactly one month before the catastrophe at Camden, a French army of 6,500 men under Jean-Baptiste-Donatien de Vimeur, comte de Rochambeau, splashed ashore in Rhode Island, sartorially resplendent in their white uniforms with black hats. The French were greeted by news of the American disaster at Charleston. A few weeks later they learned of Gates's defeat. Rochambeau had known before sailing that things were not going well for the allies—that was why he was being sent—though he had hardly expected such dire news on his arrival.

Rochambeau's appearance followed a long chain of international maneuvers and clashes. Comte de Vergennes, the French foreign minister, had brought France into the war two years earlier expecting a quick victory. To improve the odds of succeeding rapidly, Vergennes had sought to draw Spain into the war at the same time. His counterpart in Madrid, conde de

Floridablanca, was not ready to take that step in 1778. After six months at war, and with nothing to show for it but colossal expenses, Vergennes renewed his efforts to persuade Spain to enter the hostilities. Spain's price was exorbitant. It demanded a joint invasion of England. Madrid believed that only successes in such a stupendous undertaking would provide the leverage needed to force London to return Gibraltar, which Spain had lost to England seventy-five years earlier. Vergennes was unenthusiastic, but increasingly desperate, for he had inched steadily toward the troublesome conclusion that Spanish belligerence was essential if France was to obtain anything from this war. Spain's entrance into the war would immediately terminate the Royal Navy's lopsided three-to-two superiority in heavy warships over the French navy. In fact, a Franco-Spanish alliance would bring to an end the Royal Navy's control of the seas. In April 1779, just after Washington's eye-opening stay in Philadelphia, Vergennes agreed to Madrid's insistence on invading England, and Spain signed a treaty of alliance with France.[38]

The battle plan called for the French and Spanish navies to rendezvous off the northwest coast of Spain in the late spring of 1779. The armada was to include a French army of some thirty-eight thousand men, a force roughly equivalent in size to that under General Howe at the time he invaded New York. Once the allied navies gained control of the English Channel, the invasion force was to land in the far southwestern corner of England. Fear swept England that spring, a foreboding captured by an undersecretary of war who anxiously remarked that "this country was never in so perilous a situation." The next few weeks, he added, would be "as important, as ever were known in history."[39] It was fanciful to believe that the allies could conquer all of England, though with Britain's armed forces scattered about the globe and no continental ally to provide help, France and Spain could cause immense damage. Furthermore, if the French army succeeded in getting ashore, London would not easily get rid of it. If matters reached that stage, the allies believed that Great Britain would be compelled to make enormous concessions, including relinquishing Gibraltar and terminating the American war with a recognition of the independence of the United States.

Giant operations of this sort usually include diversions, and in this instance France thought an undertaking by the American sailor Commodore John Paul Jones might draw some of Britain's fleet from the English Channel. Born John Paul in Scotland thirty-two years earlier, Jones (he took the name in the 1770s) had, like many another young boy, fled to the sea looking for adventure. With several commercial voyages under his belt, he had become the captain of his own ship by age twenty-one. Five years later, he was on the run from the law, having killed a man in the West Indies. He surfaced in

Virginia. A couple of years later, the Revolutionary War erupted. The war was a godsend for many a man who was adrift or ambitious, or both. Jones was just such a man and he seized the opportunity, entering the newly founded American navy. Jones did not gain prominence until 1778, when sailing in the *Ranger*, a yellow and black frigate, he conducted raids in Whitehaven and Kirkcudbright Bay in Scotland, the first enemy sailor to carry out wartime attacks on sites within Britain's homeland in 111 years. What is more, during that mission, Jones captured the HMS *Drake* in a slugfest, the first instance of an American navy ship defeating a British warship of similar size.

France invested heavily in the intrepid American sailor in 1779, putting a quarter as many livres into his mission as it had given or loaned to the United States over the past four years. Jones was furnished with a squadron consisting of three frigates, a corvette, a cutter, and 1,071 men, many of them French. Jones's ship, and the flagship of the enterprise, was the old and slow *Bonhomme Richard*, a nine-hundred-ton vessel outfitted with forty guns. Jones put to sea from L'Orient during the sultry days of summer and sailed around Scotland. His destination was the east coast of England. In four weeks he captured several prizes and attempted, without success, a raid on Leith, near Edinburgh. Next, he planned a raid on Newcastle upon Tyne, the source of London's coal supply. Before reaching it, however, he spotted a fleet of nearly fifty commercial vessels returning from Scandinavia. Jones knew those ships were sailing in convoy. He knew as well that they would be escorted by powerful Royal Navy craft. He did not hesitate. Pulsing as always with a warrior's taste for battle, Jones went after the convoy realizing that he would have a fight on his hands.

A titanic clash with the HMS *Serapis*, a copper-bottomed frigate carrying fifty guns, soon followed. The late-September bloodbath commenced when the sun hung low in the western sky. Dark shadows cast by the tall gray cliffs along the nearby shoreline shrouded both vessels. When the first shot was fired the vessels were so close that Jones's crew could hear the orders being shouted by *Serapis*'s officers. The gunners on both ships were firing at point-blank range. Some guns fired eighteen-pound cast-iron balls, others bar shot designed to destroy masts and rigging, and still others hurled case shot (similar to grapeshot) made for killing and maiming. Atop all this, each ship was equipped with coehorns, or mortars, that lobbed bombs into the laps of its adversary. How anyone survived this maelstrom is a mystery. Many did not. Half of the six hundred men in the brawl were killed or wounded, and many of the injuries were hideous. Within seconds of the initial shots, the decks of both vessels were laden with bodies and body parts, and awash with blood. The carnage only worsened during the next two hours. The battle terminated after nightfall when one of Jones's sailors succeeded in hurling a grenade through an open hatch on the *Serapis*, igniting powder cartridges down below and touching off a series of explosions and a fire that spread in a flash from one end of the ship to the other. The *Serapis* was destroyed. The *Bonhomme Richard* had long since been fatally damaged.

Others in Jones's squadron took the *Countess of Scarborough*, one of the other Royal Navy vessels that had escorted the convoy, so that Jones returned from his venture with several vessels and more than five hundred prisoners. He was briefly acclaimed for his daring, courage, and valor. Then he was forgotten. A century later John Paul Jones was elevated to iconic status by ultranationalist Americans who felt that the nation's fledgling empire needed a naval hero. They made Jones into a figure familiar to every schoolchild, clinching his exalted reputation by retooling one of his less-than-catchy utterances at a desperate moment in the battle with the *Serapis*. When his adversary had demanded his surrender, Jones, according to witnesses, had said something like, "I may sink, but I'll be damned if I strike." His response was transformed into the pithy and immortal line: "I have not yet begun to fight."[40]

Jones's exploit may have been the stuff of legend, but it had not made the invasion of England a successful venture. Nothing could have. Seemingly troubled by every imaginable problem, the French fleet was weeks late in sailing to meet its ally. By the time the armada approached England, disease had reached pandemic proportions among the armada's sailors. With over one thousand dead or near death, the French government—at nearly the same time as Jones's epic battle—ordered the fleet home. Not a single allied soldier had set foot on English soil. John Adams dejectedly thought the only major outcome of the episode had been that the allied failure had given disheartened Great Britain "a Flash of Spirits."[41]

The flurry of activity during 1779 and 1780 had come from exhausted belligerents eager to bring an end to hostilities. Spain's entrance into the conflict, d'Estaing's campaign to retake Savannah, the abortive allied invasion of England, and Britain's invasion of South Carolina all grew from the desperate hope of breaking the stalemate with a decisive action. While under the threat of invasion, London sought to persuade Russia to enter the war against France or, at the very least, to mediate the conflict in Britain's favor. Simultaneously, Britain conducted talks with Spain at the lowest levels; though Gibraltar was not on the table, London was prepared to return other territories, including Florida, if Madrid would only make peace. The failed invasion of England and word that Savannah had weathered the Franco-American attack—which occurred not long after the clash between the *Bonhomme Richard* and

Serapis—eased the pressure on London. While the British could breathe easier, the strains borne by France only increased. As 1780 dawned, French soldiers were returning from America with stories of a war-weary ally. Some thought, perhaps without much exaggeration, that there was more enthusiasm for the American Revolution in Paris coffeehouses than in the United States.

Furthermore, Vergennes had lost patience with Washington's torpid conduct of the war. The "American army . . . before the alliance had distinguished themselves by their spirit and enterprise," he remarked, but its vigor had evaporated once France entered the war. He privately confessed that he now had only "feeble confidence" in Washington. And it ate at Vergennes that Washington's army—or so the French foreign minister claimed—devoured more livres doing nothing than would an active French army four times its size. Vergennes remained committed to his goal of American independence in order to weaken Great Britain, but he knew that something must be done or the war would be lost. Early in 1780, Vergennes, who two years earlier had thought the presence of a French navy could shift the balance in this war, decided that he must commit a French army to the war in America.[42]

Washington had known for seven weeks that the French expeditionary force under Rochambeau was coming. He also knew that it was being transported across the Atlantic by a large naval squadron—the fleet, under Chevalier de Ternay, would include seven ships of the line, three frigates, and a thousand marines—and that America would shortly obtain another French loan. (Ternay's fleet was the one that Clinton had learned of at the time of his final talks with Lincoln in besieged Charleston.) This was what Washington had awaited since d'Estaing's departure for the Caribbean nearly two years earlier. He wanted to meet with Rochambeau, and the French commander was no less eager to meet his counterpart. A meeting was scheduled for Hartford in September.

Washington spent the weeks prior to the conference honing plans for a joint siege of New York. With Britain's fleet scattered up and down the American coastline, Washington believed that Ternay could establish naval superiority. Meanwhile, a combined allied army of more than forty thousand men—some thirty-five thousand of which would be Continentals and American militia—would gradually smash the British into submission. Brimming with optimism, Washington foresaw the war ending soon. That was not to be.

His two-day meeting with Rochambeau was pleasant, as the French were "delighted" to discover that Washington was sober, thoughtful, meticulous, and methodical. But it did not lead to an autumn campaign to retake New

York. Rochambeau said that more heavy warships and another two thousand soldiers were coming, and he did not wish to act until they arrived. He was immovable. After learning both of the poor showing of the American militia in the recent engagements in the South and of his ally's extraordinarily primitive supply system, the shocked and surprised French commander wanted reinforcements and ample time to make preparations. With New York out of the question, Washington proposed a joint expedition in the South or in Canada. As Washington had twice before vetoed Canadian campaigns, once even warning Congress about the danger of France regaining the region, his sudden advocacy of such an enterprise must have been a sign of his desperation. Rochambeau declined. The "most important and the most decisive" allied undertaking, he said, must be to regain New York. As reassurance, Rochambeau told Washington that the French army would remain in America until the war ended, and he held out hope for operations in the spring against British-held Manhattan.[43]

On departing Hartford in late September, Washington was disheartened but more hopeful for the long term than in ages. He was returning to his army in New Jersey, after a planned stop at West Point, which he had not seen for ten months. That in itself was reason for inspecting the installation, but it had a new commander who had been on the job for only a month, and Washington wanted to see that every conceivable step had been taken to maintain the security of the vital post. The new commander was one of Washington's most trusted subordinates, Benedict Arnold.

Washington had always admired Arnold. Unlike many of the general officers, whose perceptivity, sluggishness, even fidelity, had kept Washington awake at nights, Arnold had been unfailingly lionhearted and his tireless dynamism had gone unquestioned. If only subliminally, Washington might have glimpsed something of himself in Arnold's enterprise and fearlessness. Arnold's leadership during the 1775 invasion of Canada had been astonishing, and his actions in the Saratoga campaign had been bold, imaginative, and intrepid. Arnold had suffered two gruesome wounds in this war, and the second—inflicted at Bemis Heights when a ball shattered his right thighbone—had necessitated a slow and painful recovery. Unable to ride a horse for a year or more, a field command was out of the question, and in the summer of 1778, when the British abandoned Philadelphia, Washington named Arnold the military commander of the city. Washington could not have chosen a worse assignment for him.

Arnold had a habit of making enemies, and he made them in abundance in Philadelphia. His expensive habits annoyed some, and so, too, did his open friendship with many who were suspected of Toryism. His marriage to Peggy

Shippen, a member of a family widely thought to be less-than-stalwart patriots, aroused further ire. But it was his shady financial transactions that got
him into deep trouble. Ultimately, the government of Pennsylvania indicted
him on eight charges of misconduct. Tried by court-martial, Arnold was
eventually acquitted of seven of the eight charges and only lightly reprim-
anded for the lone count on which he was convicted.

Arnold's year in Philadelphia had left him vexed and bitter, even more so
following his legal troubles, which he felt stained his honor. Furthermore,
already irate at having been denied back pay, he felt especially victimized
when Congress had promoted others over him, including Benjamin Lincoln,
who had entered the army after Arnold joined the officers' corps and
experienced combat. Brimming with resentment toward civilian leaders who
had never been in harm's way while he had suffered debilitating wounds in
the course of years of service, Arnold, in the spring or summer of 1779, initiated clandestine talks with the British high command. If the price was right,
Arnold suggested, he would engage in a treasonous act. The talks dragged on
and on. That Arnold's commitment to perfidy was finally sealed in the immediate wake of the American disaster at Charleston suggests that his decision
to turn his coat was perhaps due as much to a belief that America could not
win the war as to outrage or lust for wealth.

According to the bargain he struck, Arnold was to seek command of the
post at West Point. If successful, he was to relinquish it to the British. In
return, he would receive £20,000, an amount in specie that today would be
the equivalent of around $1 million. Furthermore, as Clinton thought him
"the boldest and more enterprising of the rebel generals," the British
commander promised Arnold the command of a Loyalist regiment.

Early in the summer of 1780, Arnold called on Washington at Morristown.
Already anticipating Rochambeau's arrival and an autumn campaign to
retake New York, Washington offered Arnold a field command in the operation. Pleading infirmity, Arnold asked to be named commander of the army
in the Hudson Highland. Washington consented. Arnold had successfully
completed the first step of his conspiracy. West Point was under his command.
In September, on learning at the last moment that Washington would spend
an evening in Peekskill, New York, while on his trek to the Hartford meeting
with Rochambeau, Arnold alerted the British, who rapidly hatched a plan to
capture the American commander and his traveling party. Alas for Arnold,
things went awry and the scheme to nab the unsuspecting Washington was
not acted on.

Washington expected to reach the vicinity of West Point early on the
morning of the third day of his return trip from Hartford, and he sent aides

ahead to notify Arnold that he would join him for breakfast at the Robinson House, which served as Arnold's headquarters. Washington reached the Robinson House on September 25. Arnold was nowhere to be seen. Washington dined alone. By the end of the leisurely meal, Arnold still had not appeared. Fearing an emergency, Washington was rowed across the Hudson to the fort. He thoroughly scoured the installation and the area around it. Everything seemed to be in order, though Arnold could not be found. Deep into the afternoon, Washington once again was rowed across the river. Arnold had not shown up at the Robinson House. Around four P.M. the mystery of Arnold's absence was solved. A dispatch rider arrived bearing papers found two days earlier on Major John André, a British officer who had been detained behind American lines by suspicious militiamen. Though attired in civilian clothing, André had been searched. Papers were found hidden in his boot. He was immediately taken into custody. The papers that André was carrying meant nothing to the militiamen. Nor were their superiors sure of their meaning. But Washington had only to glance at them to unravel what was afoot: Arnold was bent on treason and André had been the go-between sent from British headquarters to make the final arrangements for his treacherous act.

Taking charge, Washington swiftly questioned Arnold's principal officers and staff. No one appeared to know a thing. Accompanied by the Marquis de Lafayette, Washington hurried upstairs to the bedchamber of Arnold's wife. Awkwardly, perhaps with misgivings, Washington entered Peggy Shippen Arnold's bedroom. The room was unkempt and she was disheveled, attired in a rumpled nightgown, her eyes red and swollen from crying, her hair unattended. Washington tried to calm her. It was to no avail. She paced the floor, seemingly neither comprehending Washington's questions nor speaking coherently when responding to his queries. It was a performance that would have made an award-winning actress proud. In a few minutes, Washington gave up. When he left the room, Washington not only knew of Arnold's treason, but he likely was convinced that Mrs. Arnold had long been aware of her husband's plans as well. "Arnold has betrayed me," Washington roared. "Whom can we trust now?" His shock had given way to despair, but just as quickly it morphed into unbridled fury. Washington wanted to get his hands on the traitor and make him pay for his monstrous act. He sent a party to capture Arnold. It was too late. The turncoat had made his getaway after being notified of André's seizure.[44]

Already shaken by the disasters in South Carolina, the nation was stunned by the news of Arnold's treason. The disloyalty of one person had come close to handing the British military all that it might need to gain control of the

Hudson River and crush the rebellion. For some time, essayists had contended that America's fortunes were threatened by the spirit of luxury and greed that much of the citizenry found more appealing than sacrificing for victory. Now, Arnold's treachery had been purchased, a sordid act that had come within a whisker of spelling disaster for the American Revolution. Some essayists depicted Arnold as the very symbol of the deadly corruption eating at America's soul, an enemy even more threatening than Britain's military prowess. There were those, however, who saw a ray of hope in Arnold's treason. Perhaps his act of betrayal was what was needed to resurrect the earnest spirit of the early months of the war.[45]

This was close to the low point of the war for Washington, and he responded with boundless fury. He literally wanted to kill Arnold, and in fact Washington found a volunteer to go to Manhattan and attempt to capture or assassinate the traitor. That mission failed. However, with André in his possession, Washington tried to get hold of Arnold through a swap. Clinton would have none it. Early in October, André was executed as a spy.[46]

Given what Rochambeau had said, and with winter approaching, Washington knew that his army outside New York would remain inactive for months. With no army in the South to stop Cornwallis, Washington also now admitted that the British were waging war in South Carolina with a "severity" not previously exhibited, a fact that he was reminded of by Governor Rutledge, who, after complaining that national assistance "has been trifling," begged the commander to bring his army to the Low Country and drive the British away. Rutledge also complained to Congress that from the beginning Washington's attitude toward the war in the South had been "scarcely credible." South Carolina's lieutenant governor wondered out loud if the behavior of Washington and northern congressmen could be taken to mean that the "Southern States are meant to be sacrificed." Washington was unaware of all that was being said. But even had he known, the American commander was not about to leave the vicinity of Manhattan at the very time when his long-cherished campaign to retake New York appeared likely to soon become a reality. Nevertheless, Washington did something he had not previously done.[47]

Gates's flight from the battlefield at Camden had led to his censure from many quarters, especially from those close to Washington who hoped to eliminate the commander's last rival. Benjamin Rush, in fact, quipped that "Gates is now suffering not for his defeat at Camden, but for *taking General Burgoyne.*"[48] As criticism grew, Congress suspended Gates pending an inquiry. A new commander of the remnants of the Continental army in the

Southern Department would have to be named immediately. Congress asked Washington to make the choice. On other occasions Congress had asked for Washington's recommendations when a commander was to be appointed, but he had always declined. It was Congress's responsibility to name the commanders of armies, and Washington had not wanted to enter what he correctly saw as a political minefield. This time, however, Washington responded by recommending Nathanael Greene.

The perilous situation in the South caused Washington to overcome his reservations about naming a commander, but he also acted because he thought Greene by far the best man for the job. For at least four years Washington had looked on Greene as his most trusted advisor, finding him to be prudent, savvy, industrious, bold, daring, and a stickler for details and logistics. Two additional attributes appeared to make Greene the perfect choice. He was an exponent of Fabian strategy, a way of war that clearly might have been the wiser course for both Generals Lincoln and Gates to have pursued. In addition, while Greene could be tough, he was also tactful. Washington had successfully turned to him to mollify d'Estaing, whose feathers had been ruffled during the Rhode Island endeavor in 1778, and as the quartermaster general, Greene had judiciously handled numerous delicate situations. His sensitivity would be useful in dealing with prickly Southern governors.[49]

Greene hurried from West Point to army headquarters at Totowa, New Jersey, where he met with Washington on October 22. The two talked privately for hours. To the bitter disappointment of historians, no transcript was kept, though it is likely that Washington offered counsel on dealing with the Southern governors, including Jefferson, and that he urged adherence to the Fabian way of war, a strategy aimed at bleeding the British to death and tying down Cornwallis far from New York. The following day, Greene set off, aware that the "greatest confusion" prevailed in the southern army, that Cornwallis was already "penetrating into North Carolina," and that yet another large enemy force was about to strike in Virginia. What Greene knew filled him with "the greatest degree of anxiety," for beyond a doubt he was about to enter a whirlwind while faced with "insurmountable difficulties."[50]

CHAPTER 14

"A WAR OF DESOLATION SHOCKING TO HUMANITY"

THE SOUTHERN THEATER IN 1780–1781

EACH YEAR SEEMED TO BEGIN badly for the American cause, often worse than the previous year. But none was as bad as 1781. Atop the military setbacks of the past eight months, a bankrupt economy, warnings from John Adams and others that an economically beleaguered France could not remain in the war for more than another year, and Benedict Arnold's treason, the year 1781 opened with a dangerous mutiny within the Continental army.

More than a thousand soldiers in General Anthony Wayne's brigade in the Pennsylvania Line mutinied on New Year's Day at Mount Kemble, near Morristown. The rebellion commenced with the wounding of two officers. The mutineers listed an array of grievances, all legitimate: they had not been paid for twelve months, their food and clothing was inadequate, and the three-year enlistment period of many men had expired.

Mutinies had long been Washington's nightmare of nightmares, and he now feared that the rebellion among the Pennsylvanians would trigger insurgencies throughout the army. So uneasy was Washington that he refused to leave his headquarters in New Windsor, New York, to deal personally with the crisis, fearing that the men in his own camp would revolt in his absence. The commander additionally worried that General Clinton would exploit the uprising, not so much by attacking as by seeking to induce other Continentals to mutiny or to persuade Pennsylvania's insurgents to flee to safety behind British lines. In fact, Clinton tried his best to do so, sending two agents to meet with the rebellious soldiers. But from the beginning, the mutineers declared, "We are not Arnolds." They insisted that their objective was not to sabotage the American Revolution but to obtain a fair shake for themselves. True to their word, the rebel soldiers seized Clinton's agents and turned them over to the army, which shot them as spies. A tense week passed before the disorder was quelled. An accommodation was reached after lengthy negotiations between a committee of sergeants and a panel of Pennsylvania's civilian leaders that included Joseph Reed, the chief executive of the state, which in turn conferred with a four-member committee sent by Congress. The men were promised back pay, a shirt and shoes, and a ninety-day furlough; those who had served for three years were granted hearings before a civilian board that was to determine their eligibility to be discharged. Those who were granted a discharge could reenlist for a bounty, the choice that many soldiers made, though Wayne eventually reported to Washington that his army was reduced by roughly one-third. Finally, the accord provided for a general amnesty for all mutineers, an agreement that Congress approved two weeks later.[1]

Washington hardly had time to heave a sigh of relief before word arrived a few days later in January of yet another mutiny, this by two hundred men in the New Jersey Line. These rebel soldiers, posted in Pompton, were marching on Trenton, hopeful of negotiating a deal similar to that obtained by the Pennsylvania mutineers. During the first crisis, Washington had feared that a heavy-handed response might only spawn more disturbances, and he ordered Wayne not to use force unless the mutineers tried to rendezvous with the British army. But the New Jersey mutiny was different. Not only was it smaller, but also Washington now feared that there was an "infection" in the army that would spread and end "all subordination." Concluding that "this dangerous spirit" must "be suppressed by force," Washington selected General Robert Howe—who had not shrunk from danger when faced with overwhelming odds at Savannah two years earlier—for the gruesome assignment of crushing the mutiny. Howe was given five hundred carefully selected men from West Point and ordered to "instantly execute a few of the most active and most incendiary leaders." Howe carried out his orders to the letter, compelling a dozen of the mutineers to form a firing squad and shoot two ringleaders of the insurrection. The ruthless "exemplary punishment" that Washington had ordered did the trick. Soon, the American commander wrote to Rochambeau confessing his "mortification" at the disorders but assuring him that "the spirit of mutiny is now completely subdued and will not again show itself."[2]

Washington was correct. There were no additional mutinies. But Washington had other grave anxieties. Over the past few months, the sense had grown in Congress and at army headquarters that 1781 was likely to be America's last chance to win this war and gain true independence. The rosy glow of optimism that had followed the French alliance three long years before had vanished. Some of the blame for the collapse of America's fortunes should be laid at Washington's doorstep. Thinking time was on his side, the American commander had remained largely inactive year after year since Brandywine in 1777. But Great Britain had withstood the passage of time better than its adversary, scoring victories in the South and watching as American morale waned and French disillusionment grew.

By 1781 the war had become a stalemate. Congress and Washington were awash with apprehension that if a pivotal victory was not won before that year's campaign season ended, the outcome of the war would likely be determined by a European peace conference, one that an economically beleaguered France would welcome as an honorable means of escaping a hopeless conflict. On three occasions during the past thirty months, various neutral nations had offered to mediate the conflict. Nothing had come of those proffers, as neither France nor Britain had been ready to call it quits. In 1780 several European nations had formed the League of Armed Neutrality, an alliance of sorts designed for the purpose of collectively protecting the neutral nations' ocean commerce from blockades imposed by the belligerents. Early in 1781 two of its members, Russia and Austria, proposed a mediation conference to be held in Vienna. Vergennes once again spurned such a conference, gambling that the armies of Rochambeau and Washington, and the Franco-Spanish navies, could turn the tide in the looming campaign. But for a time, John Adams, now an American diplomat in Europe, had feared the worst. He called the proposed conference the greatest threat America had faced during the war. Should a host of monarchical powers decide the outcome of the war, Adams knew the result would be the "chicaning the United States of their independence."[3]

With the American Revolution on the line, Congress in January 1781 requested another loan from France and an augmentation of the French navy in North America. There was nothing unusual about Congress pleading for further help. But this time Congress sent Colonel John Laurens, Washington's former aide, as its emissary, bypassing its minister to France, Benjamin Franklin, whom some thought too obsequious and neglectful of his duties to exert the necessary pressure on America's ally. (Franklin pitched in nevertheless, telling the French foreign minister that if Great Britain won the war, America would not again have an opportunity "in the Course of Ages" to break away from London's control.) On this occasion, too, Washington—who had never intruded in the previous approaches to France—counseled Laurens on the forthcoming talks with Vergennes. In a long and plangent letter, Washington was alternately remarkably candid and deceptive. He advised young Laurens to maintain that America's economic problems had arisen from the destruction of its commerce and congressional inexperience with

financial matters, and that the resulting fiscal woes had posed "an insuperable obstacle" to supplying the army and waging war. Tell the French,
Washington continued, that the "patience of the army" was "nearly
exhausted" and that morale on the home front had eroded because of "the
feeble and oppressive mode of conducting the war" that had been imposed
on him by the economic crisis. Finally, Laurens was to urge France to send
more warships and request that Rochambeau's army be increased to fifteen
thousand men.[4]

Congress and Washington were not alone in thinking that the American
Revolution faced its greatest crisis. Sir Henry Clinton thought so as well. The
British commander continued to believe that the suppression of the rebellion
in the Carolinas had been made inevitable by his conquest of Charleston.
Indeed, when Clinton had departed Charleston the previous June, leaving
Earl Cornwallis in charge, the British commander had told his successor that
rebel resistance in South Carolina was broken save for "a few scattering
militia."[5]

    Not quite. Following Clinton's return to New York, the upcountry—seem-
ingly indifferent to Charleston's plight in the first half of 1780—stirred in the
second half of the year, much as backcountry Massachusetts had risen up in
1774 and 1775. No one factor led those in South Carolina's upcountry to activism. Some took up arms in defense of their homeland. Others acted to save
the American Revolution, which they believed offered them hope of escaping
Charleston's political stranglehold. Not a few were Scots-Irish Presbyterians
who hated Great Britain and its Anglican Church. Old Indian fighters, and
others with a restless appetite for adventure, needed little coaxing to go into
action. Many remained detached until assailed by vindictive Tories. Britain's
policy of liberating slaves stirred some to act, as did the enemy's ruthlessness,
of which Tarleton's massacre in the Waxhaws was but one example. There
were also the opportunists—men who saw fighting as the means of plundering property and slaves from those on the other side.

    The upcountry uprising may have begun in the New Acquisition District,
not far from the Waxhaws and Camden, where a rebel militia unit was
founded during the summer of 1780. The British Legion, sent to cope with
this local defiance, responded in a heavy-handed fashion, murdering and
pillaging, taking away ninety slaves, and burning mills, ironworks, and
churches. In response, the militia swelled, growing into a regiment, and it
struck back, triggering cycles of violence. To a degree unknown in other
sections of the United States, a civil war had begun in the South, one like
many civil wars that was waged with pitiless savagery. Not for nothing would

General Nathanael Greene remark of the war in the South that "the whole Country is in Danger of being laid waste by the Whigs and Tories who pursue each other with as much relentless Fury as Beasts of Prey."[6]

During the scorching summer of 1780, bands of rebel guerrilla fighters formed in the upcountry. These mounted troopers moved rapidly, emerging from nowhere to strike small detached British parties or waylay enemy supply trains, and just as suddenly to disappear into the fastness of dark swamps, thick forests, and tall green hills. In the wake of Charleston's fall, Thomas Sumter was appointed commander of all militia in the state; Andrew Pickens and Francis Marion (who came to be known by the sobriquet "Swamp Fox") emerged to organize irregular forces in western and eastern South Carolina, respectively. Their brigades sometimes contained as many as four hundred men, including blacksmiths who repaired weapons and doctored the horses. Most of these partisans were South Carolinians, but men from North Carolina and Georgia volunteered as well. They did not wear uniforms, though nearly all donned a "hunting shirt," made of durable linsey-woolsey or osnaburg, and either a wide-brimmed hat or a leather jockey cap adorned on top with a ridge of horsehair and in back with feathers or a white deer's tail. According to one trooper, the partisans inveighed "the old women of the country" to surrender their spoons and pewter plates, which were melted down for making musket balls. Sumter paid the men with slaves seized on Tory estates.[7]

For a very long time, Washington and Congress were unaware of what was happening in South Carolina. Cornwallis knew soon enough, however. Within ninety days of Charleston's fall, he reported that the "whole country" was "in an absolute state of rebellion." After another month the British had been involved in more than a score of upcountry engagements. One, in the New Acquisition District, came to be known as the Battle of Huck's Defeat, a bloody encounter between rebels and a detachment of British Legion forces commanded by Captain Christian Huck, a Philadelphia Tory. The Legionnaires suffered a terrible beating. Huck and some 85 percent of his men were killed, many hunted down and butchered in the first of numerous reprisals for the Waxhaw massacre; afterward, a guerrilla remarked that bodies were strewn about "like dead hogs." A month later Sumter surprised an enemy supply convoy, capturing fifty wagons loaded with spoils. He took 250 prisoners. The British were experiencing an alarming rate of attrition at the hands of the partisans. By the time the summer-worn leaves took on their autumn hues, Cornwallis had lost nearly a thousand men, a third in the Battle of Camden, the remainder to the guerrillas. Nearly 15 percent of the men he had commanded in July were gone. In the wake of such heavy losses, it became increasingly difficult for the British to prevail on the Tories to bear arms.[8]

Cornwallis responded to the gathering calamity with a brutality seldom evinced by British commanders in this war. He deployed a force of some three hundred cavalry to search for guerrillas and destroy the homesteads of known partisans, ordered that parole violators be immediately hanged, threated to execute two partisans for every Tory they put to death, and unleashed Loyalist regiments already stained with a reputation as "banditti." In addition to Tarleton, units commanded by the likes of Major Patrick Ferguson roamed the upcountry, certain that only the severest measures would subdue the rebels and encourage more Tories to step forth. At age thirty-six, Ferguson had served in the British army for twenty-one years; his right arm had been shattered at Brandywine, leading the Americans to thereafter dub him the "one-armed devil." As tough as they came, Ferguson was on record as stating that only a "war of desolation" that was "shocking to Humanity" could subdue the Carolina uprising.[9]

The partisan war also drove Cornwallis to an expedient filled with epochal consequences. Britain had been plagued by commanders who were slow to act, if they acted at all. Cornwallis was cut from different cloth. Though ordered by Clinton not to leave South Carolina until the state was fully pacified, Cornwallis in the late summer of 1780 decided he must carry the war into North Carolina, staunching the flow of supplies southward to the partisans. If successful, the guerrillas would be squeezed in the fashion that an anaconda destroyed its prey. Leaving behind two-thirds of his army to hold on to what the British already possessed in South Carolina, Cornwallis in September set out with 2,200 men from Camden. He was marching for Charlotte, where he planned to rendezvous with Major Ferguson and his force of 350 men that had been sent to beat the bushes in western Carolina in search of Tory volunteers. When the two British divisions reunited, Cornwallis planned to advance to Hillsborough, where the remnants of Gates's devastated army languished. To minimize the danger that the two British forces might walk into a trap, Clinton—at Cornwallis's behest—simultaneously sent Major General Alexander Leslie with 2,200 men to raid Virginia, a diversion designed to prevent the Old Dominion from reinforcing Gates.[10]

Cornwallis's foray got off to a good start. Leslie's men landed in October at Portsmouth, Newport News, and Hampton. During the next three weeks, the raiders pillaged estates and liberated slaves. Meanwhile, Cornwallis occupied Charlotte with little difficulty. He paused there to await Ferguson, who was enjoying a bountiful harvest of Tories among frontier inhabitants who may have been in the dark about the guerrilla war against the Loyalists in South Carolina. Ferguson had distributed a proclamation in which he advised would-be Tories to do nothing if they "choose to be pissed on forever and ever," but "if [they] wish to . . . live, and bear the name of men, grasp [their] arms" and join his Loyalist force. The force known as Ferguson's Volunteers nearly tripled in size in two weeks. Carried away by his success, Ferguson, like Clinton earlier in the summer, could not resist the temptation to issue another bombastic proclamation. Ferguson vowed that if the rebels deep in western North Carolina—including portions of today's Tennessee—did not abandon their insurgency, he would "march over the mountains, hang their leader, and lay their country waste with fire and sword." His edict had an impact, though not what Ferguson envisaged. As had nothing in recent years, the promulgation aroused these hardy frontiersmen to take up arms against the king's soldiers. Partisan bands gathered in North Carolina, joined by Sumter with four hundred South Carolinians and men from western Virginia. In no time, Ferguson's buoyancy turned to anxiety. Fearing that he would be outnumbered by "Back Water Men" that he variously characterized as "barbarians," "mongrels," and the "dregs of mankind," Ferguson cut short his recruiting and set off for Charlotte to link up with Cornwallis. He never made it.[11]

Ferguson got to within about twenty miles of Cornwallis's army. He might even have reached it, but with rebel fighters sprouting like summer weeds, Ferguson decided not to chance it. He marched his 1,200 man army to the top of King's Mountain. Unlike Bunker Hill, King's Mountain was a true hill with steep, craggy, heavily wooded slopes. Although he knew he would be outnumbered—the rebels would have a two-to-one advantage—Ferguson gambled that the inexperienced enemy fighters could never reach the summit in the face of the withering fire laid down by his Tories. He was wrong.

The rebel battle plan was simple: "every man [was] to raise a whoop, rush forward, and fight his way as best he could." One of the Virginians said they were ordered to "Shout like hell and fight like devils." They launched their attack on October 11, rising up with a hair-raising war cry learned from Indians, one that in the Civil War would be known as the "rebel yell." They advanced on the summit from three sides. Unlike the redcoats, who had marched smartly up the grassy slopes of Bunker Hill, these southerners scrambled up the sharply sloping hill, running, falling, rising, and charging again, at times taking cover behind rocks and trees, and squeezing off a shot before advancing again. It was the first taste of combat for James Collins, a sixteen-year-old rebel. He was more frightened of being thought a coward than of getting shot. The first time he took aim at another man, Collins said later, "I really had a shake on me." It got easier each time thereafter when he drew a bead on an enemy soldier.[12] When the rebels neared the summit, they laid down a deadly triangulated fire. Seeing that the end was near, Ferguson— the only British regular (indeed, the only non-American) in this fight—sought to escape, making a mad dash that some interpreted as a suicidal wish. Astride his white horse and, as was his habit, wearing a plaid shirt over his British uniform, Ferguson was instantly recognized. His big charger had taken only a few steps before Ferguson, shot seven times, tumbled from the saddle.

This was the signal for the carnage to really begin. Crying "Buford! Buford! Tarleton's quarter," the rebels were merciless, killing many Tories who pleaded and waved white flags. Scores of the victors took turns urinating on Ferguson's lifeless body. This crude act may have been spontaneous. Or it may have been inspired, at least subliminally, by Ferguson's earlier inflammatory proclamation about Tories living under the patriots' degrading oppression. The Tory dead and those who were too seriously wounded to be moved were left behind, soon to be prey for packs of wolves and wild dogs. Some seven hundred were taken captive. The prisoners were stripped of their shoes and most of their clothing and made to walk to Gilbert Town, forty miles away. At the end of their tortuous tramp, a drumhead court sentenced thirty-six of the Tories to death. Nine were hanged that night in the orange glow of light provided by torches held by rebel soldiers. The remainder were spared only because of a report that Tarleton's British Legion was coming. The Battle of King's Mountain was a British catastrophe. Against only 92 rebel casualties, Cornwallis lost 320 in the battle itself and 700 others who were captured. Some immediately thought King's Mountain more than just another setback. Clinton saw it as a turning point in the war in the South, and indeed in the Revolutionary War, telling one of his generals that "all his Dreams of Conquest quite vanish'd."[13]

King's Mountain was an American victory on the scale of Washington's triumph at Trenton five long years before. Trenton-Princeton had been the first rebel success in nearly a year, while King's Mountain came at the end of a four-year dry spell. Washington's victory was important in recruiting a new army for 1777, and the rebel triumph at King's Mountain squelched Britain's recruitment of southern Tories. The manpower losses suffered by the enemy in the two engagements were nearly identical. The president of Congress rejoiced that not only was morale rising in the Carolinas but also the Tories were "not a little displeased" with their chastened "British Master." Styling the victory a demonstration of the American "spirit," Washington predicted that King's Mountain would have a "very happy influence on the successive operations" in the South.[14] He did not know the half of it.

*   *   *

Following his meeting with Washington at army headquarters in Totowa—
ten days after King's Mountain but before news of the victory reached the
northern states—General Greene rode south. After conferring with General
Steuben, who had been sent to Virginia to help reconstruct the southern
army, Greene met with Maryland's governor, Thomas Sim Lee, and sat down
in Richmond with Thomas Jefferson. Like Gates before him, Greene appealed
for every conceivable means of support. Greene did his best to frighten
Jefferson, reminding him that if the Carolinas fell, the British would target
Virginia next and that "numerous blacks and other valuable Property . . .
must inevitably fall into their Hands." He also told Jefferson, "On your
Exertions hang the Freedom and Independence of the Southern States." From
Richmond, Greene descended into North Carolina, where he relieved Gates
and took command of the army—"if it deserves the name of one," as he put it
to Washington. Greene found about 2,200 men "starving with cold and
hunger, without tents and camp equipage," and many "literally naked" and
"totally unfit for any kind of duty."[15]

Greene had been among the first batch of general officers selected by
Congress in 1775. He hailed from an affluent Rhode Island family that had
gained its wealth, and influence, through the success of its iron foundries,
sawmill, and farm in Potowomut. Raised a Quaker, and kept at work at the
family forge, young Greene experienced only a few years of formal education at
a local academy. He may have been drawn to the American insurgency through
opposition to Britain's restrictions on colonial trade, though it was the *Gaspee*
incident in 1772, when Greene was already thirty years old, that turned him
into an activist. Two years later, he was drilling with a local military company
as a private, but when Rhode Island created a provincial army in 1775, it elevated Greene to the rank of brigadier general and named him the commander
of the new army. As the colony's Army of Observation was part of the Grand
American Army in the siege of Boston, the Continental Congress could hardly
pass over Greene when it created the Continental army. Greene was thirty-
three years old, stood a burly five feet ten inches tall, walked with a slight limp
that likely stemmed from a childhood accident, and aside from marching
about on pastoral drill fields, had no military experience. Henry Knox, in fact,
thought Greene "the rawest, the most untutored" of all the original generals.
But Washington, an extraordinary judge of others, saw promise in Greene and
early on turned to the Rhode Islander as a dependable officer and his most
trusted advisor. (Within a year, Knox changed his tune, concluding that
Greene was "very superior" to most of Washington's generals.)[16]

When he took command of the southern army in North Carolina in
December 1780, Greene was thirty-eight, by now a veteran soldier who had

seen action and led men in numerous engagements. Given the series of catastrophes that had befallen the Continental army in the South, Greene was
under no illusions when he took command, but soon enough he found that
his army likely faced even greater peril than he had imagined. About four
weeks after his arrival in North Carolina, at the dawn of 1781, a British naval
squadron sporting a ship of war, four frigates, and twenty-one additional
vessels appeared and sailed unopposed up the James River. The armada
carried Benedict Arnold's green-clad American Legion, a force composed of
1,600 Tories. Though warned days earlier by Washington that the naval
force's destination might be Virginia, and also alerted the day before the
warships made landfall, December 31, that the fleet had been spotted in
Chesapeake Bay, Governor Jefferson inexplicably failed to act for more than
twenty-four precious hours. By the time Jefferson summoned the militia, the
fast-moving Arnold, transported by what an American general called
Britain's "canvass wings," was already landing men at Jamestown, fifty miles
up the James River. Three days later, the American Legion was in Richmond.
While Jefferson watched through a spyglass from the other side of the James,
Arnold's force looted and burned portions of the town. For the second time
in seventy-five days—and the third time in eighteen months—British raiders
had sowed destruction in Virginia. By mid-January, Arnold's force, as
ordered, had withdrawn to Portsmouth. But as it remained in the Old
Dominion, Greene had to know that he could not expect as much help from
Virginia as he might have wished.[17]

While Virginia was under the gun a couple of hundred miles to the north,
Greene organized his thoughts. He rapidly reached out to the guerrilla
leaders. The partisan bands had seldom acted in concert with the Continental
army, but Greene wanted to utilize this ancillary force. In the coming months
the fighters under Sumter and Marion, and others, aided the regulars in
myriad ways, including serving as foragers, scouts, and "cowboys" who drove
cattle to the hungry soldiers. Greene also planned his strategy. It would be
unconventional. He would divide his army in the face of a superior foe.
Greene would send a division of some six hundred men under General
Daniel Morgan to operate west and south of Charlotte, where not only
would foraging be better, but also it was hoped that rebel militia, inspired by
King's Mountain, would take the field. Greene would take the remainder of
his tiny army—some eight hundred men—into eastern South Carolina.
Greene reasoned that if Cornwallis came after one of the two American
forces, the other would be free to strike at lightly defended British posts in the
interior. It was both an extremely risky gamble and a daringly imaginative
plan.[18]

While Greene thought through the steps he would take, Cornwallis rested and nursed his army in the wake of King's Mountain. On learning of Ferguson's fate, the British commander had pulled back to Winnsboro, in the upcountry not far from Camden, where his army spent a miserable autumn. Almost everyone, including Cornwallis, fell ill and the usually adequately equipped British army was so poorly supplied that its soldiers had to rub along in clothing and shoes long since worn threadbare after nearly a year in the field. Nevertheless, Cornwallis was optimistic. He was certain that Greene had erred egregiously in dividing his army. Furthermore, Cornwallis had been joined in November by General Leslie, who with his 2,200 men had been summoned from Virginia in the wake of the King's Mountain disaster. Cornwallis once again had more than four thousand men, several times the size of Greene's combined forces. In January, Cornwallis was ready to destroy the latest American army sent to the southern theater. Focusing first on Morgan, Cornwallis detached Tarleton with a thousand men to find him. Tarleton was to stay on the west side of the Broad River, Cornwallis on the east. When Tarleton spotted his prey, Cornwallis planned to join him for the rout. With Morgan disposed of, the full British army would go after Greene.[19]

Morgan, in command of what was being called a "Flying Army," had been moving swiftly and gaining manpower. By early January, he commanded about a thousand men, a quarter of whom were Continentals, the remainder partisans and militiamen. More than eighty of his men were dragoons, or light cavalry, under Lieutenant Colonel William Washington, a cousin of the commander in chief. Morgan knew that Tarleton had set off to find him, and he pulled back a bit, though he was not running. Far from it. A fighter to the core, Morgan wanted to take on Tarleton's force.

A six-foot-tall, heavily muscled Virginia frontiersman, Morgan had entered the Continental army as a forty-year-old captain in 1775. Earlier, he had battled Indians. Already in the Revolutionary War, Morgan had fought the British at Quebec, Saratoga, and Monmouth, often commanding Virginia riflemen, the elite soldiery in the Continental army. These men were equipped with rifles rather than notoriously inaccurate muskets; rifles were long-range weapons, an American creation suited to meet the needs of hunters and those fighting Indians, for these guns could be fired with extreme accuracy well beyond one hundred yards. Morgan positioned and repositioned his riflemen during battles by issuing commands via a turkey call. Morgan had no love for the British. While working as a teamster in the Seven Years' War, Morgan had lost his temper and struck a British officer. He paid for it with a flogging of several hundred lashes, and for the rest of his life Morgan carried the scars of that scourging on his back.[20]

Now, Morgan retreated in search of a good place to fight. He found it in mid-January at Cowpens, twenty-five miles west of King's Mountain—a long, wide, open meadow that sloped upward to a crest at the north end. Furthermore, unlike Camden, it was devoid of thick forests on both sides. To Morgan, that meant that there was no safe haven to which a panicked militiaman could flee. Morgan positioned his army on the knoll. He posted Carolina and Georgia riflemen in the most forward positions. These shock troops were to lay down a few volleys before retreating the 150 yards to a second line of militiamen. The men in the second line were instructed to fire two times, always targeting an officer, then to retreat behind a third line composed mostly of the Delaware and Maryland Continentals. Washington's horse soldiers were situated behind that line, hidden by a slight knoll, available to be deployed when Morgan was ready. Given what had occurred at Camden, Morgan's plan was audacious, but once a militiaman himself, the rebel general believed these men would fight well if they were well led, and he knew that many of these backcountry citizen-soldiers were very good marksmen, having honed their skills on squirrels and grouse.

Tarleton's British Legion arrived in the cold, inky darkness on January 17. An hour later the fight was on. Some green-clad Tories were gunned down by Morgan's riflemen, but Tarleton kept his infantrymen moving, marching and huzzahing as drums beat and fifes sounded. Drawing near, the Legionnaires charged "as if they intended to eat us up," Morgan said later. They rushed forward into a thunderous barrage laid down by the rebels' second line. As instructed, these men got off their two shots, killing and wounding two-thirds of Tarleton's infantry officers and wiping out 90 percent of the men in four companies. When the militiamen in Morgan's second line retreated as planned, the British thought they were taking flight. Tarleton's men advanced again, this time into the maw of the Continentals. At the pivotal moment of what may have been the most furious fighting of any encounter in this war, Washington's cavalry was unleashed, springing seemingly out of nowhere from behind the knoll and shouting "Buford's play" and "Tarleton's quarter." Now it was Tarleton's soldiers who fled and cried for mercy when overtaken. No mercy was shown. Tarleton may have been the last British soldier to flee, but he too eventually took flight, barely escaping his hate-maddened enemy. When it was over, Morgan roamed the blood-soaked battlefield crying out, "Old Morgan never was beaten," and proclaiming that he had given Tarleton "a devil of a whipping." Indeed, he had. Morgan had lost seventy-three men, Tarleton some eight hundred, together with a cornucopia of weaponry, ammunition, horses, and "plenty of hard cash."[21]

Cornwallis got the bad news on the following morning. A rebel prisoner, watching as Tarleton himself reported the disagreeable details to his commander, later recounted that Cornwallis, leaning on his sword as he listened, grew so furious that he broke his saber.[22] Cornwallis had lost about one-sixth of his army. Not only could his army not endure such a rate of attrition, but also the British commander understood in a flash that if Morgan rendezvoused with Greene, the rebel army would be nearly equal in size to his own. Cornwallis acted without hesitation to prevent a reunion of the enemy armies. Gathering three times the number of men that Morgan was thought to possess, Cornwallis set out to find his adversary. He might have pounced on his prey, but for two days Cornwallis tracked to the northwest while Morgan hurried to the northeast. By the time Cornwallis realized his mistake, Morgan was twenty miles away. Nevertheless, Cornwallis was as much of a fighter as his adversary, and he was resourceful. Stripping his army of all luxuries—liquor, clothing, beds, and tents were burned, including those that had belonged to Cornwallis—the lean redcoat force set off. Morgan's men ran hard too. Cornwallis cut the gap between the two forces. At times, only a river separated the armies. But the rebels escaped, and when they rapidly crossed the Yadkin River in boats that Greene had waiting for them, Morgan's little rebel army was safe for a time.

Early in February, Morgan joined with Greene's army at Guilford Courthouse. Greene considered making a stand as Cornwallis drew near, but he soon jettisoned the thought. While Greene knew that he would receive no further reinforcements, it was entirely possible that Arnold's American Legion might descend from Virginia and link up with Cornwallis. Now it was Greene who ran, retreating northward toward the Dan River. Once across, the rebel soldiers would be in Virginia, home to numerous militiamen. But first, the rebels had to reach the Dan. They began their run for Virginia as Cornwallis's tattered, bone-tired men drew near. The British commander never paused. He knew that if he could catch and destroy his prey, there would be no American army south of the Potomac River.

The chase was on. Both armies were up and on the move long before dawn every morning. Each covered several miles a day. Each marched until nightfall. The men on each side got only a few cherished hours of sleep every night. Cornwallis's men moved faster than Greene's. In five days they cut Greene's lead from twenty miles to just four. But day five was the last day of the chase. In the final moments of sunlight on February 17, with shadows blanketing the winter landscape, the rebels began crossing the Dan into Virginia. Cornwallis's men reached the southern bank of the river as day was breaking the next morning. Greene had won the race. He was gone. All Cornwallis had to show for his valiant, dogged pursuit of the past few weeks was the loss of 250 men, one-tenth of those with him when he had set out after Morgan just after Cowpens. Cornwallis issued a hollow proclamation claiming victory, after which he led his army on a retreat of its own to Hillsborough.[23]

Just as Washington had been pursued by Cornwallis across New Jersey in 1776, Morgan and Greene had been in the same British general's crosshairs during the 250 mile chase through North Carolina in 1781. Greene's next step also resembled what Washington had done five years earlier. After scoring his Christmas victory at Trenton, Washington had abandoned his Pennsylvania sanctuary and crossed the Delaware River yet again, reentering New Jersey and harm's way. After ten days in Virginia, Greene recrossed the Dan into North Carolina. Washington had been reinforced during his stay in Pennsylvania; Greene returned with six hundred fresh Virginia militiamen. The American army had inched toward two thousand men and Greene was optimistic that additional militia would be joining him from throughout the South. Greene was a fighter, but a prudent one, and his choice to return to action was well taken. His presence, he hoped, would discourage Tories who might have been taken in by Cornwallis's bombastic proclamation. If the promised militia arrived, Greene additionally thought his army might be numerically superior. Furthermore, the redcoats were deep in the backcountry "amongst timid friends and adjoining inveterate rebels," as Cornwallis acknowledged. Greene believed that British forage parties, far from their supply base, would be vulnerable to debilitating raids by partisan bands and Continental cavalry, led by the likes of Colonels Washington and Henry Lee.[24]

Not long passed until the wisdom of Greene's thinking was borne out. Before February ended, Colonel Lee's troopers surprised and cut to pieces a four-hundred-man force of Tory cavalry under Colonel John Pyle, a local physician. Nearly every Loyalist cavalryman—most of whom were without their weapons when caught off guard—was killed or wounded in what even the rebels soon referred to as "Pyle's Massacre" and "Pyle's Hacking Match." In a carnival frenzy of retribution, Lee's bloodthirsty men screamed "Remember Buford" as they "hewed to death" their helpless, mostly teenage victims, with broadsides. It was vicious, but as an unsympathetic partisan leader remarked: "It has knocked up Toryism altogether in this part of the state." It also spurred Cornwallis to act. He emerged from his lair to hunt for Greene's army. He had no trouble finding it, but two weeks elapsed before he could bring Greene to fight. Greene remained elusive, awaiting the arrival of militia and searching for a suitable site to at last face Cornwallis. By the second week in March, the American army had ballooned to 4,400 men and Greene was carefully reconnoitering a site at Guilford Courthouse.[25]

Half or more of Greene's men were militiamen. Greene cared no more for militia than did Washington, though he knew that at times—along Battle Road, atop Bunker Hill, at Saratoga's two battles, and more recently at Cowpens, for instance—the militiamen had performed ably. Like a handful of other American commanders, Greene must have thought that their performance depended on the quality of leadership, but he also knew that at this late stage of the war, many militia companies included men who had earlier served in the Continental army, and many of them were combat-hardened veterans. Greene might have concurred with Cornwallis had he been familiar with the British commander's assessment of American militia-men: "I will not say much in praise of the [rebel] militia . . . but the list of British officers and soldiers killed and wounded by them . . . proves . . . they are not wholly contemptible."[26]

On March 15, a southern spring-soft day, Cornwallis's army—barely half the size that Greene commanded—reached the vicinity of Guilford Courthouse. Greene had positioned his men several hours earlier, utilizing a pattern that somewhat resembled Morgan's plan at Cowpens. Greene, however deployed his men in three battle lines situated hundreds of yards apart, placing riflemen and light infantry on his flanks, and cavalry on still more distant flanks. Morgan had advised Greene to station some carefully selected men in the rear with orders to gun down any militiamen who fled the battlefield. Greene did not act on that macabre advice, and in fact Morgan had done nothing of the sort in his engagement two months earlier.

The Americans waited nervously for their adversary to appear. In the early morning darkness, Cornwallis gave the order for his men to move out. They were still a considerable ways from Greene and his men. As the sun rose higher, the British force, with flags fluttering and drums beating, drew nearer and nearer to the bucolic farmland and unspoiled forest that would be the battlefield. Around noon, the redcoat army emerged from thick woods and began to cross muddy, freshly plowed fields some four hundred yards from Greene's forward line. The edgy North Carolina militiamen in that line waited, nervously thinking all the things that soldiers think on the cusp of battle. They had been ordered not to fire until the enemy was "at a *killing distance.*" That meant fifty yards, possibly only thirty. Time seemed to stop. The redcoats came on, slowly, inexorably, and in an incredibly orderly fashion, though not in the close, crowded formation characteristic of European warfare and that Howe had utilized to his detriment at Bunker Hill. Cornwallis had learned a lesson or two about fighting in America. Nevertheless, the redcoats were marching into the face of a partially hidden enemy about to open up with massed firepower. When the British soldiery drew so close that their features were readily discernible, a thousand rebel muskets and rifles erupted. Many militiamen fired buck and ball, a combination of buckshot and a thirty caliber ball that was virtually guaranteed to hit something at such close range. Many of the British fell, wounded or dead. The survivors hastily regrouped and charged. Many were cut down by a second American volley. Some militiamen fled without firing. Some ran after their first shot. Some reloaded and fired again, and then bolted for the rear. Some held their ground.

Those who stood firm found that the enemy was on them in a flash. Americans and British, wielding their muskets as clubs, fought for their lives in desperate hand-to-hand combat. The redcoats who were still on their feet after fighting through the Americans' first line of defense advanced to the second line. The fighting there broke down into dozens of skirmishes in woods and dense underbrush. Men suffered ghastly wounds—shot, knifed, hacked with swords, beaten with muskets, run over by horses. In what was a common occurrence in battle, men were wounded by friendly artillery fire that took out them and the enemy simultaneously. Deep into the brawl, smoldering cartridge paper set fire to the woods. Many who were disabled by severe wounds were consumed in the flames.

In such fierce and chaotic fighting, men were down everywhere. Cornwallis was fortunate not to be one of the wounded. He had a horse shot from beneath him, but commandeered another and continued to ride about the battlefield impervious to peril. The nature of the fighting varied from sector to sector, depending on leaders, the performance of the units, and the terrain. In some areas, the British continued to advance; in others, they were driven back. After ninety minutes on the smoke-clogged field, the frayed British left sagged. A sudden charge by the rebel infantry and cavalry might have obliterated those redcoats; Greene may have had within his grasp the opportunity to break through and envelop a substantial portion of his adversary. But Greene hesitated, perhaps wisely given the uncertainties of battle and concerns about his unseasoned men and their leaders. The opportunity passed quickly. Not long afterward, with Maryland troops giving way, Greene ordered a withdrawal. He had seen and done enough. What he called the "long, bloody, and severe" Battle of Guilford Courthouse was over.[27]

Paradoxically, the British had both won and lost the battle. They won the field, taking control of it when Greene retreated, and in the process the British captured all the rebel artillery and 1,300 muskets and rifles. But Cornwallis had lost 532 men, a staggering 28 percent of those he had led onto the battlefield. His losses were twice those suffered by the Americans, who were more capable of replacing those who had fallen. Both Cornwallis and

Greene claimed victory. Nearly everyone thought Greene's claim was more valid, a sentiment perhaps best captured by Charles James Fox, long a leading voice of opposition to the war in the House of Commons, who echoed comments made six years earlier in the wake of Bunker Hill: "Another such [British] victory would ruin the British army."[28]

Indeed, Britain's army had already sustained appalling losses in the gruesome campaigning in the South. The British army had landed on South Carolina's barren and desolate coast thirteen months before. In five major engagements—Charleston, Camden, King's Mountain, Cowpens, and Guilford Courthouse—the British had lost some 3,500 men. Another 1,000, more or less, had been lost in long forgotten skirmishes and small actions, to diseases that flourished in the miasmic southern climate, and in the arduous chases after Morgan and Greene. From the time he took command in June 1780 until March 1781, when he tallied his losses in the mournful days following Guilford Courthouse, Cornwallis had commanded approximately 8,500 men. Roughly half had been lost. As Horace Walpole in London caustically observed: "Lord Cornwallis has conquered . . . himself out of troops."[29]

CHAPTER 15

"WE HAVE GOT CORNWALLIS IN A PUDDING BAG"

THE DECISIVE VICTORY AT YORKTOWN

THE MOOD AT Continental army headquarters had brightened as news arrived of what Washington called the "brilliant action" in the southern theater. Britain's heavy losses, he thought, should "retard or injure" Cornwallis's "future movements and operations." All the same, word also arrived in the spring of 1781 that a British force of some two thousand men was sailing south from New York. The American commander did not know whether those troops were to join Benedict Arnold in Virginia or whether they were reinforcements for Cornwallis in the Carolinas.[1]

Washington's thinking only slowly came into focus during the winter and spring, evolving through many twists and turns, each dictated by what America's French ally did and did not do. In December, a few weeks before the battle at Cowpens, Washington implored the French to appeal to their Spanish ally to engage in joint naval operations to liberate Florida, Georgia, and South Carolina. Neither Rochambeau nor the French admirals wanted any part of such a campaign, but when a huge winter storm severely damaged the British fleet in New York, the French in early February hastily dispatched a small squadron to Virginia to seek out and destroy Arnold. Overjoyed, Washington pitched in by ordering Lafayette to march to Virginia with 1,200 men, adding that Arnold was to be executed if captured. This promising endeavor, like so many others in this war, netted nothing. To get Arnold, the fleet had to sail up the Elizabeth River to Portsmouth, but the river was too shallow to accommodate the French vessels, and the allied naval force returned to New England empty-handed. Perhaps embarrassed, the French agreed to try again, and in March, on the day after the Battle of Guilford Courthouse, a much larger French squadron reached the Chesapeake Bay—only to discover that its entrance was shielded by a roughly equal number of British warships. A clash ensued. The French got the worst of it and broke off the fight. For a second time in a month, a French fleet turned for New England after failing to achieve its objective. Despite its disappointment, Congress loudly praised the French. It was a step Congress had to take to smooth over ruffled feathers, as a private letter in which Washington complained of French procrastination having ruined both naval enterprises fell into the hands of Tories, who gleefully saw to its publication.[2]

While Washington's spirits were buoyed in anticipation of a summer campaign to retake New York, Cornwallis at the same moment was in the dark about which way to turn after the events at Guilford Courthouse. His army spent a dreadful night on the battlefield following Nathanael Greene's retreat. The heavy scent of battle hung over the killing ground, which remained littered with the detritus of the fighting, including scores of bodies. Throughout what seemed to be an endless night, the wounded cried out in despair and agony, and many died. The appalling sights and sounds "exceeded all description," said one young, inexperienced British officer, who prayed such a "scene of horror and distress . . . rarely occurs . . . in a military life." Cornwallis and his army remained amid the carnage for seventy-two hours, mostly waiting until some of the wounded could be moved. Those incapable of making a long trek were handed over to neighboring Quakers who had offered to care for them. The Quakers also brought milk, eggs, barnyard animals, and candles to the weary, shaken redcoats. Finally, after issuing his customary pronouncement claiming to have won another "compleat victory," Cornwallis set his army in motion for coastal Wilmington, North Carolina, where it could be replenished from British-held Charleston. It was a horrendous trek, during which still more soldiers died and others had to be left with civilians who agreed to provide care. So tattered were these redcoats that some men were barefoot throughout the interminable march.[3]

While the army was refitted, Cornwallis spent a month pondering his choices. Although Clinton had ordered him not to leave South Carolina until it was pacified, Cornwallis knew that during the year since Charleston's fall, he had not come close to subduing the rebellion in the Carolina backcountry. Indeed, campaigning in the hinterland during the past ten months had been worse than fruitless. The army's presence had only nourished the insurgency. Furthermore, the British had suffered an unsustainable rate of attrition. Despite his public claim of victory, Cornwallis privately acknowledged that "every part of our army was beat repeatedly" in his contests with Greene's rebel forces. In addition, Cornwallis had so soured on the ministry's notion that southern Tories would rush to join the British army that he likely would have endorsed the comment of one of his generals who said with disgust that the redcoats would be fortunate to raise one hundred southern Tories in the course of a thousand-mile march. In reality, Tories had turned out in considerable numbers during 1780, but the defeats that the British suffered, beginning with King's Mountain, had stymied recruiting, so that by the spring of 1781 Cornwallis was convinced, probably correctly, that he could no longer replace his losses with freshly raised Tories in the Carolinas.

For Cornwallis, everything added up to the conclusion that the sole hope of suppressing the rebellion in the Low Country lay in closing the supply routes in the Upper South through which men, arms, and munitions flowed to both the partisans and Greene's army. While in Wilmington, Cornwallis thought he glimpsed the means of achieving this end. He learned that Clinton had sent an army to Virginia to augment Arnold. This was the army that Washington in March had learned was about to sail south. A 2,000-man force under General William Phillips would bring the total number of British soldiers in Virginia to 3,500. Cornwallis reasoned that if he marched north with his 1,400 men, the British would have a sizable army in the Old Dominion. Should Clinton see fit to further shore up that army, Cornwallis believed he would possess the means of sealing the supply routes and possibly even scoring a pivotal victory. Abandoning the Carolinas would violate Clinton's orders. However, commanders who were in the field and aware of the situation always had some latitude in determining the proper course to follow. On the other hand, Clinton was the commander of the army, and among royal officials in America, he alone was responsible for formulating Britain's grand strategy.

Cornwallis had made his decision. He would march into Virginia. He wrote to Clinton that his choice was the "most solid plan" available, the only one that offered hope of being "attended with important consequences." Given the lag in communications, he knew that he would be in Virginia when his commander in chief finally became aware of what had transpired. Cornwallis had made the most important choice of his military career and perhaps the most fateful decision of this war.[4]

As Cornwallis readied his army to march to Virginia, Washington prepared for his third meeting with Rochambeau during the ten months—the ten inactive months—that the French army had been in the United States. On the cusp of the meeting to plan the campaign of 1781, Washington remarked, "Now or never our deliverance must come."[5]

The commanders met for two days in May in Wethersfield, Connecticut, in sessions that were tense and acrimonious, even bruising. Happily, Rochambeau revealed that France was bestowing six million livres on the Continental army. (Pointedly, it was to be given to the army, not to Congress.) The friction between the two commanders came over what to do that summer. Washington remained intransigently committed to a campaign to retake New York. Rochambeau was not keen on such an endeavor, as he knew that during their five-year occupation of the city, the British would have stockpiled supplies and erected formidable, perhaps impenetrable, defenses. Certain that an assault on the British lines was unlikely to succeed, Rochambeau felt that the city could be retaken only through a siege operation that could be expected to take a year or longer. If a French fleet arrived to assist, it would never remain that long. Moreover, the rule of thumb in European warfare was that, to be successful, a siege army must possess upwards of a three-to-one numerical superiority over the besieged. With American militia serving only three- to six-month tours of duty, Rochambeau was persuaded that achieving—and sustaining— the requisite manpower superiority was out of the question.

Given these considerations, Rochambeau argued in favor of a Virginia campaign. Neither he nor Washington were aware in May that Cornwallis's army would also be in Virginia, but Rochambeau felt that the odds of scoring a pivotal victory over the combined forces of Phillips and Arnold were good. Washington—who, according to Rochambeau's subsequent account, was unable to "conceive the affairs of the south to be of such urgency"—remained inflexible. The two generals argued. According to a witness, Rochambeau treated Washington with "ungraciousness and all the unpleasantness possible." But Washington would not budge, and Rochambeau's orders from Versailles were to defer to him. The conference ended with the decision "to make an attempt upon New York."

Rochambeau had been candid with Washington, though for security reasons the French commander had kept one item under wraps. He had known that the West Indian fleet of comte de Grasse had been ordered to sail to North America sometime that summer. The moment that Washington departed Wethersfield, Rochambeau—despite what he had just agreed to—wrote de Grasse asking him to sail to the Chesapeake, not to New York. A month later, Rochambeau gave the order to march from Rhode Island to New York, and over eighteen mercilessly scorching summer days, the French army slogged westward in great swirling clouds of dust. On July 6, one year almost to the day since disembarking in America, the French soldiers at last united with Washington's Continentals near White Plains, just north of New York City.[6]

By then, Cornwallis had been in Virginia for nearly six weeks. Greene had neither followed him nor retreated ahead of him back across the Dan. In fact,

THE DECISIVE VICTORY AT YORKTOWN 297

even before Cornwallis arrived in Wilmington, Greene led 1,300 men into the Low Country, home to 8,000 British troops. Most were garrisoned in Charleston and Savannah, but a quarter or more were posted in scattered and vulnerable backcountry posts. Cornwallis had turned his back on the redcoats in the backcountry. He foresaw that Greene and his "Mountaineers"— Cornwallis's term for the guerrillas—would "beat in detail" those garrisons, and on this score, the British commander was prescient. Greene took all eight British backcountry outposts within only ninety days. Greene additionally fought two major battles. He lost the first at Hobkirk's Hill outside Camden, prompting him to memorably remark: "We fight[,] get beat[,] rise and fight again." He fought next in September at Eutaw Springs, and as at Guilford Courthouse, the British paid a heavy price for winning the contested field. The British lost about 1,125 men in the two engagements.[7]

By late May, around the time that Washington's meeting with Rochambeau concluded, Clinton learned that Cornwallis had taken his army to Virginia. The British commander was incensed. Clinton understood better than Cornwallis that America's "exigencies . . . put it out of her power to continue . . . the war . . . much longer," and that realization led him to cling to a policy of "avoiding all risks," of holding on to what Britain had recovered and buying time because time was on Britain's side.[8] In addition, Clinton anticipated a Franco-American attempt to retake New York. That would be the war's epic battle, and Clinton believed that he would need the forces under Phillips and Arnold when the showdown occurred. Clinton could have recalled the British troops in Virginia in June. At the same moment, he could also have ordered Cornwallis back to South Carolina. But in one of the great mysteries of this war, Clinton did neither of those things. Instead, he sent still more reinforcements to Virginia.

The Virginia that Cornwallis entered was weary of war. During the past twenty-four months, it had suffered devastating coastal raids and damaging enemy forays up the James River. Threats at home and in the Carolinas had led Governor Jefferson and his predecessor, Patrick Henry, to summon the militia to duty on numerous occasions. But 1781 was Virginia's worst year. Arnold's destructive raid on Richmond occurred in January. Phillips arrived in the spring with a force that doubled the size of the British army in the Old Dominion, and he was accompanied by a small but powerful fleet.

Phillips wasted no time. During his first week in the state, the British general sent a flotilla of six heavily armed vessels up the Potomac. For fourteen days the expedition—which Washington characterized as a "parcel of plundering Scoundrels"—spread terror, ransacking and burning residences, and destroying shipyards and tobacco warehouses on both the Virginia and

Maryland sides of the river. One of the sites it visited was Washington's Mount Vernon, where the sloop of war the HMS *Savage* confiscated property and liberated seventeen slaves, though the mansion was left unscathed. Mere hours after that raid, Phillips dispatched yet another force up the James, hoping to do even more damage than Arnold had caused three months earlier. The raid resulted in the destruction of yet more tobacco warehouses and plantations, and the killing of large numbers of horses and cattle, but Phillips's hope of wreaking further destruction in Richmond was frustrated when Lafayette rushed defenders to the capital city.[9]

No war governor faced greater trials than Jefferson, and by the spring of 1781 he was at his wit's end. He had been forced to flee from Richmond twice, viciously assailed for his tardy response to Arnold's arrival at the beginning of the year, and pressured relentlessly for men and materials by Lincoln, then by Gates, and finally by Greene. Jefferson's frustrations gushed out in his correspondence. He complained to Congress that in the first years of the war, Virginia had sacrificed to dispatch aid to the northern states, but now in its hour of need those states were doing little to assist their southern brethren, even though the "Northern States are safe." Nor did Jefferson understand Washington's thinking. Equating the American commander's obsession with New York with Spain's fixation on Gibraltar, Jefferson maintained that the Allies should undertake a concerted campaign in the South. If they did so, he predicted, "the face of the Continental War would be totally changed."[10]

Jefferson's worries only increased when Cornwallis crossed unopposed into Virginia. On May 20, the day before the Wethersfield conference began, Cornwallis linked up with Phillips's army and took command in Virginia. Soon, too, Cornwallis found a good location for a naval base, something he would need should Clinton send aid and reinforcements. It was at Yorktown on the peninsula between the York and James Rivers. Situated on a bluff overlooking the York, Cornwallis characterized Yorktown as a "safe defensive" site.[11]

Nor did Cornwallis drag his feet before commencing his hunt for Lafayette. But if Cornwallis thought Lafayette could be induced to fight, he was mistaken. With only a third the number of men that his adversary possessed, Lafayette fell back on the Fabian tactics that had served Washington well when Cornwallis had sought to engage him in 1776. "Was I to fight a Battle I'll be Cut to pieces," the young French general confessed to Washington. Lafayette's plan was to skirmish and retreat, always careful that his militia never faced British cavalry, "whom [the militiamen] fear like they would So Many wild Beasts." Cornwallis, revitalized by being back in the fray, relished the challenge. "The Boy cannot escape me," he allegedly declared. But Lafayette did elude him, crossing the South Anna River northwest of

Richmond and withdrawing deeper into the state's interior. Cornwallis stalked his prey for only six days. He had no stomach for another protracted chase that would waste his army and, in all likelihood, end in futility.[12]

Late in May, Cornwallis shifted to a new strategy occasioned by Lafayette's retreat. As the Continentals withdrew to the north, the southern and western portions of Virginia—the region to which the state had moved nearly all its military stores—had been left nearly defenseless. Magazines dotted the area near Point of Fork, where the Rivanna and Fluvanna Rivers met to form the James. Not only were those precious supplies ripe for the plundering, but also Cornwallis had learned that General Steuben with several hundred men was at Point of Fork removing arms and equipment. Simultaneously, Cornwallis discovered that the Virginia legislature had fled the imperiled capital and was meeting in what was thought to be the secure village of Charlottesville, just a stone's throw from Monticello, the home of Governor Jefferson. Cornwallis responded by dispatching 500 men under Lieutenant Colonel John Simcoe, commander of the Queen's Rangers, to the head of the James. He ordered Colonel Tarleton with 250 of his British Legionnaires to ride hard for Charlottesville.

Simcoe failed to bag Steuben's force, but he captured or destroyed a treasure trove of military hardware. With the enemy in its midst, Virginia lost 2,500 muskets, a "large quantity" of powder, ten artillery pieces, and numerous casks loaded with materials used in making gunpowder. Under Virginia's warm summer sun, Simcoe roamed the riverbanks for a week, setting the torch to countless hogsheads of tobacco.[13]

Tarleton, meanwhile, set off for Charlottesville on Sunday, June 3, the last full day of Jefferson's second, and last, term as governor. Sometime that night, Jack Jouett, a Charlottesville native who was enjoying the libation at the Cuckoo Tavern in Louisa, spotted the fast-moving, green-clad Legionnaires as they thundered past his watering hole. Guessing correctly that they were headed for Charlottesville, some twenty-five miles away, Jouett grabbed his horse and rode like the wind—much as Paul Revere had done on another dark night six years before—to warn Jefferson and the legislators. Aware of shortcuts, Jouett outraced the soldiers by a considerable margin. He pounded on Jefferson's door at four thirty A.M., and a bit later Jouett alerted the legislators.

After posting reliable slaves as lookouts, Jefferson spent his remaining time—probably upwards of an hour—gathering or burning important papers and arranging for his wife and daughters to travel by carriage to a neighboring estate. With the sun peeping through the green summer foliage, Jefferson at last made his getaway, riding Caractacus, reputedly one of the fastest horses in the state, into the dense forest that surrounded his mountaintop lair. Jefferson had probably departed fifteen minutes, possibly thirty, before twenty of Tarleton's horse soldiers reached the summit of the mountain and stormed into the mansion. A slave who greeted the troopers fibbed that Jefferson had been gone for hours. They believed him. Thinking it a fool's errand to give pursuit, the soldiers spent nearly a full day at Monticello, apparently doing little else aside from drinking Jefferson's wine. They liberated no slaves, stole nothing, and "preserved every thing with sacred care," as Jefferson said later. Most of the legislators got away too. Only seven assembly-men who tarried fell into the hands of the enemy.[14]

Cornwallis, whose zeal for fighting had previously known no bounds, and who had come to Virginia to fight, was largely done. The reinforcements sent by Clinton had raised his strength to 7,000 men, against which Lafayette— who had also been reinforced—commanded some 3,500 Continentals and however many militiamen could be raised. If Clinton's behavior in tolerating Cornwallis's presence in Virginia is puzzling, Cornwallis's inactivity after early June is no less perplexing. Immediately after Simcoe's and Tarleton's raids, Cornwallis marched his army eastward to Yorktown, arriving just after the armies of Rochambeau and Washington rendezvoused in White Plains. Once he was in Yorktown, Cornwallis became immobile. He had to have been bewildered by the array of contradictory orders he received from Clinton. In dispatches written over a span of twenty-five days, Clinton first ordered Cornwallis to march his army to Philadelphia. Next, he instructed Cornwallis to stay in Virginia but to send two thousand of his men to New York. Finally, Clinton told Cornwallis to keep all of his men and fortify a base that was accessible to the Royal Navy. Cornwallis had not always followed Clinton's orders, but he chose to adhere scrupulously to his commander's last order. Cornwallis settled in at Yorktown. He must have come to the realization that further campaigning in Virginia, and probably throughout the South, would be unavailing unless a much larger British army was committed to the theater. Furthermore, during the summer of 1781 all signs pointed to an imminent— and in all likelihood a climactic—battle for New York. Cornwallis wished to be part of what might be an historic engagement, an epochal battle that future generations might see as even more significant than the fight for Quebec in the Seven Year's War. With a candor born from the hope that Clinton would summon him to New York, Cornwallis confided that his army in Yorktown was doing little more than guarding "some Acres of an unhealthy swamp" that was "ever liable to become a prey to a foreign" navy. If Cornwallis was hinting, it was to no avail. Clinton left him in Yorktown.[15]

*   *   *

When the French army marched into White Plains under a warm July sun, America's soldiers cheered them. Over the next couple of days, the two armies paraded for one another. Some French observers thought their ally looked "rather good," but others were alarmed at finding that many of Washington's troops were barefoot, and that some were too old for the demanding life of a soldier, while others were disquietingly young. Some seemed startled at discovering that numerous African Americans were serving in the Continental army, and one guessed that blacks composed 25 percent of the American soldiery. But one French soldier thought the African Americans were "strong, robust men" who made "a very good appearance." Still another remarked that a Rhode Island regiment made up largely of blacks was the "most neatly dressed, the best under arms, and the most precise in its maneuver" of all the Continental units.[16]

A couple of weeks before the armies linked up, Rochambeau finally revealed to Washington that de Grasse was bringing his fleet northward. Aware by then that Cornwallis was in Virginia with a large and growing army—it would top out at 8,500 men—Washington grew more flexible. Perhaps a Virginia campaign was preferable to fighting for New York, he said, though he vacillated on the matter. Given the chance that de Grasse would never arrive, the Allied commanders kept their focus on preparations for retaking New York. And they waited. Everything depended on de Grasse. He might be coming to New York. He might be coming to Virginia. He might never leave the Caribbean. Or, he might sail northward, but something—the enemy, a hurricane—might prevent his ever reaching North America. Days passed. Weeks went by without word. Finally, on August 14, the thirty-ninth day after the two allied armies came together, a dispatch rider brought word from de Grasse. His fleet had arrived at the entrance to Chesapeake Bay.[17]

Through the spring and summer Clinton's intelligence had been so good that he, too, was aware that de Grasse planned to come north. Indeed, Clinton had probably known it before Washington. Like his adversaries, however, Clinton did not know de Grasse's destination. Drawing on the information that he possessed—some of which was erroneous, as is often the case with military intelligence—Clinton and the naval officials in New York made a series of educated guesses. They assumed that de Grasse was most likely to sail for New York. They also believed he would leave some of his warships in the Caribbean and send others to France. As Clinton had requested naval reinforcements from the West Indies, he surmised that the Royal Navy would remain superior in North American waters, even after de Grasse was joined by the French squadron in New England. Some conclusions reached by those in Britain's high command in New York were mistaken, though the errors were largely due to faulty and incomplete information. In retrospect, Clinton's most egregious error was not in his judgment about the size of the rival fleets but in his failure to summon Cornwallis's army to New York. Even so, Clinton's decision was understandable, if flawed. London had long since embraced a southern strategy and stressed waging aggressive war in the South, and early in the summer Clinton had been reproached by Lord Germain for having paid insufficient attention to the Chesapeake. Furthermore, while Cornwallis might accomplish little in Virginia, his presence at least tied down large numbers of Continentals who otherwise would have joined Washington's army outside New York.[18]

Soon after de Grasse's message arrived, Washington ordered Lafayette in Virginia to do all within his power to prevent Cornwallis's escape from the Peninsula.[19] At about the same moment, the Allied soldiers began crossing from New York into New Jersey. Their commanders had done what they could to convince Clinton that they continued to plan a campaign to retake New York. They built field ovens, essential for a siege army, permitted misleading correspondence to fall into British hands, and for the first days of the march to Virginia, the armies followed the route they would have taken had their intention been to rendezvous with de Grasse at Sandy Hook for a joint attack on New York. Their hope was to forestall until it was too late for Clinton to opt to take his army to Virginia or to call Cornwallis to New York. The Allies' deception worked, though Clinton's hand was stayed mostly by his belief that de Grasse would never achieve superiority in the Chesapeake.

The French and American soldiers trudged south under a searing August sun. Crowds of onlookers gathered throughout New Jersey to see the spectacle. Learning from the spectators that the French had given Washington hard currency with which to pay for this operation, the American soldiers somewhere in New Jersey refused to take another step until they were paid a month's wages, something they had not received in well over a year. Washington paid them and the trek resumed.[20]

The armies were now following the route that Washington had taken in his disconsolate retreat from New York five years before. The gloom of 1776 was gone, however. It had been replaced by an optimism that grew when word arrived during the march that de Grasse's fleet had successfully linked with the French naval force that had descended from New England. The French squadron would indeed be superior to the Royal fleet. The soldiers marched through Princeton and Trenton. A day later, under a warm blue sky, they began crossing the Delaware River.[21]

Over three days in early September the two armies paraded through Philadelphia, "raising a dust like a smothering snow-storm," according to one soldier. The last time the Continental army had marched through Philadelphia had been in 1777 when it was en route to Brandywine. Congressman John Adams, who had watched the army's pass-by on that occasion, had been struck by the soldiers' lack of precision and absence of jauntiness, and when the last man disappeared from his sight, Adams had fretfully hurried to a church to pray. The mood was different in 1781. The French were not only going into the looming fight alongside the Continentals, but resplendent in their spit and polish white coats faced with green, they also looked like "the perfection . . . of discipline as soldiers," according to one member of Congress. James Lovell, Adams's successor in the Massachusetts delegation, thought the mood among congressmen who had watched the show of arms was one of "high Glee."[22]

On reaching Wilmington, Washington learned that Cornwallis was in Yorktown and that Lafayette, with more than two thousand Continentals and four thousand Virginia and Maryland militia, was nearby.[23] Washington was reassured about Lafayette's chances of confining Cornwallis until the Allied armies arrived. Swept with euphoria, Washington, who normally exhibited an implacably grave and reserved manner, suddenly smiled, laughed, and waved his hat, and when Rochambeau arrived, the American commander hugged him with unrestrained passion. An astonished French officer said that Washington had "put aside his character as arbiter of North America and contented himself for the moment with that of a citizen, happy at the good fortune of his country. A child, whose every wish had been gratified, would not have experienced a sensation more lively."[24] Until Lafayette's letters arrived, Washington and Rochambeau had only known that their destination was Virginia. Now they knew it was Yorktown.

The French and American soldiers marched to Head of Elk, where some allied units boarded vessels that would rapidly convey them to Virginia. But there were not enough boats for everyone. Telling his Continentals that the "success, or disgrace of our expedition depends absolutely upon the celerity of our movements," Washington ordered others to "hurry . . . upon the wind of speed" to Annapolis and Baltimore, where more vessels could be found.[25] By September 26, thirty-eight days after setting out from Dobbs Ferry, the last allied soldier was ashore near Yorktown. Long before then—in fact, while Washington was at Head of Elk—de Grasse, with an overarching superiority of nine warships, had defeated a British fleet in what came to be known as the Battle of the Virginia Capes. Perhaps deservedly called by one historian "the most important . . . naval engagement of the eighteenth century," de Grasse was in control of the Chesapeake.[26] Cornwallis could no longer be rescued by sea.

Early in September, well before the first Allied troops debouched onto Virginia soil, Cornwallis discovered that the enemy armies were coming after him. Nearly two additional weeks passed before he learned that de Grasse had slammed shut his seagoing portal to safety. During that crucial stretch, some of Cornwallis's officers urged him to try to fight through Lafayette's lines and escape. The British enjoyed a slight numerical advantage, and Cornwallis also had far more regulars under his command than Lafayette possessed. Cornwallis contemplated the advice, though in the end he spurned it. Aside from the crushing humiliation of fleeing Virginia after abandoning the Carolinas, Cornwallis knew that he was safer in Yorktown than on the run. To have to forage for food while dogged by Lafayette—and ultimately by a huge Allied army—was a formula for disaster. Besides, he continued to hope that Clinton would send assistance. After making his decision to stay put in Yorktown, Cornwallis had received word that a relief expedition consisting of four thousand men was being sent and should arrive on October 5.

Alas, for the umpteenth time in this war when speedy British action was essential, it was not forthcoming. The relief expedition's departure from New York was held up for a month while repairs were made to vessels damaged in the Battle of the Virginia Capes. As September faded into October, Cornwallis found himself alone and under siege.[27]

Under normal circumstances, the Allied commanders might have opted to simply try to starve Cornwallis into submission. However, a protracted siege was not an option. De Grasse promised to remain until the end of October, but no longer, as his orders were to move on in November. The Allies had six weeks to force Cornwallis's capitulation, and they might not have even that long. Should a great storm churn through the Chesapeake—and hurricanes were not unknown in October—de Grasse's squadron could be ruined, much as d'Estaing's had been badly damaged off Rhode Island in 1778. Rochambeau thought it imperative to act with speed, and with every advantage on the side of the Allies, he radiated optimism. The Allies had some nineteen thousand men, more than double the number that Cornwallis commanded, and a third more cannon than the British possessed. From the outset, the confident French commander assured Washington that the outcome was "reducible to calculation." It was a sentiment shared by the American troops. "[W]e have got [Cornwallis] in a pudding bag," one exclaimed, while another, as if on a rabbit hunt, boasted that the Allies had "holed him and nothing remained but to dig him out." From the beginning, General Anthony Wayne believed victory was a "most glorious certainty."[28]

The cheer within the Allied lines was not misplaced. The beginning of the end for Cornwallis came on October 5. Allied sappers, working at night in "great silence and secrecy," began digging the first artillery parallels, soon to be the initial home of the Allies' siege guns. On the American side, Washington struck a few ceremonial blows with a pickax to kick off the work. After four nights, the Allied field guns were in place, the French to the west of Yorktown, the Americans on the east side. When all was ready for the first shot to be fired, Washington once again did the honors in mid-afternoon on October 9. Scuttlebutt had it that the ball he fired tore through a house in town in which several British officers had gathered for mess; supposedly, the redcoat seated at the head of the table had been killed. After that initial shot, all the guns erupted with a mighty blast. Day after day, nearly a hundred guns laid down a thunderous barrage that went on around the clock. Every day approximately 3,600 rounds slammed into Yorktown, a tiny village that could have fit into one little corner of a large city such as Boston or Philadelphia. In no time, every house and building was reduced to rubble and bodies of men and horses littered the landscape. Cornwallis's soldiers sought shelter in trenches and basements, and the commander himself moved his headquarters into an underground bunker. The artillery in the initial parallel was about 350 yards from nearest British soldier. When the second parallel opened about a week later, the allied gunners were only 150 yards away.[29]

Cornwallis did everything he could to protract the siege, hoping that with time something, anything, might save him and his army. He reduced his men's rations, then cut them even more. To save his scant supplies, Cornwallis also ordered the slaughter of hundreds of horses, directing that their bodies be dragged down to the York River, and he banished the runaway slaves who had fled to what they thought would be the secure haven provided by the British army. These African Americans had never soldiered, but they had toiled throughout the preceding weeks as cooks, maids, and laborers on behalf of the British army, accompanying it like "a wandering Arabian or Tartar horde," in the words of a German officer. Some of Cornwallis' officers condemned his decision as shameless and "harsh," and others spoke of "herds of Negroes," many of them "trembling" with fear, setting off across the unfamiliar landscape, running once again in what for most was to be a forlorn quest of their freedom. Cornwallis saw it not only as necessary for the salvation of his army but also as the sole chance these unfortunates had of escaping certain capture by the rebel soldiers.[30]

With the guns now capable of blasting away at almost point-blank range, all that remained to bring the operation to a speedy end was to seize the British redoubts at each end of the Allied lines, steps that would make the steady bombardment fully efficient. The French were assigned responsibility for taking redoubt Number 9 in their sector; the Americans were to take

Number 10 in their area. Alexander Hamilton, who was once Washington's aide but since July had commanded a New York light infantry battalion, beseeched the American commander to put him in charge of the American operation. Doubtless hoping to reward Hamilton for years of service at headquarters, but also wishing to further the young colonel's postwar political ambitions by giving him the opportunity to win glory, Washington acquiesced. Shortly before the attack, possibly while sitting in a trench redolent with fresh-turned dirt, Hamilton wrote his pregnant bride of ten months: "Five days more the enemy must capitulate . . . then I fly home to you. Prepare to receive me in your bosom."[31]

Hamilton had volunteered for a dangerous mission. He was given three infantry battalions numbering about five hundred men, black and white. Hamilton's force would have a huge numerical superiority, as it was known that only about fifty redcoats were in the redoubt. The attackers carried empty muskets, but their bayonets were in place; as the fighting would be in close quarters, the Continentals might do immense damage to one another if they fired their weapons. Some officers were armed with swords. A few men carried a spontoon. Sappers and miners, armed with axes, were in the van of the assault force; their job was to remove abatis and clear other impediments that the British defenders had installed on the redoubt's periphery. Hamilton sounded the order to move out into the black night at seven P.M.

Catching sight of the approaching enemy at nearly the last moment, the redcoats laid down a heavy fire with musket and small field guns. The Americans charged full bore, leaping into the redoubt; some rushed in through holes that had been opened during the previous days of shelling. The fight that followed was desperate, a hand-to-hand battle between men who fought like savage animals. Soldiers used their bayonets as knives, their guns as clubs. Some swung axes and some fought with their fists. It was brutal. When it was over and the redoubt was taken, 10 percent of Hamilton's men were casualties. Three-quarters of the British defenders were dead or wounded. Hamilton was unscathed. On the same night, and at virtually the same moment, the French took redoubt Number 9.[32]

Now, as Hamilton had told his wife, it was almost over. The heavy guns pounded away for two more days, October 16 and 17, before Cornwallis waved a flag of truce. It was the ninth day of the merciless bombardment. About 7 percent of Cornwallis's men had been killed or wounded, and his situation was nearly hopeless. He wanted to talk. In reality, he wanted to spin out the discussions, stalling for more time, hoping for a miracle. The Allied commanders would not give Cornwallis the luxury of time. They demanded that he agree to surrender the next day or the guns would open up again. That next day, October 18, Cornwallis signed the surrender accord. The terms were tough, nearly identical to those that Clinton had imposed on Lincoln in the American surrender at Charleston, except that this accord provided that the Americans could recover their property from Yorktown—that is, they were entitled to reclaim the slaves they had lost.[33]

At two P.M. on October 19—six and one-half years to the day since someone had fired the first shot of this war on the village Green at Lexington, Massachusetts—Cornwallis's army formally surrendered in Yorktown, Virginia. The defeated British troops, tired, hungry, and sullen, marched somberly from the utterly destroyed little village to the field of surrender. They passed between a long row of French troops on their left, neatly attired in their white parade uniforms and exhilarated by their victory—and at having survived the siege in which some four hundred of their comrades had been casualties—and a line of bedraggled Americans on their right, equally happy to be among the living at the end of this siege that had left some three hundred Americans dead or wounded. (Ironically, fewer British than Allied soldiers were casualties, though 556 were killed or wounded.) Oddly, the defeated British soldiers were neatly attired, having turned out in newly furnished uniforms. Some observers thought the proud redcoats did not hide their mortification at having to surrender to upstart colonial soldiers. Music from a British army band filled the air. The anecdote later caught on that the musicians played the contemporary favorite "The World Turned Upside Down." In all likelihood, the story is not true, though it is known that the band—performing with drums draped with black cloth and ebony ribbons dangling from fifes—played sorrowful music throughout much of the ceremony. It was a gorgeous fall day, warm and sunny, and the leaves were hurrying toward the peak of their autumn splendor. Many residents of nearby Williamsburg, frequent victims of British raiders during the past eighteen months, had gleefully come to witness the British capitulation, and not incidentally to search for slaves who during recent months had fled to the presumed safety offered by the redcoats.

In time, the principal officers of the three armies at Yorktown rode to the surrender site. Cornwallis was not to be seen. He remained at his shattered headquarters pleading sickness, though no one then or subsequently believed his professions of indisposition. Cornwallis was more likely humiliated than ill, and he would have been less than human had he not been angry as well. He had been given the nearly impossible task of pacifying a huge region awash with the enemy's regulars, militia, and partisans, and at least in his judgment he had never possessed adequate manpower for doing the job. Nor was that all. He had been left twisting in the wind in Virginia by Clinton and those around him long after they should have seen that it was reckless to keep large numbers of troops anywhere other than in and around New York. Cornwallis placed the onus of surrendering on Brigadier Charles O'Hara, a British officer for a quarter century who had suffered two serious wounds at Guilford Courthouse.

Washington must have dreamed of this moment a thousand times, but when it at last arrived, he refused to accept the surrender of an officer who held a rank subordinate to his. By rigidly adhering to a European code of martial etiquette, Washington denied himself the delicious ecstasy of accepting the decisive British capitulation. His second in command, General Lincoln, accepted O'Hara's sword, after which that hearty British officer rode from the field with tears in his eyes. Next, the soldiers who had served under Cornwallis came forward in an orderly manner to lay down their arms. Glum and quiet, these men faced an uncertain future; they now were prisoners of war in the care of an enemy that at times had been unable to properly feed, clothe, and house its own soldiers. A French band belted out upbeat tunes as these drawn and troubled soldiers passed into captivity.[34]

More than eight thousand prisoners were taken at Yorktown, of whom close to 15 percent were Germans. Roughly five hundred men who had soldiered under Cornwallis were not among the prisoners. According to the surrender terms, Cornwallis had been permitted to dispatch one vessel to New York, a ship that was supposed to carry only letters from the soldiers. Cornwallis cheated. Not entirely unexpectedly, he loaded the ship with his Loyalist soldiers and a few Continental army deserters.

No one knows how many African Americans had come to Yorktown with Cornwallis. Upwards of ten thousand slaves in Virginia had fled to the British army, almost all during 1780 and 1781. The runaways had died in droves, mostly of smallpox and typhoid fever. It is possible that some, though no one knows how many, may have had the good fortune to have been shipped to New York or Charleston prior to the siege. Many who came to Yorktown with Cornwallis perished in the course of the siege, mostly from diseases, though some were victims of the Allied shelling.

The victors who entered the rubble-strewn remains of Yorktown found corpses "all over the place," including the bodies of "an immense number of Negroes" who had died "in the most miserable manner" from smallpox. Meanwhile, many soldiers, hot for booty, were hired by local slave owners to scour the area in search of their runaway chattel. Some Continental army officers joined the search, looking for African Americans they had once owned. General Washington was one who spent some time combing the countryside. He found two of his slaves who had escaped in the raid of the HMS *Savage*. He sent them back to Mount Vernon and a lifetime of servitude.[35]

In this hour of triumph for a revolution waged for life, liberty, and the pursuit of happiness, Washington also found the time to congratulate his army on the victory that had brought "Joy" to "every Breast."[36]

CHAPTER 16

"Oh God, It Is All Over"

Peace, Conspiracy, Demobilization, Change, 1781–1783

FITTINGLY, THE FIRST DEFINITIVE WORD of the catastrophe at Yorktown was delivered to the London residence of Lord Germain. The American secretary summoned a coach for a brief, uneasy ride to Downing Street, where he broke the bad news to Lord North. The prime minister, according to a witness, reacted as if he had "taken a ball in the breast." Wringing his hands and pacing the floor, North reportedly cried, "Oh God, it is all over!" Whether he meant his ministry or the war, or both, was not clear.[1]

Opposition to war with America had existed in Parliament since before the order to use force went out early in 1775, but North's government had always rested on a comfortable majority. Nearly four out of five MPs supported the government's policies at the outset of hostilities, and after a snap election in the autumn of 1780—hard on the heels of word of the surrender of Charleston—the ministry still enjoyed a two-to-one majority. Yorktown changed things. A motion in December that decried the war as "contrary to the true interests of this kingdom" was defeated by only a narrow margin, failing because the king and Germain still supported the war. "Take away America, and we should sink into perfect insignificance," said the American secretary. The monarch insisted that losing America "would annihilate the rank in which the British Empire stands among the European states."[2] But support for their war steadily waned. Not even North any longer wanted the war to continue, though he thought it must in order for Great Britain to exercise leverage in the looming peace negotiations.

North's ministry fell piece by piece over a span of four months. In December, Sir Henry Clinton, on whose watch the war was finally lost, was replaced by General Sir Guy Carleton, the fourth commander of Britain's army in America in six years. Germain was gone in January in a gust of nearly universal antipathy. Six attempts were made to censure North's ministry during the early weeks of 1782. Each failed, but the government's majority steadily dwindled. North survived the last vote of no confidence by only a dozen votes. Late in February a motion stipulating that the war "may no longer be pursued" failed by a single vote. A week later a motion carried that labeled all who supported "the further prosecution of the war" as enemies of the realm. North stayed on for a few more days, telling the MPs that he would remain at the head of the ministry until the king asked him to resign or Parliament removed him with a vote of no confidence. The Hosue of Commons in effect did just that on March 27, prompting North's immediate resignation in one last speech as prime minister, remarks delivered "with that placid temper that never forsook him," according to an observer. With that, North hurried outdoors to a waiting carriage and was gone, bringing to an end his twelve years as prime minister.[3]

A melancholy spirit pervaded drab and dismal London throughout the weeks that North's ministry teetered and fell, but following Yorktown a festive mood prevailed in Philadelphia. Word of Cornwallis's surrender reached the city late in the night of October 22. Philadelphia's night watchman, one of the first to know, immediately walked the dark, lonely streets delivering his long-awaited announcement in a mixture of English and his native German: "Basht dree o'clock, und Gorn-wal-lis isht da-ken." Congress ordered a day of celebration that included a worship service and an evening when most Philadelphians put a candle in at least one window, a simple and unpretentious way of expressing their joy and thanksgiving.[4] As the news of Yorktown spread across the land—followed in the spring by the arrival of the text of the Commons' condemnation of the war—the sense grew that Cornwallis's surrender meant that peace was at hand. Long and sticky peace negotiations were certain to come, and small-scale skirmishing would continue in the southern Low Country, but big campaigns and battles were a thing of the past in North America.

De Grasse sailed away immediately after the British capitulation at Yorktown. Rochambeau's army stayed in Virginia until the following June, when it commenced a leisurely march to Massachusetts that consumed nearly three months. The French soldiers were honored and entertained in nearly every hamlet through which they passed. On Christmas Eve 1782, convinced that the war was really over, the French army boarded troop transports in Boston and sailed for home.[5] The Continental army, on the other hand, had left Yorktown almost immediately after Cornwallis's surrender. It marched north and spent most of 1782 on the Hudson above Manhattan. About eight thousand men, all unpaid and eager to go home, remained on duty, but

America's army could hardly be disbanded. Some twenty-five thousand British troops were still in the United States, most in New York, the remainder in Charleston and Savannah. The soldiers in both armies would remain in place until the peace talks concluded.

Not long after North's fall, the Earl of Shelburne formed a ministry. The presumption in London was that peace talks were imminent.[6] Nearly two decades earlier, Shelburne, at the time the secretary responsible for American affairs, had pursued an enlightened Western policy linked to a scheme for staunching further parliamentary taxation. Had he been able to realize his plans, the Anglo-American crisis might never have returned to fever pitch. But Shelburne had not lasted long before he was supplanted by obdurate Lord Hillsborough. In the run-up to war, Shelburne, though coy, had appeared to favor negotiations with the Continental Congress; after Saratoga, he seemed to think a military solution was beyond Britain's reach, at least so long as Germain was involved in the strategic planning. Word of Shelburne's ministry was greeted with optimism by perceptive colonists. John Adams thought peace inevitable no matter who headed the ministry, but he welcomed Shelburne as thoughtful and reasonable. Benjamin Franklin saw Shelburne as a welcome replacement for the "unclean Spirits" who had presided for years.[7]

America's diplomats in Europe had seemingly waited forever for the moment when peace talks would begin. Congress had declared independence in 1776, but for three years thereafter it never determined what it hoped to gain from the war. The most plausible reason for its failure to tackle that thorny issue was that Congress feared that such divisiveness would result among the disparate states that the war effort would be harmed, possibly fatally. In 1779, France forced Congress to act. As Spain early that year proposed to mediate the war, the French minister to the United States asked Congress in February to determine its peace terms and appoint a minister plenipotentiary who could join in the negotiations, if and when they occurred.[8]

Congress had no difficulty agreeing on several terms: British recognition of American independence must be a precondition of peace talks; the British army must withdraw from the United States; Nova Scotia was to be ceded to the United States; and all territory extending westward to the Mississippi River—between the thirty-first parallel in the South and a line that ran from just below Montreal to the Mississippi—was to be recognized as belonging to the United States. Congress initially wished to adopt two additional demands: recognition of American fishing rights in and around Newfoundland and, secondly, the right of navigation on the Mississippi River to the thirty-first parallel and access to a port in Spanish territory below that parallel. The northern states favored the former demand, the southern states the latter. France, however, favored neither, as it sought to prohibit American competition in the fisheries and was bent on protecting the interests of Spain, its tenuous ally, on the Mississippi. Congress dared not antagonize France. Although its debates were rancorous and lasted for weeks, and some threats were made to quit the war if state and regional interests were not protected, Congress acquiesced to French wishes.[9]

Congress's deliberations over its selection of a minister plenipotentiary to negotiate peace were not as bitter, but there were dustups. The delegations from New England backed John Adams, hoping he could protect their fishing industry. The mid-Atlantic states backed John Jay, in the hope that he could look after their commercial interests. The French minister once again intruded. France preferred Jay, thinking him more malleable than the fiercely independent Adams. But Congress defied the French on this issue. After a lengthy battle, Adams was appointed and Jay was sent to Madrid to seek an alliance with Spain. Congress also dispatched Henry Laurens, its former president, to Holland, hopeful of obtaining recognition and assistance.

Adams arrived in Europe late in 1779, fortunate to have survived a danger-laden Atlantic crossing on which his ship, *La Sensible*, was badly damaged in a storm. Adams's hazardous crossing turned out to be considerably premature. Peace was hardly imminent. When the war continued through 1780 and 1781, Adams—after learning that Laurens had been captured by the Royal Navy during his Atlantic crossing—scurried to Amsterdam where he spent nearly two years seeking a Dutch loan. During his absence, Foreign Minister Vergennes moved to have Congress dump Adams as America's peace commissioner. The two had clashed often during the six months that Adams lived in Paris and Vergennes heartily disliked him. But Vergennes feared Adams more than he hated him, and he continued to want a less resolute American envoy, one who might be manipulated to French ends. The perfect choice, Vergennes believed, was Franklin, the American minister to France since 1778, a figure who abhorred confrontation as much as Adams appeared to relish it. Congress was willing to concede control of the eventual peace negotiations to Vergennes, but it was unwilling to humiliate Adams, though it stripped him of sole responsibility for negotiating peace. In June 1781—just as Rochambeau's army began its march from Rhode Island to link up with Washington's Continentals for the anticipated campaign for New York—Congress named Franklin, Jay, Laurens, and Thomas Jefferson as Adams's fellow peace commissioners, after which it foolishly instructed its envoys "to

govern yourself by [France's] advice and opinion" whenever a peace conference got under way.[10]

The first step toward peace occurred nine months later. It was North who
made the initial move, acting in the twilight period between the news of
Yorktown and his ministry's fall. At North's behest, David Hartley, an MP,
wrote to his old friend Franklin in January 1782. It was an amicable letter, but
one in which Hartley sought to persuade the Americans to negotiate a separate peace treaty, a step that would leave Britain to fight France alone. North
had Hartley tell Franklin that Britain would fight "to the last man, and the
last shilling, rather than be dictated to by France," raising the prospect that if
the Americans did not seize the moment and make peace, the war would
continue indefinitely. However, if the American commissioners would come
alone to the peace table, Hartley continued, Britain was ready to sign a treaty
with *"liberal constructions."* Franklin did not take the bait. Thankful for the
help that France had provided and mindful that the United States would need
its friendship in the postwar period, Franklin told Hartley that no American
patriot would desert its "noble and generous Friend for the sake of [peace]
with an unjust and cruel Enemy." Franklin shared with Vergennes what
North had been up to, leading France's foreign minister to make clear to
London that the Allies would negotiate in concert. Vergennes also informed
the British that he wished merely to annul France's losses in the previous war,
not to humiliate Great Britain.[11]

Immediately after the collapse of North's government, the new ministry
sent Thomas Grenville—the son of the prime minister responsible for the
Sugar and Stamp Acts—to Paris to negotiate with Vergennes and Richard
Oswald, a seventy-six-year-old Scottish merchant and onetime resident of
America, to meet with the American commissioners. Oswald's assignment
was to learn what the Americans wanted and what they might concede. By a
stroke of luck, Oswald conferred solely with Franklin for four months beginning in April. Adams remained in Amsterdam; Laurens, though recently
released from confinement in the Tower in London, did not participate;
Jefferson had declined his appointment; and Jay, who had hurried to Paris
from Madrid for the negotiations, straightaway fell ill with influenza and was
incapacitated for weeks. Franklin's separate negotiations were conducted
with the approval of Vergennes, who anticipated—or at least hoped—that the
accords reached with Great Britain by the United States, France, and Spain
would be concluded and signed simultaneously.[12]

Franklin and Oswald at once got on well together. They shared much in
common. They were about the same age, and both had been businessmen and
exhibited a penchant for pragmatism and common sense. No less important,

each was good-natured and polite, and Franklin was soon gratified to discover that his counterpart was a gentleman of "Candour, Probity, good Understanding, and good Will to both Countries." After several meetings, Franklin divulged the peace terms that the Americans would accept, dividing them into two categories. One list, labeled "necessary," was largely a compilation of the terms that Congress had stipulated three years earlier, though Franklin added demands for American fishing rights off Newfoundland "& elsewhere," the restoration of the Canadian boundaries "to what they were" prior to the Quebec Act, and—mostly by implication—the requirement that the peace settlement acknowledge the new United States' right of navigation on the Mississippi River. His second list, designated as "advisable," included the cession of Canada to the United States and reparations totaling £600,000 for the damages Britain had caused to American towns and farms.[13] When Shelburne saw what Franklin had produced, he correctly deduced that the advisable items constituted a wish list and that the Americans would not prolong negotiations to attain them. Anxious for peace, Shelburne also saw Franklin's essential demands as either acceptable or inevitable, and late in July the prime minister conceded American independence.

Franklin had skillfully conducted the talks with Oswald to reach this point, but Shelburne had proceeded adroitly as well. The prime minister knew that if the Americans could be brought to the point of settling, pressure would build on France and Spain to accept suitable terms, lest the United States—wearied, and frustrated, by their ally's plodding manner—was tempted to conclude a separate treaty.

As autumn beckoned, Adams was summoned to Paris by Franklin and Jay, and a team of three British diplomats crossed to France. Some in the British delegation joined Oswald to hammer out the details of the stubborn, lingering issues with the Americans; their colleagues, meanwhile, commenced negotiations with Britain's European adversaries. Beginning late in October, tense Anglo-American discussions ensued nearly every day, often lasting for eight hours or more and continuing until well after darkness engulfed Paris. These talks alternated between the residences of Oswald and his American counterparts. As Franklin was suffering horribly from kidney stones, he was unable to participate in every session, and Laurens was present only on the last day. Thus, it fell to Jay and Adams to deal with the sticky particulars, a daily "Scuffle Morning noon and night about Cod and Haddock on the Grand Bank Deer Skins on the Ohio and Pine Trees at Penobscot, and ... all the Refugees," as Adams put it.[14]

In the end, the Americans came away with an accord that was nothing less than a triumph of diplomacy, an achievement secured through the envoys' negotiating skills, the strong bargaining position afforded by the victory at Yorktown, and the eagerness of Shelburne to get the war behind him. Employing a team of diplomats was all-important, for Franklin was a crucial counterweight to Jay and Adams, both of whom distrusted France more than England. Exuberant at America's triumph over one of the world's great powers, Adams was put in mind of an old allegorical story of a powerful eagle that seized a small cat and soared into the sky. "The Eagle finding Herself scratched and pressed, bids the Cat let go and fall down. No says the Cat: I wont let go and fall, you shall stoop and set me down."[15]

Through the Treaty of Paris of 1783, the United States gained the opportunity to become truly independent and not merely a French client state. If the infant nation could resolve its incorrigible financial woes, and doubtless myriad other strains that would test the fragile union of states, this settlement would furnish the United States with the wherewithal to grow in strength and security.

The treaty specified that Canada would remain in British hands and Britain was to return East and West Florida to Spain, but otherwise the United States acquired the boundaries that Congress had wanted, a huge domain that stretched to the Mississippi River and would eventually encompass ten trans-Appalachian states. The United States (together with Great Britain) was to have the right of navigation on the Mississippi River and to enjoy fishing rights off Newfoundland. Britain agreed to remove its "Armies, Garrisons and Fleets" from the United States "with all convenient speed." It would do so, it pledged, "without . . . carrying away any Negroes or other property of the American inhabitants." (The latter clause was inserted at the behest of Laurens, his sole contribution.) The lone American concession of consequence was an agreement that the colonists' prewar debts owed to British creditors were to be paid and "in Sterling Money."

The talks might have concluded earlier had it not been for the question of American compensation for the Loyalists. From compassion and domestic political pressure, Shelburne was desperate to include a stipulation mandating American indemnification for the losses suffered by the Tories. Jay and Adams were willing, but Franklin, despite having a son who had remained loyal to Great Britain, refused. He was unable to put aside his scorn for all things British that had lingered in his heart since his humiliation in the Cockpit nearly nine years earlier. In the end, London buckled. The accord simply called for Congress to recommend to the states that they make restitution for all "Rights & Properties which have been confiscated," an article that the Americans knew, and the British suspected, was meaningless.

When the talks at last were done, on November 30, thirteen months after Cornwallis's surrender at Yorktown, the diplomats gathered one last time. They met in private in Oswald's spacious suite in the Grand Hotel Muscovite and, without fanfare, signed the accord. Thereafter, all climbed into carriages and under gloomy wintry clouds rode to Valentinois, an eighteen-acre estate in suburban Passy that included Franklin's villa, for a celebratory dinner.[16]

The American diplomats had disregarded Congress's directive to permit Vergennes to negotiate the treaty for them. By insisting on fishing rights and navigational rights on the Mississippi, they additionally ignored the terms that Congress—under the thumb of Vergennes—had stipulated in 1779. Furthermore, the envoys turned a blind eye toward the commitment their country had made in the Treaty of Alliance to never make a separate peace. While France was still negotiating with its adversaries, the American diplomatic team signed the peace accord with their British counterparts. It was a defiant act that may have compelled Vergennes—who was suddenly faced with the possibility of fighting on without his American ally—to make concessions that he otherwise would not have made. The Americans may have betrayed their ally, but immediately after the negotiations concluded, the unflappable Franklin met with Vergennes and apologized for "this little misunderstanding" that he termed a "breach of etiquette." He also asked for another loan. Incredibly, he got one for six million livres.[17]

The terms of the accord were appropriately, though coincidentally, carried to Philadelphia by the *Washington*, which docked on March 12, 1783. Congress reacted with relief and joy, but also with restraint, given that what had been signed in Paris were preliminary articles that required the approval of each signatory's government. In sober tones the congressmen said things like the terms "come up to the full wish of every American," the treaty was "Equal to the most Sanguine Expectation," and it was a "favorable" pact. Congress ordered no celebrations and no city witnessed spontaneous revelry as had occurred after Saratoga and Yorktown. It may have been, as Thomas Paine remarked, that peace "requires a gradual composure of the senses to receive it."[18] What is more, coming so long after Cornwallis's surrender, for many it was as if the peace settlement was anticlimactic.

Washington, fearing that word of a peace treaty would provoke mutinies or massive desertions among his unpaid soldiers, sat on the news for ten days before informing the army, and he accompanied his announcement with word that he was "pleased" to order that "no relaxation in the Discipline or police of the Army shall be suffered." The preliminary peace treaties also instituted an armistice, news that Washington announced on April 19, 1783, the eighth anniversary of the beginning of the war. The army, posted now at Newburgh on the Hudson, briefly celebrated the "Cessation of Hostilities," though as Washington carefully pointed out, the soldiers were not marking "the annunciation of a general peace."[19] The festivities concluded with the singing of the new anthem "Independence," a song of joy and hope for "Harmony and Peace"—though looking toward the future expansion into trans-Appalachia, it anticipated having the "Natives bow" to "America victorious."[20]

Although the response to the peace accord was muted, many felt that a corner had been turned. "'The times that tried men's souls,' are over," Thomas Paine exclaimed. When Franklin learned that some of his countrymen were quibbling over this or that item in the peace treaty, he declared that *there never was a good war or a bad peace.*" In time, his countrymen would understand the treaty for what Adams understood it to be in the last days of the negotiations: an accord that made being "completely independent" a reality, ending the days when America would be "a Football between contending [European] nations" and affording the possibility—if the Americans were wise enough to take advantage of it—that the new nation would no longer be dragged into "the Wars of Europe."[21]

After Yorktown, the British and American armies had begun doing something they had previously haggled over but seldom undertaken. They began swapping prisoners. The issue had been discussed off and on since 1775, and in 1780 an exchange formula had been adopted. It included one-for-one swaps—a corporal for a corporal, a lieutenant for a lieutenant—and also sanctioned numerous complicated equivalencies, such as 372 privates for one major general or one colonel for one lieutenant colonel and a major. Few exchanges occurred, largely because of American obstinacy. Washington feared that liberated American soldiers whose terms of service had expired during a long captivity would go home, while redcoats and Hessians, soldiers for the long haul, would return to their army.

In the aftermath of Yorktown, General Clinton informed authorities in London that the Americans held twelve thousand British prisoners while only five hundred American captives were in his hands.[22] His was a guess that should not be taken at face value. But not long thereafter—around the time that the talks between Franklin and Oswald pointed toward a peace settlement—Great Britain took the first step toward ending the stalemate concerning prisoners of war by freeing those Americans held captive in Britain. Exchanges in America soon occurred with some frequency, but it was the armistice that produced the breakthrough. Within one hundred days of the promulgation of the cease-fire in April 1783, the two sides exchanged the last of their prisoners.

Sadly, many prisoners taken by both sides perished in captivity. Historians estimate that at least 8,500 of the 18,154 Continental soldiers and sailors who were captured in this war died in confinement, and to their numbers may be added as many as 2,500 American militiamen and privateers. Figures are lacking for British and Hessian prisoners, but some died while in American hands, and considerable numbers of captive Loyalist soldiers, who all too often were subjected to inhuman treatment, are believed to have perished. The principal causes of the mortality rate on both sides were inadequate diet and unsanitary conditions. The former stemmed largely from food shortages that plagued both armies while the latter not uncommonly arose from callous, even inhuman, indifference.[23]

Prisoners of war were not the only ones on the move as the war wound down. Some sixty thousand Loyalists went into exile. Some left early in the war, but most remained, hoping for a British victory. In the course of the war, many Tories fled to British-occupied cities, especially New York, which had become home to upwards of thirty thousand Loyalists by 1783. When the British army evacuated Savannah and Charleston in the summer and fall of 1782, well over six thousand Loyalists left as well, accompanied by their slaves. The British also took with them the surviving former slaves who had bolted to freedom behind the redcoats' lines. It was a huge exodus. Counting the soldiery, some twenty thousand embarked from those two cities within twelve months of Cornwallis' surrender.[24]

The discussions concerning prisoner swaps in the wake of Yorktown had been handled by the commanders' subordinates. But once the armistice took effect and the British evinced no hint of evacuating New York anytime soon, Washington arranged a meeting with Carleton in Tappan, a Hudson River village above Manhattan. Washington hoped to negotiate a date for the British army's departure. Aware that the British had taken former slaves with them when evacuating Savannah and Charleston, Washington additionally hoped to pry from Carleton a pledge that he would not leave New York with African Americans who once had been enslaved. Washington came away frustrated on both counts. Carleton was not going to sail from the United States until ordered to do so by London—which would not occur until after the preliminary peace treaty was final and official—and he adamantly refused to return the fugitive slaves. Carleton accurately pointed out that virtually all the runaway slaves had fled to the British years before the preliminary peace was negotiated, some as long ago as 1775, when Lord Dunmore had issued his proclamation. Should Carleton return these freemen to the Americans, and to slavery, some would probably be executed and many would doubtless face harsh punishments.[25]

Washington was disappointed. He was eager to conclude his service and return home. His meeting with Carleton occurred close to the eighth anniversary of the day he had departed Mount Vernon in 1775 to journey to the Second Continental Congress, and to war. He had gotten home for the first time during the war while en route to Yorktown, for a four-day visit, and he had spent a few additional days there following Cornwallis's surrender. But as much as he wished to get home, Washington wanted to get the war behind him for another reason. He was all too aware that the Continental army was a powder keg.

The officers had caused endless trouble, beginning with their threat to quit the army during the first autumn of the war if their pay was not increased. Congress had obliged. Many did quit during the Valley Forge winter two years later. Those who stayed on throughout that miserable winter had demanded a half-pay pension for life following the war or they too, they said, would leave the army. In a bind, Congress agreed to a half-pay pension for seven years. The officers consented, but two years later, using as leverage the crisis created by the loss of the southern army at Charleston, they renewed their demand for a half-pension for life. In the wake of the disaster at Camden and Benedict Arnold's treason, and pressed by Washington's warnings that "the temper of the Army . . . requires great caution" and that "the Officers are held by the feeblest ties," Congress capitulated.[26]

By late 1782, with peace on the horizon and the nation in dire financial straits, the officers knew the chances were remote that Congress would fund their half-pay pension or see that they received their back pay. In fact, Congress that year had sought an amendment to the Articles of Confederation empowering it to levy an impost, a tax on imported goods to raise revenue. But unanimity of the states was required for amending the constitution, and by Christmas all knew that the proposed amendment had failed. This was the signal for the officers to change step. In a plan concocted at the army's camp in Newburgh, the officers petitioned Congress. They asked for their back pay and what they called "commutation." Instead of a lifetime half-pay pension, the officers now asked for a full-pay pension for five years following peace. They sent their appeal to Philadelphia with a delegation of officers who buttonholed congressmen in dark corners and, in surly and embittered tones, whispered vague threats. Among other things, they warned of the possibility of a mutiny in which Washington would be thrown overboard and replaced by a successor who would use the Continental army to secure the ends sought by the desperate officers. The anger within the officers' corps was such, the congressmen were advised, that it had made "wise men mad."[27]

While in Philadelphia, if not before, the officers joined hands with civilian plotters who saw the army's threat as a means for stampeding recalcitrant states into agreeing to empower Congress to levy an impost. Robert Morris, the superintendent of finance, was certainly involved, together with some congressmen, including Alexander Hamilton, now a twenty-eight-year-old member of the New York delegation. These individuals spread alarming rumors and warned that no one knew what the officers might do if thwarted. James Madison, a young Virginia congressman, spoke of hearing "very highly colored expressions." Not a few in Congress, for whom the American Revolution had begun as an insurgency to save the colonies from further encroachment by Great Britain's powerful central government, saw what was occurring as an attempt to use the "terror of a mutinying Army" as the means of increasing the power of America's national government. Some came to believe that the plotters harbored "tory designs" to roll back the political and social changes that had occurred since 1776. The delegation of officers remained in Philadelphia for six weeks, all the while stirring the pot. They did not succeed. Congress took no action.[28]

Early in March 1783 things came to a head within the army. An unsigned manifesto, soon known as the Newburgh Address, was circulated among the officers at Newburgh. It proposed that if the officers' back pay and commutation were not immediately forthcoming, the army would disband should the peace talks fail and the war continue, but if peace broke out, the army would refuse to dissolve. Either step would pose a threat to the American Revolution and national security.[29]

A meeting of officers was called for March 15 to discuss the Newburgh Address and decide on a course of action. Just as the conclave was beginning, Washington burst into the room through a side door. Having been alerted by Hamilton to what was coming, Washington had prepared an address of his own. He took the podium and read a powerful statement, one of the best of his career. Washington called the author of the address "an insidious foe" of the American Revolution and reminded the officers that the army was subordinate to civilian authority. He pleaded with the officers to be patient, reminding them that legislative bodies moved slowly, but predicting that in the end the officers would receive "compleat justice" from Congress.

Washington's speech had not been what most officers had wanted to hear. The room fell into an awkward, sullen silence as Washington closed. Aware that he had failed to win over the officers, Washington, a consummate thespian, called on his theatrical skills to save the day. Saying that he wished to read something to the audience, Washington slowly extracted a letter from his coat pocket, meticulously unfolded it, and began reading. He stumbled over the first sentence, then faltered again as he tried to continue. He seemed to be having trouble seeing. After a lengthy pause, Washington yet again reached into his coat pocket, this time pulling out a pair of spectacles, which he slowly and deliberately put on. Few men in the audience had seen Washington—this virile, robust man of action—wearing glasses. After carefully adjusting the wire-rimmed glasses, Washington, in the soft tone of a man grown weary from years of military sacrifice, said, "Gentlemen, you must pardon me. I have grown gray in your service and now find myself growing blind."[30]

In an instant, the mood of the room was transformed. Sturdy, redoubtable men who had been to hell and back in this war, broke down weeping. The officers' plot was over. Following their commander's departure, the officers adopted a statement of loyalty to Congress, which Washington dispatched to Philadelphia. With a straight face, he told Congress that it was the officers' "last glorious proof of Patriotism." He also pleaded for the back pay of the "whole army," an army which he said had "done and suffered more than any other Army ever did in the defence of the rights and liberties of human nature." But back pay alone was insufficient for the officers, Washington continued. They deserved a pension, lest they "are to grow old in poverty wretchedness and contempt," forced to trade honor for charity and "to wade thro' the vile mire of dependency" late in their lives. (Although Washington repeatedly appealed to Congress on behalf of the officers and their families, he objected to public assistance for the wives and children of enlisted men, saying that such a practice "Would be robbing the public and encouraging idleness.") On the day that Washington's letter reached Philadelphia, Congress voted for commutation. When funds became available, the officers were to receive a full-pay pension for five years. Money was at hand in the 1790s during Washington's presidency and the tenure of Alexander Hamilton as treasury secretary. Congress did not provide pensions for the enlisted men until 1818, however, and a half century passed after the Newburgh Conspiracy before pensions were voted for those who had served in the militia and state lines.[31]

The Newburgh Conspiracy was a dark intrigue, conducted in such secrecy that few officers were fully aware of its depth, and fewer still knew all the machinations involved. The general public knew even less. To this day, no one can say with assurance whether the threat was real or a bluff, who orchestrated the conspiracy, or the precise level of involvement of anyone concerned with the affair, including even Washington.[32]

The results of the conspiracy can be seen with greater clarity. Having learned from the experience, the officers soon thereafter formed the Society of the Cincinnati, an organization for officers that was to be partially fraternal in nature and partly a political vehicle. Furthermore, Washington's already iconic status was enhanced, as he came to be seen as the bulwark of the American Revolution and savior of republicanism. In a sense, too, the affair was the seedtime of the campaign for a stronger national government, with the next step taken by Washington, who in June sent a "Circular to the States" warning that unless reforms to strengthen the central government were forthcoming, "the Union cannot be of long duration."[33]

The Newburgh Conspiracy also hastened demobilization. The officers may have threatened mutiny, but there was a history of actual mutinies by enlisted men and the army still bulged with ten thousand men who had not been paid for months. With fear abounding that Congress's concessions to the officers might spark unrest among these already restive men, both Congress and Washington were eager to reduce the army to a less-threatening size. In May, after it was reported that disorder was rampant at West Point—the soldiers were allegedly "yelling indecent expressions" at the officers—Congress authorized Washington to furlough most of the men. Before June was out, the Continental army had shrunk by more than 80 percent, to about 1,800 men. Even so, in June about 80 unpaid furloughed soldiers in the Pennsylvania Line marched on Congress to demand their back pay. The frightened congressmen ran for their lives, quitting Philadelphia for the third time in this war and ultimately reconvening in Princeton.

Meanwhile, furloughed officers and men left Newburgh and other posts and headed home, their pockets stuffed with so-called Morris notes, certificates named after the superintendent of finance that were supposedly redeemable within six months.[34] Nearly all regarded this "money" as worthless and a great many soldiers, probably most, sold their certificates to speculators. For penniless soldiers, the money realized from the sale of the promissory notes was often their only means of paying for food and lodging on their long trek home, and even then many soldiers had to find work to earn sufficient money to get home. Some furloughed soldiers did not reach their families until a year or more after their journey commenced, long after General Washington and the British redcoats did.

On November 1, newspapers in four American cities broke the news that the definitive peace treaty had been signed in Paris eight weeks earlier. The next day Washington released a farewell address to the army. Though he called the American victory an "astonishing" miracle, Washington said that, in the end, America was triumphant because the men in the army believed in America and America's cause. Men from throughout America, who at the outset had been filled with "the most violent local prejudices" toward those from "different parts of the Continent," had in time become "one patriotic band of brothers" united in the hope of winning "such a wonderful revolution." Throughout the "glorious period" since 1775 the "hardy Soldiers" had persevered, and now they would be "retiring victorious from the field of War" to enjoy "all the blessings" of "the rights of Citizens."[35] Soon thereafter Congress discharged all troops, save for those garrisoned at Fort Pitt and West Point, and Carleton at last set a date—November 22—for relinquishing what he called "York Island."

Four days prior to Carleton's expected departure, Washington and the roughly eight hundred Continentals remaining at West Point began their final march. They came south, past bygone encampments, down roads once used in times of hasty withdrawals, near the places of desperate earlier battles, and through the site where the Franco-American armies had rendezvoused in 1781, now empty save for the litter left behind by soldiers who had hurriedly departed for Virginia. On November 21, the Continentals crossed the Harlem River. For the first time in seven years, American soldiers were back on Manhattan Island.

The British army was running late, perhaps a fitting end to its war in America. Quitting the city was a stupendous operation. The last four German regiments in America, plus 20,000 British troops (including 5,818 Americans, black and white, who had served the king in provincial units), vast amounts of ordinance and supplies, and large numbers of Loyalists had to be loaded onto scores of ships.[36] Late on the morning of November 25 the last of the British soldiers embarked in small craft for their troop transports.

At one P.M., as a stinging late-autumn wind blew across the city, the Continental army began its victory parade. Under a flawless blue sky, Washington and New York governor George Clinton led the procession. Army officers and civilian officials followed, some on horseback, some on foot. The soldiers came next, marching to music played by an army band; the artillerymen among them proudly conveyed four captured British field pieces. On and on they came down Manhattan's east side to the lower end of New York, past throngs that lined the streets and solitary individuals who looked down from upstairs windows along the route.[37]

A few days after the parade, Washington rode to Annapolis, where the peripatetic Congress was meeting. Only one member of Congress, Thomas Jefferson, had served with Washington in the Continental Congress prior to his departure in June 1775 to take command of the army. Now that the war was over, Washington had returned to formally resign from the army. At noon on December 23, he entered the hushed congressional chamber still wearing his familiar buff and blue uniform. With difficulty, Washington read a brief address to the congressmen and a large crowd of onlookers in the gallery. This time he was not acting. He was overcome with emotion. Characteristically, he took no credit for America's victory, which he attributed to his officers, the will of the American people, and the hand of God. He said nothing of the help provided by France or of the sacrifices made by thousands of enlisted soldiers and militiamen.[38]

When he was done, Washington drew his commission from his pocket and relinquished it to the president of Congress. A civilian once again and anxious to get home, Washington quickly left for Mount Vernon, accompanied by two military aides and Billy Lee, his personal slave. He reached his estate as the sun was setting on Christmas Eve 1783.

The war was really over. The end came almost nine years after North's ministry sent orders to General Gage to use force to suppress the American rebellion. More than one hundred thousand men had served in the Continental army, and many thousands more in the Continental navy and state militias, and not a few aboard privateering vessels. It is probable that approximately two hundred thousand men served in some capacity, an aggregate that is astoundingly close to the number of free Americans of military age. Most students of the war believe that about thirty thousand who served in the Continental army perished while on duty, a percentage roughly equal to the toll of regulars in the Civil War and nearly ten times greater than among those who soldiered for the United States in World War II. If these conservative estimates are correct, about one in sixteen free American males of military age died in the Revolutionary War, compared with one in ten in the Civil War and one in seventy-five in World War II. No one knows how many militiamen died while on duty, but as they faced the same hazards as the Continentals, the number of militiamen who perished must have been considerable, adding to an incredible death toll among young American males.[39]

There were civilian casualties as well, though the number of United States residents that perished from war-related causes is impossible to quantify. Unlike modern wars, battles in the Revolutionary War were rarely fought in populous areas, though fighting did exact heavy tolls among those who dwelled along Battle Road on the bloody first day of hostilities and later in Charleston and Savannah. Civilians were additionally victims of indiscriminate naval bombardments and coastal raids. Some who lived on the frontier died in Indian attacks, while the savage civil war in the southern backcountry claimed an untold number of victims. However, far more civilians died from diseases unwittingly spread by nearby armies or furloughed and discharged soldiers who carried camp maladies to loved ones and neighbors at home. Smallpox was the major culprit, but assorted fevers and pneumonia, always a danger to the vulnerable, were killers as well. There were instances when diseases spread from the army to civilians must have led to death rates that equaled, or surpassed, the mortality rate experience by the soldiery. (But this was a two-way street of carnage. Civilians who left home to join the army, or to serve as militiamen in conjunction with the army, sometimes inadvertently carried afflictions into the camps of the Continentals, spreading sickness and death.) Rebels, Tories, neutrals, slaves, and Indians who never took up arms suffered from the spread of disease. Historian Elizabeth Fenn concluded that smallpox—first transmitted in this war from soldiers to civilians during the siege of Boston in 1775—spread relentlessly. *Variola*, the virus that causes smallpox, coursed throughout every state, into Canada and Florida, beyond the Appalachians and across the Mississippi, striking one Indian tribe after another all the way to the Pacific coast; by 1782, according to her estimate, some 130,000 noncombatants had perished in the maelstrom, the lion's share the victim of someone else's war, a war waged between belligerents that most who died had no knowledge of.[40]

America's ally and its enemies also paid a heavy price. One-quarter of all British and German soldiers deployed in North America—roughly ten thousand redcoats and seventy-five hundred mercenaries—died there, and to their number must be added approximately four thousand Americans who lost their lives while bearing arms for the Crown. This war, which began in a small hamlet in Massachusetts, grew into a conflict that saw fighting between the British and their French and Spanish foes in the Caribbean, Africa, India, and around the world on the high seas. Taken as a whole, in excess of fifty thousand who served Great Britain and more than twenty thousand Frenchmen died. Spaniards died, too, so that ultimately close to one hundred thousand who served in British and European armies lost their lives in this widespread conflagration.[41]

That figure does not include the death toll suffered by enemy noncombatants as a result of direct military actions, though it must have been extensive. Both Continentals and militia carried out attacks on Native American settlements. Countless numbers of women, children, and elderly were killed in these actions. Most such incidents are no longer remembered, but some may have resembled the massacre perpetrated by 160 Pennsylvania militiamen at Gnadenhutten, a Lenape (Delaware) Indian town that was part of a cluster of Moravian mission settlements in present-day Ohio. Six months after Yorktown, the Pennsylvania troopers clubbed to death twenty-eight men, twenty-seven women, and thirty-nine children "while they were praying, singing, and kissing." The victims were unarmed and, as the Continental officer in command at nearby Fort Pitt remarked, they "have always given us the most convincing proofs of their attachment to the cause of America." It was a despicable act that a century later led Theodore Roosevelt to aptly characterize the militiamen as "inhuman cowards."[42] Elsewhere, untold numbers of Indians perished in the wake of the destruction of their housing and food supply by American soldiers, and it is likely that many Loyalists, confronted with the hardships of flight and relocation, became casualties of this war. Similarly, numerous slaves who fled in search of freedom were either captured and executed or ran headlong into the maw of unfamiliar diseases that proved fatal.

With peace, many in England concluded that the war had never been winnable. That was soothing balm for failure. The reality was that at the dawn of 1781 Great Britain was on the cusp of coming out of the war with a considerable American empire. If this stalemated war ended as deadlocked conflicts often concluded—in a peace conference in which the major powers settled the outstanding territorial issues on the principle of *uti possidetis*, that is, each belligerent retaining possession of what it held at the moment of the armistice—Great Britain might have emerged with all of Canada, New York City, the trans-Appalachian West, Florida, Georgia, and South Carolina, and many of its prewar sugar islands in the West Indies. Had that occurred, the new United States would have been small, weak, encircled, and faced with what likely would be insuperable difficulties in remaining independent. In fact, even six months after Yorktown, Rochambeau's aide-de-camp thought it unlikely that the United States could last long as a nation before it reunited with Great Britain in some manner or other, perhaps something along the lines of what Lord North had proposed in peace plan in 1778.[43]

But Great Britain had in the end been defeated. It might never have come to that had its armed forces in America in 1775 been adequate for launching devastating first strikes against the rebellious Yankees, or had its army in 1776 and 1777 been commanded by a general capable of seizing the many opportunities that existed to visit stunning, possibly mortal, blows on its adversary. However, General Howe was Britain's commander in America and time and again in 1776 he permitted favorable moments to slip through his fingers, while in 1777 he scuttled a well-considered strategic plan in favor of a misguided stratagem that put General Burgoyne on a path to ruin. In the wake of Saratoga, France entered the war, a development that previously had been far from assured, and Britain's difficulties grew by quantum leaps. Yet, despite France's intervention—and Spain's a year later—the British had only to avoid defeat in 1781 to emerge from hostilities with a partial, though considerable, victory and an honorable peace settlement. Indeed, had Cornwallis remained in the Carolinas, leaving the Allies with the option of attacking New York, 1781 might be remembered as the year of Franco-America's decisive defeat rather than as the year of its decisive victory at Yorktown.

To some degree, the outcome of the conflict was more a case of Britain having lost the war rather than America having won it. Nevertheless, the rebels, with French help—assistance that Congress had come to understand in 1776 was America's linchpin for success—earned their victory. Congress replaced the Grand American Army with the truly national Continental army in 1775, and two years later refashioned it as a standing army, a body of regulars that was generally well led, performed capably under fire, and stood up to unimaginable misery and deprivation with superhuman endurance. From start to finish, militiamen also played a major role in America's military effort. Sometimes they fought well. Sometimes they did not. But in one campaign after another, these citizen-soldiers provided numbers for the endless tasks necessary for maintaining a functional army.

America's top military leaders were mostly amateurs who all too often owed their selection to politics, and many failed the fiery trials they faced. However, General Lee's presence in 1776 was crucial in extricating the army from the coffinlike trap of Manhattan Island, Generals Schuyler and Gates each played seminal roles in the pivotal defeat of Burgoyne the following year, and General Greene's southern campaign in 1781 was a master stroke without which the war would have come to a different ending.

The war's iconic commander, General Washington, was temperamentally incapable of making rapid decisions and in the early going he openly admitted that he was unschooled in commanding a large army in a big battle or a massive campaign. His inexperience led him to blunder frequently, most egregiously in 1776 and 1777 when he came within a hair of suffering fatal defeats. Until Yorktown four years later, he never again fought a major battle, whether from shrewd military calculations or from fear of his own deficiencies. At times, Washington's strategic vision was flawed, nearly fatally so with regard to his obsession with retaking New York. On the other hand, Washington brought crucially important traits of leadership to his position as commander. He was sober, industrious, and virtuous, not given to unnecessarily risky conduct, a decent administrator, an extraordinary judge of men, and an excellent politician and diplomat. Not for nothing did Rochambeau's aide-de-camp wax lyrical that Washington was a "*true soldier in his bearing*" and laud him for "his *gentle* and *affable* nature; his *very simple* manners, his *very easy* accessibility; his *even* temper; his great *presence of mind*," his "*penetrating ... calculations.*" In sum, said Baron Ludwig von Closen, Washington was "a *great man* and a *brave one.*"[44] Washington was the best man that Congress could have chosen to lead the army and, all things considered, a better leader than any who commanded the British army. America was at once fortunate to have had Washington and lucky to have survived him.

The Revolutionary War may have been over, but not the American Revolution. Some contemporaries understood that to be true. Shortly after the coming of peace, Benjamin Rush noted that Europeans thought "the American Revolution is *over*. This is ... far from being the case. ... [W]e have only finished the first act of the great drama."[45] That first act had witnessed breathtaking political changes, as the American provinces were transformed from dependencies of monarchical and aristocratic Britain into states in an independent republic. Between 1776 and 1783, the citizenry in America came to be recognized as the creators of government, their constitutions were fundamental laws that could not be altered at the whim of legislatures, and the combination of those constitutions and revolutionary laws subverted hereditary privilege and the seemingly inviolable clout of elite families. Through the broadening of suffrage rights and more equal legislative representation, not only did the people wield influence to a degree that was unimaginable before the insurgency, but sometimes men who would have been unlikely to hold any office of consequence prior to the Revolution were elevated to important offices. That was true in state assemblies, now and then on judicial benches, and especially on popularly chosen committees of safety and price control panels that exerted significant influences over the day-to-day lives of many Americans. This popular activism raised political sensibilities, often leading those who wielded newfound authority to demand equal treatment or at least to be treated with respect. Even in planter-dominated southern states, the elite at times were compelled to listen to the wishes of the populace to a degree unknown before 1776.[46]

But, just as Rush envisaged, that was merely the beginning. For some, the American Revolution from the outset had been about securing fundamental changes, and not merely in America. The feelings of some insurgents, imbued with both rage against the old order and radiant hopes for the future, had been captured by Thomas Paine. In *Common Sense*, Paine had lashed out at a "world overrun with oppression" and dared to dream that the American Revolution would "begin the world over again."[47] Most Americans may never have been that radical. Happy with being part of the British Empire, most were only slowly transformed into revolutionaries. Like John Adams, they experienced a gradual alteration of "hearts and minds" brought on by London's actions and provocations after 1765. Their conversion was often accompanied by a sense that the mother country was hopelessly corrupt, and by a desire not merely to break with England, but to purge America of those venal qualities that had supposedly led Great Britain down the path of oppression. Seeing events and the mother country through the prism of pervasive Whig ideas transmitted through the pamphlet literature of the age, many Americans in the decade after the Stamp Act came to believe that their values and institutions were fundamentally unlike those in the mother country. It was a discovery that first moved them to break with Great Britain, and once free of London and the restraints imposed by war, caused many to want to bring to germination the American seedlings planted during the long colonial era.

But just as the thinking of many colonists had been profoundly transformed by July 1776, events and experiences thereafter were transformative for others. The war—a long, deadly struggle widely seen as waged to achieve liberty and equality—not only nurtured hopes for fundamental transformations, but also sparked changes in the way that many Americans saw themselves. For instance, before the war George Robert Twelves Hewes, a poor Boston shoemaker, had exhibited a meek and submissive deference to his social betters. But Hewes put his life on the line as a militiaman and privateer during the war, serving for twenty months, seeing combat on land and twice coming face to face with death at sea. Risking his life for his country led Hewes to see himself and others in a different light. Late in the war, when a social superior commanded Hewes to remove his hat to him—a customary show of respect by one from a lower class toward one of an exalted class—the once-deferential shoemaker refused. He was no longer willing to humble himself "for any man," he said. Hewes had come to egalitarianism less through natural rights philosophy than from a feeling of having earned an equal status with others through soldiering. He had abandoned his once-deferential manner toward social betters, as in all probability had a great many soldiers.[48]

The outlook of Private Joseph Plumb Martin, who twice enlisted in the Continental army, soldiering almost continuously from 1776 until demobilization, was changed by the harsh and exploitive conditions he endured. He had thought uncritically of society prior to the war, but years of service led him to loathe many officers, mostly men from more elevated social backgrounds than the enlisted soldiers, and men who throughout the war had lived much more comfortably than the troopers beneath them. Moved to enlist at least in part by his patriotic feelings, Martin grew embittered by the indifference of elite-dominated governments. Well after the war, while in his middle years, Martin became a Jeffersonian Republican and was twice elected to the Massachusetts legislature. As an assemblyman, Martin battled a Federalist Party that he must have seen as dominated by an uncaring elite that bore a striking resemblance to the officers in the Continental army that he had grown to despise.[49] Few ordinary soldiers recorded their thoughts, but it is not difficult to imagine that the transformative experiences of Hewes and Martin were shared by many of their fellow soldiers.

A captured British army officer, interned in Virginia, subsequently told of being present at Tuckahoe, the grand James River mansion of the Randolph family, when three or four years into the war "three country peasants . . . came upon business." Without waiting to be invited, they took seats, removed "their country boots all over mud," spit into the fireplace, and taking "great liberties" conversed with the planter-owner as if they were his equal. After they departed, Colonel Randolph explained to his guest, who was affronted by such behavior, that it "was unavoidable," for "the spirit of independency was converted into equality, and everyone who bore arms esteemed himself upon a footing with his neighbor." To that, Randolph added: "No doubt, each of these men conceives himself, in every respect, my equal."[50]

Those who did not soldier were also buffeted by the woes of war. The burden of paying taxes and meeting the interminable requisitions for food and supplies for the army often fell disproportionately on those in the lowest strata of society, fueling aspirations for fundamental political and social changes, not least of which were a more widespread suffrage and equal representation.[51] Democracy was only in the throes of being born at war's end, but it was alive and growing, and a part of the new world brought on by the American Revolution.

One can reckon up these political and social changes, though doing so fails to capture what a novelty the new United States was in the immediate postwar world. But those who lived in Revolutionary America understood. They were aware that they had achieved more than simply breaking away from Great Britain. They recognized that they had brought into being a new-model experimental polity—a nation in which power was thought to flow up from the people, a dynamic unlike anything the world had seen. Thomas Jefferson liked to remind his countrymen that in Europe there were only "wolves and sheep," and that Voltaire had gotten it right when he said that throughout the expanse of the continent "every man . . . must be the hammer or the anvil." The great promise of America was that it really had begun the world anew. "My countrymen," said Jefferson, possess "precious blessings" of "equality, liberty, laws . . . which no other people on earth enjoy." Within five years of the end of the war, the most enlightened Europeans had begun to understand what Jefferson meant. The English radical Richard Price discerned a "spirit" in America that could not be confined to the New World. The quintessence of the new American Republic was that its governing system, and its people's adoration of liberty, promised "a State of Society more favourable to peace, virtue, Science, and liberty (and consequently to human happiness and dignity than has yet been known" in the annals of history.[52]

The Revolution unleashed important changes in nonpolitical realms as well. By casting off British restraints on America's economy, the American Revolution accelerated trends already under way in the northern provinces. Chiefly, it expedited capitalist development, paving the way for the emergence in subsequent generations of a modern and comprehensive market society characterized by a capitalist class and a working class.

Although the pace varied, nearly every state also reshaped its church-state relationship. Religious tests for holding office were modified or eliminated, the Anglican Church was disestablished throughout the South, Virginia in 1776 terminated its persecution of dissenters, and in New England the Congregationalist Church ceased to be the established church, though the change occurred years after the war. The Declaration of Independence had included ringing assertions of humankind's natural rights, though it said nothing of religious freedom. However, in 1779 the Declaration's principal author, Thomas Jefferson, proposed the bill Establishing Religious Freedom in Virginia and seven years later it was enacted. It both prohibited governmental compulsion to "support any religious worship" and stated that no one could be made to "suffer on account of his religious opinions or belief." Less than a decade later, the Bill of Rights did for the nation what Jefferson and his allies had accomplished in Virginia.[53]

Slavery, like religion, felt the winds of the American Revolution. The spirit of the Enlightenment led some to reconsider slavery, but the natural rights philosophy that was part and parcel of the ideology of the American insurgency also provoked questioning of the slave trade and the practice of holding other humans in bondage. With justification, the British Tory Samuel Johnson famously asked during the war: "How is it that we hear the loudest yelps for liberty among the drivers of negroes" in America. Although Johnson's stinging query was not misplaced, a great many rebels who cherished the belief that all humankind possessed God-given rights, including life, liberty, and the freedom to pursue happiness, did rethink much about their world, including slavery. But some rumination was brought on not solely because of the Revolution's rhetoric, but also from a knowledge that so many African Americans soldiered, and indeed had soldiered just as effectually as white troopers, and from the realization that so many thousands of slaves demonstrated an irrepressible desire to gain their freedom. Some awakened to the inescapable truth that African Americans had seen the American Revolution and its war as what historian Benjamin Quarles called a "black Declaration of Independence," and that they too had "viewed the war as an ongoing revolution for freedom's cause."[54]

The upshot was that some whites abandoned ingrained attitudes about African Americans or slavery, leading to substantial change. Within thirty years of Lexington and Concord, every northern state had acted to end slavery, either immediately or gradually. Change was less spectacular in slavery's heartland, the southern states. Nevertheless, throughout the Upper South state laws were revised making it easier for slave owners to manumit their slaves, with the result that the free black population witnessed a dramatic growth. Whereas only 1 percent of blacks in pre-Revolutionary Virginia had been free, more than 7 percent were free by 1810. The percentage of free blacks within the United States doubled in that same period, jumping to nearly 14 percent of the total number of African Americans.[55] What is more, the Founding generation took steps that it thought would lead to slavery's gradual end. Four years after the war ended, slavery was forbidden in the Northwest Territory, essentially the region the colonists had called the Ohio Country. With tobacco on the skids, upland cotton not yet a viable crop, and slavery's axis confined to five southeastern states, the Founders were confident at the time of the Constitutional Convention in 1787 that this "evil of Colossal magnitude"—as John Adams put it—could not, would not, expand. The Founders were certain, too, that if slavery could not spread, it would die. Their optimism proved to be illusory.[56] Slavery continued to exist and to grow, but as historian Gordon Wood noted, the American Revolution "ended the cultural climate that had allowed black slavery ... to exist ... without serious challenge," a reality that "led inexorably to the Civil War."[57]

Some Americans gained much from the Revolution, some not so much. As historian Jan Lewis has written, "neither women nor gender were central to the Revolution or Revolutionary thought," and with the exception of enslaved females, "it is hard to point to dramatic changes wrought by Revolutionary ideals in the daily lives of women." But the forces set in motion by the American Revolution were not always realized at once. For instance, the escape from Britain's restrictive economic policies let loose and brought to flower capitalist impulses within America, and the far-reaching economic changes that resulted—in conjunction with the democratic revolution spawned by the Revolution—began to dramatically affect the lives of many American women early in the nineteenth century.[58]

Loyalists, and Indians, suffered most as a result of the American Revolution. Tories lost careers, jobs, property, and in many instances their homeland. A larger percentage of the American population fled into exile than would become expatriates during the volcanic French Revolution. The bulk of the Loyalists, about thirty thousand in all, went to Nova Scotia and New Brunswick. Another five thousand moved to Quebec and an equal number migrated to East Florida. A bit more than twenty-five hundred wound up in the Bahamas and Jamaica. Some eight thousand white Loyalists and five thousand black Loyalists crossed to Great Britain. It has been estimated that Tory slave owners took some fifteen thousand of their chattel with them into exile.[59]

Some Indian tribes fought and sustained heavy losses. Worst of all, perhaps, was their betrayal by the British, who rewarded the loyalty and sacrifices of their Indian allies by surrendering their traditional homelands east and west of the mountains in the Treaty of Paris.

Change often seems more profound to contemporaries than to those in subsequent generations who look back. The political changes that had occurred rapidly from 1774 onward were not accompanied by a similarly swift social transformation, and the customary hierarchical society of colonial days remained largely intact at war's end. But fermentation was seen, or felt, following the war that had not been sensed earlier. For some conservative-minded Americans, a deeply-seated belief emerged that the Revolutionary changes had gone far enough, if not too far. Indeed, three months before independence was declared, John Adams noted that conservatives in the colonies were already complaining to Congress that "our Struggles has loosened the bands of Government every where. That Children and Apprentices were disobedient—that Indians slighted their Guardians and Negroes grew insolent to their Masters." What anguished the conservatives early in 1776 proved to be merely the tip of the iceberg. Fifteen years later, the most conservative Americans, such as Fisher Ames, a Massachusetts congressman, were convinced that the American Revolution had "turned the world upside down." Ames and like-minded conservatives were mortified to find that "the spirit of independency was converted into equality," and many such as Alexander Hamilton thought "our real Disease . . . is DEMOCRACY," which he characterized as a "poison."[60]

Much of American politics in the two decades after the Treaty of Paris of 1783 involved the question of how much more the American Revolution would change America and, even, whether some revolutionary political and social changes could be undone. The pivotal election of 1800 resolved the matter. Calling his election to the presidency "the revolution of 1800," Thomas Jefferson—drawing on Paine's 1776 dream of an American Revolution that would start the world anew—envisaged his electoral triumph as the inauguration of a new "chapter in the history of man." Jefferson added that his election meant the American Revolution visualized by the "wisdom of our sages" and won by the "blood of our heroes" would survive and proceed. Indeed, his presidency, said Jefferson, would unleash "as real a revolution in the principles of our government as that of 1776 was in its form." Assured from the outset that there had never been a cause of greater worth than the struggle against British monarchy and for independence and republicanism, Jefferson in his inaugural address said that henceforth the new nation was committed to what he called the most "sacred" principles of the American Revolution: man can "be trusted with the government of himself"; "the right of election by the people"; "absolute acquiescence in the decisions of the majority"; and "Equal and exact justice to all men."[61]

In his first days as president, Jefferson, using a nautical metaphor, reflected in letters to friends that although the American Revolution had sailed through heavy seas, it "stood the waves into which she was steered with a view to sink her." But the American Revolution had at last arrived safely in port. The birthday of a new world was indeed at hand. America, President Jefferson continued, had "returned ... to sentiments worthy of former times"—those of 1776.[62]

SELECT BIBLIOGRAPHY

ABBREVIATIONS

AA	Abigail Adams
AFC	L. H. Butterfield, et al., eds., *Adams Family Correspondence.* Harvard University Press: Cambridge, Mass. 1963–.
AJL	Lestor J. Cappon, ed., *The Adams-Jefferson Letters: The Complete Correspondence Between Thomas Jefferson and Abigail and John Adams.* 2 vols. Chapel Hill, N.C., University of North Carolina Press, 1959.
AH	Alexander Hamilton
Am Archives 4	Peter Force, ed., *American Archives*, 4th series. 6 vols. Washington, D.C.: U.S. Government Printing Office, 1837–1846.
Am Archives 5	Peter Force, ed., *American Archives*, 5th series. 3 vols. Washington, D.C.: U.S. Government Printing Office, 1847–1853.
CGTG	Clarence Edwin Carter, ed., *The Correspondence of General Thomas Gage with the Secretaries of State and with the War Office and the Treasury, 1763–1775.* New Haven, Conn.: Yale University Press, 1933.
DAJA	L. H. Butterfield, et al., eds., *The Diary and Autobiography of John Adams.* 4 vols. Cambridge, Mass.: Harvard University Press, 1961.
DAR	K. G. Davies, ed., *Documents of the American Revolution.* Dublin: Irish University Press, 1972–1981.
EHD	David C. Douglas, et al., eds., *English Historical Documents.* London, Eyre & Spottiswoode, Ltd., 1956–1970.
FLTJ	E. M. Betts and J. A. Bear Jr., eds., *The Family Letters of Thomas Jefferson.* Columbia, Mo.: University of Missouri Press, 1966.
Ford, *WTJ*	Paul Leicester Ford, ed., *The Writings of Thomas Jefferson.* 10 vols. New York, G. P. Putnam's, 1892–1899.
GW	George Washington
JA	John Adams

JCC   Worthington C. Ford, ed., *Journals of the Continental Congress, 1774–1789*. 34 vols. Washington, D.C., Government Printing Office, 1905–37.

JMB   James A. Bear and Lucia Stanton, eds., *Jefferson's Memorandum Books: Accounts, with Legal Records and Miscellany, 1767–1826*. 2 vols. Princeton, N.J.: Princeton University Press, 1997.

L & B, *WTJ*   A. A. Lipscomb and A. E. Bergh, eds., *The Writings of Thomas Jefferson*. 20 vols. Washington, D.C.: Thomas Jefferson Memorial Association of the United States, 1900–1904.

LDC   Paul H. Smith, ed., *Letters of Delegates to Congress, 1774–1789*. 29 vols. Washington, D.C.: Library of Congress, 1976–2000.

LLP   Stanley J. Idzerda, et. al., eds., *Lafayette in the Age of the American Revolution: Selected Letters and Papers*. 5 vols. Ithaca, N.Y.: 1977–1983.

LP   *Lee Papers, Collections of the New-York Historical Society for The Year 1871, . . . 1872, . . . 1873, . . . 1874*. New York: New-York Historical Society, 1872–1875.

NG   Nathanael Greene

PAH   Harold C. Syrett and Jacob E. Cooke, eds., *The Papers of Alexander Hamilton*. 27 vols. New York: Columbia University Press, 1961–1987.

PGWC   W. W. Abbot, et al., eds., *The Papers of George Washington: Colonial Series*. 10 vols. Charlottesville: University Press of Virginia, 1983–95.

PGWCfed   W. W. Abbot, et al., eds., *The Papers of George Washington: Confederation Series*. 6 vols. Charlottesville: University Press of Virginia, 1985–1997.

PGWP   Dorothy Twohig, et al., eds., *The Papers of George Washington: Presidential Series*. Charlottesville: University Press of Virginia, 1987–.

PGWR   Philander Chase, et al., eds., *The Papers of George Washington: Revolutionary War Series*. Charlottesville: University Press of Virginia, 1985–.

PGWRet   Dorothy Twohig, et al., eds., *The Papers of George Washington: Retirement Series*. 4 vols. Charlottesville: University Press of Virginia, 1998–1999.

PH   T. C. Hansard, ed., *The Parliamentary History of England . . . The Parliamentary Debates*. London, 1806–1820.

PJA   Robert J. Taylor, et al., eds., *Papers of John Adams*. Cambridge, Mass.: Harvard University Press, 1977–.

PNG   Richard K Showman, ed., *The Papers of Nathanael Greene*. 13 vols. Chapel Hill: University of North Carolina Press, 1976–2005.

PTJ   Julian P. Boyd, et al., eds., *The Papers of Thomas Jefferson*. Princeton, N.J.: Princeton University Press, 1950–.

PTJ: Ret. Ser. J. Jefferson Looney, et al., eds., *The Papers of Thomas Jefferson: Retirement Series*. Princeton, N.J., Princeton University Press, 2004–.

SOS Henry Steele Commager and Richard B. Morris, eds., *The Spirit of '76: The Story of the American Revolution as Told by Participants*. 2 vols. Indianapolis: Bobbs-Merrill, 1958.

TJ Thomas Jefferson

WMQ *William and Mary Quarterly*

WSA Harry Alonzo Cushing, ed., *The Writings of Samuel Adams*. (New York: Octagon Books, 1968).

WW John C. Fitzpatrick, ed., *The Writings of Washington*. 39 vols. Washington, D.C.: U. S. Government Printing Office, 1931–1944.

PAPERS AND DOCUMENTARY COLLECTIONS

Adams, John: Robert J. Taylor, et al., eds., *Papers of John Adams* (Cambridge, Mass.: 1977–); L. H. Butterfield, et al., eds., *Adams Family Correspondence* (Cambridge, Mass., 1963–); L. H. Butterfield, et al., eds., *The Diary and Autobiography of John Adams*, 4 vols. (Cambridge, Mass.: 1961).

Adams, Samuel: Harry Alonzo Cushing, ed., *The Writings of Samuel Adams*, 4 vols. (New York, 1904–1908).

British Government: K. G. Davies, ed., *Documents of the American Revolution*, 21 vols. (Dublin, 1972–1981).

Continental Congress: Worthington C. Ford, et al., eds., *The Journals of the Continental Congress*, 34 vols. (Washington, D.C., 1904–1937); Paul H. Smith, ed., *Letters of Delegates to Congress, 1774–1789*, 26 vols. (Washington, D.C., 1976–2000).

Dickinson, John: Paul Leicester Ford, ed., *The Writings of John Dickinson* (Philadelphia, 1895).

Franklin, Benjamin: Leonard Labaree, et al., eds., *The Papers of Benjamin Franklin* (New Haven, Conn., 1959–).

Gage, Thomas: Clarence Carter, ed., *The Correspondence of General Thomas Gage with the Secretaries of State, and the War Office and the Treasury, 1763–1775*, 2 vols. (reprint, New York, 1969).

Greene, Nathanael: Richard Showman, et al., eds., *The Papers of Nathanael Greene*, 13 vols. (Chapel Hill, N.C., 1976–2005).

Hamilton, Alexander: Harold C. Syrett and Jacob E. Cooke, eds., *The Papers of Alexander Hamilton*, 27 vols. (New York, 1961–1979).

Jefferson, Thomas: Julian P. Boyd, et al., eds., *The Papers of Thomas Jefferson* (Princeton, N.J., 1950–).

Lafayette, Marquis de: Stanley J. Idzerda, et al., eds., *Lafayette in the Age of the American Revolution: Selected Letters and Papers, 1776–1790*, 5 vols. (Ithaca, N.Y., 1976–1983).

Laurens, Henry: Philip M. Hamer, et al., eds., *The Papers of Henry Laurens* (Columbia, S.C., 1968–).

Lee, Charles: *Lee Papers, Collections of the New-York Historical Society for the Year 1871 . . . 1872, . . . 1873, . . . 1874*, 4 vols. (New York, 1871–1874).

Paine, Thomas: Philip S. Foner, ed., *The Complete Writings of Thomas Paine*, 2 vols. (New York, 1945).

Parliament: T. C. Hansard, ed., *The Parliamentary History of England . . . The Parliamentary Debates*, 36 vols. (London, 1806–1820).

Sullivan, John: Otis G. Hammond, ed., *Letters and Papers of Maj. General John Sullivan*, 3 vols. (Concord, N.H., 1930–1939).

Washington, George: Philander Chase, et al., eds., *The Papers of George Washington: Revolutionary War Series* (Charlottesville, Va., 1985–); John C. Fitzpatrick, ed., *Writings of Washington*, 39 vols. (Washington, D.C., 1931–1944); Donald Jackson, et al., eds., *The Diaries of George Washington*, 6 vols. (Charlottesville, Va., 1976–1979).

150 SECONDARY BOOKS ON THE AMERICAN REVOLUTION

The literature on the American Revolution and its war is massive. The following is a list of 150 books that I found particularly useful in teaching courses on the subject or in writing this and other books on the American Revolution. These books span the period covered in this history, 1763–1783. For many additional good books on the topic see the endnotes in this volume.

Histories and Analyses of the American Revolution

John Alden, *The American Revolution, 1775–1783* (New York, 1954); Edward Countryman, *The American Revolution* (New York, 1983); John Ferling, *A Leap in the Dark: The Struggle to Create the American Republic* (New York, 2003); Patrick Griffin, *America's Revolution* (New York, 2013); Merrill Jensen, *The Founding of a Nation: A History of the American Revolution* (New York, 1967); Robert Middlekauff, *The Glorious Cause: The American Revolution, 1763–1789* (revised edition, New York, 2005); Gary B. Nash, *The Unknown American Revolution: The Unruly Birth of Democracy and the Struggle to Create America* (New York, 2005); Jack Rakove, *Revolutionaries: A New History of the Invention of America* (New York, 2010); Thomas P. Slaughter, *Independence: The Tangled Roots of the American Revolution* (New York, 2013); Gordon S. Wood, *The Creation of the American Republic, 1776–1787* (Chapel Hill, N.C., 1969); idem., *The Radicalism of the American Revolution* (New York, 1992); idem., *The American Revolution: A History* (New York, 2002).

Leaders and Other Key Figures

Adams, John: Joseph J. Ellis, *Passionate Sage: The Character and Legacy of John Adams* (New York, 1993); John Ferling, *John Adams: A Life* (reprint, New York, 2010). Edith B. Gelles, *Abigail and John: Portrait of a Marriage* (New York, 2009).

Adams, Samuel: John K. Alexander, *Samuel Adams: The Life of an American Revolutionary* (Lanham, Md., 2011).

Arnold, Benedict: James Kirby Martin, *Benedict Arnold, Revolutionary Hero: An American Warrior Reconsidered* (New York, 1997); Willard Sterne Randall, *Benedict Arnold: Patriot and Traitor* (New York, 1990).

Burgoyne, John: Richard J. Hargrove, *General John Burgoyne* (Newark, Del., 1983).

Clinton, Henry: William B. Willcox, *Portrait of a General: Sir Henry Clinton in the War of Independence* (New York, 1964).

Cornwallis, Earl: Franklin and Mary Wickwire, *Cornwallis and the War of Independence* (London, 1971).

Dickinson, John: Milton E. Flower, *John Dickinson: Conservative Revolutionary* (Charlottesville, Va., 1983).

Franklin, Benjamin: H. W. Brands, *The First American: The Life and Times of Benjamin Franklin* (New York, 2010); Edmund S. Morgan, *Benjamin Franklin* (New Haven, Conn., 2002); Gordon S. Wood, *The Americanization of Benjamin Franklin* (New York, 2004).

Gage, Thomas: John R. Alden, *General Gage in America: Being Principally a History of His Role in the American Revolution* (Baton Rouge, La., 1948).

Gates, Horatio: Paul David Nelson, *General Horatio Gates: A Biography* (Baton Rouge, La., 1976).

Germain, Lord George: Alan Valentine, *Lord George Germain* (Oxford, Eng., 1962).

Greene, Nathanael: Theodore Thayer, *Nathanael Greene: Strategist of the American Revolution* (New York, 1960).

Hamilton, Alexander: Ron Chernow, *Alexander Hamilton* (New York, 2004).

Henry, Patrick: Richard R. Beeman, *Patrick Henry: A Biography* (New York, 1974).

Howe, Sir William: Ira D. Gruber, *The Howe Brothers and the American Revolution* (New York, 1972).

Jefferson, Thomas: Dumas Malone, *Jefferson: The Virginian* (Boston, 1948); Merrill Peterson, *Thomas Jefferson and the New Nation: A Biography* (New York, 1970).

Jones, John Paul: Samuel Eliot Morison, *John Paul Jones: A Sailor's Biography* (Boston, 1959).

Knox, Henry: North Callahan, *Henry Knox: George Washington's General* (New York, 1958).

Lee, Charles: John Alden, *Charles Lee, Traitor or Patriot?* (Baton Rouge, La., 1951).

Lincoln, Benjamin: David Mattern, *Benjamin Lincoln and the American Revolution* (Columbia, S.C., 1995).

Morgan, Daniel: Don Higginbotham, *Daniel Morgan: Revolutionary Rifleman* (Chapel Hill, N.C., 1961).

North, Frederick Lord: Alan Valentine, *Lord North*, 2 vols. (Norman, Okla., 1967);

Schuyler, Philip: Martin Bush, *Revolutionary Enigma: A Re-Appraisal of General Philip Schuyler of New York* (Port Washington, N.Y., 1969); Don Gerlach, *Proud Patriot: Philip Schuyler and the War of Independence, 1775–1783* (Syracuse, N.Y., 1987).

Sullivan, John: Charles P. Whittemore, *General of the Revolution: John Sullivan of New Hampshire* (New York, 1961).

Washington, George: Stephen Brumwell, *George Washington: Gentleman Warrior* (New York, 2012); Ron Chernow, *George Washington: A Life* (New York, 2010); Joseph J. Ellis, *His Excellency: George Washington* (New York, 2004); John Ferling, *The First of Men: A Life of George Washington* (reprint, New York, 2010); idem., *The Ascent of George Washington: The Hidden Political Genius of an American Icon* (New York, 2009); James Thomas Flexner, *George Washington and the American Revolution* (Boston, 1967); Douglas Southall Freeman, *George Washington: A Biography*, 7 vols. (New York, 1948–1957) [vols. 3, 4, and 5 deal with the American Revolution]; Edward Lengel, *General George Washington: A Military Life* (New York, 2005).

Wayne, Anthony: Paul David Nelson, *Anthony Wayne: Soldier of the Early Republic* (Bloomington, Ind., 1985).

The Coming of the American Revolution

David Ammerman, *In the Common Cause: American Response to the Coercive Acts of 1774* (Charlottesville, Va., 1974); Richard Archer, *As If an Enemy's Country: The British Occupation of Boston and the Origins of Revolution* (New York, 2010); Bernard Bailyn, *The Ideological Origins of the American Revolution* (Cambridge, Mass., 1967); T. H. Breen, *American Insurgents, American Patriots: The Revolution of the People* (New York, 2010); Benjamin Carp, *Defiance of the Patriots: The Boston Tea Party and the Making of America* (New Haven, Conn., 2010); idem., *Rebels Rising: Cities and the American Revolution* (New York, 2007); Ian Christie and Benjamin Labaree, *Empire or Independence: A British-American Dialogue on the Coming of the American Revolution* (New York, 1976); Bernard Donahue, *British Politics and the American Revolution: The Path to War, 1773–1775* (London, 1964); Woody Holton, *Forced Founders: Indians, Debtors, Slaves, and the Making of the American Revolution in Virginia* (Chapel Hill, N.C., 1999); Benjamin Labaree, *The Boston Tea Party* (New York, 1964); Pauline Maier, *From Resistance to Revolution: Colonial Radicals and the Development of Opposition to Great Britain, 1765–1776* (New York, 1972); Edmund S. and Helen Morgan, *The Stamp Act Crisis: Prologue to Revolution* (Chapel Hill, N.C., 1953); Gary B. Nash, *The Urban Crucible: Social Change, Political Consciousness, and the Origins of the American Revolution* (Cambridge, Mass., 1979); Richard Alan Ryerson, *The Revolution Is Now Begun: The Radical Committees of Philadelphia, 1765–1776* (Philadelphia, 1978); Peter D. G. Thomas, *British Politics and the Stamp Act Crisis: The First Phase of the American Revolution, 1763–1767* (New York, 1975); idem., *The Townshend Duty Crisis: The Second Phase of the American Revolution, 1767–1773* (New York, 1987); idem., *Tea Party to Independence: The Third Phase of the American Revolution, 1773–1776* (New York, 1991); Hiller B. Zobel, *The Boston Massacre* (New York, 1970).

The Continental Congress and the Declaration of Independence

Carl Becker, *The Declaration of Independence: A Study in the History of Political Ideas* (New York, 1960); John Ferling, *Independence: The Struggle to Set America Free* (New York, 2011); H. James Henderson, *Party Politics in the Continental Congress* (New York, 1974); Pauline Maier, *American Scripture: Making the Declaration of Independence* (New York, 1998); Jerrilyn Greene Marston, *King and Congress: The Transfer of Political Legitimacy, 1774–1776* (Princeton, N.J., 1987); Jack N. Rakove, *The Beginnings of National Politics: An Interpretive History of the Continental Congress* (Baltimore, Md., 1982).

Histories of the War of Independence

John Ferling, *Almost a Miracle: The American Victory in the War of Independence* (New York, 2007); Don Higginbotham, *The War of American Independence: Military Attitude, Policies, and Practice, 1763–1789* (New York, 1971); Piers Mackesy, *The War for America, 1775–1783* (Cambridge, Mass., 1965); Christopher Ward, *The War of the Revolution*, 2 vols. (New York, 1952).

Analyses of the War, Its Leaders, and Its Battles

George A. Billias, ed., *George Washington's Generals* (New York, 1964); idem., *George Washington's Opponents* (New York, 1969); John Buchanan, *The Road to Guilford Courthouse: The American Revolution in the Carolinas* (New York, 1997); Don Higginbotham, ed., *Reconsiderations on the Revolutionary War: Selected Essays* (Westport, Conn., 1978); Andrew Jackson O'Shaughnessy, *The Men Who Lost America: British Leadership, the American*

Revolution and the Fate of the Empire (New Haven, Conn., 2013); Jim Piecuch, *Three Peoples, One King: Loyalists, Indians, and Slaves in the Revolutionary South, 1775–1782* (Columbia, S.C., 2008); Eric Robson, *The American Revolution: In Its Political and Military Aspects, 1763–1783* (Hamden, Conn., 1965); John Shy, *A People Numerous and Armed: Reflections on the Military Struggle for American Independence* (New York, 1976); W. J. Wood, *Battles of the Revolutionary War, 1775–1781* (Chapel Hill, N.C., 1990).

The Armies, Navies, Militias, and Soldiers in the Revolutionary War

Rodney Atwood, *The Hessians: Mercenaries from Hessen-Kassel in the American Revolution* (Cambridge, 1980); R. Arthur Bowler, *Logistics and the Failure of the British Army in America, 1775–1783* (Princeton, N.J., 1975); Larry G. Bowman, *Captive Americans: Prisoners During the American Revolution* (Athens, Ohio, 1977); Caroline Cox, *A Proper Sense of Honor: Service and Sacrifice in George Washington's Army* (Chapel Hill, N.C., 2004); E. Wayne Carp, *To Starve the Honor at Pleasure: Continental Army Administration and American Political Culture, 1775–1783* (Chapel Hill, N.C., 1984); William M. Fowler, *Rebels Under Sail: The American Navy During the American Revolution* (New York, 1976); Sylvia Frey, *The British Soldier in America: A Social History of Military Life in the Revolutionary Period* (Austin, Tex., 1981); Robert Gross, *The Minutemen and Their World* (New York, 1976); Lee Kennett, *The French Forces in America, 1780–1783* (Westport, Conn., 1977); Charles Lesser, ed., *The Sinews of Independence: Monthly Strength Reports of the Continental Army* (Chicago, 1976); James Kirby Martin and Mark Edward Lender, *A Respectable Army: The Military Origins of the Republic, 1763–1789* (Arlington Heights, Ill., 1982); Charles Neimeyer, *America Goes to War: A Social History of the Continental Army* (New York, 1996); Howard Peckham, *The Toll of Independence: Engagements and Battle Casualties of the American Revolution* (Chicago, 1974); Jonathan G. Rossie, *The Politics of Command in the American Revolution* (Syracuse, N.Y., 1975); Charles Royster, *A Revolutionary People at War: The Continental Army and American Character, 1775–1783* (Chapel Hill, N.C., 1979); David Syrett, *The Royal Navy in American Waters, 1775–1783* (Aldershot, Eng., 1989); Harry M. Ward, *George Washington's Enforcers: Policing the Continental Army* (Carbondale, Ill., 2006).

Battles, Events, and Campaigns of the War of Independence (in chronological order)

Lexington-Concord: David Hackett Fischer, *Paul Revere's Ride* (New York, 1994).
Bunker Hill: Richard Ketchum, *Decisive Day: The Battle for Bunker Hill* (Boston, 1974); Nathaniel Philbrick, *Bunker Hill: A City, a Siege, a Revolution* (New York, 2013).
Canadian Campaign: Arthur Lefkowitz, *Benedict Arnold's Army: The 1775 American Invasion of Canada During the Revolutionary War* (New York, 2008).
New York Campaign: Barry Schecter, *The Battle for New York: The City as the Heart of the American Revolution* (New York, 2002).
Trenton-Princeton: David Hackett Fischer, *Washington's Crossing* (New York, 2004).
Saratoga: Richard M. Ketchum, *Saratoga: Turning Point of the Revolutionary War* (New York, 1997); Max Mintz, *The Generals of Saratoga* (New Haven, Conn., 1990); Gavin K. Watt, *Rebellion in the Mohawk Valley: The St. Leger Expedition of 1777* (Toronto, 2002).
Philadelphia Campaign: Stephen R. Taaffe, *The Philadelphia Campaign, 1777–1778* (Lawrence, Kan., 2002).

Valley Forge: Wayne K. Bodle, *Valley Forge Winter: Civilians and Soldiers in War* (University Park, Pa., 2002); Thomas Fleming, *Washington's Secret War: The Hidden History of Valley Forge* (New York, 2005).

Monmouth: Theodore Thayer, *Washington and Lee: The Making of a Scapegoat* (Port Washington, N.Y., 1976).

Newport: Paul F. Dearden, *The Rhode Island Campaign of 1778: Inauspicious Dawn of Alliance* (Providence, R.I., 1980).

Sullivan Expedition: Joseph R. Fischer, *A Well-Executed Failure: The Sullivan Campaign Against the Iroquois, July–September 1779* (Columbia, S.C., 1997); Glenn F. Williams, *Year of the Hangman: George Washington's Campaign Against the Iroquois* (Yardley, Pa., 2005).

Southern Campaign: Walter Edgar, *Partisans and Redcoats: The Southern Conflict That Turned the Tide of the American Revolution* (New York, 2001); David K. Wilson, *The Southern Strategy: Britain's Conquest of South Carolina and Georgia, 1775–1780* (Columbia, S.C., 2005).

Siege of Savannah: Alexander A. Lawrence, *Storm over Savannah: The Story of Count d'Estaing and the Siege of the Town in 1779* (Athens, Ga., 1951).

Siege of Charleston: Carl P. Borick, *A Gallant Defense: The Siege of Charleston, 1780* (Columbia, S.C., 2003).

King's Mountain: Hank Messick, *King's Mountain: The Epic of the Blue Ridge "Mountain Men" in the American Revolution* (Boston, 1976).

Cowpens: Lawrence E. Babits, *A Devil of a Whipping: The Battle of Cowpens* (Chapel Hill, N.C., 1998).

Guilford Courthouse: Lawrence E. Babits and Joshua Howard, *Long, Obstinate and Bloody: The Battle of Guilford Courthouse* (Chapel Hill, N.C., 2009).

Yorktown: Jerome A. Greene, *The Guns of Independence: The Siege of Yorktown* (New York, 2005).

The Diplomacy of the American Revolution

Jonathan Dull, *A Diplomatic History of the American Revolution* (New Haven, Conn., 1983); Richard B. Morris, *The Peacemakers: The Great Powers and American Independence* (New York, 1965); Orville T. Murphy, *Charles Gravier, Comte de Vergennes: French Diplomacy in the American Revolution* (Albany, 1982); William Stinchcombe, *The American Revolution and the French Alliance* (Syracuse, N.Y., 1969).

Native Americans and the American Revolution

James H. O'Donnell, III, *Southern Indians in the American Revolution* (Knoxville, Tenn., 1972); Alan Taylor, *The Divided Ground: Indians, Settlers, and the Northern Borderland of the American Revolution* (New York, 2006).

Women and the American Revolution

Holly A. Meyer, *Belonging to the Army: Camp Followers and Community During the American Revolution* (Columbia, S.C., 1996); Mary Beth Norton, *Liberty's Daughters: The Revolutionary Experience of American Women, 1750–1800* (Boston, 1980).

African Americans and the American Revolution

Douglas R. Egerton, *Death or Liberty: African Americans and Revolutionary America* (New York, 2009); Alan Gilbert, *Black Patriots and Loyalists: Fighting for Emancipation in the War of Independence* (Chicago, 2012); Cassandra Pybus, *Epic Journeys of Freedom: Runaway Slaves of the American Revolution and Their Global Quest for Liberty* (Boston, 2006); Benjamin Quarles, *The Negro in the American Revolution* (Chapel Hill, N.C., 1961).

Loyalists

Wallace Brown, *The Good Americans: The Loyalists in the American Revolution* (New York, 1969); Maya Jasanoff, *Liberty's Exiles: American Loyalists in the Revolutionary World* (New York, 2011); William Nelson, *The American Tory* (Oxford, 1961).

The Home Front During the War

E. James Ferguson, *The Power of the Purse: A History of American Public Finance, 1776–1790* (Chapel Hill, N.C., 1961); Merrill Jensen, *The American Revolution Within America* (New York, 1974); Michael A. McDonnell, *The Politics of War: Race, Class, and Conflict in Revolutionary Virginia* (Chapel Hill, N.C., 2007); Jackson Turner Main, *The Sovereign States, 1775–1783* (New York, 1973); Ray Raphael, *A People's History of the American Revolution: How Common People Shaped the Fight for Independence* (New York, 2001).

NOTES

INTRODUCTION: "I SEE NOTHING BEFORE US BUT ACCUMULATING DISTRESS"

1. Quoted in Douglas Southall Freeman, *George Washington* (New York, 1948–1957), 5:232.

2. GW to George Mason, March 27, 1779, *PGWR* 19:627–28.

3. AH to John Laurens, May 22, 1779, June 30, 1780, *PAH* 2:53, 347; TJ to Virginia Delegates in Congress, October 27, 1780, *PTJ* 4:77; Arthur Lee to JA, September 28, 1780, *PJA* 10:185.

4. Nathaniel Peabody to Richard Henry Lee, October 27, 1780, *LDC* 16:281; John Hanson to Charles Carroll of Carrollton, October 30, 1780, ibid., 16:285; SA to Samuel Cooper, November 7, 1780, ibid., 16:303; James Madison to Edmund Pendleton, November 7, 1780, ibid., 305; John Sullivan to Meshech Weare, November 15, 1780, ibid., 16:339; Sullivan to John Hancock, November 18, 1780, ibid., 16:353; Thomas Burke to JA, December 20, 1780, ibid., 16:472; Artemas Ward to Unknown, December 14 and December [?], 1780, ibid., 16:446, 522.

5. JA to Elbridge Gerry, June 24, 1780, *PJA* 9:470; JA to PC, December 14, 1780, ibid., 10: 410–11; Joan Derk van der Capellen tot de Pol to JA, December 24, 1780, ibid., 431; JA to Edmund Jenings, January 3, 1781, ibid., 11:10; William Stinchcombe, *The American Revolution and the French Alliance* (Syracuse, N.Y., 1969), 153–59; Richard B. Morris, *The Peacemakers: The Great Powers and American Independence* (New York, 1965), 180–1; Jonathan Dull, *A Diplomatic History of the American Revolution* (New Haven, Conn., 1983), 123; Edward Corwin, *French Policy and the American Alliance of 1778* (New York, 1916), 284–95; Orville T. Murphy, "The View from Versailles: Charles Gravier Comte de Vergennes's Perceptions of the American Revolution," in Ronald Hoffman and Peter J. Albert, eds., *Diplomacy and the Revolution: The Franco-American Alliance of 1778* (Charlottesville, Va., 1981), 140–41.

6. GW to John Cadwalader, October 5, 1780, *WW* 20:122; GW to George Mason, October 22, 1780, ibid., 20:242; GW to PC, October 11, December 15, 1780, ibid., 20:158, 478.

7. GW to George Clinton, January 4, 1781, ibid., 21:59: GW to PC, January 23, 1781, ibid., 21:136.

8. Madison to TJ, January 9, 1781, *LDC* 16:581; James Lovell to JA, January 2, 1781, ibid., 16:537.

CHAPTER 1: "I AM A BRITON": ON THE BRINK

1. The preceding draws largely on Merrill Jensen, *The Founding of a Nation: A History of the American Revolution* (New York, 1968), 3–35; R. C. Simmons, *The American Colonies:*

From Settlement to Independence (New York, 1976), 150–205; Gordon S. Wood, *The Radicalism of the American Revolution* (New York, 1992), 77–92; John W. Tyler, *Smugglers and Patriots: Boston Merchants and the Advent of the American Revolution* (Boston, 1986), 9–10, 16–17. Joyce Appleby, *Capitalism and a New Social Order: The Republican Vision of the 1790s* (New York, 1984), 10–11. For an introduction to imperial trade laws, see the "Forum" titled "Rethinking Mercantilism," in which historians Steve Pincus, Cathy Matson, Christain J. Koot, Susan D. Amussen, Trevor Burnard, and Margaret Ellen Newell discussed assorted issues on the topic in *WMQ* 69 (2012): 3–70. The quotations on the strife over Anglicanism can be found in Thomas S. Kidd, *God of Liberty: A Religious History of the American Revolution* (New York, 2010), 53, 59–60. The "master or a servant" quotation can be found in Rhys Isaac, *The Transformation of Virginia, 1740–1790* (Chapel Hill, N.C., 1982), 132.

2. Governor Robert Dinwiddie, Instructions to GW, [January 1754], *PGWC* 1:65; GW to John Augustine Washington, May 31, 1754, ibid., 1:118.

3. Quoted, Kidd, *God of Liberty*, 29.

4. On colonial warfare and its dislocations, see John Ferling, *Struggle for a Continent: The Wars of Early America* (Arlington Heights, Ill., 1993); Fred Anderson, *Crucible of War: The Seven Years' War and the Fate of British North America, 1754–1766* (New York, 2000); Fred Anderson, *A People's Army: Massachusetts' Soldiers and Society in the Seven Years' War* (Chapel Hill, N.C., 1984); William M. Fowler Jr., *Empires at War: The French and Indian War and the Struggle for North America, 1754–1763* (New York, 2005); John Ferling, *The Ascent of George Washington: The Hidden Political Genius of an American Icon* (New York, 2009), 9–45; Edward G. Lengel, *General George Washington: A Military Life* (New York, 2005), 19–80; Ron Chernow, *George Washington: A Life* (New York, 2010), 29–93; Gary B. Nash, *The Urban Crucible: Social Change, Political Consciousness, and the Origins of the American Revolution* (Cambridge, Mass., 1979), 161–97, 233–63. For the figures on military service, casualties, and the cost of the war, see Anderson, *Crucible of War*, 198, 244–46, 317–18; John Ferling, *The First of Men: A Life of George Washington* (reprint, New York, 2010), 46; James Titus, *The Old Dominion at War: Society, Politics, and Warfare in Late Colonial Virginia* (Columbia, S.C., 1991), 113–14.

5. Quoted in Ian R. Christie and Benjamin W. Labaree, *Empire or Independence, 1760–1776* (New York, 1976), 19.

6. The quotations can be found in Jack P. Greene, *Understanding the American Revolution: Issues and Actors* (Charlottesville, Va., 1995), 49–50; BF to Lord Kames, January 3, 1760, *PBF* 9:6–7. On many colonists speaking of England as "home," see Edmund S. Morgan, *The Birth of the Republic, 1763–1789* (Chicago, 1956), 6.

7. Quoted in Greene, *Understanding the American Revolution*, 49–50.

CHAPTER 2: "LOYAL BUT JEALOUS OF THEIR LIBERTIES": CHANGES IN IMPERIAL POLICY AND THE COLONISTS' THINKING, 1759–1766

1. Margaret Ellen Newell, *From Dependency to Independence: Economic Revolution in Colonial New England* (Ithaca, N.Y., 1998), 4.

2. Quoted in Theodore Draper, *A Struggle for Power: The American Revolution* (New York, 1996), 97.

3. Carl Degler, *Out of Our Past: The Forces That Shaped Modern America* (New York, 1959), 69–71; David Hackett Fischer, *Albion's Seed: Four British Folkways in America* (New York, 1989), 57–62, 256–64, 470–75.

4. Francis Bernard to Lord Barrington, November 23, 1765, in Edward Channing and Archibald Cary Coolidge, eds., *The Barrington-Bernard Correspondence and Illustrative Matter, 1760–1770* (Cambridge, Mass., 1912), 93.

5. Quoted in Draper, *Struggle for Power*, 156.

6. Examination [of Benjamin Franklin] before the ... House of Commons, February 13, 1766, *PBF* 13:135.

7. J. M. Bumstead, " 'Things in the Womb of Time': Ideas of American Independence, 1633 to 1763," *WMQ* 31 (1974): 533–64.

8. Quoted in Fred Anderson, *Crucible of War: The Seven Years' War and the Fate of Empire in British North America, 1754–1766* (New York, 2000), 520.

9. Sir Lewis Namier, *England in the Age of the American Revolution* (New York, 1966), 273–82.

10. Draper, *Struggle for Power*, 15; JA to Nathan Webb, October 12, [1755?], *PJA* 1:5.

11. Jack P. Greene, "An Uneasy Connection: An Analysis of the Preconditions of the American Revolution," in Stephen G. Kurtz and James H. Hutson, eds., *Essays on the American Revolution* (Chapel Hill, N.C., 1973), 32–80; Draper, *Struggle for Power*, 157.

12. John W. Tyler, *Smugglers and Patriots: Boston Merchants and the Advent of the American Revolution* (Boston, 1986), 13.

13. Newell, *From Dependency to Independence*, 269.

14. The Proclamation of 1763, *EHD* 9:642; John Shy, *Toward Lexington: The Role of the British Army in the Coming of the American Revolution* (Princeton, N.J., 1965), 45–83, 114; Bernhard Knollenberg, *Origin of the American Revolution, 1759–1766* (New York, 1960), 87–115; Edward Countryman, *The American Revolution* (New York, 1985), 50.

15. Newell, *From Dependency to Independence*, 214–35; Joseph Albert Ernst, *Money and Politics in America, 1755–1775* (Chapel Hill, N.C., 1973), 3–88, 353–62; Merrill Jensen, *The Founding of a Nation: A History of the American Revolution, 1763–1776* (New York, 1968), 51–55; Woody Holton, *Forced Founders: Indians, Debtors, Slaves, and the Making of the American Revolution in Virginia* (Chapel Hill, N.C., 1999), 62.

16. Anderson, *Crucible of War*, 487; Jensen, *Founding of a Nation*, 41–42; Ian R. Christie and Benjamin W. Labaree, *Empire or Independence, 1760–1776* (New York, 1976), 25–26; P. Langford, *The First Rockingham Administration, 1765–1766* (London, 1973), 6; Ian R. Christie, *Wars and Revolutions: Britain, 1760–1815* (Cambridge, Mass., 1982), 56; Lawrence Henry Gipson, *The British Empire Before the American Revolution* (New York, 1936–1968), 9:7–8; Alan Valentine, *Lord North* (Norman, Okla., 1967), 1:113.

17. Gregory Evans Dowd, *War Under Heaven: Pontiac, the Indian Nations, and the British Empire* (Baltimore, 2002), 114–74; Brendan Simms, *Three Victories and a Defeat: The Rise and Fall of the First British Empire, 1714–1783* (New York, 2007), 505, 533.

18. Quoted in Peter D. G. Thomas, *British Politics and the Stamp Act Crisis: The First Phase of the American Revolution, 1763–1767* (Oxford, Eng., 1975), 53.

19. JA to Webb, October 12, [1755], *PJA* 1:5.

20. Gary B. Nash, *The Urban Crucible: Social Change, Political Consciousness, and the Origins of the American Revolution* (Cambridge, Mass., 1979), 233–63; Benjamin L. Carp, *Rebels Rising: Cities and the American Revolution* (New York, 2007), 38–39; Newell, *From Dependency to Independence*, 245, 266.

21. Bernard to Barrington, May 1, 1762, November 23, 1765, Channing and Coolidge, eds., *Barrington-Bernard Correspondence*, 53, 95. Bernard even told the ministry that obedience to the trade laws by Massachusetts's merchants was the "most commendable" of any colony

in America, and that when they did resort to smuggling, it was done in order to compete with the "unbounded" violations by Rhode Island's merchants. See Bernard to William Pitt, May 5, October 5, 1761, in Colin Nicolson, ed., *The Papers of Francis Bernard: Governor of Colonial Massachusetts, 1760–1769* (Boston, 2007), 1:114–15, 155–56.

22. For an explanation of the case and Otis's argument, see L. Kinvin Wroth and Hiller B. Zobel, eds., *Legal Papers of John Adams* (Cambridge, Mass., 1965), 2:106–44. See also, M. H. Smith, *The Writs of Assistance Case* (Berkeley, Calif., 1978), 312–86. The quotation is taken from a pamphlet subsequently written by Otis, though Smith's careful analysis demonstrates that Otis's argument in the Writs of Assistance case formed the basis for the position he took in that pamphlet. See James Otis, *The Rights of the British Colonies Asserted and Proved* (1764), in Bernard Bailyn, ed., *Pamphlets of the American Revolution, 1750–1776* (Cambridge, Mass., 1965), 1:419–82. See, too, Bailyn's introductory essay in ibid., especially 1:411–13. For more on Otis, see Mark Mayo Boatner III, ed., *Encyclopedia of the American Revolution* (New York, 1966), 821–23.

23. The quotations are from Otis, *The Rights of the British Colonies Asserted and Proved* in Bailyn, *Pamphlets of the American Revolution*, 1:461, 470. See also Newell, *From Dependency to Independence*, 278.

24. Tyler, *Smugglers and Patriots*, 91. The governor's characterization of Otis is in Bernard to Richard Jackson, January 25, 1763, Nicolson, *Papers of Bernard*, 1:319.

25. JA to William Tudor, March 29, 1817, *WJA* 10:247–48. JA's reflection that the New England insurgency commenced in response to the Currency Act of 1759 is in Newell, *From Dependency to Independence*, 228.

26. Newell, *From Dependency to Independence*, 270–78. See also Stephen Hopkins, *The Rights of Colonies Examined* (1764), in Bailyn, *Pamphlets of the American Revolution*, 507–22.

27. Newell, *From Dependency to Independence*, 245, 267.

28. Jensen, *Founding of a Nation*, 70–97.

29. Instructions of the Town of Boston to its Representatives in the General Court, May 1764, *WSA* 1:3–5; Edmund S. Morgan and Helen M. Morgan, *The Stamp Act Crisis: Prologue to Revolution* (Chapel Hill, N.C., 1953), 53–54; John K. Alexander, *Samuel Adams: The Life of an American Revolutionary* (Lanham, Md., 2011), 25–26.

30. Bernard to Barrington, June 23, 1764, November 23, 1765, Channing and Coolidge, eds., *Barrington-Bernard Correspondence*, 76, 94–95; BF to Joseph Galloway, October 11, 1766, *PBF* 12:48n; BF to Richard Jackson, January 16, 1764, ibid., 11:19, 13:127n. The "chopt hay" quotation is in Lawrence Henry Gipson, *American Loyalist: Jared Ingersoll* (New Haven, Conn., 1920), 123.

31. Jeremy Black, *Pitt the Elder* (Cambridge, Eng., 1992), 226.

32. The foregoing draws on Morgan and Morgan, *Stamp Act Crisis*, 53–115; Jensen, *Founding of a Nation*, 63; Thomas, *British Politics and the Stamp Act Crisis*, 85–100; Anderson, *Crucible of War*, 641–46.

33. Jensen, *Founding of a Nation*, 66–69.

34. Quoted in Thomas, *British Politics and the Stamp Act Crisis*, 130.

35. Anderson, *Crucible of War*, 657–58.

36. *DGW* 1:338–40; TJ on Patrick Henry (c. 1811), in Saul K. Padover, ed., *The Complete Thomas Jefferson* (Freeport, N.Y., 1969), 897–98; TJ, *Autobiography* (January 6–July 21, 1821), ibid., 1121; Kevin J. Hayes, *The Road to Monticello: The Life and Mind of Thomas Jefferson* (New York, 2008), 75. On Patrick Henry, see Robert Dourthat Meade, *Patrick Henry: Patriot*

in the Making (Philadelphia, 1957); 35–182, 255–56; Richard R. Beeman, *Patrick Henry: A Biography* (New York, 1974), 1–41; and Kevin J. Hayes, *The Mind of a Patriot: Patrick Henry and the World of Ideas* (Charlottesville, Va., 2008), 1–62. The assessments of Henry's manner of speaking are in Hayes, 56–57.

37. The Virginia Stamp Act Resolutions (May 30, 1765), *EHD* 9:669–70.

38. Nash, *Urban Crucible*, 244, 247, 254.

39. *DAJA* 1:238, 239n.

40. Bernard to Board of Trade, August 15, 1765, Nicolson, *Papers of Francis Bernard*, 2:304; Bernard to John Pownall, November 26, 1765, March 5, 10, 1767, ibid., 2:422; 3:110, 342; Bernard to Richard Jackson, August 30, 1767, ibid., 3:394; Bernard to Earl of Shelburne, December 22, 1766, January 24, 1767, ibid., 3:276, 316; John A. Schutz and Douglass Adair, eds., *Spur of Fame: Dialogues of John Adams and Benjamin Rush, 1805–1813* (San Marino, Calif., 1966), 74–75.

41. Andrew Oliver to John Spooner, January 18, 1769, Hutchinson and Oliver Papers Coll., Massachusetts Historical Society; Thomas Hutchinson to [?], August 16, 1765, Thomas Hutchinson Letterbooks, ibid.; Hutchinson to Richard Jackson, August 30, 1765, ibid.; Bernard to Board of Trade, August 15, November 30, 1765, Nicolson, *Papers of Francis Bernard*, 2:302, 427; Bernard to Earl of Halifax, August 31, 1765, ibid., 2:337–38; Jensen, *Founding of a Nation*, 109; Hiller B. Zobel, *The Boston Massacre* (New York, 1970), 29–31; Dirk Hoerder, *Crowd Action in Revolutionary Massachusetts, 1765–1780* (New York, 1977), 92, 97–110; Nash, *Urban Crucible*, 297, 300; Morgan, *Stamp Act Crisis*, 144–58; Bernard to Earl of Halifax, August 31, 1765, *EHD* 9:676.

42. Oliver to Jackson, March 1, 1769, Andrew Oliver Letterbook, Massachusetts Historical Society; Oliver to Henry Bromfield, April 20, 1771, ibid.; Oliver to Bernard, August 31, 1772, ibid.; Hutchinson to Thomas Whatley, April 30, 1770, Thomas Hutchinson Letterbooks; Hutchinson to Bernard, March 10, 1773, ibid.; Adair and Schutz, *Peter Oliver's Origin and Progress of the American Rebellion*, 39–40; JA to William Tudor, June 5, 1817, *WJA* 10:263; JA to Jedidiah Morse, December 5, 1815, ibid., 10:190; JA to Benjamin Rush, August 1, 1812, John A. Schutz and Douglass Adair, eds., *Spur of Fame*, 235; *DAJA* 1:271. On the life of SA, see Alexander, *Samuel Adams*, 1–23; William M. Fowler, *Samuel Adams: Radical Puritan* (New York, 1997), 1–42; John C. Miller, *Sam Adams: Pioneer in Propaganda* (Stanford, Calif., 1936), 3–47; Benjamin H. Irvin, *Samuel Adams: Son of Liberty, Father of Revolution* (New York, 2002), 24–49; Pauline Maier, *The Old Revolutionaries: Political Leaders in the Age of Samuel Adams* (New York, 1982), 3–50.

43. Morgan, *Stamp Act Crisis*, 144–58; Jensen, *Founding of a Nation*, 111–22; Joseph Galloway to BF, July 18, 1765, *PBF* 12:218; John Hughes to BF, September 8–17, 1765, PBF 12:264–66; Samuel Wharton to BF, October 13, 1765, ibid., 12:315–16; Deborah Franklin to BF, September 22, 1765, ibid., 12:271.

44. Edward Countryman, *A People in Revolution: The American Revolution in New York, 1760–1790* (Baltimore, 1981), 37–39; Edward Countryman, *The American Revolution* (New York, 1985), 89.

45. Jensen, *Founding of a Nation*, 129–30.

46. *EHD* 9:672–73. Its statement on rights of the colonists is also available in Morgan, *Stamp Act Crisis*, 105–7.

47. Morgan, *Stamp Act Crisis*, 159–204; Nash, *Urban Crucible*, 303–11.

48. Edmund S. Morgan, *The Birth of the Republic, 1763–1789* (Chicago, 1956), 27.

49. Quoted in Thomas, *British Politics and the Stamp Act Crisis*, 136.

50. Thomas Gage to Sir Henry Conway, September 23, October 12, 1765, *CGTG* 1:67, 69–70; Thomas, *British Politics and the Stamp Act Crisis*, 135, 139.

51. Anderson, *Crucible of War*, 67–68; Thomas, *British Politics and the Stamp Act Crisis*, 139–40.

52. Gage to Conway, November 4, 1765, *CGTG* 1:71; Editor's Note, PBF 13:66–70; Jensen, *Founding of a Nation*, 160–62; Thomas, *British Politics and the Stamp Act Crisis*, 142–43; Staughton Lynd and David Waldstreicher, "Free Trade, Sovereignty, and Slavery: Toward an Economic Interpretation of American Independence," *WMQ* 68 (2011): 602.

53. Thomas, *British Politics and the Stamp Act Crisis*, 143–50; Nicole Eustace, *Passion Is the Gale: Emotion, Power, and the Coming of the American Revolution* (Chapel Hill, N.C., 2008), 395.

54. Daniel Baugh, *The Global Seven Years' War, 1754–1763* (London, 2011), 24; Black, *Pitt the Elder*, 48, 60, 63, 112–15, 226, 230–31, 255–56; Anderson, *Crucible of War*, 698–701; Andrew Jackson O'Shaughnessy, *The Men Who Lost America: British Leadership, the American Revolution and the Fate of the Empire* (New Haven, Conn., 2013), 73; Stanley Ayling, *The Elder Pitt: Earl of Chatham* (New York, 1976), 169, 308, 340; Simms, *Three Victories and a Defeat*, 544, 549, 573.

55. Thomas, *British Politics and the Stamp Act Crisis*, 154–84; Francis D. Cogliano, *Revolutionary America, 1763–1815* (London, 2000), 37.

56. Thomas, *British Politics and the Stamp Act Crisis*, 218.

57. *The Examination of Doctor Benjamin Franklin before an August Assembly . . .*, February 13, 1766, *PBF* 13:129–59. The quotations can be found on pages 134, 135, 136, 137, 139, 142, 143, and 151.

58. *EHD* 9:695–96; Thomas, *British Politics and the Stamp Act Crisis*, 244–52; Jensen, *Founding of a Nation*, 178–79; Newell, *From Dependency to Independence*, 283. The quotations can be found in Thomas, *British Politics and the Stamp Act Crisis*, 244, 245.

59. Quoted in Thomas, *British Politics and the Stamp Act Crisis*, 232.

60. Alexander, *Samuel Adams*, 41–42; Irvin, *Samuel Adams*, 63, 67; *DAJA* 1:263.

61. J. Kent McGaughy, *Richard Henry Lee of Virginia: A Portrait of an American Revolutionary* (Lanham, Md., 2004), 16–78; Oliver Perry Chitwood, *Richard Henry Lee: Statesman of the Revolution* (Morgantown, W.V., 1967), 7–59; Beeman, *Patrick Henry*, 41; Hayes, *Mind of a Patriot*, 57. The "fasten the chains" quotation can be found in McCaughy, page 78.

62. Quoted in Morgan, *Stamp Act Crisis*, 295.

63. Jensen, *Founding of a Nation*, 189.

64. Morgan, *Stamp Act Crisis*, 285. The JA quotations can be found in *DAJA* 1:263, 309.

CHAPTER 3: "A PLAN FOR GOVERNING AND QUIETING THEM": THE SECOND GREAT CRISIS, 1767–1770

1. BF to Joseph Galloway, March 14, April 14, 1767, *PBF* 14:88, 124.

2. Alan Valentine, *Lord North* (Norman, Okla., 1967), 1:136; Christopher Hobhouse, *Fox* (London, 1964), 60; Leland J. Bellot, *William Knox: The Life and Thought of an Eighteenth Century Imperialist* (Austin, Tex., 1977), 44; Charles R. Ritcheson, *British Politics and the American Revolution* (Norman, Okla., 1954), 94; Carl B. Cone, *Burke and the Nature of Politics: The Age of the American Revolution* (Lexington, Ky., 1957), 60; Sir Lewis Namier, *England in the Age of the American Revolution* (New York, 1966), 401–2; Sir Lewis Namier

and John Brooke, *Charles Townshend* (New York, 1964), 1, 2, 8–9; John Brooke, *The Chatham Administration, 1766–1768* (New York, 1968), 93; William Burke to Edmund Burke, [post September 4, 1767], in Thomas W. Copeland, ed., *The Correspondence of Edmund Burke* (Chicago, 1958–78), 1:326; Sir William R. Anson, ed., *Autobiography and Political Correspondence of Augustus Henry, Third Duke of Grafton* (Reprint, Milwood, N.Y., 1973), 128.

3. Chatham to Duke of Grafton, December 7, 1766, Anson, *Autobiography . . . of Grafton*, 110; Ian R. Christie, *Wars and Revolutions: Britain, 1760–1815* (Cambridge, Mass., 1982), 56.

4. Bernard to Barrington, September 1, 1766, in Colin Nicolson, ed., *The Papers of Francis Bernard: Governor of Colonial Massachusetts, 1760–1769* (Boston, 2007–), 3:21–15; Thomas Gage to Lord Barrington, January 17, 1767, *CGTG* 2:406.

5. Quoted in Theodore Draper, *A Struggle for Power: The American Revolution* (New York, 1996), 303.

6. Quoted in Namier and Brooke, *Charles Townshend*, 140–41.

7. Quoted in ibid., 115, 129. On the death of his brother, see ibid., 2.

8. P. D. G. Thomas, *British Politics and the Stamp Act Crisis: The First Phase of the American Revolution, 1763–1767* (Oxford, Eng., 1975), 300–309; Merrill Jensen, *The Founding of a Nation: A History of the American Revolution, 1763–1776* (New York, 1968), 227; BF to Galloway, June 13, 1767, *PBF* 14:184; *EHD* 9:703–4. Chatham's "hands of their enemies" remark is in Jack M. Sosin, *Whitehall and the Wilderness: The Middle West in British Colonial Policy, 1760–1775* (Lincoln, Neb., 1961), 130.

9. *EHD* 9:702–3; Jensen, *Founding of a Nation*, 227–28.

10. John Shy, *Toward Lexington: The Role of the British Army in the Coming of the American Revolution* (Princeton, N.J., 1965), 232–60; Ritcheson, *British Politics and the American Revolution*, 64–65; Sosin, *Whitehall and the Wilderness*, 99–121.

11. *EHD* 9:701–2; Ian R. Christie and Benjamin Labaree, *Empire or Independence, 1760–1776* (New York, 1976), 48, 103; Francis D. Cogliano, *Revolutionary America, 1763–1815: A Political History* (New York, 2000), 40.

12. Shy, *Toward Lexington*, 258–66; Sosin, *Whitehall and the Wilderness*, 136–64; Ritcheson, *British Politics and the American Revolution*, 110–11.

13. *DAJA* 1:324.

14. The preceding paragraphs draw on Richard Archer, *As If an Enemy's Country: The British Occupation of Boston and the Origins of Revolution* (New York, 2010), 68–71; John Tyler, *Smugglers and Patriots: Boston Merchants and the Advent of the American Revolution* (Boston, 1986), 111–12; Jensen, *Founding of a Nation*, 243–48.

15. John Dickinson, *The Late Regulations respecting the British Colonies* (1765), in Bernard Bailyn, ed., *Pamphlets of the American Revolution, 1750–1776* (Cambridge, Mass., 1965), 1:669–91; John Dickinson, *Letters from a Farmer in Pennsylvania* (1768), in Merrill Jensen, ed., *Tracts of the American Revolution, 1763–1776* (Indianapolis, 1967), 127–63. The quotations can be found in Jensen on pages 133, 135, 139–40, 152. On Dickinson's life, see Milton E. Flower, *John Dickinson: Conservative Revolutionary* (Charlottesville, Va., 1983).

16. Petition by the House of Representatives of Massachusetts to the King, January 20, 1768, *WSA* 1:162–66; Massachusetts Circular Letter to the Colonial Legislatures, February 11, 1768, *EHD* 9:714–16.

17. The Duke of Newcastle is quoted in Brooke, *Chatham Administration*, 373.

18. Peter D. G. Thomas, *The Townshend Duties Crisis: The Second Phase of the American Revolution, 1767–1773* (Oxford, Eng., 1987) 49; BF to Joseph Galloway, January 9, July 2, 1768, *PBF* 15: 16, 164.

19. BF to Thomas Cushing, June 10, 1771, *PBF* 18:121–22; BF to Samuel Cooper, February 5, 1771, ibid., 18:24; Shy, *Toward Lexington*, 294.

20. BF to William Franklin, December 29, 1767, *PBF* 14:349; BF to Cushing, June 10, 1771, ibid., 18:122. The "peaceable subjects" quote can be found in Thomas, *Townshend Duties Crisis*, 82.

21. Lord Hillsborough, Circular Letter to the Governors, April 21, 1768, *EHD* 9:716–17; Archer, *As If an Enemy's Country*, 91.

22. Jensen, *Founding of a Nation*, 252–87; Tyler, *Smugglers and Patriots*, 111–16; T. H. Breen, *The Marketplace of Revolution: How Consumer Politics Shaped American Independence* (New York, 2004), 61, 99; Margaret Ellen Newell, *From Dependence to Independence: Economic Revolution in Colonial New England* (Ithaca, N.Y., 1998), 283–94.

23. GW to George Mason, April 5, 1769, *PGWC* 8:177–80; Arthur Lee to GW, June 15, 1777, *PGWR* 10:43.

24. Woody Holton, *Forced Founders: Indians, Debtors, Slaves, and the Making of the Revolution in Virginia* (Chapel Hill, N.C., 1999), 85, 89–90. The Ramsay quotation is in Kevin Phillips, *1775: A Good Year for Revolution* (New York, 2012), 109. For a sample of GW's trials and tribulations with English merchants, see GW to Richard Washington, May 7, 1759, August 10, 1760, *PGWC* 6:319, 452; GW to Capel & Osgood Co., June 12, 1759, ibid., 6:322; GW to James Gildart, June 12, 1759, ibid., 6:325; GW to Robert Cary & Co., September 20, 1759, August 10, 1760, ibid., 6:348–50, 448–49; GW to Farell & Jones, July 30, 1760, ibid., 6:442; GW to Charles Lawrence, September 28, 1760, ibid., 6:458–60.

25. GW to George Mason, April 5, 1769, *PGWC* 8:178–80, 180–81n.

26. Bernard to Barrington, March 4, July 20, 1768, Edward Channing and Archibald Cary Coolidge, eds., *The Barrington-Bernard Correspondence and Illustrative Matter, 1760–1770* (Cambridge, Mass., 1912), 147–48, 167; Archer, *As If an Enemy's Country*, 75–89; Thomas, *Townshend Duties Crisis*, 82.

27. BF to William Franklin, March 13, 1768, *PBF* 15:75–76; Gage to Barrington, March 10, 1768, Carter, ed., *CGTG* 2:450.

28. Hillsborough to Thomas Gage, June 8, July 30, 1768, *CGTG* 2:68–69, 72–73; Gage to Hillsborough, June 17, 1768, ibid., 1:180.

29. Archer, *As If an Enemy's Country*, 99. The "little Difference" quotation is in Eliga H. Gould, "Fears of War, Fantasies of Peace: British Politics and the Coming of the American Revolution," in Eliga H. Gould and Peter S. Onuf, eds., *Empire and Nation: The American Revolution in the Atlantic World* (Baltimore, 2005), 28.

30. Quoted in Ira Stoll, *Samuel Adams: A Life* (New York, 2008), 73.

31. Archer, *As If an Enemy's Country*, 100–104.

32. John K. Alexander, *Samuel Adams: The Life of an America's Revolutionary* (Lanham, Md., 2002), 83–89. On incidents between soldiers and civilians in Boston, see Archer, *As If an Enemy's Country*, 127–33.

33. For an excellent summary of Enlightenment political thought, see James MacGregor Burns, *Fire and Light: How the Enlightenment Transformed Our World* (New York, 2013), 31–38, 56, 60–62.

34. Bernard Bailyn, *The Ideological Origins of the American Revolution* (Cambridge, Mass., 1967), 22–94, and Robert E. Shalhope, *The Roots of Democracy: American Thought and Culture, 1760–1800* (Boston, 1990), 39–44.

35. James P. Byrd, *Sacred Scripture, Sacred War: The Bible and the American Revolution* (New York, 2013), 39–63; T. H. Breen, *American Insurgents, American Patriots: The Revolution*

of the People (New York, 2010), 242, 249–51. The JA and TJ quotes are in Patricia U. Bonomi, *Under the Cope of Heaven: Religion, Society, and Politics in Colonial America* (New York, 1986), 209–10.

36. Bailyn, *Ideological Origins of the American Revolution*, 107.

37. On Wilkes, see Pauline Maier, *From Resistance to Revolution: Colonial Radicals and the Development of American Opposition to Britain, 1765–1776* (New York, 1972), 183–90; Bailyn, *Ideological Origins of the American Revolution*, 110–12; and Jensen, *Founding of a Nation*, 155–58, 317–20. The "design . . . to enslave them" quote can be found in Bailyn, page 144. The "sacred number" quote is in Jensen, page 317.

38. L. Kinvin Wroth and Hiller B. Zobel, eds., *Legal Papers of John Adams* (Cambridge, Mass., 1965), 2:103, 183; *DAJA* 1:52, 211–16, 331, 337–38, 341–43, 349, 352; 3:289–91; JA, Instructions to Braintree's Representative concerning the Stamp Act [ante September 24—October 10, 1765], *PJA* 1:129–43; JA to William Tudor, March 11, 1818, *WJA* 10:295–96. For a string of JA's propaganda pieces, see *PJA* 1:211–35.

39. BF to Lord Kames, February 25, 1767, *PBF* 14:69–70; BF, "A Horrid Spectacle to Men and Angels," January 17, 1769, ibid., 16:19; idem., "Purported Letter from Paris," January 1769, ibid., 16:20; idem., "An Account Stated Against GG," January 17, 1769, ibid., 22–25; BF to Galloway, January 9, 1769, ibid., 16:17; BF, "Causes of the American Discontents before 1768," January 5–7, 1768, ibid., 16:15:12–13; Gordon S. Wood, *The Americanization of Benjamin Franklin* (New York, 2004), 120–24.

40. Thomas, *Townshend Duty Crisis*, 76–160. The quotation is on page 118.

41. The quotes can be found in Christie and Labaree, *Empire or Independence*, 144, and Peter Whiteley, *Lord North: The Prime Minister Who Lost America* (London, 1996), 94.

42. Jensen, *Founding of a Nation*, 354–63. The "farce" quote is on page 355.

43. BF to Galloway, March 9, 1769, *PBF* 16:64; BF to James Bowdoin, July 13, 1769, ibid., 16:176–77.

44. Archer, *As If an Enemy's Country*, 166–81.

45. The best accounts of the Boston Massacre, and the events leading to it, can be found in Archer, *As If an Enemy's Country,* 182–202, and Hiller B. Zobel, *The Boston Massacre* (New York, 1970), 164–205. On the events of March 5, 1770, as something other than "a spontaneous accident," see Thomas, *Townshend Duty Crisis*, 180.

46. Quoted in Alexander, *Samuel Adams*, 107.

47. Quoted in Jensen, *Founding of a Nation*, 413. Dr. Joseph Warren wore the toga in 1775. See Nathaniel Philbrick, *Bunker Hill: A City, a Siege, a Revolution* (New York, 2013), 97.

48. See Archer, *As If an Enemy's Country*, 228.

CHAPTER 4: "I AM UNWILLING TO GIVE UP THAT DUTY TO AMERICA": TO THE TEA PARTY, 1770–1773

1. Alan Valentine, *Lord North* (Norman, Okla., 1967), 1:3–189; Peter Whitley, *Lord North: The Prime Minister Who Lost America* (London, 1996), 1–84; Peter D. G. Thomas, *Lord North* (London, 1967), 3–18.

2. Andrew Jackson O'Shaughnessy, *The Men Who Lost America: British Leadership, the American Revolution and the Fate of the Empire* (New Haven, Conn., 2013), 49, 71–72.

3. *PH* 16:719–20.

4. Peter D. G. Thomas, *The Townshend Duty Crisis: The Second Phase of the American Revolution, 1767–1773* (Oxford, Eng., 1987), 180–213; Ian R. Christie and Benjamin W.

Labaree, *Empire or Independence, 1760–1776* (New York, 1976), 145–50. The "democratical" quote is in Thomas, page 185.

5. Benjamin Woods Labaree, *The Boston Tea Party* (New York, 1964), 52.

6. Hiller B. Zobel, *The Boston Massacre* (New York, 1970), 26–94, 214, 217–21, 242, 267–94; *DAJA* 3:292–94; *PJA* 1:238n. For the lawyers' notes and minutes of the trials, see the entire third volume of L. Kinvin Wroth and Hiller B. Zobel, eds., *Legal Papers of John Adams* (Cambridge, Mass., 1965).

7. Bernard Bailyn, *The Ordeal of Thomas Hutchinson* (Cambridge, Mass., 1974), 169–84. The quotations can be found on pages 169, 174, and 175.

8. Thomas, *Townshend Duty Crisis,* 225–30; Christie and Labaree, *Empire or Independence,* 156. For an in-depth account, see David S. Lovejoy, *Rhode Island Politics and the American Revolution, 1760–1776* (Providence, R.I., 1958), 158–59.

9. Samuel Cooper to BF, January 1, 1771, *PBF* 18:3–4.

10. GW to Thomas Lewis, February 17, 1774, *PGWC* 9:483.

11. GW to William Preston, February 28, 1774, ibid., 9:500–501. On the trans-Appalachia lands and British officialdom, see Thomas, *Townshend Duty Crisis,* 60–75; Charles R. Ritcheson, *British Politics and the American Revolution* (Norman, Okla., 1954), 144–49; Merrill Jensen, *The Founding of a Nation: A History of the American Revolution, 1763–1776* (New York, 1968), 386–93; Thomas P. Abernethy, *Western Lands and the American Revolution* (Charlottesville, Va., 1937), 1–58; Woody Holton, *Forced Founders: Indians, Debtors, Slaves, and the Making of the American Revolution in Virginia* (Chapel Hill, N.C., 1999), 3–32.

12. John Ferling, *The Ascent of George Washington: The Hidden Political Genius of an American Icon* (New York, 62–66; Earl of Dartmouth to Governors, February 5, 1774, *DAR* 8:42–45.

13. GW to Lewis, February 17, 1774, *PGWC* 9:483; GW to James Wood, February 20, 1774, ibid., 9:490; GW to William Preston, February 28, 1774, ibid., 9:501; GW to William Crawford, September 25, 1773, ibid., 9:329.

14. T. H. Breen, *Tobacco Culture: The Mentality of the Great Tidewater Planters on the Eve of Revolution* (Princeton, N.J., 1985), 175–78.

15. Holton, *Forced Founders,* 49, 53, 57.

16. Breen, *Tobacco Culture,* 128. GW is quoted in Kevin Phillips, *1775: A Good Year for Revolution* (New York, 2012), 108. The TJ quotation can be found in Merrill D. Peterson, *Thomas Jefferson and the New Nation: A Biography* (New York, 1970), 40. The "pay double" quote is in Holton, *Forced Founders,* 63.

17. Holton, *Forced Founders,* 62, 66–73; Thomas Jefferson, Autobiography, in Saul K. Padover, ed., *The Complete Thomas Jefferson: Containing His Writings, Published and Unpublished* (Freeport, N.Y., 1969), 1122; [Thomas Jefferson], *A Summary View of the Rights of British America* (Williamsburg, Va., 1775), *PTJ* 1:135.

18. John K. Alexander, *Samuel Adams: The Life of an American Revolutionary* (Lanham, Md., 2011), 119–37; Irvin, *Samuel Adams,* 96–100; John C. Miller, *Sam Adams: Pioneer in Propaganda* (Stanford, Calif., 1936), 227–55; William M. Fowler Jr., *Samuel Adams: Radical Puritan* (New York, 1997), 55–127; Ira Stoll, *Samuel Adams: A Life* (New York, 2008), 91–93.

19. John Ferling, *Setting the World Ablaze: Washington, Adams, Jefferson and the American Revolution* (New York, 2000), 78, 83; *DAJA* 2:35; JA to Isaac Smith, April 11, 1771, *AFC* 1:74; Alexander, *Samuel Adams,* 139. For JA's comments about his experiences in the assembly, see *DAJA* 1:350–51, 362–63; 2:1–2, 10–12, 15, 42–43, 54–55, 66.

20. Richard D. Brown, *Revolutionary Politics in Massachusetts: The Boston Committee of Correspondence and the Towns, 1772–1774* (Cambridge, Mass., 1978), 122.

21. Brown, *Revolutionary Politics in Massachusetts*, 44–46; SA to Arthur Lee, September 27, 1771, *WSA* 2:230–37; Alexander, *Samuel Adams*, 139–41; Jensen, *Founding of a Nation*, 415–16; [Samuel Adams?], A State of the Rights of the Colonists (1772), in Merrill Jensen, ed., *Tracts of the American Revolution, 1763–1776* (Indianapolis, 1967), 233–55.

22. Brown, *Revolutionary Politics in Massachusetts*, 51–55; The House of Representatives of Massachusetts to the Governor, January 26, 1773, *WSA* 2:401–26; Bernard Bailyn, *The Ordeal of Thomas Hutchinson* (Cambridge, Mass., 1974), 208; Jensen, *Founding of a Nation*, 417–19; Alexander, *Samuel Adams*, 96, 106, 145–46.

23. *DAJA* 2:77; Alexander, *Samuel Adams*, 143–45.

24. Alexander, *Samuel Adams*, 150–52; Bailyn, *Ordeal of Thomas Hutchinson*, 241–42; JA to Benjamin Rush, February 27, 18–5, May 1, 21, 1807, in John A. Schutz and Douglass Adair, eds., *The Spur of Fame: Dialogues of John Adams and Benjamin Rush, 1805–1813* (San Marino, Calif., 1966), 35–36, 80, 88; *DAJA* 2:74.

25. Jensen, *Founding of a Nation*, 430–31; SA to Richard Henry Lee, April 10, 1773, *WSA* 3:25; Peterson, *Thomas Jefferson and the New Nation*, 69.

26. Alexander, *Samuel Adams*, 149.

27. Valentine, *Lord North*, 1:260; BF to Cushing, April 3, 1770, *PBF* 20:129; BF to William Franklin, August 17, 1772, ibid., 19:244; Dartmouth to Thomas Hutchinston, *DAR* 5:239.

28. Dartmouth to Cushing, June 19, 1773, in Benjamin F. Stevens, comp., *Facsimiles of Manuscripts in European Archives, Relating to America, 1773–1783* (London, 1889–1895), 24:[Document #] 2025.

29. BF to Galloway, November 3, 1773, *PBF* 20:462.

30. The foregoing draws on Labaree, *Boston Tea Party*, 58–79; Thomas, *Townshend Duty Crisis*, 246–57; and Benjamin L. Carp, *Defiance of the Patriots: The Boston Tea Party and the Making of America* (New Haven, Conn., 2010), 7–20. On the consumption of tea, see Arthur Meier Schlesinger, *The Colonial Merchants and the American Revolution, 1763–1776* (New York, 1957), 246. The East India Company's imports of tea into Boston were greater by some £80,000 in the five years after the Townshend Duties went into effect than they had been during the five years preceding the tea tax. Obviously, the company's troubles were not due solely to dutied tea. For the figures on imports, see Staughton Lynd and David Waldstreicher, "Free Trade, Sovereignty, and Slavery: Toward an Economic Interpretation of American Independence," *WMQ* 68 (2011): 608.

31. BF to Thomas Cushing, June 4, 1773, *PBF* 20:228; William Tryon to Dartmouth, November 3, 1773, *DAR* 6:238–39.

32. Carp, *Defiance of the Patriots*, 79–80; John W. Tyler, *Smugglers and Patriots: Boston Merchants and the Advent of the American Revolution* (Boston, 1986), 196.

33. Labaree, *Boston Tea Party*, 80–103, 152–54. The "make a Goose" quote is in Irvin, *Samuel Adams*, 106.

34. Bailyn, *Ordeal of Thomas Hutchinson*, 259.

35. This account of the preparation for the Boston Tea Party, and the actual event, draws on Carp, *Defiance of the Patriots*, 100–140; Alfred Young, "George Robert Twelves Hewes (1742–1840): A Boston Shoemaker and the Memory of the American Revolution," *WMQ* 38 (1981): 562–623; Alfred Young, *The Shoemaker and the Tea Party: Memory and the American Revolution* (New York, 1992), 42–45. The older, brief account in Labaree, *Boston*

Tea Party, 126–45, remains useful. For a list of known participants, see Carp, *Defiance of the Patriots*, 234–39. Almost all the participants were in their twenties or thirties. The description of the gathering at the Old South Church on the day of the Boston Tea Party draws on Nathaniel Philbrick, *Bunker Hill: A City, a Siege, a Revolution* (New York, 2013), 3. The quote about young men who would not be easily recognized is in Young, *Shoemaker and the Tea Party*, 43.

36. Montagu is quoted in Carp, *Defiance of the Patriots*, 139. JA's comments are in *DAJA* 2:85–86.

CHAPTER 5: "BEHOLD AMERICANS WHERE MATTERS ARE DRIVING": 1774, YEAR OF MOMENTOUS DECISIONS

1. Fred Junkin Hinkhouse, *The Preliminaries of the American Revolution as Seen in the English Press, 1763–1775* (reprint, New York, 1969), 159, 162, 168; Solomon Lutnick, *The American Revolution and the British Press, 1775–1783* (Columbia, Mo., 1967), 36–41; Troy Bickham, *Making Headlines: The American Revolution as Seen Through the British Press* (DeKalb, Ill., 2009), 60, 74; William Allen, *The American Crisis: A Letter . . .* (1774), in Harry T. Dickerson, ed., *British Pamphlets on the American Revolution, 1763–1785* (London, 2007), 2:354, 405; [Anon.], *A Letter to a Member of Parliament on the Unhappy Dispute between Great Britain and the Colonies* (1774), ibid., 3:117, 125; David H. Murdoch, ed., *Rebellion in America: A Contemporary British Viewpoint, 1765–1783* (Santa Barbara, Calif., 1979), 129–30; Benjamin L. Carp, *Defiance of the Patriots: The Boston Tea Party and the Making of America* (New Haven, Conn., 2010), 185–87.

2. The text of Wedderburn's attack on Franklin can be found in *PBF* 21:43–68. See also the editor's note in ibid., 21:19–23. For BF's written responses, see BF, "A Letter from London," *Boston Gazette*, April 25, 1774, ibid., 21:79–83. The "Bull-baiting" quotation can be found in BF, "Extract of a Letter from London," *Pennsylvania Gazette*, April 20, 1774, ibid., 21:112. For excellent descriptions of BF's ordeal in the Cockpit, see Edmund S. Morgan, *Benjamin Franklin* (New Haven, Conn., 2002), 200–203; H. W. Brands, *The First American: The Life and Times of Benjamin Franklin* (New York, 2000), 1–2, 4–5, 469–75; Carl Van Doren, *Benjamin Franklin* (New York, 1938), 467–68; Esmond Wright, *Franklin of Philadelphia* (Cambridge, Mass., 1986), 226–27.

3. Lord North's quote is in Alan Valentine, *Lord North* (Norman, Okla., 1967), 1:320. See also Peter Whitley, *Lord North: The Prime Minister Who Lost America* (London, 1996), 137–41; Peter D. G. Thomas, *Tea Party to Independence: The Third Phase of the American Revolution, 1773–1776* (Oxford, Eng., 1991), 26–61.

4. On Burke in these years, see Jesse Norman, *Edmund Burke: The First Conservative* (New York, 2013), 10–69, 96–97.

5. The foregoing draws on Thomas, *Tea Party to Independence*, 48–87; Bernard Donahue, *British Politics and the American Revolution: The Path to War, 1773–1775* (London, 1964), 73–104; Benjamin Woods Labaree, *The Boston Tea Party* (New York, 1964), 200–203; Carl Cone, *Burke and the Nature of Politics: The Age of the American Revolution* (Lexington, Ky., 1957), 1–194; John Derry, *English Politics and the American Revolution* (New York, 1976), 78–80; Peter D. G. Thomas, *The Townshend Duty Crisis: The Second Phase of the American Revolution, 1767–1773* (Oxford, Eng., 1987), 188; Brendan Simms, *Three Victories and a Defeat: The Rise and Fall of the First British Empire, 1714–1783* (New York, 2007), 591, 596–97. For the

content of the Intolerable Acts, see *EHD* 9:779–85; and *PH* 18:486–87, 1215–70. My analysis on Burke's speech draws in part on the insights provided in Jack Rakove, *Revolutionaries: A New History of the Invention of America* (Boston, 2010), 68–70.

6. Quoted in Whitley, *Lord North*, 145.

7. Thomas, *Tea Party to Independence*, 26–47.

8. Richard D. Brown, *Revolutionary Politics in Massachusetts: The Boston Committee of Correspondence and the Towns, 1772-1774* (Cambridge, Mass., 1970), 190–91, 200; Merrill Jensen, *The Founding of a Nation: A History of the American Revolution, 1763-1776* (New York, 1968), 468–69.

9. Carp, *Defiance of the Patriots*, 182–83; Labaree, *The Boston Tea Party*, 147–48; Samuel Adams to Arthur Lee, December 31, 1773, *WSA* 3:76.

10. BF to Cushing, February 15[–19], March 22, 1774, *PBF* 21:95, 152; Labaree, *Boston Tea Party*, 218.

11. The Town of Boston to the Colonies, May 13, 1774, *WSA* 3:107–8; The Committee of Correspondence to the Committee of Correspondence of Philadelphia, May 13, 1774, ibid., 3:110–11; *American Archives* 4, 1:331, 331n; David Ammerman, *In the Common Cause: American Response to the Coercive Acts of 1774* (Charlottesville, Va., 1974), 19; T. H. Breen, *American Insurgents, American Patriots: The Revolution of the People* (New York, 2010), 116–18.

12. Jack Rakove, *The Beginnings of National Politics: An Interpretive History of the Continental Congress* (Baltimore, 1979), 23; Labaree, *Boston Tea Party*, 231–32.

13. Bernard Bailyn, *The Ideological Origins of the American Revolution* (Cambridge, Mass., 1967), 192–93. For the Massachusetts Bay Company Charter of 1629, see *EHD* 9:81–82. Religious freedom in Pennsylvania went back to the Frame of Government of 1782, which William Penn had concluded with the first immigrants to Pennsylvania in the years after the charter was granted. See Joseph E. Illick, *Colonial Pennsylvania: A History* (New York, 1976), 14.

14. Woody Holton, *Forced Founders: Indians, Debtors, Slaves, and the Making of the American Revolution in Virginia* (Chapel Hill, N.C., 1999), 35–38. The *Connecticut Courant* is quoted in Thomas S. Kidd, *God of Liberty: A Religious History of the American Revolution* (New York, 2010), 67. Arthur Lee is quoted in Simms, *Three Victories and a Defeat*, 584.

15. Brown, *Revolutionary Politics in Massachusetts*, 191–93, 200n; Breen, *American Insurgents, American Patriots*, 81.

16. On the turmoil in the Massachusetts backcountry, see Breen, *American Insurgents, American Patriots*, 76–98, 256, and Ray Raphael, *The First American Revolution: Before Lexington and Concord* (New York, 2002). The Raphael quote is on page 168.

17. John E. Selby, *The Revolution in Virginia, 1775-1783* (Williamsburg, Va., 1988), 8; Ammerman, *In the Common Cause*, 19–34.

18. Richard Alan Ryerson, *The Revolution Is Now Begun: The Radical Committees of Philadelphia, 1765-1776* (Philadelphia, 1978), 25–63. See also, John Ferling, *A Leap in the Dark: The Struggle to Create the American Republic* (New York, 2003), 47–51, 111–12; John Ferling, *Independence: The Struggle to Set America Free* (New York, 2011), 60–66; Charles S. Olton, *Artisans for Independence: Philadelphia Mechanics and the American Revolution* (Syracuse, N.Y., 1975), 33–72; Milton E. Flower, *John Dickinson: Conservative Revolutionary* (Charlottesville, Va., 1983), 110–10; Benjamin H. Newcomb, *Franklin and Galloway: A Political Partnership* (New Haven, Conn., 1972), 5–104, 243–47.

19. John K. Alexander, *Samuel Adams: The Life of an American Revolutionary* (Lanham, Md., 2011), 177–78.

20. Richard R. Beeman, *Our Lives, Our Fortunes and Our Sacred Honor: The Forging of American Independence, 1774–1776* (New York, 2013), 57–60, 170.

21. Breen, *American Insurgents, American Patriots*, 134–39; David Hackett Fischer, *Paul Revere's Ride* (New York, 1994), 44–45; *DAJA* 2:124; Silas Deane to Elizabeth Deane, September 6, 7, 1774, *LDC* 1:29, 34; JA to AA, September 8, 1774, *AFC* 1:150.

22. *DAJA* 2:124; Silas Deane to Elizabeth Deane, September 6, 7, 1774, *LDC* 1:29, 34; JA to AA, September 8, 1774, *AFC* 1:150.

23. James Duane, Notes of Debates, September 7, 1774, *LDC* 1:35.

24. On Dr. Warren, see John Cary, *Joseph Warren: Physician, Politician, Patriot* (Urbana, Ill., 1961), 1–157.

25. Thomas Cushing to Joseph Warren, September 17, 1774, *LDC* 1:76; Joseph Galloway on the First Continental Congress (1780), *EHD* 9:802. The text of the Suffolk Resolves can be found in *JCC* 1:31–37.

26. Galloway on the First Continental Congress (1780), *EHD* 9:801.

27. Thomas Cushing to Joseph Warren, September 17, 1774, *LDC* 1:76; Joseph Galloway on the First Continental Congress (1780), *EHD* 9:802; *DAJA*, 2:134–35.

28. *DAJA* 2:137–40; Jensen, *Founding of a Nation*, 496–97.

29. Galloway's Proposed Resolution, September 28, 1774, *LDC* 1:112; Plan of Union, September 28, 1774, ibid., 1:117–19; Galloway Statement on His Plan of Union, ibid., 1;119–27; *DAJA* 2:141–44. Galloway fleshed out, or rehashed, his lengthy speech in Congress in a pamphlet that he soon thereafter published. See Joseph Galloway, *A Candid Examination of the Mutual Claims of Great Britain and the Colonies* (1775), in Merrill Jensen, ed., *Tracts of the American Revolution, 1763–1776* (Indianapolis, 1967), 350–99.

30. *DAJA* 2:142–43; Samuel Ward, Diary, *LDC* 1:234.

31. JA to AA, September 14, 1774, *AFC* 1:155.

32. Jensen, *Founding of a Nation*, 500–507; The Association, October 20, 1774, *EHD* 9:813–16.

33. The Declaration of Colonial Rights and Grievances, October 1, 1774, *EHD* 9:805–8; *JCC* 1:63–73.

34. Lee's Proposed Resolution, October 3, 1774, *LDC* 1:140; Silas Deane, Diary, ibid., 1:138–39.

35. *JCC* 1:115–22.

36. JA to Richard Cranch, September 18, 1774, *AFC* 1:160; JA to William Tudor, October 7, 1770, *PJA* 2:188.

CHAPTER 6: "BLOWS MUST DECIDE WHETHER THEY ARE TO BE SUBJECT TO THIS COUNTRY": THE WAR BEGINS

1. Quoted in Bernard Bailyn, *The Ordeal of Thomas Hutchinson* (Cambridge, Mass., 1974), 304.

2. BF, Arthur Lee, and William Bollan to the Speaker of the Pennsylvania Assembly, December 24, 1774, *PBF* 21:399; George III to North, September 11, November 18, December 15, 1774, in Sir John Fortescue, ed., *The Correspondence of George III, 1760–1783* (London, 1927), 3:131, 153, 156; B. D. Bargar, *Lord Dartmouth and the American Revolution* (Columbia,

S.C., 1965), 146–48; Peter D. G. Thomas, *Tea Party to Independence: The Third Phase of the American Revolution, 1773–1776* (Oxford, Eng., 1991), 1660–70; Peter Whitely, *Lord North: The Prime Minister Who Lost America* (London, 1996), 146–47; Bernard Donoughue, *British Politics and the American Revolution: The Path to War, 1773–1775* (London, 1964), 217; Jeremy Black, *George III: America's Last King* (New Haven, Conn., 2006), 81–82, 108–43, 209–16.

3. George III to North, December 18, 1774, in W. Bodham Donne, ed., *The Correspondence of King George the Third with Lord North, 1768 to 1783* (reprint, New York, 1971), 1:220; Dora Mae Clark, *British Opinion and the American Revolution* (reprint, New York, 1966), 76–92; Solomon Lutnick, *The American Revolution and the British Press, 1775–1783* (Columbia, Mo., 1967), 42–45, 42n; H. W. Brand, *The First American: The Life and Times of Benjamin Franklin* (New York, 2000), 481.

4. John Penn to Dartmouth, July 5, 1774, *DAR* 8:142; Earl of Dunmore to Dartmouth, June 6, 1774, ibid., 8:128; Josiah Martin to Dartmouth, September 1, 1774, 8:172; William Bull to Dartmouth, July 31, 1774, ibid., 8:154; James Wright to Dartmouth, August 24, 1774, ibid., 8:162.

5. Gage to Dartmouth, August 27, September 2, 12, October 3, 17, 30, 1774, in Clarence Carter, ed., *The Correspondence of General Thomas Gage with the Secretaries of State, and the War Office and Treasury, 1763–1775* (reprint, New York, 1969), 1:366, 367, 370, 371, 374, 378, 380, 383; Gage to Lord Barrington, September 25, October 3, November 2, 1774, ibid., 2:654, 656, 659. The figure for the size of the British army under Gage in late 1774 can be found in David Hackett Fischer, *Paul Revere's Ride* (New York, 1994), 309. Gage's comment that a year or two might be required to suppress the rebellion can be found in John Richard Alden, *General Gage in America: Being Principally a History of His Role in the American Revolution* (Baton Rouge, La., 1948), 212.

6. Alan Valentine, *Lord North* (Norman, Okla., 1967), 1:310, 319; Troyer Steele Anderson, *The Command of the Howe Brothers During the American Revolution* (New York, 1936), 30; John Shy, *A People Numerous and Armed: Reflections on the Military Struggle for American Independence* (New York, 1976), 40; Julie Flavell, "British Perceptions of New England and the Decision for a Coercive Colonial Policy, 1774–1775," in Julie Flavell and Stephen Conway, eds., *Britain and American Go to War: The Impact of War and Warfare in Anglo-America, 1754–1815* (Gainsville, Fla., 2004), 95–115; Mark Urban, *Fusiliers: The Saga of a British Redcoat Regiment in the American Revolution* (New York, 2007), 81; Eric Robson, *The American Revolution: In Its Political and Military Aspects, 1763–1783* (Hamden, Conn., 1965), 127; Andrew Jackson O'Shaughnessy, *The Men Who Lost America: British Leadership, the American Revolution and the Fate of the Empire* (New Haven, Conn., 2013), 84. For how British officers viewed colonial soldiers and officers, see Douglas Edward Leach, *Roots of Conflict: British Armed Forces and Colonial Americans, 1677–1763* (Chapel Hill, N.C., 1986), 130–32.

7. BF, Hints for . . . a durable Union, [between December 4 and 6, 1774], *PBF* 21:366–68.

8. BF, Proposals to Lord Howe, [December 31, 1774], ibid., 21:409–11; editor's note, ibid., 21:408–9.

9. Thomas, *Tea Party to Independence*, 176–81; Ian R. Christie and Benjamin W. Labaree, *Empire or Independence, 1760–1776* (New York, 1976), 231; Fischer, *Paul Revere's Ride*, 51. On George III's comment about this being a justifiable war, see Robson, *American Revolution*, 29.

10. Dartmouth to Gage, January 27, 1775, in Carter, *Correspondence of General Thomas Gage*, 2:179–81.

11. Two accounts of Chatham's speech can be found in *PH* 18:149–60 and 149–56n.

12. Ibid., 18:222–24, 319–21, 438–33, 447; Thomas, *Tea Party to Independence*, 191–97, 201; Dartmouth, Circular Letter to the Governors, March 3, 1775, *DAR* 9:60–62; North to the King, February 19, 1775, Fortescue, *Correspondence of George III*, 3:177; Valentine, *Lord North* 1:347; John Derry, *English Politics and the American Revolution* (New York, 1976), 129–48; BF to William Franklin, Journal of Negotiations in London, March 22, 1775, *PBF* 21:581. The quote on North's chicanery can be found in Richard R. Beeman, *Our Lives, Our Fortunes and Our Sacred Honor: The Forging of American Independence, 1774–1776* (New York, 2013), 178.

13. *PH* 18:478–538. The "fierce spirit" quote can be found in Patricia U. Bonomi, *Under the Cope of Heaven: Religion, Society, and Politics in Colonial America* (New York, 1986), 187.

14. John Galvin, *The Minutemen: The First Fight: Myths and Realities of the American Revolution* (Washington, D.C., 1989), 42–67; Richard Henry Lee's Proposed Resolution, October 3, 1774, *LDC* 1:140; JA's Proposed Resolutions, September 30, 1774, ibid., 1:132; Richard Buel Jr., *Dear Liberty: Connecticut's Mobilization for the Revolutionary War* (Middletown, Conn., 1980), 30; *PGWC* 10:345–47, 349–50; Kevin Phillips, *1775: A Good Year for Revolution* (New York, 2012), 304, 310. The stipulations for the riflemen in Fairfax County, Virginia, can be found in Rhys Isaac, *The Transformation of Virginia, 1740–1790* (Chapel Hill, N.C., 1982), 256.

15. The "committee for the detection of conspiracy" is in Douglas Bradburn, *The Citizenship Revolution: Politics and the Creation of the American Union, 1774–1804* (Charlottesville, Va., 2009), 57.

16. The quotations can be found in Beeman, *Our Lives, Our Fortunes, and Our Sacred Honor*, 189, and Bradburn, *Citizenship Revolution*, 58.

17. T. H. Breen, *The Marketplace of Revolution: How Consumer Politics Shaped American Independence* (New York, 2004), 292; T. H. Breen, *American Insurgents, American Patriots: The Revolution of the People* (New York, 2010), 160–206; Phillips, *1775*, 260–61; David Ammerman, *In the Common Cause: American Response to the Coercive Acts of 1774* (Charlottesville, Va., 1974), 103–8; John W. Tyler, *Smugglers and Patriots: Boston Merchants and the Advent of the American Revolution* (Boston, 1986), 231–32; Merrill Jensen, *The Founding of a Nation: A History of the American Revolution, 1763–1776* (New York, 1968), 515–29.

18. These two paragraphs draw on Jensen, *Founding of a Nation*, 525–34. See also Benjamin H. Newcomb, *Franklin and Galloway: A Political Partnership* (New Haven, 1972), 258–59, and Alexander C. Flick, ed., *The American Revolution in New York: Its Political, Social and Economic Significance* (reprint, Port Washington, N.Y., 1967), 47–48.

19. JA's Novanglus essays can be found in *PJA* 2:216–387. Three of Massachusettensis's seventeen essays can be found in Merrill Jensen, ed., *Tracts of the American Revolution, 1763–1776* (Indianapolis, 1967), 278–96, 341–49.

20. For a more detailed summary see John Ferling, *Jefferson and Hamilton: The Rivalry That Forged a Nation* (New York, 2013), 34–38. Hamilton's two pamphlets, titled *A Full Vindication of the Measures of the Congress* and *The Farmer Refuted*, can be found in *PAH* 1:45–78, 81–165.

21. Joseph Galloway, *A Candid Examination of the Mutual Claims of Great Britain and the Colonies* (1775), in Jensen, *Tracts of the American Revolution*, 350–99. On Galloway's life and thought see John Ferling, *The Loyalist Mind: Joseph Galloway and the American Revolution* (State College, Pa., 1977), 7–80. Jensen's quote on Galloway can be found in Jensen, *Founding of a Nation*, 512–13.

22. TJ, Draft of Instructions to the Virginia Delegates in the Continental Congress, [July 1774], *PTJ* 1:121–35. These instructions were published in Williamsburg late in 1774 as *A Summary View of the Rights of British America*. Hereafter it is cited as *A Summary View*.

23. [Charles Lee], *Strictures on "A Friendly Address to All Reasonable Americans"* (1775), [Readex Microprint, Early American Imprint Series I: Evans 1639–1800, no. 13372].

24. TJ, *A Summary View, PTJ* 1:126, 134.

25. Alden, *General Gage in America*, 205–32; David Hackett Fischer, *Paul Revere's Ride* (New York, 1994), 58–64.

26. Nathaniel Philbrick, *Bunker Hill: A City, a Siege, a Revolution* (New York, 2013), 88.

27. Gage to Barrington, April 22, 1775, Carter, *Correspondence of Gage*, 2:674; Patrick Griffin, *America's Revolution* (New York, 2013), 125.

28. Urban, *Fusiliers*, 27; Diary, Amos Farnsworth, Massachusetts Historical Society, *Proceedings*, 2d Series, 12 (1897–1899): 78.

29. The account of this fateful day, from Gage's preparations through the day's end, draws on Fischer, *Paul Revere's Ride*, 78–260, 400–401, and Philbrick, *Bunker Hill*, 109–60. The quotations can be found in Fischer, pages 163–64, 189, 191, and Philbrick, pages 154–55.

CHAPTER 7: "GREAT BRITAIN IS EQUAL TO THE CONTEST": WAR BRINGS CRUCIAL CHANGES IN 1775

1. GW to George William Fairfax, May 31, 1775, *PGWC* 10:368; JA to AA, May 8, 29, 1775, *AFC* 1:195, 207.

2. Lee to William Lee, May 10, 1775, *LDC* 1:337; John Dickinson to Arthur Lee, April 29, 1775, ibid., 1:331; Robert R. Livingston to John Stevens, April 23, 1775, ibid., 1:331; JA to Joseph Palmer, May 2, 1775, *PJA* 3:1.

3. David Hackett Fischer, *Paul Revere's Ride* (New York, 1994), 267–79; Frank L. Mott, "The Newspaper Coverage of Lexington and Concord," *New England Quarterly* 17 (1944): 489–505; Phillip Davidson, *Propaganda and the American Revolution, 1763–1776* (Chapel Hill, N.C., 1941), 150–52; Arthur M. Schlesinger, *Prelude to Independence: The Newspaper War on the Britain, 1764–1776* (New York, 1966), 232–33; *Am. Archives* 4, 2:489–502; "Intercepted Letters of the Soldiery in Boston," April 28, 1775, ibid., 2:440–41. The quote from the *Cape Fear Mercury* can be found in T. H. Breen, *American Insurgents, American Patriots: The Revolution of the People* (New York, 2010), 284. The New Englanders got their version of events to London before General Gage got his across the Atlantic, and briefly some English newspapers denounced the behavior of the regulars on the first day of war. See James Warren, "To the Inhabitants of Great Britain," April 26, 1775, ibid., 2:487–88; Robert S. Rantoul, "The Cruise of the 'Quero': How We Carried the News to the King," *Essex Institute Historical Collections* 36 (1900): 5–18; Fred Junkin Hinkhouse, *The Preliminaries of the American Revolution as Seen in the English Press, 1763–1775* (reprint, New York, 1969), 188; Troy Bickham, *Making Headlines: The American Revolution as Seen Through the British Press* (DeKalb, Ill., 2009), 71–72.

4. Silas Deane Diary, *LDC* 1:351.

5. Gordon S. Wood, *The Radicalism of the American Revolution* (New York, 1992), 95–109, 169–89. The quotation is on page 169. See also JA to Henry, June 3, 1776, *PJA* 4:2234–35.

6. *DAJA* 1:7, 8, 23; JA to Jonathan Sewall, February [?], 1760, *PJA* 1:41–42; John Hazleton, *The Declaration of Independence: Its History* (New York, 1906), 161–62; John Ferling, *John*

Adams: A Life (reprint, New York, 2010), 9–130, 169; Joseph J. Ellis, *Passionate Sage: The Character and Legacy of John Adams* (New York, 1993), 42–43. Also good on JA is Peter Shaw, *The Character of John Adams* (Chapel Hill, N.C., 1976).

7. Dickinson, "Notes for a Speech in Congress," [May 23–25?] 1775, *LDC* 1:371–82; Brendan Simms, *Three Victories and a Defeat: The Rise and Fall of the First British Empire, 1714–1783* (New York, 2007), 587–88.

8. Silas Deane Diary, *LDC* 1:352; Connecticut Delegates to Jonathan Trumbull Sr., May 31, 1775, ibid., 1:422–23; Connecticut Delegates to William Williams, May 31, 1775, ibid., 1:423; John Hancock to the New York Provincial Congress, June 1, 1775, ibid., 2:64–65, 73–75.

9. JA to Moses Gill, June 10, 1775, *PJA* 3:21; SA to Joseph Warren, June 10, 1775, *LDC* 1:468; *DAJA* 3:321–323; *JCC* 2:89–93, 96–97.

10. Cushing to James Bowdoin Sr., June 21, 1775, *LDC* 1:530; Deane to Elizabeth Deane, June 16, 1775, ibid., 1:494; Eliphalet Dyer to Jonathan Trumbull, June 16, 1775, ibid., 1:496; Dyer to Joseph Trumbull, June 17, 1775, ibid., 1:499–500; Hancock to Elbridge Gerry, June 18, 1775, ibid., 1:507; JA to AA, June 17, 1775, *AFC* 1:215–16; AA to JA, July 16, 1775, ibid., 1:246; Benjamin Rush to Thomas Rushton, October 29, 1775, in L. H. Butterfield, ed., *Letters of Benjamin Rush* (Princeton, N.J., 1951), 1:92. On GW's background and preparation for assuming command, see John Ferling, *The First of Men: A Life of George Washington* (reprint, New York, 2010), 31–61; John Ferling, "School for Command: Young George Washington and the Virginia Regiment," in Warren R. Hofstra, ed., *George Washington and the Virginia Backcountry* (Madison, Wisc., 1998), 195–222; Douglas Southall Freeman, *George Washington: A Biography* (New York, 1948–57), 1:274–437; 2:1–399; James Thomas Flexner, *George Washington: The Forge of Experience, 1732–1775* (Boston, 1965), 59–223; Joseph Ellis, *His Excellency: George Washington* (New York, 2004), 3–39; Stephen Brumwell, *George Washington: Gentleman Warrior* (New York, 2012), 49–154; Edward Lengel, *General George Washington: A Military Life* (New York, 2005), 19–80; Ron Chernow, *Washington: A Life* (New York, 2010), 29–93.

11. *JCC* 2:93–103; JA to Gerry, June 18, 1775, *PJA* 3:26; Jonathan G. Rossie, *The Politics of Command in the American Revolution* (Syracuse, N.Y., 1975), 17–30.

12. JA to AA, June 23, 1775, *AFC* 1:226; Freeman, *George Washington*, 3:458–59; Chernow, *Washington*, 191; James T. Flexner, *George Washington and the American Revolution* (Boston, 1967), 23.

13. *JCC* 2:182. GW is quoted in Chernow, *Washington*, 359.

14. Gage to Dartmouth, September 20, 1775, *CGTG* 1:415; James H. O'Donnell, *Southern Indians in the American Revolution* (Knoxville, Tenn., 1973), 30–53.

15. Richard Frothingham, *History of the Siege of Boston* (Boston, 1849), 116–23; Richard M. Ketchum, *Decisive Day: The Battle for Bunker Hill* (New York, 1974), 64, 77–79, 111; Nathaniel Philbrick, *Bunker Hill: A City, a Siege, a Revolution* (New York, 2013), 188–207, 337; Allen French, *The Siege of Boston* (New York, 1911), 257; Louis Birnbaum, *Red Dawn at Lexington: "If They Mean to Have a War, Let It Begin Here"* (Boston, 1986), 210–28. On General Ward, see Charles Martyn, *The Life of Artemas Ward* (New York, 1921). The colonists had actually invested Breed's Hill, adjacent to Bunker Hill, but the engagement is known to history as the Battle of Bunker Hill.

16. Ira D. Gruber, *The Command of the Howe Brothers During the American Revolution* (New York, 1972), 45–48, 56–58; Sir Maldwyn A. Jones, "Sir William Howe: Conventional Strategist," in George A. Billias, ed., *George Washington's Opponents* (New York, 1969), 43–46; David Hackett Fischer, *Washington's Crossing* (New York, 2004), 67–71.

17. Douglas Edward Leach, *Arms for Empire: A Military History of the British Colonies in North America, 1607–1763* (New York, 1973), 427–35.

18. Amos Farnsworth, Diary, *SOS* 1:122; William Howe to the British Adjutant General, June 22, 24, 1775, ibid., 1:131–32; Samuel Blachley Webb to Joseph Webb, June 19, 1775, in Dennis P. Ryan, ed., *A Salute to Courage: The American Revolution as Seen Through Wartime Writings of Officers of the Continental Army and Navy* (New York, 1979), 7; Ketchum, *Decisive Day*, 125–26, 154; French, *Siege of Boston*, 261, 267–68.

19. The "majestic terrors" quoted can be found in Thomas S. Kidd, *God of Liberty: A Religious History of the American Revolution* (New York, 2010), 2. Lucy Trumbull is quoted in Patrick Griffin, *America's Revolution* (New York, 2013), 142.

20. Philbrick, *Bunker Hill*, 208–30; Don Higginbotham, *The War of American Independence: Military Attitudes, Policies, and Practices, 1763–1789* (New York, 1960), 75; Account of Adjutant Waller, June 23, 1775, in Samuel Adams Drake, ed., *Bunker Hill: The Story Told in Letters from the Battle Field by British Officers Engaged* (Boston, 1875), 28–29; "Historical Record of the Royal Marines," ibid., 32; George H. Scheer and Hugh F. Rankin, *Rebels and Redcoats* (Cleveland, 1957), 59, 63; Ketchum, *Decisive Day*, 137–83; Birnbaum, *Red Dawn at Lexington*, 227–54.

21. Ketchum, *Decisive Day*, 183; William Howe to Adjutant General, June 24, 28, 1775, *SOS* 1:132; Letter of a British Officer, July 5, 1775, ibid., 1:136; "A British Officer to a Friend in England," n.d., Massachusetts Historical Society *Proceedings* 44 (1910–1911): 102–3; Gage to Barrington, June 26, 1775, Carter, *Correspondence of Gage*, 2:686. The "day will never be out of my mind" quote is in Sarah J. Purcell, *Sealed with Blood: War, Sacrifice, and Memory in Revolutionary America* (Philadelphia, 2002), 19.

22. Hancock to GW, June 28, 1775, *LDC* 1:155, 430n; Jack N. Rakove, *The Beginnings of National Politics: An Interpretive History of the Continental Congress* (Baltimore, 1979), 78, 417.

23. The Declaration on the Causes and Necessity for Taking Up Arms can be found in both *JCC* 2:128–57 and *PTJ* 1:213–18. For Congress on the North Peace Plan, see The Resolution as Adopted by Congress, July 31, 1775, *PTJ* 1:230–33.

24. Draft Petition to the King [June 3–19], 1775, *LDC* 1:440–41; Jerrilyn Greene Marston, *King and Congress: The Transfer of Political Legitimacy, 1774–1776* (Princeton, N.J., 1987), 211–13; Rakove, *Beginnings of National Politics*, 73–79.

25. JA to Warren, July 11, 1775, *PJA* 3:72; JA, Autobiography, *DAJA* 3:89; John Dickinson's Notes of Debates, May 23–25, 1775, *LDC* 1:390–91.

26. Dyer to Joseph Trumbull, July 10, 1775, *LDC* 1:620; *DAJA* 2:140; JA to AA, June 17, 1775, *AFC* 1:216; JA to Warren, July 6, 1775, *PJA* 3:61; JA to Josiah Quincy, October 6, 1775, ibid., 3:187; JA to Moses Gill, June 10, 1775, ibid., 3:21.

27. Peter D. G. Thomas, *Tea Party to Independence: The Third Phase of the American Revolution, 1773–1776* (Oxford, Eng., 1991), 238–411; Piers Mackesy, *The War for America, 1775–1783* (Cambridge, Mass., 1965), 38; B. D. Bargar, *Lord Dartmouth and the American Revolution* (Columbia, S.C., 1965), 170; Dartmouth to Governor Earl of Dunmore, July 5, 1775, *DAR* 10:24; Dartmouth to Guy Carleton, July 24, 1775, ibid., 10:42; Dartmouth to Guy Johnson, July 24, 1775, ibid., 11:56. On British mobilization in 1775 and later see Stephen Conway, *The British Isles and the War of American Independence* (New York, 2000), 11–44.

28. Alan Valentine, *Lord North* (Norman, Okla., 1967), 378–79; Stephen Conway, *The War of American Independence, 1775–1783* (London, 1995), 44; Thomas, *Tea Party to Independence*, 254–56.

29. Dartmouth to Gage, August 2, 1775, in Clarence Carter, ed., *The Correspondence of General Thomas Gage with the Secretaries of State, and the War Office and Treasury, 1763–1775* (reprint, New York, 1969), 1:203; Bargar, *Lord Dartmouth and the American Revolution*, 176–81; Valentine, *Lord North*, 1:389–95, 407–8.

30. Mackesy, *War for America*, 50; Alan Valentine, *Lord George Germain* (Oxford, Eng. 1962), 1–96; Gerald Saxon Brown, *The American Secretary: The Colonial Policy of Lord George Germain, 1775–1778* (Ann Arbor, Mich., 1963), 1–30; Andrew Jackson O'Shaughnessy, *The Men Who Lost America: British Leadership, the American Revolution, and the Fate of the Empire* (New Haven, Conn., 2013), 167–77; *PH* 17:1196, 1312–13; 18:990; Valentine, *Lord North*, 1:403. The "buggering hero" quote is in O'Shaughnessy, page 171.

31. Thomas, *Tea Party to Independence*, 260–63; Jeremy Black, *George III: America's Last King* (New Haven, Conn., 2006), 215–22; Proclamation for Suppressing Rebellion and Sedition, August 23, 1775, *EHD* 9:850–51.

32. David McCullough, *1776* (New York, 2005), 3–10; The King's Speech to Parliament, October 26, 1775, *EHD* 9:851–52.

33. *PH* 18:710–13, 722–23, 769–79, 907, 916–27, 930–34; Simms, *Three Victories and a Defeat*, 596–97.

34. *PH* 18: 963–82.

35. Thomas, *Tea Party to Independence*, 294; *PH* 18:989–92.

36. *PH* 18:993–94; Peter Whiteley, *Lord North: The Prime Minister Who Lost America* (London, 1996), 161; Thomas, *Tea Party to Independence*, 298–99; Ira Gruber, *The Howe Brothers and the American Revolution* (New York, 1972), 37–38; American Prohibitory Act, December 22, 1775, *EHD* 9:853.

37. GW to Hancock, September 21, 1775, *PGWR* 2:26; Marston, *King and Congress*, 158–64; Committee of Conference Minutes of Proceedings, October 223–24, 1775, *LDC* 2:233–38.

38. GW to Nicholas Cooke, August 4, 1775, *PGWR* 1:221–22; GW to Hancock, August 4[–5], 1775, ibid., 1:227. On the issue of munitions, see Kevin Phillips, *1775: A Good Year for Revolution* (New York, 2012), 297–329.

39. GW to Joseph Reed, November 28, 1775, ibid., 2:449; GW to Hancock, December 18, 1775, ibid., 2:574; John Ferling, *Independence: The Struggle to Set America Free* (New York, 2011), 187; Charles Lesser, ed., *The Sinews of Independence: Monthly Strength Reports of the Continental Army* (Chicago, 1976), 8.

40. William M. Fowler Jr., *Rebels Under Sail: The American Navy During the American Revolution* (New York, 1976), 16–38; GW to Hancock, October 5, 1775, *PGWR* 2:100; GW to John A. Washington, October 13, 1775, ibid., 2:161; GW to Reed, November 20, 30, 1775, ibid., 2:409, 463; James Morgan, "American Privateering in America's War for Independence, 1775–1783," *American Neptune*, 35 (April 1976): 80; Nathan Miller, *Sea of Glory: The Continental Navy Fights for Independence, 1775–1783* (New York, 1974), 71.

41. *DAJA* 2:198–202, 205, 214–17; Marston, *King and Congress*, 173–77; Silas Deane, Proposals, [October 16?, 1775], *LDC* 2:182–87; David Syrett, *The Royal Navy in American Waters, 1775–1783* (Aldershot, Eng., 1989), 7–8; Miller, *Sea of Glory*, 52–55; Fowler, *Rebels Under Sail*, 42–72.

42. The foregoing draws on John E. Selby, *The Revolution in Virginia, 1775–1783* (Williamsburg, Va., 1988), 14–15, 41–85; Merrill Jensen, *The Founding of a Nation: A History of the American Revolution, 1763–1776* (New York, 1968), 644–45; Michael A. McDonnell, *The*

Politics of War: Race, Class, and Conflict in Revolutionary Virginia (Chapel Hill, N.C., 2007), 52–53, 55, 61, 65, 118, 133–74; Gary B. Nash, *The Forgotten Fifth: African Americans in the Age of Revolution* (Cambridge, Mass., 2006), 28–29; Alan Gilbert, *Black Patriots and Loyalists: Fighting for Emancipation in the War for Independence* (Chicago, 2012), 21–28; Douglas R. Egerton, *Death or Liberty: African Americans and Revolutionary America* (New York, 2009), 70–71; Cassandra Pybus, *Epic Journeys of Freedom: Runaway Slaves of the American Revolution and Their Global Quest for Liberty* (Boston, 2006), 8–9; Edward Countryman, *Enjoy the Same Liberty: Black Americans and the Revolutionary Era* (Lanham, Md., 2012), 47; Elizabeth A. Fenn, *Pox Americana: The Great Smallpox Epidemic of 1775–82* (New York, 2001), 57–59; GW to Richard Henry Lee, December 26, 1775, *PGWR* 2:611; GW to Joseph Reed, December 15, 1775, ibid., 2:553; Francis Lightfoot Lee to Landon Carter, February 12, 1776, *LDC* 3:237; Thomas Nelson to Mann Page, January 4, 1776, ibid., 3:30; Edward Rutledge to Ralph Izard, December 8, 1775, ibid., 2:462.

43. SA to Warren, November 4, 1775, *LDC* 2:298. The "piss upon him" quotation is in Rhys Isaac, *The Transformation of Virginia, 1740–1790* (Chapel Hill, N.C., 1982), 259.

44. *JCC* 3:319, 326; New Hampshire Delegates to Matthew Thornton, October 2, November 3, 1775, *LDC* 2:98–99, 292–93; Jensen, *Founding of a Nation*, 620–28, 638–41; Marsten, *King and Congress*, 256–73.

45. BF to David Harley, October 3, 1775, *PBF* 22:217; TJ to John Randolph, November 29, 1775, *PTJ* 1:269.

CHAPTER 8: "THE BIRTHDAY OF A NEW WORLD": AMERICA DECLARES INDEPENDENCE

1. JA to AA, February 18, 1776, *AFC* 1:348.

2. Samuel Ward to Nicholas Cooke, January 7, 1776, *LDC* 3:54; SA to John Pitts, January 12, 1776, ibid., 3:84.

3. Thomas Paine, *Common Sense* (1776), in Philip Foner, ed., *The Complete Writings of Thomas Paine* (New York, 1945), 1:3–46. The quotations can be found on pages 8, 20, 26, and 30. For the sales figures, see Gordon S. Wood, *The American Revolution: A History* (New York, 2003), 55; Isaac Kramnick, ed., Thomas Paine, *Common Sense* (New York, 1986), 8–9; and Nicole Eustace, *Passion Is the Gale: Emotion, Power, and the Coming of the American Revolution* (Chapel Hill, N.C., 2008), 441. On the intellectual roots of the tract, and of the notion of "common sense," see Sophia Rosenfeld, "Tom Paine's Common Sense and Ours," *WMQ* 65 (2008): 633–68. On pastors reading *Common Sense* to their congregations, see Douglas Bradburn, *The Citizenship Revolution: Politics and the Creation of the American Union, 1774–1804* (Charlottesville, Va., 2009), 39.

4. Josiah Bartlett to John Langdon, January 13, 1776, *LDC* 3:88; GW to Joseph Reed, April 1, 1776, *PGWR* 4:11.

5. Richard Smith Diary, *LDC* 3:72, 148, 167; SA to JA, January 15, 1776, ibid., 3:92–93; John Dickinson's Proposed Resolutions on a Petition to the King, [January 9–24, 1776], ibid., 3:63; John Dickinson's Proposed Resolutions for Negotiating with Great Britain, [January 9–24, 1776], ibid., 3:64–65; John Dickinson's Proposed Instructions for Commissioners to Negotiate with Great Britain, [January 9–24, 1776], ibid., 3:66–68; JA to AA, February [13], 1776, *AFC* 1:347; JCC 4:134–46; Milton E. Flower, *John Dickinson: Conservative Revolutionary* (Charlottesville, Va., 1983), 129, 134, 143–46; Charles Page Smith, *James Wilson: Founding*

Father, 1742–1798 (Chapel Hill, N.C., 75–76; Jerrilyn Greene Marston, *King and Congress: The Transfer of Political Legitimacy, 1774–1776* (Princeton, N.J., 1987), 180.

6. Francis Lightfoot Lee to John Page, January 30, 1776, *LDC* 3:168–69.

7. GW, General Orders, September 5, 1775, *PGWR* 1:415. On Arnold's background, see James Kirby Martin, *Benedict Arnold, Revolutionary Hero: An American Warrior Reconsidered* (New York, 1997); Willard Sterne Randall, *Benedict Arnold* (New York, 1997); and Willard M. Wallace, *Traitorous Hero: The Life and Fortunes of Benedict Arnold* (Freeport, N.Y., 1964).

8. Philip Schuyler to GW, September 26, 1775, *PGWR* 2:54.

9. The story of the American invasion draws on Hal T. Shelton, *General Richard Montgomery and the American Revolution* (New York, 1994), 68–150; Martin, *Benedict Arnold*, 104–74; Thomas A. Desjardin, *Through a Howling Wilderness: Benedict Arnold's March to Quebec, 1775* (New York, 2006); Arthur Lefkowitz, *Benedict Arnold's Army: The 1775 American Invasion of Canada During the Revolutionary War* (New York, 2008); John Ferling, *Almost a Miracle: The American Victory in the War of Independence* (New York, 2007), 80–99; Christopher Ward, *The War of the Revolution* (New York, 1952), 1:135–201; Don R. Gerlach, *Proud Patriot: Philip Schuyler and the War of Independence, 1775–1783* (Syracuse, N.Y., 1987), 35–49; Martin H. Bush, *Revolutionary Enigma: A Re-Appraisal of General Philip Schuyler of New York* (Port Washington, N.Y., 1969), 3–39. Many of the journals and diaries kept by those who make the trek through Maine are reprinted in Kenneth Roberts, ed., *March on Quebec: Journals of the Members of Arnold's Expedition* (New York, 1946).

10. Paine, *Common Sense*, in Foner, *Complete Writings of Thomas Paine*, 1:39.

11. Orville T. Murphy, *Charles Gravier, Comte de Vergennes: French Diplomacy in the Age of Revolution, 1719–1787* (Albany, N.Y., 1982), 232–33; Marston, *King and Congress*, 220; *PBF* 22:280–81n; Minutes, Secret Committee, February 14, 1776, *LDC* 3:256; Richard Smith Diary, ibid., 3:72.

12. JA to AA, April 28, 1776, *AFC* 1:401.

13. For an excellent, and succinct, appraisal of the yearlong congressional deliberations over opening American ports, see Staughton Lynd and David Waldstreicher, "Free Trade, Sovereignty, and Slavery: Toward an Economic Interpretation of American Independence," *WMQ* 68 (2011): 620–29.

14. Hancock to Certain Colonies, April 12, 1776, *LDC* 3:514; SA to Hawley, April 15, 1776, ibid., 3:528; Whipple to Brackett, April 11, 1776, ibid., 3:509; Hewes to Samuel Johnston, March 20, 1776, ibid., 3:416; Elbridge Gerry to Warren, March 26, 1776, ibid., 3:442; Committee of Secret Correspondence Minutes of Proceedings, March 2, 1776, ibid., 3:320–23; Robert Morris to Silas Deane, March 30, 1776, ibid., 3:466–68; JA to Horatio Gates, March 23, 1776, *PJA* 4:59; JA to AA, April 6, 1776, ibid., 3:492; JA to AA, April 12, 1776, *AFC* 1:377; *JCC* 4:214, 229–32; Patricia U. Bonomi, *Under the Cope of Heaven: Religion, Society, and Politics in Colonial America* (New York, 1986), 211; James Morgan, "American Privateering in America's War for Independence, 1775–1783," *American Neptune* 35 (April 1976): 80–85.

15. GW, Circular to the General Officers, September 8, 1775, *PGWR* 1:432–34; Council of War, September 11, 1775, ibid., 1:450–51; GW, Instructions to Colonel Henry Knox, November 16, 1775, ibid., 2:384–85; Knox to GW, November 27, December 5, 17, 1775, January 5, 1776, ibid., 2:434, 495–96, 563–66; North Callahan, *Henry Knox: George Washington's General* (New York, 1958), 16–56.

16. Council of War, February 16, 1776, *PGWR* 3:320–22, 323–24n; GW to Joseph Reed, February 26[–March 9], 1776, ibid., 3:373; Plan for Attacking Boston, [February 18–25, 1776], ibid., 3:332–33; editorial note, ibid., 3:333–35n.

17. AA to JA, March 16, 1776, *AFC* 1:358; Ward, *War of the Revolution*, 1:128

18. *PGWR* 3:377–78n; 4:2n; GW to Reed, February 26[—March 9], 1776, ibid., 3:376; *Am. Archives* 4, 5:644, 794–95.

19. BF to Anthony Todd, March 29, 1776, *PBF* 22:393; *Am. Archives* 4, 3:133, 322, 682, 692; Brendan McConville, *The King's Three Faces: The Rise and Fall of Royal America, 1688–1776* (Chapel Hill, N.C., 2006), 247–311; Maya Jasanoff, *Liberty's Exiles: American Loyalists in the Revolutionary World* (Cambridge, Mass., 2011), 6–7, 21–23.

20. *Pennsylvania Gazette*, May 1, 1776. For additional anti-independence essays, see those by "Civis," "Cato," "Hampden," "CS," and an anonymous writer in *Am. Archives* 4, 5:445, 514, 803–4, 976, 992, 1037, 1141–42, 1158–59. For pro-independence tracts, see those by "Salus Populi," "An American," "FA," "Somers," Thomas Paine as "The Forester," and anonymous pieces in ibid., 4th Series, 5:98–99, 122–23, 131, 214, 227, 450, 1015, 1020, 1034–35, 1078, 1134.

21. *Am. Archives* 4, 5:608–14, 1025–32; Pauline Maier, *American Scripture: Making the Declaration of Independence* (New York, 1997), 69–72; JA to Warren, April 22, 1776, *PJA* 4:135.

22. Hancock to the Massachusetts Assembly, May 16, 1776, *LDC* 4:7; Hewes to James Iredell, May 17, 1776, ibid., 4:27; Bartlett to John Langdon, May 19, 1776, ibid., 4:39; Oliver Wolcott to Laura Wolcott, May 25, 1776, ibid., 4:72; Hancock to Certain Colonies, June 4, 1776, ibid., 4:136; TJ to Thomas Nelson, May 16, 1776, *PTJ* 1:292.

23. *Am. Archives* 4, 5:1034–35, 6:1524; Merrill Jensen, *The Founding of a Nation: A History of the American Revolution, 1763–1776* (New York, 1968), 678–79.

24. JA to John Winthrop, May 6, 1776, *PJA* 4:175; JA to Warren, May 20, 1776, ibid., 4:195; Richard Henry Lee to Charles Lee, May 11, 1776, *LDC* 3:655; Thomas Stone to James Hollyday[?], May 20, 1776, ibid., 4:47; *JCC* 4:342, 357–58; William Hogeland, *Declaration: The Nine Tumultuous Weeks When America Became Independent, May 1–July 4, 1776* (New York, 2010), 97–100; Richard Alan Ryerson, *The Revolution Is Now Begun: The Radical Committees of Philadelphia, 1765–1776* (Philadelphia, 1978), 171–75.

25. Ryerson, *The Revolution Is Now Begun*, 211–26; Jensen, *Founding of a Nation*, 686–87; Hogeland, *Declaration*, 129–57.

26. [John Adams], *Thoughts on Government* (1776), *PJA* 4:86–93. See also the editor's note, ibid., 4:65–68n. For JA on Paine, see John Ferling, *John Adams: A Life* (reprint, New York, 2010), 155.

27. John W. Gordon, *South Carolina and the American Revolution: A Battlefield History* (Columbia, S.C., 2003), 15–36; Hugh T. Lefler and William S. Powell, *Colonial North Carolina: A History* (New York, 1973), 269–77; Don Higginbotham, *The War of American Independence: Military Attitudes, Policies, and Practice, 1763–1789* (New York, 1971), 135; Piers Mackesy, *The War for America, 1775–1783* (Cambridge, Mass., 1965), 63–64; Clinton to Germain, July 8, 1776, *DAR* 12:163.

28. SA to Warren, June 6, 1776, *LDC* 4:150.

29. Commissioners to Canada to Hancock, May 27, 1776, ibid., 4:81–82; Carleton to Germain, May 14, 1776, *DAR* 12:137–38; Thomas Ainslie Journal, *SOS* 1:211; John Sullivan to Hancock, ibid., 1:215.

30. Charles P. Whittemore, *A General of the Revolution: John Sullivan of New Hampshire* (New York, 1961), 1–31; Ferling, *Almost a Miracle*, 109–11; Paul H. Smith, "Sir Guy Carleton:

Soldier-Statesman," in George A. Billias, ed., *George Washington's Opponents: British Generals and Admirals in the American Revolution* (New York, 1969), 103–41. The "wicked tyrannical Brute" quote is in Elizabeth A. Fenn, *Pox Americana: The Great Smallpox Epidemic of 1775–82* (New York, 2001), 76.

31. Hewes to Samuel Johnston, June 4, 1776, *LDC* 4:139; Commissioners to Canada to Hancock, May 10, 17, 27, 1776, ibid., 3:646–47; 4:22–24, 80–82; Hancock to Certain Colonies, June 4, 1776, ibid., 4:136.

32. The Paine quotation is from *Common Sense*, in Foner, *Complete Writings of Thomas Paine*, 1:19.

33. AH, *The Farmer Refuted, &c.*, February 23, 1776, *PAH* 1:165. The Rakove quotation is in Jack Rakove, *Revolutionaries: A New History of the Invention of America* (Boston, 2010), 17.

34. Edmund S. Morgan, *Prologue to Revolution: Sources and Documents on the Stamp Act Crisis, 1764–1766* (Chapel Hill, N.C., 1966), 103, 131; Alan Valentine, *Lord North* (Norman, Okla., 1967), 1:314, 319–20; Brendan Simms, *Three Victories and a Defeat: The Rise and Fall of the First British Empire, 1714–1783* (New York, 2009), 550, 580, 590.

35. Hancock to GW, June 7, 1776, *LDC* 4:156; *JCC* 5:428–29, 431, 433; *PJA*, 342n. For the arguments offered by both sides in the debate, see Dickinson, Notes for a Speech in Congress [June 8–10?, 1776], *LDC* 4:165–69, and TJ, "Notes of Proceedings," [June 7–28, 1776], *PTJ* 1:309–13.

36. Thomas Jefferson, *Notes on the State of Virginia*, ed., William Peden (Chapel Hill, N.C., 1955), 128. On TJ's inheritance, see Dumas Malone, *Jefferson and His Time* (Boston, 1948–1981), 1:440.

37. Samuel Ward to Henry Ward, June 22, 1775, *LDC* 1:535; William Maclay, *The Journal of William Maclay: United States Senator from Pennsylvania, 1789–1791* (New York, 1927), 265–66; JA to Timothy Pickering, August 6, 1822, in Charles Francis Adams, ed., *The Works of John Adams. . . .* (Boston, 1850–56), 2:514n.

38. JA, Autobiography, *DAJA* 3:336–37; JA to Timothy Pickering, August 6, 1822, Adams, *Writings of John Adams*, 2:512–14n; TJ to James Madison, August 30, 1823, Paul Leicester Ford, ed., *The Writings of Thomas Jefferson* (New York, 1892–1899), 10:267–69. For the circumstantial evidence pointing to TJ's better memory, see Maier, *American Scripture*, 99–105.

39. TJ to Henry Lee, May 8, 1825, in A. A. Lipscomb and A. E. Bergh, eds., *The Writings of Thomas Jefferson* (Washington, D.C., 1903), 7:407.

40. Among other things, the Virginia Declaration of Rights stated that "all men are born equally free and independent, and have certain inherent natural rights . . . among which are the enjoyment of life and liberty, with the means of acquiring and possessing property." See Maier, *American Scripture*, 124–28. On the influences that shaped Jefferson's composition, see Carl Becker, *The Declaration of Independence: A Study in the History of Political Ideas* (New York, 1922), and Garry Wills, *Inventing America: Jefferson's Declaration of Independence* (New York, 1978).

41. For TJ's draft, see "Jefferson 'original Rough draft,'" *PTJ* 1:423–28.

42. For other important works on aspects of the Declaration of Independence, see David Armitage, *The Declaration of Independence: A Global History* (Cambridge, Mass., 2007); Julian P. Boyd, *The Declaration of Independence: The Evolution of the Text* (Washington, D.C., 1999); and Robert G. Parkinson, "The Declaration of Independence," in Francis D. Cogliano, ed., *A Companion to Thomas Jefferson* (New York, 2012), 44–59.

43. Jay Fliegelman, *Declaring Independence: Jefferson, Natural Language, and the Culture of Performance* (Stanford, Calif., 1993), 4–28; Andrew Burstein and Nancy Isenberg, *Madison and Jefferson* (New York, 2010), 36–39.

44. On the queries about the meaning of "all men are created equal," see Maier, *American Scripture*, 136, 191–208. On the idea that TJ meant political equality, see Danielle Allen, *Our Declaration: A Reading of the Declaration of Independence in Defense of Equality* (New York, 2014). On the idea of social equality, see Gordon S. Wood, "The Radicalism of Jefferson and Paine Considered," in Gordon S. Wood, *The Idea of America: Reflections on the Birth of the United States* (New York, 2011), 213–28, and Gordon S. Wood, "A Different Idea of Our Declaration," *New York Review of Books* (August 14, 2014), 37–38. The quote about the idea of egalitarianism tearing through American society and culture can be found in Gordon S. Wood, *The Radicalism of the American Revolution* (New York, 1992), 232. In pages 233–43 Wood follows with an important elaboration of the conjunction of equalitarianism and republicanism.

45. JA to Archibald Bulloch, July 1, 1776, *PJA* 4:352.

46. John Dickinson, Notes for a Speech in Congress, [July 1, 1776], *LDC* 4:351–56, 356n; JA to Zabdiel Adams, July 1, 1776, *PJA* 4:353.

47. John Hazleton, *The Declaration of Independence: Its History* (New York, 1906), 161–62; Ferling, *John Adams*, 169.

48. Jefferson, Notes of Proceeding in the Continental Congress, [June 7–August 1, 1776], *PTJ* 1:314.

49. Milton E. Flower, *John Dickinson: Conservative Revolutionary* (Charlottesville, Va., 1983), 153–57. On the saga of Caesar Rodney and the breakdown of votes in each delegation, see John Ferling, *Independence: The Struggle to Set America Free* (New York, 2011), 327–35. On July 9 New York's Provincial Convention authorized its congressmen to approve independence.

50. On the editing of the document, both by the committee and by Congress, see Maier, *American Scripture*, 97–153.

51. JA to AA, *AFC* 2:28. For the comments of comments SA, Paine, and numerous other delegates, see Hazleton, *Declaration of Independence*, 193–219.

52. JA to AA, July 3, 1776, *AFC* 2:30.

CHAPTER 9: "THE AMERICAN CAUSE IS IN A CRITICAL SITUATION": THE NEW YORK CAMPAIGN IN 1776

1. JA to Samuel Chase, July 1, 1776, *LDC* 4:347; Josiah Bartlett to Nathaniel Folsom, July 1, 1776, ibid., 4:350.

2. John Alden, *General Charles Lee: Traitor or Patriot?* (Baton Rouge, La., 1951), 1–75; John W. Shy, "Charles Lee: The Soldier as Radical," in George A. Billias, ed., *George Washington's Generals* (New York, 1964), 22–53; JA to James Warren, June 20, 1775, *PJA* 3:34; JA to Josiah Quincy, July 29, 1775, ibid. 3:106; AA to JA, July 16, 1775, *AFC* 1:246. Lee's "doggism" quote can be found on page 77 in Alden's biography.

3. GW to Joseph Read, January 4, 1776, *PGWR* 3:25; GW, Instructions to Major General Charles Lee, January 8, 1776, ibid., 3:53–54; GW to John Augustine Washington, March 31, 1776, ibid., 3:570; Lee to GW, February 19, 1776, ibid., 3:339–40; Lee, Report on the Defence of New York, March 1776, *LP* 1:347–57. Hereafter John Augustine Washington is cited as J. A. Washington.

4. GW to Hancock, March 13, June 23, 1776, *PGWR* 3:462; 5:79; GW to J. A. Washington, May 31[–June 4], 1776, ibid., 4:413; GW to Adam Stephen, July 20, 1776, ibid., 5:408–9; New York Convention to GW, July 16, 1776, ibid., 5:348; David Hackett Fischer, *Washington's Crossing* (New York, 2004), 83–84.

5. John Ferling, *Almost a Miracle: The American Victory in the War of Independence* (New York, 2007), 125–26.

6. Alan Valentine, *Lord North* (Norman, Okla., 1967), 1:07–8; Ira Gruber, *The Howe Brothers and the American Revolution* (New York, 1972), 31–67; Gerald Saxon Brown, *The American Secretary: The Colonial Policy of Lord George Germain, 1775–1778* (Ann Arbor, Mich., 1963), 64–72; Peter D. G. Thomas, *Tea Party to Independence: The Third Phase of the American Revolution, 1773–1776* (Oxford, Eng., 1991), 303–17; Weldon A. Brown, *Empire or Independence: A Study in the Failure of Reconciliation, 1774–1783* (reprint, Port Washington, N.Y., 1966), 82–85; *PH* 18:1144–56, 1248–55, 1284–86.

7. Memorandum of an Interview with Lieutenant Colonel James Paterson, July 20, 1776, *PGWR* 5:398–401, 401–3n; Lord Howe to BF, June 20[–July 12], 1776, *PBF* 22:483–84; BF to Lord Howe, July 20, 1776, ibid., 22:519–21.

8. Gruber, *Howe Brothers*, 117; JA to James Warren, September 4, 1776, *PJA* 3:12; JA to SA, September 14, 1776, *LDC* 5:159–62; Henry Strachey's Notes on Lord Howe's Meeting with a Committee of Congress, September 11, 1776, ibid., 5:137–42; JA to AA, September 6, 1776, *AFC* 2:120–21; JA, Autobiography, *DAJA* 3:419–20.

9. GW to Field Officers of the Connecticut Light Horse, July 16, 1776, *PGWR* 5:336–37. GW's "could not be of use" remark was communicated to the governor of Connecticut by an intermediary. See ibid., 5:337n.

10. Eric Robson, *The American Revolution: In Its Political and Military Aspects, 1763–1783* (Hamden, Conn., 1965), 103; Rodney Atwood, *The Hessians: Mercenaries from Hessen–Kassel in the American Revolution* (Cambridge, Eng., 1980), 52–57. On Clinton's failure off Charleston, see William B. Willcox, *Portrait of a General: Sir Henry Clinton in the War of Independence* (New York, 1962), 79–93; John Buchanan, *The Road to Guilford Courthouse: The American Revolution in the Carolinas* (New York, 1997), 11–16.

11. Edward H. Tatum Jr., ed., *The American Journal of Ambrose Serle: Secretary to Lord Howe, 1776–1778* (San Marino, Calif., 1940), 35; Ferling, *Almost a Miracle*, 122, 130–34; GW to Trumbull, August 14, 1776, *PGWR* 6:123; GW to Hancock, June 17, August 22, 23, 1776, ibid., 5:21; 6:102, 111; GW to William Heath, August 23, 1776, ibid., 6:113; GW to Israel Putnam, August 25, 1776, ibid., 6:127; GW, General Orders, August 20, 1776, ibid., 6:89; Edward G. Lengel, *General George Washington* (New York, 2005), 141; Fischer, *Washington's Crossing*, 88, 92–93; Ira D. Gruber, "America's First Battle: Long Island, 27 August 1776," in Charles E. Heller and William A. Stofft, eds., *America's First Battles, 1776–1965* (Lawrence, Kans., 1986), 15–17, 22.

12. Christopher Ward, *The War of the Revolution* (New York, 1952), 1:211–37; Douglas Southall Freeman, *George Washington* (New York, 1948–57), 4:153–57; Ron Chernow, *Washington: A Life* (New York, 2010), 248; John J. Gallagher, *The Battle of Brooklyn, 1776* (Edison, N.J., 2002), 101–34; Barnet Schecter, *The Battle for New York: The City at the Heart of the American Revolution* (New York, 2002), 126–54.

13. Robson, *American Revolution*, 135–36.

14. Gruber, "America's First Battle," in Heller and Stofft, *America's First Battles*, 28–29; Henry P. Johnson, *The Campaign of 1776 Around New York and Brooklyn* (Brooklyn, 1878), part 2, 36–39; Fischer, *Washington's Crossing*, 100; Schecter, *Battle for New York*, 155–67;

Council of War, August 29, 1776, *PGWR* 6:153; GW to Hancock, August 31, 1776, ibid., 6:177; George A. Billias, *John Glover and His Marblehead Men* (New York, 1960), 100–103.

15. Richard M. Ketchum, "Men of the Revolution: Israel Putnam," *American Heritage* 24 (June 1973), 27; GW to Hancock, September 2, 1776, *PGWR* 6:199–200.

16. GW to Hancock, September 2, 8, 1776, *PGWR* 6:200, 248–52; Certain general officers to GW, September 11, 1776, ibid., 6:279; Council of War, September 12, 1776, ibid., 6:288–89; Hancock to GW, September 3, 1776, ibid., 6:207.

17. Schecter, *Battle for New York*, 179–93.

18. GW to Lund Washington, October 6, 1776, *PGWR* 6:494; GW to Hancock, September 22, 1776, ibid., 6:369; Hans Huth, "Letters from a Hessian Mercenary," *Pennsylvania Magazine of History and Biography* 62 (1938): 494–95; Chernow, *Washington*, 255; Governor William Tryon to Germain, September 24, 1776, *DAR* 112:230–31.

19. GW to Hancock, September 8, 19, 1776, *PGWR* 6:248, 341; GW to Lund Washington, October 6, 1776, ibid., 6:493; GW to Samuel Washington, October 5, 1776, ibid., 6:486; GW, General Orders, September 30, 1776, ibid., 6:432.

20. GW to Lund Washington, September 30, 1776, ibid., 6:441–42; GW to J. A. Washington, September 22, 1776, ibid., 6:371–74; GW to Hancock, September 24, 25, 1776, ibid., 6:389, 396–97; GW to Samuel Washington, October 5, 1776, ibid., 6:486–87.

21. GW to Abraham Yates, September 23, 1776, ibid., 6:383; GW to Trumbull, September 23, 1776, ibid., 6:382; Schecter, *Battle for New York*, 219–24.

22. James Smith to Eleanor Smith, October 7, 1776, *LDC* 5:315; George A. Billias, *John Glover and His Marblehead Men* (New York, 1960), 110–19; Ward, *War of the Revolution*, 1:256–59; Fischer, *Washington's Crossing*, 110; *PGWR* 6:593n.

23. Ward, *War of the Revolution*, 1:261–66; Gruber, *Howe Brothers*, 132–33; Chernow, *Washington*, 258–59; Schecter, *Battle for New York*, 231–42; *PGWR* 7:52–54n.

24. Council of War, October 16, November 6, 1776, *PGWR* 6:576; 7:92; GW to Hancock, November 6, 1776, ibid., 7:97; Richard M. Ketchum, *The Winter Soldiers* (Garden City, N.Y., 1973), 108–9; Schecter, *Battle for New York*, 117, 245–46; John Richard Alden, *General Charles Lee: Traitor or Patriot?* (Baton Rouge, La., 1951), 145.

25. GW to Greene, November 8, 1776, *PGWR* 7:115–16; GW to Reed, August 22, 1779, ibid., 7:106n; GW to J. A. Washington, November 6[–19], 1776, ibid., 7:105.

26. Ward, *War of the Revolution*, 1:267–74; Schecter, *Battle for New York*, 248–55.

27. GW to Hancock, November 19[–21], 1776, *PGWR* 7:180–83, 186n; GW to William Livingston, November 21, 1776, ibid., 7:195; Schecter, *Battle for New York*, 255–57; Robson, *American Revolution*, 160; Fischer, *Washington's Crossing*, 121–23.

28. SA to Elizabeth Adams, December 9, 1776, *LDC* 5:590–91. Gerry to Unknown, December 12, 1776, ibid., 5:602. The "shudder" quotation is in Charles Royster, *A Revolutionary People at War: The Continental Army and American Character, 1775–1783* (Chapel Hill, N.C., 1979), 111.

29. GW to Reed, November 30, 1776, *PGWR* 7:237, 237–38n.

30. GW to Lee, November 21, 24, 27, ibid., 7:194–96, 207–10, 224–25; Ferling, *Almost a Miracle*, 164; Andrew Jackson O'Shaughnessy, *The Men Who Lost America: British Leadership, the American Revolution, and the Fate of the Empire* (New Haven, Conn., 2013), 249–51. On Gates's orders, see *PGWR* 7:146n.

31. GW to Hancock, November 23, 27, 30, December 1, 2, 3, 4, 5, 6, 8, 1776, *PGWR* 7:196–98, 223–24, 232–34, 243–45, 245–47, 251–52, 255–56, 262–64, 266, 273–75; Ferling, *Almost a*

Miracle, 164–70; Fischer, *Washington's Crossing*, 115–37; Arthur F. Lefkowitz, *The Long Retreat: The Calamitous American Defense of New Jersey, 1776* (Metuchen, N.J., 1998), 54–126; Chernow, *Washington*, 264–70.

32. GW to Samuel Washington, December 18, 1776, *PGWR* 7:371; GW to Robert Morris, December 22, 1776, ibid., 7:412; Paul David Nelson, *General Horatio Gates: A Biography* (Baton Rouge, La., 1976), 72, 75; Fischer, *Washington's Crossing*, 129–35, 381; Charles H. Lesser, ed., *The Sinews of Independence: Monthly Strength Reports of the Continental Army* (Chicago, 1976), 43; William M. Dwyer, *The Day Is Ours!: An Inside View of the Battles of Trenton and Princeton* (New York, 1983), 16–17.

33. NG to President of Congress, December 21, 1776, *PNG* 1:370.

34. Hancock to Morris, December 23, 1776, *LDC* 5:642–43; Hancock to GW, December 27, 1776, *PGWR* 7:461–62, 262–63n.

35. David F. Hawke, *Paine* (New York, 1974), 52–62. Paine produced two of his thirteen *American Crisis* essays within about three weeks and two others in 1777. For the two that appeared during the end of the year crisis, see Thomas Paine, *The American Crisis*, in Philip S. Foner, ed., *The Complete Writings of Thomas Paine* (New York, 1945), 1:50–72. The "try men's souls" quote can be found on page 50.

36. Fischer, *Washington's Crossing*, 264–66.

37. On the planning of the attack and the battle, see GW to Heath, December 14, 1776, *PGWR* 7:334; GW to Hancock, December 24, 27, 1776, ibid., 7:429–31, 454–56, 456–61n; GW to Reed, December 23, 1776, ibid., 7:423; GW, General Orders, December 25, 1776, ibid., 7:434–38; Chernow, *Washington*, 269–76; Ferling, *Almost a Miracle*, 173–79; Fischer, *Washington's Crossing*, 160–262.

38. GW to Morris, December 31, 1776, *PGWR* 7:497; GW to Hancock, January 1, 5, 1776, ibid., 7:504, 519; Fischer, *Washington's Crossing*, 270–93; Dwyer, *The Day Is Ours!*, 320.

39. "Diary of Captain Thomas Rodney, January 2, 1777, Rodney Family Papers, Library of Congress; "The Good Soldier [Joseph] White," *American Heritage* 7 (June 1956): 77; Chernow, *Washington*, 280; Fischer, *Washington's Crossing*, 290–307; Ketchum, *Winter Soldiers*, 291.

40. Fischer, *Washington's Crossing*, 326–40, 413–15; Dwyer, *This Day Is Ours*, 342; Ketchum, *Winter Soldiers*, 292, 303, 313.

41. Fischer, *Washington's Crossing*, 405–6, 412–15.

CHAPTER 10: "ACROSS AMERICA IN A HOP, STEP, AND A JUMP": THE CAMPAIGNS OF 1777

1. Morris to Deane, January 8, 1777, *LDC* 6:62; William to Joseph Hewes, February 15, 1777, ibid., 6:290.

2. GW to Hancock, February 9, September 2, 1776, *PGWR* 3:275–76; 6:199; GW, Circular Recruiting Instructions to the Colonels of the Sixteen Additional Continental Regiments, January 12[–27], 1777, ibid., 8:44; *JCC* 2:11–22; 3:331–34; 5:729, 747, 749, 751, 756–57, 762–63, 788–807; Charles Royster, *A Revolutionary People at War: The Continental Army and American Character, 1775–1783* (Chapel Hill, N.C., 1979), 35, 64–65; James Kirby Martin and Mark Lender, *A Respectable Army: The Military Origins of the Republic, 1763–1789* (Arlington Heights, Ill., 1982), 73, 88; Walter Sargent, "The Massachusetts Rank and File of 1777," in John

Resch and Walter Sargent, eds., *War and Society in the American Revolution: Mobilization and Home Fronts* (DeKalb, Ill., 2007), 46, 55; Richard Buel Jr., *Dear Liberty: Connecticut's Mobilization for the Revolutionary War* (Middletown, Conn., 1980), 53, 68–70, 101–2, 117–18; Robert Gross, *The Minutemen and Their World* (New York, 1976), 135; John Resch, *Suffering Soldiers: Revolutionary War Veterans, Moral Sentiment, and Political Culture in the Early Republic* (Amherst, Mass., 1999), 19–25, 34; Gregory T. Knouff, *The Soldiers' Revolution: Pennsylvanians in Arms and the Forging of Early American Identity* (University Park, Pa., 2004), 35–36; John Ferling, *Almost a Miracle: The American Victory in the War of Independence* (New York, 2007), 193–97; Don Higginbotham, *The War of American Independence: Military Attitudes, Policies, and Practices, 1763–1789* (New York, 1971), 391–93; Charles P. Neimeyer, *America Goes to War: A Social History of the Continental Army* (New York, 1996), 52–53, 56–57; John R. Sellers, "The Common Soldier in the American Revolution," in S. J. Underdal, ed., *Military History of the American Revolution: Proceedings of the Sixth Military History Symposium, USAF Academy* (Washington, D.C., 1976), 155; Charles H. Lesser, ed., *The Sinews of Independence: Monthly Strength Reports of the Continental Army* (Chicago, 1976), 38, 50.

3. Alan Valentine, *Lord North* (Norman, Okla., 1967), 421–27; Alan Valentine, *Lord George Germain* (Oxford, Eng., 1962), 148–61; Andrew Jackson O'Shaughnessy, *The Men Who Lost America: British Leadership, the American Revolution and the Fate of the Empire* (New Haven, Conn., 2013), 92.

4. Howe to Germain, November 30, 1776, *DAR* 12:264–66.

5. Valentine, *Lord George Germain*, 151; Ira Gruber, *The Howe Brothers and the American Revolution* (New York, 1972), 192.

6. Piers Mackesy, *The War for America 1775–1783* (Cambridge, Mass., 1964), 115; O'Shaughnessy, *The Men Who Lost America*, 105–6, 112, 186.

7. Mackesy, *War for America*, 125; GW to J. A. Washington, June 29, 1777, *PGWR* 10:150; GW to Hancock, July 25, 1777, ibid., 10:410; GW to Trumbull, July 31, 1777, ibid., 10:472; O'Shaughnessy, *The Men Who Lost America*, 253; Stephen R. Taaffe, *The Philadelphia Campaign, 1777–1778* (Lawrence, Kans., 2003), 45.

8. Max Mintz, *The Generals of Saratoga* (New Haven, Conn., 1990), 3–11; Richard J. Hargrove, *General John Burgoyne* (Newark, Del., 1983), 17–68; George A. Billias, "John Burgoyne: Ambitious General," in George A. Billias, ed., *George Washington's Opponents* (New York, 1969), 142–64; John S. Pancake, *1777: The Year of the Hangman* (University, Ala., 1977), 88–94; Mackesy, *War for America*, 108, 113; O'Shaughnessy, *The Men Who Lost America*, 124–34. The quotes on Burgoyne's showmanship are in O'Shaughnessy, page 124.

9. Burgoyne to Germain, June 22, 26, 1777, *DAR* 14:119, 121; Carlton to Burgoyne, May 29, 1777, ibid., 14:101; Mackesy, *War for America*, 115, 131; Hargrove, *General John Burgoyne*, 117–23; Christopher Ward, *The War of the Revolution* (New York, 1952), 1:402–3; Ferling, *Almost a Miracle*, 211–13; Richard Ketchum, *Saratoga: Turning Point of America's Revolutionary War* (New York, 1997), 107–11.

10. Paul H. Smith, "Sir Guy Carleton: Soldier-Statesman," in George A. Billias, ed., *George Washington's Opponents* (New York, 1969), 123–25; James Kirby Martin, *Benedict Arnold, Revolutionary Hero: An American Warrior Reconsidered* (New York, 1997), 219–84; Willard Sterne Randall, *Benedict Arnold: Patriot and Traitor* (New York, 1990), 296–317; Don R. Gerlach, *Proud Patriot: Philip Schuyler and the War of Independence, 1775–1783*

(Syracuse, N.Y., 1987), 158–87; Christopher Ward, *War of the Revolution* (New York, 1952), 1:384–97. The "American cause . . . was saved" quotation can be found in Claude van Tyne, *The War of Independence: American Phase* (Boston, 1929), 373–74.

11. O'Shaughnessy, *The Men Who Lost America*, 177. Howe's letter can be found in *SOS* 1:543–44.

12. Ward, *War of the Revolution*, 1:405–7; Ketchum, *Saratoga*, 116, 160; Mintz, *Generals of Saratoga*, 107, 142.

13. Ketchum, *Saratoga*, 167–84; Ward, *War of the Revolution*, 1:410–11; Ferling, *Almost a Miracle*, 215–19; Schuyler to GW, July 7, 1777, *PGWR* 10:219–21.

14. Ferling, *Almost a Miracle*, 219–23.

15. GW to Putnam, July 1, 22, 1777, *PGWR* 10:166, 362; Schuyler to GW, July 14, 21, 26[–27], August 1, 1777, ibid., 280, 348, 482; Mintz, *Generals of Saratoga*, 160; O'Shaughnessy, *The Men Who Lost America*, 148, 150; Eric Robson, *The American Revolution: In Its Political and Military Aspects, 1763–1783* (Hamden, Conn., 1965), 99–100. The "no men of military science quote is in Billias, "John Burgoyne," Billias, *George Washington's Opponents*, 175.

16. Schuyler to GW, July 10, 17, 1777, *PGWR* 10:245, 312; Hargrove, *General John Burgoyne*, 147, Ketchum, *Saratoga*, 246–48; John H. G. Pell, "Philip Schuyler: The General as Aristocrat," in George A. Billias, ed., *George Washington's Generals* (New York, 1964), 67. GW is quoted in Don R. Gerlach, *Proud Patriot: Philip Schuyler and the War of Independence, 1775–1783* (Syracuse, N.Y., 1987), 217.

17. Gates to Burgoyne, September 2, 1777, *SOS* 1:560; Mintz, *Generals of Saratoga*, 162, 182; Ketchum, *Saratoga*, 274–77; Paul David Nelson, *General Horatio Gates* (Baton Rouge, La., 1976), 110–11.

18. Ketchum, *Saratoga*, 291–328, 341; Ward, *War of the Revolution*, 1:417–31.

19. Gavin K. Watt, *Rebellion in the Mohawk Valley: The St. Leger Expedition of 1777* (Toronto, 2002), 154–261; Isabel T. Kelsay, *Joseph Brant, 1743–1807: Man of Two Worlds* (Syracuse, N.Y., 1984), 194–208; Ward, *War of the Revolution*, 1:477–91; Glen F. Williams, *Year of the Hangman: George Washington's Campaign Against the Iroquois* (Yardley, Pa., 2005), 54–57.

20. SA to Samuel Cooper, July 15, 1777, *LDC* 7:343; SA to Richard Henry Lee, July 15, 1777, ibid., 7:344; JA to AA, July 18, 1777, *AFC* 2:284.

21. Charles Thomson's Notes of Debates, July 26, 28, 1777, *LDC* 7:382–83, 388–89; Nelson, *General Horatio Gates*, 94–103; Jonathan Rossie, *The Politics of Command in the American Revolution* (Syracuse, N.Y., 1975), 159–65.

22. SA to Samuel Freeman, August 5, 1777, *LDC* 7:413–14. On Gates's background, see Nelson, *General Horatio Gates*, 1–103, and see pages 5–6 on his appearance and manner. See also Mintz, *Generals of Saratoga*, 1–2.

23. Nelson, *General Horatio Gates*, 106–13; Ward, *War of the Revolution*, 1:502; Ketchum, *Saratoga*, 394–404; Mintz, *Generals of Saratoga*, 204–13; William C. Stinchcombe, *The American Revolution and the French Alliance* (Syracuse, N.Y., 1969), 9.

24. On the battles and the Arnold-Gates clash, see Nelson, *General Horatio Gates*, 122–37; James Kirby Martin, *Benedict Arnold, Revolutionary Hero: An American Warrior Reconsidered* (New York, 1997), 369–402; Willard Sterne Randall, *Benedict Arnold: Patriot and Traitor* (New York, 1990), 351–68, 375; Ketchum, *Saratoga*, 363–405; Mintz, *Generals of Saratoga*, 187–213. For the biographer's description of Arnold going into battle, see Willard M. Wallace, *Traitorous Hero: The Life and Fortunes of Benedict Arnold* (reprint, Freeport, N.Y., 1970), 155.

25. Minutes of the Council of War, October 12–15, 1777, *DAR* 14:212–15; Burgoyne to Germain, October 20, 1777, ibid., 14:233–34; Ketchum, *Saratoga*, 418–20.

26. Mintz, *Generals of Saratoga*, 204, 220–23; Ketchum, *Saratoga*, 420–25; Nelson, *General Horatio Gates*, 138–41; Ferling, *Almost a Miracle*, 240; Hargrove, *General John Burgoyne*, 200–201. For Burgoyne's lengthy account of his campaign, see Burgoyne to Germain, October 20, 1777, *DAR* 14:228–36.

27. Ketchum, *Saratoga*, 426–33; O'Shaughnessy, *The Men Who Lost America*, 158.

28. GW to George Clinton, July 1, 1777, *PGWR* 10:163; GW to Hancock, July 2, 1777, ibid., 169; GW to William Livingston, July 12, 1777, ibid., 10:256; GW to Heath, July 19, 1777, ibid., 10:339; Hamilton to Hugh Knox, [July 1777], *PAH* 1:300.

29. Robson, *American Revolution*, 98.

30. Bruce Burgoyne, ed., *Enemy Views: The American Revolutionary War as Recorded by the Hessian Participants* (Bowie, Md., 1996), 164–65; Baron Karl Leopold Baurmeister, *Revolution in America: Confidential Letters and Journals, 1776–1784* (Westport, Conn., 1973), 93, 98; "Before and After the Battle of Brandywine. Extracts from the Journal of Sergeant Thomas Sullivan of H. M. Forty-Ninth Regiment of Foot," *Pennsylvania Magazine of History and Biography* 31 (1907): 408; Taaffe, *Philadelphia Campaign*, 53.

31. Hamilton to Hugh Knox, [July 1777], *PAH* 1:300.

32. Enoch Anderson, *Personal Recollections of Enoch Anderson* (New York, 1971), 38.

33. Charles P. Whittemore, *A General of the Revolution: John Sullivan of New Hampshire* (New York, 1961), 58; Jim Piecuch, ed., *Cavalry of the American Revolution* (Yardley, Pa., 2012), 4–8.

34. Edward G. Lengel, *General George Washington: A Military Life* (New York, 2005), 229–41; Ward, *War of the Revolution*, 1:342–54; Ferling, *Almost a Miracle*, 246–50; Taafe, *Philadelphia Campaign*, 63–78; Editor's Note, *PGWR* 11:187–93; Editor's Note, *PNG* 2:157–62n; Journal of Sergeant Sullivan, *Pennsylvania Magazine of History and Biography* 31:416.

35. Quoted in Royster, *A Revolutionary People at War*, 225.

36. GW to Samuel Washington, October 27, 1777, *PGWR* 12:35; GW to Hancock, September 11, 13, 15, 17, 19, 23, 1777, ibid., 11:200, 213, 237, 253, 268, 301; Lengel, *General Washington*, 242; Ferling, *Almost a Miracle*, 251–52, 310; James Thomas Flexner, *George Washington* (Boston, 1965–72), 2:227–30; Douglas Southall Freeman, *George Washington* (New York, 1948–57), 4:490–99. On Paoli, see Taaffe, *Philadelphia Campaign*, 84–87.

37. "The Diary of Robert Morton," *Pennsylvania Magazine of History and Biography* 1 (1877): 3–4; Sarah Fisher, " 'A Diary of Trifling Occurrences': Philadelphia, 1776–1778," ibid., 82 (1958):450; JA to AA, September 30, 1777, *AFC* 2:349; *DAJA* 2:117, 118n, 256n, 262, 265.

38. GW to Gates, September 24, 1777, *PGWR* 11:310; Gates to GW, October 5, 1777, ibid., 11:392–93.

39. Council of War, September 28, 1777, ibid., 11:338–39; GW to Hancock, October 5, 1777, ibid., 11:393; Taaffe, *Philadelphia Campaign*, 94.

40. Taaffe, *Philadelphia Campaign*, 93–107; Ward, *War of the Revolution*, 1:362–71; Ferling, *Almost a Miracle*, 253–56; John Ferling, *The Ascent of George Washington: The Hidden Political Genius of an American Icon* (New York, 2009), 134–35; GW to Hancock, October 5, 1777, *PGWR* 11:393–94.

41. Elbridge Gerry to JA, December 3, 1777, *LDC* 8:373–74; Taaffe, *Philadelphia Campaign*, 108–31; Council of War, October 29, 1777, *PGWR* 12:46–48. On Gates's response to the request for manpower, see John Ferling, *Jefferson and Hamilton: The Rivalry That*

Forged a Nation (New York, 2013), 72–73. Private Martin's account of his trials in a Delaware River fort can be found in George F. Scheer, ed., *Private Yankee Doodle: Being a Narrative of Some of the Adventures, Dangers and Sufferings of a Revolutionary Soldier, by Joseph Plumb Martin* (Boston, 1962), 84–92.

42. Taaffe, *Campaign for Philadelphia*, 131–44; Committee at Headquarters to George Washington, December 10, 1777, *LDC* 8:399–400; Gerry to James Warren, December 12, 1777, ibid., 8:404–5; GW, Circular to the General Officers of the Continental Army, December 3, 1777, *PGWR* 12:506. GW asked for written responses concerning the recommendations of the general officers. Their replies can be found in ibid., 12:379–84, 387–88, 391–94, 396–404.

43. NG to GW, November 24, 1777, *PGWR* 12:378.

44. GW to Henry Laurens, December 22, 23, 1777, ibid., 12:669–70, 685; editor's note, ibid., 12:642–44n.

CHAPTER 11: "THE CENTRAL STONE IN THE GEOMETRICAL ARCH": THE WAR IS TRANSFORMED IN 1778

1. Wayne K. Bodle, *Valley Forge Winter: Civilians and Soldiers in War* (University Park, Pa., 2002), 5–10, 103–4, 116; GW, General Orders, December 20, 1777, *PGWR* 12:641, 644n; Paine to BF, May 16, 1778, *PBF* 26:487; John Ferling, *Almost a Miracle: The American Victory in the War of Independence* (New York, 2007), 275–76.

2. GW to Henry Laurens, December 23, 1777, March 12, 1778, *PGWR* 12:683–87; 14:161; Benjamin Rush to GW, December 26, 1777, ibid., 13:7; NG to GW, January 1, 1778, *PNG* 2:241; NG to Christopher Greene, January 5, 1778, ibid., 2:247; Committee at Camp to Laurens, February 11, 12, 14, 20, 24, 25, 1778, *LDC* 9:73–75, 79–82, 95, 143–45, 163–64, 168–75, 206, 219–21; Ferling, *Almost a Miracle*, 276–81; Bodle, *Valley Forge Winter*, 103–42; Noel F. Busch, *Winter Quarters: George Washington and the Continental Army at Valley Forge* (New York, 1974), 49–53; Stephen R. Taaffe, *The Philadelphia Campaign, 1777–1778* (Lawrence, Kans., 2003), 148–53; George Scheer, ed., *Private Yankee Doodle: Being a Narrative of Some of the Adventures, Dangers and Sufferings of a Revolutionary Soldier* (Boston, 1962), 101–2; Charles Royster, *A Revolutionary People at War: The Continental Army and American Character, 1775–1783* (Chapel Hill, N.C., 1979), 191, 193; Charles H. Lesser, ed., *The Sinews of Independence: Monthly Strength Reports of the Continental Army* (Chicago, 1976), 55; Eric Robson, *The American Revolution: In Its Political and Military Aspects, 1763–1783* (Hamden, Conn., 1965), 160; "Diary of Albigence Waldo, of the Connecticut Line," *Pennsylvania Magazine of History and Biography* 21 (1897): 304–10; John Ferling, "Joseph Galloway's Military Advice: A Loyalist's View of the Revolution," ibid., 99 (1974): 174–76.

3. Edward G. Lengel, *General George Washington* (New York, 2005), 272.

4. Anthony Wayne to GW, February 26, 1778, *PGWR* 13:678; Taaffe, *Philadelphia Campaign*, 153–54; E. Wayne Carp, *To Starve the Army at Pleasure: Continental Army Administration and American Political Culture, 1775–1783* (Chapel Hill, N.C., 1984), 44, 55–73; James A. Huston, *Logistics of Liberty: American Services of Supply in the Revolutionary War and After* (Newark, Del., 1991), 67–68, 75, 82.

5. GW to Laurens, December 23, 1777, *PGWR* 12:683–87; GW to Henry, December 27, 1777, ibid., 13:17; GW to William Livingston, December 31, 1777, ibid., 13:86; GW to William Buchanan, February 7, 1778, ibid., 13:465; GW to George Greene, February 21, 1777, ibid., 13:619; GW to NG, February 12, 1778, ibid., 13:514; Bodle, *Valley Forge Winter*, 123, 165–220;

Taaffe, *Philadelphia Campaign*, 154; Carp, *To Starve the Army at Pleasure*, 81–85; NG to GW, February 15, 1777, *PNG* 2:285. For GW on Howe winning the war had he attacked, see Robson, *American Revolution*, 160.

6. Robson, *American Revolution*, 165–66.

7. See the useful discussion in Royster, *A Revolutionary People at War*, 373–78.

8. GW to Laurens, November 26[–27], 1777, *PGWR* 12:420.

9. Jonathan Dull, *A Diplomatic History of the American Revolution* (New Haven, Conn., 1985), 51–55.

10. Virginia Resolutions for Independence, June 7, 1776, *EHD* 9:868; Dull, *Diplomatic History of the American Revolution*, 53; *PJA* 4:260–302; William C. Stinchcombe, *The American Revolution and the French Alliance* (Syracuse, N.Y., 1969), 7–8.

11. JA to James Lovell, July 26, 1778, *PJA* 6:318–19; Vegennes to Marquis de Lafayette, August 7, 1780, April 19, 1781, *LLP* 3:129, 4:47; American Commissioners to the Committee for Foreign Affairs, December 18, 1777, *PBF* 25:305–6; editors notes, ibid., 25:234n, 306n; Dull, *Diplomatic History of the American Revolution*, 75–91; Orville T. Murphy, "The Battle of Germantown and the Franco-American Alliance of 1778," *Pennsylvania Magazine of History and Biography*, 82 (1958): 55–64.

12. The Franco-American Treaty of Alliance, February 6, 1778, *PBF* 25:585–625; BF and Deane to the President of Congress, February 8, 1778, ibid., 25:635; BF to David Hartley, February 12, 1778, ibid., 25:651; Dull, *Diplomatic History of the American Revolution*, 93–96; Carl Van Doren, *Benjamin Franklin* (New York, 1938), 594.

13. Alan Valentine, *Lord George Germain* (Oxford, Eng., 1962), 261, 263, 265; *PH* 19:540.

14. Piers Mackesy, *The War for America, 1775–1783* (Cambridge, Mass., 1965), 180; *PH* 19:488, 525, 538, 1200.

15. On Britain's logistical nightmare, see Arthur Bowler, *Logistics and the Failure of the British Army in America, 1775–1783* (Princeton, N.J., 1975).

16. The two preceding paragraphs draw on Brendan Simms, *Three Victories and a Defeat: The Rise and Fall of the First British Empire* (New York, 2007), 618–21; Piers Mackesy, *War for America*, 153; Stephen Conway, "The British Army, 'Military Europe,' and the American War of Independence," *WMQ* 67 (2010): 73–75, 78; Edward S. Curtis, *The Organization of the British Army in the American Revolution* (New Haven, Conn., 1926), 56–60.

17. Valentine, *Lord North*, 473–549; Charles R. Ritcheson, *British Politics and the American Revolution* (Norman, Okla., 1964), 233–86; Mackesy, *War for America*, 153–61, 165–70, 181–86; Jim Piecuch, *Three Peoples, One King: Loyalists, Indians, and Slaves in the Revolutionary South, 1775–1782* (Columbia, S.C., 2008), 127.

18. Editor's notes, *PBF* 26:94–95n, 334–35n. BF is quoted in Eliga H. Gould, *Among the Powers of the Earth: The American Revolution and the Making of a New World Empire* (Cambridge, Mass., 2012), 79.

19. Ritcheson, *British Politics and the American Revolution*, 258; Valentine, *Lord North*, 473–500; Peter D. G. Thomas, *Lord North* (London, 1976), 116; Peter Whitely, *Lord North: The Prime Minister Who Lost America* (London, 1996), 174; Andrew Jackson O'Shaughnessy, *The Men Who Lost America: British Leadership, the American Revolution and the Fate of the Empire* (New Haven, Conn., 2013), 62; *PH* 19:762–67; Weldon Brown, *Empire or Independence: A Study in the Failure of Reconciliation, 1774–1783* (Baton Rouge, La., 1941), 225–26.

20. Ritcheson, *British Politics and the American Revolution*, 268–69.

21. GW, Circular to the States, December 29, 1777, *PGWR* 13:36–37; GW to John Banister, April 21, 1778, ibid., 14:575–76.

22. GW to Nicholas Cooke, May 26, 1778, *PGWR* 15:223; GW to J. A. Washington, May [?], 1778, ibid., 15:286; Richard Henry Lee to TJ, May 3, 1778, *LDC* 9:586; John Banister to Theodorick Bland, May 3, 1778, ibid., 9:569.

23. GW to Laurens, March 24, 1778, *PGWR* 14:292–93; From a Board of General Officers, November 10, 1777, ibid., 12:188–89; JA to AA, June 3, 1776, May 22, 1777, *AFC* 2:5, 245; Taaffe, *Philadelphia Campaign*, 154–56.

24. Royster, *A Revolutionary People at War*, 231, 240–41.

25. Laurens to Lafayette, January 12, 1778, *LDC* 8:572; *PGWR* 13:695n, 14:551n; GW to a Continental Camp Committee, January 29, 1778, ibid., 13:376–404; GW to Laurens, April 30, 1778, ibid., 14:682; Gouverneur Morris to GW, May 15, 1778, ibid., 15:127–28; Ferling, *Almost a Miracle*, 284–88; Lengel, *General George Washington*, 275–76; Royster, *A Revolutionary People at War*, 198–201, 213–38.

26. JA to Rush, March 19, 1812, in John A. Schutz and Douglass Adair, eds., *The Spur of Fame: Dialogues of John Adams and Benjamin Rush, 1805–1813* (San Marino, Calif., 1966), 213; Rush to JA, January 6, 1806, February 12, 1812, ibid., 46, 207–8; Laurens to John Laurens, October 16, 1777, January 8, 1778, in Philip M. Hamer, et al., eds., *The Papers of Henry Laurens* (Columbia, S.C., 1968–), 11:554–55, 12:275; Alexander Hamilton to Schuyler, February 18, 1781, *PAH* 2:565–67; AH to James McHenry, February 18, 1781, ibid., 2:569; Jonathan G. Rossie, *The Politics of Command in the American Revolution* (Syracuse, N.Y., 1975), 192.

27. GW to Thomas Conway, November 5, 16, 1777, *PGWR* 12:129, 277; Conway to GW, November 5, 1777, ibid., 12:130–31; GW to Laurens, January 2, 1778, ibid., 13:119; John Ferling, *The Ascent of George Washington: The Hidden Political Genius of an American Icon* (New York, 2009), 140–55; Bernard Knollenberg, *Washington and the Revolution: A Reappraisal* (New York, 1941), 40–41; Laurens to Lafayette, January 12, 1778, *LDC* 8:572; *PGWR* 13:695n, 14:551n; GW to a Continental Camp Committee, January 29, 1778, ibid., 13:376–404; GW to Laurens, April 30, 1778, ibid., 14:682; Gouverneur Morris to GW, May 15, 1778, ibid., 15:127–28; Ferling, *Almost a Miracle*, 284–88; Lengel, *General George Washington*, 275–76; Royster, *A Revolutionary People at War*, 198–201, 213–38.

28. Laurens to John Lewis Gervais, September 5, 1777, Hamer, *Papers of Henry Laurens*, 11:498–99; John Laurens to Laurens, January 3, 1778, ibid., 12:246; Laurens to John Laurens, January 8, 1778, ibid., 12:273; Abraham Clark to William Alexander, January 15, 1778, *LDC* 8:597; Knollenberg, *Washington and the Revolution*, 58.

29. Royster, *A Revolutionary People at War*, 193–213; GW to John Banister, April 21, 1778, *PGWR* 14:577.

30. Rush to William Gordon, December 10, 1778, in Lyman H. Butterfield, ed., *Letters of Benjamin Rush* (Princeton, N.J., 1951), 1:221; JA to Rush, March 19, 1812, Schutz and Adair, *Spur of Fame*, 212. See also Laurens to Isaac Motte, January 26, 1778, Hamer, *Papers of Henry Laurens*, 12:346, 348; Laurens to John Laurens, January 8, 1778, ibid., 12:272; Laurens to William Smith, September 12, 1778, ibid., 14:302.

31. Thomas Fleming, *Washington's Secret War: The Hidden History of Valley Forge* (New York, 2005), 191–92; Paul K. Longmore, *The Invention of George Washington* (Berkeley, Calif., 1988), 204–5; Barry Schwartz, *George Washington: The Making of an American Symbol* (New York, 1987), 23–33.

32. GW, General Orders, April 20, May 7, 1778, *PGWR* 14:567, 15:70; GW to Alexander McDougall, March 31, 1778, ibid., 14:370; Washington's Thoughts upon a Plan of Operations

for Campaign 1778, [April 26–29], 1778, ibid., 14:641–48; GW to Thomas Nelson, February 8, 1778, ibid., 13:481; Council of War, May 8, 1778, ibid., 15:79–81; From a Council of War, May 9, 1778, ibid., 15:83–87; James Duane to Gates, December 16, 1777, *LDC* 8:421; Laurens to Augustin de La Balme, January 11, 1778, ibid, 8:559–60; Laurens to Lafayette, January 22, 1778, ibid., 8:634–35; Paul David Nelson, *General Horatio Gates: A Biography* (Baton Rouge, La., 1976), 172.

33. Germain to Clinton, September 25, 1778, *DAR* 15:208; O'Shaughnessy, *Men Who Lost America*, 213.

34. Council of War, June 24, 1778, *PGWR* 15:520–21; ibid., 15:522n; Lee to GW, June 18, 1778, ibid., 15:457–58; Wayne to GW, June 24, 1778, ibid., 15:534–35; AH to Elias Boudinot, July 5, 1778, *PAH* 1:510; NG to GW, June 24, 1778, *PNG* 2:446–47; John Richard Alden, *General Charles Lee: Traitor or Patriot?* (Baton Rouge, La., 1951), 205–6, 208–10.

35. *PGWR*, 15:573–75n; GW to Laurens, July 1, 1778, ibid., 16:2–6; Mackesy, *War for America*, 215; Paul David Nelson, *Anthony Wayne: Soldier of the Early Republic* (Bloomington, Ind., 77–80; Christopher Ward, *The War of the Revolution* (New York, 1952), 2:579; Theodore Thayer, *The Making of a Scapegoat: Washington and Lee at Monmouth* (Port Washington, N.Y., 1976), 36–56; Taaffe, *Philadelphia Campaign*, 196–224.

36. Lengel, *General George Washington*, 300; Testimony of Colonel Richard Harrison, in *SOS*, 2:712; George F. Scheer and Hugh F. Rankin, *Rebels and Redcoats* (Cleveland, Ohio, 1957), 331; Harry Ward, *Charles Scott and the "Spirit of '76"* (Charlottesville, Va., 1988), 50–51.

37. Lafayette, "Memoirs of 1779," *LLP* 2:11; AH to Boudinot, July 5, 1778, *PAH* 1:512; Taaffe, *Campaign for Philadelphia*, 218–19; GW, General Orders, June 29, 1778, *PGWR* 15:583–84; editor's note, ibid., 573–76n.

38. GW to J. A. Washington, July 4, 1778, *PGWR* 16:25–26; GW to Laurens, June 28, July 1, 1778, ibid., 15:578–79; 16:2–6; Ward, *Charles Scott*, 49–51; Lengel, *General George Washington*, 297–304; Thayer, *Making of a Scapegoat*, 36–58; Taaffe, *Campaign for Philadelphia*, 212–24; Ward, *War of the Revolution*, 2:576–85. The most detailed account of the engagement is that of William S. Stryker and William S. Myers, *The Battle of Monmouth* (Princeton, N.J., 1927).

39. GW, Loose Thoughts about an Attack on New York, ND, *PGWR* 16:68–71n; GW to Laurens, July 12, 1778, ibid., 16:59–60; GW to Trumbull Sr., July 22, 1778, ibid., 16:136–37; GW to John Parke Custis, [August 4–8, 1778], ibid., 16:242.

40. GW to J. A. Washington, September 23, 1778, ibid., 17:110–12; James Thomas Flexner, *George Washington in the American Revolution, 1775–1783* (Boston, 1968), 324; Ward, *War of the Revolution*, 2:588.

41. Charles P. Whittemore, *General of the Revolution: John Sullivan of New Hampshire* (New York, 1961), 64–68; NG to Charles Pettit, August 22, 1778, *PNG* 2:491, 2:485n; Ira Gruber, *The Howe Brothers and the American Revolution* (New York, 1972), 316–17. For the most detailed account of the campaign, see Paul F. Darden, *The Rhode Island Campaign of 1778: Inauspicious Dawn of Alliance* (Providence, R.I., 1980).

CHAPTER 12: "THE LONGEST PURSE WILL WIN THE WAR": REFORM AT HOME WHILE THE WAR TAKES A NEW TURN

1. Barbara Clark Smith, *The Freedoms We Lost: Consent and Resistance in Revolutionary America* (New York, 2010), 3–18. The quotation is on page 14.

2. JA to Henry, June 3, 1776, *PJA* 4:234–35.

3. JA, The Earl of Clarendon to William Pym, January 27, 1766, ibid., 1:165; JA to Henry, June 3, 1776, ibid., 4:234–35; JA, Humphrey Ploughjogger to Philanthrop, [ante January 5, 1767], ibid., 1:179; JA, "U" to the *Boston Gazette,* July 18, 1763, ibid., 1:71; *DAJA* 1:207; JA to AA, July 3, 1776, *AFC* 2:28; Gordon S. Wood, *The Radicalism of the American Revolution* (New York, 1991), 169–89, 229–32.

4. Thomas Paine, *Common Sense* (1776), in Philip Foner, ed., *The Complete Writings of Thomas Paine* (New York, 1945), 1:27.

5. Jackson Turner Main, *The Sovereign States, 1775–1783* (New York, 1973), 143–221; Gordon S. Wood, *The American Revolution: A History* (New York, 2003), 65–70; Elisha P. Douglass, *Rebels and Democrats: The Struggle for Equal Political Rights and Majority Rule During the American Revolution* (Chapel Hill, N.C., 1955), 296.

6. Main, *Sovereign States,* 151–54; Gary B. Nash, *The Unknown American Revolution: The Unruly Birth of Democracy and the Struggle to Create America* (New York, 2005), 268–77.

7. Theodore Thayer, *Pennsylvania Politics and the Growth of Democracy, 1740–1776* (Harrisburg, Pa., 1953), 184–97. Rush is quoted in Nash, *Unknown American Revolution,* 277. On JA, see JA to Warren, February 3, June 11, 1777, *PJA* 5:76, 221; JA to Francis Dana, August 16, 1776, ibid., 4:466; JA to AA, October 4, 1776, *AFC* 2:138.

8. JA to AA, April 28, 1776, *AFC* 1:401.

9. JA to AA, July 10, 1776, ibid., 2:43.

10. David Conroy, *Public Houses: Drink and the Revolution of Authority in Colonial Massachusetts* (Chapel Hill, N.C., 1995), 254, 276.

11. Bernard Bailyn, *The Ideological Origins of the American Revolution* (Cambridge, Mass., 1967), 94–95.

12. Wood, *Radicalism of the American Revolution,* 190.

13. Michael A. McDonnell, *The Politics of War: Race, Class, and Conflict in Revolutionary Virginia* (Chapel Hill, N.C., 2007), 90–124, 149–50, 197–98, 253–54, 276–85, 353, 377–80, 389. McDonnell's quote is on page 312. The "ensure success" quotation is in Harry M. Ward, *The War for Independence and the Transformation of American Society* (London, 1999), 111.

14. Jackson Turner Main, "The American Revolution and the Democratization of the Legislatures," *WMQ* 23 (1966): 391–406. The quotes are on pages 406–7.

15. Maya Jasanoff, *Liberty's Exiles: American Loyalists in the Revolutionary World* (New York, 2011), 357. The Warren quotation is from Wood, *Radicalism of the American Revolution,* 177.

16. TJ to JA, October 28, 1813, *AJL* 2:389; TJ, Third Draft by Jefferson of a Constitution [before June 13, 1776], *PTJ* 1:362; TJ to George Wythe, November 1, 1778, August 13, 1786, ibid., 1:230, 10:244; TJ, Bill No. 20, ibid., 2:391–93, 393n; TJ, Bill No. 82, ibid., 2:545–47; TJ to James Madison, December 16, 1786, ibid., 10:603–4; TJ, Autobiography, in Saul K. Padover, ed., *The Complete Thomas Jefferson* (reprint, Freeport, N.Y., 1969), 1144–46; John Selby, *The Revolution in Virginia* (Charlottesville, Va., 1980), 145, 160; R. B. Bernstein, *Thomas Jefferson* (New York, 2003), 38–40; Merrill D. Peterson, "Jefferson and Religious Freedom," *Atlantic Monthly* 272 (December 1994): 113–24.

17. Wood, *Radicalism of the American Revolution,* 234.

18. AA to JA, March 31, 1776, *AFC* 1:370; JA to AA, April 14, 1776, ibid., 1:382; Mary Beth Norton, *Liberty's Daughters: The Revolutionary Experience of American Women, 1750–1800* (Boston, 1980), 50, 110. Hannah Corbin is quoted in Douglas Bradburn, *The Citizenship*

Revolution: Politics and the Creation of the American Political Union, 1774-1804 (Charlottesville, Va., 2009), 52.

19. Peter Kolchin, *American Slavery, 1619-1877* (New York, 1993), 63-70.

20. Hopkins is quoted in David Waldstreicher, *Runaway America: Benjamin Franklin, Slavery, and the American Revolution* (New York, 2004), 176. Otis, Lee, and Rush are quoted in Douglas R. Egerton, *Death or Liberty: African Americans and Revolutionary America* (New York, 2009), 44-45, 47, 48. See also Thomas Paine, "African Slavery in America" (1775), in Philip S. Foner, ed., *Complete Writings of Thomas Paine* (New York, 1945), 2:16-19. Paine's quote is on page 16.

21. Bernard Bailyn, *The Ideological Origins of the American Revolution* (Cambridge, Mass., 1967), 230-46; Benjamin Quarles, *The Negro in the American Revolution* (Chapel Hill, N.C., 1961), 40-41; GW, Address to the Inhabitants of Canada, September 1, 1775, *PGWR* 1:461.

22. Milton E. Flower, *John Dickinson: Conservative Revolutionary* (Charlottesville, Va., 1983), 175-79; John Dickinson, "Notes," July 1, 1776, *LDC* 4:354; *DAJA* 2:245-46; Merrill Jensen, *The Articles of Confederation: The Interpretation of the Social-Constitutional History of the American Revolution, 1774-1781* (Madison, Wisc., 1940), 144-48.

23. The foregoing draws on Main, *Sovereign States*, 222-52; E. James Ferguson, *The Power of the Purse* (Chapel Hill, N.C., 1961), 25-100; Richard D. Brown, "The Confiscation and Disposition of Loyalists' Estates in Suffolk County, Massachusetts, *WMQ* 21 (1964): 534-50; Staughton Lynd, "Who Shall Rule at Home? Dutchess County, New York, in the American Revolution," *WMQ* 18 (1961): 352-53. The "wagon load" quotation can be found in GW to John Jay, April 23, 1779, *PGWR* 20:176.

24. These two paragraphs draw on GW to George Mason, March 27, 1779, *PGWR* 19:627; GW to Benjamin Harrison, December 18[-30], 1778, ibid., 18:449-50.

25. GW to Mason, March 27, 1779, ibid., 19:627-28.

26. GW to John Jay, April 14, 1779, ibid., 20:57-64; GW to Laurens, November 11, 14, 1778, ibid., 20:94-105, 149-51, 105-12n.

27. Laurens to GW, November 20, 1778, ibid., 18:230-33.

28. Commissioners for Quieting Disorders to Germain, November 16, 1778, *DAR* 15:258-59; Germain to Clinton, March 8, 1778, ibid., 15:60; Jim Piecuch, *Three Peoples, One King: Loyalists, Indians, and Slaves in the Revolutionary South, 1775-1782* (Columbia, S.C., 2008), 134; David K. Wilson, *The Southern Strategy: Britain's Conquest of South Carolina and Georgia, 1775-1780* (Columbia, S.C., 2005), 65-80; Christopher Ward, *The War of the Revolution* (New York, 1952), 2:679-83; Cassandra Pybus, "Jefferson's Faulty Math: The Question of Slave Defections in the American Revolution," *WMQ* 62 (2005): 253.

29. John Henry to Thomas Johnson, January 30, 1779, *LDC* 11:538; Laurens to Reed, February 9, 1779, ibid., 12:39; John Ferling, *Almost a Miracle: The American Victory in the War of Independence* (New York, 2007), 345, 385.

30. Gage to Lord Shelburne, June 13, 1767, *CGTG* 1:141-42; TJ to George Rogers Clark, December 25, 1780, *PTJ* 4:237-38; Jack M. Sosin, *The Revolutionary Frontier, 1763-1783* (Albuquerque, New Mexico, 1967), 111-20; Gregory Evans Dowd, *A Spirited Resistance: The North American Indian Struggle for Unity, 1745-1815* (Baltimore, 1992), 68-83; John E. Selby, *The Revolution in Virginia, 1775-1783* (Williamsburg, Va., 1988), 184-203. Selby's quote is on page 203.

31. John Stark to GW, September 28, 1778, *PGWR* 17:169; ibid., 18:181n; Isabel T. Kelsay, *Joseph Brant, 1743-1807: Man of Two Worlds* (Syracuse, N.Y., 1984), 43-67, 109-15, 134, 155,

160–73, 279; Glenn F. Williams, *Year of the Hangman: George Washington's Campaign Against the Iroquois* (Yardley, Pa., 2005), 18–19, 32–34, 185, 298; Max Mintz, *Seeds of Empire: The American Revolutionary Conquest of the Iroquois* (New York, 1999), 7–8, 14–20, 72–73; Joseph R. Fischer, *A Well-Executed Failure: The Sullivan Campaign Against the Iroquois, July-September 1779* (Columbia, S.C., 1997), 9–33; Alan Taylor, *The Divided Ground: Indians, Settlers, and the Northern Borderland of the American Revolution* (New York, 2006), 3–94; Dale Van Every, *A Company of Heroes: The American Frontier, 1775–1783* (New York, 1962), 88–92; Ward, *War of the Revolution*, 2:633–37. See also Barbara Graymont, *The Iroquois in the American Revolution* (Syracuse, N.Y., 1972). The notion that Brant snatched the leadership role from sachem chief was Graymont's. See ibid., 115–16. For an overview of the above, and much more, see Colin Calloway, *The American Revolution in Indian Country* (Cambridge, Eng., 1995). The quote "We mind nothing but Peace" is taken from Calloway, page 29.

32. GW to General Edward Hand, October 19, 1778, *PGWR* 17:462; GW to Schuyler, January 25, 1779, ibid., 19:73; GW to General Lachlan McIntosh, January 31, 1779, ibid., 19:114, 116.

33. GW to Sullivan, May 31, 1779, ibid., 20:716, 718.

34. Fischer, *A Well-Executed Failure*, 1–2, 43–80; Sullivan to Congress, August 15, 1779, Otis G. Hammond, ed., *Letters and Papers of Major-General John Sullivan, Continental Army* (Concord, N.H., 1930–1939), 3:97; Taylor, *Divided Ground*, 97–108; Ward, *War of the Revolution*, 2:638–45; Kelsay, *Joseph Brant*, 254–71. Brant's letter is in Kelsay, *Joseph Brant*, 286.

35. TJ to Jay, June 19, 1779, *PTJ* 3:5; Michael Kranish, *Flight from Monticello: Thomas Jefferson at War* (New York, 2010), 114–17; Michael A. McDonnell, *The Politics of War: Race, Class, and Conflict in Revolutionary Virginia* (Chapel Hill, N.C., 2007), 343–44; David Syrett, *The Royal Navy in American Waters, 1775–1783* (Aldershot, Eng., 1989), 121–23, 129.

36. William B. Willcox, *Portrait of a General: Sir Henry Clinton in the War of Independence* (New York, 1964), 276; GW to Schuyler, June 9, 1779, *PGWR* 21:117–18; Syrett, *Royal Navy in American Waters*, 124–25.

37. Douglas Southall Freeman, *George Washington: A Biography* (New York, 1948–1957), 5:109; Andrew Jackson O'Shaughnessy, *The Men Who Lost America: British Leadership, the American Revolution, and the Fate of the Empire* (New Haven, Conn., 2013), 224–28; Henry Clinton, *The American Rebellion: Sir Henry Clinton's Narrative of His Campaigns, 1775–1782*, ed., William B. Willcox (New Haven, Conn., 1954), 190–94.

38. Ward, *War of the Revolution*, 2:596–603; Paul David Nelson, *Anthony Wayne: Soldier of the Early Republic* (Bloomington, Ind., 1985), 94–100; Chernow, *Washington*, 362–63; GW to Jay, July 21, 1779, *PGWR* 21:596–600; Gates to GW, July 25, 1779, ibid., 21:645.

39. Ferling, *Almost a Miracle*, 382–88.

40. Piecuch, *Three Peoples, One King*, 146–48, 169; Wilson, *Southern Strategy*, 133–77; Ward, *War of the Revolution*, 2:688–94; Henry Lumpkin, *From Savannah to Yorktown: The American Revolution in the South* (Columbia, S.C., 1981), 27–40.

41. GW to Joseph Reed, May 28, 1780, WW: 18:436–38.

CHAPTER 13: "WHOM CAN WE TRUST NOW?": A YEAR OF DISASTERS, 1780

1. GW to Lafayette, March 18, 1780, WW 18:126; Schuyler, January 30, 1780, ibid., 17:467; George F. Scheer, ed., *Private Yankee Doodle: Being a Narrative of Some of the Adventures and Sufferings of a Revolutionary Soldier* (Boston, 1962), 169–70, 172; James Thacher, *Military*

Journal of the American Revolution (reprint, New York, 1969), 184–85; NG to Moore Freeman, January 4, 1780, *PNG* 5:230; NG to Christopher Greene, February 10, 1780, ibid., 5:363; NG to Jeremiah Wadsworth, March 17, 1780, ibid., 5:460; NG to Griffin Greene, April 25, 1780, ibid., 5:531–32; Edward G. Lengel, *General George Washington* (New York, 2005), 319; James T. Flexner, *George Washington in the American Revolution* (Boston, 1967), 354–56; Douglas Southall Freeman, *George Washington: A Biography* (New York, 1948–1957), 5:143–53.

2. E. Wayne Carp, *To Starve the Army at Pleasure: Continental Army Administration and American Political Culture, 1775-1783* (Chapel Hill, N.C., 1984), 171–73; GW to Fielding Lewis, May 5[–July 6], 1780, *WW* 19:132; GW to President of Congress, April 3, 1780, ibid., 18:209; GW to Henry Champion, May 26, 1780, ibid., 18:424; GW to William Heath, December 21, 1779, ibid., 17:295; GW to Livingston, December 21, 1779, ibid., 17:293; GW to Steuben, April 2, 1780, ibid., 18:203; Lengel, *General George Washington*, 320–21; Ron Chernow, *Washington: A Life* (New York, 2010), 368; Stephen Brumwell, *George Washington: Gentleman Warrior* (New York, 2012), 358–59.

3. Scheer, *Private Yankee Doodle*, 68–69, 107, 111–12, 186, 198, 285; Don Higginbotham, *The War of Independence: Military Attitudes, Policies, and Practice, 1776-1789* (New York, 1971), 399–401; Charles Royster, *A Revolutionary People at War: The Continental Army and American Character, 1775-1783* (Chapel Hill, N.C., 1979), 71; Charles H. Lesser, *The Sinews of Independence: Monthly Strength Reports of the Continental Army* (Chicago, 1976), 59–61, 101, 149, 194; Allen Bowman, *The Morale of the Revolutionary Army* (Washington, D.C., 1943), 63–92; Daniel Barber, *The History of My Own Times* (Washington, D.C., 1827), 16; Herbert T. Wade and Robert A. Lively, eds., *The Glorious Cause: The Adventures of Two Company Officers in Washington's Army* (Princeton, N.J., 1958), 174; "Itinerary of the Pennsylvania Line from Pennsylvania to South Carolina, 1781-1782," *Pennsylvania Magazine of History and Biography* 36 (1912): 273–92; James McMichael, "Diary of Lt. James McMichael, of the Pennsylvania Line, 1776-1778," ibid., 16:153; John Ferling, *A Wilderness of Miseries: War and Warriors in Early America* (Westport, Conn., 1980), 100–101; Harry M. Ward, *George Washington's Enforcers: Policing the Continental Army* (Carbondale, Ill., 2006), 92–98, 102–5; Charles Bolton, *The Private Soldier under Washington* (London, 1902), 77, 143, 145, 151.

4. Caroline Cox, *A Proper Sense of Honor: Service and Sacrifice in George Washington's Army* (Chapel Hill, N.C., 2004), 76–117; Jim Piecuch, ed., *Cavalry of the American Revolution* (Yardley, Pa., 2012), 13; Ward, *George Washington's Enforcers*, 156–57, 163, 175, 183–84, 186; Scheer, *Private Yankee Doodle*, 255–56.

5. Howard H. Peckham, *The Toll of Independence: Engagements and Battle Casualties of the American Revolution* (Chicago, 1974), 11, 28, 46, 56, 66, 78, 93, 99, 108, 113, 117, 120, 123, 125–27, 130–34; Elizabeth A. Fenn, *Pox Americana: The Great Smallpox Epidemic of 1775-1782* (New York, 2001), 14–79, 87–92; GW to William Shippen, January 28, 1777, *PGWR* 8:174; GW to Hancock, February 5, 1777, ibid., 8:251.

6. Robert Wright, *The Continental Army* (Washington, D.C., 1983), 105-7, 128–46; Brumwell, *George Washington*, 325–28; Charles Neimeyer, *America Goes to War: A Social History of the Continental Army* (New York, 1996), 27–64; Ward, *George Washington's Enforcers*, 140–43; Scheer, *Private Yankee Doodle*, 197–98.

7. Council of War, July 9, October 8, 1775, *PGWR* 1:79–80; 2:125; GW, General Orders, November 12, 1775, ibid., 2:354–55; GW to Hancock, July 10[–11], December 31, 1775, ibid., 1:90, 2:624; Henry Wiencek, *An Imperfect God: George Washington, His Slaves, and the Creation of America* (New York, 2003), 196–205; Joyce Lee Malcolm, "Slavery in

Massachusetts and the American Revolution," *Journal of the Historical Society* 10 (210): 429–34.

8. Benjamin Quarles, *The Negro in the American Revolution* (Chapel Hill, N.C., 1961), ix, 52–57; Alan Gilbert, *Black Patriots and Loyalists: Fighting for Emancipation in the War of Independence* (Chicago, 2012), 95–115; Judith L. Van Buskirk, "Claiming Their Due: African Americans in the Revolutionary War and Its Aftermath," in John Resch and Walter Sargent, eds., *War and Society in the American Revolution: Mobilization and Home Fronts* (DeKalb, Ill., 2007), 134–35, 138; Gary B. Nash, *The Forgotten Fifth: African Americans in the Age of Revolution* (Cambridge, Mass., 2006), 12–13; Douglas R. Egerton, *Death or Liberty: African Americans and Revolutionary America* (New York, 2009), 75–85; Wiencek, *An Imperfect God*, 223–32; Gregory D. Massey, *John Laurens and the American Revolution* (Columbia, S.C., 2000), 93–97, 130–31; Neimeyer, *America Goes to War*, 65–88; Ray Raphael, *A People's History of the American Revolution: How Common People Shaped the Fight for Independence* (New York, 2001), 261–62, 290; Philip D. Morgan and Andrew Jackson O'Shaughnessy, "Arming Slaves in the American Revolution," in Christopher Leslie Brown and Philip D. Morgan, eds., *Arming Slaves: From Classical Times to the Modern Age* (New Haven, Conn., 2006), 192–94; Thomas Burke's Draft Committee Report, [ante March 25, 1779], *LDC* 12:242–44, 244n; Henry Laurens's Draft Committee Report, [ante March 25, 1779], ibid., 12:247; Burke to GW, March 24, 1779, March 24, 1779, ibid., 12:238–39; H. Laurens to GW, March 16, 1779, ibid., 12:200; AH to Jay, March 14, 1779, *PAH* 2:17–19 GW to H. Laurens, March 20, 1779, *WW* 14:267.

9. See Holly Mayer, *Belonging to the Army: Camp Followers and Community During the American Revolution* (Columbia, S.C., 1996); Walter Blumenthal, *Women Camp Followers of the American Revolution* (reprint, New York, 1974); John Rees, " 'The Multitude of Women': An Examination of the Number of Female Camp Followers with the Continental Army," *Minerva* 14 (1996): 3–30; Harry M. Ward, *The War of Independence and the Transformation of American Society* (London, 1999), 117–22.

10. Raphael, *People's History of the American Revolution*, 112; Dorothy Denneen Volo and James M. Volo, *Daily Life During the American Revolution* (Westport, Conn., 2003), 232–34; Ward, *War of Independence*, 148; Elizabeth Cometti, "Women in the American Revolution," *New England Quarterly* 20 (1947): 329–46; Linda Grant DePauw and Conover Hunt, *Remember the Ladies: Women in America, 1750–1815* (New York, 1976), 86.

11. AA to JA, July 12, August 10, September 16, 25, October 1, 9, 1775, March 31, 1776, *AFC* 1:243, 272, 279, 284, 288, 297–98, 370.

12. Raphael, *People's History of the American Revolution*, 113–14; Mary Beth Norton, *Liberty's Daughters: The Revolutionary Experience of American Women, 1750–1800* (Boston, 1980), 219; Ward, *War of Independence*, 84, 109; Robert Middlekauff, *The Glorious Cause: The American Revolution, 1763–1789* (revised edition, New York, 2005), 545–51. For a good example of the travail of a woman left behind and her alternating temperament, see the letters of Sarah Hodgkins to her absent husband in Herbert T. Wade and Robert A. Lively, eds., *This Glorious Cause: The Adventures of Two Company Officers in Washington's Army* (Princeton, N.J., 1958). On Abigail Adams, see Edith B. Gelles, *Abigail and John: Portrait of a Marriage* (New York, 2009), 61–109; Woody Holton, "Abigail Adams, Bond Speculator," *WMQ* 64 (2007): 821–38, and Woody Holton, *Abigail Adams* (New York, 2009).

13. Sarah Hodgkins to Joseph Hodgkins, October 9, November 19, December 10, 1775, February 1, 11, May 23, October 19, 1776, April 26, 1778, in Herbert T. Wade and Robert A.

Lively, eds., *This Glorious Cause: The Adventures of Two Company Officers in Washington's Army* (Princeton, N.J., 1958), 178, 184, 186, 191, 192, 203, 224, 239–40; AA to JA, August 5, 1782, *AFC* 4:358.

14. Raymond C. Werner, ed., *Diary of Grace Growden Galloway* (New York, 1971), 54, 60, 80, 85, 87, 158, 167, 172, 177, 178, 180, 189.

15. Prevost to Clinton, March 1, May 21, 1779, *DAR* 17:69–70, 127–29; Prevost to Germain, June 10, 1779, ibid., 17:141–43; Clinton to Germain, April 4, May 22, December 15, 1779, ibid., 17:97, 129–30, 259–60; William B. Willcox, *Portrait of a General: Sir Henry Clinton in the War of Independence* (New York, 1962), 289–99; David Ramsay, *The History of the American Revolution* (reprint, Indianapolis, Ind., 1990), 2:27; David K. Wilson, *The Southern Strategy: Britain's Conquest of South Carolina and Georgia, 1775–1780* (Columbia, S.C., 2005), 81–13; James Lovell to Gates, November 11, 1779, *LDC* 14:179.

16. Andrew Jackson O'Shaughnessy, *The Men Who Lost America: British Leadership, the American Revolution, and the Fate of Empire* (New Haven, Conn., 2013), 230. The quotation is in John Ferling, *Almost a Miracle: The American Victory in the War of Independence* (New York, 2007), 411.

17. Carl P. Borick, *A Gallant Defense: The Siege of Charleston, 1780* (Columbia, S.C., 2003), 34–36, 39–40, 66; Samuel Huntington to GW, November 10, 1779, *LDC* 14:173; GW to Congress, November 29, 1779, *WW* 17:206; Wilson, *Southern Strategy*, 196, 208; Lincoln to TJ, January 7, 1780, *PTJ* 3:260–61.

18. Ferling, *Almost a Miracle*, 415; John Buchanan, *The Road to Guilford Courthouse: The American Revolution in the Carolinas* (New York, 1997), 27; Paul H. Smith, *Loyalists and Redcoats: A Study in British Revolutionary Policy* (Chapel Hill, N.C., 1964), 13–78.

19. Peter Russell, "The Siege of Charleston: Journal of Peter Russell, December 25, 1779, to May 2, 1780," *American Historical Review* 4 (1899): 484; Borick, *A Gallant Defense*, 49–65; Anthony Allaire, *Diary of Lieut. Anthony Allaire* (reprint, New York, 1968), 10.

20. David Mattern, *Benjamin Lincoln and the American Revolution* (Columbia, S.C., 1995), 6–58.

21. Borick, *A Gallant Defense*, 115–18; Mattern, *Benjamin Lincoln*, 93, 96.

22. GW to Congress, April 2, 1780, *WW* 18:198–99.

23. Willcox, *Portrait of a General*, 303–8; Borick, *A Gallant Defense*, 66, 71–73, 96–108, 121–26, 130–34, 145–60; Wilson, *Southern Strategy*, 200–225, 246–47; Robert D. Bass, *The Green Dragoon: The Lives of Banastre Tarleton and Mary Robinson* (reprint, Orangeburg, S.C., 1973), 11–31; Buchanan, *Road to Guilford Courthouse*, 58–60, 196–98, 202; Elizabeth A. Fenn, *Pox Americana: The Great Smallpox Epidemic of 1775–82* (New York, 2001), 117; Clinton to Germain, May 13, 1780, *DAR* 18:87.

24. Borick, *A Gallant Defense*, 152–54; Lachlan McIntosh, "Journal of the Siege of Charleston, 1780," Lilla Hawes, ed., *University of Georgia Libraries Miscellanea Publications* 7 (Athens, 1968), 104–5, 107.

25. Borick, *A Gallant Defense*, 136–38, 172–73; Johann Ewald, *Diary of the American War: A Hessian Soldier*, ed., Joseph P. Tustin (New Haven, Conn., 1979), 237; Uhlendorf, *Siege of Charleston*, 287, 395; Memoirs of General William Moultrie, in *SOS* 2:1109; Hugh Rankin, *The North Carolina Continentals* (Chapel Hill, N.C. . 1971), 228–29; Clinton to Lincoln, May 8, 1780, in *Original Papers Relating to the Siege of Charleston, 1780* (Charleston, S.C., 1898), 39; Mark Urban, *Fusiliers: The Saga of a British Redcoat Regiment in the American Revolution* (New York, 2007), 189. Clinton's "Blockheads" comment can be found in Stephen Conway,

"The British Army, 'Military Europe,' and the American War of Independence," *WMQ* 67 (2010): 95.

26. Clinton to Germain, May 13, 1780, *DAR* 18:88–89; Wilson, *Southern Strategy*, 234–35, 241, 315–16n; Borick, *A Gallant Defense*, 126, 137–41, 159–76, 197–219, 222; Urban, *Fusiliers*, 189. For the surrender negotiations and the final terms of the capitulation, see *Original Papers Relating to the Siege of Charleston*, 43–55. The quote about Clinton becoming the most popular man in England can be found in Jim Piecuch, *Three Peoples, One King: Loyalists, Indians, and Slaves in the Revolutionary South, 1775–1782* (Columbia, S.C., 2008), 181.

27. Morgan and O'Shaughnessy, "Arming Slaves in the American Revolution," in Brown and Morgan, *Arming Slaves*, 190–91; Piecuch, *Three Peoples, One King*, 216–17; Gilbert, *Black Patriots and Loyalists*, 117–18, 120–21; Egerton, *Death or Liberty*, 85–86; Nash, *Forgotten Fifth*, 35–36; Neimeyer, *America Goes to War*, 79; Sylvia R. Frey, *The British Soldier in America: A Social History of Military Life in the Revolutionary Period* (Austin, Tex., 1981), 18–19; Sylvia R. Frey, *Water from the Rock: Black Resistance in a Revolutionary Age* (Princeton, N.J., 1991), 118–20; Cassandra Pybus, "Jefferson's Faulty Math: The Question of Slave Defections in the American Revolution," *WMQ* 62 (2005): 255. The "quitted the plantation" quote is in Cassandra Pybus, *Epic Journeys of Freedom: Runaway Slaves of the American Revolution and Their Global Quest for Liberty* (Boston, 2006), 43

28. Ward, *War of the Revolution*, 2:704–5; Franklin and Mary Wickwire, *Cornwallis and the War of Independence* (London, 1971), 135; Piecuch, *Three Peoples, One King*, 179–95; Thomas B. Allen, *Tories: Fighting for the King in America's First Civil War* (New York, 2010), 281–82; Urban, *Fusiliers*, 193–94; O'Shaughnessy, *The Men Who Lost America*, 231. The "Military Law" quotation is in Piecuch, *Three Peoples, One King*, 183.

29. Buchanan, *Road to Guilford Courthouse*, 81–82.

30. Bass, *The Green Dragoon*, 11–31, 79–83; Wilson, *Southern Strategy*, 141–61. On the composition of the British Legion, see Lawrence E. Babits and Joshua B. Howard, "Continentals in Tarleton's British Legion, May 1780–October 1781," in Piecuch, *Cavalry of the American Revolution*, 184–85.

31. William Churchill Houston to William Livingston, June 2, 4, 1780, *LDC* 15:234, 245; Schuyler to GW, June 18, 1780, ibid., 15:345; John Hanson to Philip Thomas, June 21, 1780, ibid., 15:355; Thomas McKean to William Atlee, June 12, 1780, ibid., 15:304; James Madison to TJ, June 23, 1780, *PTJ* 3:461.

32. The "affairs to the Southward look blue" quote can be found in Paul David Nelson, *General Horatio Gates: A Biography* (Baton Rouge, La., 1976), 219. See also GW to Congress, August 20, 1780, *WW* 18:403.

33. TJ to Gates, August 4, September 3, 1780, *PTJ* 3:526, 588; TJ to GW, July 2, 1780, ibid., 3:478.

34. Gates to TJ, July 19, 1780, *PTJ* 3:495–96; Nelson, *General Horatio Gates*, 220–21, 227.

35. Buchanan, *Road to Guilford Courthouse*, 153.

36. Nelson, *General Horatio Gates*, 224, 229; Gates to TJ, August 3, 1780, *PTJ* 3:525; Buchanan, *Road to Guilford Courthouse*, 155.

37. Nelson, *General Horatio Gates*, 229–39; Buchanan, *Road to Guilford Courthouse*, 161–72; John Richard Alden, *The American Revolution, 1775–1783* (New York, 1954), 233–34; Urban, *Fusiliers*, 200–213; "A Narrative of the Campaign of 1780, by Colonel Otho Holland Williams, Adjutant General," in William Johnson, *Sketches of the Life and Correspondence of General Nathanael Greene* (Charleston, S.C., 1822), 1:487–88, 494–98; NG to William

Greene, September 5, 1780, *PNG* 6:257; ibid., 513-14n; John Pancake, *This Destructive War: The British Campaign in the Carolinas* (Tuscaloosa, Ala., 1985), 103-6; John C. Dann, ed., *Revolution Remembered: Eyewitness Accounts of the War of Independence* (Chicago, 1980), 195; Ward, *War of the Revolution*, 2:725-30.

38. Jonathan Dull, *A Diplomatic History of the American Revolution* (New Haven, Conn., 1983), 125-43; Edward Corwin, *French Policy and the American Alliance of 1778* (New York, 1916), 173-217; Samuel Flagg Bemis, *The Diplomacy of the American Revolution* (New York, 1935), 70-93.

39. Quoted in Brendan Simms, *Three Victories and a Defeat: The Rise and Fall of the First British Empire* (New York, 2007), 629.

40. On Jones's life and exploits, see Samuel Eliot Morison, *John Paul Jones: A Sailor's Biography* (Boston, 1959), and Evan Thomas, *John Paul Jones: Sailor, Hero, Father of the American Navy* (New York, 2003). On what Jones was alleged to have said during the battle, see Morison, 240-42. For riveting narratives of the epic sea battle between the *Bonhomme Richard* and the *Serapis*, see Morison, 200-240, and Thomas, 168-205. For America's war at sea in general, see William M. Fowler Jr., *Rebels Under Sail: The American Navy During the American Revolution* (New York, 1976).

41. Jonathan Dull, *The French Navy and American Independence: A Study of Arms and Diplomacy, 1774-1787* (Princeton, N.J., 1975), 142-58; Piers Mackesy, *The War for America, 1775-1784* (Cambridge, Mass., 1965), 278-97; JA to President of Congress, February 19, 1780, *PJA* 8:336.

42. Mackesy, *War for America*, 306-18; Samuel Flagg Bemis, *The Hussey-Cumberland Mission and the American Revolution* (Princeton, N.J., 1931); Lee Kennett, *The French Forces in America, 1780-1783* (Westport, Conn., 1977), 7-12; William Stinchcombe, *The American Revolution and the French Alliance* (Syracuse, N.Y., 1969), 153-59; Orville T. Murphy, "The View from Versailles: Charles Gravier Comte de Vergennes's Perceptions of the American Revolution," in Ronald Hoffman and Peter J. Albert, eds., *Diplomacy and Revolution: The Franco-American Alliance of 1778* (Charlottesville, Va., 1981), 140-41; Vergennes to Lafayette, August 7, 1780, April 19, 1781, *LLP* 3:129, 4:47.

43. GW, Memorandum for Concerting a Plan of Operations, July 15, 1780, *WW* 19:174-76; Lafayette to GW, August 3, 1780, ibid., 19:314; Conference at Hartford, September 22, 1780, ibid., 20:76-81; Lafayette to GW, July 29, 31, 1780, *LLP* 3:113-15, 116-19; Lafayette to Rochambeau and Ternay, August 9, 1780, ibid., 3:131, 133-34; Rochambeau to Lafayette, August 12, 1780, ibid., 3:140; Rochambeau to Chevalier de La Luzerne, August 14, 1780, ibid., 3:141; Summary of the Hartford Conference, September 22, 1780, ibid., 3:175-78; Lafayette to Adrienne de Lafayette, February 2, 1781, ibid., 3:311; Lafayette to Luzerne, February 7, 1781, ibid., 3:317; Lafayette to Vergennes, October 4, 1780, ibid., 3:188.

44. On Arnold's treason, see Willard Sterne Randall, *Benedict Arnold: Patriot and Traitor* (New York, 1990), 453-83; Willard Sterne Randall, "Why Benedict Arnold Did It," *American Heritage* 41 (September-October, 1990), 60-73; Willard M. Wallace, *Traitorous Hero: The Life and Fortunes of Benedict Arnold* (Freeport, N.Y., 1964), 128-259.

45. Charles Royster, " 'The Nature of Treason': Revolutionary Virtue and American Reactions to Benedict Arnold," *WMQ* 36 (1979): 163-93.

46. George F. Sheer, "The Sergeant Major's Strange Mission," *American Heritage* 8 (October 1957): 26-29, 98; Carl Van Doren, *Secret History of the American Revolution* (New York, 1941), 392-94; John Evangelist Walsh, *The Execution of Major Andre* (New York, 2001).

47. GW to TJ, June 29, October 10, 1780, *WW* 19:97, 20:147; GW to James Henry, June 29, 1780, ibid., 19:92; James Haw, *John and Edward Rutledge of South Carolina* (Athens, Ga., 1997), 148.

48. Rush to JA, October 23, 1780, *PJA* 10:303.

49. On Greene's character and attributes, see Theodore Thayer, *Nathanael Greene: Strategist of the American Revolution* (New York, 1960), 24–26; Terry Golway, *Washington's General: Nathanael Greene and the Triumph of the American Revolution* (New York, 2005), 81, 89, 162–63, 171.

50. GW to NG, October 14, 22, 1780, *PNG* 6:385–86, 424–25; NG to Catherine Greene, October 21, 28, 1780, ibid., 6:415, 439; NG to GW, November 19, 1780, ibid., 6:488.

CHAPTER 14: "A WAR OF DESOLATION SHOCKING TO HUMANITY": THE SOUTHERN THEATER IN 1780-1781

1. Paul David Nelson, *Soldier of the Early Republic* (Bloomington, Ind., 1985), 120–23; GW to Wayne, January 3[–4], 1781, *WW* 21:55; GW, Circular to the New England States, January 5, 1781, ibid., 21:62. See also Carl Van Doren, *Mutiny in January* (New York, 1943), 41–203. Wayne's estimate of having lost one-third of his men is in Van Doren, page 202.

2. GW to George Clinton, January 13, 1781, *WW* 21:95; GW to Congress, January 23, 1781, ibid., 21:136; GW to Robert Howe, January 22, 1781, ibid., 21:128; GW to Rochambeau, January 24, 28, 1781, ibid., 21:137, 151.

3. Samuel Flagg Bemis, *The Diplomacy of the American Revolution* (New York, 1935), 172–86; JA to President of Congress, July 11, 15, August 3, 4, 1781, *PJA* 11:410–12, 419–20, 436–37, 438–40; JA to Vergennes, July 7, 13, 16, 18, 19, 21, 1781, ibid., 11:405–6, 413–17, 420–22, 424–30. See also the editor's note and a string of documents, including the terms of the Russo-Austrian mediation proposal in *PJA* 11:368–465, and John Ferling, *John Adams: A Life* (reprint, New York, 2010), 235–36.

4. John Witherspoon to William Livingston, December 16, 1780, *LDC* 16:452; BF to Vergennes, February 13, 1781, *PBF* 34:373; GW to John Laurens, January 15, 1781, *WW* 21:105–10.

5. Quoted in Carl P. Borick, *A Gallant Defense: The Siege of Charleston, 1780* (Columbia, S.C., 2003), 230, 233.

6. Quoted in Ray Raphael, *A People's History of the American Revolution: How Common People Shaped the Fight for Independence* (New York, 2001), 82.

7. Michael C. Scoggins, "South Carolina's Backcountry Rangers in the American Revolution," in Jim Piecuch, ed., *Cavalry of the American Revolution* (Yardley, Pa., 2012), 145–73. The quote is on page 165.

8. Cornwallis to Clinton, August 6, 1780, in Charles Ross, ed., *Correspondence of Charles, First Marquis Cornwallis* (London, 1859), 1:54; Walter Edgar, *Partisans and Redcoats: The Southern Conflict That Turned the Tide of the American Revolution* (New York, 2001), 73–90, 97–106; Robert D. Bass, *The Green Dragoon: The Lives of Banastre Tarleton and Mary Robinson* (New York, 1957), 84–94, 104–26; John Buchanan, *The Road to Guilford Courthouse: The American Revolution in the Carolinas* (New York, 1997), 131–41, 173–86. On the partisan warfare, see also Russell F. Weigley, *The Partisan War: The South Carolina Campaign of 1780-1782* (Columbia, S.C., 1970) and the essays in Ronald Hoffman, Thad Tate, and Peter J. Albert, eds., *An Uncivil War: The Southern Backcountry During the American Revolution* (Charlottesville, Va., 1985).

9. Cornwallis to Germain, August 21, 1780, *DAR* 18:151; Franklin and Mary Wickwire, *Cornwallis and the War of Independence* (London, 1971), 175, 179; Edgar, *Partisans and Redcoats*, 60, 123, 136; Buchanan, *Road to Guilford Courthouse*, 201–2; Andrew Jackson O'Shaughnessy, *The Men Who Lost America: British Leadership, the American Revolution, and the Fate of the Empire* (New Haven, Conn., 2013), 259, 263–64.

10. Cornwallis to Clinton, July 14, August 6, 10, 1780, Ross, *Correspondence of Cornwallis*, 1:52, 54, 55.

11. Ferguson's edicts can be found in Thomas B. Allen, *Tories: Fighting for the King in America's First Civil War* (New York, 2010), 288, and Lyman C. Draper, *King's Mountain and Its Heroes: History of the Battle of King's Mountain, October 7, 1780, and the Events Which Led to It* (Cincinnati, 1881), 169. Also see Buchanan, *Road to Guilford Courthouse*, 208–21; Edgar, *Partisans and Redcoats*, 116; W. J. Wood, *Battles of the Revolutionary War, 1775–1781* (Chapel Hill, N.C., 1990), 189–94.

12. "Memoir of Thomas Young," *Orion* 3 (1843): 86; James Collins, *A Revolutionary Soldier* (Clinton, La., 1859), 52–53.

13. Anthony Allaire, *Diary of Lieut. Anthony Allaire* (reprint, New York, 1968), 31–32; Account of Isaac Shelby, in *SOS*, 2:1142; Account of Ensign Robert Campbell, ibid., 2:1142; Christopher Ward, *The War of the Revolution* (New York, 1952), 2:739–45; Hank Messick, *King's Mountain: The Epic of the Blue Ridge "Mountain Men" in the American Revolution* (Boston, 1976), 107–55; Wood, *Battles of the Revolutionary War*, 196–202; *PNG* 6:408n. Clinton is quoted in O'Shaughnessy, *The Men Who Lost America*, 239.

14. Samuel Huntington to Jonathan Trumbull Sr., October 23, 1780, *LDC* 16:237; GW, General Orders, October 27, 1780, *WW* 20:258.

15. NG to TJ, November 20, 1780, *PNG* 6:491; NG to GW December 7, 1780, ibid., 6:543. See also NG to Thomas Sim Lee, November 10, 1780, ibid., 6:473–74.

16. Theodore Thayer, *Nathanael Greene: Strategist of the American Revolution* (New York, 1960), 15–51. Knox's quotes are on page 67.

17. GW to TJ, November 8, December 9, 1780, *PTJ* 4:105, 195; TJ, Diary of Arnold's Invasion and Notes on Subsequent Events in 1781 [The 1796? Version], December 31, 1780, January 1, 1781, PTJ 4:258–59; Arnold's Invasion as Reported by TJ in the *Virginia Gazette*, January 13, 1781, ibid., 4:269–70; TJ to GW, January 10, 1781, ibid., 4:333–35; Michael Kranish, *Flight from Monticello: Thomas Jefferson at War* (New York, 2010), 167–99. General Charles Lee's "canvass wings" comments is in Eric Robson, *The American Revolution: In Its Political and Military Aspects, 1763–1783* (Hamden, Conn., 1965), 107.

18. *PNG* 6:xviii, 587–88; NG to Daniel Morgan, December 16, 1780, ibid., 6:589–90; NG to Steuben, December 28, 1780, ibid., 7:11; NG to Marion, December 4, 24, 1780, ibid., 6:519–20, 607; NG to [?], January 1–23, 1781, ibid., 7:175l; NG to Samuel Huntington, December 28, 1781, ibid., 7:7–9.

19. Cornwallis to Tarleton, January 2, 1781, *SOS*, 2:1155; Cornwallis to Clinton, December 3, 1780, *DAR* 18:244; Cornwallis to Clinton, January 6, 1781, Ross, *Correspondence of Cornwallis*, 1:80–82; Wickwires, *Cornwallis and the War of Independence*, 230 48; Arthur Bowler, *Logistics and the Failure of the British Army in America, 1775–1783* (Princeton, N.J., 1975), 151, 200–201; Wood, *Battles of the Revolutionary War*, 212.

20. Don Higginbotham, *Daniel Morgan: Revolutionary Rifleman* (Chapel Hill, N.C., 1961), 1–26.

21. The best account of the Battle of Cowpens, on which this narrative draws, is Lawrence E. Babits, *A Devil of a Whipping: The Battle of Cowpens* (Chapel Hill, N.C., 1998). Crucial, too, is Lawrence E. Babits and Joshua B. Howard, "Continentals in Tarleton's British Legion: May 1780–October 1781," in Piecuch, *Cavalry of the American Revolution*, 182–202. Good shorter accounts can be found Higginbotham, *Daniel Morgan*, 135–55; Bass, *Green Dragoon*, 152–62; Buchanan, *Road to Guilford Courthouse*, 319–26; Wood, *Battles of the American Revolution*, 221–26.

22. Wickwires, *Cornwallis*, 269.

23. Ibid., 274–81; Buchanan, *Road to Guilford Courthouse*, 337–58; Ward, *War of the Revolution*, 2:764–78; Higginbotham, *Daniel Morgan*, 145–54; Lawrence E. Babits and Joshua B. Howard, *Long, Obstinate, and Bloody: The Battle of Guilford Courthouse* (Chapel Hill, N.C., 2009), 13–36; Thayer, *Nathanael Greene*, 308–18; Morgan to NG, January 23, 25, 28, 29, 1781, *PNG* 7:178, 199, 200–201, 211, 215; NG to Congress, January 31, 1781, ibid., 7:225; NG to Militia Commanders in the Salisbury District, January 31, 1781, ibid., 7:227–28; Proceedings of a Council of War, February 9, 1781, ibid., 7:261–62; Otho Holland Williams to NG, February 13, 1781, ibid., 7:285; NG to Williams, February 14, 1781, ibid., 7:287, 287n.

24. NG to Colonel Alexander Martin, February 23, 1781, *PNG* 7:335; NG to GW, February 28, 1781, ibid., 7:369–70; NG to TJ, March 10, 1781, ibid., 7:419–20; Ward, *War of the Revolution*, 2:779–80. The Cornwallis quote is in Babits and Howard, *Long, Obstinate, and Bloody*, 42; Harry M. Ward, *Between the Lines: Banditti of the American Revolution* (Westport, Conn., 2003), 226.

25. Pickens to NG, February 26, 1781, *PNG* 7:358; Babits and Howard, *Long, Obstinate, and Bloody*, 37–51, 220–21; Buchanan, *Road to Guilford Courthouse*, 362–72; Wickwires, *Cornwallis*, 288–91; Thayer, *Nathanael Greene*, 326–27; Harry M. Ward, *Between the Lines: Banditti of the American Revolution* (Westport, Conn., 2002), 226.

26. Babits and Howard, *Long, Obstinate, and Bloody*, 57. Cornwallis is quoted in Don Higginbotham, "American Militia," in Don Higginbotham, ed., *Reconsiderations on the Revolutionary War: Selected Essays* (Westport, Conn., 1978), 99.

27. NG to Congress, March 16, 1781, *PNG* 7:434; NG to TJ, March 16, 1781, ibid., 7:441; NG to Catherine Greene, March 18, 1781, ibid., 7:446; editor's notes, ibid., 7:436–41n; Journal of Sergeant Roger Lamb, *SOS*, 2:1164–65; Ward, *War of the Revolution*, 2:784–94; Wood, *Battles of the American Revolution*, 246–56; Buchanan, *Road to Guilford Courthouse*, 374–83; Wickwires, *Cornwallis*, 305–10; Thayer, *Nathanael Greene*, 327–31. The most detailed account of the battle can be found in Babits and Howard, *Long, Obstinate, and Bloody*, 100–169. The section on Cornwallis having learned new tactical approaches draws on Stephen Conway, "The British Army, 'Military Europe,' and the American War of Independence, *WMQ* 67 (2010): 77.

28. Babits and Howard, *Long, Obstinate, and Bloody*, 173. Fox is quoted in Terry Golway, *Washington's General: Nathanael Greene and the Triumph of the American Revolution* (New York, 2005), 260.

29. Quoted in O'Shaughnessy, *The Men Who Lost America*, 271.

CHAPTER 15: "WE HAVE GOT CORNWALLIS IN A PUDDING BAG": THE DECISIVE VICTORY AT YORKTOWN

1. GW to Rochambeau, April 3, 1781, *WW* 21:402; GW to John Laurens, April 9, 1781, ibid., 21:437; GW to TJ, April 4, 1781, ibid., 21:417–18.

2. GW to Lafayette, February 20, 1781, *LLP* 3:333–34; GW, Instructions to Lafayette, February 20, 1781, ibid., 3:334–36; GW to Rochambeau, February 15, 1781, *WW* 21:230; GW to Lafayette, March 1, 1781, ibid., 21:322; GW to Lund Washington, March 28, 1781, ibid., 21:386; Lee Kennett, *The French Forces in America, 1780–1783* (Westport, Conn., 1977), 83–84, 94–97, 99–100; James Thomas Flexner, *George Washington in the American Revolution, 1775–1783* (Boston, 1967), 414–15; Douglas Southall Freeman, *George Washington: A Biography* (New York, 1968), 251–74; John Ferling, *The First of Men: A Life of George Washington* (Knoxville, Tenn., 1988), 292.

3. Lawrence E. Babits and Joshua B. Howard, *Long, Obstinate, and Bloody: The Battle of Guilford Courthouse* (Chapel Hill, N.C., 2009), 171–80. The "scene of horror" quotation is from Sylvia R. Frey, *The British Soldier in America: A Social History of Military Life in the Revolutionary Period* (Austin, Tex., 1981), 110.

4. The foregoing paragraphs draw on Franklin and Mary Wickwire, *Cornwallis and the War of Independence* (London, 1971), 311–19; Andrew Jackson O'Shaughnessy, *The Men Who Lost America: British Leadership, the American Revolution, and the Fate of Empire* (New Haven, Conn., 2013), 269; Cornwallis to Clinton, April 10, 23, 1781, in Sir Henry Clinton, *Observations on Some Parts of Earl Cornwallis's Answer to Sir Henry Clinton's Narrative* (1783), in Benjamin F. Stevens, ed., *The Campaign in Virginia, 1781: An Exact Reprint of Six Rare Pamphlets on the Clinton-Cornwallis Controversy* (London, 1888), 1:398, 424–25; Cornwallis to William Phillips, April 24, 1781, ibid., 1:428; Cornwallis to Germain, April 18, 1781, ibid., 1:417–18; Earl Cornwallis, An Answer to . . . the Narrative of . . . Henry Clinton, ibid., 1:65, 67. On Loyalist recruiting in the Carolinas, see Jim Piecuch, *Three Peoples, One King: Loyalists, Indians, and Slaves in the Revolutionary South, 1775–1782* (Columbia, S.C., 2008), which persuasively argues that Loyalist recruiting in the Carolinas demonstrated the wisdom of British officials who envisaged a considerable turnout of southern Tories to bear arms for the king.

5. GW to J. Laurens, April 9, 1781, *WW* 21:439.

6. GW to Congress, May 17, 1781, ibid., 22:97–98; Conference with Rochambeau, May 23, 1781, ibid., 22:105–7; GW to NG, June 1, 1781, ibid., 22:146; Kennett, *The French Forces in America*, 78; Baron Ludwig von Closen, *The Revolutionary Journal of Baron Ludwig von Closen, 1780–1783*, ed., Evelyn Acomb (Chapel Hill, N.C., 1958); Edward G. Lengel, *General George Washington* (New York, 2005), 329–30; Flexner, *George Washington in the American Revolution*, 418–19, 429–30.

7. John Ferling, *Almost a Miracle: The American Victory in the War of Independence* (New York, 2007), 509, 516–20; Christopher Ward, *The War of the Revolution* (New York, 1952), 2:798, 801, 824–25, 823–34; Terry Golway, *Washington's General: Nathanael Greene and the Triumph of the American Revolution* (New York, 2005), 271–76, 280–84; PNG 8:160n.

8. Henry Clinton, *The American Rebellion: Sir Henry Clinton's Narrative of His Campaigns, 1775–1782*, ed., William B. Willcox (New Haven, Conn., 1954), 274, 284, 293, 305–6; William B. Willcox, "Sir Henry Clinton: Paralysis of Command," in George A. Billias, ed., *George Washington's Opponents* (New York, 1969), 91–92.

9. GW to Lund Washington, April 30, 1781, *WW* 22:15; Ferling, *Almost a Miracle*, 503, 511; John E. Selby, *The Revolution in Virginia, 1775–1783* (Williamsburg, Va., 1988), 270–74.

10. TJ to Samuel Huntington (President of Congress), January 15, 1781, *PTJ* 4:370; TJ to Chevalier de la Luzerne, April 12, 1781, ibid., 5:422.

11. Cornwallis to Clinton, May 26, June 30, 1781, Stevens, *Campaign in Virginia*, 1:488; 2:35–36.

12. Lafayette to GW, May 24, 1781, *LLP* 4:130–31; Ward, *War of the Revolution*, 2:873.

13. Selby, *Revolution in Virginia*, 276–81; Wickwires, *Cornwallis and the War of Independence*, 330–34.

14. TJ, Diary of Arnold's Invasion [The 1796? Version], *PTJ* 4:261; TJ to William Gordon, July 16, 1788, ibid., 13:363; James A. Bear and Lucia Stanton, eds., *Jefferson's Memorandum Books: Accounts, with Legal Records and Miscellany, 1767–1826* (Princeton, N.J., 1997) 1:510–11n; Annette Gordon-Reed, *The Hemingses of Monticello: An American Family* (New York, 2008), 138–39; Michael Kranish, *Flight from Monticello: Thomas Jefferson at War* (New York, 2010), 283–86; Dumas Malone, *Jefferson and His Time* (Boston, 1948–1981), 1:357.

15. Clinton to Cornwallis, May 29, June 8, 19, 28, July 11, 1781, Stevens, *Campaign in Virginia*, 1:493–98; 2:14–17, 26–28, 29–30, 62–65; Cornwallis to Clinton, July 8, 27, 1781, ibid., 2:57, 104.

16. Claude Blanchard, *The Journal of Claude Blanchard, 1780–1783*, ed., Thomas Bulch (reprint New York, 1969), 107; Kennett, *French Forces in America*, 114; von Closen, *Revolutionary Journal of Baron Ludwig von Closen*, 91–92; "Journal of Comte de Clerment-Crevecoeuer," in Howard C. Rice and Anne S. K. Brown, eds., *The American Campaigns of Rochambeau's Army, 1780, 1781, 1782, 1783* (Princeton, N.J., 1972), 1:33; Marquis De Chastellux, *Travels in North America in the Years 1780, 1781, and 1782*, ed., Howard C. Rice (Chapel Hill, N.C., 1963), 2:229. The "most neatly dressed" quotation is in Charles Patrick Neimeyer, *America Goes to War: A Social History of the Continental Army* (New York, 1996), 83.

17. Edward G. Lengel, *General George Washington: A Military Life* (New York, 2005), 332; GW to Rochambeau, June 13, 1781, *WW* 22:208.

18. Richard M. Ketchum, *Victory at Yorktown: The Campaign That Won the Revolution* (New York, 2004), 159; David Syrett, *The Royal Navy in American Waters, 1775–1783* (Aldershot, Eng., 1989), 178, 181, 191; O'Shaughnessy, *Men Who Lost America*, 241, 261–62; William B. Willcox, *Portrait of a General: Sir Henry Clinton in the War of Independence* (New York, 1962), 392–408.

19. GW to Lafayette, August 21, 1781, *WW* 23:34.

20. Lengel, *General George Washington*, 335.

21. Daniel Jackson et al., eds., *The Diaries of George Washington* (Charlottesville, Va., 1976–1979), 3:414–16; Ketchum, *Victory at Yorktown*, 159.

22. James Thacher, *Military Journal of the American Revolution* (reprint, New York, 1969), 273–78 JA to AA, August 14, 1777, *AFC* 2:327–28; James Lovell to AA, [September] 4, 1781, *LDC* 18:8; Virginia Delegates to Thomas Nelson, September 4, 1781, ibid., 18:15.

23. Lafayette to GW, August 24, 25, 1781, *LLP* 4:349–51, 356–59.

24. Gilbert Chinard, *George Washington as the French Knew Him* (Princeton, N.J., 1940), 42.

25. GW to Lincoln, September 7, 1781, *WW* 23:101; The "wind of speed" quote is in David B. Mattern, *Benjamin Lincoln and the American Revolution* (Columbia, S.C., 1995), 118.

26. William B. Willcox, "Arbuthnot, Gambier, and Graves: 'Old Women' of the Navy," in Billias, *George Washington's Opponents*, 280.

27. O'Shaughnessy, *The Men Who Lost America*, 242, 279–80; Wickwires, *Cornwallis and the War of Independence*, 364; Clinton to Cornwallis, September 6, 1781, Stevens, *Campaign in Virginia*, 2:152–53; Cornwallis to Clinton, September 16–17, 1781, ibid., 2:157.

28. Ward, *War of the Revolution*, 2:887–88; Ketchum, *Victory at Yorktown*, 198, 217; Ferling, *Almost a Miracle*, 531; George Weedon to NG, September 5, 1781, *PNG* 9:300–301;

Journal of John Trumbull, in *SOS*, 2:1227. Wayne is quoted in Jerome A. Greene, *The Guns of Independence: The Siege of Yorktown* (New York, 2005), 70.

29. Mattern, *Benjamin Lincoln*, 119; George Scheer, ed., *Private Yankee Doodle: Being a Narrative of Some of the Adventures, Dangers and Sufferings of a Revolutionary Soldier* (Boston, 1962), 230, 233–34; Ketchum, *Victory at Yorktown*, 222, 227; Lengel, *General George Washington*, 337–38.

30. Gary B. Nash, *The Forgotten Fifth: African Americans in the Age of Revolution* (Cambridge, Mass., 2006), 37; Cassandra Pybus, *Epic Journeys of Freedom: Runaway Slaves of the American Revolution and Their Global Quest for Liberty* (Boston, 2006), 48–53.

31. AH to Elizabeth Schuyler Hamilton, October 12, 1781, *PAH* 2:678.

32. Ibid., 2:679n; Greene, *Guns of Independence*, 240–45.

33. Cornwallis to GW, October 17, 18, 1781, Stevens, *Campaign in Virginia*, 2:189, 195–96; Cornwallis to Clinton, October 20, 1781, ibid., 2:215; Articles of Capitulation, October 19, 1781, ibid., 2:199–203; GW to Cornwallis, October 17, 18, 1781, *WW* 23:236–37, 237–38; Wickwires, *Cornwallis and the War of Independence*, 385–86.

34. The foregoing on the surrender draws on Ketchum, *Victory at Yorktown*, 244; Greene, *Guns of Independence*, 296; Eric Robson, *The American Revolution: In Its Political and Military Aspects, 1763-1783* (Hamden, Conn., 1965), 129; John Buchanan, *The Road to Guilford Courthouse: The American Revolution in the Carolinas* (New York, 1997), 335; Scheer, *Private Yankee Doodle*, 240; Closen, *Journal*, 153–54; Thacher, *Journal*, 298.

35. Alan Gilbert, *Black Patriots and Loyalists: Fighting for Emancipation in the War of Independence* (Chicago, 2012), 175; Nash, *Forgotten Fifth*, 38–39; Douglas R. Egerton, *Death or Liberty: African Americans and Revolutionary America* (New York, 2009), 90–91; Sylvia R. Frey, *Water from the Rock: Black Resistance in a Revolutionary Age* (Princeton, N.J., 1991), 164–71; Cassandra Pybus, "Jefferson's Faulty Math: The Question of Slave Defections in the American Revolution," *WMQ*, 62 (2005): 254–58; Henry Wiencek, *An Imperfect God: George Washington, His Slaves, and the Creation of America* (New York, 2003), 247–48.

36. GW, General Orders, October 20, 1781, *WW*, 23:144–47.

CHAPTER 16: "OH GOD, IT IS ALL OVER": PEACE, CONSPIRACY, DEMOBILIZATION, CHANGE, 1781-1783

1. Alan Valentine, *Lord North* (Norman, Okla., 1967), 2:274.

2. Quoted in Brendan Simms, *Three Victories and a Defeat: The Rise and Fall of the First British Empire, 1714-1783* (New York, 2009), 654–55.

3. Peter Whiteley, *Lord North: The Prime Minister Who Lost America* (London, 1996), 195–208; Valentine, *Lord North*, 274–328; Andrew Jackson O'Shaughnessy, *The Men Who Lost America: British Leadership, the American Revolution and the Fate of the Empire* (New Haven, Conn., 2013), 76–78; *PH* 22:636, 680, 705–7, 723, 726, 729, 802–3, 808, 812, 831, 1028–48, 1076–80, 1085–90; Stanley Weintraub, *Iron Tears: America's Battle for Freedom, Britain's Quagmire, 1775-1783* (New York, 2005), 306–16.

4. Elias Boudinot to Hannah Boudinot, October 21, 1781, *LDC* 18:151; Connecticut Delegates to Jonathan Trumbull Sr., October 25, 1781, ibid., 18:165; John Ferling, *A Leap in the Dark: The Struggle to Create the American Republic* (New York, 2003), 240–41.

5. William M. Fowler Jr., *American Crisis: George Washington and the Dangerous Two Years After Yorktown, 1781-1783* (New York, 2011), 104–6.

6. The Marquis of Rockingham, who in 1766 had formed an administration that repealed the troublesome Stamp Act, put together a ministry in the spring of 1782 that supplanted Lord North's government. His secretary for American affairs was the Earl of Shelburne. However, when Rockingham died after only a few weeks in power, the king in July asked Shelburne to form a government.

7. John Ferling, *John Adams: A Life* (reprint, New York, 2010), 244; BF to GW, April 8, 1782, *PBF* 37:116; BF to Robert Livingston, March 30, 1782, ibid., 37:71.

8. William Stinchcombe, *The American Revolution and the French Alliance* (Syracuse, N.Y., 1969), 62–63; William Henry Drayton's Notes of Proceedings, February 15, 1779, *LDC* 12:171–73.

9. *JCC* 13:239–44; John Fell's Diary, March 24, 1779, *LDC* 12:239; North Carolina Delegates to Richard Caswell, April 2, 1779, ibid., 12:275–76; Lovell to Gates, April 5[?], 1779, ibid., 12:299; SA to Samuel Cooper, April 29, 1779, ibid., 12;402; Henry Laurens's Notes of Debates, June 19, July 1, 1779, ibid., 13:82–84, 133–43; John Armstrong to GW, June 25, 1779, ibid., 13:108; Gouverneur Morris to Benjamin Towne, July 9, 1779, ibid., 13:180; Daniel of St. Thoms Jenifer to Charles Carroll, June 30, 1779, ibid., 13:139; Richard B. Morris, *The Peacemakers: The Great Powers and American Independence* (New York, 1965), 11–14; Stinchcombe, *American Revolution and the French Alliance*, 66–72; Joseph L. Davis, *Sectionalism in American Politics, 1774–1787* (Madison, Wisc., 1977), 17, 21; Jack Rakove, *The Beginnings of National Politics: An Interpretive History of the Continental Congress* (Baltimore, 1979), 256–58; H. James Henderson, *Party Politics in the Continental Congress* (New York, 1974), 197.

10. *DAJA* 2:403–4; 4:191–203; *JCC* 20:614–15, 618–19, 627, 648; Stinchcombe, *American Revolution and the French Alliance*, 153–62; John Ferling, "John Adams, Diplomat," *WMQ*, 51 (1994): 242–44.

11. David Hartley to BF, January 2[–8], 1782, *PBF* 36:360–64; BF to Hartley, January 15, April 13, 1782, ibid., 36:435, 37:143–44; Morris, *The Peacemakers*, 252–54; Stacy Schiff, *A Great Improvisation: Franklin, France, and the Birth of America* (New York, 2005), 298; Orville T. Murphy, *Charles Gravier, Comte de Vergennes: French Diplomacy in the Age of Revolution, 1719–1787* (Albany, N.Y., 1982), 322.

12. Jonathan Dull, *A Diplomatic History of the American Revolution* (New Haven, Conn., 1985), 139, 142.

13. BF to Richard Oswald, June 27, 1782, *PBF* 37:558; BF to Lafayette, July 9, 1782, ibid., 37:600. Oswald's account of BF's terms can be found in ibid., 37:599–600n.

14. JA to Richard Cranch, December 15, 1782, *AFC* 5:47.

15. *DAJA* 3:45.

16. Dull, *Diplomatic History of the American Revolution*, 137–51; *DAJA* 3:82; David McCullough, *John Adams* (New York, 2001), 283–85; John Ferling, *John Adams: A Life* (reprint, New York, 2010), 245–56; Schiff, *The Great Improvisation*, 52–53, 316; John Ferling, *Setting the World Ablaze: Washington, Adams, Jefferson and the American Revolution* (New York, 2001), 256–65. For the complete text of the preliminary accord signed on November 30, 1782, see Dull, *Diplomatic History*, 170–74.

17. BF to Vergennes, December 17, 1782, *SOS*, 2:1271–72; Dull, *Diplomatic History*, 151.

18. Gunning Bedford to Nicholas Van Dyke, March 12, 1783, *LDC* 20:3; John Taylor Gilman to Meshech Weare, March 12, 1783, ibid., 20:10; William Floyd to George Clinton, March 12, 1783, ibid., 20:9; Thomas Paine, "The American Crisis, XIII," April 19, 1783, in Philip S. Foner, ed., *The Complete Writings of Thomas Paine* (New York, 1945), 1:230.

19. GW, General Orders, March 28, April 18, 1783, *WW* 26:264, 334.

20. Quoted in Fowler, *American Crisis*, 192.

21. Paine, "The American Crisis, XIII," April 19, 1783, Foner, *Complete Writings of Thomas Paine*, 1:230; BF to Joseph Banks, July 27, 1783, *SOS*, 2:1275; *DAJA* 3:52.

22. Linda Colley, *Captives: Britain, Empire, and the World, 1600–1850* (New York, 2002), 210.

23. Larry Bowman, *Captive Americans: Prisoners During the American Revolution* (Athens, Ohio, 1977), 109–15; Memorandum of Agreement for Liberation of British Prisoners of War, April 19, 1783, *WW* 26:341; Howard H. Peckham, *The Toll of Independence: Engagements and Battle Casualties of the American Revolution* (Chicago, 1974), 11, 28, 46, 56, 66, 78, 93, 98, 99, 108, 113, 117, 120, 123, 125–27, 130–32; David Sterling, ed., "American Prisoners of War in New York: A Report by Elias Boudinot," *WMQ* 13 (1956): 380–81, 385.

24. Maya Jasanoff, *Liberty's Exiles: American Loyalists in the Revolutionary World* (New York, 2011), 63–81.

25. Fowler, *American Crisis*, 200–203.

26. GW to President of Congress, October 11, 1780, *WW* 20:158.

27. Quoted in Richard Kohn, "The Inside History of the Newburgh Conspiracy: America and the Coup d'Etat," *WMQ* 27 (1970): 194.

28. Arthur Lee to SA, January 29, 1783, *LDC* 19:639; E. James Ferguson, *The Power of the Purse: A History of American Public Finance, 1776–1790* (Chapel Hill, N.C., 1961), 158; Thomas Fleming, *The Perils of Peace: America's Struggle for Survival After Yorktown* (New York, 2007), 264.

29. *JCC* 24:295–97.

30. GW, To the Officers of the Army, March 15, 1783, *WW* 26:222–27; Josiah Quincy, ed., *The Journal of Major Samuel Shaw* (Boston, 1843), 101–105.

31. GW to President of Congress, March 18, 1783, *WW* 26:229–32; GW to John Stark, August 5, 1778, *PGWR* 16:256. On pensions see Judith L. Van Buskirk, "Claiming Their Due: African Americans in the Revolutionary War and Its Aftermath," in John Resch and Walter Sargent, eds., *War and Society in the American Revolution: Mobilization and Home Fronts* (DeKalb, Ill., 2007), 132–60.

32. On the so-called Newburgh Conspiracy, see Kohn, "Inside History of the Newburgh Conspiracy," *WMQ* 27 (1970): 187–220; Paul David Nelson, with a rebuttal by Richard H. Kohn, "Horatio Gates at Newburgh, 1783: A Misunderstood Role," ibid., 29 (1972): 143–55; C. Edward Skeen, with a rebuttal by Richard H. Kohn, "The Newburgh Conspiracy Reconsidered," ibid., 31 (1974): 273–98; Fowler, *American Crisis*, 146–88.

33. GW, Circular to the States, June 8, 1783, *WW* 26:483–96.

34. Fowler, *American Crisis*, 203; Fleming, *Perils of Peace*, 286–87.

35. GW, Farewell Orders to the Armies of the United States, November 2, 1783, *WW* 27:222–27.

36. Jasanoff, *Liberty's Exiles*, 86.

37. Fowler, *American Crisis*, 227–33.

38. GW, Address to Congress, December 23, 1783, *WW* 27:284–85.

39. These figures draw on Peckham, *Toll of Independence*, 130–34, though scholars now believe that his calculations, which were made in the early 1970s, were far too low.

40. Elizabeth A. Fenn, *Pox Americana: The Great Smallpox Epidemic of 1775–82* (New York, 2001), 259–77.

41. Michael Clodfelter, *Warfare and Armed Conflict: A Statistical Reference to Casualty and Other Figures, 1618–1991* (Jefferson, N.C., 1992), 1:197–98; Neil Cantlie, *A History of the Army Medical Department* (Edinburgh, 1974), 1:156; Rodney Atwood, *The Hessians: Mercenaries from Hessen-Kassel in the American Revolution* (Cambridge, Eng., 1980), 255; Paul H. Smith, "The American Loyalists: Notes on Their Organization and Numerical Strength," *WMQ* 25 (1968): 264, 266, 268, 275n.

42. Gregory Evans Dowd, *A Spirited Resistance: The North American Indian Struggle for Unity, 1745–1815* (Baltimore, 1992), 83–87; Rob Harper, "Looking the Other Way: The Gnadenhutten Massacre and the Contextual Interpretation of Violence," *WMQ* 64 (2007): 621–44. The "praying, singing" quotation is in Harper, page 621.

43. Eric Robson, *The American Revolution: In Its Political and Military Aspects, 1763–1783* (Hamden, Conn., 1965), 164.

44. Evelyn M. Acomb, ed., *The Revolutionary Journal of Baron Ludwig von Closen, 1780–1783* (Chapel Hill, N.C., 1958), 64.

45. Benjamin Rush to Richard Price, May 25, 1786, in L. H. Butterfield, ed., *Letters of Benjamin Rush* (Princeton, N.J., 1951), 1:388.

46. Gary B. Nash, *The Unknown American Revolution: The Unruly Birth of Democracy and the Struggle to Create America* (New York, 2005), 283, 316–17; Jean B. Lee, "Lessons in Humility: The Revolutionary Transformation of the Governing Elite of Charles County, Maryland," in Ronald Hoffman and Peter J. Albert, eds., *The Transforming Hand of Revolution: Reconsidering the American Revolution as a Social Movement* (Charlottesville, Va., 1995), 90–117; Ronald Hoffman, "The 'Disaffected' in the Revolutionary South," in Alfred F. Young, ed., *The American Revolution: Explorations in the History of American Radicalism* (DeKalb, Ill., 1976), 273–316.

47. Thomas Paine, *Common Sense* (1776) in Foner, *Complete Writings of Thomas Paine*, 1:30, 41, 45.

48. Alfred F. Young, *The Shoemaker and the Tea Party: Memory and the American Revolution* (Boston, 1999), 3–4, 58–66.

49. For Private Martin's long account, see George F. Scheer, ed., *Private Yankee Doodle: Being a Narrative of Some of the Adventures, Dangers and Sufferings of a Revolutionary Soldier* (Boston, 1962). For an excellent summary, including a narrative of Martin's postwar years, see Philip Mead, " 'Adventures, Dangers and Sufferings': The Betrayals of Private Joseph Plumb Martin, Continental Soldier," in Alfred F. Young, Gary B. Nash, and Ray Raphael, eds., *Revolutionary Founders: Rebels, Radicals, and Reformers in the Making of the Nation* (New York, 2011), 117–34.

50. Quoted in Merrill Jensen, *The American Revolution Within America* (New York, 1974), 104–5.

51. Michael A. McDonnell, " 'The Spirit of Levelling': James Cleveland, Edward Wright, and the Militiamen's Struggle for Equality in Revolutionary Virginia," in Young, et. al., *Revolutionary Founders*, 135–54.

52. TJ to Edward Carrington, January 16, 1787, *PTJ* 11:49; TJ to Charles Bellini, September 30, 1785, ibid., 8:568; TJ to James Monroe, June 17, 1785, ibid., 8:233. The Richard Price quote can be found in Gordon S. Wood, *Empire of Liberty: A History of the Early Republic, 1789–1815* (New York, 2009), 46.

53. See Rhys Isaac, *The Transformation of Virginia, 1740–1790* (Chapel Hill, N.C., 1992); Allan Kulikoff, *Tobacco and Slaves: The Development of Southern Culture in the Chesapeake,*

555

1680–1800 (Chapel Hill, N.C., 1986); and Jon Butler, "James Ireland, John Leland, John 'Swearing Jack' Waller, and the Baptist Campaign for Religious Freedom in Revolutionary Virginia," in Alfred F. Young, et al., *Revolutionary Founders*, 169–84. For an excellent survey of the alterations in church–state relationships, see Thomas S. Kidd, *God of Liberty: A Religious History of the American Revolution* (New York, 2010), 167–86.

54. Benjamin Quarles, "The Revolutionary War as a Black Declaration of Independence," in Ira Berlin and Ronald Hoffman, eds., *Slavery and Freedom in the Age of the American Revolution* (Charlottesville, Va., 1983), 283–301. The quotation is on page 301.

55. Peter Kolchin, *American Slavery, 1619–1877* (New York, 1993), 63–92. The Samuel Johnson quote can be found on pages 76–77.

56. JA is quoted in John Ferling, *Setting the World Ablaze: Washington, Adams, Jefferson, and the American Revolution* (New York, 2000), 287.

57. Gordon S. Wood, *The Radicalism of the American Revolution* (New York, 1992), 186–87.

58. Jan E. Lewis, "A Revolution for Whom? Women in the Era of the American Revolution," in Nancy A. Hewitt, ed., *A Companion to Women's History* (Oxford, Eng., 2002), 83–99. The quotations can be found on pages 87 and 97.

59. Jasanoff, *Liberty's Exiles*, 351–58.

60. JA to AA, April 14, 1776, *AFC* 1:381–82. Fisher Ames's quotation is in Seth Ames, ed., *Works of Fisher Ames* (Boston, 1854), 2:101. See also Jensen, *American Revolution Within America*, 105; and AH to Theodore Sedgwick, July 10, 1804, *PAH* 26:309.

61. TJ to Spencer Roane, September 6, 1819, Paul Leicester Ford, ed., *The Writings of Thomas Jefferson* (New York, 1892–1899), 12:136, 140; TJ to Priestley, March 21, 1801, *PTJ* 33:394; TJ, First Inaugural Address, March 4, 1801, ibid., 33:150–51; TJ to Paine, March 18, 1801, ibid., 33:358–59. On the election of 1800, see John Ferling, *Adams vs. Jefferson: The Tumultuous Election of 1800* (New York, 2004).

62. TJ to John Dickinson, March 6, 1801, *PTJ* 33:196–97; TJ to Paine, March 18, 1801, ibid., 33:358–59.

INDEX

A NOTE ON THE AUTHOR

John Ferling is professor emeritus of history at the University of West Georgia. A leading authority on American Revolutionary history, he is the author of eleven books, including *Jefferson and Hamilton: The Rivalry That Forged a Nation*; *The First of Men: A Life of George Washington*; the award-winning *A Leap in the Dark: The Struggle to Create the American Republic*; *Adams vs. Jefferson: The Tumultuous Election of 1800*; *Almost a Miracle: The American Victory in the War of Independence*; *The Ascent of George Washington: The Hidden Political Genius of an American Icon*, named one of the best books of 2009 by the *Washington Post*; and *Independence: The Struggle to Set America Free*. He and his wife, Carol, live in metropolitan Atlanta.